Guide to State Procurement

A 50-State Primer on Purchasing Laws, Processes, and Procedures

THIRD EDITION

Melissa Javon Copeland, Editor

AMERICAN BAR ASSOCIATION
Public Contract Law Section

Cover design by Jill Tedhams/ABA Design

Printed in the United States of America.

26 25 24 23 5 4 3 2

A catalog record for this book is available from the Library of Congress.

Contents

Colorado Procurement Rules and Regulations 55

Connecticut Procurement Rules and Regulations 69

Idaho Procurement Rules and Regulations 163

Maine Procurement Rules and Regulations 253

Montana Procurement Rules and Regulations 331

Nebraska Procurement Rules and Regulations 341

North Carolina Procurement Rules and Regulations 407

North Dakota Procurement Rules and Regulations 423

Ohio Procurement Rules and Regulations 445

Oklahoma Procurement Rules and Regulations 463

Pennsylvania Procurement Rules and Regulations 491

Puerto Rico Procurement Rules and Regulations 501

Rhode Island Procurement Rules and Regulations 517

Acknowledgments

State	Authors
Alabama	Peter D. LeJeune Jesse S. Unkenholz
Alaska	Connor Smith
Arizona	James J. Sienicki Emily Parker Josh Grabel
Arkansas	Luke Vance Nicole Gore
California	Joshua Deitz Aaron Silberman
Colorado	Eric Whytsell Judith Araujo
Connecticut	Antionette Webster
Delaware	Richard A. Forsten
Florida	Karen D. Walker Joseph M. Goldstein Andrew Schwartz
Georgia	Melissa J. Copeland
Hawaii	Anna H. Oshiro
Idaho	Frederick J. Hahn III
Illinois	Jeff H. Eckland Mark J. Blando Vince Reuter Robert Dube
Indiana	Barbara A. Duncombe Erin R. Davis
Iowa	Willard L. Boyd III
Kansas	Brian E. Sobczyk
Kentucky	Amanda S. Johnson Erin R. Davis Christina Heidecker

State	Authors
Louisiana	Gerard E. Wimberly, Jr. Angelina Christina Elizabeth S. Horn Melissa Harris
Maine	A. Robert Ruesch
Maryland	C. Scott Maravilla
Massachusetts	Brian J. O'Rourke
Michigan	Jeff H. Eckland Mark J. Blando Vince Reuter Robert Dube
Minnesota	Jeff H. Eckland Mark J. Blando Vince Reuter Robert Dube
Mississippi	Adam Stone Kaytie M. Pickett Amber L. Kipfmiller
Missouri	Diana C. (Farr) Carter Melissa J. Copeland
Montana	Meghan Holmlund
Nebraska	William T. Foley Blake S. Schneiderwind
Nevada	Michael B. Brown Max S. Fujii
New Hampshire	Richard Parsons
New Jersey	Kristopher Berr
New Mexico	Joshua Grabel
New York	C. Scott Maravilla
North Carolina	Jackson W. Moore Jeffrey J. Truitt
North Dakota	Jeff H. Eckland Mark J. Blando Vince Reuter Robert Dube
Ohio	Barbara A. Duncombe Sean A. Graves Erin R. Davis
Oklahoma	Melissa J. Copeland
Oregon	Thomas A. Larkin Grant N. Margeson
Pennsylvania	Kristopher Berr
Rhode Island	Robert E. Craven, Jr.
South Carolina	Keith C. McCook

State	Authors
South Dakota	Jeff H. Eckland Mark J. Blando Vince Reuter Robert Dube
Tennessee	Erica Bell Vick David R. Esquivel Ramon J. Ryan
Texas	Sandy D. Hellums-Gomez
Utah	Brian D. Bolinder
Vermont	William T. Clark
Virginia	John S. Pachter Edmund M. Amorosi Michael T. Gwinn
Washington	Karl F. Oles Danika Duffy
West Virginia	Eric Whytsell
Wisconsin	Jeff H. Eckland Mark J. Blando Vince Reuter Robert Dube
Wyoming	John L. Skari, Jr. Eric Whytsell
District of Columbia	James C. McKay, Jr.
Puerto Rico	María C. Cartagena-Cancel José A. Irizarry-Castro

Introduction

The First Edition of this Guide was published in 2011 and was very well received. The Second Edition was published in 2016 and replaced and superseded the First Edition. In the Second Edition, we also added summaries for the District of Columbia and Puerto Rico. Each summary also contained a new section about each government's use and implementation of the Model Procurement Code. This Third Edition updates and supersedes the prior editions. In this edition, we added a new section on cooperative purchasing. Just like the Second Edition, this Guide will be available in electronic format, which was a feature that was widely requested. We hope having the Guide available in this format will allow even more users to have this resource readily available to them for use in their everyday work.

As those involved in state purchasing are well aware, purchasing laws and regulations can change quickly. Therefore, the reader should check the current status of the laws and regulations cited in these summaries before relying on them in legal briefs and arguments. These summaries are not intended to be, nor should they be construed as, legal advice or as a comprehensive collection of all relevant laws.

The summaries generally focus on purchasing at the state level and provide information about procurement statutes and regulations, bid processes, bid protest procedures, and administrative and judicial remedies. The Section hopes that this book becomes a staple in your library and that you will find it to be an invaluable resource. We welcome your ideas on how the Section can assist you in the future.

I want to thank the Section leadership and especially the members of the Section's Publications Board for their support and commitment to this project. Although the entire Section has been supportive of this effort from the First Edition, there are a few individuals who require a special mention for their original and continued support of this Guide and of state and local procurement efforts in general: Don Featherstun, Michael Hordell, Aaron Silberman, and Professor Chris Yukins—thank you for your support and encouragement! Finally, I want to thank every author in this publication for their time and effort in drafting the summaries.

Melissa J. "Missy" Copeland
Email: Missy@SchmidtCopeland.com

Introductio

Alabama Procurement Rules and Regulations

Prepared by Peter D. LeJeune and Jesse S. Unkenholz
Balch & Bingham LLP
Email: plejeune@balch.com and junkenholz@balch.com

I. Statutory Reference

A. Procurement/Purchasing Statutes[1]

State and local public contracts are governed by title 41 of the Code of Alabama, chapter 16. Public works contracts are governed by title 39 of the Code of Alabama, chapters 1, 2, 3, 5, 6, 7, and 8.

In April 2021, the governor of Alabama signed into law Senate Bill 77, which is meant to establish the Office of Chief Procurement Officer and revamp the Alabama Competitive Bid Law. (See Act No. 2021-296, https://arc-sos.state.al.us/ucp/L0604004.AI1.pdf.) The effective date is October 1, 2022. A full summary of the new law and related regulations will be included in the next publication of this Guide.

Under Act 2021-296, the Division of Purchasing in the Department of Finance will be abolished and replaced with the Office of the Chief Procurement Officer within the Department of Finance. The act repeals the following articles of chapter 16 of title 41, Code of Alabama 1975: article 2 (commencing with section 41-16-20), article 3A (commencing with section 41-16-70), and Division 1 (commencing with section 41-4-110) of article 5 of chapter 4 of title 41. These will be replaced by new article 5 (commencing with section 41-4-110) that will create the Office of the Chief Procurement Officer in the Department of Finance and the position of chief procurement officer; to authorize the chief procurement officer to make or supervise the purchase of supplies or services by the state; and to provide for the appointment, qualifications, duties, and authority of the chief procurement officer.

B. Other Applicable Statutes

Alabama's ethics rules, governing, inter alia, lobbying activities, are codified in title 36 of the Code of Alabama, chapter 25.

1. Information compiled from the Code of Alabama (1975) and the State of Alabama Department of Examiners of Public Accounts, Alabama Competitive Bid and Public Works Law Manual (2021), https://examiners.alabama.gov/PDF/publications/Al_Bid_Law_2021.pdf.

II. Regulations

The Alabama Department of Finance, Purchasing Division's rules related to vendors and competitive bidding are contained in Alabama Administrative Code Regulations 355-4-1-.01 *et seq.* and 355-5-1-.01 *et seq.* This is the state agency generally responsible for any purchases made by or on behalf of the state or a state agency. The Purchasing Division posts relevant statutes, regulations, and attorney general opinions on its website at http://www.purchasing.alabama.gov.

The rules that apply to public construction and improvement projects assigned to the Alabama Building Commission by state law for its supervision and administration are contained in Alabama Administrative Code Regulation 170-X-5-.01 *et seq.*

III. Source Selection

The Alabama Competitive Bid Law generally governs the bid process for goods and services and requires that contracts awarded through competitive bidding be awarded to the lowest responsible bidder. (See Alabama Code §§ 41-16-20 and 41-16-50.) The source selection techniques used generally follow those of the federal system. The procurement can be accomplished either through an invitation to bid (ITB), a request for proposals (RFP), or, in limited circumstances, sole source. The threshold for competitive bid is $15,000 for state contracts and $15,000 for certain state and local agencies. (*Id.*)

The Alabama Competitive Bid Law does make a concession for awarding contracts for goods or services to one other than the lowest bidder where the lowest bidder is a foreign entity and another bidder with certain characteristics (e.g., located in local preference zone, minority-owned enterprise, woman-owned enterprise, etc.) submits a bid that is no more than 10 percent greater than the bid of the foreign entity. (See Alabama Code § 41-16-50.)

There are exceptions to the competitive bidding requirement, which are listed in Alabama Code sections 41-16-21, 41-16-22, and 41-16-23 as well as section 41-16-51. These include certain departments or agencies whose principal business is honorariums from competitive bid laws, federal government purchases, and exemption from public advertisement in cases of emergencies affecting public health and safety.

The Public Works Law governs the bid process for contracts covering construction, repair, renovation, or maintenance of public buildings, structures, sewers, roads, bridges, and so on, and requires that projects in excess of $50,000 be awarded by sealed bid. There is a sole source exception and an exception for Department of Transportation contracts of less than $250,000 that follow certain prescribed notice requirements. (See Alabama Code §§ 39-2-2(f) and 39-2-2(j), respectively.) Public works contracts must be awarded to the lowest responsible and responsive bidder. (See Alabama Code § 39-2-6.) However, if the awarding authority finds all bids to be unreasonable or that it is not in the interest of the awarding authority to accept any of the bids, the awarding authority may direct that the work be done by force account. (*Id.*)

IV. Bid Protests and Contract Disputes

A. Bid Protests

The Alabama Code does not provide for a formal process for bid protests and contract disputes. There is, however, a protest process outlined in the Alabama Administrative

Code for the Division of Purchasing within the Department of Finance. (See Alabama Administrative Code r. 355-4-1-.04.) The process requires that any bidder adversely affected by an intent to award a contract let by competitive bid file with the director of purchasing a notice of protest within five calendar days after the notice of intent to award the contract. A formal written protest must then be filed within seven days, excluding Saturday, Sunday, and state holidays, after the notice of protest is filed. Within 30 calendar days of submission of the protest, the director of purchasing will issue a written decision. If an adverse decision is issued, the bidder may seek relief in accordance with Alabama Code section 41-16-31. This section provides for potential injunctive relief:

> Any taxpayer of the area within the jurisdiction of the awarding authority and any bona fide unsuccessful bidder on a particular contract shall be empowered to bring a civil action in the appropriate court to enjoin execution of any contract entered into in violation of the provisions of this article.

Alabama Code section 41-16-31.

However, according to the Alabama Supreme Court, section 41-16-31 does not confer upon an unsuccessful bidder a right to sue for monetary damages or recover bid preparation costs (see *Vinson Guard Service, Inc. v. Retirement System of Alabama*, 836 So. 2d 807, 810 (Ala. 2002)), rather the remedy is limited to enjoining the execution of the contract. (See *Urban Sanitation Corp. v. Pell City*, 662 F. Supp. 1041, 1044 (D. Ala. 1986) ("There is no indication in [§ 41-16-31], however, that an unsuccessful bidder has any right or expectancy to insist upon the award of a contract. To the contrary, the statute is carefully crafted to limit the remedy to 'enjoin[ing] execution of any contract entered into in violation of the provisions of this article.'").) Regardless, injunctive relief is rarely granted. (See *Spring Hill Lighting & Supply Co. v. Square D Co.*, 662 So. 2d 1141, 1147 (Ala. 1995) (reviewing several state and federal applications of Alabama Bid Law and determining that "[i]njunctive relief is seldom granted in actions alleging violations of the Competitive Bid Law").)[2]

B. Bid Protest Appeals

An unsuccessful bidder who seeks to enforce an injunction based upon Alabama Competitive Bid Law, but fails at the trial court level, may appeal to the court of

2. *See also id.* at 1147–48. *Compare* Crest Constr. Corp. v. Shelby County Bd. of Educ., 612 So. 2d 425 (Ala. 1992); Steeley v. Nolen, 578 So. 2d 1278 (Ala. 1991); Horne Wrecker Serv., Inc. v. City of Florence, 567 So. 2d 1285 (Ala. 1990); Advance Tank & Constr. Co. v. Arab Water Works, 910 F.2d 761 (11th Cir. 1990) (applying Alabama law); Hosp. Sys., Inc. v. Hill Rom, Inc., 545 So. 2d 1324 (Ala. 1989); McCord Contract Floors, Inc. v. City of Dothan, 492 So. 2d 996 (Ala. 1986); 1 F. Pate Contractors v. Mobile Airport Auth., 484 So. 2d 418 (Ala. 1986); Mobile Dodge, Inc. v. Mobile Cnty., 442 So. 2d 56 (Ala. 1983); Int'l Telecomm. Sys. v. State, 359 So. 2d 364 (Ala. 1978); White v. McDonald Ford Tractor Co., 248 So. 2d 121 (Ala. 1971); Townsend v. McCall, 80 So. 2d 262 (Ala. 1955); Mitchell v. Walden Motor Co., 177 So. 151 (Ala. 1937); and Carson Cadillac Corp. v. City of Birmingham, 167 So. 794 (Ala. 1936), all denying injunctive relief, *with* Kennedy v. City of Prichard, 484 So. 2d 432 (Ala. 1986), and Arrington v. Associated Gen. Contractors of Am., 403 So. 2d 893 (Ala. 1981), *cert. denied*, 455 U.S. 913 (1982), both granting injunctive relief. While it is appropriate to create a restrictive standard for interfering with the normal progress of government works, the statements in the cases discussed above indicating that the injunctive remedy is the only remedy for violation of the Competitive Bid Law were not intended to create a license for persons to commit fraud and other intentional torts.

appeals only if he or she has also requested a stay of the judgment. Otherwise, if the contract was awarded and performance is begun under the contract, the appeal will be deemed moot. (See *Masonry Arts, Inc. v. Mobile County Commission*, 628 So. 2d 334 (Ala. 1993).)

C. Contract Disputes

Because the Alabama Code does not provide a formal process for bid protests or contract disputes, the procedures described above are the only procedures available to dispute a contract award. (See Alabama Code § 41-16-31 (providing for limited injunctive relief).)

D. Suspension and Debarment

Neither the Alabama Code nor Alabama Administrative Code contains procedures or processes for debarment or suspension. However, there are various provisions within the Alabama Administrative Code that prohibit awarding contracts or entering agreements with debarred and/or suspended contractors. These provisions generally rely on the federal list of debarred contractors or individual actions of state and local governmental bodies. (See, e.g., Alabama Administrative Code rr. 305-0-2-.01 and 335-15-7-.30.)

V. Administrative and Judicial Review

A. Administrative Review

Generally, aggrieved parties must seek administrative review from the contracting agency and exhaust all available administrative remedies before seeking judicial review.[3]

B. Judicial Review

In Alabama, courts have generally granted deferential review of the agency's decision-making process. For example, the Alabama Supreme Court stated:

> We think that *State authorities should have discretion in determining who the lowest responsible bidder is*. This discretion should not be interfered with by any court unless it is exercised arbitrarily or capriciously, or unless it is based upon a misconception of the law or upon ignorance through lack of inquiry or in violation of law or is the result of improper influence. . . .
>
> It is fair to say that the legislative intent in passing the Competitive Bid Law was to get the best quality equipment at the lowest possible price, and the executive authorities should carry out this intent of the legislature. *These officials must have discretion, not an unbridled discretion, but one exercised within the bounds we have tried to delineate in this opinion*. The single most important requirement of the Competitive Bid Law is the good faith of the officials

3. Ala. Code § 41-22-20 ("A person who has exhausted all administrative remedies available within the agency, other than rehearing, and who is aggrieved by a final decision in a contested case is entitled to judicial review under this chapter. A preliminary, procedural, or intermediate agency action or ruling is immediately reviewable if review of the final agency decision would not provide an adequate remedy.").

> charged in executing the requirements of the law. A bad motive, fraud or a gross abuse of discretion will vitiate an award whether made with specifications which are quite general or very precise.

White v. McDonald Ford Tractor Co., 248 So. 2d 121, 129 (Ala. 1971) (emphasis added).

Historically, the Alabama Supreme Court has given the awarding agencies great discretion in contract disputes. In *Vinson Guard Service, Inc. v. Retirement System of Alabama*, 836 So. 2d 807, 811–12 (Ala. 2002), the Alabama Supreme Court held that a trial court did not err in refusing to compel a state agency to award a contract for security services to a firm that entered a bid at the state agency's invitation when the agency's invitation to bid contained errors and the state agency sought to rebid the contract. The court also held that the firm that submitted the bid was not entitled to an injunction prohibiting the state agency from rebidding the contract. (*Id.*)

VI. Extent of State's Adoption or Adaptation of ABA Model Procurement Code

Act 2021-296, referenced above, is based upon portions of the American Bar Association's Model Procurement Act.

VII. Cooperative Purchasing

A. Authority

Alabama law authorizes a cooperative purchasing model, wherein state agencies and county and city boards of education may "piggyback" on contracts without engaging in a separate bidding process, provided that certain conditions are met. (See Alabama Code §§ 41-16-51 and 16-13B-2.) Both sections 41-16-51 and 16-13B-2 of the Alabama Code exempt the purchase of goods made as a part of the purchasing cooperative sponsored by the National Association of Counties, its successor organization, or any other competitive bid nationwide cooperative purchasing program.

B. Requirements

State agencies may "piggyback" on purchases of goods other than voice or data wireless communication services as a part of any purchasing cooperative sponsored by the National Association of Counties, provided the following conditions are met:

- The goods or services being purchased are available as a result of a competitive bid process conducted by a governmental entity and approved by the Alabama Department of Examiners of Public Accounts for each bid
- The goods or services are either not at the time available to counties on the state purchasing program or are available at a price equal to or less than that on the state purchasing program
- The purchase is made through a participating Alabama vendor holding an Alabama business license if such a vendor exists
- The entity purchasing goods or services under this provision has been notified by the Department of Examiners of Public Accounts that the competitive bid process utilized by the cooperative program offering the goods complies with the above requirements

See Alabama Code section 41-16-51. Materially similar conditions also apply to cooperative purchases made by county and city boards of education. See Alabama Code section 16-13B-2.[4]

4. The sole distinction between the requirements in Alabama Code section 41-16-51 and section 16-13B-2 is that the former requires notification of compliance from the Department of Examiners of Public Accounts, while the latter does not.

Alaska Procurement Rules and Regulations

Prepared by Connor Smith
Stoel Rives LLP
Email: connor.smith@stoel.com

I. Statutory Reference

A. Procurement/Purchasing Statutes

The State of Alaska purchasing and procurement is generally managed by the Alaska Department of Administration, Division of Administrative Services (DAS). Information about the Department of Administration can be accessed through the website at http://www.doa.alaska.gov/das/. In addition, the DAS provides a Procurement Section within an Alaska Administrative Manual (AAM) that gives general guidance as to the state's procurement system and procedures, available at https://doa.alaska.gov/dof/manuals/aam/index.html?msclkid=a255b1f2d0c011ecad0e556cd2098576. Purchasing is governed by the Alaska State Procurement Code, title 36, chapter 30, Alaska Statutes sections 36.30.005 *et seq*.

A table of contents for the State Procurement Code is below:

Chapter 30. State Procurement Code

Article 8. Legal and Contractual Remedies
Sections 36.30.550–.699

Article 9. Intergovernmental Relations
Sections 36.30.700–.790

Article 10. General Provisions
Sections 36.30.850–.995

B. Other Applicable Statutes

1. Alaska Online Public Notice System (Alaska Statutes § 44.62.175)
2. Executive Branch Ethics Act (Alaska Statutes § 39.52.010 *et seq.*)
3. Fiscal Procedures Act, title 37, chapter 5, Payment for State Purchases (Alaska Statutes § 37.05.285)
4. Administrative Procedure Act (Alaska Statutes § 44.62 *et seq.*)

II. Regulations

The State of Alaska purchasing regulations are promulgated pursuant to the statutory authority of the Administrative Procedure Act (Alaska Statutes § 44.62) and are found in the Alaska Administrative Code (AAC), title 2, chapter 12.

The regulations are available online at http://www.legis.state.ak.us/basis/aac.asp.

A table of contents for the procurement regulations follows below:

Title 2 Administration, Chapter 12 Procurement

Source Selection (AAC tit. 2, §§ 12.010–.060)

Specifications (AAC tit. 2, §§ 12.070–.110)

Competitive Sealed Bidding; Multistep Bidding (AAC tit. 2, §§ 12.120–.210)

Competitive Sealed Proposals (AAC tit. 2, §§ 12.215–.315)

Competitive Sealed Proposals for Architect, Engineer, or Land Surveying Services (AAC tit. 2, §§ 12.320–.390)

Small Purchases (AAC tit. 2, § 12.400)

Single Source Procurement (AAC tit. 2, §§ 12.410–.420)

Limited Competition Procurements (AAC tit. 2, § 12.430)

Emergency Procurements (AAC tit. 2, §§ 12.440–.460)

Contract Formation and Modification (AAC tit. 2, §§ 12.470–.570)

Innovative Procurement (AAC tit. 2, §§ 12.575–.577)

Supply Management (AAC tit. 2, §§ 12.580–.610)

Legal and Contractual Remedies (AAC tit. 2, §§ 12.615–.695)

Intergovernmental Relations (AAC tit. 2, §§ 12.700–.710)

Miscellaneous Provisions (AAC tit. 2, §§ 12.720–.920)

Design-Build Construction Contracts (AAC tit. 2, §§ 12.931–.949)

Construction Arbitration Procedures (AAC tit. 2, §§ 12.950–.989)

General Provisions (AAC tit. 2, § 12.990)

III. Source Selection

The general methods of procurement include:

A. Small Procurements (Alaska Statutes § 36.30.320)

A procurement for supplies, services, or professional services that does not exceed an aggregate dollar amount of $100,000, construction that does not exceed an aggregate dollar amount of $200,000, or lease of space that does not exceed 7,000 square feet may be made in accordance with the regulations for small procurements. Small procurements need not be made through competitive sealed bidding or competitive sealed proposals, but shall be made with competition that is practicable under the circumstances. Procurement requirements may not be artificially divided or fragmented so as to constitute a purchase under this section or to circumvent the source selection procedures required by Alaska Statutes sections 36.30.100–.270. The procurement officer shall give adequate public notice of intent to make a procurement under this section in accordance with regulations. *Note*: Although this requirement is in the statute, there is no corresponding regulation requiring public notice of "intent" to make a small procurement.

Under the threshold for small procurements there are several methods for procurement of supplies, services, and professional services according to varying dollar amounts:

1. Written or Oral Quotations for Procurements between $10,000 and $50,000

Agencies may solicit written or oral quotes or informal proposals from at least three firms when soliciting procurements of supplies, services, professional services, or construction estimated to cost between $10,000 and $50,000, and concession contracts estimated to have gross receipts between $10,000 and $50,000. The solicitation may be made verbally or in writing and shall include the specifications, award criteria, and date and time responses are due.[1]

2. Written Quotations for Procurements between $50,000 and $100,000

Agencies must seek written quotations from at least three firms using a request for quotations form when making small procurements estimated to exceed $50,000, but not more than $100,000, for supplies, services, professional services, concession contracts estimated to have gross receipts between $50,000 and $100,000, and construction contracts between $50,000 and $200,000. The solicitation shall be made in writing and include the specifications, award criteria, and date and time responses are due.[2]

3. Award Notification

A written notice of award is required for small procurements above $50,000. The notice must be provided to each firm or person providing a quotation or informal proposal, describe protest rights under AAC title 2, section 12.695, and the time limitations within which a protest must be received by the purchasing agency.[3]

---

1. Alaska Admin. Code tit. 2, § 12.400(c) (2014).
2. *Id.* § 12.400(d); AAM 81.240.
3. AAM 81.200.

B. Invitation to Bid (Alaska Statutes § 36.30.110)

When competitive sealed bidding is used, the procurement officer shall issue an invitation to bid. It must include a time, place, and date by which the bid must be received, instructions and information to bidders concerning the bid submission requirements (AAC tit. 2, § 12.120(a)(1)), address of the office to which bids are to be delivered (AAC tit. 2, § 12.120(a)(1)), purchase description, a description of all contractual terms and conditions applicable to the procurement, maximum time for bid acceptance by the state, and other specific information (AAC tit. 2, § 12.120(a)(1)), evaluation factors (AAC tit. 2, § 12.120(a)(2)), delivery or performance schedule (AAC tit. 2, § 12.120(a)(2)), and inspection and acceptance requirements that are not included in the purchase or project description (AAC tit. 2, § 12.120(a)(2)).

The bidder must have a valid Alaska business license at the time designated in the invitation to bid for bid opening.

Pursuant to Alaska Statutes section 36.30.130, the procurement officer shall give adequate public notice of the invitation to bid at least 21 days before the date for the opening of bids. If the procurement officer determines *in writing* that a shorter notice period is advantageous for a particular bid and adequate competition is anticipated, the period may be shortened. Notice shall be posted on the Alaska Online Public Notice System.[4]

When practicable, notice may include publication in a newspaper calculated to reach prospective bidders or notice posted in public places within the area where the work is to be performed or the material furnished.

Failure to comply with the notice requirements of this section does not invalidate a bid or the award of a contract. If the state fails to substantially comply with the requirements of a notice of invitation to bid, the state is liable for damages caused by that failure.

C. Request for Proposals

When the procurement officer determines in writing, with particularity, that the use of the competitive sealed proposals is more advantageous to the state than competitive sealed bidding, a contract may be entered into by competitive sealed proposals. In addition, an agency contract shall be awarded by competitive sealed proposals if it is not awarded by competitive sealed bidding.[5]

A request for competitive sealed proposals under Alaska Statutes section 36.30.210(a) must contain the date, time, and place for delivering proposals; a specific description of the supplies, construction, services, or professional services to be provided under the contract; and the terms under which the supplies, construction, services, or professional services are to be provided.

A request for proposals under Alaska Statutes section 36.30.210(c) must contain that information necessary for an offeror to submit a proposal or contain references to any information that cannot reasonably be included with the request. The request must provide a description of the factors that will be considered by the procurement officer when evaluating the proposals received, including the relative importance of price and other evaluation factors.

4. ALASKA STAT. § 44.62.175 (2018).
5. *Id.* § 36.30.200.

Notice of a request for proposals under Alaska Statutes section 36.30.210(d) shall be given in accordance with procedures under section 36.30.130. The procurement officer may use additional means considered appropriate to notify prospective offerors of the intent to enter into a contract through competitive sealed proposals.

The offeror must have a valid Alaska business license at the time designated, in the request for proposals, for opening of the proposals.[6]

1. Discussion with Responsible Offerors and Revisions to Proposals

Discussions may be conducted with responsible offerors who submit proposals determined to be reasonably susceptible of being selected for award for the purpose of clarification to assure full understanding of, and responsiveness to, the solicitation requirements. Offerors reasonably susceptible of being selected for award shall be accorded fair and equal treatment with respect to any opportunity for discussion and revision of proposals, and revisions may be permitted after submissions and before the award of the contract for the purpose of obtaining best and final offers. In conducting discussions, the procurement officer may not disclose information derived from proposals submitted by competing offerors.[7]

D. Limited Competition Procurements (Alaska Statutes § 36.30.305)

A construction contract under $100,000, or a contract for supplies, services, or professional services, may be awarded without competitive sealed bidding or competitive sealed proposals. A contract may be awarded through limited competition procurement only when the chief procurement officer determines *in writing* that a situation exists that makes competitive sealed bidding or competitive sealed proposals impractical or contrary to the public interest, except that the attorney general, the public defender, or the director of the office of public advocacy as provided in Alaska Statutes section 36.30.015(k) may make the determination for services of legal counsel, and the commissioner of transportation and public facilities may make the determination for construction contracts under $100,000 or procurements for the state equipment fleet.

Limited competition procurements shall be made with competition that is practicable under the circumstance. Except for procurements of supplies, services, professional services, or construction that does not exceed the amount for small procurements under Alaska Statutes section 36.30.320(a), as applicable, the authority to make a determination required by this section may not be delegated. The using agency shall submit written evidence to support a determination under this section. Single source procurements may not be made under this section.

E. Single Source Procurements (Alaska Statutes § 36.30.300)

A contract may be awarded for supplies, services, professional services, or construction without competitive sealed bidding, competitive sealed proposals, or other competition in accordance with regulations only when the chief procurement officer or, for construction contracts or procurements for the state equipment fleet, the commissioner of transportation and public facilities determines in writing that (1) it is not practicable to award a contract by competitive sealed bidding under Alaska Statutes

6. *Id.* § 36.30.210(e).
7. *Id.* § 36.30.240.

section 36.30.100, competitive sealed proposals under section 36.30.200, or limited competition under section 36.30.305; and (2) award of the contract is in the state's best interest.

The using agency shall submit written evidence to support a request for a single source procurement. The commissioner of administration or the commissioner of transportation and public facilities, as appropriate, may also require the submission of cost or pricing data in connection with an award under this section.

To the extent practicable, the procurement officer shall negotiate with the single source to obtain contract terms advantageous to the state. Procurement requirements may not be aggregated or structured so as to constitute a purchase or to circumvent the source selection procedures required by Alaska Statutes sections 36.30.100–.270.

F. Construction Manager General Contractor Contract (Alaska Statutes § 36.30.309)

The Department of Transportation and Public Facilities (DOT), only, may award by competitive sealed proposals a construction manager general contractor contract in which DOT awards a two-phase contract for a construction manager to be responsible for providing preconstruction services during the design phase of the project and, if an agreed-on price for constructing the project is reached, general contractor services during the construction phase. Under Alaska Statutes section 36.30.990(28), "preconstruction services" are "information, research, advice, and related tasks regarding the impacts of design on the physical construction of a project," but not "architectural, engineering, or land surveying services." Alaska Statutes section 36.30.309(a) enables DOT to award the contractor providing "preconstruction services" under the contract with the second phase of the contract to provide construction services without further competitive sealed bidding or competitive sealed proposal process. Once awarded a construction manager general contractor contract, the contractor may negotiate with DOT to provide construction services for the applicable project. If the contractor and DOT reach an agreed-on price for the construction services under the second phase of the contract, DOT shall award the contractor phase two of the contract. If agreement is not reached, DOT may seek an alternative contractor. In doing so, DOT may prohibit the contractor providing "preconstruction services" from participating in the subsequent procurement process.

G. Emergency Procurements (Alaska Statutes § 36.30.310)

An emergency procurement need not be made through competitive sealed bidding or competitive sealed proposals but shall be made with competition that is practicable under the circumstances. Procurements may be made under emergency conditions as defined in regulations adopted by the commissioner when there exists a threat to public health, welfare, or safety, when a situation exists that makes a procurement through competitive sealed bidding or competitive sealed proposals impracticable or contrary to the public interest, or to protect public or private property. Emergency procurement may be limited to supplies, services, professional services, or construction necessary to meet the emergency under AAC title 2, section 12.450.

Under AAC title 2, section 12.440, emergency conditions include fire, flood, epidemic, riot, environmental accident, or similar compelling reason; equipment failure, if the need for timely repair is essential; a situation in which procurement through competitive sealed bidding or competitive sealed proposals is impracticable or contrary to the public interest; or a need to protect public or private property.

A written determination by the chief procurement officer of the basis for the emergency and for the selection of the particular contractor shall be included in the contract file. The written determination must include findings of fact that support the determination. Except where there is insufficient time for the chief procurement officer to make the written determination required by this section, the chief procurement officer may not delegate the authority to make the determination.

IV. Bid Protests and Contract Disputes

A. Bid Protests

1. Filing of a Protest (Alaska Statutes § 36.30.560)

An interested party may protest the award of a contract, the proposed award of a contract, or a solicitation for supplies, services, professional services, or construction by an agency. The protest shall be filed with the procurement officer of the contracting agency *in writing* and include the following information: (1) the name, address, and telephone number of the protester; (2) the signature of the protester or the protester's representative; (3) identification of the contracting agency and the solicitation or contract at issue; (4) a detailed statement of the legal and factual grounds of the protest, including copies of relevant documents; and (5) the form of relief requested.

2. Time for Filing a Protest (Alaska Statutes § 36.30.565)

A protest based on alleged improprieties or ambiguities in a solicitation must be filed at least ten days before the due date of the bid or proposal, unless a later protest due date is specifically allowed in the solicitation.

The protest of an invitation to bid or a request for proposals in which a pre-bid or pre-proposal conference is held within 12 days of the due date must be filed before the due date of the bid or proposal if the protest is based on alleged improprieties or ambiguities in the solicitation.

A protest based upon alleged improprieties in an award of a contract or a proposed award of a contract must be filed within ten days after a notice of intent to award the contract is issued by the procurement officer.

If the protester shows good cause, the procurement officer of the contracting agency may consider a filed protest that is not timely.

If a solicitation is made with a shortened public notice period and the protest is based on alleged improprieties or ambiguities in the solicitation, the protest must be filed before the due date of the bid or proposal.

3. Notice of a Protest (Alaska Statutes § 36.30.570)

The procurement officer shall immediately give notice of a protest filed under Alaska Statutes section 36.30.565 to the contractor if a contract has been awarded or, if no award has been made, to all interested parties.

4. Stay of Award (Alaska Statutes § 36.30.575)

If a protest is filed, the award may be made unless the procurement officer of the contracting agency determines *in writing* that a reasonable probability exists that the protest will be sustained; or a stay of the award is not contrary to the best interests of the state.

5. Decision by the Procurement Officer (Alaska Statutes § 36.30.580)

The procurement officer of the contracting agency shall issue a written decision containing the basis of the decision within 15 days after a protest has been filed. A copy of the decision shall be furnished to the protester by certified mail or other method that provides evidence of receipt. If a decision is not made by the date it is due, the protester may proceed as if the procurement officer had issued a decision adverse to the protester.

The time for decision may be extended up to 30 days for good cause by the commissioner of administration, or, for protests involving construction or procurements for the state equipment fleet, by the commissioner of transportation and public facilities. If an extension is granted, the procurement officer shall notify the protester in writing of the date that the decision is due.

6. Protest Remedies (Alaska Statutes § 36.30.585)

If the procurement officer sustains a protest in whole or in part, the procurement officer shall implement an appropriate remedy. In determining an appropriate remedy, the procurement officer shall consider (1) the circumstances surrounding the solicitation or procurement including the seriousness of the procurement deficiencies; (2) the degree of prejudice to other interested parties or to (3) the integrity of the procurement system; (4) the good faith of the parties; (5) the extent the procurement has been accomplished; (6) the costs to the agency and other impacts on the agency of a proposed remedy; and (7) the urgency of the procurement to the welfare of the state.

If a protest is sustained in whole or in part, the protester's damages are limited to reasonable bid or proposal preparation costs.

B. Bid Protest Appeal (Alaska Statutes § 36.30.590)

An appeal from a decision of a procurement officer on a protest may be filed by the protester with the commissioner of administration. An appeal shall be filed within ten days after the decision is received by the protester. The protester shall file a copy of the appeal with the procurement officer. An appeal must contain the information required under Alaska Statutes section 36.30.560. In addition, the appeal must include a copy of the decision being appealed and the identification of the factual or legal errors in the decision that form the basis for the appeal.

Note: An appeal from a decision of a procurement officer on a protest involving construction or procurements for the state equipment fleet may be filed with the commissioner of transportation and public facilities.

1. Notice and Copy of Protest Appeal (Alaska Statutes § 36.30.595)

The procurement officer shall immediately give notice of an appeal filed under Alaska Statutes section 36.30.590 to the contractor if a contract has been awarded, or, if no award has been made, to all interested parties. The commissioner shall, on request, furnish a copy of the appeal to all persons notified of the protest appeal. Confidential material shall be deleted from the copy.

2. Stay of Award during Protest Appeal (Alaska Statutes § 36.30.600)

If a protest appeal is filed before a contract is awarded and the award was stayed under Alaska Statutes section 36.30.575, the filing of the appeal automatically continues the stay until the commissioner of administration or the commissioner of transportation and public facilities, as appropriate, makes a written determination that the award of the contract without further delay is necessary to protect substantial interests of the state.

C. Contract Disputes

1. Contract Claims (Alaska Statutes § 36.30.620)

A contractor shall file a claim concerning a contract awarded with the procurement officer. A claim must be filed within 90 days after the contractor becomes aware of the basis of the claim, or should have known the basis of the claim, whichever is earlier. The contractor shall certify that (1) the claim is made in good faith; (2) the supporting data is accurate and complete to the best of the contractor's knowledge and belief; and (3) the amount requested accurately reflects the contract adjustment for which the contractor believes the state is liable. *Note*: A lease rate adjustment called for in the lease must be filed prior to the expiration date of the lease.

a. Procedure

If a claim asserted concerning a contract awarded cannot be resolved by agreement, the procurement officer shall, after receiving a written request by the contractor for a decision, issue a written decision. The procurement officer shall make the decision not more than 90 days after receipt of all necessary information from the contractor. If the contractor fails to furnish necessary information requested by the procurement officer, the procurement officer shall proceed to decide the claim and may, in the procurement officer's discretion, deny all or part of the claim because of the failure to furnish necessary information. During an appeal the contractor may not rely on or introduce information that the contractor has failed to furnish to the procurement officer in support of the claim. Before issuing the decision, the procurement officer shall review the facts relating to the claim and obtain necessary assistance from legal, fiscal, and other advisors. If the procurement officer does not issue a written decision by the date it is due, the contractor may proceed as if the procurement officer had issued a decision adverse to the contractor.

b. Contents of Decision

The procurement officer shall furnish a copy of a contract claim decision to the contractor by certified mail or other method that provides evidence of receipt. The decision must include (1) a description of the claim; (2) a reference to the pertinent contract provisions; (3) a statement of the agreed upon and disputed facts; (4) findings of fact about the claim; (5) a determination of any amount payable; (6) a statement of reasons supporting the decision; and (7) a statement substantially as follows: "This is the final decision of the procurement officer. This decision may be appealed to the commissioner of (administration/transportation and public facilities). If you appeal, you must file a written notice of appeal with the commissioner within 14 days after you receive this decision."

c. Interest on Certain Claims

The amount on a contract claim that is ultimately due accrues interest from the date that a claim that meets all the requirements is filed, until the final decision.[8]

---

8. *Id.* § 36.30.623.

d. Time Extensions for Decisions

First Time Extension: Upon written request of the procurement officer, the time for issuing the decision may be extended up to 60 additional days by the commissioner if the claim concerns an amount in excess of $50,000.

Second Time Extension: Upon the written request of the procurement officer showing that good cause exists for a second extension, the commissioner may extend the time for issuing a decision up to 90 additional days after the first extension. The contractor shall be provided with an opportunity to oppose or otherwise respond to the request for a second extension. If a second extension is granted, the commissioner shall notify the contractor and the procurement officer in writing that the time for the issuance of a decision has been extended and give the date by which a decision shall be issued.

2. Contract Claims Appeals (Alaska Statutes § 36.30.625)

An appeal from a decision of the procurement officer on a contract claim may be filed by the contractor with the commissioner of administration or, for a claim involving a construction contract or procurement for the state equipment fleet, the commissioner of transportation and public facilities. The appeal shall be filed within 14 days after the decision is received by the contractor. An appeal by a contractor of DOT may not raise any new factual issues or theories of recovery that were not presented to and decided by the procurement officer in the decision under Alaska Statutes section 36.30.620(b), except that a contractor may increase the contractor's calculation of damages if the increase arises out of the same operative facts on which the original claim was based. The contractor shall file a copy of the appeal with the procurement officer. An appeal must contain a copy of the decision being appealed and identification of the factual or legal errors in the decision that form the basis for the appeal.

DOT, or a contracting agency to which the responsibility for handling the claim is delegated by DOT under Alaska Statutes section 36.30.632, shall handle the appeal of a claim under this section expeditiously.

a. Construction Contract Claim Appeals (Alaska Statutes § 36.30.627)

An appeal from a decision of the procurement officer of a claim involving a construction contract shall be resolved, if not by a hearing, by binding and final arbitration under Alaska Statutes sections 09.43.010–.180 if the claim is (1) less than $250,000 and the contractor requests arbitration of the claim; or (2) $250,000 or more and both the agency and the contractor agree to arbitration of the claim.

D. Suspension and Debarment

1. Authority (Alaska Statutes § 36.30.635)

The commissioner of administration may, after consultation with the using agency and the attorney general, suspend or debar a person for cause from consideration for award of contracts.

2. Notice (Alaska Statutes § 36.30.645)

The commissioner of administration shall issue a written decision to debar or suspend. The decision must (1) state the reasons for the action taken; and (2) inform the debarred person of rights to judicial appeal or inform the suspended person of rights to administrative and judicial appeal.

3. Hearing (Alaska Statutes § 36.30.650)

A person suspended under Alaska Statutes section 36.30.635 is entitled to a hearing conducted according to section 36.30.670 if the suspended party files a written request for a hearing with the commissioner of administration within seven days after receipt of the notice of suspension. A hearing may not be delayed longer than six months after notice of the suspension.

4. Period of Effect (Alaska Statutes § 36.30.635)

The suspension may not be for a period exceeding three months. The debarment may not be for a period exceeding three years.

V. Administrative and Judicial Review

A. Administrative Review

A hearing on a protest appeal shall be conducted in accordance with Alaska Statutes section 36.30.670. A decision by the commissioner of administration or the commissioner of transportation and public facilities after a hearing is final. A decision shall be sent within 20 days after the hearing to all parties by personal service or certified mail, except that a decision by the commissioner of transportation and public facilities involving procurement of construction shall be sent to all parties by personal service or certified mail within 45 days after receipt by the commissioner of transportation and public facilities of the hearing officer's decision.

The provisions of the Administrative Procedure Act (Alaska Statutes § 44.62 *et seq.*) do not apply to a hearing conducted under the State Procurement Code.[9]

B. Judicial Review

1. Judicial Appeal (Alaska Statutes § 36.30.685)

A final decision of the commissioner of administration or the commissioner of transportation and public facilities may be appealed to the superior court.

2. Judicial Decisions

In a lease between the State of Alaska and a private building owner, the procurement code covers a rent dispute over an ongoing lease, and the landlord contractor must exhaust its administrative remedies before filing suit in court.[10]

Public entities are required to reject bids that vary materially from the specifications set forth in published requests for proposals. A variance is material if it gives one bidder a substantial advantage over other bidders, which in turn restricts or stifles competition.[11]

If an administrative agency's findings are supported by substantial evidence, the reviewing court will not choose between competing inferences or independently evaluate the strength of the evidence.[12]

---

9. *Id.* § 36.30.670(a).

10. Bachner Co. Inc. v. State, 387 P.3d 16, 18 (Alaska 2016).

11. Gunderson v. Univ. of Alaska, 922 P.2d 229, 235 (Alaska 1996) (internal citations omitted).

12. Handley v. State, Dep't of Revenue, 838 P.2d 1231, 1233 (Alaska 1992).

VI. Extent of State's Adoption or Adaptation of ABA Model Procurement Code

The Alaska State Procurement Code, originally adopted in 1988, is closely modeled after the American Bar Association's (ABA's) initial version of the Model Procurement Code for State and Local Governments.

VII. Cooperative Purchasing

A. Authority (Alaska Statutes § 36.30.700)

Any local or state public procurement unit may participate in, sponsor, conduct, or administer a cooperative purchasing agreement for the procurement of supplies, services, professional services, or construction, including joint or multi-party contracts between public procurement units and open-ended state public procurement unit contracts that are made available to local public procurement units.

B. Requirements

Under Alaska Statutes section 36.30.700, a public procurement unit's participation in, sponsorship of, or administration of a cooperative purchasing agreement must be in accordance with an agreement entered into between the participants in the cooperative. Participants in a cooperative purchasing agreement may include a municipality, another subdivision of the state, another entity that expends public funds for procurement, any nonprofit corporation operating a charitable hospital, and any buying organization not located in the state that if located in the state would qualify under section 36.30.790(4) as a public procurement unit. Under Alaska Statutes section 36.30.750(a), when claims arise under a cooperative purchasing agreement between an administering public procurement unit and its bidders, offerors, or contractors, they are to be resolved under the existing bid protest and contract dispute procedures codified at Alaska Statutes sections 36.30.560–.699.

Arizona Procurement Rules and Regulations

Prepared by James J. Sienicki and Emily Parker[1]
Snell & Wilmer, L.L.P.
Email: jsienicki@swlaw.com and eparker@swlaw.com
and
Josh Grabel
Dickinson Wright PLLC
Email: jgrabel@dickinsonwright.com

I. Statutory Reference

A. Procurement/Purchasing Statutes

In 1984, the Arizona Legislature adopted the Arizona Administrative Procedure Act (AAPA), which is largely based on the model state procurement code. (See Arizona Revised Statutes tit. 41, State Government.). The majority of state agencies are governed by the AAPA, and administrative rules and regulations set forth in the Arizona Administrative Code (AAC), specifically AAC title 2, Administration, and chapter 7, Department of Administration, Finance Division—Purchasing Office.

Although the majority of state procurements are governed by the AAPA, a number of state agencies have their own statutory schemes and/or specifications that control procurements. For instance, the Arizona Department of Transportation (ADOT) has a separate set of statutes, Arizona Revised Statutes title 28, that govern its procurements. ADOT has also adopted regulations, known as ADOT Specifications, that further govern its procurements. They are available online at https://www.azleg.gov/arsDetail/?title=28.

Similarly, a few other state agencies (including but not limited to the Board of Regents, State Board of Education, and Judicial Branch) are also exempt from title 41 procurement laws and are governed by their own rules and regulations. (See Arizona Revised Statutes § 41-2501.) Those procurement policies can be found as follows:

1. The authors would like to thank Byron Sarhangian and Nicole Sornsin for their contributions in helping to write the previous editions of this chapter. They would also like to thank Juan Zazueta, law clerk, for his assistance in working on this edition.

- The Board of Regents: Policy Manual, chapter 3, Business and Finance, section H, University Procurement Code (3-801) (https://www.azregents.edu/policy-manual)
- The State Board of Education: AAC title 7, Education, chapter 2, State Board of Education, article 10, School District Procurement (https://apps.azsos.gov/public_services/CodeTOC.htm#ID7)
- The Judicial Branch: Procurement Rules for the Judicial Branch (https://www.azcourts.gov/adminservices/Procurement)

With regard to local government procurements for construction projects, cities, towns, counties, or quasi-governmental agencies are generally controlled by two sources: (1) Arizona Revised Statutes title 34 (Public Buildings and Improvements), and (2) codes or ordinances that are adopted by the individual governmental agencies. Non-construction procurements may also be impacted by other statutory schemes, including Arizona Revised Statutes titles 9 (Cities and Towns) and 11 (Counties), depending upon the procurement at issue. Thus, when considering any public procurement issue in Arizona, it is initially important to determine who is conducting the procurement to ensure that you contact the appropriate governmental entity to obtain the relevant procurement documents, and understand the relevant underlying statutory and/or regulatory scheme that governs the procurement. Failure to do so can be fatal to your objectives with respect to such procurement.

With regard to the majority of Arizona state public procurements, Arizona Revised Statutes title 41 dictates that the Arizona Department of Administration (ADOA) oversees all state procurements. The director of the ADOA is the primary procurement officer for the State of Arizona, is appointed by the governor, and is responsible for regulations related to the procurement process. The director is also responsible for delegating procurement authority to the proper state governmental agencies. Each agency within the state that does any procurement also has its own procurement department, and a chief procurement officer who oversees procurements for that particular agency.

With regard to compliance with the state's procurement code, the director has delegated adherence to the state procurement statutes to the state procurement administrator who is responsible for most procedural matters relating to state procurement.

State law requires that the Arizona State Procurement Office review their rules and regulations once every five years. The State Procurement Office uses an online procurement program, ProcureAZ, for revising their regulations. ProcureAZ can be accessed through the following link: https://spo.az.gov/contracts/upcoming-bids. The ProcureAZ program encompasses vendor selection, issuing solicitations, and contract management. The latest July 2015 revisions can be found at https://spo.az.gov/sites/default/files/documents/files/Arizona%20Procurement%20Code%20-%20July%202015.pdf.

Arizona Revised Statutes are organized into titles. Each title is categorized into chapters that are subcategorized into articles.

- Statutes pertaining to state procurement are found under title 41, State Government, chapter 23, Arizona Procurement Code.
- Statutes pertaining to local government agency procurement for public works are located in title 34, Public Buildings and Improvements.
- Statutes pertaining to ADOT are found under title 28, Transportation.

Arizona Revised Statutes can be found through the following link: https://www.azleg.gov/arstitle/.

B. Other Applicable Statutes

1. Lobbying Laws

The Arizona Constitution authorizes the legislature to create laws governing state lobbying. Arizona Revised Statutes title 41, State Government, chapter 7, Legislature, article 8.1, Registration and Regulation of Lobbyists, states that entities and their respective lobbyists involved in the act of lobbying must register with the Secretary of State "no later than 5:00pm on the second Monday in January of each even numbered year." Persons who contact a state officer or employee in connection with the procurement or attempted procurement of materials, services, or construction are exempt from registration regulations. All lobbying expenditures must be reported annually by both the entity and the lobbyist. Violations of lobbying regulations carry penalties of a Class 1 misdemeanor punishable by up to six months in jail and/or up to a $2,500 fine.

The Arizona Secretary of State governs lobbyists and publishes a handbook outlining the guidelines for lobbyists and containing registration forms and reporting samples. (See *Arizona Department of State, Arizona Lobbying Handbook* (2020), https://azsos.gov/sites/default/files/2020.02.04%20Lobbying%20Handbook.pdf.)

2. Ethics Laws

Statutes pertaining to ethical conduct for employees of public agencies are located in Arizona Revised Statutes title 38, which provides guidelines for various matters, including conflict of interest, confidentiality of privileged information, coercion, and self-profiting. (See *id.*) Pursuant to Arizona Revised Statutes section 38-503, any public officer or employee of a public agency who has, or whose relative has, a substantial interest in any decision of a public agency or any contract, sale, purchase or service to such public agency, shall make known that interest in the official records of such public agency and shall refrain from voting upon or otherwise participating in any manner as an officer or employee in such contract, sale, or purchase. If an agency enters into a contract that violates these guidelines, the contract is voidable and the involved parties may be subject to civil suit. (Arizona Revised Statutes § 38-506.)

3. Anti-Bribery Statutes

The Arizona Revised Statutes define bribery as the corrupt intent to offer benefit to a public servant with the intent to influence his or her opinion and/or action. The statutes also define the criminal punishment for bribery of a public servant as a Class 4 felony. (See Arizona Revised Statutes tit. 13, Criminal Code, ch. 26, Bribery.) Bribery is a cause for debarment or suspension from consideration for contract procurement. The duration of such disciplinary actions is not to exceed three years for debarment and six months for suspension.

C. Opinions of the Office of the Attorney General

The Office of Attorney General issues opinions that could impact Arizona procurement at https://www.azag.gov/opinions. Opinions issued since 1999 related to state and local procurement include:

- Opinion re: Arizona Board of Regents and Design-Build Construction
- Opinion re: Arizona Board of Regents and Design-Build Construction Projects (July 30, 1999) (https://www.azag.gov/opinions/i99-015-r99-010)

- Opinion re: School District Procurement of Architectural Services (Nov. 24, 1999) (https://www.azag.gov/opinions/i99-024-r99-053)
- Opinion re: Ban on Lobbyists Paying for Entertainment for State Officers or Employees (Dec. 22, 2000) (https://www.azag.gov/opinions/i00-031-r00-047)
- Opinion re: Restrictions on Qualifying Contributions by Lobbyists during Legislative Session (Jan. 10, 2002) (https://www.azag.gov/opinions/i02-001-r01-050)
- Opinion re: Use of Building Renewal Fund Balances for Preventative Maintenance (Dec. 19, 2003) (https://www.azag.gov/opinions/i03-011-r03-041)
- Opinion re: Inflation Adjustment of Square Footage Cost for New School Construction (Dec. 3, 2004) (https://www.azag.gov/opinions/i04-011-r04-029)
- Opinion re: County Use of Highway User Revenue Funds (May 23, 2005) (https://www.azag.gov/opinions/i05-003-r04-011)
- Opinion re: Statutes Requiring Paving or Stabilization of Parking Lots and Driveways as Air Pollution Control Measures (Dec. 12, 2008) (https://www.azag.gov/opinions/i08-011r08-017)
- Opinion re: Cancellation of Contracts Pursuant to Arizona Revised Statutes section 38-511 (Dec. 12, 2008) (https://www.azag.gov/opinions/i08-010-r08-026)
- Opinion re: Application of Arizona Merchandising Businesses for the Blind Act (Mar. 27, 2009) (https://www.azag.gov/opinions/i09-002-r08-048)
- Opinion re: Lobbying (Sept. 18, 2013) (https://www.azag.gov/opinions/i13-009-r13-014)
- Opinion re: Zoning Rights of Charter School Leasing Facilities (Feb. 23, 2015) (https://www.azag.gov/opinions/i15-001-r14-017)
- Opinion re: Recent Legislation concerning School Procurement Practices (Nov. 9, 2018) (https://www.azag.gov/opinions/i18-012-r18-017)
- Opinion re: Concerns Relating to COVID-19 and Procurement Procedures That Apply to School Districts under Arizona Law (Mar. 23, 2020) (https://www.azag.gov/opinions/i20-003)

II. Regulations

The AAC is organized into titles, chapters, and articles. State procurement-related regulations are found under title 2, Administration, chapter 7, Department of Administration, State Procurement Office. Regulations related to school district procurement are found under title 7, Education, chapter 2, State Board of Education. The AAC can be found through the following link: https://apps.azsos.gov/public_services/CodeTOC.htm#ID7.

State procurement regulations from the AAC are currently organized to follow the same order as related Arizona Revised Statutes. The following is a listing of articles that outline the structure of both state procurement statutes and administrative codes:

Article 1 General Provisions
Article 2 Procurement Organization
Article 3 Source Selection and Contract Formation
- Part A General Provisions
- Part B Competitive Sealed Bidding
- Part C Competitive Seed Proposals
- Part D Procurements Not Exceeding the Amount Prescribed in A.R.S. § 41-2535

III. Source Selection

Arizona state departments (i.e., ADOT, Board of Regents, and Department of Corrections) have their own procurement regulations that govern their procurements. This section explains specific statutes and rules related to such procurements and outlines generally how state agencies conduct their procurements in Arizona.

Arizona provides formal solicitations for state contracts when the anticipated value of the contract exceeds $100,000. (Arizona Revised Statutes § 41-2535.) Contracts valued between $5,000 and $100,000 are solicited through the State of Arizona's informal bid solicitation process. (See AAC § R2-7-D301 *et seq.*) Contracts valued below $5,000 are directly solicited by the department to a minimum of three vendors on the State Procurement Office's vendor listing. (See *id.*) For these contracts, the selection of vendors to solicit is done on a rotating basis in order to give all listed vendors opportunities for such contracts. (See Arizona Revised Statutes § 41-2578.)

As outlined above, Arizona uses multiple methods for procurement (those over $100,000). Because it is the least complicated and appropriate in most circumstances, many procurements are issued through a competitive sealed bidding process (also referred to as an "invitation for bid" (IFB)). In certain cases, at the discretion of the director of the ADOA, multi-step sealed bidding or competitive sealed proposal methods may be used. Construction contracts or contracts for certain professional services follow a different procurement method, which is further described below. Contracts based on a cost plus a percentage of cost basis are prohibited unless it is determined that this method is the least costly to the state or that it is impracticable to procure under an alternative method.

A. Traditional Bid Process

Arizona procurement contracts were traditionally offered through an IFB notification process and awarded via competitive sealed bidding. Special rules and a simplified construction procurement program could be used for construction procurements that are less than $150,000 (see AAC sections R2-7-501 through -511; or Arizona Revised Statutes title 41, chapter 23, articles 3 and 5), but all state contracts executed before the year 2000 were awarded using this traditional method.

Generally, there is no prequalification requirement for the majority of state contract procurement other than meeting the requirements of the particular procurement (i.e., being responsive to the bid request and a responsible bidder) and complying with basic Arizona statutes to perform work in the state (i.e., having appropriate licenses where necessary prior to bidding). However, a number of state agencies (particularly ADOT) require potential state contractors to go through a prequalification process, through which the contractors must demonstrate that they are properly licensed and meet certain minimum requirements with regard to financial strength, experience, training, and capabilities to perform certain work on state procurement jobs. All bids are open and become public record after a contract has been awarded.

B. Alternative Methods of Project Delivery

In 2000, the Arizona Legislature adopted statutes allowing state agencies (including ADOT) to start using alternative methods of project delivery for public procurement. These methods include (1) design-build, (2) construction manager at risk (CMAR), and (3) job order contracting. They were adopted in hopes of providing better flexibility and/or increased communication and input (especially from the contractor) during the procurement process, and a substantial number of state projects, especially those procured through ADOT, are now done using the design-build or CMAR project delivery method. Under Arizona Revised Statutes section 41-2579, an agency may use any of the new alternative methods of project delivery or the traditional design-bid-build method when procuring design and construction services.

Until recently, when using CMAR, price was not a factor that a state or municipal entity could consider in evaluating the procurement. In 2009, to conform with the requirements of the American Recovery and Reinvestment Act (ARRA), the state legislature amended the CMAR statutes to allow a contracting agency to consider price as a factor for awarding the contract if the contract involves federal funds, but that provision was sunsetted when the ARRA funds were depleted. (See Arizona Revised Statutes § 41-2578.) Obviously, if there is a new stimulus package, there is a possibility that the price factor will be reinstituted in Arizona.

C. Public-Private Partnerships

Statutes pertaining to ADOT are found under title 28, Transportation. Since 2009, ADOT has used public-private partnerships as a tool to address Arizona's transportation requirements. Arizona Revised Statutes section 28-7702 grants ADOT broad authority to partner with the private sector to build or improve Arizona transportation facilities. ADOT has the authority after a competitive procurement process to award a project based on best value to the state, or to reject all proposals. The best value can be based on price, financial proposal, or other factors, although ADOT is required to disclose its criteria as part of the project procurement. Public-private partnerships can be initiated either by ADOT or through an unsolicited proposal. In the case of unsolicited proposals, if ADOT feels the proposal has merit, then it is required to go through a competitive procurement process.

D. Requests for Proposals

Alternatively, a request for proposals (RFP) is used for formal bids if the state needs to conduct technical negotiations related to the project requirements or compares suitability of various potential vendors. The formal RFP process is often utilized to acquire goods or services that will cost the state agencies more than $50,000. The state utilizes the RFP process when the state agency intends to award a contract to a responsible supplier whose proposal is determined to be the most advantageous to the state while taking into consideration the evaluation factors announced in the RFP. RFPs are generally used when qualifications, performance levels, expertise, quality of service, and/or product performance are more important than the cost. When using the RFP process, agencies may conduct negotiations or allow proposal modifications to obtain the best value. (See Arizona Revised Statutes § 41-2578.)

E. Construction Delivery Methods

A contract offering commences with an IFB that outlines bid submission requirements, contract requirements, contract terms, and any evaluation criteria to be used for contractor selection. Vendors with questions regarding a certain proposal can request a debriefing from the contracting agency or submit requests for information (RFIs), which are answered by addendums before the deadline for bid or proposal submission. Procurement officers are authorized to execute contracts that are priced on either a fixed-price (with no cost incentive), lease, or lease-purchase basis. Cost-reimbursed or cost-incentive contracts may only be entered into by the state with approval from the state procurement administrator. Contracts for materials or services may be up to five years long. Job-order-contracting construction services contracts may be up to three years long. (See Arizona Revised Statutes § 41-2503.)

1. Design-Bid-Build

The design-bid-build is the traditional construction procurement method. For competitive sealed bids, contracts are awarded to the lowest cost, responsive, and responsible vendor who meets the requirements and evaluation criteria outlined in the IFB. Only objectively measurable costs can be used in determining the lowest cost vendor. Responsibility of the vendor is based on such factors as financial, physical, and personnel resources, as well as the vendor's historical record and legal qualifications to provide services to the state.

2. Design-Build

This method combines the duties and obligations of the architect/engineer and provides for one contract between the design-builder and the owner and allows for increased speed and communication between the designer and builder. This method requires greater and more sophisticated communication between the owner and design-builder and therefore may be best suited for sophisticated owners. The design-builder is responsible for both the design and construction and therefore owners enjoy the benefit of not being responsible for the design (as owners generally are pursuant to the *Spearin* doctrine). Although proposals become public record upon the awarding of the contract, a vendor can request that confidential "trade secret" information be concealed from public record.

3. CMAR

The CMAR is similar to the traditional design-bid-build method in that there are separate contracts between the owner and architect and between the owner and contractor. Often there are two contracts between the owner and contractor, one for preconstruction services and one for construction services. This method allows the owner to hire the CMAR simultaneously with the architect so that the CMAR can be involved during the design and preconstruction phase. After the preconstruction phase, the CMAR and the owner enter into the construction contract and agree to a guaranteed maximum price, and the CMAR takes on the established role of the general contractor.

4. Job-Order-Contracting

This method allows the owner to have a contractor on call for smaller jobs. The maximum dollar amount for an individual project using job-order-contracting is $1,000,000. The job-order-contracting method saves the expenses and delays of forcing the owner to bid on every small project.

A listing of current solicitations as well as current contracts is available through the ADOA, State Procurement Office website at https://spo.az.gov/contracts.

F. Bonds

1. Bid Security Bonds

Bid security is required for all construction procured under Arizona Revised Statutes sections 41-2533 and 41-2578. Bid security requirements typically allow the bidder the choice of posting a bid bond, certified check, or cashier's check. The bid security amount is 10 percent of the amount of the bid. If the RFP requires security, noncompliance requires that the agent reject the proposal for noncompliance with the security requirement, unless the agent determines that the bid fails to comply in a non-substantial manner with the security requirements. (See Arizona Revised Statutes § 41-2573.)

2. Payment Bonds

A payment bond that is executed and furnished in an amount equal to 100 percent of the price specified in the contract for the protection of all persons supplying labor or materials to the contractor or its subcontractors for the performance of the construction provided for in the contract is required under Arizona Revised Statutes section 41-2574.

3. Performance Bonds

A performance bond is required in an amount equal to 100 percent of the price specified in the contract conditioned on the faithful performance of the contract in accordance with the plans, specifications, and conditions of the contract. (See Arizona Revised Statutes § 41-2574.)

4. Retention

Ten percent of all construction contract payments shall be retained by the state as insurance of proper performance of the contract for the initial work on a project. After 50 percent of the project is complete, half of the retention monies may be released to the contractor, if the contractor is making satisfactory progress and there is no specific reason to require a larger amount be retained. For the remainder of the project, the retention rate shall be 5 percent. For job-order-contracting contracts, initial retention of payments may be reduced to 5 percent, at the discretion of the agent. Contractors have the option of offering alternative securities in lieu of project retention. The contractor is entitled to all interest from any such substitute security account. (See Arizona Revised Statutes § 41-2576.)

G. Mandatory Contract Provisions

The following are brief summaries of provisions for certain types of contracts.

Contract Price Ceilings: For job-order-contracting services, individual job orders may be limited to maximum amounts set out by the agent. All such contracts are limited to an individual job ceiling of $1,000,000.

Certain Professional Services Contracts: For contracts related to certain professional services, the state solicits a request for qualifications. Aside from a public solicitation, the procurement officer uses a qualifications database containing annual qualification statements from registered vendors interested in contracting for related services. A selection committee is formed to hold discussions with vendors. The committee then creates a list of "most qualified" vendors. The contract may be awarded through either a single negotiated fee method where the procurement officer attempts to negotiate a contract with the most preferred vendor, or through a multiple fee proposal method where the selected vendors are requested to submit pricing bids. An informational brochure further explaining procurement for these professional services is published by the State Procurement Office.

Emergency Procurement: Statutes allow for emergency procurements to be made when there is a threat to public health, welfare, or safety. These procurements are to be made with such competition that is practicable under the circumstances.

Legal Counsel, Accountant Services Contracts, and Other Services: Procurement of legal counsel, certified public accountants, or other services described in Arizona Revised Statutes section 41-2513 are done on an RFP basis through the public solicitation process and through an annual qualifications listing maintained by the procurement officer. All contracts for legal or accounting services must be approved by the state attorney general and state auditor general, respectively.

Sole Source Procurement: Sole source procurements are only made in instances where there is only one source for the required material or services and there are no acceptable substitutes. In the event that a procurement agency determines that a sole source procurement is necessary, a written request must be made to the director for approval. Sole source vendors will negotiate contract terms directly with the procurement officer. (*See* Arizona Revised Statutes § 41-2536.)

Change Orders: Any change order greater than $100,000 or over $10,000 and exceeding 10 percent of the contract price must be determined to be advantageous to the state and approved by the state procurement administrator or, for construction contracts, the assistant director of facility management.

Contract Duration: Job-order-contracting contracts may be multi-term, with a maximum duration limit of five years.

H. Procurement Pointers

Void Contract Provisions: Any contract provision that indemnifies the contractor from or against liability from the negligence of the contractor or its employees, or that subjects the contract to laws of another state, or requires any dispute resolution to be conducted in another state is void and unenforceable. (*See* Arizona Revised Statutes § 41-2586.)

Bond Conditions and Provisions: Statutes provide the form of conditions and provisions for performance and payment bonds that contractors should follow in submitting proper bonds. (*See* Arizona Revised Statutes § 41-2574.)

Subcontractor Payments: Payments to subcontractors must follow the guidelines of timeliness expressed in Arizona Revised Statutes section 41-2577.

I. Socioeconomic Policies

Mandatory Purchase List: A departmental committee annually reviews materials and services offered by both the Arizona Industries for the Blind and Arizona Correctional Industries and determines whether they meet quality, availability, and pricing criteria for state procurement. Upon qualification, the committee may direct the State Procurement Office to sign a contract for such materials and/or services and place these on the state's mandatory purchase listing.

Small Business Set-Aside: Contracts not exceeding $50,000 are restricted to small businesses, if practicable, and are solicited through the state's online notification system. Under Arizona Revised Statutes section 41-1001(21), a "small business means a concern, including its affiliates, which is independently owned and operated, which is not dominant in its field and which employs fewer than one hundred full-time employees or which had gross annual receipts of less than four million dollars in its last fiscal year. For purposes of a specific rule, an agency may define small business to include more persons if it finds that such a definition is necessary to adapt the rule to the needs and problems of small businesses and organizations."

Veteran-Owned Business: Since 2011, the ADOA has been required to report on veteran-owned businesses and state contracts. A new business indicator classification has been established in ProcureAZ to allow vendors to register as a veteran-owned business. Certain enumerated requirements must be met.

Disadvantaged Business Enterprises (DBEs): Companies that meet the requirements found in the *Code of Federal Regulations* (C.F.R.) title 49, part 26 can be certified as a DBE to work on transportation projects in the state of Arizona. Some of the requirements include, but are not limited to, these conditions:

- The company owner must be a U.S. citizen (or resident alien) and be a member of a socially or economically disadvantaged group, as defined in 49 C.F.R. part 26.
- The disadvantaged individual must have a personal net worth (PNW) of less than $1,320,000.
- For construction-related work, a company (including its affiliates) must not have average annual gross receipts over the company's previous three fiscal years in excess of $22,410,000. The company must be a for-profit, ongoing

small business where socially and economically DBE owner(s) own at least a 51 percent interest and have managerial and operational control of the business operations.

- The socially and economically DBE owner(s) must possess the power to direct or cause the direction to the management and policies of the company and to make both day-to-day and long-term decisions on matters of management, policy, and operations.

IV. Bid Protests and Contract Disputes

A. Bid Protests

Bid protests are to be made to the procurement officer of the state agency offering the contract. For most state agencies, a written protest must be made within ten days of knowledge of the protest basis and is to include all of the information outlined in AAC section R2-7-A901.[2] ADOT requires this protest be filed within seven days of knowledge of the basis for protest. Various municipalities and counties have other deadlines that can be as short as three days (City of Phoenix). Therefore, if a protest is contemplated, the protesting party must investigate the underlying issue as soon as possible after learning of the basis for the protest (which can be as simple as not being the low bidder) and contact a knowledgeable attorney as soon as possible so they can make independent evaluation of timing, contents, basis, and procedure for the protest.

Depending on feasibility, protests related to solicitation improprieties are to be made before bid opening or the closing date for submittal of the proposal. The procurement officer is responsible for making a decision on the protest within 14 days of filing, unless the procurement officer has been granted an extension of time from the director. If the protest is sustained, the procurement officer is also responsible for determining the remedy. Appropriate remedies at the discretion of the procurement officer include contract termination, decline to exercise an option under the contract to renew, amendment to the solicitation, or issue a new solicitation.

B. Bid Protest Appeals

For state procurements, an appeals process is available for decisions on bid protests. Appeals are to be made to the director of the ADOA within 30 days of the procurement officer's decision. The appellant must file a copy of the appeal with both the director and the procurement officer. The appeal must contain the information set forth in AAC section R2-7-A901(B), as well as a copy of the decision of the agency chief procurement officer and the precise factual or legal error in the decision of the agency chief procurement officer from which an appeal is taken. (See AAC § R2-7-A905.) The procurement officer must furnish the appellant with an agency report including all related documents as well as a statement summarizing findings, actions, recommendations, and any other evidence to assist in the appeal decision. Upon receipt of the agency report, the appellant then has five days to file an answer to the report with the director.

2. Under section 103.10 of the ADOT Standard Specifications for Road and Bridge Construction 2008, a bid protest must be received by the state engineer no later than seven calendar days after the opening of bids.

The director may dismiss an appeal if it is untimely or does not state a valid basis for protest. It is the director's responsibility to make a decision and, if applicable, an appropriate remedy. If the director finds an appeal has merit, the director may either decide the appeal on the protest, or assign the matter to an administrative law judge for a hearing on a particular issue. After delegation, the director may in its discretion reject the administrative law judge's decision; however, such a rejection has an increased chance of being appealed by an abuse of discretion standard.

C. Contract Disputes

1. Contract Claims

Contract claims are to be made to the procurement officer of the government agency offering the contract within 180 days after the claim arises and a lawsuit must be filed within one year of that date unless the contract in question has a mandatory alternative dispute resolution (ADR) provision. In most instances, efforts will be made by the procurement officer to reach a mutually agreed settlement with the vendor. If a mutual agreement is not reached, the vendor must file a request for final decision. The procurement officer has 60 days from the request filing to issue a written decision. Settlements in excess of $10,000 require the written approval of the state procurement administrator. Contract claims are not subject to the laws of another state and potential litigation or arbitration must be conducted within the state.

If a mandatory ADR provision exists, the time to file a notice of claim or a lawsuit does not begin to run until the ADR is completed. This is an area filled with landmines and you should promptly contact a knowledgeable public construction claims attorney to avoid missing any deadlines and losing your claim.

2. Contract Claims Appeals

Similar to bid protests, an appeals process is available for decisions on contract claims and must be made to the director of the ADOA within five days of the procurement officer's decision. The appellant must file the appeal with both the director and the procurement officer. The appeal must contain a copy of the procurement officer's decision as well as the factual or legal premise for which the appeal is being made.

D. Suspension and Debarment

The director of the ADOA has sole authority to debar or suspend a person from participating in state procurement. Any person is subject to suspension or debarment for the following actions:

- Conviction of a criminal offense related to procurement of a private or public contract
- Conviction by the federal government or any state for any offense indicating a lack of business integrity that affects responsibility as a state contractor
- Conviction of any offense under state or federal antitrust statutes
- Violations of contract provisions that justify debarment action

Debarment and suspension terms cannot exceed three years and six months, respectively.

The director must notify any party under consideration of debarment and assign a hearing for such debarment. The party under consideration must file a written notice to appear within 30 days of receiving debarment notice. For matters involving suspension, a request for hearing must be made to the director. The director will act as or will appoint the hearing officer. The director will make final determination of debarment or suspension either directly or by means of reviewing the hearing officer's recommendations. A request for rehearing is available for parties aggrieved by the director's final decision.

Statutes define liability of persons who contract for or purchase in a manner contrary to the procurement statutes. Such persons are personally liable for all public monies paid out plus 20 percent, interest on such monies, and all costs and damages arising out of the violation. The criminal penalty for such action is a Class 4 felony.

V. Administrative and Judicial Review

A. Administrative Review

The administrative review process is detailed above.

B. Judicial Review

The procurement statute, Arizona Revised Statutes section 41-2614, subjugates any final decision of the director to judicial review pursuant to title 12, Courts and Civil Proceedings, chapter 7, Special Actions and Proceedings in Which the State Is a Party, article 6, Judicial Review of Administrative Decisions. These statutes appoint the state superior court with jurisdiction to review final administrative decisions. Assigned venues depend on the administrative decision being reviewed and where the subject matter involved is situated. A formal complaint must be filed within 35 days from the date of the decision being contested.

The complaint must contain a statement of the findings and decision on which the matter is being challenged, as well as the legal grounds on which the review is being sought. Within 30 days of the complaint, either party may request an evidentiary hearing in which supplemental testimony may be made if no record was made of the preliminary administrative decision, and a trial by jury de novo can be requested in the complaint or answer filed with the court.

The court may stay, affirm, reverse, modify, or vacate and remand the agency decision and action. The court will review the decision using an abuse of discretion standard. (See *Arizona's Towing Professionals v. State*, 993 P.2d 1037 (Ariz. Ct. App. 1999).) If the underlying dispute arises out of the contract or the bid documents allow for it, attorney costs may be awarded to the defendant if a judgment adverse to the plaintiff is rendered. An appellate review of the superior court decisions can be made to the Arizona Supreme Court.

The following are court cases that have helped shape the government procurement law in Arizona:

- *County of Greenlee v. Webster*, 215 P. 161 (Ariz. 1923)—Clarification of what contract variances are considered compensable alterations under contract, as well as what authority government employees have of ordering such alternations
- *Berryhill Office Equipment Co. v. Phillips*, 276 P. 4 (Ariz. 1929)—Clarification of solicitation requirements for proper bidding; other issues addressed include purchasing agency required to offer complete information during solicitation, fixed-price contracts, unduly restrictive contract requirements, and specification changes during bidding period

- *Brown v. City of Phoenix*, 272 P. 2d 358 (Ariz. 1954)—Proper governmental use of discretion to award contracts to the lowest "responsible" bidder
- *Gamewell Co. v. City of Phoenix*, 216 F.2d 928 (9th Cir. 1954), *modified*, 219 F.2d 180 (9th Cir. 1955)—Payment for work performed under a contract that had not undergone proper competitive bidding
- *Sulphur Springs Valley Electric Coop v. City of Tombstone*, 401 P.2d 753 (Ariz. Ct. App. 1965)—The standardization of plans and specifications for all bidders for a contract, allowing comparability of bids
- *City of Scottsdale v. Deem*, 556 P.2d 328 (Ariz. Ct. App. 1976)—Contractors are not entitled to lost profits when unjustifiably denied a contract as the lowest bidder. (See also *Grand Canyon Pipe Lines, Inc. v. City of Tempe*, 816 P. 2d 247 (Ariz. Ct. App. 1991).)
- *Wyatt v. Ruck Construction, Inc.*, 517 P.2d 683 (Ariz. Ct. App. 1977)—Challenging the right of a public officer to make a negative statement against a subcontractor while acting within his or her duties
- *Ruck Construction Co. v. City of Tucson*, 570 P.2d 220 (Ariz. Ct. App. 1977)—The extent of agency liability for increased contractor costs due by agency-imposed restrictions
- *Smith v. Graham County Community College District*, 600 P.2d 44 (Ariz. Ct. App. 1979)—Authority of purchasing agency to use government employees on procurement contracts
- *Marana Unified School District No. 6 v. Aetna Casualty & Surety Co.*, 696 P.2d 711 (Ariz. Ct. App. 1984)—Contractor refusal to perform based on an error in its bid
- *Central Arizona Water & Ditching Co. v. City of Tempe*, 680 P.2d 829 (Ariz. Ct. App. 1984)—Clarification whether nonprofit corporations are bound by procurement purchasing regulations
- *New Pueblo Constructors, Inc. v. State*, 696 P.2d 185 (Ariz. 1985)—Issues related to claims against the government, including proper notice, government waiver of liquidated damages, proper calculation of damages, and attorney fees against the state
- *Big D Construction Corp. v. Court of Appeals*, 789 P.2d 1061 (Ariz. 1990)—Five percent preference set forth in Arizona Revised Statutes section 34-241(A) not constitutional
- *Achen-Gardner, Inc. v. Superior Court*, 839 P.2d 1093 (Ariz. 1992)—Even if private money is used for improvements, street improvements or public property are "structures" and competitive bidding statutes must be followed; purpose of public procurement law is to "promote competition, guard against favoritism, fraud and corruption, and secure the best work at the lowest possible price"
- *Canon School District No. 50 v. W.E.S. Construction Co.*, 869 P.2d 500 (Ariz. 1994)—Validity of an arbitration clause included in the procurement contract
- *R.L. Augustine Construction Co. v. Peoria Unified School District*, 904 P.2d 462 (Ariz. Ct. App. 1995), *reversed on other grounds*, 936 P.2d 554 (Ariz. 1997)—Constitutionality of school board procurement rules and applicability of Administrative Review Act to school districts
- *Arizona's Towing Professionals, Inc. v. State*, 993 P.2d 1037 (Ariz. Ct. App. 1999)—State improperly considered an untimely bid protest without a showing of good cause for tardiness; bidders must raise any issue that they know or should know before bids are submitted pre-bid, or they waive their objections

- *Ry-Tan Construction, Inc. v. Washington Elementary School District No. 6*, 111 P.3d 1019 (Ariz. 2005)—School district's board vote to accept a contractor's bid does not constitute a formal contract; contract with a public agency is not binding on the public agency until a formal contract is executed
- *Martinez v. Goddard*, 521 F. Supp. 2d 1002 (D. Ariz. 2007)—In upholding the Arizona licensing scheme, the court held that the purpose of the licensing scheme was to protect the public from unscrupulous, unqualified, and financially irresponsible contractors; the court found that the scheme's requirements were constitutional in that it required contractors to meet numerous qualifications, which included a written examination, relevant experience, posting a bond based on business volume, submitting a detailed financial statement, demonstrating good character, and paying an application/renewal fee ranging from $200 to $675 a year
- *Kaman Aerospace Corp. v. Arizona Board of Regents*, 171 P.3d 599 (Ariz. Ct. App. 2007)—Change orders not officially authorized by the Arizona Board of Regents not binding on the board despite approval from project manager
- *Flagstaff Affordable Housing L.P. v. Design Alliance, Inc.*, 223 P.3d 664 (Ariz. 2010)—Parties to a contract in construction defect cases (regardless of whether one party is an architect or design professional) will be limited to their contractual remedies for purely economic losses
- *Gorman v. Pima County*, 287 P.3d 800 (Ariz. Ct. App. 2012)—There was no contract between parents of bicyclist killed on highway and county to cooperatively construct memorial park; although parents and county administrator exchanged letters regarding location of proposed park and potential funding options, county administrator was not authorized to accept a contract offer or grant funding on behalf of county
- *A. Miner Contracting, Inc. v. Toho-Tolani County Improvement District*, 311 P.3d 1062 (Ariz. Ct. App. 2013), *review denied* (Mar. 21, 2014)—Adjudicative determination by board of directors of county improvement district that contractor was in default on road and drainage improvement project barred contractor from later litigating whether contractor was "excused" from performance by district's purported breach of contract before contractor terminated its work; contractor could have appeared at hearing before board and presented evidence that it was unable to continue or perform work due to a breach by district.
- *Falcone Bros. & Associates, Inc. v. City of Tucson*, 381 P.3d 276 (Ariz. Ct. App. 2016)—The city's procurement code was invalid insofar as it attempted to make decisions by the city's director of procurement binding and limit access to the superior court by restricting parties to special action review
- *Rodgers v. Huckelberry*, 450 P.3d 1279 (Ariz. Ct. App. 2019)—Although taxpayers may have standing to challenge a government's procurement of services, the challenge becomes moot once the services are rendered and the government pays for them
- *MD Helicopters Inc. v. United States*, 435 F. Supp. 3d 1003 (D. Ariz. 2020)—Arizona federal court lacks jurisdiction over claim by aerospace manufacturer that it was unfairly excluded from government prototype deal because the government has other transaction authority (OTA), which allows it to enter into prototype deals with private companies without it being considered a procurement contract

VI. Extent of State's Adoption or Adaptation of ABA Model Procurement Code

The AAPA, originally adopted in 1984, is closely modeled after the American Bar Association's (ABA's) initial version of the Model Procurement Code for State and Local Governments. In 2000, the ABA updated the Model Code. Arizona has partially adopted the amendments. (Arizona Revised Statutes Annotated § 41-2501 *et seq.*)

VII. Cooperative Purchasing

One procurement method that states use to meet their contracting needs is cooperative purchasing. There are three commonly used models of cooperative purchasing: third-party aggressors, piggyback contracts, and formal cooperatives. Arizona uses a piggyback scheme, whereby the state handles all contract administration, and Arizona cities, counties, and school districts order off of that contract under the same contractual provisions. Arizona's cooperative purchasing efforts are managed through the Arizona Cooperative Program, which has more than 800 members and more than 900 contracts.

A. Authority

The Arizona Cooperative Program is run by the ADOA State Procurement Office as authorized under Arizona Revised Statutes section 41-2631 *et seq.*, article 10, Intergovernmental Procurement, which authorizes cooperative purchasing for public procurement units and nonprofits, and AAC section R2-7-1001, which permits the governing body of any eligible procurement unit to enter into an agreement with the state for the purpose of utilizing state contracts.

B. Requirements

Only members of the Arizona Cooperative Program can take advantage of state contracts. Membership in the cooperative is available to all Arizona political subdivisions including cities, counties, school districts, and special districts. Membership is also available to all nonprofit organizations, state governments, the U.S. federal government, and tribal nations. (See Arizona Revised Statutes § 41-2631(3)–(5).) Nonprofit organizations are defined in Arizona Revised Statutes section 41-2631(4) as any nonprofit corporation as designated by section 501(c)(3) through 501(c)(6) of the Internal Revenue Code.

To join the Arizona Cooperative Program, eligible entities must fill out the Arizona State Purchasing Cooperative Agreement and return it to the State Procurement Office. Nonprofit entities must also attach proof of nonprofit status. The Arizona State Purchasing Cooperative Agreement can be found at the following link: https://azadoagov.na1.echosign.com/public/esignWidget?wid=CBFCIBAA3AAABLblqZhBiC7p3mAN7-HczqL7P3r3nw0dimIpjgZTmzXOUIE_TpqE6EV6ciVi0XcRve2BXEsM*.

Arkansas Procurement Rules and Regulations

Prepared by Luke Vance and Nicole Gore
Rose Law Firm, a Professional Association
Email: lvance@roselawfirm.com; ngore@roselawfirm.com

I. Statutory Reference

A. Procurement/Purchasing Statutes

The Office of State Procurement (OSP) is managed by the Arkansas Department of Finance and Administration and it has primary responsibility and oversight for the statewide procurement of commodities and technical and professional services for all state agencies, boards and commissions, and colleges and universities. OSP also provides training in procurement law, regulations, and policies, and it is responsible, through its Marketing and Redistribution Department, for the disposal of state surplus property and equipment. Information about OSP can be found at https://www.transform.ar.gov/procurement/.

Purchasing is governed by Arkansas Code Annotated section 19-11-101 *et seq*. A table of contents of the purchasing statutes is listed below.

Subchapter 3—Bidding—State Industry Priority
Tit. 19, Ch. 11, Subch. 3 Note
19-11-301. Intent.
19-11-302. Definitions.
19-11-303. Preference of Provisions.
19-11-304. Priority to State Industries.
19-11-305. Multiple Private Industry Bids.
19-11-306. Under Bid by Out-of-State Industry.

Subchapter 4—Bidding—Bonds
19-11-401–19-11-405. [Repealed.]

Subchapter 5—Purchases of Workshop-Made Products and Services.
19-11-501–19-11-504. [Repealed.]

Subchapter 6—Federal Government Surplus Property
Tit. 19, Ch. 11, Subch. 6 Note
19-11-601. Authority to Transfer to State and Local Agencies.
19-11-602. Purchase for Schools and School Districts.
19-11-603. Service Charge.
19-11-604. Rural Water Associations.
19-11-605. Authority to Transfer Excess Military Property to State and Local Agencies—Service Charge.

Subchapter 7—Ethics
Tit. 19, Ch. 11, Subch. 7 Note
19-11-701. Definitions.
19-11-702. Penalties.
19-11-703. State Policy and Objective.
19-11-704. General Ethical Standards.
19-11-705. Employee's Financial Interest—Breach.
19-11-706. Employee Disclosure Requirements.
19-11-707. Gratuities and Kickbacks—Breach.
19-11-708. Retainment for Commission—Prohibition.
19-11-709. Employment Restrictions.
19-11-710. Confidential Information Use—Breach.
19-11-711. Procurement Information—Public Record.
19-11-712. Remedies against Breaching Employees.
19-11-713. Remedies against Breaching Nonemployees.
19-11-714. Recovery—Transferred Value—Kickbacks.
19-11-715. Duties of Secretary of the Department of Finance and Administration.
19-11-716. Admittance to Business Incubators.
19-11-717. State-Supported Institutions of Higher Education.
19-11-718. Special State Employees—Conflicts of Interest.

19-11-1205. Evaluation of Responses to Solicitations.
19-11-1206. Guaranteed Energy Cost Savings Contract Requirements.
19-11-1207. Administration of Subchapter—Fees.
19-11-1208. Use of Maintenance and Operation Appropriations.

Subchapter 13—Partial Equity Ownership Agreements
19-11-1301. Definition.
19-11-1302. Review of Partial Equity Ownership Agreements.
19-11-1303. Imminent Need to Enter into a Partial Equity Ownership Agreement.
19-11-1304. Retrospective Review of a Partial Equity Ownership Agreement to Ensure Disclosure.

Subchapter 14—Construction Manager—General Contractor Method of Procurement Pilot Program
19-11-1401. Title.
19-11-1402. Legislative Findings.
19-11-1403. Definitions.
19-11-1404. Construction Manager—General Contractor Method of Procurement Pilot Program—Creation.
19-11-1405. Project Selection.
19-11-1406. Request for Proposals.
19-11-1407. Construction Manager—General Contractor Selection.
19-11-1408. Rules.

B. Other Applicable Statutes

1. Minority Procurement (Arkansas Code Annotated § 15-4-301 *et seq.* and § 25-36-104)
2. Disbursement of Public Funds (Arkansas Code Annotated § 19-4-1206)
3. Sale of Surplus Commodities to Not-for-Profit Organizations (Arkansas Code Annotated § 22-1-101)
4. Motor Vehicles (Arkansas Code Annotated § 22-8-101 *et seq.*)
5. Risk Management (Arkansas Code Annotated § 23-61-601 *et seq.*)
6. OSP—Marketing and Redistribution Section—Marketing and Redistribution of Surplus State Personal Property (Arkansas Code Annotated § 25-8-106)
7. Information Technology Access for the Blind (Arkansas Code Annotated § 25-26-201 *et seq.*)
8. Prison Made Goods (Arkansas Code Annotated § 12-30-201 *et seq.*)
9. Surplus Equipment Not Sold (Arkansas Code Annotated § 25-34-107)
10. Disbursement of Revenues (Arkansas Code Annotated § 25-34-108)

II. Regulations

The Department of Finance and Administration has promulgated regulations regarding procurement that can be found on its website at https://www.dfa.arkansas.gov/regulations-links.

III. Source Selection

The following source selection methods are available:

Small Procurements: These may be made on the open market at $10,000 or less.

Competitive Bidding: This method is used for purchases greater than $10,000 and less than or equal to $50,000 by soliciting informally at least three competitive quotations.

Competitive Sealed Bidding: This bidding is used for purchases exceeding $50,000. An award is made to the lowest responsive and responsible bidder.

Competitive Sealed Proposals: Competitive sealed proposals are used when competitive sealed bidding is not practicable or advantageous, and when the evaluation involves the relative abilities to perform and other factors and price is not the only consideration. The request for proposals (RFP) describes in general terms the needs of the state and allows offerors the opportunity to propose solutions. An award is made to the highest ranked responsible offeror based on evaluation criteria set forth in the RFP.

Competitive Request for Qualifications: The state procurement director may provide for prequalification of suppliers as responsible prospective contractors for particular types of commodities, technical and general services, and professional and consultant services. (Arkansas Code Annotated § 19-11-236.)

Proprietary or Sole Source: These may be awarded for a required or designated commodity or service to a sole or mandatory supplier when the state procurement director, the head of a procurement agency, or a designee of either officer above the level of agency procurement official determines in writing that it is not practicable to use other than the required or designated commodity or service. (Arkansas Code Annotated § 19-11-232.)

Emergency Procurements: Emergency procurements means the acquisition of commodities or services, which if not immediately initiated, will endanger human life or health, state property, or the functional capability of a state agency. (Arkansas Code Annotated § 19-11-204.) The state procurement director, the head of a procurement agency, or a designee of either officer may make or authorize others to make emergency procurements in accordance with rules promulgated by the director. A person or state agency that makes an emergency procurement shall receive at least three competitive bids unless the emergency is a critical emergency; and complete a quotation abstract that includes the names of the firms contacted; time that each firm was contacted; quoted price obtained from each contacted firm; and method used for contacting each firm. (Arkansas Code Annotated § 19-11-233.)

IV. Bid Protests and Contract Disputes

A. Bid Protests

1. Deadlines

a. Specification Protest

Any actual or prospective bidder, offeror, or contractor who is aggrieved in connection with the solicitation of a contract may protest by presenting a written notice at least 72 hours before the filing deadline for the solicitation response to the state procurement director or the head of a procurement agency. A protest pertaining to events or facts arising during the solicitation process must be filed within 14 calendar days after the protesting party knew or should have known of the facts giving rise to the protest.

b. Protest of Award

Any actual bidder, offeror, or contractor who is aggrieved in connection with the award of a contract may protest to the state procurement director or the head of a procurement agency. A protest of an award must be filed within 14 calendar days after the protesting party knew or should have known of the facts giving rise to the protest. Only those parties who participated as bidders may protest. (Arkansas Code Annotated § 19-11-244(a).)

2. Form and Filing

No particular form is required. The protest must be submitted in writing to the director of state procurement or the head of the procurement agency. (Arkansas Code Annotated § 19-11-244.)

3. Stay of Procurement

Once a timely protest has been submitted, the procurement or award is stayed until a final decision is issued unless the director or head of a procurement agency makes a written determination that the award or performance of the contract without delay is necessary to protect substantial interests of the state. (Arkansas Code Annotated § 19-11-244(f).)

4. Decision

Pursuant to Arkansas Code Annotated section 19-11-244, if the protest is not resolved by agreement, notice will be given to the person involved and such person will be given an opportunity to respond to protest issues and thereafter a decision will be issued promptly and mailed within five days after it is written to the protestor and any intervening party. The decision is final and conclusive. (Arkansas Code Annotated § 19-11-244(c)–(d).)

5. Costs

When a protest is sustained and the successfully protesting bidder or offeror was denied the contract award, the protesting bidder or offeror may be entitled to the reasonable costs incurred in connection with the solicitation, including bid preparation costs, through the Arkansas State Claims Commission. (Arkansas Code Annotated § 19-11-244(g).)

6. Private Action

When an actual or prospective bidder is aggrieved by a meritless protest or a protest intended purely to delay the award of a contract, the actual or prospective bidder may bring a private cause of action for tortious interference with a business expectancy against the person or entity that submitted the meritless protest. (Arkansas Code Annotated § 19-11-244(h).)

B. Contract Disputes

Controversies between the state and a contractor that arise by virtue of a contract between them should be brought to the director of state procurement or the head of a procurement agency that has the authority to resolve such controversy. If the controversy is not resolved, after notice and an opportunity to be heard, the director or agency head will issue a written decision. If a decision is not issued within 120 days or such later agreed upon time frame, the contractor may proceed as if an adverse decision had been rendered. The decision is final and conclusive. (Arkansas Code Annotated § 19-11-246.)

C. Suspension and Debarment

1. Suspension

The director of the OSP or the head of a procurement agency shall have the authority to suspend a person from consideration for award of contracts provided that doing so is in the best interest of the state and there is probable cause for debarment. Prior to suspension, the contractor shall be given an opportunity to discuss the issue and potentially reach a settlement. A suspension shall not exceed three months.

2. Debarment

After reasonable notice and an opportunity to be heard before a committee according to regulations promulgated by the state procurement director, the director or the head of a procurement agency shall have authority to debar a person for cause from consideration for award of contracts, provided that doing so is in the best interests of the state. Debarment shall not exceed three years.

V. Administrative and Judicial Review

A. Administrative Review

The administrative review process applicable to bid protests, contract controversies, and suspension and debarment proceedings is set forth in Section IV (Bid Protests and Contract Disputes) above.

Determinations of the director of the OSP (or the relevant procurement officer, director, or designee) pursuant to Arkansas Code Annotated section 19-11-244(c), which refers to resolution of protested solicitations and awards; Arkansas Code Annotated section 19-11-246(e), which refers to resolution of contract and breach of contract controversies, finality of decision; and Arkansas Code Annotated section 19-11-245(d), which refers to debarment or suspension, are final and conclusive.

Determinations of the director of the OSP (or the relevant procurement officer, director, or designee) pursuant to Arkansas Code Annotated section 19-11-229(h), which refers to competitive sealed bidding, award; Arkansas Code Annotated section 19-11-230(b), which refers to competitive sealed proposals, conditions for use; Arkansas Code Annotated section 19-11-230(f), which refers to competitive sealed proposals, award; Arkansas Code Annotated section 19-11-232, which refers to proprietary or sole source procurements; Arkansas Code Annotated section 19-11-233, which refers to emergency procurements; Arkansas Code Annotated section 19-11-234, which refers to competitive bidding; Arkansas Code Annotated section 19-11-235, which refers to responsibility of bidders and offerors, determination of responsibility; Arkansas Code Annotated section 19-11-238(b), which refers to multiyear contracts, determination prior to use; and Arkansas Code Annotated section 19-11-263, which refers to special procurements, are all final and conclusive, unless they are clearly erroneous, arbitrary, capricious, or contrary to law.

B. Judicial Review

There is limited Arkansas case law addressing procurement issues, all of which pertain to the exhaustion of administrative remedies. However, there is ample, well-established case law addressing procurement issues in the construction law context, which does cite and cover procurement law cited above.

- *Conway Corp. v. Construction Engineers, Inc.*, 782 S.W.2d 36 (Ark. 1989). The Arkansas Supreme Court held that the public utility company was permitted the discretion to reject a low bid on a contract as long as the rejection was for good cause and made in good faith. Bad faith, according to the court, consists of dishonest, malicious, or oppressive conduct with a state of mind characterized by hatred, ill will, or a spirit of revenge.
- *Mountain Home School District No. 9 v. T.M.J. Builders, Inc.*, 858 S.W.2d 74 (Ark. 1993). The chancellor's finding of fact may not be set aside on appeal unless clearly erroneous, even though chancery cases are reviewed de novo. The court also held that a general contractor's mistaken bid that totaled 3.9 percent of the bid was not of the magnitude to render enforcement of the contract unconscionable. Therefore, the contractor was not entitled to rescission based on its own unilateral mistake.

VI. Extent of State's Adoption or Adaptation of ABA Model Procurement Code

The Arkansas Procurement Code is closely modeled after the American Bar Association's (ABA's) initial version of the Model Procurement Code for State and Local Governments.

VII. Cooperative Purchasing

A. Authority

A public procurement unit may participate in, sponsor, conduct, or administer a cooperative purchasing agreement for the acquisition of commodities or services in accordance with an agreement entered into between participants. A cooperative purchasing agreement is limited to commodities and services for which the public procurement unit may realize savings or material economic value, or both. (Arkansas Code Annotated § 19-11-249(a).)

B. Requirements

For any cooperative purchasing agreements entered into by a state agency, the state procurement director is required to consider the economic justifications for using a cooperative purchasing agreement when granting or withholding approval for the cooperative purchasing agreement. That director shall adopt rules to create a review policy outlining how the economic justification required may be demonstrated. This includes, but is not limited to, current state contract pricing and the pricing under a cooperative purchasing agreement or information obtained from a request for information and pricing under a cooperative purchasing agreement. (Arkansas Code Annotated § 19-11-249(a)(2)(B).)

5. Requirements

California Procurement Rules and Regulations

Prepared by Joshua Deitz and Aaron Silberman
Rogers Joseph O'Donnell
Email: jdeitz@rjo.com and asilberman@rjo.com

I. Statutory Reference

A. Procurement/Purchasing Statutes[1]

1. Public Contract Code (PCC) sections 10100–10111.2—State Contract Act
2. PCC sections 10300–10334—Competitive bidding and other acquisition procedures
3. PCC sections 10335–10381—Contracts for services
4. PCC sections 12100–12113—Acquisition of information technology (IT) goods and services
5. PCC section 12120—Acquisition of telecommunications goods and services
6. Government Code (GC) sections 4000–4563—Public work and public purchases

B. Other Applicable Statutes

1. GC section 19130—Standards for the use of personal services contracts, including conflicts of interest, and PCC sections 10410–10412 regarding conflicts of interest of current and former officers, employees, or appointees
2. GC section 8350 *et seq.*—Drug-Free Workplace Act of 1990
3. GC section 12990 *et seq.*—Nondiscrimination and compliance programs (and regulations promulgated thereunder at California Code of Regulations (CCR), title 2, division 4.1, subchapter 5, Contractor Nondiscrimination and Compliance, section 11099 *et seq.*)
4. Public Resources Code section 42460 *et seq.*—Electronic Waste Recycling Act of 2003 (see also PCC sections 12200–12217, Recycled Materials, Goods, and Supplies)
5. PCC section 6108—Sweatfree Code of Conduct (see also https://www.dir.ca.gov/sweatfreecode.htm)

---

1. All Public Contract Code and Government Code references can be found at https://leginfo.legislature.ca.gov/faces/codes.xhtml.

II. Regulations

A. CCR Title 2 (Administration), Division 2 (Financial Operations), Chapter 3 (Department of General Services)

A link to the CCR can be reached through the Office of Administrative Law (OAL) at https://oal.ca.gov/publications/ccr/, with all published regulations available at https://govt.westlaw.com/calregs/.

B. State Administrative Manual

The State Administrative Manual (SAM) is a reference source for statewide management policies generally and for specific agencies and functions. It is available online at https://www.dgs.ca.gov/Resources/SAM. Relevant sections include the following:

1. Chapter 1200—Contracts (policy direction for state agencies for services, consultant services, interagency agreements, architectural and engineering, and minor public works contracts)
2. Chapters 3500 and 3600—Purchases (and Purchases (cont'd))
3. Chapter 3700—Lease/Purchase Equipment (provides guidance on determining if it is more economical to lease or purchase equipment)
4. Chapter 5200—IT (DGS—Procurement)

C. State Contracting Manual

The State Contracting Manual (SCM) provides policies, procedures, and guidelines for use by state officers and employees involved in the contracting process.

1. SCM volume 1—Provides policies, procedures, and guidelines for procurement of services (https://www.dgs.ca.gov/OLS/Resources/Page-Content/Office-of-Legal-Services-Resources-List-Folder/State-Contracting)
2. SCM volume 2—Provides purchasing authority requirements, including statutes, regulations, policies, procedures, and best practices applicable to the acquisition of non-IT goods (https://www.dgs.ca.gov/PD/Resources/Page-Content/Procurement-Division-Resources-List-Folder/State-Contracting-Manual)
3. SCM volume 3—Provides policies, procedures, and methods for procurement of IT goods and services (https://www.dgs.ca.gov/PD/Resources/Page-Content/Procurement-Division-Resources-List-Folder/State-Contracting-Manual) *Note*: The SCM does not eliminate or override statutory requirements, or requirements implemented by way of superseding Executive Orders and Management Memos.

D. Executive Orders and Management Memos

Executive Orders are available at https://www.gov.ca.gov/category/executive-orders/. Executive Orders from prior administrations are available at https://www.library.ca.gov/government-publications/executive-orders/. SAM Management Memos are available at https://www.dgs.ca.gov/Resources/ManagementMemos.

E. Standard Contract Language and Model Language

Current versions of standard contract language for non-IT services are available at https://www.dgs.ca.gov/OLS/Resources/Page-Content/Office-of-Legal-Services-Resources-List-Folder/Standard-Contract-Language.

Required language for solicitations and contracts, including IT and non-IT terms bidder instructions, general provisions, and special provisions, is available at https://www.dgs.ca.gov/PD/Resources/Page-Content/Procurement-Division-Resources-List-Folder/Required-Language-for-Solicitations-and-Contracts.

III. Source Selection

PCC section 10301 requires that "all contracts for the acquisition or lease of goods in an amount of twenty-five thousand dollars ($25,000), or a higher amount as established by the director, shall be made or entered into with the lowest responsible bidder meeting specifications." If award will be made to other than the lowest bidder, the process is addressed at PCC section 10306. For public works procurements, awards are made to the lowest responsible bidder. (PCC § 10122.) Three competitive bids or proposals are required for contracts for services. (PCC § 10340.)

Additional detailed source selection requirements are found throughout the various codes, regulations, and policy documents, as applicable to the specific procurement. (See, for example, SCM vol. 1, ch. 5, Competitive Bidding Methods; SCM vol. 2, ch. 4, Competitive Solicitations; SCM vol. 3, ch. 4, Competitive Solicitations. See also various sections of the SAM as referenced under Bids, Competitive in the index (generally at § 3500 *et seq*. and § 5200 *et seq*.).)

IV. Bid Protests and Contract Disputes

A. Bid Protests

1. PCC Section 10306—Protests of Contracts or Purchase Orders

Whenever a contract or purchase order under this article is not to be awarded to the lowest bidder, the bidder shall be notified 24 hours prior to awarding the contract or purchase order to another bidder. Upon written request by any bidder who has submitted a bid, notice of the proposed award shall be posted in a public place in the offices of the department at least 24 hours prior to awarding the contract or purchase order. If, prior to making the award, any bidder who has submitted a bid files a protest with the department against the awarding of the contract or purchase order on the grounds that he or she is the lowest responsible bidder meeting specifications, the contract or purchase order shall not be awarded until either the protest has been withdrawn or the Department of General Services (DGS) has made a final decision as to the action to be taken relative to the protest. In computing the 24-hour periods provided for in this section, Saturdays, Sundays, and legal holidays shall be excluded.

Within ten days after filing a protest, the protesting bidder shall file with the DGS a full and complete written statement specifying in detail the grounds of the protest and the facts in support thereof.

2. PCC Section 12102.2(g)—Protest Procedures for IT Awards

Protest procedures shall be developed to provide bidders an opportunity to protest any formal, competitive acquisition conducted in accordance with this chapter. The procedures shall provide that protests must be filed no later than five working days after the issuance of an intent to award. Authority to protest may be limited to participating bidders. The director of technology, or a person designated by the director, may consider and decide on initial protests of bids for IT projects conducted by the Department of Technology and telecommunications procurement made pursuant to section 12120. The Director of DGS, or a person designated by the director, may consider and decide on initial protests of all other IT acquisitions. A decision regarding an initial protest shall be final. If, prior to the last day to protest, any bidder who has submitted an offer files a protest with the department against the awarding of the contract on the grounds that their bid or proposal should have been selected in accordance with the selection criteria in the solicitation document, the contract shall not be awarded until either the protest has been withdrawn or the DGS has made a final decision as to the action to be taken relating to the protest. Within ten calendar days after filing a protest, the protesting bidder shall file with the DGS a full and complete written statement specifying in detail the grounds of the protest and the facts in support thereof.

3. PCC Sections 12125–12129—The Alternative Protest Pilot Project

See also CCR title 1, division 2, chapter 5, Procedures for Conducting Protests under the Alternative Protest Pilot Project.

4. PCC Sections 19100–19102—Claims and Disputes

5. CCR Title 1, Division 2, Chapter 1, Section 1000 *et seq.*—General APA Hearing Procedures

6. CCR Title 2, Division 2, Chapter 3, Subchapter 1.5, Section 1195—Contract Protest Procedures; Protest Procedures for Consulting and Services Contracts

7. SCM

a. Volume 1, chapter 6—Contract Award Protests (services or consulting services contracts that are awarded through an invitation for bid (IFB) or request for proposal (RFP) process)
b. Volume 2, chapter 7—Protest and Post Award Disputes (non-IT goods)
c. Volume 3, chapter 7—Protest and Post Award Disputes (IT goods and services)

B. Bid Protest Appeals

A petition for writ of mandate can be sought in state court under the California Code of Civil Procedure (CCP). Writs of mandate are addressed at CCP sections 1084–1097. If the protest is arbitrated, petition of an arbitration award is conducted under CCP sections 1290–1294.

C. Contract Disputes

1. Contract Claims

Claims must be brought within six months of (1) the contracting agency's final written decision under contract claim provisions or (2) accrual of the cause of action, if there are no contract claim provisions. (PCC § 19100.) This section does not apply to a claim subject to PCC section 10240.1 (i.e., claims under the State Contract Act); the remedy for such claims is arbitration as set forth in PCC section 10240.

Post-award disputes are also addressed in the SCM. (See Section IV.A.7.)

See also the DGS "Dispute Resolution Unit" page at https://www.dgs.ca.gov/PD/About/Page-Content/PD-Branch-Intro-Accordion-List/Policy-Training-and-Customer-Service/Dispute-Resolution-Unit.

General Provisions (non-IT), ¶ 38(c) (Disputes)—If the state fails to render a final decision within 90 days after receipt of a contractor's demand, it shall be deemed a final decision adverse to the contractor's contentions (current versions are available at https://www.dgs.ca.gov/PD/Resources/Page-Content/Procurement-Division-Resources-List-Folder/Required-Language-for-Solicitations-and-Contracts).

General Provisions (IT), ¶ 44(a) (Disputes)—If a written decision is not rendered within 30 days after receipt of the contractor's demand, it shall be deemed a decision adverse to the contractor's contention (current versions are available at https://www.dgs.ca.gov/PD/Resources/Page-Content/Procurement-Division-Resources-List-Folder/Required-Language-for-Solicitations-and-Contracts).

2. Contract Claims Appeals

A party may petition the court to confirm, correct, or vacate an award rendered by the arbitrator under PCC section 10240. (PCC § 10240.12.)

A petition for writ of mandate can be sought in the courts under the CCP. Writs of mandate are addressed at CCP sections 1084–1097. If the protest is arbitrated, petition of an arbitration award is conducted under CCP sections 1290–1294.

General Provisions (non-IT), ¶ 38(c) (Disputes)—The state's final decision is conclusive and binding regarding the dispute unless the contractor commenced an action in a court of competent jurisdiction to contest such decision within 90 days following the date of final decision or one year following accrual of the cause of action, whichever is later (current versions are available at https://www.dgs.ca.gov/PD/Resources/Page-Content/Procurement-Division-Resources-List-Folder/Required-Language-for-Solicitations-and-Contracts).

General Provisions (IT), ¶ 44(c) (Disputes)—The same result (current versions are available at https://www.dgs.ca.gov/PD/Resources/Page-Content/Procurement-Division-Resources-List-Folder/Required-Language-for-Solicitations-and-Contracts).

D. Suspension and Debarment

The state and local agencies can both issue suspensions and debarments, and different jurisdictions maintain separate lists of suspended and debarred contractors. State debarment and suspension is primarily overseen by the Department of Industrial Relations, Division of Labor Standards Enforcement (DLSE). Various state laws and regulations prohibit contracting with entities that are debarred or suspended at the federal, state, and/or local level. A list of DLSE debarred contractors can be found at http://www.dir.ca.gov/dlse/debar.html.

DGS oversees suspension and debarment related to violations of small business and disabled veteran business enterprise violations at https://www.dgs.ca.gov/PD/Resources/Page-Content/Procurement-Division-Resources-List-Folder/SB-DVBE-Program-Violations-and-Sanctions.

V. Administrative and Judicial Review

A. Administrative Review

Contractors can appeal decisions of the relevant department director or their designee. The contractor can appeal the decision to the DGS, deputy director, Procurement Division. (See General Provisions (Non-IT) ¶ 38(a), and General Provisions (IT) ¶ 44 (current versions are available at https://www.dgs.ca.gov/PD/Resources/Page-Content/Procurement-Division-Resources-List-Folder/Required-Language-for-Solicitations-and-Contracts).)

Decisions regarding IT goods and/or services may be appealed to the DGS, deputy director, Procurement Division. (See General Provisions (IT) ¶ 44(a) (current versions are available at https://www.dgs.ca.gov/PD/Resources/Page-Content/Procurement-Division-Resources-List-Folder/Required-Language-for-Solicitations-and-Contracts).)

B. Judicial Review

A petition for writ of mandate can be sought in the courts under the CCP. Writs of mandate are addressed at CCP sections 1084–1097. If the protest is arbitrated, petition of an arbitration award is conducted under CCP sections 1290–1294.

VI. Extent of State's Adoption or Adaptation of ABA Model Procurement Code

California has not adopted the American Bar Association (ABA) Model Procurement Code. (See National Association of State Procurement Officials, 2020 Survey of State Procurement Practices, https://www.naspo.org/research-innovation/publications/survey-state-procurement-practices/.)

VII. Cooperative Purchasing

A. Authority

California provides for cooperative purchasing through various types of leveraged purchase agreements in PCC section 10290 *et seq*. Specific cooperative purchasing provisions for IT procurements are provided for in PCC section 10299. Numerous cooperative purchasing entities are operating at state and local levels in California. California permits public agencies to enter into joint powers agreements for cooperative purchasing via the authority in GC sections 6500 and 6502.

B. Requirements

California utilizes state-level cooperative purchasing agreements to avoid competition for repetitive procurements and leverage buying power. California participates in a variety of cooperative purchasing agreements for IT and non-IT goods and services. Information is available through DGS at https://www.dgs.ca.gov/PD/About/Page-Content/PD-Branch-Intro-Accordion-List/Acquisitions/Cooperative-Agreements. California uses a number of different types of cooperative purchasing agreements—multiple award schedules, master agreements, software licensing agreements, statewide contracts, and one-time acquisitions, among others.

The SCM provides additional information in volume 1, chapter 3.13, available at https://www.dgs.ca.gov/OLS/Resources/Page-Content/Office-of-Legal-Services-Resources-List-Folder/State-Contracting, and volume 2, chapter 6, available at https://www.dgs.ca.gov/PD/Resources/Page-Content/Procurement-Division-Resources-List-Folder/State-Contracting-Manual. The various types of leveraged purchase agreements have thresholds ranging from $500,000 for master agreement and cooperative agreement contracts to unlimited purchase from statewide contracts.

Colorado Procurement Rules and Regulations

Prepared by Eric Whytsell and Judith Araujo
Stinson LLP
Email: eric.whytsell@stinson.com and judith.araujo@stinson.com

I. Statutory Reference

Colorado purchasing is managed by the Department of Personnel and Administration, Office of the State Controller. Within that office, the State Purchasing and Contracts Office (SPCO) sets the state's procurement rules (except for bridge and highway construction), handles vendor appeals related to bid protest decisions, sources and administers the state's price agreements, maintains the online solicitation publication systems for all statewide competitive procurements, conducts procurements for various state departments, manages the state's procurement card program, conducts statewide training in public procurement, runs the small business development program for state procurement, and performs oversight and generally establishes policy relating to public procurement by the State of Colorado. The SPCO is responsible for the oversight of state government procurements. The Department of Personnel and Administration maintains a website containing resources about procurement in Colorado: https://osc.colorado.gov/spco/procurement-resources.

A. Procurement/Purchasing Statutes

The table of contents of the Colorado Revised Statutes (CRS) governing procurement follows:

PROCUREMENT CODE

ARTICLE 101—GENERAL PROVISIONS

<u>Part 1: Purposes, Construction, and Application</u>

§ 24-101-101	Short title
§ 24-101-102	Purposes—rules of construction
§ 24-101-103	Supplementary general principles of law applicable (Repealed)
§ 24-101-104	Requirement of good faith
§ 24-101-105	Application of this code
§ 24-101-106	Procurement training
§ 24-101-107	Procurement ethics

Part 2: Determinations

§ 24-101-201 Determinations

Part 3: Definitions

§ 24-101-301 Definitions

Part 4: Procurement Records and Information

§ 24-101-401 Public access to procurement information (Repealed)

§ 24-101-402 Retention of procurement records

ARTICLE 102—PROCUREMENT ORGANIZATION

Part 1: Executive Director of the Department of Personnel

§ 24-102-101 Authority and duties of the executive director

Part 2: Purchasing

§ 24-102-201 Purchasing

§ 24-102-202 Authority of the executive director and chief procurement officer—delegation of authority—rules

§ 24-102-202.5 Supplier database—fees—cash fund—program account

§ 24-102-203 Special duties regarding state-owned motor vehicles (Repealed)

§ 24-102-204 Delegation of purchasing authority by the executive director of the department of personnel (Repealed)

§ 24-102-205 Centralized contract management system—personal services contracts—legislative declaration—definitions (Repealed)

§ 24-102-206 Contract performance outside the United States or Colorado—notice—penalty

§ 24-102-206.5 Contract performance outside the United States or Colorado—annual report

§ 24-102-207 Statewide procurement card agreement—definition

Part 3: Organization of Public Procurement

§ 24-102-301 Centralization of procurement authority

§ 24-102-302 Purchasing agencies—establishment—authority

Part 4: State Procurement Rules (Repealed)

§ 24-102-401 State Procurement Rules (Repealed)

Part 5: Coordination

§ 24-102-501 Collection of data concerning public procurement

§ 24-102-502 Procurement advisory council—sunset review (Repealed)

ARTICLE 103—SOURCE SELECTION AND CONTRACT FORMATION

Part 1: Definitions (Repealed)

§ 24-103-101 Definitions (Repealed)

Part 2: Methods of Source Selection

§ 24-103-201	Methods of source selection
§ 24-103-201.5	Market research—request for information
§ 24-103-202	Invitation for bids
§ 24-103-202.3	Invitation for best value bids
§ 24-103.202.5	Low tie bids—award procedure and determination—bid preference (Repealed)
§ 24-103-203	Request for proposals
§ 24-103-204	Small purchases
§ 24-103-205	Sole-source procurement
§ 24-103-206	Emergency procurement
§ 24-103-206.5	Procurements funded with federal "American Recovery and Reinvestment Act of 2009" moneys—wavier of "Procurement Code"—requirements—repeal (Repealed)
§ 24-103-207	State purchases of recycled paper and paper products (Repealed)
§ 24-103-207.5	Purchasing preference for environmentally preferable products—definitions (Repealed)
§ 24-103-208	Other procurement methods
§ 24-103-209	Purchase of compost by government bodies—definitions (Repealed)
§ 24-103-210	Use of foreign-produced goods—iron, steel, and related manufactured products–disclosure—report (Repealed)
§ 24-103-211	Service-disabled veteran owned small businesses—state procurement set aside—definitions (Repealed)

Part 3: Cancellation of Invitations for Bids or Requests for Proposals

§ 24-103-301	Cancellation of invitation for bids or requests for proposals

Part 4: Qualifications and Duties

§ 24-103-401	Responsibility of bidding and offerors
§ 24-103-402	Prequalification of suppliers
§ 24-103-403	Cost or pricing data
§ 24-103-404	Motor carriers (Repealed)

Part 5: Types of Contracts (Repealed)

§ 24-103-501	Types of contracts (Repealed)
§ 24-103-502	Approval of accounting system (Repealed)
§ 24-103-503	Multiyear contracts (Repealed)

Part 6: Audit of Records (Repealed)

§ 24-103-601	Right to audit records (Repealed)

Part 7: Determination and Reports

§ 24-103-701	Finality of determinations
§ 24-103-702	Reporting of anticompetitive practices

§ 24-106-103 Centralized contract management system—personal services contracts—legislative declaration—definitions
§ 24-106-104 Types of contracts
§ 24-106-105 Multiyear contracts
§ 24-106-106 Right to audit records
§ 24-106-107 Monitoring of vendor performance—definitions
§ 24-106-108 Administrative rules—cost reimbursement
§ 24-106-109 Terms and conditions in contracts

ARTICLE 107—COST PRINCIPLES (Repealed)
§ 24-107-101 Administrative rules—cost reimbursement (Repealed)

ARTICLE 108—SUPPLY MANAGEMENT (Repealed)
§§ 24-108-101 to 24-108-401 (Repealed)

ARTICLE 109—REMEDIES
Part 1: Prelitigation Resolution of Controversies
§ 24-109-101 Resolution of controversies (Repealed)
§ 24-109-101.1 Definitions
§ 24-109-101.5 Resolution of controversies
§ 24-109-102 Protested solicitations and awards
§ 24-109-103 Stay of procurements
§ 24-109-104 Entitlement to costs (Repealed)
§ 24-109-105 Debarment and suspension
§ 24-109-106 Resolution of contract and breach of contract controversies—applicability—authority
§ 24-109-107 Issuance and appeal of decision
§ 24-109-108 Computation of time

Part 2: Appeals
§ 24-109-201 Appeal to the executive director—stay of procurements
§ 24-109-202 Rules of procedure
§ 24-109-203 Time limitation for appeals
§ 24-109-204 Decisions of the executive director
§ 24-109-205 Appeals to district court
§ 24-109-206 Time limitations on appeals to the district court

Part 3: Interest
§ 24-109-301 Interest

Part 4: Solicitations and Awards in Violation of the Law
§ 24-109-401 Applicability (Repealed)
§ 24-109-402 Remedies prior to an award (Repealed)
§ 24-109-403 Remedies after an award (Repealed)
§ 24-109-404 Liability of public employees

Part 5: Remedies

§ 24-109-501 Applicability

§ 24-109-502 Protests—remedies prior to an award

§ 24-109-503 Protest—remedies following an award—ratification by chief procurement officer

§ 24-109-504 Appeals—remedies following an award

§ 24-109-505 Costs

ARTICLE 110—INTERGOVERNMENTAL RELATIONS

Part 1: Definitions

§ 24-110-101 Definitions (Repealed)

Part 2: Cooperative Purchasing

§ 24-110-201 Cooperative purchasing authorized

§ 24-110-202 Sale, acquisition, or use of supplies by a public procurement unit

§ 24-110-203 Cooperative use of supplies or services

§ 24-110-204 Joint use of facilities

§ 24-110-205 Supply of personnel, information, and technical services

§ 24-110-206 Use of payments received by a supplying public procurement unit

§ 24-110-207 Public procurement units—compliance with code

§ 24-110-207.5 Certification of certain entities as local public procurement units—rules—report

§ 24-110-208 Review of procurement requirements

Part 3: Contact Controversies

§ 24-110-301 Contract controversies

ARTICLE 111—PREFERENCES IN AWARDING CONTRACTS—FEDERAL ASSISTANCE REQUIREMENTS

§ 24-111-101 Exemptions from prescribed methods of source selection

§ 24-111-102 Priorities among preferences

§ 24-111-103 Compliance with federal requirements (Repealed)

ARTICLE 112—EFFECTIVE DATE—APPLICABILITY

§ 24-112-101 Effective date—applicability

These statutes are current through all laws passed during the 2021 First Regular Session of the 73d General Assembly of the State of Colorado.

B. Other Applicable Law

Unless otherwise precluded, principles of law and equity, such as the Uniform Commercial Code, and laws relating to capacity to contract, agency, fraud, misrepresentation, duress, coercion, mistake, or bankruptcy, may supplement the Procurement

Code. The Procurement Code requires all parties involved in the negotiation, performance, or administration of state contracts to act in good faith. (CRS § 24-101-104.)

Article 29, Ethics in Government, of the Colorado Constitution, applies to the conduct of public officers and government employees, including independent contractors. (Colorado Constitution art. XXIX, § 2.) Article 29 imposes a gift ban and states that no public officer, member of the general assembly, local government official, or government employee shall accept or receive any money, forbearance, or forgiveness of indebtedness from any person, without such person receiving lawful consideration of equal or greater value in return from the public officer, member of the general assembly, local government official, or government employee who accepted or received the money, forbearance, or forgiveness of indebtedness. (Colorado Constitution art. XXIX, § 3.) The article is designed to hold the respect and confidence of the people of Colorado and to avoid conduct that created a justifiable impression among members of the public that such trust is being violated. (Colorado Constitution art. XXIX, § 1(1), (2).)

The Colorado Open Records Act applies to the procurement process, and allows for certain records to be open to the public for inspection by any person at reasonable times as specified in CRS section 24-72-200.1 *et seq*. Trade secrets and proprietary information may not be considered a public record where notated on any bid documents and where such documents are readily separable from the bid in order to facilitate public inspection. (See, e.g., Colorado Procurement Rules, 1 Code of Colorado Regulations (CCR) § 101-9, Rules R-24-103-202a-08, R-24-103-202b-08, and R-24-103-202b-11.) All procurement records are retained and disposed of in accordance with the records and retention guidelines at CRS section 24-80-105.

The Colorado Procurement Code and its attendant rules (1 CCR § 101-9 *et seq.*) do not apply to procurements where (1) no state funds are expended or the contract is revenue-producing; agencies shall maximize the return to the state when revenue-producing contracts are involved; competitive bidding is encouraged to ensure fair and open competition; (2) the procurement is made by the legislative or judicial branch of state government; (3) the procurement is for highway and/or bridge construction; (4) the contract is between state agencies, between the state and a political subdivision, another state, or the federal government, or any combination as described in the procurement rules, CCR volume 1, § 101-9 *et seq.*; (5) the procurement is for public printing that meets the requirements of article 109, title 24, of the CRS, as amended; (6) the procurement is for services provided by architects, engineers, landscape architects, industrial hygienists, and land surveyors (CRS §§ 24-30-1401 through 24-30-1407); (7) after approval of a written determination, a supplier's item is to be procured for resale; (8) where the procurement of services from a specific vendor(s) is necessary to comply with the specific terms and conditions of a grant award; or (9) the awarding of grants, as the term is defined in CRS section 24-101-301(19).

II. Regulations

The regulations implementing procurement statutes establish procedures for state procurement. The Procurement Rules, CCR volume 1, section 101-9 *et seq.*, are promulgated by the Department of Personnel and Administration, and can be found through the Secretary of State's website: http://www.sos.state.co.us/.

III. Source Selection

A. Qualification and Duties of Bidders and Offerors

1. Responsibility and Prequalification

Determinations of responsibility or non-responsibility are governed by rule. The prospective contractor must supply information requested by the procurement officer concerning the responsibility of such contractor. If a bidder or offeror who otherwise would have been awarded a contract is found non-responsible, a written determination of non-responsibility setting forth the basis of the finding shall be prepared by the director or head of a purchasing agency. A copy of the determination shall be sent promptly to the non-responsible bidder or offeror. (CRS § 24-103-401.)

The director, or head of a purchasing agency, may develop prequalification procedures for specific solicitations. (CRS § 24-103-402.)

2. Cost or Pricing Data

Cost or pricing data must be submitted in support of a proposal when adjusting the price of any contract, where an emergency procurement is made in excess of $25,000, or when the procurement officer determines in writing that such data is warranted. However, cost or pricing data shall not be required where the contract price is based on adequate price competition, based on established catalog or market prices, set by law or rule, or where such requirements are waived. Refusal to supply cost or pricing data may disqualify the noncomplying offeror. (CRS § 24-103-403.)

B. Invitation for Bids

Contracts are awarded by an invitation for bids as provided in CRS section 24-103-201, except as delineated in CRS section 24-103-201 where the procurement concerns awards by request for proposals (CRS § 24-103-203), invitation for best value bids (CRS § 24-103-202.3), small purchases (CRS § 24-103-204), sole source procurements (CRS § 24-103-205), emergency procurements (CRS § 24-103-206), and several other types of procurements listed in CRS section 24-103-201. It is state policy to purchase products, commodities, services, and construction in a manner that affords businesses a fair and equal opportunity to compete. (1 CCR § 101-9, R-24-103-901.)

Contracts shall be solicited using an invitation for bids. The procuring agency shall issue an invitation for bids, including a purchase description and all contractual terms and conditions applicable to the procurement. Adequate public notice must be provided. Bids will be opened publicly with one or more witnesses at the designated time and place. The criteria for evaluation, such as discounts, transportation costs, and total or life-cycle costs, must be identified in the invitation for bids. Criteria not set forth in the bid may not be used. An inadvertently erroneous bid may be withdrawn. The contract will be awarded by written notice to the low responsible bidder with reasonable promptness. There are special guidelines for situations where all bids exceed available funds, as well as for requests for the submission of unpriced offers as a first step in an invitation for bids. (CRS § 24-103-202.)

C. Request for Proposals

When it is determined that the use of invitation for bids is either not practicable or not advantageous to the state, a contract may be entered into by request for proposals. This type of procurement method may be used for the procurement of professional services as well as specified types of supplies, services, or construction. (CRS § 24-103-203.)

D. Invitation for Best Value Bids

When the chief procurement officer or a procurement official determines in writing that the use of an invitation for best value bids is advantageous to the state, a contract may be solicited by invitation for best value bids. A bidder may be allowed to submit prices for enhancements, options, or alternatives to the base bid for a commodity or service that will result in a product or service to the state having the best value at the lowest cost. These enhancements, options, or alternatives must be clearly stated in the invitation as well as the purchase description. The functional specification may not be reduced. The awarded contract may actually be higher than the total of another bidder if the higher total amount provides a contract with the best value at the lowest cost to the state. The executive director of the Department of Personnel has established rules for the evaluation of these bids in CCR volume 1, section 101-9, which provides criteria for objectively measuring prices, and criteria of objectively determining if the proposed extras provide the best value at the lowest cost to the state. (CRS § 24-103-202.3 and 1 CCR § 101-9.)

E. Small Purchases

Any procurement less than the specified amount established by rule may be made in accordance with small purchase procedures established by the rules, but procurement requirements shall not be artificially divided so as to constitute a small purchase under this section. (CRS § 24-103-204.) Small purchases are goods and services purchases costing less than $150,000 and construction projects costing less than $150,000. (1 CCR § 101-9.)

F. Sole Source Procurements

A contract may be awarded for a supply, service, or construction item without competition when the person entitled to make this decision determines that there is only one good or service that can reasonably meet the need and there is only one vendor who can provide the good or service. (CRS § 24-103-205.) A requirement for a particular proprietary item (i.e., a brand-name specification) does not justify a sole source procurement if there is more than one potential bidder or offeror for that item. (1 CCR § 101-9.)

G. Emergency Procurements

An emergency procurement may be made when it is determined by the executive director of the Department of Personnel, the chief procurement officer, the procurement official, or a designee of any such officer that there exists a threat to public health, welfare, or safety under emergency conditions, per the rules. Emergency procurements shall be limited to a quantity of those supplies, services, or construction items necessary to meet the emergency. (1 CCR § 101-9.) Such procurements will be made with as much competition as is practicable under the circumstances. (CRS § 24-103-208.)

H. Other Possible Procurement

The executive director of the Department of Personnel may establish, by rule, other competitive procurement methods. The state auditor shall review these methods every fiscal year. These methods must be in the best interest of the state and consistent with the provisions of CRS section 24-101-102. (CRS § 24-103-208.) Current alternative methods of other competitive procurement are competitive reverse auctions and competitive negotiation. (1 CCR § 101-9.)

I. Legislative Declaration—Nonprofit Set-Asides

There are set-asides for nonprofits employing persons with severe disabilities bidding on certain service solicitations. (CRS §§ 24-103-801 through -807.)

J. Special Considerations

When feasible and practical, state purchase of recycled paper products is required to be 50 percent of the total volume. (CRS § 24-103-903.) Likewise, selection of "environmentally preferable products" is the goal, provided products meet the conditions specified. The bid price will not exceed by more than 5 percent the lowest bid price for products that are not environmentally preferable. A bidder may submit documentation that the products offered are environmentally preferable, which may include a life-cycle analysis conducted on the applicable product in accordance with applicable standards; reference to an existing product list of the state or federal government; or a reference to a nationally recognized third-party certification. When the purchase of a product involves the replacement of existing electrical, natural gas, or steam service, the cost analysis will consider any stranded utility costs. (CRS § 24-103-904.)

When it is in the best interests of the state, pursuant to the rules, the state may cancel any invitation for bids or request for proposals or solicitations, and bids or proposals may be rejected. (CRS § 24-103-301.)

Use of a cost-plus-a-percentage-of-cost contract is prohibited. Limitations apply to a cost-reimbursement contract. (CRS § 24-106-104.) Multiyear contracts are allowed. (CRS § 24-106-105.)

The state is entitled to audit the books and records of any contractor or subcontractor who has a negotiated contract or subcontract with the state. (CRS § 24-106-106.)

If any anticompetitive practices are suspected among any bidders or offerors, relevant facts shall be transmitted to the attorney general. (CRS § 24-103-702.)

All specifications will seek to promote overall economy for the intended purpose and encourage competition in satisfying the state's needs and will not be unduly restrictive. (CRS § 24-104-205.) When feasible, specifications will incorporate the concepts of energy efficiency, value analysis, and life-cycle cost. (CRS § 24-104-206.)

Priorities among preferences when two or more socioeconomic procurement programs are applicable to the same procurement, businesses benefitting from such programs shall be considered in the following order of precedence: correctional industries; industries for the visually impaired; and industries for persons with severe disabilities. (CRS § 24-111-102.)

Any material the bidder wishes to designate as a trade secret or other proprietary data intended to remain confidential and not subject to public inspection must be identified and readily separable from the bid in order to facilitate public inspection of the nonconfidential portions of the bid. (CRS § 24-72-200.1 *et seq.*)

Colorado labor shall be employed on a public works project unless a waiver is allowed pursuant to CRS section 8-17-101.

IV. Bid Protests and Contract Disputes

A. Bid Protests

Protestors may file a protest on any phase of solicitation or award, including but not limited to, specifications, award, or disclosure of information marked confidential in the bid offer. The protest of an invitation for bids or a request for proposals must be submitted in writing within ten business days after such aggrieved person knows or should have known of the facts giving rise thereto; for small purchase solicitations or awards, protests must be submitted in writing within three business days after the aggrieved person knows or should have known of the facts giving rise thereto. Protests should include, at a minimum, the name and address of the protestor; appropriate identification of the procurement by bid or award number; a statement of the reasons for the protest; and any available exhibits, evidence, or documents substantiating the protest. A contract resulting from a request for proposals is not awarded until any protest made in connection with the request for proposals has been resolved. An agency decision shall inform the protester of his or her right to appeal administratively or judicially in accordance with article 109 (Remedies) of the Colorado Procurement Code. (CRS § 24-109-101 *et seq.*)

The procurement official or designee is authorized to settle and resolve any questions regarding any protest concerning the solicitation or award of a contract, debarment or suspension from consideration for award of contracts, and any contract controversy including those controversies based on breach of contract, mistake, misrepresentation, or any other cause for contract modification or rescission. (CRS § 24-109-101.5.)

B. Bid Protest Appeals

An appeal of an adverse decision arising from a bid protest may be made to the executive director of the Department of Personnel or the District Court of the City and County of Denver. Unless an action has been initiated previously in the District Court of the City and County of Denver, the executive director reviews and determines de novo any appeal by an aggrieved person from a decision of the procurement official. (CRS § 24-109-201.) An appeal of a decision by the executive director or by the procurement official must be filed with the District Court for the City and County of Denver, which has exclusive jurisdiction to hear such appeals. Judicial actions are subject to de novo review. Judicial review under the Colorado Administrative Procedure Act does not apply to bid protest appeals. (CRS § 24-109-205.)

C. Contract Disputes

The procurement official or designee is authorized to settle and resolve any controversy between the state and the contractor arising from a contract between them including those controversies based on breach of contract, mistake, misrepresentations, or any other cause for contract modification or rescission. (CRS § 24-109-101.5.)

D. Suspension and Debarment

The procurement official or designee may decide to suspend a person from consideration for award of contracts if there is probable cause to believe that said person has engaged in activities that may lead to debarment. Before a person can be debarred, the person involved is entitled to reasonable notice and reasonable opportunity to be heard. A person may be debarred for any of the following reasons:

- Conviction of a criminal offense as an incident to obtaining or attempting to obtain a public or private contract or subcontract or in the performance of such contract or subcontract
- Conviction under state or federal statutes of embezzlement, theft, forgery, bribery, falsification or destruction of records, or receiving stolen property
- Conviction under state or federal antitrust statutes arising out of the submission of bids or proposals
- Willful material failure to perform in accordance with the terms of one or more contracts, following notice of such failure, or a history of material failure to perform, or of materially unsatisfactory performance of, one or more contracts
- The person is currently under debarment by any other governmental entity that is based upon a settlement agreement or a final administrative or judicial determination issued by a federal, state, or local governmental entity
- The Department of Labor and Employment has imposed three fines on a contractor within five years pursuant to CRS section 8-17-104 for failure to satisfy Colorado labor requirements

After consultation with the affected using agency, the attorney general, and, where practicable, the contractor or potential contractor who is to be suspended, the director may issue a written determination to suspend a person from consideration of contracts pending an investigation to determine whether cause exists for debarment. A notice of suspension, including a copy of the determination, shall be sent to the suspended contractor or prospective contractor. A contractor or prospective contractor is suspended upon issuance of the notice of suspension. The suspension shall remain in effect during any appeals but will not exceed three months, unless the person has a criminal charge issued that may be cause for debarment. At the attorney general's request the suspension will remain in effect until after the trial. (CRS § 24-109-105; 1 CCR § 101-9, R-24-109-105-01.)

A debarment is similar, but the period of debarment may last up to three years. Following completion of the investigation to determine whether a contractor or prospective contractor has engaged in activities that are a cause for debarment, and after consultation with the affected using agencies and attorney general, the director may debar a contractor or prospective contractor with written notice. The reasons for debarment include conviction of a criminal offense as an incident to obtaining or attempting to obtain a public or private contract or subcontract; conviction under state or federal statutes of embezzlement, theft, forgery, bribery, falsification or destruction of records, or receiving stolen property; conviction under antitrust statutes; willful failure to perform; or being under debarment by any other government entity. A contractor may also be debarred if the Department of Labor and Employment has imposed three fines on a contractor within five years for failure to satisfy Colorado labor requirements. (CRS § 24-109-105; 1 CCR § 101-9, R-24-109-105-02.)

V. Administrative and Judicial Review

A. Administrative Review

The executive director of the Department of Personnel or designee will determine if there is entitlement to reimbursement of reasonable costs incurred in the solicitation if a protest is sustained administratively or upon administrative or judicial review. The executive director or designee will decide the contract controversy, suspension or debarment, or whether the solicitation or award was in accordance the procedures. (CRS § 24-109-505; CRS § 24-109-204.)

B. Judicial Review

Decisions by the executive director of the Department of Personnel or designee or the head of a purchasing agency or designee may be appealed to the District Court for the City and County of Denver, which will have exclusive jurisdiction to hear such appeals. Any judicial action under this section shall be de novo. (CRS § 24-109-205.)

There is limited Colorado case law addressing procurement issues. The older cases from the 19th and first half of the 20th century have largely been incorporated into statutory regime. However, there are two cases from the past 50 years that may guide the user:

- *Powder Horn Constructors, Inc. v. City of Florence*, 754 P.2d 356 (Colo. 1988) (holding that bidder for a public construction contract who submitted a bid containing a mistake could rescind the bid only where the bidder establishes by a preponderance of the evidence that the mistake is of a clerical or mathematical nature, that the mistake was made in good faith and relates to a material aspect of the bid, and that the public authority did not rely to its detriment on the mistaken bid)
- *Heritage Pools, Inc. v. Foothills Metropolitan Recreation & Park District*, 701 P.2d 1260 (Colo. App. 1985) (holding that in the absence of any other agreement, the mere listing of a subcontractor on the prime bid pursuant to the public entity's bidding rules and instruction did not constitute an independent bid to the public entity by the subcontractor and therefore the acceptance of the general contractor's bid did not create a contract between the public entity and the subcontractor, nor did it confer on the subcontractor third-party beneficiary status)

VI. Extent of State's Adoption or Adaptation of ABA Model Procurement Code

Colorado adopted the American Bar Association (ABA) Model Procurement Code in 1982 and has made state-specific changes to it since.

VII. Cooperative Purchasing

A. Authority

Any public procurement unit is authorized to participate in, sponsor, conduct, or administer a cooperative purchasing agreement for the procurement of any supplies, services, or construction with one or more public procurement units, external procurement activities, or procurement consortiums, which include 501(c)(3) tax-exempt organizations, in accordance with an agreement entered into between the participants. Such cooperative purchasing may include, but is not limited to, joint or multiparty contracts between public procurement units and open-ended state public procurement unit contracts, which are made available to local public procurement units. (CRS § 24-110-201.)

B. Requirements

The state's chief procurement officer must approve the use of a cooperative purchasing agreement, except that prior approval is not required for the use of state price agreements such as National Association of State Procurement Officials (NASPO) agreements included on the SPCO price agreement website. (CRS § 24-101-105(1)(f); CRS § 24-110-201.) A list of the state price agreements can be accessed here: https://www.bidscolorado.com/co/portal.nsf/xpPriceAgreementsByCategory.xsp.

The SPCO created ACCESSColorado as a resource to provide additional guidance regarding the procurement process, which is accessible via https://osc.colorado.gov/spco/accesscolorado. ACCESSColorado lists the following local purchasing and national cooperative associations: (1) Cooperative Educational Purchasing Council; (2) Multiple Assembly of Procurement Officials; (3) NASPO; (4) National Institute of Governmental Purchasing; and (5) Rocky Mountain Governmental Purchasing Association.

Connecticut Procurement Rules and Regulations

Prepared by Antoinette M. Webster
State of Connecticut, Department of Administrative Services
Email: antoinette.webster@ct.gov

I. Statutory Reference

A. Procurement/Purchasing Statutes

The relevant sections of the General Statutes of Connecticut are as follows:

§§ 2-71p–2-71v	General Assembly and Legislative Agencies; Purchases and Contracts for Supplies, Materials, Equipment and Contractual Services
§§ 4a-1–4a-67h	Administrative Services; Commissioner; Purchases and Printing
§§ 4b-1–4b-50	State Real Property, State Properties Review Board
§§ 4b-51–4b-102	Construction, Alternations, Repairs, Additions and Demolition
§§ 4d-1–4d-48	State Information and Telecommunication Systems Management and Contracts
§§ 4e-1–4e-50	State Contracting; State Contracting Standards Board
§§ 4e-70–4e-76	State Contracting: General Provisions
§§ 10a-151b	Purchases of Equipment, Supplies, and Contractual Services by Constituent Units and Their Institutions

1. Department of Administrative Services, Division of Procurement Services

The Department of Administrative Services (DAS) commissioner is responsible for purchasing, leasing, or contracting for all supplies, materials, equipment, and contractual services required by any state agency as described in Connecticut General Statutes (CGS) section 4a-50. The commissioner's powers are established under CGS section 4a-2(a)(2). The DAS website provides information on procurement procedures at https://portal.ct.gov/das.

Chapter 58, title 4a of the CGS governs the state's procurement and printing practices. This chapter is available at http://www.cga.ct.gov/current/pub/chap_058.htm.

Title 4a. Purchasing and Printing.

§ 4a-1.	Department of Administrative Services. Commissioner.
§ 4a-2.	Commissioner's general powers and responsibilities.
§ 4a-50.	(Formerly Sec. 4-109). Definitions.
§ 4a-51.	(Formerly Sec. 4-110). Duties of Administrative Services Commissioner re purchases.
§ 4a-52.	(Formerly Sec. 4-111). Regulations.
§ 4a-52a.	Purchases by constituent units of the state system of higher education. Disqualification from bidding. Delegation of purchasing authority to state agencies.
§ 4a-52b.	Circumstances in which constituent units authorized to purchase by negotiation.
§ 4a-53.	(Formerly Sec. 4-110c). Cooperative purchasing plans. Purchase from person having contract to sell to other government or nonprofit entities or public purchasing consortia.
§ 4a-53a.	Contracting agent for group of municipalities.
§ 4a-54.	(Formerly Sec. 4-110a). Purchasing by certain institutions through administrative services commissioner.
§ 4a-56.	(Formerly Sec. 4-123). Purchasing standards and specifications.
§ 4a-57.	(Formerly Sec. 4-112). Competitive bidding or competitive negotiation for purchases and contracts. Regulations. Waivers. Exception.
§ 4a-57a.	Distribution of surplus state property. Lease of property to municipalities.
§ 4a-57b.	Program to encourage bidding on state contracts by businesses that trade with African countries.
§ 4a-57d.	Report re resident bidders. Program to increase state contract awards to resident bidders.
§ 4a-58.	(Formerly Sec. 4-113). Standardization committee. Waiver of bid or proposal requirement.
§ 4a-59.	(Formerly Sec. 4-114). Award of contracts.
§ 4a-59a.	Restrictions on contract extensions. Exception.
§ 4a-60.	(Formerly Sec. 4-114a). Nondiscrimination and affirmative action provisions in awarding agency, municipal public works, and quasi-public agency project contracts.
§ 4a-60a.	Provisions re nondiscrimination on the basis of sexual orientation required in awarding agency, municipal public works, and quasi-public agency project contracts.
§ 4a-60b.	Reverse auctions. Use by contracting agencies authorized.
§ 4a-60g.	(Formerly Sec. 32-9e). Set-aside program for small contractors and minority business enterprises.
§ 4a-60h.	(Formerly Sec. 32-9f). Administration of set-aside program. Administration of set-aside program for municipal public works and quasi-public agency project contracts. Regulations.
§ 4a-60i.	(Formerly Sec. 32-9g). Responsibilities of agency heads to negotiate and approve contracts not affected.

§ 4a-60j. (Formerly Sec. 32-9h). Time for payment of contractors.

§ 4a-61. (Formerly Sec. 4-114b). Award of contracts concerning minority business enterprises.

§ 4a-62. (Formerly Sec. 4-114c). Minority business enterprise review committee.

§ 4a-63. Disqualification from bidding on contracts. Suspension.

§ 4a-64. (Formerly Sec. 4-116). Persons not to be interested in contract.

§ 4a-65. (Formerly Sec. 4-115). Unlawful purchases.

§ 4a-66. (Formerly Sec. 4-25). Acquisition of federal property. Contracts with federal agencies concerning health services. Exemption from statutes or municipal charter. Purchasing from federal contractors.

§ 4a-67. (Formerly Sec. 4-120a). Acquisition of federal surplus property.

§ 4a-67a. Efforts to increase state purchase of goods containing recyclable materials and goods capable of being recycled or remanufactured.

§ 4a-67b. Elimination of use of disposable and single-use products in state government.

§ 4a-67c. Equipment and appliances for state use, energy standards.

§ 4a-67d. Purchase of cars, light duty trucks, and buses. Gasoline mileage ratings. Alternative-fueled, hybrid electric, or plug-in electric vehicles. Zero-emission vehicles and buses. Requirements. Exemptions. Definitions. Reports.

§ 4a-67e. Standards for purchase of recycled paper.

§ 4a-67f. Specifications for printing and writing paper.

§ 4a-67g. Recycling and remanufacture of laser printer toner cartridges.

§ 4a-67h. Procedures promoting the procurement and use of recycled products and environmentally preferable products and services by state agencies.

§ 4a-70a. Prohibition on printing state stationery containing party symbol.

§ 4a-71. (Formerly Sec. 4-121a). Prompt payment by state departments and agencies.

§ 4a-72. (Formerly Sec. 4-121b). Prompt payment. Exceptions.

§ 4a-73. (Formerly Sec. 4-121c). Administration of prompt payment provisions.

§ 4a-74. (Formerly Sec. 4-110d). Governmental exemption from public utility late payment charge.

§ 4a-75. (Formerly Sec. 4-122). Payment of obligations. Department of Administrative Services revolving fund.

§ 4a-76. (Formerly Sec. 4-122a). Recording of estimated requirements.

§ 4a-77. Definitions.

§ 4a-78. State policy with respect to providing Social Security numbers and federal employer identification numbers.

§ 4a-79. Federal Social Security number or employer identification number required on each license issued by a public agency.

§ 4a-81. Contracts for goods and services over fifty thousand dollars. Affidavit by bidder or vendor re consulting agreements. Failure to submit. Disqualification.

§ 4a-82. Janitorial work program for persons with a disability and persons with a disadvantage. Inclusion of contractual services in program.

Chapter 58a. Prequalification and Evaluation of Contractors 2

§ 4a-100. Prequalification of contractors and substantial subcontractors. Fees. Application. Regulations. Renewal. Revocation. Notice re state contractors or substantial contractors. Appeal. Notice re bond guarantee program.

§ 4a-101. Standard contractor evaluation form. Public agency to submit completed evaluation form. Contractor response. Definitions. Preliminary evaluation. Exemption from liability. Failure to submit form.

2. DAS, Division of Construction

Pursuant to CGS title 4b, the commissioner of the DAS is responsible for the procurement of contracts to construct, reconstruct, alter, remodel, repair, or demolish any public building or other public work by the state except a public highway or bridge project or any other construction project administered by the Department of Transportation, and the purchase, acquisition, sale, and lease of land and buildings.

Title 4b. State Real Property.

Chapter 59. State Real Property.

Chapter 60. Construction and Alterations of State Buildings.

§ 4b-1. Duties of Commissioner of Administrative Services.

§ 4b-1a. Public works capital projects revolving fund.

§ 4b-2. Commissioner of Administrative Services' reports and records of realty transactions; authorized consultations.

§ 4b-3. State properties review board established. Commissioner of Administrative Services' powers in state realty transactions. Review by board of transactions, contracts and acquisition of development rights. Appeals.

§ 4b-4. Filing of statements of financial interests.

§ 4b-36. Contracts for construction of buildings or facilities on state-owned land. Lease to state with provision to purchase.

§ 4b-51. Alterations, repairs, or additions to real assets. Selection of consultants for certain projects.

§ 4b-51a. Recycled content requirements for construction materials.

§ 4b-52. Repairs or changes to state premises. Exception for emergency conditions. Renegotiation of leases.

§ 4b-55a. Contracting for environmental evaluations for priority higher education facility projects.

§ 4b-56. State construction services selection panels, and Connecticut health education facilities authority construction services panels, established. Membership.

§ 4b-57. Consultant Services. Invitation of responses. Consideration by selection panel.

§ 4b-58. Contracting for consultant services.

§ 4b-59. Commissioner to adopt regulations.
§ 4b-61. Contracting for design professional services.
§ 4b-91. Process for bidding for public works contracts. Prequalification requirements. Exceptions.
§ 4b-92. "Lowest responsible and qualified bidder" defined. Bid bonds, certified checks, when forfeited.
§ 4b-93. Contract specifications; subtrades, subcontracts.
§ 4b-94. Rejection of bids.
§ 4b-95. General bid form requirements. Selection by awarding authority. Subcontractors.
§ 4b-95a. Listing of general bidder as a subcontractor on bid form.
§ 4b-96. Subcontract, form. Procedure on failure of subcontractor to execute subcontract. General bidder's responsibilities.
§ 4b-100. Regulations.
§ 4b-100a. Construction services award panels. Screening, interview, and selection of contractors. Memoranda re selection. Regulations.
§ 4b-102. Bidding for certain construction contracts for the Connecticut State University System.
§ 4b-103. Construction manager at-risk project delivery contracts.

3. DAS, Division of Information Technology

Pursuant to title 4d, there is established a Division of Information Technology (BEST), which is responsible for purchasing, leasing, and contracting for all information systems and telecommunication system facilities, equipment, and services for state agencies. A chief information officer oversees BEST and is responsible for approval/disapproval of the acquisition of hardware/software for information technology systems and is authorized to establish guidelines and regulations. BEST also governs contracts for consultants for information and telecommunication systems for state agencies.

Title 4d. State Information and Telecommunication Systems.
Chapter 61. State Information and Telecommunication Systems Management and Contracts.
§ 4d-1. Definitions.
§ 4d-2. Division of Information Technology within Department of Administrative Services. Chief Information Officer. Duties. Review of state agency contracts.
§ 4d-3. Regulations.
§ 4d-5. Telecommunication facilities, equipment, services, and infrastructure.
§ 4d-8. Information and telecommunication systems. Purchase, lease, contracts for, sale, and disposal.
§ 4d-9. Technical Services Revolving Fund.
§ 4d-30. Definitions.
§ 4d-31. Contracts, subcontracts, amendments to include State Comptroller's specifications.

§ 4d-32. Approval of subcontract awards.
§ 4d-33. "Public record" defined.
§ 4d-34. Ownership rights and integrity of public records under a contract, subcontract, or amendment.
§ 4d-35. Application of Freedom of Information Act to public records provided to contractor or subcontractor.
§ 4d-36. Nondisclosure of public records by contractor or subcontractor.
§ 4d-37. Prohibition on selling, marketing, or otherwise profiting from public records.
§ 4d-38. Notice to commissioner of violations.
§ 4d-39. Remedies and penalties for violations.
§ 4d-40. General Assembly access to state agency records under contracts, subcontracts, and amendments thereto.
§ 4d-44. Continuity of systems in event of expiration or termination of contract, amendment or subcontract, or default of contractor or subcontractor.
§ 4d-47. Hiring of state employees by contractors and subcontractors.
§ 4d-48. Disqualification of potential contracts and subcontractors for past nonperformance.

4. State Contracting Standards Board

Pursuant to CGS title 4e, there is established a State Contracting Standards Board, which has oversight and is the policy body for all state procurement. The Standards Board shall appoint a chief procurement officer to assist the Board in implementing its programs, policies, and procedures. The State Contracting Standards Board has the power to, including but not limited to, assist state agencies in complying with procurement statutes; review and make recommendations concerning proposed legislation concerning procurement, management, control, and disposal of any and all supplies, services, and construction to be procured by the state; review and certify a state agency's procurement processes; for cause, review, terminate, or recommend termination of any contract or procurement agreement undertaken by the state agency; disqualify any contractor(s), bidder(s), or proposer(s) for up to five years and restrict or terminate the authority of an employee or agent of a state contracting agency to enter into a contract or procurement agreement.

Title 4e. State Contracting.
Chapter 62. State Contracting Standards Board.
Chapter 62a. State Contracting: General Provisions
§ 4e-1. Definitions.
§ 4e-2. State Contracting Standards Board. Established. Members. Chairperson. Executive director. Chief Procurement Officer. Duties. Prohibited activities of employees. Rules of the board. Quorum.
§ 4e-3. Exercise of rights, powers, duties, and authority relating to the procurement policies of the state by the board.
§ 4e-4. Authority and responsibilities of the board with respect to procurements by state contracting agencies.

§ 4e-26.	Regulations for the establishment of standards for the preparation, maintenance, and content of specifications for supplies, services, and construction.
§ 4e-27.	Regulations for the use of cost-reimbursement contracts.
§ 4e-28.	Regulations concerning the submission of accounting system documentation by contractors to state contracting agencies.
§ 4e-29.	Inspection of contractor's or subcontractor's plant or place of business by state contracting agency.
§ 4e-30.	Audit of contractor's or subcontractor's books and records by state contracting agency.
§ 4e-31.	Notice of suspected collusion or other anticompetitive practice to the Attorney General.
§ 4e-32.	Retention and disposal of procurement records by state contracting agencies.
§ 4e-33.	Record of contracts awarded for certain small purchases, minor, nonrecurring, or emergency purchases, and under waiver of competitive bid or proposal requirements.
§ 4e-34.	Disqualification of contractor, bidder, or proposer by State Contracting Standards Board. Causes for disqualification.
§ 4e-35.	Suspension of contractor, bidder, or proposer by department head of state contracting agency. Causes for suspension.
§ 4e-36.	Contest of the solicitation or award of a contract by bidder or proposer.
§ 4e-37.	Contractor's, bidder's, or proposer's appeal of suspension decision issued by department head.
§ 4e-38.	Issuance of decision on appeal by board.
§ 4e-39.	Determination by board of violation of law in solicitation or proposed award of a contract prior to award. Options.
§ 4e-40.	Determination of violation of law in solicitation or award of contract after award. Options.
§ 4e-41.	Regulations concerning the procurement of architectural and engineering services.
§ 4e-42.	Regulations concerning bid security for certain competitive sealed bidding.
§ 4e-43.	Regulations concerning errors and omissions insurance.
§ 4e-44.	Regulations concerning the procurement of consultant services.
§ 4e-45.	Regulations concerning infrastructure facilities.
§ 4e-46.	Regulations for contract modifications, change orders, and price adjustments for construction contracts in excess of fifty thousand dollars.
§ 4e-47.	Regulations concerning application of certain contracting statutes to each constituent unit of the state system of higher education.
§ 4e-48.	Reciprocal preference provision in award of state contracts. Definitions. Application of provision. List of states with in-state preference published by the State Contracting Standards Board.

§ 4e-49.	Regulations concerning contracting procedures for the Metropolitan District of Hartford County.
§ 4e-50.	Contracts for environmental remediation of brownfields.
§ 4e-70.	Requirements for state contractors who receive confidential information. Definitions. Minimum requirements. Prohibitions. Breach. Violation. Ban. Effect of other applicable laws.
§ 4e-71.	Additional protections and alternate measures of security assurance for sharing of confidential information.
§ 4e-76.	Modification of contracts.

B. Other Applicable Statutes

1. Connecticut Code of Ethics—Chapter 10 of Title 1

a. The Code of Ethics for Public Officials (CGS §§ 1-79 through 1-83)
b. The Code of Ethics for Lobbyists (CGS §§ 1-91 through 1-101a)
c. Ethical Considerations concerning Bidding and State Contracts (CGS §§ 1-101mm through 101rr)

2. Large State Contracts: Certifications—CGS Sections 4-250 and 4-252 and Governor M. Jodi Rell's Executive Order No. 1, Section 8

3. Connecticut Campaign Contribution Certification—CGS Section 9-612(g)

4. In-State Contracting Preferences

a. Correctional Enterprises of Connecticut (CGS § 18-88(g))
b. In accordance with CGS section 4a-51(b), DAS shall give a preference to dairy products, poultry, eggs, beef, pork, lamb, farm-raised fish, fruits, or vegetables grown or produced in Connecticut when such products are comparable in cost to other dairy products, poultry, eggs, beef, pork, lamb, farm-raised fish, fruits, or vegetables grown or produced in another state
c. In accordance with CGS section 4a-59(c), DAS provides for preferences of up to 10 percent for:
    i. The purchase of goods with recycled materials or the purchase of recyclable or remanufactured products
    ii. The purchase of motor vehicles powered by clean alternative fuel
    iii. The purchase of motor vehicles powered by fuel other than a clean alternative fuel and conversion equipment to convert such motor vehicles to be powered by either the exclusive use of clean alternative fuel or dual use of a clean alternative fuel and a fuel other than a clean alternative fuel
    iv. A micro-business price preference, except in the case of a veteran-owned business, of up to 15 percent. "Micro-business" means a business with gross revenues not exceeding three million dollars in the most recently completed fiscal year

d. CGS section 4a-60g (establishes a set-aside program for Connecticut small contractors and minority business enterprises)
e. CGS section 4a-82 (establishes a janitorial work program for persons with a disability and persons with a disadvantage; inclusion of contractual services in program)
f. CGS section 4e-48 (provides for a reciprocal preference provision in the award of state contracts)
g. All other things being equal, a preference to Connecticut-based contractors

II. Regulations

Regs., Administrative Services §§ 4a-52-1 through 4a-52-22	State Purchasing Procedures
§§ 4a-60h-1 through 4a-60h-6	Set-Aside Program
§§ 4a-63-1 through 4a-63-5	Procedure for Disqualification or Suspension
§§ 4a-100-1 through 4a-101-1	Prequalification and Evaluation of Contractors
Regs., State Real Property §§ 4b-100-1 through 4b-100-10	Procedure for Alleged Violation or Violations of Part II Chapter 60 of Connecticut General Statutes
Regs., State Information and Telecommunication Systems §§ 4d-3-1 through 4d-3-19	Procurement of Information and Telecommunication Systems

III. Source Selection

The general methods of procurement include the following:

A. Competitive Sealed Bidding (CGS § 4a-57)

B. Competitive Sealed Proposals and Negotiations (CGS § 4a-57 and Regulations of Connecticut State Agencies § 4a-52-16)

C. Sole Source Procurement (Regulations of Connecticut State Agencies § 4a-52-15)

D. Waiver of Bid or Proposal Requirement for Emergency Purchases or for Extraordinary Conditions (CGS § 4a-58 and Regulations of Connecticut State Agencies § 4a-52-20)

E. Cooperative Purchasing (CGS §§ 4a-53 and 4a-53a)

F. Small Purchases (General Letter No. 71)

Pursuant to the authority granted in title 4a, chapter 58 of the CGS, purchases of goods and/or services may be made, subject to limitations.

IV. Bid Protests and Contract Disputes

A. Bid Protests

The DAS does not have an administrative bid protest process. An unsuccessful bidder may request an appointment to talk with the commissioner or designee in procurement.

B. Bid Protest Appeals

There is no administrative bid protest appeal process.

C. Contract Claims

Contract claims are filed directly in state court.

D. Suspension and Debarment

CGS section 4a-63 and Regulations of Connecticut State Agencies sections 4a-63-1 through 4a-63-5 govern disqualifications from bidding on contracts and suspension. The commissioner of DAS, after consultation with the Connecticut attorney general, may disqualify any person, firm, or corporation, for up to five years from bidding on contracts, for supplies, materials, equipment, and contractual services required by any state agency, for one or more causes:

1. Conviction or entry of a plea of guilty for commission of a criminal offense as an incident to obtaining or attempting to obtain a public or private contract or subcontract, or in the performance of such contract or subcontract
2. Conviction or entry of a plea of guilty under state or federal law for embezzlement, theft, forgery, bribery, falsification or destruction of records, receiving stolen property, or any other offense indicating a lack of business integrity or business honesty that affects responsibility as a state contractor
3. Conviction or entry of a plea of guilty under state or federal antitrust, collusion, or conspiracy statutes arising out of the submission of bids or proposals
4. Noncompliance with contract provisions, of a character regarded by the commissioner to be of such gravity as to indicate a lack of responsibility to perform as a state contractor, including deliberate failure, without good cause, to perform in accordance with specifications or time limits provided in a contract
5. A recent record of failure to perform or of unsatisfactory performance in accordance with the terms of one or more contracts, unless such failure to perform or unsatisfactory performance was caused by acts beyond the control of the contractor or supplier
6. Any other cause the commissioner determines to be so serious or compelling as to affect responsibility as a state contractor, including disqualification by another governmental entity, having caused financial loss to the state, or having caused a serious delay or inability of state officials to carry out their duties on a past contract or contracts

V. Administrative and Judicial Review

A. Administrative Review

There is no administrative review process or procedure applicable to bid protests or contract claims.

B. Judicial Review

Bid protests and contract claims may be filed in state court.

VI. Extent of State's Adoption or Adaptation of ABA Model Procurement Code

The State of Connecticut does model the American Bar Association (ABA) Model Procurement Code, but has not adopted it.

VII. Cooperative Purchasing

A. Authority

CGS section 4a-53, Cooperative purchasing plans—Purchase from person having contract to sell to other governmental or nonprofit entities or public purchasing consortia, states that the commissioner of DAS may join with federal agencies, other state governments, Connecticut political subdivisions, or nonprofit organizations in cooperative purchasing plans when the best interests of the state would be served.

B. Requirements

The DAS determines if it is in the best interests of the state to purchase equipment, supplies, materials, and services from a person who has a contract to sell such property or services to other state governments, political subdivisions of Connecticut, nonprofit organizations, or public purchasing consortia, in accordance with the terms and conditions of such contract. If it is in the best interests of the state, the DAS's Procurement Division facilitates internal approval for purchasing under the contract.

Delaware Procurement Rules and Regulations

Prepared by Richard A. Forsten
Saul Ewing Arnstein & Lehr LLP
Email: Richard.Forsten@saul.com

I. Statutory Reference

Generally speaking, Delaware's public procurement and bid laws are found in title 29, chapter 69 of the Delaware Code, entitled "State Procurement." The Delaware Code is accessible online through the state's website, http://delcode.delaware.gov. As will be discussed in greater detail below, the Delaware Code creates four categories of public procurement or bid processes, each with their own requirements and nuances: (1) central contracting, (2) materiel and nonprofessional services, (3) public works contracts, and (4) professional services. Additionally, certain contract requirements applicable to state agencies can be found in title 29, chapter 65, including, for example, interest on late payments. (See, e.g., Delaware Code tit. 29, § 6516(f).)

The Delaware Section of Government Support Services (GSS) in the Office of Management and Budget is responsible for purchasing or contracting for equipment and supplies for the State of Delaware. Further information about the GSS can be obtained through the State of Delaware website at http://gss.omb.delaware.gov/default.shtml.

The Procurement Code also establishes a Contracting and Purchasing Advisory Council, the purpose of which is, inter alia, to (1) recommend procurement policy and administrative procedure to the director of the Office of Management and Budget and the administrator of the GSS; (2) report annually to the governor regarding the effectiveness of the state's procurement process; and (3) set the dollar threshold amounts required under the Procurement Code relating to formal bidding procedures. (Delaware Code tit. 29, § 6913.)

II. Regulations

There are no regulations in Delaware regarding public procurement or bid laws.

III. Source Selection

There are four categories of goods and services under which items to be procured by the state are classified: (1) materiel;[1] (2) nonprofessional services; (3) public works;[2] and (4) professional services.[3] The Council has established thresholds relating to formal bidding procedures in each classification.

Delaware agencies are required to use formal bidding procedures only when a purchase is made in an amount that meets the following threshold limits adopted by the Council:

Materiel and nonprofessional services:	≥ $25,000
Public works:	≥ $100,000
Professional services:	≥ $50,000

For materiel and nonprofessional services, the dollar amount is a yearly cumulative limit, while public works and professional services are on a contract-by-contract basis. Below is a summary of procedures for purchases according to threshold amounts:

Materiel and nonprofessional services:	< $10,000 $10,000–$24,999 ≥ $25,000	Open market purchase Three written quotes Formal bid
Public works:	< $50,000 $50,000–$99,999 ≥ $100,000	Open market purchase Three letter bids Formal bid
Professional services:	< $50,000 ≥ $50,000	Open market Formal request for proposals process

A. Materiel and Nonprofessional Services (Delaware Code Tit. 29, §§ 6922–6939)

1. Competitive Sealed Bids or Requests for Proposals

Any state contract (other than for lodging and travel) for which an agency is a party for materiel or nonprofessional services, whose annual probable cost is at least $25,000, shall be made through competitive sealed bids. If the agency head determines that the use of competitive sealed bids is either not practical or not in the best interest of the state, then a contract may be entered into through competitive sealed proposals, otherwise known as requests for proposals (RFPs).

1. "Materiel" means materials, equipment, tools, supplies, or any other personal property, but does not include real property or electric, gas, water, telephone, or similar utilities. DEL. CODE tit. 29, § 6902(17).

2. "Public works" means construction, reconstruction, demolition, alteration and repair work, and maintenance work paid for, in whole or in part, with public funds. *Id.* §6902(22).

3. "Professional services" means services that generally require specialized education, training, or knowledge and involve intellectual skills (e.g., engineering, land surveying, geology, architecture, accounting, teaching, construction management, etc.). Professional services does not include legal services from attorneys or law firms. *Id.* § 6902(19).

2. Sole Source Procurement

Sole source procurement of materiel or nonprofessional services is permitted if the agency head determines in writing that there is only one source for the required materiel or nonprofessional service. There must be sufficient evidence that there is only one source for the required material or service and that no other type of material or service will satisfy the requirements of the agency. Sole source procurement is avoided, except when no reasonable alternative sources exist. The agency may, but is not required to, submit a request for review by the GSS to determine if sole source procurement is proper. Textbooks and related instructional materials are sole source purchases.

3. Three Written Quotes

If the contract for materiel or nonprofessional services has an estimated cost between $10,000 and $24,999.99, the procurement may be made through the solicitation of three written quotes.

4. Open Market Purchase

If the contract for materiel or nonprofessional services has an estimated cost less than $10,000, the procurement may be made via the open market. Please note, however, that procurement of materiel and nonprofessional services covered by central contracts negotiated by the GSS are mandatory for "covered agencies" (i.e., any agency other than school districts, Delaware Technical Community College, Delaware State University, and the legislative branch of state government). Thus, open market purchases are only permitted for those items not already under contract through the GSS pursuant to Delaware Code title 29, section 6911.

5. Emergency Procurement

An agency head may waive all of the requirements of the Procurement Code to meet the critical needs of the agency as required by emergencies or other conditions where it is determined to be in the best interest of the agency. Any procurement in the event of an emergency shall be limited to those materiel and nonprofessional services necessary to satisfy the emergency.

B. Public Works Contracts (Delaware Code Tit. 29, §§ 6960–6970)

1. Competitive Sealed Bids

Any state public works contract for which an agency is a party and for which the probable cost is at least $100,000 shall be made through competitive sealed bids. The Procurement Code requires that a public notice (advertisement for bids) be placed not less than once a week for two consecutive weeks in a newspaper of general circulation in the state. Notice is also to be provided on the state's electronic (internet) advertising system/web page. The notice must contain a brief description of the work and the location of the project. Additionally, the notice must provide information on the time and place of the pre-bid meeting, the time and place of the bid opening, and how to obtain bid documents. Performance bonds and payment bonds are required for all public works projects over $100,000.

2. Three Letter Bids

Public works projects with an estimated value between $50,000 and $99,999.99 do not require an advertisement for bids. In this situation, the agency is required to solicit competitive written proposals from a minimum of three contractors. Contractors are selected based on past performance and experience on projects of similar magnitude. Performance bond and payment bond requirements may be waived if the contract is less than $100,000 with approval from the agency director or administrator, as the case may be.

3. Open Market Purchase

Open market purchases are permitted on contracts for public works projects with probable costs of less than $50,000. In these circumstances, an agency usually contacts more than one contractor to create competition and promote fairness.

4. Sole Source Procurement

Sole source procurement for a public works project is permitted if the agency head determines in writing that there is only one source for the required public works project. There must be sufficient evidence that there is only one source for the required public works project and that no other type of public works project will satisfy the requirements of the agency. Sole source procurement is avoided, except when no reasonable alternative sources exist. The agency may, but is not required to, submit a request for review by the GSS to determine if sole source procurement is proper.

5. Prevailing Wage Requirements

For all publics works projects in excess of $500,000 for new construction and $45,000 for alteration, repair, renovation, rehabilitation, demolition, or reconstruction, the prevailing wage, as set by the Delaware Department of Labor pursuant to Delaware Code title 29, section 6960, is required to be paid to all laborers and mechanics working at the project site. In addition, all firms contracting with the state to work on public works projects must give preference to laborers, workers, and mechanics who are residents of the State of Delaware. If not, such firms may be assessed fines equivalent to the amount of compensation paid to any person hired in violation of this preference requirement. (See Delaware Code tit. 29, § 6962(d)(4)(b).) In 2019, the Delaware General Assembly added a requirement that all contractors and subcontractors employing ten or more persons on a project subject to prevailing wage must also offer a craft training program as defined in the act. (See Delaware Code tit. 29, § 6962(c)(13)i.)

6. Emergency Procurement

An agency head may waive all of the requirements of the Procurement Code to meet the critical needs of the agency as required by emergencies or other conditions where it is determined to be in the best interest of the agency. Any procurement in the event of an emergency shall be limited to those services necessary to satisfy the emergency. Any public works project contracted during an emergency shall still be subject to prevailing wage laws and Delaware labor preference provisions and penalties.

7. Contractor and Subcontractor Registration

In 2019, the General Assembly created a contractor and subcontractor registration system applicable to most contractors and subcontractors in the construction industry.

(See generally Laws of Delaware vol. 92, ch. 168, *codified at* Delaware Code tit. 29, § 3501 *et seq.*) A contractor placing a bid on a public works contract must now provide proof of its registration and its subcontractors' registration prior to the award of any public works contract. (Delaware Code tit. 29, § 6968.)

C. Professional Services (Delaware Code Tit. 29, §§ 6980–6987)

1. RFP

Any state contract for professional services for which an agency is a party and for which the probable cost is greater than $50,000 shall be made through an RFP process. The Procurement Code requires that a public notice (advertisement for proposals) be placed not less than once a week for two consecutive weeks in a newspaper of general circulation in the state. The agency shall make its selection based on the following criteria: (1) experience and reputation; (2) expertise; (3) capacity to meet requirements; (4) location; (5) demonstrated ability; (6) familiarity with public work and its requirements; or (7) distribution of work to individuals and firms or economic considerations.

The public notice requirement is waived where supplemental professional services within the scope of a previously awarded contract are necessary during the course of completing the contract. The public notice requirement is also waived in emergencies where there is a critical need for professional services.

2. Open Market Purchase

Open market purchases are permitted on contracts for projects with probable costs of less than $50,000.

3. Sole Source Procurement

Sole source procurement for professional services is permitted if the agency head determines in writing that there is only one source for the required professional service. There must be sufficient evidence that there is only one source for the required professional service and that no other type of professional service will satisfy the requirements of the agency. Sole source procurement is avoided, except when no reasonable alternative sources exist. The agency may, but is not required to, submit a request for review by the GSS to determine if sole source procurement is proper.

D. Violations and Penalties (Delaware Code Tit. 29, § 6903)

The following is a list of acts that are violations of the Procurement Code and could subject the person, entity, or agency official (as applicable) to fines up to $2,000 and imprisonment up to six months for the first offense, and fines up to $5,000 and imprisonment up to one year for a subsequent offense: (1) any person who willfully fragments or subdivides any contract for the purchase of materiel, nonprofessional services, public works, or professional services with the intent to avoid compliance with the Procurement Code; (2) an agency official who offers to solicit or secure (or solicits or secures) any agency or central contract and in connection therewith is paid any fee, commission, percentage, gift, or any other consideration; (3) an individual or firm who offers, agrees, or contracts to improperly influence any agency or its employees in the procurement of any agency or central contract and who is paid or is to be paid a fee, commission, percentage, gift, or any other consideration contingent upon a resulting award; and (4) any individual or firm offering materiel or services who offers to pay to an agency official, representative, or employee, or is paid any fee, commission, percentage, gift, or any other consideration contingent upon or resulting from the award or making of any agency or central contract.

E. Central Contracting (Delaware Code Tit. 29, §§ 6910–6915)

In Delaware, any organization, entity, or person who receives "grant-in-aid" is entitled to purchase materiel and nonprofessional services under any central contract negotiated by the GSS during the fiscal year that such "grant-in-aid" is appropriated, provided that the organization, entity, or person received at least $100,000 and has a staff of at least five people.

Additionally, any 501(c)(3) nonprofit organization, organization in good standing with the Delaware Association of Nonprofit Agencies, or Delaware-registered nonprofit corporation, who is under contract with the state to provide goods and services, may purchase materiel and nonprofessional services under any central contract negotiated by the GSS during the fiscal year for which said nonprofit contract is in effect.

F. Multiple Source Contracting (Delaware Code Tit. 29, §§ 6926, 6966, 6986)

An agency may award to two or more firms a contract for a particular materiel or nonprofessional service, public works project, or professional service, if the agency head makes a determination that such an award is in the best interests of the state. If such a determination is made, then the advertisement for proposals shall include a notification of the right of the agency to make such an award and the criteria upon which such an award will be based.

G. Purchase of Used Materiel or Equipment (Delaware Code Tit. 29, § 6934)

An agency may purchase used equipment or materiel by negotiated purchase no matter what the cost, if it is demonstrated to the satisfaction of the agency that the negotiated price is reasonable for the intended use.

H. Energy Performance Contracting (Delaware Code Tit. 29, §§ 6971–6976)

The Procurement Code authorizes agencies to enter into an energy performance contract with a qualified provider to reduce energy or operational costs of an agency facility through one or more energy conservation measures, if the agency finds that the amount the agency would spend on the energy conservation measures will not exceed the amount to be saved in both energy and operational costs for up to 20 years from the date of installation.

The qualified provider is selected through a formal RFP process. In executing the energy performance contract, the qualified provider must adhere to the public works contracts procedures. Performance bonds and payment bonds are required.

I. Exceptions (Delaware Code Tit. 29, § 6904)

The following are not governed by the Procurement Code: (1) the purchase of materiel or services from the federal government or from the State of Delaware; (2) contracts for the transportation of school children; (3) the purchase of library materials or the purchase of services by libraries of any agency; (4) the purchase of materiel or work in connection with the Beach Preservation Act; (5) the purchase of historical artifacts or art for public display; (6) any purchase of education materials by post-secondary schools participating in special education discount and cooperative programs; (7) the procurement of goods and services by the Wilmington Housing Authority when such goods and services are provided by primarily Wilmington Housing Authority resident-owned businesses; (8) the purchase of material or work by the Department of Elections to conduct a primary, general, or special election, or voter registration; (9) the procurement of goods and services by the Department of Education from the University of Delaware, Delaware State University, and Delaware Technical Community College; and (10) the procurement of financial services by the Board of Pension Trustees relating to any fund administered by the Delaware Public Employees' Retirement System.

IV. Bid Protests and Contract Disputes

There is no Delaware statute governing bid protests or contract disputes. Rather, bid protests are typically handled by Delaware's famous Court of Chancery, which has the equitable power to issue injunctions. Contract disputes are ordinarily handled in the Delaware Superior Court, as monetary damages can usually provide an adequate remedy for the aggrieved party.

A. Bid Protests

Bid protests usually arise out of two circumstances: (1) the apparent low bidder is not awarded the contract; or (2) a higher bidder believes the lower bidder(s) should not be awarded the contract for failure to comply with all applicable requirements. Depending on the situation and time pressures, the disappointed bidder usually first complains to the government agency before proceeding to court. In court, the matter will be handled on an expedited basis (the Court of Chancery is very responsive and accustomed to expedited proceedings).

As a general rule, contracting agencies enjoy broad discretion, and their decisions to award a contract that complies with state law will not be overturned unless the decision is arbitrary, capricious, or made in bad faith. (See, e.g., *Dunvir Corp. v. City of Wilmington*, 2008 WL 4560903, at *5 (Del. Ch. Oct. 6, 2008) ("A state-contracting agency is vested with broad discretion. This court will not overturn an agency decision to award a contract that complies with the law unless that decision was made arbitrarily, capriciously, or in bad faith.").) Over the years, a small but significant body of case law has developed to determine statutory requirements that are mandatory and cannot be waived, as compared to other nonmandatory items or issues that may be waived or ignored by an agency. (Compare *Asphalt Paving Systems, Inc. v. Department of Transportation*, 2008 WL 852817, at *4 (Del. Ch. Mar. 20, 2009) (holding that the Procurement Code requires the use of an agency pre-approved bid bond form), and *George & Lynch, Inc. v. Division of Parks & Recreation*, 465 A.2d 345, 351 (Del. 1983) (holding that a proper subcontractor list is required under the Procurement Code), with *Lockheed Martin IMS Corp. v. Delaware Department of Transportation*, 1997 WL 252641, at *5 (Del. Ch. May 5, 1997) (holding that statutory language does not require approval from the Department of Transportation to proceed under statute).)

B. Bid Protest Appeals

There is no administrative bid protest process, and hence no administrative appeal process. Rather, disappointed bidders pursue injunctive relief directly in the Court of Chancery. Appeals from the Court of Chancery are made directly to the Delaware Supreme Court.

C. Contract Disputes

With no statutory requirements for contract disputes, breach of contract claims are handled as any ordinary breach of contract claim is handled—typically in court. Because Delaware's equity and law courts were never merged, contract disputes are most often heard in the Delaware Superior Court. (See, e.g., *Commonwealth Construction Co. v. Red Clay Consolidated School District*, 2010 WL 4657165 (Del. Super. Ct. Nov. 15, 2010); *State Use of Certain-Teed Products Corp. v. United Pacific Insurance Co.*, 389 A.2d 777 (Del. Super. Ct. 1978); *O'Neill, Inc. v. Mayor*, 1963 WL 65233 (Del. Super. Ct. June 26, 1963).)

D. Suspension and Debarment (Delaware Code Tit. 29, § 6962(d)(14))

Any contractor who fails to perform a public works contract or fails to complete a public works project within the time established by the agency may be subject to suspension or debarment for one or more of the following reasons: (1) failure to supply the adequate labor supply ratio for the project; (2) inadequate financial resources; or (3) poor performance on the project. Upon such failure for the foregoing reasons, the agency may petition the director of the Office of Management and Budget for suspension or debarment of the contractor. If the director believes that the petition has merit, he or she will hold a hearing at which the agency shall have the burden of proving, by a preponderance of evidence, that the contractor failed to perform for one of the foregoing reasons.

If the director finds in favor of the agency, he or she may suspend a contractor from bidding on any public works project for up to one year for a first offense, up to three years for a second offense, or permanently debar the contractor for a third offense. The director's decision may be appealed by the contractor to the Delaware Superior Court within 30 days.

V. Administrative and Judicial Review

A. Administrative Review

There is no administrative review process for bid protests or contract disputes.

B. Judicial Review

The judicial review process is discussed above.

VI. Extent of State's Adoption or Adaptation of ABA Model Procurement Code

Delaware has not adopted the American Bar Association's (ABA's) Model Procurement Code.

VII. Cooperative Purchasing

A. Authority

Delaware does allow for "central contracting," whereby the state will procure certain material and nonprofessional services below the threshold for participating agencies. Organizations receiving "grant-in-aid" money from the state and nonprofit organizations may participate in these contracts. (See Delaware Code tit. 29, §§ 6910–6915.)

B. Requirements

The Division of Support Services in the Department of Administrative Services is responsible for central contracting, including forming advisory groups to determine the type of material and services to be subject to such contracts. (See Delaware Code tit. 29, §§ 6911(a), 6912.)

District of Columbia Procurement Rules and Regulations

Prepared by James C. McKay, Jr.
Senior Assistant Attorney General
Office of the Attorney General for the District of Columbia
Email: james.mckay@dc.gov

I. Statutory Reference

A. Procurement/Purchasing Statutes

1. District of Columbia Procurement Practices Reform Act

Procurement by agencies of the District of Columbia government (the "District government") is governed primarily by the District of Columbia Procurement Practices Reform Act of 2010 (PPRA), District of Columbia Official Code (D.C. Code) section 2-351.01 *et seq.* (2012). The PPRA is a limited revision, minor reorganization, and complete recodification of a prior statute, the District of Columbia Procurement Practices Act of 1985, D.C. Code section 2-301.01 *et seq.* (2001). Most of the sections of the PPRA are identical to the prior statute. Hence, administrative and judicial decisions interpreting sections of the prior statute should be equally applicable to the corresponding sections of the PPRA.

The PPRA applies to "all subordinate agencies, instrumentalities, and employees of the District government, independent agencies, boards, and commissions." (D.C. Code § 2-351.05(a).) However, there are exceptions for certain types of contracts and for certain agencies. There are wholesale exemptions for "[t]he acquisition, disposition, or transfer of a real property asset or interest in a real property asset by lease, purchase, sale, or other method"; a contract involving the "rental and utilization of public space"; and "[a] contract or agreement receiving or making grants or loans or for federal financial assistance." (D.C. Code § 2-351.05(c)(1), (2), (12).) In addition, the other two branches of the District government (the Council of the District of Columbia and the District of Columbia Courts), and several independent agencies, are exempt from the PPRA in whole or in part. These agencies include the D.C. Housing Finance Agency, the Public Defender Service, the D.C. Water and Sewer Authority, the Washington Convention and Sports Authority, the Not-for-Profit Hospital Corporation, the D.C. Retirement Board, the D.C. Health Benefit Exchange Authority, the Captive Insurance Agency, and the Green Finance Authority. A complete list is at D.C. Code section 2-351.05(b), (c). These agencies have their own procurement procedures, which are published in the District of Columbia Municipal Regulations (DCMR). References to these procedures are in Section II.C.

A unique feature of the PPRA, compared to procurement laws of statewide applicability, is that the Council of the District of Columbia has the right to review and approve or disapprove multiyear contracts and contracts in excess of $1 million. (See D.C. Code § 2-352.02.) Multiyear contracts must be approved by resolution of the Council within 45 days of receipt; contacts in excess of $1 million are deemed approved unless disapproved by the Council within ten days of receipt.

The text of all sections of the D.C. Code may be accessed on the website of the Council of the District of Columbia at https://code.dccouncil.us/us/dc/council/code. The PPRA is codified under title 2 (Government Administration) in chapter 3A (Government Procurement) of the D.C. Code. The sections of the PPRA, as codified, are as follows:

Chapter 3A. Government Procurement.
Subchapter I. General Provisions.
§ 2-351.01. Purposes and policies.
§ 2-351.02. Supplementary general principles of law applicable.
§ 2-351.03. Obligation of good faith.
§ 2-351.04. Definitions.
§ 2-351.05. Application; exemptions.
Subchapter II. Procurement Organization.
§ 2-352.01. Office of Contracting and Procurement; authority.
§ 2-352.02. Criteria for Council review of multiyear contracts and contracts in excess of $1 million.
§ 2-352.03. Office of Contracting and Procurement.
§ 2-352.04. Duties of the Chief Procurement Officer.
§ 2-352.05. Privatization contracts and procedures requirements.
§ 2-352.06. Procurement training institute.
§ 2-352.07. Ombudsman for contracting and procurement.
Subchapter III. Contractor Standards.
§ 2-353.01. Contractor standards.
§ 2-353.02. Determination of contractor responsibility.
Subchapter IV. Source Selection and Contract Formation.
§ 2-354.01. Source selection methods.
§ 2-354.02. Competitive sealed bids.
§ 2-354.03. Competitive sealed proposals.
§ 2-354.04. Sole source procurements.
§ 2-354.05. Emergency procurements.
§ 2-354.06. Human care procurements.
§ 2-354.07. Small purchase procurements.
§ 2-354.08. Special pilot procurements.
§ 2-354.09. Auctions.
§ 2-354.10. General Services Administration schedules.
§ 2-354.11. Cooperative purchasing.

§ 2-354.12. District of Columbia Supply Schedule.
§ 2-354.13. Competition exemptions.
§ 2-354.14. Cancellation of solicitations.
§ 2-354.15. Collusion.
§ 2-354.16. Contingent fees.
§ 2-354.17. Confidentiality.
§ 2-354.18. Right to audit records; right to inspect.
§ 2-354.19. Reasonable prices.
§ 2-354.20. Prequalification.
Subchapter V. Types of Contracts.
§ 2-355.01. Cost-plus-a-percentage-of-cost contract prohibited.
§ 2-355.02. Cost-reimbursement contracts.
§ 2-355.03. Use of other types of contracts.
§ 2-355.04. Multiyear contracts.
Subchapter VI. Procurement of Construction Projects and Related Services.
§ 2-356.01. Project delivery methods authorized.
§ 2-356.02. Source selection methods assigned to project delivery methods.
§ 2-356.03. Prequalification process for construction.
§ 2-356.04. Architectural and engineering services.
§ 2-356.05. Estimate of construction costs.
§ 2-356.06. Use of project labor agreements for construction contracts.
Subchapter VII. Bonds and Other Forms of Security.
§ 2-357.01. Bid security in construction contracts.
§ 2-357.02. Contract performance and payment bonds in construction contracts.
§ 2-357.03. Bond forms and copies.
§ 2-357.04. Other forms of security.
§ 2-357.05. Authority to require bonds.
§ 2-357.06. Fiscal responsibility.
Subchapter VIII. Supply Management.
§ 2-358.01. Supply management rules.
§ 2-358.02. Disposition of surplus goods.
§ 2-358.03. Electronic Inventory Control System.
§ 2-358.04. Repealed.
§ 2-358.05. Surplus Property Sales Fund.
Subchapter IX. Prohibited Actions; Remedies.
§ 2-359.01. Oral agreements.
§ 2-359.02. Improper contracts.
§ 2-359.03. Termination of contracts.
§ 2-359.04. Sovereign immunity defense not available.
§ 2-359.05. District government not liable for punitive damages.
§ 2-359.06. Claims by District government against contractors.
§ 2-359.07. Debarment and suspension.
§ 2-359.08. Claims by contractors against the District government.

§ 2-359.09. Interest.
§ 2-359.10. Employees subject to employee conduct standards of Merit Personnel Act.
Subchapter X. Contract Appeals Board.
§ 2-360.01. Creation of Contract Appeals Board.
§ 2-360.02. Terms and qualifications of members.
§ 2-360.03. Jurisdiction of Board.
§ 2-360.04. Contractor's right of appeal to Board.
§ 2-360.05. Appeal of Board decisions.
§ 2-360.06. Oaths, discovery, and subpoena power.
§ 2-360.07. Actions in court; judicial review of Board decisions.
§ 2-360.08. Protest procedures.
Subchapter XI. Miscellaneous Provisions.
§ 2-361.01. Green procurement.
§ 2-361.02. Payment of stipends authorized.
§ 2-361.03. Supply schedule, purchase card, and training fund.
§ 2-361.04. Transparency in contracting.
§ 2-361.05. Acquisition planning.
§ 2-361.06. Rules.
Subchapter XII. Repealed Provisions; Transfers and Continuation.
§ 2-362.02. Transfers and continuation.

2. Public-Private Partnership Act

The Public-Private Partnership Act of 2014 (PPPA) (D.C. Code §§ 2-271.01 to 2-275.01), established the Office of Public-Private Partnership. It provides a framework for solicitation of public-private partnership projects by the Office and a process for the Office to receive and consider unsolicited proposals.

A "public-private partnership" is defined as "the method in the District for delivering a qualified project using a long-term, performance-based agreement between a public entity and a private entity or entities where appropriate risks and benefits can be allocated in a cost-effective manner between the public and private entities in which: (A) [a] private entity performs functions normally undertaken by the government, but the public entity remains ultimately accountable for the qualified project and its public function; and (B) [t]he District may retain ownership or control in the project asset and the private entity may be given additional decision-making rights in determining how the asset is financed, developed, constructed, operated, and maintained over its life cycle." (D.C. Code § 2-271.01(11).)

Parties to agreements with the Office of Public-Private Partnerships are exempt from the PPRA, subject to specific exceptions. The exceptions are as follows: D.C. Code section 2-352.02 (Council review of multiyear contracts and contracts in excess of $1 million); D.C. Code section 2-354.15 (collusion); D.C. Code sections 2-357.01 to 2-357.06 (bonds and other forms of security); and D.C. Code sections 2-360.01 to 2-360.08 (review by the Contract Appeals Board (CAB)). (See D.C. Code §§ 2-273.08(a), 2-351.05(c)(19).) These provisions of the PPRA apply to public-private partnership agreements.

The private entities involved are subject, to the extent applicable, to certain District and federal laws, including those related to first source employment; living wage requirements; small, local, and disadvantaged businesses; the general license law; green building requirements; and the Davis-Bacon Act. (D.C. Code § 2-273.08(b).)

The PPPA is codified under title 2 (Government Administration) in chapter 2A (Public-Private Partnership) of the D.C. Code. The sections of the PPPA, as codified, are as follows:

Subchapter 1. General.
§ 2-271.01. Definitions.
Subchapter 2. Office of Public-Private Partnerships Establishment.
§ 2-272.01. Establishment of the Office of Public-Private Partnerships.
§ 2-272.02. Professional Staff.
§ 2-272.03. Budget.
§ 2-272.04. Public-Private Partnership Administration Fund.
Subchapter 3. Procurement of Public-Private Partnerships.
§ 2-273.01. Requests for Information.
§ 2-273.02. Pre-Qualification.
§ 2-273.03. Solicitation through Requests for Proposals.
§ 2-273.04. Unsolicited Proposals.
§ 2-273.05. Review of Requests for Proposals.
§ 2-273.06. Public-Private Partnership Agreements.
§ 2-273.07. Legal Rights; Dispute Resolution.
§ 2-273.08. Compliance with Federal and District Law.
§ 2-273.09. Transparency.
Subchapter 4. Rules.
§ 2-274.01. Rules.
Subchapter 5. Applicability; Construction.
§ 2-275.01. Applicability; Construction.

B. Other Applicable Statutes

1. General

The PPRA is supplemented by "the principles of law and equity, including" the Uniform Commercial Code (D.C. Code § 28:101.01 *et seq.*) and "laws relative to capacity to contract, agency, fraud, misrepresentation, duress, coercion, mistake, or bankruptcy," unless they are superseded by particular provisions of the PPRA. (D.C. Code § 2-351.02.)

2. Federal Laws Related to Procurement Expressly Applicable to the District Government

Because of the District of Columbia's historic connection with the federal government, several federal statutes related to government contracting expressly apply to the District government. The primary statutes are as follows:

a. Buy American Act of 1933, 41 U.S.C. §§ 8301–8305 (requiring preference for goods made in the United States)
b. Davis-Bacon Act of 1931, 40 U.S.C. §§ 3141–3148 (for contracts over $2,500, requiring that laborers and mechanics be paid the local prevailing wage,

established by the Department of Labor, for contracts for the construction, alteration, or repair of public buildings or public works)

c. Service Contract Act of 1965, 41 U.S.C. §§ 6701–6707 (for contracts over $2,500, requiring that service employees in various classes be paid the local prevailing wage determined by the Department of Labor)
d. Walsh-Healey Public Contracts Act of 1936, 41 U.S.C. §§ 35–45 (for contracts over $15,000, for manufacture or furnishing of goods, requiring that contractor employees be paid the prevailing local wage determined by the Department of Labor, and setting job health and safety standards)

3. Federal Laws Related to Procurement That District of Columbia Government Requires Contractors to Follow

The District government requires contractors to follow a number of general federal laws, including the following: (1) Americans with Disabilities Act of 1990 (ADA), 42 U.S.C. §§ 12101 to 12213 (prohibiting discrimination based on disability); (2) Buy American Act of 1933 (described above); (3) Davis-Bacon Act of 1931 (described above); (4) Drug-Free Workplace Act of 1988, 41 U.S.C. §§ 8101 to 8106 (requiring contractors to promise to provide drug-free workplaces as a precondition of receiving a contract); (5) Fair Labor Standards Act of 1938, 29 U.S.C. §§ 201 to 219 (requiring minimum wages and time-and-a-half overtime pay for employees working more than 40 hours a week); (6) Health Insurance Portability and Accountability Act of 1996 (HIPAA), 42 U.S.C. §§ 1320d to 1320d-9 (protecting health insurance coverage when a worker changes jobs, providing standards for how personally identifiable healthcare and health insurance information is protected from disclosure and preventing healthcare fraud and abuse; setting standards for pre-tax medical spending accounts; establishing standards for group health plans; and governing company-owned life insurance policies); (7) Rehabilitation Act of 1973, 29 U.S.C. §§ 701 to 7961 (requiring affirmative action in employment, and prohibiting discrimination, based on disability, using standards similar to the ADA); (8) Service Contract Act of 1965 (described above); and (9) Walsh-Healey Act of 1936 (described above).

4. District of Columbia Laws Related to Procurement That District Contractors Are Required to Follow

The PPRA is supplemented by District of Columbia statutes relating to certain types of contracts and contractors. In many cases, these statutes also apply to District agencies that are excluded from the PPRA.

A bond is required for a "contract, exceeding $25,000 in amount, for the construction, alteration, or repair of any public building or public work of the District of Columbia," at an amount that varies depending on the size of the contract, with a maximum of $2.5 million. Laborers and materialmen have a right to sue on the bond. (See D.C. Code §§ 2-201.01 to 2-201.03, 2-201.11.)

On contracts for construction work for the District government, 10 percent of the total amount of the contract may be retained as a guaranty fund to ensure that the terms of the contract are strictly and faithfully performed, with discretion to release this amount after 50 percent of the work is complete. (See D.C. Code § 2-203.01.)

Under the Small, Local, and Disadvantaged Business Enterprise Development and Assistance Act of 2005, the District government has a program for certifying qualifying businesses. (See D.C. Code §§ 2-218.01 to 2-218.82.) Businesses certified under this program receive certain preferences in evaluating their bids and proposals. (See D.C. Code § 2-218.43; DCMR tit. 27, ch. 8.)

The District has a "first source agreement" program under the First Source Employment Agreement Act of 1974 to ensure that residents of the District of Columbia receive priority for new jobs created by municipal financing and development programs by requiring all construction projects funded in whole or in part with District of Columbia funds, or other funds that the District administers, provide for increased employment opportunities for District residents. (See D.C. Code §§ 2-219.01 to 2-219.52.)

Under the Living Wage Act of 2006, contractors with the District government that have contracts in the amount of $100,000 or more, are required to pay to their affiliated employees, at minimum, the living wage required by the act. (See D.C. Code §§ 2-220.01 to 2-220.11; DCMR tit. 7, ch. 10.)

Under the Quick Payment Act of 1984, District government agencies under the direct control of the mayor may be liable for interests and penalties if vendors are not paid within prescribed periods. (See D.C. Code §§ 2-221.01 to 2-221.06; DCMR tit. 1, § 1700 *et seq*. See also D.C. Code § 2-359.09 (incorporating interest rate set forth in D.C. Code § 28-3302(b) and providing that interest accrues from when the contracting officer receives the claim until it is paid).)

The Office of the Chief Technology Officer of the District of Columbia is authorized to "[r]eview and approve all agency proposals, purchase orders, and contracts for the acquisition of information technology and telecommunications systems, resources, and services, and recommend approval or disapproval to the Chief Procurement Officer." (D.C. Code § 1-1403(2).) This process applies to all such contracts valued at more than $25,000. (DCMR tit. 1, § 5602. See also D.C. Code §§ 2-213.01 to 2-213.02 (automatic data processing contracts).)

The Green Finance Authority, also referred to as the Green Bank, was established as an instrumentality of the District government to increase private investment in clean energy, clean transportation vehicles and infrastructure, clean water, stormwater management, energy efficiency, water efficiency, and green infrastructure projects in the District of Columbia. The act established a fund for the Authority and a board of directors and authorized the Authority to issue bonds. (See D.C. Code §§ 8-173.01 to 8-173.64.)

5. District of Columbia Laws Imposing Criminal or Civil Liability

Contractors, bidders, and prospective bidders with respect to contracts with the District government are subject to general criminal laws prohibiting bribery or corrupt influence. (D.C. Code § 22-704.)

The PPRA itself imposes civil liability for submitting an unsupported claim to a contracting officer. (D.C. Code § 2-359.08(d)(1).)

Contractors or others who make false claims to a District government officer, employee, or agent are liable for treble damages and civil penalties. (See D.C. Code §§ 2-381.01 to 2-381.10.) Civil penalties are between $5,500 and $11,000 for each false claim. (D.C. Code § 2-381.02.) The penalty for a knowingly false, fictitious, or fraudulent representation is a fine of $100,000. (D.C. Code § 2-381.09.)

Contractors in construction contracts that misclassify employees as independent contractors are liable for civil and administrative penalties. (D.C. Code §§ 32-1307 to 32-1331.07.)

6. General District of Columbia Laws That Contractors Are Required to Follow

In addition, contractors are subject to general District laws, including the following: (1) District of Columbia Freedom of Information Act (FOIA), D.C. Code sections 2-531 to 2-539; (2) District of Columbia Human Rights Act, D.C. Code sections 2-1401.01 to 2-1431.08; (3) Fair Criminal Record Screening Act of 2014, D.C. Code sections 32-1341 to 32-1346; (4) Language Access Act of 2004, D.C. Code sections 2-1931 to 2-1936; (5) Protecting Pregnant Workers Fairness Act of 2014, D.C. Code sections 32-1231 to 32-1231.15; and (6) Unemployed Anti-Discrimination Act of 2012, D.C. Code sections 32-1361 to 32-1368.

II. Regulations

A. Authority to Issue Procurement Rules

Under prior law (the D.C. Procurement Practices Act of 1985), regulations (called "rules" under District of Columbia law) pertaining to procurement under that statute were promulgated by the mayor of the District of Columbia. (D.C. Code §§ 2-302.02, 2-302.04 (2001).) However, under the PPRA, with two exceptions, rulemaking authority has been vested in the chief procurement officer (CPO) of the District of Columbia. (D.C. Code § 2-361.06(a)(1).) The exceptions are as follows: Rules concerning procurement of construction projects and related services under D.C. Code sections 2-356.01 to 2-356.04 are issued by the Department of General Services. (D.C. Code § 2-361.06(a)(2).) Rules concerning matters under the jurisdiction of the CAB, D.C. Code sections 2-360.01 to 2-360.08, are issued by the Board. (D.C. Code § 2-361.06(a)(3).) All rules must be issued pursuant to the D.C. Administrative Procedure Act. (D.C. Code §§ 2-501 to 2-510.) However, the PPRA has a savings clause for existing rules; they will remain in effect until superseded, unless they are inconsistent with the PPRA. (D.C. Code § 2-361.06(b).) The great bulk of the current procurement rules were issued under prior law, whose provisions, as noted, are for the most part identical to the PPRA.

B. Procurement Rules Pertaining to the PPRA and Related Statutes

The procurement rules concerning the PPRA and related statutes, including the PPPA, are codified in title 27 of the DCMR, entitled "Contracts and Procurement." They are on Westlaw and LexisNexis and also on the website of the D.C. Office of Documents at http://www.dcregs.dc.gov. The chapters in title 27, with links to each, can be displayed by typing the number 27 in the field entitled "By Chapter Number" and pressing the magnifying glass icon. In addition, chapters 1 to 4 are also available on the website of the CAB, https://cab.dc.gov. Go to the tab "Rules and Regulations." The chapters of DCMR title 27 are as follows:

- Chapter 1. General Rules of the Contract Appeals Board
- Chapter 2. Appeal Procedures of the Contract Board
- Chapter 3. Protest Procedures of the Contract Appeals Board
- Chapter 4. Electronic Filing
- Chapter 5. Criminal Background and Traffic Records Checks for District Government Contractors That Provide Direct Services to Children or Youth
- Chapter 6. Minority Business Development

Chapter 7. Minority Business Enterprises
Chapter 8. Local, Small, and Disadvantaged Business Enterprises Contracting
Chapter 9. Surplus Property
Chapter 10. District of Columbia Procurement System
Chapter 11. Minority and Other Business Preferences
Chapter 12. Contract Management and Administration
Chapter 13. Publicizing Contract Actions
Chapter 14. Use of Electronic Commerce
Chapter 15. Procurement by Competitive Sealed Bidding
Chapter 16. Procurement by Competitive Sealed Proposals
Chapter 17. Sole Source and Emergency Procurements
Chapter 18. Small Purchase and Other Simplified Purchase Procedures
Chapter 19. Contracting for Services
Chapter 20. Special Contracting Methods
Chapter 21. Required Sources of Goods and Services
Chapter 22. Contractors
Chapter 23. Delivery and Performance
Chapter 24. Types of Contracts
Chapter 25. Specifications, Standards, and Other Purchase Descriptions
Chapter 26. Construction and Architect-Engineer Contracts
Chapter 27. Bonds, Other Security, and Insurance
Chapter 28. Subcontracting
Chapter 29. Special Pilot Project Procurements
Chapter 30. Inherently Governmental Functions
Chapter 31. Patents, Copyrights, and Proprietary Information
Chapter 32. Contract Financing and Funding
Chapter 33. Contract Cost Principles
Chapter 36. Contract Modifications
Chapter 37. Termination of Contracts
Chapter 38. Protests, Claims, and Disputes
Chapter 40. Quality Assurance
Chapter 41. Use of District Property and Sources by Contractors
Chapter 42. Freedom of Information and Privacy
Chapter 45. Procurement Training
Chapter 46. Not-for-Profit Hospital Corporation Procurement Rules
Chapter 47. Department of General Services Procurement Rules for Construction and Related Services
Chapter 48. Public-Private Partnerships
Chapter 50. Office of the Attorney General Procurement Rules
Chapter 51. Civil False Claims Penalty Inflation Adjustment

It should be noted that chapter 47 of title 27 of the DCMR sets forth detailed rules concerning procurement of construction and construction-related services by the District of Columbia Department of General Services, which is a major source of government contracts by the District government.

C. Procurement Rules Pertaining to District Government Agencies Exempt from the PPRA

As noted, several District government agencies are exempt in whole or in part from the PPRA. Generally, these agencies have procurement rules that are codified in the DCMR. As noted above, all of these rules are accessible at http://www.dcregs.dc.gov. These agencies, and the pertinent rules, are as follows, listed alphabetically by agency name:

District of Columbia General Hospital: DCMR title 22B, chapter 96
District of Columbia Public Schools: DCMR title 5D, chapter 1 (Office of Public Education Facilities Modernization)
District of Columbia Retirement Board: DCMR title 7, chapter 16
District of Columbia School of Law: DCMR title 8A, chapter 25
District of Columbia Water and Sewer Authority: DCMR title 21, chapter 53
Not-for-Profit Hospital Corporation: DCMR title 27, chapter 46
Office of the Attorney General for the District of Columbia: DCMR title 27, chapter 50
Public Service Commission of the District of Columbia: DCMR title 15, chapter 22
University of the District of Columbia: DCMR title 8B, chapter 30
Washington Convention and Sports Authority: DCMR title 19, chapter 3

III. Source Selection

The methods of source selection are listed in D.C. Code section 2-354.01 and are detailed below. Contacts between bidders or offerors and District employees concerning source selection are restricted. (See D.C. Code § 2-354.01a.) Certain classes of transactions are exempt from the competition requirements under D.C. Code section 2-354.13. (See Section III.M.)

A. Competitive Sealed Bidding

Contracts over $100,000 must be awarded by competitive sealed bidding unless the CPO issues a determination and findings (D&F) that this is not practicable or not in the best interests of the District government. Bids are solicited through an invitation for bids (IFB), which may include responsibility standards, and must state whether an award is made on the lowest bid price or the lowest evaluated price. If the lowest evaluated price is used, the objective measurable criteria utilized must be set forth in the IFB. Public notice of an IFB must be given at least 14 days in advance, unless the CPO issues a D&F that it is appropriate to shorten the notice period to not less than three days. Bids are opened publicly, and each bid, the bidder, and the price offering are recorded and open to public inspection. (See D.C. Code § 2-354.02; DCMR tit. 27, ch. 15.)

B. Competitive Sealed Proposals

A contract may be awarded by competitive sealed proposals when competitive sealed bidding is not practicable or advantageous to the District government. Proposals are solicited through a request for proposals (RFP) from the maximum number of qualified sources consistent with the nature of and need for the goods or services. The RFP must set forth the evaluation factors and their relative importance, including price. The contracting officer may issue a request for qualifications (RFQ) if the CPO makes a D&F that it is advantageous to the District government. The contracting officer shall rank the prospective contractors submitting RFQs and shall issue an RFP to at least the three highest ranked prospective contractors. After ranking the prospective contractors, the contracting officer may elect to proceed with negotiations with the highest ranked contractor on price or scope of the contract and, if a satisfactory contract cannot be negotiated, may negotiate with the second most qualified contractor, and so on. (See D.C. Code § 2-354.03; DCMR tit. 27, ch. 16.)

C. Sole Source Procurements

A contract may be awarded by noncompetitive negotiations when there is only one source after the CPO makes a D&F justifying this method of procurement. Notice of intent to enter into a sole source contract must be posted on the internet at least ten days prior to award with a description of the items to be procured and the intended contractor. (See D.C. Code § 2-354.04; DCMR tit. 27, §§ 1700, 1701.)

D. Emergency Procurements

A contract may be awarded by emergency procurement (1) if there is an imminent threat to the public health, welfare, property, or safety, or (2) to prevent or minimize serious disruption in agency operations. The procurement must be made with as much competition as is practicable under the circumstances. These procedures may not be used for contracts exceeding 90 days (unless the development time exceeds 90 days, in which case the limit is 120 days). Notice of the emergency procurement must be posted on the internet at least ten days prior to award with a description of the items to be procured and the designated contractor. (See D.C. Code § 2-354.05; DCMR tit. 27, §§ 1702, 1703.) An emergency procurement may not be justified by (1) the lack of adequate advance planning; (2) delays in the procurement caused by administrative delays, lack of sufficient procurement personnel, or improper handling of procurement requests or competitive procedures; or (3) pending expiration of budget authority. (DCMR tit. 27, § 1702.3.)

E. Human Care Procurements

The CPO may enter into an agreement for human care services if the services are (1) negotiated on a fee-for-service or unit-rate basis using benchmarks and quantifiable measurements that shall be uniformly applied to providers of the same service; (2) purchased at rates adopted by rule; or (3) of the type that an agency typically purchases as needs arise, but for which the quantity, rate of utilization, delivery areas, or specific beneficiaries of the service cannot be accurately estimated at the outset of the procurement process. (D.C. Code § 3-254.06.) A "human care agreement" is defined as one for "education, special education, health, human, or social services, to be provided directly to individuals who have disabilities or are disadvantaged, displaced, elderly, indigent, mentally ill, physically ill, unemployed, or minors in the custody of the District." (D.C. Code § 2-351.04(37).) The CPO must publish an RFQ and may negotiate with any responsible service provider that submits an RFQ.

F. Small Purchase Procurements

Contracts for goods and services not exceeding $100,000 may be procured by a streamlined process, which includes requiring solicitation from multiple vendors and transparency. The CPO may establish a noncompetitive process for contracts not to exceed $10,000. (See D.C. Code § 2-354.07; DCMR tit. 27, ch. 18.) A contracting officer may award a contract not to exceed $10,000 without competitive quotations but must obtain at least three quotations for contracts over that amount and not in excess of $100,000. (DCMR tit. 27, §§ 1800.3, 1800.4.)

G. Special Pilot Procurements

The CPO may award a contract without competitive sealed bidding or competitive sealed proposals if it is determined that there is "an unusual or unique situation" that makes applications of the requirements for these procurement methods not in the public interest, including a contract made to (1) satisfy a new and unique District government requirement or (2) obtain a new technology. The procurement must be made with such competition that is practicable under the circumstances and there must be a D&F of the reasons for this type of procurement. (See D.C. Code § 2-354.08; DCMR tit. 27, § 4723.)

H. Reverse Auctions

The CPO may procure goods or services through a reverse action (i.e., "an online procurement method whereby pre-qualified suppliers compete with one another to provide a good or service, typically commodities, to a buyer or group of buyers," D.C. Code § 2-351.04(54)) upon a determination that this procurement method is the most effective for the District government. The CPO may dispose of surplus goods through this method. (See D.C. Code § 2-354.09; DCMR tit. 27, § 1566.)

I. Procurements through a General Services Administration Schedule

The CPO may procure goods and services through a General Services Administration Schedule pursuant to 40 U.S.C. §§ 502(a)(3) and 602(c), provided that the price is determined to be reasonable. (See D.C. Code § 2-354.10.)

J. Cooperative Agreements

The CPO may purchase goods and services through cooperative purchasing (i.e., "procurement conducted by the District Government with, or on behalf of, any government or public entity, including a state, county, or municipal jurisdiction or the Federal government," D.C. Code §§ 2-351.04(18), 2-354.11). (See Part VII.)

K. Procurements through the District of Columbia Supply Schedule

Agencies may procure goods and services from the District of Columbia Supply Schedule (DCSS) from certified business enterprises by any sole source selection method authorized by the PPRA or from a DCSS contractor that maintains a price agreement with a federal agency or who agrees to adopt the same pricing, provided that the price does not exceed that of the agreement with the federal agency. (See D.C. Code § 2-354.12.)

L. Infrastructure Facilities and Services

Procurements for construction projects and related management services may be awarded pursuant to D.C. Code sections 2-356.01 to 2-356.04. The types of project delivery methods authorized are (1) architectural and engineering services; (2) construction management; (3) construction management at risk; (4) design-bid-build; (5) design-build; (6) design-build-finance-operate-maintain; (7) design-build-operate-maintain; and (8) operations and maintenance.

The source selection methods depend on the type of contract. (See D.C. Code § 356.02.) Except for architectural and engineering services, prospective contractors may be selected through a prequalification process set forth in D.C. Code section 2-356.03. Architectural and engineering services may be procured by negotiated contracts on the basis of demonstrated competence and qualification fair and reasonable prices pursuant to D.C. Code section 2-356.04.

M. Exemptions from Competition Requirements

D.C. Code section 2-354.13, provides that "[c]ontracts for the following procurements shall be exempt from the competition requirements established by this act [the PPRA]": (1) artistic services or works of art; (2) commodities or contractual services if federal or District law prescribes with whom the District must contract; (3) legal services or negotiation services in connection with proceedings before administrative agencies or state or federal courts, including experts, attorneys, and mediators; (4) copyrighted or patented materials, including technical pamphlets, published books, maps, and testing or instructional materials, provided that the materials are purchased directly from the owner of the copyright or patent; (5) memberships in trade or professional organizations; (6) entertainers; (7) job-related seminars and training for District employees; (8) maintenance and support of existing software and technology to the extent that the creator of the intellectual property is still protected and is the only source of the maintenance and support of the existing software and technology; (9) public transit fare cards, passes, and tokens; (10) personal property or services provided by another public entity, agency, or authority; (11) postage; (12) purchases of advertising in all media, including electronic, print, radio, and television, provided that they are purchased directly from the media outlet; (13) trade and career fairs for District employees; (14) special event venues and related services as dictated by the establishment; (15) subscriptions for periodicals and newspapers; (16) ticket purchases for special events, tourist attractions, and amusement parks; and (17) professional development training that supports principal, teacher, and student achievement pursuant to the District of Columbia Public Schools Master Education Plan.

IV. Bid Protests and Contract Disputes

A. Bid Protests

There is no formal process within a contracting agency to determine protests.

B. Bid Protest Appeals

A protest of the solicitation or award of a contract must be filed with the District of Columbia CAB. (See Section V.B.) A protest may be filed by "any actual or prospective bidder, offeror, or contractor who is aggrieved in connection with the solicitation or award of a contract." (D.C. Code § 2-360.08(a).) A protest based on alleged improprieties in the solicitation apparent before bid opening must be filed prior to the bid opening or the time set for receipt of initial proposals, or, if the improprieties were incorporated later into the proposal, the protest must be filed no later than the closing time for receipt of proposals following the incorporation. Otherwise, a protest must be filed within ten business days after the earlier of when the basis of the protest was or should have been known. (D.C. Code § 2-360.08(b).)

If a protest is filed, the CAB is required to notify the contracting officer and the contract may not be awarded while the protest is pending. If the contract has been awarded and the contracting officer receives this notice within 11 business days after the award, the contracting officer must immediately direct the contractor to suspend work while the protest is pending. (D.C. Code § 2-360.08(c)(1).) Notwithstanding these rules, performance may proceed, or an award may be made, if the CPO makes a determination in writing supported by substantial evidence that urgent and compelling circumstances that significantly affect the interests of the District do not permit waiting for the decision of the CAB. (D.C. Code § 2-360.08(c)(2).)

The CAB decides whether the solicitation or award is in accordance with applicable laws, rules, and terms of the solicitation. The CAB may receive additional evidence, and prior decisions of administrative officials are not final or conclusive. As amended in 2016, the PPRA provides, with respect to the CAB's review of a bid protest, that "[a]n agency's determination of its minimum needs and its determination of the best method of accommodating those minimum needs are business judgments primarily within the agency's discretion," and "[t]he [CAB] may not sustain a protest on the basis of either determination unless a protester demonstrates by clear and convincing evidence that the determination lacked a reasonable basis." (D.C. Code § 2-360.08(d-1).) The amendment overrode the holding in *MorphoTrust USA, Inc. v. D.C. Contract Appeals Board*, 115 A.3d 571 (D.C. 2015), based on prior language of D.C. Code section 2-360.08(d) that the CAB's proceedings were "de novo" (which was repealed by the same amendment), which had the effect of requiring the CAB to determine from scratch whether the specifications met the agency's minimum needs. The CAB must issue a decision within 60 business days from the date the protest is filed. If the CAB determines the contract is void, it must direct that the contract be canceled and that a determination be made under D.C. Code section 2-359.02 as to whether the displaced contractor is entitled to costs actually incurred. (See D.C. Code § 2-360.08(d).)

The CAB's protest procedures are set forth in DCMR title 27, chapter 3.

C. Contract Disputes

1. Contract Claims

Claims by a contractor against the District government must be in writing and submitted to the contracting officer for decision. The contracting officer is required to issue a decision within 120 days. If a decision is not rendered within this period, the claim is deemed to have been denied, and the contractor has the right to appeal to the CAB. (D.C. Code § 2-359.08.)

2. Contract Claims Appeals

A contractor has a right to appeal the decision of a contracting officer to the CAB by filing a complaint within 90 days after the date the decision is issued or the date the claim is deemed denied (by the contracting officer's failure to issue a decision within 120 days). (D.C. Code § 2-360.04.) If the amount in dispute is $50,000 or less, the contractor may elect a procedure for the accelerated disposition of the appeal. Under this procedure, the CAB must resolve the dispute within 180 days. (D.C. Code § 2-360.04(c).) If the amount in dispute is $10,000 or less, the contractor may elect a small claims procedure. Under this procedure, the dispute may be resolved by a single member of the CAB and, whenever possible, should be resolved within 90 days. (D.C. Code § 2-360.04(d). See Section V.A for a general discussion of the CAB.)

The CAB's procedures for contract claims (including claims for interest and penalties) and disputes (including disputes concerning suspension or debarment) are set forth in DCMR title 27, chapter 2.

D. Debarment and Suspension

1. Grounds for Suspension or Debarment

Under D.C. Code section 2-359.07, the CPO may suspend or debar a person from consideration of award of contracts or subcontracts for any of the following reasons, unless the CPO finds that this action would be contrary to the best interests of the District or would be unwarranted under the circumstances: (1) conviction of a criminal offense incident to obtaining, or attempting to obtain, a public or private contract or subcontract or in the performance of the contract; (2) conviction for fraud, embezzlement, theft, forgery, bribery, falsification or destruction of records, receiving stolen property, or any other offense indicating a lack of business integrity that currently affects the contractor's responsibility as a District government contractor; (3) conviction under antitrust laws arising out of the submission of bids or proposals; (4) adjudication by a court of civil liability for filing false claims; (5) a determination by the CPO of a false assertion of certified business enterprise status or eligibility; (6) a determination by the CPO that the contractor's willful failure to perform according to specifications or within time limits or other unsatisfactory performance justifies this action; (7) a determination by the CPO of misclassification of an employee as an independent contractor; (8) any other cause the CPO determines to be sufficiently serious and compelling to affect responsibility as a District Government contractor, including debarment by another governmental entity for any cause listed in rules; (9) submission of a bid or proposal to a District agency by a person debarred or suspended under D.C. Code section 2-359.07(c)(1), (2), or (3); or (10) receipt by the CPO of notification from the chairman of the Council of the District of Columbia that a person has willfully failed to cooperate with an investigation by the Council or a committee thereof (debarment only).

2. Procedure for Suspension and Debarment

A suspension takes effect immediately. A debarment takes effect after notice and a reasonable opportunity for a hearing. A debarment may not be more than five years. (D.C. Code § 2-359.07(a), (b).) However, a person debarred twice is debarred permanently, although with the right of reinstatement after ten years. (D.C. Code § 2-359.07(k).)

The CPO must issue a written decision to suspend or debar a person. The person has the right of appeal to the CAB within 60 days of receipt of the CPO's decision, but filing a notice of appeal with the CAB does not stay the action. (D.C. Code § 2-359.07(e), (f), (g).)

Rules concerning debarment and suspension under the PPRA are set forth in DCMR title 27, sections 2210 to 2218. In addition, procurement rules pertaining to independent agencies not subject to the PPRA contain provisions on suspension and debarment for those agencies. (See Section II.C.)

V. Administrative and Judicial Review

A. Administrative Review

As noted, review of final decisions of contracting agencies and officers may be obtained by filing an appeal in the CAB. The CAB is located at 441 Fourth Street, NW, Suite 350 North, Washington, D.C., 20001. The telephone number is (202) 727-6597. Parties before the CAB may file and serve all pleadings in a secure digital environment. Documents filed in the CAB and the CAB's decisions and orders are accessible on the CAB's website, https://cab.dc.gov.

The CAB is a three-member board appointed by the mayor, and is the "exclusive hearing tribunal for, and shall review and determine de novo": (1) any protest of a solicitation or award of a contract addressed to the CAB by any actual or prospective bidder, offeror, or the contractor who is aggrieved in connection with the solicitation or award of a contract; (2) any appeal by a contractor from a final decision by the contracting officer on a claim by a contractor, when the claim arises under or relates to a contract; and (3) any claim by the District against a contractor, when such claim arises under or relates to a contract. (D.C. Code § 2-360.03(a).)

Title 27 of the DCMR (Contracts and Procurement) contains several chapters applicable to administrative review in the CAB:

Chapter 1. General Rules of the Contract Appeals Board

Chapter 2. Appeal Procedures of the Contract Appeals Board (see Section IV.C.2)

Chapter 3. Protest Procedures of the Contract Appeals Board (see Section IV.B)

Chapter 4. Electronic Filing

The DCMR is searchable on Westlaw and Lexis and is available on the website of the D.C. Office of Documents. (See Section II.B.) In addition, the CAB's rules, chapters 1 to 4 of title 27 of the DCMR, are available on the CAB's website. The link is https://cab.dc.gov. Go to the tab "Rules and Regulations."

The CAB's decisions are published in the District of Columbia Register, which is on Westlaw and Lexis and is also available at https://dcregs.dc.gov/. The CAB's decisions are also available on the CAB's website. The link is https://cab.dc.gov. Under the tab "Appeals and Protests," go to "Search for a Case."

The CAB's decisions have precedential value with respect to proceedings before the CAB, except for decisions utilizing the small claims procedure, which have no precedential value. (See D.C. Code § 2-360.04(d)(5).)

B. Judicial Review

1. Review of Contested Cases by the District of Columbia Court of Appeals

The PPRA provides that a decision of the CAB may be appealed to the District of Columbia Court of Appeals by a contractor or by the CPO, with the prior approval of the Office of the Attorney General for the District of Columbia. (D.C. Code § 2-360.05.) An appeal must be filed within 120 days of the CAB's decision. (*Id.*) This extended time period for an appeal is consistent with the rules of that court, which, while providing 30 days as the default time frame for agency appeals, defers to other time frames provided by statute. (D.C. Court of Appeals R. 15(a)(2).)

This right to appeal CAB decisions to the District of Columbia Court of Appeals, however, is limited to decisions in "contested cases" (i.e., proceedings in which the parties have a right to a trial-type hearing). (It is also limited to appeals by "contractors" or the CPO.) A disappointed bidder does not have a right to appeal a decision of the CAB directly to the District of Columbia Court of Appeals because a bid protest is not a "contested case." (See *Jones & Artis Construction Co. v. D.C. Contract Appeals Board*, 549 A.2d 315 (D.C. 1988); *accord Abadie v. D.C. Contract Appeals Board*, 916 A.2d 913 (D.C. 2007).) Moreover, a bidder is not a "contractor."

The PPRA provides that "the decision of the Board on questions of fact shall be final and conclusive and shall not be set aside unless the decision is fraudulent, arbitrary, capricious, or so grossly erroneous as to necessarily imply bad faith, or if the decision is not supported by substantial evidence." (D.C. Code § 2-360.07.) However, the District of Columbia Court of Appeals reviews questions of law and contract interpretation de novo. The court accords great weight to the CAB's interpretation of a contract, but will not defer to the CAB's interpretation if it determines that it is unreasonable. (*District of Columbia v. D.C. Contract Appeals Board*, 145 A.3d 523, 530 (D.C. 2016); *accord Tillery v. D.C. Contract Appeals Board*, 912 A.2d 1169, 1176 (D.C. 2006); *Unfoldment, Inc. v. D.C. Contract Appeals Board*, 909 A.2d 204, 208–09 (D.C. 2006); *Belcon, Inc. v. D.C. Water & Sewer Authority*, 826 A.2d 380, 384 (D.C. 2003).)

The District of Columbia Court of Appeals has noted that, in reviewing the CAB's decisions, it "look[s] not only to the case law on which the Board [CAB] relied but to other decisions of the United States Court of Appeals for the Federal Circuit, the former United States Court of Claims and its successors, and the various federal boards of contract appeals, 'all of which have particular expertise in this area.'" (*Abadie v. Organization for Environmental Growth*, 806 A.2d 1225, 1227 (D.C. 2002) (quoting *Dano Resource Recovery, Inc. v. District of Columbia*, 620 A.2d 1346, 1352 (D.C. 1993)); *accord TRG Construction, Inc. v. D.C. Water & Sewer Authority*, 70 A.3d 1164, 1167 (D.C. 2013).)

Decisions of the District of Columbia Court of Appeals are available on Westlaw and Lexis, and from the District of Columbia Courts' website at https://www.dccourts.gov/court-of-appeals/opinions-memorandum-of-judgments.

2. Review of Noncontested Cases by the Superior Court of the District of Columbia

A disappointed bidder or other person aggrieved by a decision of the CAB in a noncontested case, such as a bid protest, may obtain judicial review by filing an original action in the Superior Court of the District of Columbia, invoking that court's equitable jurisdiction. (See *Jones & Artis Construction Co. v. D.C. Contract Appeals Board*, 549 A.2d 315 (D.C. 1988).) The time limit for filing such an action is the residual, three-year statute of limitations under D.C. Code section 12-301(8). The Rules of the Superior Court do not presently provide a time frame for filing such an action. However, because such an action invokes the court's equitable jurisdiction, the equitable defense of laches may be available.

A party aggrieved by the decision of the Superior Court of D.C. may seek review in the District of Columbia Court of Appeals by filing a notice of appeal within 30 days pursuant to D.C. Court of Appeals Rule 4. The D.C. Court of Appeals reviews the decision of the D.C. Superior Court de novo and, in effect, supplants the decision of the D.C. Superior Court. (See *Eagle Maintenance Services, Inc. v. D.C. Contract Appeals Board*, 893 A.2d 569, 572 (D.C. 2006).)

VI. Extent of State's Adoption or Adaptation of ABA Model Procurement Code

The PPRA follows the American Bar Association (ABA) Model Procurement Code (MPC) in many respects, and often copies the language of sections of the MPC verbatim. In particular, the PPRA is identical, or substantively similar, to the following MPC Articles:

Article 1—General Provisions (see D.C. Code §§ 2-351.01 to 2-351.04)

Article 2—Procurement Organization (see D.C. Code § 2-352.01)

Article 3—Source Selection and Contract Formation (see D.C. Code §§ 2-354.01 to 2-364.20 and 2-355.01 to 2-355.04)

Article 5—Procurement of Infrastructure Facilities and Services (see D.C. Code §§ 2-356.01 to 2-356.04 and 2-357.01 to 2-357.06)

Article 8—Supply Management (see D.C. Code §§ 2-358.01 to 2-358.03)

Article 9—Legal and Contractual Remedies (see D.C. Code §§ 2-359.02 to 2-359.09 and 2-360.01 to 2-360.08)

Article 10—Cooperative Purchasing (see D.C. Code § 2-354.11)

VII. Cooperative Purchasing

A. Authority

The PPRA provides that "[t]he CPO may, and is encouraged to, participate in, sponsor, conduct, or administer cooperative purchasing agreements for the procurement of goods, services, or construction." (D.C. Code § 2-354.11(a).) A "cooperative purchasing agreement" is defined as "procurement conducted by the District Government with, or on behalf of, any government or public entity, including a state, county, or municipal jurisdiction or the Federal government." (D.C. Code § 2-351.04(18).)

Two agencies that are not subject to the PPRA are authorized by rules to use cooperative purchasing agreements—namely, the Not-for-Profit Hospital Corporation (see DCMR tit. 27, § 4614.1) and the Office of the Attorney General for the District of Columbia (see DCMR tit. 27, § 5028.1). The rules both provide that the agencies are "authorized and encouraged to participate in, sponsor, conduct, or administer Cooperative Purchasing Agreements and contracts with any other organization, public or private, including group purchasing organizations, hospitals and hospital consortiums, state, county, or municipal jurisdictions, for the purpose of procuring supplies and services, which shall include construction services or architectural and engineering services related to construction repairs, upgrades, restoration, alteration, and reconstruction of existing buildings and facilities." (DCMR tit. 27, §§ 4614.1(a), 5028.1(a).)

B. Requirements

The rules for cooperative purchasing agreements are general. These agreements "shall be in accordance with, to the extent practicable, all laws and rules of the District government with respect to contracting, and shall be consistent with laws and rules of the United States government that apply specifically to the District." (D.C. Code § 2-354.11(b).) Also, before an agency may enter into a cooperative purchasing agreement, it must obtain authorization from the CPO or a designee. (D.C. Code § 2-354.11(c).)

The rules authorizing the Not-for-Profit Corporation and Office of the Attorney General for the District of Columbia to enter into cooperative agreements likewise provide that they "be in accordance with, to the extent practicable, all laws, statutes, and regulations applicable to the [agency] with respect to contracting, and shall not be inconsistent with laws, statutes, and regulations of the United States government that apply specifically to the District." (DCMR tit. 27, §§ 4614.1(b), 5028.1(b).)

Florida Procurement Rules and Regulations

Prepared by
Karen D. Walker, Holland & Knight LLP
Email: karen.walker@hklaw.com
and
Joseph M. Goldstein, Shutts & Bowen LLP
Email: jgoldstein@shutts.com
and
Andrew Schwartz, Associate General Counsel, Terran Orbital
Email: andrew.schwartz@terranorbital.com

I. Statutory Reference

The State of Florida spends billions of dollars each year on contracts for goods and services. The Florida Department of Management Services develops and oversees the procedures under which state agencies purchase commodities and services. Commodities and services that are frequently purchased by numerous agencies are procured by the Department of Management Services under standard specifications resulting in state term contracts. State term contracts are required to be used by state agencies, but may also be used by eligible users, which include the legislative and judicial branches, local governments, state universities, school districts, and certain independent, non-profit colleges and universities.

Florida is not a Model Code state. Chapter 287 of the Florida Statutes governs the procurement of commodities and contractual services by Florida executive branch agencies. There are various other statutory provisions, however, throughout the Florida Statutes regarding government procurement. In addition to the statutory provisions, Florida agencies have adopted procurement regulations. The Florida Department of Management Services' general purchasing regulations are found in chapter 60A-1 of the Florida Administrative Code. The Florida Administrative Code also includes other agency rules relating to purchasing. This summary identifies the key statutory and regulatory provisions found in the Florida Statutes and Florida Administrative Code.

Some local government procurements are governed by state statute and others are governed by local ordinance, policy, or procedure. Several key statutes that apply to local government procurements include Florida Statutes section 255.20, governing local bids and contracts for public construction works, and section 287.055, the

Consultants' Competitive Negotiation Act, governing the acquisition of professional services in the areas of architecture, engineering, landscape architecture, or surveying and mapping by state and local agencies and school districts.

A. Procurement/Purchasing Statutes

1. Primary Procurement Statutes

Chapter 287	Procurement of personal property and services
Chapter 120	Administrative Procedure Act (bid protest provisions are contained specifically in section 120.57(3))
Section 255.20	Local bids and contracts for public construction works

2. Other Procurement Statutes

Agriculture

§ 591.21	Community forests

Bonds

§ 215.68	Bond sales by the state
§ 218.385	Bond sales by local governments
§ 348.0005	Bond sales by expressway authorities

Child Support

§ 61.1826	Child support, operation of State Disbursement Unit and State Case Registry

Child Welfare

§ 402.73	Department of Children and Families, contracting and performance standards
§ 402.7305	Department of Children and Families, procurement of contractual services and contract management
§ 409.987	Community-based child welfare lead agency procurement

Corrections

§ 944.597	Prisoner transportation by private companies
§§ 944.710 –944.729	Correctional facilities private construction, and operation
§ 948.11	Electronic monitoring devices for offenders on community control
Chapter 957	Correctional privatization

Educational Facilities

§ 1010.04	Purchasing
§ 1013.15	Lease, rental, and lease-purchase of educational facilities
§§ 1013.4 –1013.51	Contracting for educational facilities

<u>Elections</u>

§ 101.293 Voting equipment

<u>Environmental Cleanup</u>

§ 376.3071(6) Petroleum contamination site rehabilitation

<u>Federal Surplus Property</u>

§§ 217.15–217.20 Federal surplus property

<u>General</u>

§ 286.041 Prohibited requirements of bidders on contracts for public works relative to income tax returns

<u>Health Care</u>

§§ 394.457(3) and 409.906(8)	Community-based mental health services
§ 408.045	Certificates of need for intermediate care facility for the developmentally disabled
§ 409.016	Revenue maximization program
§§ 409.906, 409.908, 409.91188, and 409.912	Medicaid services
§ 409.91188	Specialty prepaid health plans for Medicaid recipients with HIV or AIDS
§ 409.966, 409.967, and 409.974	Medicaid managed care
§ 409.981	Long-term managed care

<u>Historic Preservation</u>

§ 267.031 Expenditures relating to historic properties

<u>Insurance</u>

§ 110.123 State group insurance program

§ 110.12301 Post-payment claims review services

§ 110.12304 Independent benefits consultant

§ 110.1234 Health insurance and Medicare supplement policies

§ 284.33 Purchase of insurance, reinsurance, and services

<u>Juvenile Justice</u>

§ 984.01 Children and families in need of services

<u>Law Enforcement</u>

§ 292.709 State agency law enforcement radio system and interoperability network

§ 321.02 Highway patrol equipment

<u>Local Government</u>

§ 125.012 Franchises at public mass transit facilities

§§ 153.10, 153.62(15), 153.73(7), and 153.79 County water and sewer system construction, reconstruction, acquisition, or improvement contracts

§ 154.215	Contracts for construction of county health facility project
§ 189.053	Special district purchases from purchasing agreements of special districts, municipalities, and counties
§§ 190.011 and 109.33	Community development district contracts
§§ 218.70–218.79	Local Government Prompt Payment Act
§ 218.80	Municipal bid proposals (Public Bid Disclosure Act)
§ 286.043	Limitation on use of funds for discriminatory contract, or bid specifications relating to local government car rental concessions at airports
§§ 336.41 and 336.44	County road construction

Lottery

§§ 24.105, 24.109, 24.111, and 24.113	Lottery contracts

Printing

§§ 283.32, 283.33, 283.34, and 283.35	Public printing

Public-Private Partnerships

§ 255.065	Public-private partnerships; public records and public meetings exemptions

Public Property

§ 255.04	Preference to home industries in building public buildings
§ 255.041	Separate specifications for building contracts
§ 255.05	Bond of contractor constructing public buildings
§ 255.0515	Prohibition against substituting subcontractors on public construction projects
§ 255.0516	Bid protests by educational boards
§§ 255.0525, 255.101, 255.102, 255.103, and 255.29	Public construction projects
§ 255.20	Local bids and contracts for public construction works
§§ 255.249 and 255.25	State leases of private buildings
§ 255.2501	Lease of space financed with local government obligations

Sewage
§ 381.00 Sewage treatment and disposal

Taxation
§ 210.12(7) Cigarette taxes, forfeited property

Technology
§ 215.964 Use of card-based technology
Chapter 282 Communications and data processing
§ 445.011(2) Workforce information systems

Telecommunications
§ 365.172 Wireless emergency 911 service system

Transportation

§ 332.007	Commercial service airports
§ 334.044(26)	Plants for roadside beautification
§§ 337.02, 337.11 337.16, 337.168, 337.17, and 337.25	Florida Department of Transportation procurements
§ 479.261(4)	Highway logo signs

Unclaimed Property
§ 717.122(1) Unclaimed property

B. Other Applicable Statutes

1. Florida's Public Records Act and Sunshine Law

Florida has a broad public records and open meeting laws founded in the state constitution and statute. (See Florida Constitution art. 1, § 24; Florida Public Records Act, Florida Statutes ch. 119; Florida Sunshine Law, Florida Statutes §§ 286.011 through 286.0114.) Additional information about Florida's Public Records Act and Sunshine Law, including a copy of the Government-in-the-Sunshine Manual prepared by the Office of the Attorney General and published by the First Amendment Foundation, is available on the Attorney General's Office website at http://myfloridalegal.com/.

2. Lobbying Laws

A person who seeks, on behalf of another person, to influence an executive branch agency with respect to a decision of the agency in the area of policy or procurement or attempts to obtain the goodwill of an agency official or employee must register with the Florida Commission on Ethics as an executive branch lobbyist and file quarterly compensation reports with the Florida Commission on Ethics. (Florida Statutes § 112.3215.)

Some local governments have adopted lobbying ordinances that are applicable to procurements and require registration and reporting by lobbyists lobbying the local government.

Under Florida's gift law, Florida Statutes section 112.3148, a vendor doing business with an agency, as well as a lobbyist, or the partner, firm, employer, or principal of a lobbyist, is prohibited from giving a gift that has a value in excess of $100 to an individual required by law to file full or limited disclosure of his or her financial interests or to a procurement employee. In addition, the gift law requires gifts valued between $25 and $100 given to a reporting individual or procurement employee to be reported on a quarterly basis to the Florida Commission on Ethics.

Florida Statutes section 112.3217 prohibits a person from giving or receiving a fee, bonus, commission, or other compensation that is dependent or in any way contingent on the enactment, defeat, modification, or other outcome of any specific executive branch action.

The entity charged with the enforcement of the lobbying laws relative to procurements is the Florida Commission on Ethics. The Florida Commission on Ethics is a nine-member commission. Five members are appointed by the governor. Two members are appointed by the speaker of the Florida House of Representatives, and two members are appointed by the president of the Florida Senate. The Florida Commission on Ethics enforces the standards of conduct for public officers and employees in Florida and functions as an independent commission responsible for investigating and issuing public reports on complaints of breaches of the public trust by public officers and employees.

3. Ethics Laws

In addition to regulating state lobbyists, Florida law includes a broader Code of Ethics for Public Officers and Employees, within part III of chapter 112 of the Florida Statutes, which contains provisions relevant to state and local procurement in Florida. Florida Statutes section 112.313 contains general standards of conduct for public officers and employees of agencies. As noted above, section 112.3148, which is also contained within the Code of Ethics, prohibits gifts above a certain value by vendors, lobbyists, or principles of lobbyists to reporting individuals or procurement employees. Further, section 112.3185 sets forth certain prohibitions on agency employees involved in procurements from being employed by a person contracting with the agency.

As noted above, the Florida Commission on Ethics is charged with enforcement of Florida's ethics laws. The Commission has adopted regulations implementing part III of section 112 of the Florida Statutes. These regulations are contained in chapter 34 of the Florida Administrative Code. The Florida Administrative Code can be accessed online at https://www.flrules.org/. The Florida Commission on Ethics' website can be accessed online at www.ethics.state.fl.us.

4. Anti-Bribery Statute

Chapter 838 of the Florida Statutes prohibits bribery of public officials. Specifically, section 838.015 prohibits a person from corruptly giving, offering, or promising to any public servant any pecuniary or other benefit with an intent or purpose to influence the performance of any act or omission that the person believes to be within the official discretion of a public servant, in violation of a public duty, or in performance of a public duty. Bribery is a third-degree felony.

In addition to bribery, there is a specific criminal statute prohibiting bid tampering at section 838.22, which is a second-degree felony.

C. Opinions of the Office of the Attorney General

Florida Statutes section 16.01(3) requires the attorney general to, at the request of certain specified public officers, "give an official opinion and legal advice in writing on any question of law relating to the official duties of the requesting officer." The attorney general is not authorized to render opinions to private individuals or entities. In addition, so that the attorney general does not intrude upon the judicial branch, attorney general opinions generally are not rendered on questions pending before the courts or on questions requiring a determination of the constitutionality of a statute or ordinance. Attorney general opinions are not law. They are advisory only and are not binding on a court of law. Various resources, including general information and legal opinions, are available on the Attorney General's Office website at http://myflorida legal.com/.

II. Regulations

The regulations adopted by Florida administrative agencies that implement certain provisions of the Florida Statutes are contained in the Florida Administrative Code. The Florida Administrative Code is organized into chapters, each of which contains individual agency rules. As noted above, the Florida Administrative Code may be accessed at https://www.flrules.org/.

Procurement regulations contained in the Florida Administrative Code include the following:

<u>Department of State</u>

Rule 1S-2.004 Department of State, Division of Elections (Purchase, Sale, and Uses of Voting Equipment and Systems)

<u>Department of Agriculture and Consumer Services</u>

Rule 5A-12.006 Department of Agriculture and Consumer Services (Designation of Informal Hearing Officer for Bid Protests)

Rule 5P-3.003 Department of Agriculture, Division of Food, Nutrition, and Wellness (Procurement Standards for Summer Food Service Program)

<u>Department of Education, School Districts, State Universities, and Community Colleges</u>

Rule 6A-1.012 School Districts (Purchasing Policies)

Rule 6A-1.013 School Districts (Pool Purchases)

Rule 6A-3.006 State Board of Education (Pool Purchase Plan for Purchase of Equipment and Contractual Needs for Transportation)

Rule 6A-14.0734 Community Colleges (Procurement Requirements)

<u>Department of Transportation</u>

Chapter 14-22 Department of Transportation (Contractors—Qualification to Bid)

Chapter 14-75 Department of Transportation (Professional Consultants)
Chapter 14-91 Department of Transportation (Design-Build Contracts)

Department of Citrus

Rule 20-104.003 Department of Citrus (Competition Announcement for Promotional and Advertising Services Contracts)
Rule 20-104.005 Department of Citrus (Selection Procedure for Promotional and Advertising Services Contracts)
Chapter 20-106 Department of Citrus (Procedures for Purchasing and MBE Program)

Public Service Commission

Chapter 25-25 Public Service Commission (Purchasing—General Purchasing Procedures)

Administration Commission

Chapter 28-110 Bid Protests (Applicable to All State Agencies)

Water Management Districts

Chapter 40A-1 Northwest Florida Water Management District (Various Purchasing Policies)
Chapter 40E-7 South Florida Water Management District (Various Purchasing Policies)
Chapter 40C-1 St. Johns River Water Management District (Various Purchasing Policies)

Department of the Lottery

Rule 53ER99-37 Department of the Lottery (Procurement of Merchandise to Be Awarded As Prizes)
Rule 53ER07-55 Department of the Lottery (Procurement of Commodities and Contractual Services)

Department of Elder Affairs

Rule 58C-1.0031 Department of Elder Affairs (Community Care for the Elderly Lead Agency Dispute Resolution)

Department of Management Services

Chapter 60A-1 Department of Management Services—General Purchasing Regulations (Applies to All State Agencies)
Chapter 60A-2 Department of Management Services (MBE)
Chapter 60A-7 Department of Management Services (State of Florida Purchasing Manual Prison Rehabilitative Industries and Diversified Enterprises (PRIDE))
Chapter 60A-9 Department of Management Services (Office of Supplier Diversity)

Chapter 60B-1	Department of Management Services (Motor Vehicles and Watercraft Acquisition, Assignment, and Use)
Chapter 60B-4	Department of Management Services (Aircraft Acquisition, Assignment, Operation, Use, and Reporting)
Chapter 60D-5	Department of Management Services (Procedures for Construction Contract Bidding, Award, Negotiation, and Changes)
Chapter 60D-13	Department of Management Services (Procedures for Contracting for Design-Build Services)
Chapter 60D-15	Department of Management Services (Utilization of Construction Management Entities)
Chapter 60E-1	Department of Management Services (Commission for Purchase from the Blind or Other Severely Handicapped)
Rule 60H-1.015	Department of Management Services (Procurement Procedures for Leases of 5,000 Square Feet or More in Privately-Owned Buildings)

Department of Environmental Protection

Rule 62-503.700	Department of Environmental Protection (Planning, Design, and Procurement Requirements for State Revolving Fund Loan Program)
Rule 62-552.700	Department of Environmental Protection (Planning, Design, Construction, and Procurement for Drinking Water State Revolving Fund Loan Program)
Rule 62-554.200	Department of Environmental Protection (General Program Requirements for Water Storage Facility Loan Program)
Chapter 62-772	Department of Environmental Protection (Procurement Procedures for Petroleum Cleanup)

Florida Housing Finance Corporation

Chapter 67-49	Florida Housing Finance Corporation (Procurement of Commodities or Contractual Services)

Freshwater Fish and Wildlife Commission

Rule 68-1.002	Freshwater Fish and Wildlife Commission (Minority Business Enterprise Procurement Activities)

Department of Financial Services

Rule 69I-44.005	Department of Financial Services (Competitive Procurement of Services and Commodities)

Department of Economic Opportunity

Rule 73C-23.0051	Department of Economic Opportunity (Florida Small Cities Community Development Block Grant Program)

III. Source Selection

A. Procurement Methods

State agencies must generally purchase goods and services in excess of $35,000 only through a competitive solicitation process, which is either (1) an invitation to bid (ITB), (2) a request for proposals (RFP), or (3) an invitation to negotiate (ITN). (Florida Statutes § 287.057(1)(a)–(c).)

An ITB is used when the agency is capable of specifically defining the scope of work for which a contractual service is required, or is capable of developing precise specifications defining the actual commodity or group of commodities required. When an ITB is used, the award is made to the lowest, responsive, and responsible bidder.

An RFP may only be used by an agency if the agency determines in writing that use of an ITB is not practicable. An RFP is used when the agency is incapable of specifically defining the scope of work for which the commodity, group of commodities, or contractual service is required and when the agency is requesting that a qualified offeror propose a commodity, group of commodities, or contractual service to meet the specifications of the solicitation document. Proposals submitted in response to an RFP are evaluated against a specified set of evaluation criteria and scored by an evaluation team using a point system. When an RFP is used, the award is made to the responsible and responsive vendor whose proposal is determined to be the most advantageous to the state, taking into consideration the price and other criteria in the RFP.

An ITN is used to determine the best method for achieving a specific goal or solving a particular problem. An ITN may only be used if any agency head determines and specifies in writing that the use of an ITB or RFP is not practicable. An ITN calls for replies that are evaluated against evaluation criteria set forth in the ITN in order to establish a competitive range of replies reasonably susceptible of award. The agency may select one or more vendors in the competitive range with which to negotiate. Following negotiations, the agency awards the contract to the responsible and responsive vendor that the agency determines will provide the best value to the state based on the selection criteria.

There are a limited number of reasons to procure goods and services without competition. (See Florida Statutes § 287.057(3).) For example, commodities or contractual services available only from a single source may be excepted from Florida's competitive procurement requirements only after notice is provided to other prospective vendors. (Florida Statutes § 287.057(3)(c).) Similarly, emergency purchases may be made without competition only where the agency head determines in writing that an immediate danger to the public health, safety, or welfare, or other substantial loss to the state requires emergency action. (Florida Statutes § 287.057(3)(a).) There are also certain commodities and contractual services that the Florida Legislature has exempted from the competitive procurement requirements of chapter 287 of the Florida Statutes. The exemptions are found in section 287.057(3)(d), (e), and (f).

B. Mandatory Contract Provisions

Florida Statutes section 287.058 sets forth terms and conditions that must be included in most competitively procured contracts. Such terms and conditions include the following: (1) a provision that bills for fees or other compensation will be submitted in detail sufficient for a proper pre-audit and post-audit; (2) a provision that bills for travel expenses will be submitted in accordance with the state per diem travel limitations set forth in Florida Statutes section 112.061; (3) a provision allowing unilateral cancellation by the agency for refusal of the contractor to comply with Florida's Public Records Act; (4) a provision specifying the scope that clearly establishes all tasks that the contractor must perform; (5) a provision dividing the contract into units of deliverables that must be received and accepted in writing by the contract manager prior to payment; (6) a provision specifying the criteria and the final date by which such criteria must be met for completion of the contract; (7) a provision stating that the contract may be renewed for a period that may not exceed three years or the term of the original contract, whichever period is longer, specifying the renewal price, specifying the costs for the renewal may not be charged, and specifying that renewals shall be contingent upon satisfactory evaluations by the agency and subject to the availability of funds; (8) a provision specifying the financial consequences the agency must apply if the contractor fails to perform per the contract terms; and (9) a provision addressing the property rights of any intellectual property related to the contract and the specific rights of the state regarding the intellectual property if the contractor fails to provide the services or is no longer providing services.

Florida Statutes section 287.0582 requires the following statement to be included in state contracts: "The State of Florida's performance and obligation to pay under this contract is contingent upon an annual appropriation by the Legislature."

Each contract for services within the scope of the practice of architecture, professional engineering, landscape architecture, or registered surveying or mapping must also contain a prohibition against contingent fees. (Florida Statutes § 287.055(6)(a).)

C. Socioeconomic Policies

1. Minority Business Enterprise Policies

On November 9, 1999, former Governor Jeb Bush announced the One Florida Initiative, which includes the One Florida Equity in Contracting Plan. This plan prohibited reserve procurement and price preferences for agencies that report directly to the governor. Other state agencies have the option to use the measures voluntarily. Many state agencies still award points for participation in procurements by entities that are certified minority business enterprises. Florida Statutes still include the ability to set-aside contracts among certified minority businesses, to use price preference, and to set aside contracts among vendors who agree to subcontract with certified minority businesses. (Florida Statutes § 287.057(7)–(8).) Florida's Office of Supplier Diversity is responsible for minority business enterprise contracting issues and for certifying minority business enterprises. The Florida Department of Transportation has a separate disadvantaged business enterprise utilization policy overseen by its Equal Opportunity Office whose mission is to ensure economic prosperity for all by, among other things, ensuring equal opportunity in contracts.

2. Preferences

<u>Florida Commodities</u>: Whenever two or more competitive sealed bids are received, one or more of which relates to commodities manufactured, grown, or produced in Florida, and whenever the bids are equal with respect to price, quality, and service, the Florida commodities shall be given preference. (Florida Statutes § 287.082.)

<u>Florida Businesses</u>: When an agency, county, municipality, school district, or other political subdivision of the state is required to make purchases of personal property through competitive solicitation and the lowest responsible and responsive bid is by a vendor whose principal place of business is in a state or political subdivision that

grants a preference for the purchase of such personal property to a person whose principal place of business is in such state, a preference may be awarded to the lowest responsible and responsive vendor having a principal place of business within Florida, which preference is equal to the preference granted by the state or political subdivision in which the lowest responsible and responsive vendor has its principal place of business. In a competitive solicitation in which the lowest bid is submitted by a vendor whose principal place of business is located outside the state and that state does not grant a preference in competitive solicitation to vendors having a principal place of business in that state, the preference to the lowest responsible and responsive vendor having a principal place of business in this state shall be 5 percent. (Florida Statutes § 287.084(1)(a).) This preference provision does not apply to transportation projects for which federal aid funds are available. (Florida Statutes § 287.084(1)(b).) The term "other political sub-division of the state" does not include counties or municipalities. (Florida Statutes § 287.084(1)(c).) Any vendor whose principal place of business is outside the state of Florida must accompany any written bid, proposal, or reply documents with a written opinion of an attorney at law licensed to practice law in that foreign state, as to the preferences, if any or none, granted by the law of that state to its own business entities whose principal places of business are in that foreign state in the letting of any or all public contracts. (Florida Statutes § 287.084(2).)

Drug-Free Workplace Programs: When two or more equal bids, proposals, or replies are received, a preference shall be given in the award process to the business that certifies that it has implemented a drug-free workplace program. (Florida Statutes § 287.087.)

Foreign Manufacturers with Florida Factories: A foreign manufacturing company with a factory in the state and employing more than 200 employees in Florida shall have preference over any other foreign company when price, quality, and service are the same, regardless of where the product is manufactured. (Florida Statutes § 287.092.)

IV. Bid Protests and Contract Disputes

A. Bid Protests

For procurements involving state agencies, as defined by section 287.012(1) of the Florida Statutes, disappointed bidders may file bid protests under the Florida Administrative Procedure Act (APA). Bidders must initiate such protests by the filing of a notice of intent to protest by an adversely affected person with the procuring agency within 72 hours (not including weekends and holidays) of the posting of the notice of decision or intended decision. A formal written protest must then be filed within ten days (including weekends and holidays) of the date the notice of intent to protest is filed. The formal written protest must state with particularity the facts and law upon which the protest is based. (Florida Statutes § 120.57(3).) For most procurements, the formal written protest must be accompanied by a bid bond in the amount of 1 percent of the contract amount. (Florida Statutes § 287.042(2)(c).) For Florida Department of Transportation procurements, the bid protest bond must be filed with the notice of intent to protest and the bond amount may vary depending on the type of contract. (Florida Statutes § 337.11(5).) Although they are not defined as state agencies under section 287.012(1), most educational boards subject themselves to the Florida APA for bid protests, and if they do so, then they may require protesters bid protest bonds in varying amounts, depending on the amount of the contract. (Florida Statutes § 255.0516.) Other agencies, such as the Department of the Lottery, have special rules regarding bid protests and bonds.

Upon receipt of a timely formal written protest, and absent emergency circumstances that involve an immediate and serious danger to the public health, safety, or welfare, the agency must stop the solicitation or contract award process until the subject of the protest has been resolved by final agency action. The agency must provide an opportunity to resolve the protest by mutual agreement between the parties within seven business days of the receipt of a formal written protest. (Florida Statutes § 120.57(3)(c).)

If the protest is not resolved by mutual agreement and there are no disputed material facts, the procuring agency must conduct an informal administrative hearing. If the protest is not resolved by mutual agreement and there are disputed issues of material fact, the procuring agency must refer the protest to the Division of Administrative Hearings (DOAH) for assignment of an administrative law judge (ALJ). (Florida Statutes § 120.57(3)(d).)

Some local governmental entities, including counties and municipalities, are not subject to the APA and the bid protest procedures therein unless they elect to be subject to such procedures. Therefore, many local governmental entities have their own bid protest procedures that are adopted by ordinance or through policy. For these entities, companies should consult the solicitation, local ordinance, and rules, and submit a public records request to the governmental entity to obtain the most current version of any bid protest policy.

B. Bid Protest Appeals

When a bid protest involving disputed issues of material fact is filed by the procuring agency with DOAH for assignment of an ALJ to conduct an evidentiary hearing, jurisdiction over the bid protest is transferred temporarily to DOAH. The ALJ presides over discovery, prehearing proceedings, and the evidentiary administrative hearing. Following the evidentiary administrative hearing, parties are provided an opportunity to submit proposed recommended orders to the ALJ. The ALJ then issues his or her recommended order, which is transmitted back to the procuring agency for entry of a final order. At that point, jurisdiction over the bid protest is transferred back to the procuring agency. (See Florida Statutes §§ 120.57(1), (3) and 120.569.)

The parties are provided an opportunity to file exceptions to the recommended order with the procuring agency. (Florida Statutes § 120.57(1)(k).) The agency then enters a final order that either adopts, rejects, or modifies the recommended order. The agency may reject or modify conclusions of law in a recommended order over which the agency has substantive jurisdiction and interpretation of administrative rules over which it has substantive jurisdiction. The agency, however, may not reject or modify findings of fact in a recommended order unless the agency first determines from a review of the entire record, and states with particularity in its final order, that the findings of fact were not based on competent substantial evidence or that the proceedings on which the findings were based did not comply with the essential requirements of law. (Florida Statutes § 120.57(1)(l).)

C. Contract Disputes

1. Contract Claims

There are no general procedures for contract claims in Florida specific to state or local government contracts. Contract claims are handled in the same manner as contract claims between private parties. Alternative dispute resolution may be required depending on the terms of a particular contract. Contract claims are typically heard by a Florida circuit court.

2. Contract Claims Appeals

As noted above, contract claims under state or local government contracts are handled in the same manner as contract claims between private parties. If a contract claim is decided by a Florida circuit court, the contract claim may be appealed to a Florida district court of appeal.

D. Suspension and Debarment

Convicted Vendor List: The Florida Department of Management Services maintains a list of the names and addresses of those who have been disqualified from public contracting and purchasing processes for conviction of a public entity crime. A "public entity crime" is "a violation of any state or federal law by a person with respect to and directly related to the transaction of business with any public entity or with an agency or political subdivision of any other state or with the United States, including, but not limited to, any bid, proposal, reply, or contract for goods or services, any lease for real property, or any contract for the construction or repair of a public building or public work, involving antitrust, fraud, theft, bribery, collusion, racketeering, conspiracy, or material misrepresentation." (Florida Statutes § 287.133(1)(g).) A "conviction" means "a finding of guilt or conviction of a public entity crime, with or without adjudication of guilt, in any federal or state trial court of record relating to charges brought by indictment or information after July 1, 1989, as a result of a jury verdict, nonjury trial, or entry of a plea of guilty or nolo contendere." (Florida Statutes § 287.133(1)(b).) The list maintained by the Florida Department of Management Services is known as the convicted vendor list.

Florida Statutes section 287.133 prohibits a person or affiliate that has been placed on the convicted vendor list from submitting a bid, proposal, or reply on a contract with a public entity and from transacting business with a public entity for $35,000 or more (Category Two under section 287.012) for a period of 36 months following the date of being placed on the convicted vendor list. Similarly, section 287.133 prohibits a public entity from accepting any bid, proposal, or reply from, awarding any contract to, or transacting any business in excess of $35,000 with any person or affiliate on the convicted vendor list for a period of 36 months following the date that person or affiliate was placed on the convicted vendor list unless the person or affiliate has been removed from the convicted vendor list.

Discriminatory Vendor List: The Florida Department of Management Services maintains a list of the names and addresses of those who have been disqualified from public contracting and purchasing processes for discrimination. "Discrimination" is defined for purposes of the discriminatory vendor list as "a determination of liability by a state circuit court or federal district court for a violation of any state or federal law prohibiting discrimination on the basis of race, gender, national origin, disability or religion." (Florida Statutes § 287.134(1)(b).) Section 287.134 prohibits an entity or affiliate that has been placed on the discriminatory vendor list from bidding on a contract with a public entity or transacting business with a public entity. Similarly, section 287.134 prohibits a public entity from transacting any business with an entity or affiliate on the discriminatory vendor list for a period of 36 months following the date that entity or affiliate was placed on the discriminatory vendor list unless the person or affiliate has been removed from the discriminatory vendor list.

V. Administrative and Judicial Review

A. Administrative Review

As noted above, administrative review in a bid protest is conducted by DOAH. As also noted, once the DOAH enters a recommended order it transfers the bid protest back to the referring agency, where the parties may file exceptions to the recommended order. The agency rules upon the exceptions, and enters a final order. There is no further administrative review once a final order is entered.

B. Judicial Review

Final orders issued by agencies in bid protests may be appealed to a Florida district court of appeal. In addition, contract disputes decided by a Florida circuit court may be appealed to a Florida district court of appeal.

Below are some procurement decisions issued by Florida district courts of appeal or the Florida Supreme Court since 2000. These decisions may be located either on the court's website, Westlaw, Lexis, Google Scholar search, or Fastcase, among other places:

- *AHF MCO of Florida, Inc. v. Agency for Healthcare Administration*, 308 So. 3d 1136 (Fla. Dist. Ct. App. 2020). Disappointed offeror who was excluded from competitive range violated statutory cone of silence during procurement, but agency did not decide whether offeror was ineligible for award at that time because offeror was not in contention for award. Agency posted award recommendation and offeror protested, claiming standing to seek a reject all because agency's handling of procurement was "fundamentally flawed." DOAH ALJ entered recommended order in favor of offeror, expressly holding that because agency did not find offeror ineligible for award during procurement it could not revisit the matter during protest proceeding to attack standing. Agency rejected recommended order and entered final order dismissing for lack of standing since offeror would be ineligible to compete in any rebid due to cone violations. Appellate court affirmed agency's final order, finding agency's failure to eliminate offeror during the competition was no bar to raising the cone violation during protest since agency had no reason to contemporaneously go through such an exercise for an offeror not in contention for award. Appellate court expressly declined to determine whether standing can be based on allegations that an agency's handling of a procurement was "fundamentally flawed."
- *Agency for Healthcare Administration v. Best Care Assurance, LLC*, 302 So. 3d 1012 (Fla. Dist. Ct. App. 2020). Successful offeror in multiple award procurement alleged award to competitor violated controlling statute, and that it had standing because it was harmed by increased competition. Appellate court found that successful offeror did not have standing to challenge other awardees based on increased competition.

- *Asphalt Paving System, Inc. v. Columbia*, 264 So. 3d 1110 (Fla. Dist. Ct. App. 2019). Appellate court found prospective offeror had standing to challenge, in a Florida Statutes section 120.57(1) "substantial interest" proceeding (which does not have an automatic stay), an allegedly "out-of-scope" modification to an existing contract as a de facto sole source procurement.
- *Heritage Oaks, LLP v. Madison Pointe, LLC*, 277 So. 3d 215 (Fla. Dist. Ct. App. 2019). Appellate court upheld final order adopting recommended order, holding that competitive solicitations must be construed according to their plain language.
- *Biscayne Marine Partners, LLC v. City of Miami*, 273 So. 3d 97 (Fla. Dist. Ct. App. 2019). Disappointed offeror alleged city was required to reject awardees' proposal as nonresponsive to requirements of RFP, arguing that administrative bid protest hearing officers and trial courts were required to conduct their own "independent review" of this matter. Appellate court affirmed lower court order denying protest, holding that arbitrary and capricious standard applies to responsiveness challenges.
- *Matheson v. Miami-Dade County*, 258 So. 3d 516 (Fla. Dist. Ct. App. 2018). Individual challenged county's proposed sale of county-owned land to third party without a competition as unlawful. Appellate court held that prospective offeror had standing based on allegations that it would have bid on the land but for allegedly unlawful failure to hold a competition.
- *Kapsch Trafficom IVHS, Inc. v. Florida Department of Transportation*, 249 So. 3d 693 (Fla. Dist. Ct. App. 2018). Agency non-competitively awarded a patent license agreement for toll collection "readers." Prospective offeror protested, alleging it would have bid but for the violation of competitive bidding requirements of chapter 287 of the Florida Statutes. Appellate court held that chapter 287 only applies to the procurement of "commodities or contractual services," and license agreements are neither.
- *Madison Highlands, LLC v. Florida Housing Finance Corp.*, 220 So. 3d 467 (Fla. Dist. Ct. App. 2017). Agency preliminarily dismissed administrative bid protest for lack of standing. Appellate court reversed, holding protester had standing because it alleged it would have won but for the agency's mishandling of the procurement.
- *Florida Department of Transportation v. Schwefringhaus*, 188 So. 3d 840 (Fla. 2016). Agency entered into a contract with private party that included an indemnity clause. Agency argued that sovereign immunity bars private party from enforcing its rights under indemnity clause. The Florida Supreme Court explained that when the state enters into a properly authorized express written contract, it waives sovereign immunity for the contract. The Supreme Court held that since the contract at issue was lawfully entered into and no separate authorization was needed for the indemnity clause, sovereign immunity did not bar enforcement of indemnity clause against the state.
- *AT&T Corp. v. State, Department of Management Services*, 201 So. 3d 852 (Fla. Dist. Ct. App. 2016). Disappointed offeror filed protest alleging that awardee should have been excluded from competitive range because its initial proposal was nonresponsive to the ITN's statement of work. DOAH ALJ denied protest, finding that the statement of work did not include any responsiveness requirements, and that responses to it were qualitatively evaluated for scoring purposes. ALJ alternatively found that disappointed offeror had waived its protest, as the inclusion of a competitor within the competitive range must

be challenged when it is posted. Appellate court affirmed ALJ's denial on the merits as to the responsiveness challenge, but noted that ALJ was incorrect as to waiver issue. Appellate court noted that Florida's administrative bid protest statutes and regulations enumerate four "decisions or intended decisions" that trigger the 72-hour deadline for filing a notice of protest: (1) the posting of a solicitation, including addenda; (2) a determination that specified procurement can be made only from a single source; (3) the rejection of an offer or all offers; and (4) an award. Appellate court noted that since the inclusion of a competitor within the competitive range is not one of the enumerated "decisions or intended decisions" it does not trigger any protest deadlines.

- *City of Ft. Lauderdale v. Israel*, 178 So. 3d 444 (Fla. Dist. Ct. App. 2015). County sheriff brought action for unjust enrichment for sheriffing services provided to city after expiration of written agreement between sheriff's office and city, and was awarded damages by trial court. Judgment was reversed. Under doctrine of sovereign immunity, Florida municipalities can only be bound by and liable under an express written contract.
- *Handi-Van, Inc. v. Broward County*, 116 So. 3d 530 (Fla. Dist. Ct. App. 2013). County exercised termination for convenience clause, and contractor sued for bad-faith termination. The appeals court held that the government is not bound by any duty of good faith and fair dealing when exercising a termination for convenience clause.
- *Pro Tech Monitoring v. Department of Corrections*, 72 So. 3d 277 (Fla. Dist. Ct. App. 2011). Contractor timely delivered its bid protest to the agency on the day it was due by courier, but courier was stopped at the security desk, which accepted the protest, and agency did not stamp the protest as filed until the next day and dismissed protest as untimely. The court held that where the agency prevents a protestor from timely delivering with the agency clerk, but otherwise accepts the protest, it is timely filed. In the alternative, the timeliness requirements of Florida Statutes section 120.57(3) are non-jurisdictional in nature, and equitable tolling would apply.
- *Martin County v. Polivka Paving, Inc.*, 44 So. 3d 126 (Fla. Dist. Ct. App. 2010). Under *Appeal of Eichleay Corp.*, ASBCA No. 5183, 60-2 B.C.A. (CCH) ¶ 2688, 1960 WL 538 (ASBCA 1960) and its progeny, a contractor seeking entitlement to recover home office overhead damages from the government must prove that a government-imposed delay required the contractor to indefinitely stand by to the point that the contractor was effectively suspended and unable to take on additional work. Here, because the contractor's evidence at trial showed that it could not meet the entitlement prerequisites, the court reversed the award of home office overhead damages to the contractor.
- *Keystone Peer Review Organization, Inc. v. Agency for Health Care Administration*, 26 So. 3d 652 (Fla. Dist. Ct. App. 2010). Court reversed agency's final order where agency dismissed protest based on health services exemption in Florida Statutes section 287.057(5)(f)6 without referring the protest to DOAH. The appellate court held that, because the protester alleged that the exemption did not apply, the agency must permit DOAH to rule on the application of the exemption.
- *Keesler v. Community Maritime Park Associates, Inc.*, 32 So. 3d 659 (Fla. Dist. Ct. App. 2010). Court affirmed summary judgment for the government, holding that the Sunshine Law does not give public the right to speak at meetings otherwise open to the public.

- *Grapski v. City of Alachua*, 31 So. 3d 193 (Fla. Dist. Ct. App. 2010), *review denied*, No. SC10-798, 2010 WL 4016980 (Fla. Oct. 13, 2010). Use of consent agenda did not violate the Sunshine Law because public has no right to participate in decision-making process.
- *First Quality Home Care, Inc. v. Alliance for Aging, Inc.*, 14 So. 3d 1149 (Fla. Dist. Ct. App. 2009). Court denied a writ of mandamus compelling the area agency on aging to forward disappointed bidder's protest to DOAH, certifying a conflict with Florida's Fourth District Court of Appeal in *Mae Volen Senior Center, Inc. v. Area Agency on Aging Palm Beach/Treasure Coast, Inc.*, 978 So. 2d 191 (Fla. Dist. Ct. App. 2008).
- *Mae Volen Senior Center, Inc. v. Area Agency on Aging Palm Beach/Treasure Coast, Inc.*, 978 So. 2d 191 (Fla. Dist. Ct. App. 2008). Nonprofit corporation that acted as an area agency on aging for multicounty area acted as a state agency, and thus DOAH had jurisdiction to hear bid protest.
- *Accela, Inc. v. Sarasota County*, 993 So. 2d 1035 (Fla. Dist. Ct. App. 2008). The court held that a "piggyback" contract was improper, reasoning that the terms of the new contract must be substantially the same as those of the existing contract.
- *Blu-Med Response Systems v. Florida Department of Health*, 993 So. 2d 150 (Fla. Dist. Ct. App. 2008). Court upheld emergency award of contract, concluding that governor's declaration of an emergency under Florida Statutes section 252.36(5)(a) excused agency from complying with emergency procurement rules under Florida Statutes sections 287.057(5)(a) or 120.569(2)(n).
- *Florida Department of Environmental Protection v. Contractpoint Florida Parks, LLC*, 986 So. 2d 1260 (Fla. 2008). State agency must pay a valid judgment arising from a breach of contract and cannot avoid such judgment based on Florida Statutes section 11.066, which generally requires a specific legislative appropriation before a governmental entity can be required to make a payment.
- *Emerald Correctional Management v. Bay County Board of County Commissioners*, 955 So. 2d 647 (Fla. Dist. Ct. App. 2007). Court reversed dismissal of complaint regarding circuit court bid protest, holding that prospective contractor's allegations of impermissible favoritism were sufficient to state a cause of action challenging county's award of contract to another contractor in RFP process.
- *Coastal Fuels Marketing, Inc. v. Canaveral Port Authority*, 962 So. 2d 942 (Fla. Dist. Ct. App. 2007). The Port Authority was not an agency under the Florida APA subject to chapter 120 bid protest procedures.
- *American Home Assurance Co. v. Plaza Materials Corp.*, 908 So. 2d 360 (Fla. 2005). Court discussed public construction bonds under Florida Statutes section 255.05.
- *Broward County v. Brooks Builders, Inc.*, 908 So. 2d 536 (Fla. Dist. Ct. App. 2005). Court held that public contractor was not entitled to delay damages under *Eichleay* and its progeny.
- *General Electric v. Department of Transportation*, 869 So. 2d 1273 (Fla. Dist. Ct. App. 2004). Court held that notice and an opportunity to cure are required before a bid protest is dismissed solely due to a deficient bond.
- *Helicopter Applicators, Inc. v. South Florida Water Management District*, 892 So. 2d 1114 (Fla. Dist. Ct. App. 2004). Court affirmed dismissal of untimely bid protest when bidder filed protest months after bid opening.

- *Miami-Dade County School Board v. J. Ruiz School Bus Service*, 874 So. 2d 59 (Fla. Dist. Ct. App. 2004). In circuit court bid protest action, lost profits are not permitted, but government may award future comparable contracts to protester.
- *Consultech of Jacksonville, Inc. v. Department of Health*, 876 So. 2d 731 (Fla. Dist. Ct. App. 2004). Unsuccessful bidder's appeal of agency's acceptance of other bidder's proposal was an abuse of the appellate process and warranted an award of appellate attorney fees to successful bidder, where unsuccessful bidder's principal strategy on appeal was to reargue facts previously presented to the ALJ.
- *MRO Software, Inc. v. Miami-Dade County*, 895 So. 2d 1086 (Fla. Dist. Ct. App. 2004). Court held that in county procurement a contract award was an executive function that may be challenged in a direct action in circuit court, rather than a quasi-judicial act subject to writ certiorari review in circuit court.
- *Sutron Corp. v. Lake County Water Authority*, 870 So. 2d 930 (Fla. Dist. Ct. App. 2004). Court upheld agency's decision to reject all bids where the low bidder was involved in specification development based on Florida Statutes section 287.057(18), even though statutory prohibition was not applicable to the Water Authority.
- *Grace v. Jenne*, 855 So. 2d 262 (Fla. Dist. Ct. App. 2003). Court held that when one files suit challenging an agency's denial of public records under Florida Statutes section 119.11, trial court must hold an evidentiary hearing, and it is improper to dismiss complaint without doing so.
- *Everett Painting Co. v. Padula & Wadsworth Construction, Inc.*, 856 So. 2d 1059 (Fla. Dist. Ct. App. 2003). Surety bonds could not be conditional payment bond on public construction project under Florida Statutes section 255.05, because there are no provisions for such bonds within that statute equivalent to conditional payment bond under section 713.245 for private construction projects.
- *White Construction Co. v. Florida Department of Transportation*, 860 So. 2d 1064 (Fla. Dist. Ct. App. 2003). Under sections 337.185 and 337.19, regarding state arbitration board and circuit court actions against Department of Transportation, court upheld dismissal of arbitration where contractor had timely filed circuit court action, but then untimely requested arbitration, but case could remain in circuit court to determine whether initial demand amount was made in good faith.
- *Santa Rosa Island Authority v. Pensacola Beach Pier, Inc.*, 834 So. 2d 261 (Fla. Dist. Ct. App. 2002). Local governmental authority appealed a final judgment requiring it to reinstitute negotiations with the firm that ranked the highest following an RFP process even though the authority rescinded negotiations and re-advertised for proposals when faced with threatened litigation. The court held that there was no evidence of illegality, fraud, oppression, or misconduct by the authority, and, therefore, the authority's decision to rescind negotiations and re-advertise for proposals was not subject to judicial interference.
- *City of Sweetwater v. Solo Construction Corp.*, 823 So. 2d 798 (Fla. Dist. Ct. App. 2002). Unsuccessful bidder, which was the lowest responsive, responsible bidder, challenged award of contract to other than the lowest responsive, responsible bidder following review by bid committee members selected by mayor. Although the city received negative comments about the unsuccessful bidder, none would deem the bidder to be non-responsible. The court held that the

city acted outside of its discretion in awarding the contract to other than the lowest responsive, responsible bidder because the evaluation process was not contemplated by the bid documents.

- *Avmed, Inc. v. School Board of Broward County*, 790 So. 2d 571 (Fla. Dist. Ct. App. 2001). After bid protest was filed, school board voted to override the mandatory, statutory stay of contract award process with respect to health insurance contract because any delay in the contract award process would result in loss of health insurance for school board employees. The court held that the school board stated with sufficient particularity facts that evidenced a serious and immediate danger to the public health, safety, or welfare that justified an override of the automatic stay.
- *Engineering Contractors Association of South Florida, Inc. v. Broward County*, 789 So. 2d 445 (Fla. Dist. Ct. App. 2001). Unsuccessful bidders on county road construction project challenged amendment to county procurement code providing for sealed bidding to be conducted following short-listing of prospective bidders by county staff. Plaintiffs alleged that Florida Statutes section 336.41 requires the county to let road construction contracts to the lowest responsible bidder and that the new requirement excludes qualified bidders. The court held that the amendment to the county procurement code was contrary to the dictates of Florida Statutes chapter 336; circumvented the purposes of competitive bidding; and the procedure injected into the procurement subjectivity and personal preferences that the bidding statutes were designed to eliminate.
- *Department of Lottery v. GTECH Corp.*, 816 So. 2d 648 (Fla. Dist. Ct. App. 2001). Unsuccessful bidder challenged agreement between the Department of the Lottery and successful bidder to provide systems and services to the Florida Lottery on the basis that the contract ultimately negotiated between the parties omitted or altered material provisions required by the RFP. The court held that an agency cannot use the RFP process for ranking purposes only and then negotiate a contract that differs from the bidder's proposal.
- *Department of Transportation v. OHM Remediation Services Corp.*, 772 So. 2d 572 (Fla. Dist. Ct. App. 2000). Florida Department of Transportation petitioned for judicial review of an administrative order denying its motion for protective order after bidder on state contract sought to depose agency lawyers in a bid protest. The court held that ALJ's refusal to issue protective order warranted remand given ALJ's failure to rule on whether fact or opinion work product was at issue and whether, if the former, bidder had need of facts at issue and was unable, without undue hardship, to obtain facts from a source other than agency attorneys.
- *Department of Corrections v. C&W Food Service, Inc.*, 765 So. 2d 728 (Fla. Dist. Ct. App. 2000). Plaintiff was the successful bidder on a contract for food storage and delivery service with state agency. The parties signed a one-year contract with a renewal clause for two additional one-year periods. The renewal clause provided that renewal was to be based on mutual agreement, subject to satisfactory performance and the availability of funds. When the agency unilaterally decided not to renew the contract beyond the initial one-year term, plaintiff sued for damages. The court held that Florida Statutes section 287.058, which governs renewal of contracts with state agencies, provides that a contract is not renewable as a matter of right.

VI. Extent of State's Adoption or Adaptation of ABA Model Procurement Code

Florida is not a Model Procurement Code state. Florida first adopted procurement statutes in 1969 governing state agency procurements and they have been amended numerous times since.

VII. Cooperative Purchasing

A. Authority

At the state level, Florida authorizes cooperative purchasing through state term contracts and alternate contract source contracts. The relevant statutory provisions are Florida Statutes sections 287.042(16), 287.012(28)–(29), and 287.056. The relevant regulatory provisions are Florida Administrative Code Rules 60A-1.002(4)(*l*) and (m) and 60A-1.045(5).

At the local level, Florida local governments may have their own cooperative purchasing or "piggybacking" procedures that are reflected in ordinance, policy, or procedure. These can vary from jurisdiction to jurisdiction.

B. Requirements

State term contracts are indefinite quantity contracts that state agencies must use and other eligible users may use to purchase commodities or contractual services available from such purchasing agreements. (Florida Statutes §§ 287.012(28), (29), 287.056(1).) Each state term contract must include (1) a provision specifying a scope of work that clearly establishes all tasks that the contractor is required to perform; and (2) a provision dividing the contract into quantifiable, measurable, and verifiable units of deliverables that must be received and accepted in writing by the contract manager before payment, and each deliverable must be directly related to the scope of work and specify the required minimum level of service to be performed and the criteria for evaluating the successful completion of each deliverable. (Florida Statutes § 287.056(1).) Each underlying state term contract must be competitively procured using one of the procedures authorized by section 287.057 (an ITB, RFP, or ITN). (Florida Statutes § 287.056(1).) When agencies or eligible users procure commodities or contractual services under a state term contract with 25 or fewer approved vendors, they must send a request for quotes to all approved vendors for the commodity or contractual services being procured. (Florida Statutes § 287.056(2).) For any term contracts with more than 25 approved vendors, a request for quotes must be issued to at least 25 of the approved vendors. (Florida Statutes § 287.056(2).) The purpose of the request for quotes is to determine whether a price, term, or condition more favorable to the agency or eligible user than that provided in the state term contract is available. Section 287.056(2) provides that "use of a request for quotes" may not be challenged in an administrative bid protest under Florida Statutes section 120.57(3). Section 287.056(2) is silent as to whether any decision made pursuant to a request for quotes (e.g., the rejection of one or more quotes, or an award) may be challenged in an administrative bid protest.

The "alternate contract source" process is a "piggybacking" procedure. Florida Statutes section 287.042(16) authorizes the Department of Management Services to "evaluate contracts let by the Federal Government, another state, or a political subdivision for the provision of commodities and contract services, and, if it is determined in writing to be cost-effective and in the best interest of the state, to enter into a written agreement authorizing an agency to make purchases under such contract." To make an alternate contract source award, an agency must obtain approval from the Department of Management Services, which maintains a list of current alternate contract source contracts on its website. (Florida Administrative Code R. 60A-1.045(5).) An alternative contract source contract must contain specific language authorizing third parties to make purchases from the contract with the vendor's consent. The Department of Management Services maintains a list on its website of current Alternative Contract Source contracts for use by all agencies. The Department of Management Services also maintains a web page for the federal General Services Administration Cooperative Purchasing Program, indicating it has pre-approved the use of this federal program.

Georgia Procurement Rules and Regulations

Prepared by Melissa J. Copeland
Schmidt & Copeland LLC
Email: Missy@SchmidtCopeland.com

I. Statutory Reference

A. Procurement/Purchasing Statutes

The majority of purchasing in Georgia is managed by the Department of Administrative Services (DOAS). Information about DOAS can be accessed through their website at https://doas.ga.gov. Purchasing is governed by Georgia Code Annotated section 50-5-50 *et seq*. A table of contents of these purchasing statutes is set forth below:

§ 50-5-80. Unlawful to use resources or methods established pursuant to this article to obtain anything of value for personal benefit or gain; penalties for violators; applicability
§ 50-5-81. Unlawful for agencies or subdivisions to purchase other than United States produced beef; exceptions; penalty
§ 50-5-82. "State agency" defined; limitations on contracting for goods; role of Department of Revenue
§ 50-5-83. Definitions; requirements for state purchasing card program
§ 50-5-84. Contracting with companies having business operations in Sudan; scrutinized companies; certifications
§ 50-5-85. State prohibited from entering into certain contracts without certification that boycott of Israel not to be conducted by other party

PART 2. LOCAL POLITICAL SUBDIVISION PURCHASES

§ 50-5-100. Local political subdivision purchases through state authorized
§ 50-5-101. Notice to department; establishment of uniform standard specifications; report of annual requirements
§ 50-5-102. Competitive bidding procedure; bidder information; establishment of regulations and standards
§ 50 5 103. Purchase of motor vehicles, material, equipment, or supplies in name of state; procedure

PART 3. SMALL BUSINESS ASSISTANCE

§ 50-5-120. Short title
§ 50-5-121. Definitions
§ 50-5-122. Legislative intent
§ 50-5-123. Creation of advisory council; membership; meetings; chairman; executive director
§ 50-5-124. Reports required of advisory council

PART 4. MINORITY BUSINESS ENTERPRISE DEVELOPMENT

§ 50-5-130. Purpose
§ 50-5-131. Definitions
§ 50-5-132. Eligibility and procedures for certification; appeal of denial
§ 50-5-133. Fraud in certification process; penalty; effect of multiple violations

PART 5. STATE USE COUNCIL

§ 50-5-135. Creation; membership; terms; appointments; compensation; existence
§ 50-5-136. Powers and authority of council
§ 50-5-137. Participation of certified community based rehabilitation programs
§ 50-5-138. Procurement of contracts with central nonprofit agencies; fees; cancellation or modification; existing contracts grandfathered

B. Other Applicable Statutes

1. Georgia Department of Transportation has the ability to procure certain "design-build" services, Georgia Code Annotated section 32-2-81
2. Public works contracting requirements, Georgia Code Annotated section 13-10-1 *et seq.*
3. Offenses against public administration, Georgia Code Annotated section 16-10-1 *et seq.*
4. Ethics in Government Act, Georgia Code Annotated section 21-5-1 *et seq.*
5. Trading with the State Employees Act, Georgia Code Annotated section 45-10-20 *et seq.*
6. Georgia Code Annotated section 48-7-38, which provides tax incentives for contracting with minorities
7. Georgia Taxpayer Protection against False Claims Act, Georgia Code Annotated section 23-3-120 *et seq.*

II. Regulations

Regulations are promulgated pursuant to the statutory authority of Georgia Code Annotated section 50-5-54 and are found in the Georgia Procurement Manual, which is available online at https://doas.ga.gov/assets/State%20Purchasing/GPM%20Documents/GPM-V9-January%202021.pdf. The Georgia Procurement Manual governs all solicitations publicly posted on or after the date of the manual. (See Georgia Procurement Manual § I.1.1.)

III. Source Selection

The general methods of procurement include:

A. Request for Quotes

A request for quotes (RFQ) is a competitive procurement method used to solicit bids for the supply of goods or services. In the RFQ process, the state entity prescribes both the specification and solutions for its needs. An award should be made to the lowest price responsive and responsible bidder.

B. Request for Proposals

A request for proposals (RFP) is only used when a determination has been made that sealed bidding (i.e., RFQ) is not practicable or advantageous to the state. The RFP describes in general terms the needs of the state and allows offerors to propose solutions. Award is made to the highest ranked responsible offeror based on evaluation criteria set forth in the RFP.

C. Request for Qualified Contractors

A request for qualified contractors (RFQC) is a process to prequalify suppliers with respect to a particular service, goods, material, or equipment. The required qualifications are known and each supplier is judged on the supplier's ability to meet or surpass the required qualifications. The supplier is not issued an award based on the RFQC but is eligible to submit a response to any future RFQ or RFP for the particular goods, materials, or services for which they are qualified.

D. Reverse Auctions

Reverse auctions may be used as an alternative to sealed bidding, are performed in real time via the internet, and allow the vendors to see the lowest bid but not the identity of the bidders. Once the auction is closed, the state evaluates the bids and awards to the lowest responsive and responsible vendor.

The state may also contract with vendors under the following methods when circumstances allow:

E. Emergency Purchases

Emergency purchases may be made in accordance with Georgia Code Annotated section 50-5-71 to purchase urgently needed items arising from unforeseen causes, including, but not limited to, extreme weather conditions or official declared emergencies.

F. Sole Source Purchases

Sole source purchases may be made when it is determined that only one source of supply is available to provide the requested goods or services.

G. Cooperative Purchasing

This purchasing may be used by DOAS to enter into or authorize state entities to enter into contracts with sources of supply already established by competitive bidding conducted by other governmental entities or cooperative purchasing groups. DOAS must first advertise its intent to contract with such consortia or cooperative approved suppliers before entering into a contract. (See Georgia Code Annotated § 50-5-51 and Georgia Procurement Manual § 1.3.4.4.)

IV. Bid Protests and Contract Disputes

A. Bid Protests

1. Deadlines

Protests must be received within ten calendar days after the protesting party knows or should have known of the occurrence of the action that is protested or the specific protest deadlines as set forth below.

Specification Protest: A protest pertaining to events or facts arising during the solicitation process must be filed no later than two business days prior to the bid closing or proposal due date for procurements with a dollar threshold of $250,000 or greater and one business day prior for procurements with a dollar threshold of $25,000 to $249,999.99.

Protest of Sole Source Notice: A challenge to a sole source notice must be submitted prior to the closing date and time on the notice.

Protest of Results of RFQC: A challenge to the results of an RFQC must be filed within ten calendar days of the posting of the list of qualified suppliers.

Challenge to Consortium/Cooperative Purchase Notice: A challenge must be submitted prior to the closing date and time in the notice of intent to purchase.

Protest of Notice of Intent to Award (NOIA): A protest of an NOIA must be filed no later than five calendar days following the date of the NOIA for purchases with a dollar threshold of $25,000 to $249,999.99; for those purchases with a dollar threshold of $100,000 to $249,999.99, the protester has an additional five calendar days to submit supporting exhibits, evidence, or documents. Protests of purchases with a dollar threshold of $250,000 or greater must be filed within ten calendar days of posting of the NOIA.

Protests of Award Where NOIA Not Required: The protest notice must be filed within ten calendar days of the date the notice of award is posted.

DOAS will not consider untimely protests absent evidence of malfeasance or administrative error by the state entity that substantially impaired an interested supplier's ability to file a timely protest. In the event that a state entity does not provide access to records included in the register of proposals or the administrative review within one business day of issuance of the NOIA, the interested supplier may file, within the filing period, a request for extension of the filing period to extend the protest period by the number of days that it takes for the state entity to produce the records beyond the first business day. In the event that a state entity does not provide timely access to records other than those that comprise the register of proposals or administrative review, the interested supplier is required to file a protest within the filing period, indicating the failure of the state entity to provide timely access to records and reserving the right to file an amended protest upon production of such records.

2. Standing

Specification Protest: An interested supplier capable of responding to a solicitation may assert a specification protest.

Sole Source Protest: An interested supplier capable of providing the goods or services identified in a sole source notice may protest such notice.

RFQC Protest: An interested supplier submitting a timely written response to an RFQC may protest the results of the RFQC.

Cooperative Purchase Protest: Any interested supplier capable of providing the goods/services identified in a consortia/cooperative notice may file a protest challenging the consortia or cooperative notice determination.

Award Protest: An interested supplier submitting a timely written response to solicitation may protest an actual or intended award of the solicitation.

3. Form and Filing

The protest must state the name and address of the protestor, appropriate identification of the solicitation, sole source notice, consortia/cooperative purchase notice, or award that is the subject of the protest; a statement of reasons for the protest; and the desired remedy. The protest must include all supporting exhibits, evidence, and documents unless such materials are not available by the protest deadline, in which case they must be identified and the date of the expected availability of the materials given. The protest must be signed by a company officer authorized to sign contracts on behalf of the vendor or legal counsel that has been engaged by the supplier. The protest, in order to be considered filed, must be received by the deputy commissioner within the filing period. The protest must be submitted via email to protests@doas.ga.gov.

4. Stay of Procurement

Once a timely protest has been submitted, the procurement or award is stayed until a final decision is issued unless the State Purchasing Division deputy commissioner makes a written determination after consulting with the user agency that the award or performance of the contract without delay is necessary to protect the interests of the state.

5. Hearing

No hearing is provided for under the rules.

6. Decision

A decision will be issued as expeditiously as possible. This decision is final unless a request for formal review is filed.

7. Remedies

In no event will protesting parties be entitled to recover costs or attorneys' fees incurred in connection with the solicitation or protest. Available remedies include the following:

Specification Protest: Remedies include modification of the solicitation, extension of the solicitation closing date and time, or cancellation of the solicitation.

Sole Source or Consortia/Cooperative Procurement Protest: Remedies include revision or cancellation of sole source or consortia/cooperative notice.

RFQC Protest: Remedies include revisions or cancellation of the list of qualified contractors, re-evaluation, cancellation, or resolicitation.

Award Protest: Remedies include revision or cancellation of the award, re-evaluation and re-award, cancellation, or resolicitation.

B. Bid Protest Appeals

1. Deadline

A request for formal review/appeal must be requested within three business days of the date of the protest decision. All protest decisions concerning solicitations, sole source awards, consortia/cooperative purchasing notices, and awards with an estimated value of $100,000 or more will be subject to formal review. If the solicitation or intended award has an estimated value of less than $100,000, the commissioner of DOAS has discretion to allow a formal review.

2. Standing

Specification Protest: The supplier filing the protest, any supplier adversely affected by the decision (if the supplier is interested in and capable of providing the goods and services at issue), and the state entity identified in the solicitation may appeal.

Sole Source Protest: The supplier filing the protest, the supplier identified in the sole source notice, and the state entity identified in the sole source notice may appeal.

RFQC Protest: The supplier filing the protest, any supplier adversely affected by the decision (provided the supplier submitted a timely response to the RFQC), and the state entity identified in the RFQC may appeal.

Award Protest: The supplier filing the protest, any supplier adversely affected by the decision (provided that the supplier submitted a timely response to the solicitation), and the state entity identified in the solicitation may appeal.

3. Form and Filing

The request for formal review must identify any errors in the protest decision and any factual and legal grounds for reversal or modification. The request for formal review must be filed with the commissioner of DOAS via email at protests@doas.ga.gov.

4. Stay of Procurement

The stay continues until the commissioner of DOAS makes a decision on the final appeal unless the State Purchasing Division deputy commissioner makes a written determination after consulting with the user agency that the award or performance of the contract without delay is necessary to protect the interests of the state.

5. Hearing

The parties involved in the protest have a right to a hearing before the DOAS Commission. If a hearing is requested, the DOAS commissioner, or his or her designee, shall issue a procedural order, scheduling and providing details for a hearing. The parties may submit documentary evidence and witness testimony in the form of affidavits prior to the hearing. The DOAS commissioner may solicit additional information from the parties at any time prior to the issuing of the final decision. Issues not raised in the initial protest or issues not raised in the initial request for formal review may, at the discretion of the DOAS commissioner, be deemed voluntarily relinquished. The protesting party may request that the hearing be conducted before a court reporter. Such request must be in writing and include an agreement by the protesting party that it shall secure and pay for the court reporting services for such hearing. To be made part of the record, the original transcript of any such proceedings shall be submitted to the DOAS commissioner as soon as the transcript is available, without cost. The DOAS commissioner will make a decision on the protest as expeditiously as possible after receiving all relevant requested information.

6. Decision

The decision of the commissioner is final.

C. Contract Disputes

There are no statutes or regulations that govern a dispute arising between a contractor and the state during the performance of a public contract. Either the contractor or the state is permitted to bring an action in state court for breach of contract.

D. Suspension and Debarment

1. Suspension

Suspension is initiated by a written determination by the State Purchasing Division deputy commissioner after consultation with the state purchasing agent(s) or agency procurement officer(s), the Office of Legal Services, the Attorney General's

Office, other state entity representatives, and, where practicable, the supplier who is to be suspended. A notice of the suspension shall be sent to the suspended supplier and shall provide that (1) the suspension is for the period necessary to complete an investigation into possible debarment including any appeal of a debarment decision, but not longer than 120 days; and (2) the supplier shall be ineligible as a prime contractor or a subcontractor for award of any new contracts during the period of suspension. The suspended person may request a hearing within ten days of notice of the suspension.

2. Debarment

A request for debarment must be submitted in writing along with supporting documentation to the State Purchasing Division deputy commissioner. The deputy commissioner will review the documentation and stated reasons for debarment and issue a written determination as to whether suspension or debarment is appropriate. The vendor must request a hearing within ten calendar days after the vendor receives the notice of debarment.

Hearings will only be conducted if requested as set forth above. The hearings will be as informal as may be reasonable and appropriate under the circumstances. The State Purchasing Division deputy commissioner (or his or her designee) will serve as the hearing officer. Parties are allowed to present evidence and argument and stipulations of fact. The hearing may be recorded but will not be transcribed except at the request and expense of the vendor. A record of attendees, identification of any written evidence, copies of all written statements, and a summary of the hearing will be sufficient record. Opening statements may be made unless a party waives this right.

The hearing officer will issue a final decision no later than 120 days after the date of the issuance of the suspension. If debarment is recommended or ordered, the decision will include the length of debarment (no less than six months but not to exceed five years), the reason for the debarment, the extent to which the supplier's affiliates are included in the debarment, and a statement regarding the debarred supplier's right to judicial review. A debarment decision will take effect upon issuance and receipt by the supplier.

The supplier may appeal the decision to the DOAS commissioner no later than ten calendar days following the date of the hearing officer's decision The commissioner may in his or her sole discretion request oral argument. The commissioner's decision will be final.

V. Administrative and Judicial Review

A. Administrative Review

The administrative review process applicable to bid protests and suspension and debarment proceedings is set forth above.

B. Judicial Review

Decisions of DOAS are specifically exempted from the application of the Georgia Administrative Procedures Act. (Georgia Code Annotated § 50-13-2(1).) Therefore, a vendor may seek judicial review of a DOAS decision in any court of competent jurisdiction.

1. Judicial Decisions

- Even in competitive sealed proposals under Georgia Code Annotated section 50-5-67(a), a rejected bidder who alleges the proposal was conducted in an arbitrary and unfair manner falls within the zone of interest to be protected by the procurement laws. *Amdahl Corp. v. Georgia Department of Administrative Services*, 398 S.E.2d 540 (Ga. 1990).
- Sovereign immunity bars a claim for injunctive relief against the state. *Georgia Department of Natural Resources v. Center for a Sustainable Coast, Inc.*, 755 S.E.2d 184 (Ga. 2014) (overruling *IBM v. Georgia Department of Administrative Services*, 453 S.E.2d 706 (Ga. 1995)).

Sovereign immunity bars claims for declaratory relief and including declaratory relief from officials' acts that are alleged to be unconstitutional. *Lathrop v. Deal*, 801 S.E.2d 867, 869 (Ga. 2017) ("Simply put, the constitutional doctrine of sovereign immunity forbids our courts to entertain a lawsuit against the State without its consent. In *Georgia Dept. of Natural Resources v. Center for a Sustainable Coast*, 294 Ga. 593, 602 (2) (755 SE2d 184) (2014), we held that the doctrine extends to suits for injunctive relief, and in *Olvera v. Univ. System of Ga. Board of Regents*, 298 Ga. 425, 428 n.4 (782 SE2d 436) (2016), we held that it likewise extends to suits for declaratory relief. But those decisions involved no constitutional claims, and since *Sustainable Coast*, we have not had occasion to consider whether the doctrine of sovereign immunity extends to claims for injunctive or declaratory relief that rest upon constitutional grounds. See *State of Ga. v. Intl. Keystone Knights of the Ku Klux Klan*, 299 Ga. 392, 395 (1) n.11 (788 SE2d 455) (2016). In this case, we are confronted squarely with that question. We hold today that the doctrine of sovereign immunity extends generally to suits against the State, its departments and agencies, and its officers in their official capacities for injunctive and declaratory relief from official acts that are alleged to be unconstitutional. In so holding, however, we recognize the availability of other means by which aggrieved citizens may obtain relief from unconstitutional acts, including prospective relief from the threatened enforcement of unconstitutional laws.").

2. Attorney General Decisions

- Opinion No. 74-16 discusses DOAS's authority under the purchasing laws.
- Opinion No. 71-114 authorizes DOAS to establish federal General Services Administration as a source of supply.

VI. Extent of State's Adoption or Adaptation of ABA Model Procurement Code

Georgia reports that it has partially adopted the American Bar Association (ABA) Model Procurement Code (MPC). (See the 2015 Survey of State Procurement Practices, compiled by the National Association of State Procurement Officials (NASPO).) Georgia's procurement rules and regulations generally and loosely follow the outline of the MPC in that Georgia has a centralized procurement authority, has similar source selection methods, and provides for a two-step protest process. However, it does not appear to have wholesale adopted any of the provisions of the MPC.

VII. Cooperative Purchasing

A. Authority

The Department of Administrative Services shall have the power and authority and it shall be the department's duty, subject to this part:

* * *

(9) To enter into or authorize agreements with cooperative purchasing organizations or other states and their political subdivisions to effectuate the purposes and policies of this chapter;

(Georgia Code Annotated § 50-5-51.)

B. Requirements

The Georgia Procurement Manual provides as follows:

> In accordance with [Georgia Code Annotated] Section 50-5-51, DOAS has both the *authority and duty to canvass all sources of supply to establish contracts for needed goods and services as well as enter into or authorize agreements with private non-profit organizations or other states and their political subdivisions*. Pursuant to this authority, DOAS may enter into and/or authorize state entities to enter into contracts with sources of supply established pursuant to competitive bidding conducted by other governmental entities or cooperative purchasing groups. However, prior to designating a supplier approved by a consortium or purchasing cooperative as an authorized source of supply, the state entity *must publicly advertise its intent to contract with the consortium-approved/cooperative-approved supplier in accordance with the following procedures. . .*

(Georgia Procurement Manual § 1.3.4.4. (emphases added).) The procurement professional must complete the following steps before finalizing a cooperative purchase: (1) conduct market research to determine the appropriateness of a cooperative purchase; (2) prepare cooperative purchase justification; (3) estimate expected contract value and route to State Purchasing Division if it exceeds the agency's purchasing authority; (4) post public notice; (5) invite market response (through the public posting); (6) complete any protest process; and (7) award contract.

The consortia/cooperative procurement process does not apply to any of the following purchases: (1) purchases that are exempt from the competitive solicitation process and/or the State Purchasing Act purchases; (2) purchases from mandatory or convenience statewide contracts; (3) purchases from existing state entity contracts; (4) purchases pursuant to Tier 3 of the Order of Precedence; (5) State Purchasing Division-approved "piggyback" purchases; or (6) any contract resulting from a competitive solicitation conducted in accordance with the provisions of the manual even if only one responsive and responsible bid/proposal is received. (Georgia Procurement Manual § 1.3.4.4.) Below is the sample notice required before a consortium contract is entered:

> [Insert State Entity Name] is providing public notice of its intent to award a contract to [Insert Name of Consortia/Cooperative] to provide [Insert Description of Goods/Services]. [Insert Name of Consortia/Cooperative] has been identified as the supplier for this purchase for the reasons stated in the

> attached Consortia/Cooperative Justification Form. Any supplier capable of providing the identified goods/services at the same or better value may challenge this determination by filing a written protest with the Deputy Commissioner of the State Purchasing Division (SPD) in accordance with the protest procedures outlined in Section 6.5. Step 4—Supplier Participates in Protest Process. The protest must be received prior to the closing date and time identified herein.

(*Id.*) "The total posting period for a consortium or cooperative purchase notice is determined by the estimated contract value. If the estimated contract value is $25,000–$249,999.99, the notice is to be posted for a minimum of five (5) business days. If the estimated contract value is $250,000 or greater, the notice is to be posted for a minimum of fifteen (15) calendar days." (*Id.*)

Hawaii Procurement Rules and Regulations

Prepared by[1] *Anna H. Oshiro*
Director, Damon Key Leon Kupchak Hastert
Email: aho@hawaiilawyer.com

I. Statutory Reference[2]

A. Procurement/Purchasing Statutes

The State Procurement Office (SPO) is the central authority on the statutes and regulations governing procurement activities by the state and its counties. While actual procurement is decentralized within state government and among the state and counties, the SPO is the central authority on all matters of government procurement policy. Information about the SPO and the rulemaking Procurement Policy Board is available at https://spo.hawaii.gov.

Hawaii's Public Procurement Code, Hawaii Revised Statutes (HRS) chapter 103D, applies to state and county procurement of goods, services, or construction, and also provides for the management of government inventory and surplus property. Government procurement of health and human services is separately codified at HRS chapter 103F and applies to all state contracts for direct services to families, communities, or individuals. Counties have discretion to implement the health and human services procurement provision. Hawaii's procurement laws are based upon the 1979 American Bar Association's (ABA's) Model Procurement Code for State and Local Governments (MPC), with numerous revisions.

The provisions of chapter 103D, Hawaii Public Procurement Code, and chapter 103F, Purchases of Health and Human Services, can be accessed at https://spo.hawaii.gov/references/hrs/. The table of contents for both chapters is set forth below.

Chapter 103D, Hawaii Public Procurement Code, Table of Contents

PART I. General Provisions

1. Prior editions were prepared by Danielle M. Conway with assistance from Joy S. Naifeh.
2. All citations to the Hawaii Revised Statutes are current through December 28, 2015.

Chapter 103F, Purchases of Health and Human Services, Table of Contents

PART III. Procurement Organization

§ 103F-301. Powers and duties of the administrator.

§ 103F-302. Delegation of authority of the administrator of the state procurement office.

PART IV. Source Selection and Contract Formation

§ 103F-401. Methods of selection.

§ 103F-401.5. Proposals and awards.

§ 103F-402. Competitive purchase of services.

§ 103F-403. Restrictive purchase of services.

§ 103F-404. Treatment purchase of services.

§ 103F-405. Small purchases.

§ 103F-406. Crisis purchase of services.

§ 103F-407. Amendment and cancellation of requests.

§ 103F-408. Modification and termination of contracts.

§ 103F-409. Types of contracts.

§ 103F-410. Multi-term contracts.

§ 103F-411. Multiple awards.

§ 103F-412. Time line.

§ 103F-413. Interim measure for assuring continuation of services.

§ 103F-414. Allotment.

PART V. Protests

§ 103F-501. Protested awards.

§ 103F-502. Right to request reconsideration.

§ 103F-503. Award of contract suspended during a protest.

§ 103F-504. Exclusivity of remedies.

B. Other Applicable Statutes

- HRS chapter 103, Expenditure of Public Money and Public Contracts
- HRS chapter 104, Wages and Hours of Employees on Public Works
- HRS chapter 125, Procurement and Control of Distribution of Necessary Commodities
- HRS chapter 125C, Procurement, Control, Distribution, and Sale of Petroleum Products

II. Regulations[3]

Hawaii Administrative Rules (HAR) sections 3-120 to 3-132, implement HRS chapter 103D, Public Procurement Code, and HAR sections 3-140 to 3-149 implement HRS chapter 103F, Purchases of Health and Human Services.

3. All citations to the Hawaii Administrative Rules are current through December 28, 2015.

These rules can be accessed at https://spo.hawaii.gov/references/har/goods/ and https://spo.hawaii.gov/references/har/hhs/, respectively. The table of contents for both sets of rules are set forth below.

Implementing Chapter 103D, Hawaii Public Procurement Code

§ 3-120. General Provisions
§ 3-121. Procurement Organization
§ 3-122. Source Selection and Contract Formation
§ 3-123. Cost Principles
§ 3-124. Preferences
§ 3-125. Modifications and Terminations of Contracts
§ 3-126. Legal and Contractual Remedies
§ 3-128. Government Relations and Cooperative Purchasing
§ 3-129. Surplus Property
§ 3-130. Inventory Management
§ 3-131. Compliance
§ 3-132. Value Engineering Incentives in Construction Contracts
Exhibit A: Value Engineering Change Proposal

Implementing Chapter 103F, Purchases of Health and Human Services

§ 3-140. Definitions
§ 3-141. General Provisions
§ 3-142. Planning
§ 3-143. Competitive Purchase of Service
§ 3-144. Restrictive Purchase of Service
§ 3-145. Treatment Purchase of Service
§ 3-146. Small Purchase of Service
§ 3-147. Crisis Purchase of Service
§ 3-148. Protest and Request for Reconsideration
§ 3-149. Contracting

While statutes authorize state and county agencies to adopt regulations further implementing the state procurement laws, no state or county agency has done so. Instead, state and county agencies have developed standard contract terms and conditions applicable to public construction projects. Some examples include the Interim General Conditions issued by the Department of Accounting and General Services, available at https://pwd.hawaii.gov/wp-content/uploads/2014/12/InterimGeneralConditions1999Edition.pdf, General Terms and Conditions issued by the City and County of Honolulu, available at https://www.honolulu.gov/pur/itc.html and General Provisions for Construction Projects issued by the Hawaii Department of Transportation, Air and Water Transportation Facilities Division, available at https://hidot.hawaii.gov/administration/files/2014/09/entire.pdf. These terms and conditions are nearly always included by reference in public bid documents, and are modified by special provisions included in the bid documents.

III. Source Selection

A. Methods for Purchases of Goods, Services, and Construction

1. Competitive Sealed Bidding (Invitation for Bids)

Competitive sealed bidding, or invitation for bids (IFB), is the preferred solicitation method for contracts estimated at greater than $25,000.[4] Bids are publicly opened at a time and place designated in the solicitation. Award is made on the basis of the lowest bid price, provided the bidder is responsive and responsible. (HRS §§ 103D-302, 103D-303.5; HAR § 3-122, subchs. 4 and 5.)

2. Competitive Sealed Proposals (Request for Proposals)

The request for proposals (RFP) process is used when designated by rule or when the agency determines that sealed bidding is not practicable nor advantageous to the state. An agency may conduct discussions with responsible offerors, and revisions may be allowed after submission but before the award in order to obtain the final and best offers. Award is made to the responsible offeror and is based on various criteria set forth in the RFP; price may be a factor. (HRS §§ 103D-303, 103D-303.5; HAR §§ 3-122, subchs. 4 and 6, 3-132 exhibit A.)

3. Multi-Step IFB

The multi-step IFB is a combination of the IFB and RFP, and may be used when an initial preparation of a purchase description to support an award based on price is not practicable. An IFB is issued inviting submission of unpriced technical proposals, followed by a second IFB limited to those bidders whose offers are qualified under the initial IFB. If a multi-step IFB is used, the notice and IFB must describe each step used in soliciting, evaluating, and selecting the unpriced technical proposals. Award is made to the bidder offering the lowest priced acceptable proposal. (HRS § 103D-302(i); HAR § 3-122, subchs. 4 and 6.5.)

4. Professional Services

This provision requires a purchasing agency to publish notice of the professional services it anticipates requiring that year, to invite interested providers to submit current statements of qualifications and interest to the agency, and to negotiate with qualified providers as needs arise. Contracts are awarded based on demonstrated competence and qualifications for services required, at fair and reasonable prices. Design professional services of engineers, architects, surveyors, and landscape architects (HRS ch. 464) must be procured by this method or, when applicable, as an emergency purchase.

While purchases of other professional services also may be solicited by any other procurement method, agencies typically utilize the professional services procurement option in lieu of sealed bids or proposals. (HRS § 103D-304; HAR § 3-122, subchs. 4 and 7.)

---

4. Small purchases exception: this amount is raised to $100,000 for goods and services and $250,000 for construction. Haw. Rev. Stat. § 103D-305 (2015). Additionally, this section permits an exemption for professional services, sole source, and emergency procurements from this process. *Id.* §§ 103D-304, 103D-306, 103D-307.

5. Small Purchases

Originally small purchases were procurements of any good, service, or construction estimated at less than $25,000. The amount that qualifies as a small purchase for goods and services is now up to $100,000 and a construction small purchase is less than $250,000. The change requires a performance bond for purchases of construction exceeding $50,000. Small purchases do not require public notice or public bid opening. Award is made based on best value to the government. (HRS § 103D-305; HAR § 3-122, subchs. 4 and 8.)

6. Sole Source

The head of the purchasing agency must justify in writing that the good, service, or construction has a unique feature or capability essential to meeting agency needs, and those needs can be met by a purchase from one source only and no other. Public comment must be invited and considered before a sole source contract is awarded. (HRS § 103D-306; HAR § 3-122 subchs. 4 and 9. See also SPO, Sole Source Procurement Method, https://spo.hawaii.gov/for-vendors/vendor-guide/methods-of-procurement/goods-services-construction/sole-source-procurement-method/.)

7. Emergency Procurements

The head of the purchasing agency is authorized to procure goods, services, and construction under the emergency procurement provision when an emergency condition exists that threatens the health, welfare, or safety of any person; the continued functioning of government; and/or the preservation and protection of irreplaceable property. Competition is required when practicable. (HRS § 103D-307; HAR § 3-122, subchs. 4 and 10.)

B. Methods for Purchases of Health and Human Services

The preferred method of solicitation for health and human services is the *competitive purchase of services* through an *RFP*. (HRS § 103F-402; HAR §§ 3-141, 3-143.)

Restrictive purchase of services, or award without competition, is authorized when the head of the agency determines in writing that only one provider meets the agency's or funding source's requirements. (HRS § 103F-403; HAR §§ 3-141, 3-144.)

Treatment purchase of services may be procured under a request for qualifications process similar to the procurement of professional services provided for in Section III.A.4. The provision applies when treatment services cannot be anticipated accurately on an annual basis but may become necessary from time to time, and a delay in treatment to allow for solicitation and contract formation would exacerbate the condition needing treatment. (HRS § 103F-404; HAR §§ 3-141, 3-145.)

Small purchases of less than $25,000 are made in accordance with the small purchases provision under the Public Procurement Code. (HRS §§ 103F-405, 103D-305; HAR §§ 3-141, 3-146.)

Purchase of crisis services is authorized when a crisis arises under specified conditions and services are otherwise unavailable from the Departments of Health or Human services. Competition is required when practicable. (HRS § 103F-406; HAR §§ 3-141, 3-147.)

C. Exemptions

Routine governmental operational expenses are exempted from the provisions of the Public Procurement Code. The statutes also provide for, and the rules establish additional exemptions of, specific goods, services, and construction that while potentially available from multiple sources, the competitive procurement of which would not be "practicable" or "advantageous" to the state. (HRS § 103D-102; HAR § 3-120-4(b).) Exemptions to competitive bidding procurement of health and human services are provided for at HRS section 103F-101(a) and HAR section 3-141-503.

Programmatic statutory exemptions to competitive procurement further are provided for and include emergency management (HRS § 127A-12); financing agreements (HRS § 37D-2); Hawaii Tourism Authority (HRS § 201B-12); and the Research Corporation of the University of Hawaii (HRS § 304A-3005).

All grants of exemption are posted online. The chapter 103D exemptions are available at https://spo.hawaii.gov/for-state-county-personnel/programs/procurement/solicitation/goods-services-construction/exemptions/ and those for chapter 103F are at https://spo.hawaii.gov/for-state-county-personnel/programs/procurement/solicitation/health-human-services/methods-of-procurement/competitive-procurement/cost-principles-hrs-chapter-103f-purchases-of-health-and-human-services/.

D. Preferences

The Public Procurement Code provides for certain preferences and that any preferences shall be applied to bids submitted pursuant to IFB and RFP solicitations only. Preferences are extended through percentage adjustments of bid price upward or downward, as applicable. Preferences attach to purchases of in-state agricultural, mined, and manufactured products; printing, binding, and stationery work; and software development. The code provides additional preferences for use of recycled products and for bids and offers that utilize the services of qualified community rehabilitation programs. Statutes further authorize imposition of a reciprocal preference against out-of-state bidders when those states apply residential preferences, and also require that bids and offers submitted by not-for-profit entities, for evaluation purposes, be increased by the applicable retail rate of Hawaii's general excise and use taxes. (HRS §§ 103D-1001 to 103D-1011, 103D-1301 to 103D-1304; HAR § 3-124.)

Hawaii statutes also authorize the establishment of rules and practices providing for preferences to small business. (HRS §§ 103D-901 to 103D-906.) Implementing regulations are presently in draft form but have not yet been submitted to the Procurement Policy Board. Thus, in practice, Hawaii does not currently afford any small business preference. However, where required as part of the conditions for partial federal funding, the state will implement small and disadvantaged business enterprise (DBE) requirements on state projects. These jobs will be governed by the requirements of 49 C.F.R. Part 26.

The U.S. Department of Housing and Urban Development (HUD) indicated that Act 17 of 2009, codified as HRS section 103-55.6, and Act 68 of 2010, codified as HRS section 103B, are in violation of federal housing and development rules. Section 103-55.6 gives an edge to bidders with apprentice programs. Section 103B requires that 80 percent of workers hired for state construction projects be Hawaii residents. Section 103B-4 does stipulate that the statute will not apply when in conflict with federal law or if application of the statute will disqualify a state or county agency from receiving federal funds.[5] In practice, the apprentice preference and the Hawaii resident workforce rules are used on all state and county projects.

E. Modes of Procurement

1. E-Quote Bidding

The 2006 Hawaii Legislature authorized the Procurement Policy Board to draft regulations to implement e-procurement for purchases of less than $50,000. Consequently, there is now an electronic procurement system, known as HIePRO (pronounced HI-Pro). Through HIePRO, vendor competition for state contracts is via an open and transparent electronic format. Everything is online: solicitations, addenda, questions and answers, offers, bid/quote opening, and contract awards. HIePRO is required for solicitations of $15,000 and above, although solicitations for less are posted in the system. The SPO uses HIePRO for all its solicitations and many other state agencies do as well. Some agencies, however, continue to post to other websites. (HRS § 103D-305.[6])

2. Price/Vendor List

Pursuant to statute, chief procurement officers (CPOs) may establish "price lists" (vendor schedules) for goods and services by using any appropriate source selection method for the purposes of entering into an indefinite delivery/indefinite quantity contract. Once established, use of the established price list is mandatory for all agencies subordinate to the CPO who established the list. (HAR § 3-121-6(b). See also SPO, Price & Vendor List Contracts, https://spo.hawaii.gov/for-vendors/contract-awards/price-vendor-lists/.)

5. As of 2021, the state has not augmented the statutes to meet HUD's concerns. There are currently proposed amendments to section 103-55.6, which restrict the benefits apprenticeship programs confer on qualified contractors to jobs in counties with populations of 500,000 or more. H.B. 517, H.D. 1, 28th Leg., Reg. Sess. (Haw. 2015). Articles regarding the conflict include Alan Yonan, Jr., *HUD Flags Local-hire Laws*, Honolulu Star-Advertiser (Sept. 25, 2010), https://www.staradvertiser.com/business/hud-flags-local-hire-laws/; *HUD Notifies Hawaii About Problems with Act 17, Act 68*, Pac. Bus. News (Sept. 24, 2010), http://www.bizjournals.com/pacific/stories/2010/09/20/daily46.html. The full text of the original acts are available at https://www.capitol.hawaii.gov/Archives/measure_indiv_Archives.aspx?billtype=SB&billnumber=19&year=2009 and http://www.capitol.hawaii.gov/session2010/bills/SB2840_ACT68_.pdf.

6. For more information on HIePRO, see https://hiepro.ehawaii.gov/welcome.html. The main web page with links to of all the platforms for the state's bidding opportunities is available at SPO, *Procurement Notices/Bidding Opportunities*, https://spo.hawaii.gov/for-vendors/bidding-opportunities/ (last visited May 22, 2022).

IV. Bid Protests and Contract Disputes

A. Bid Protests

1. Deadlines, Form, and Filing

a. Protests of Solicitations

"Any actual or prospective bidder, offeror, or contractor who is aggrieved in connection with" a solicitation or award may protest. Protests to solicitations under any procurement method must be submitted in writing to the CPO or a designee specified in the solicitation within five working days after the protestor "knows or should have known of the facts giving rise thereto." Protests to solicitations also must be submitted prior to the date set for receipt of offers. The protest must state reasons for the protest and include exhibits, evidence, or documents supporting the protest. Prior to award, if it is determined that a solicitation or proposed award of a contract is contrary to law, the solicitation or proposed award shall be cancelled or revised. The finding by a CPO or designee, after consultation with the attorney general or corporation counsel, that a solicitation or award violates the law, "will constitute a cogent and compelling reason to cancel, or revise a solicitation or proposed award." (HRS §§ 103D-701, 103D-704 to 103D-708; HAR § 3-126, subchs. 1 and 4.)

b. Protests of Awards

Protests to awards issued pursuant to an IFB, multi-step IFB, small purchase, or sole source procurement must be submitted in writing within five working days of the posting of the award to the CPO or a designee specified in the solicitation. Protests to awards issued pursuant to an RFP for professional services must be within five working days of posting of the award, or if pursuant to a non-selected offeror's request for a debriefing, within five working days after last debriefing. After the last debriefing, the debriefing is complete. (HRS § 103D-701(a); HAR § 3-126-4.) If after award of a contract it is determined that the solicitation or award is contrary to law, the contract may be ratified, affirmed, modified, or declared null and void based on the best interests of the state and whether or not the contractor acted fraudulently or in bad faith. (HRS § 103D-707; HAR § 3-126-38.)

c. Protests of Health and Human Services Solicitations and Awards

"A person who is aggrieved by an award of a contract" made pursuant only to a competitive or restrictive purchase of service may protest a purchasing agency's failure to follow procedures set forth in HRS chapter 103F, procurement rules, or the RFP. A notice of protest shall be submitted in writing to the head of the purchasing agency and CPO within five working days after the dated postmark on the award notice. The head of the purchasing agency shall schedule a settlement and scheduling conference within three working days of receipt of the protest notice. A written decision shall be issued within five working days, if practicable. A party may request reconsideration of a decision by the head of a purchasing agency by submitting to the CPO within five days of receiving the agency's written decision a "specific statement of the factual and legal grounds upon which reversal or modification is sought." The CPO's decision shall be issued within 15 calendar days of receipt of the request for reconsideration. (HRS §§ 103F-501, 103F-502; HAR § 3-148.)

2. Stay of Procurement

Action on a solicitation or issuance of an award shall be stayed upon the receipt of a timely protest until the issue is resolved or "until the chief procurement officer makes a written determination that the award of the contract without delay is necessary to protect the substantial interests of the State." (HRS § 103D-701(f); HAR § 3-126-5.) Upon the timely filing of a health and human services award protest or request for reconsideration of decision, contract award is suspended until the issue is resolved or the CPO determines that the award of the contract without delay is necessary. (HRS § 103F-503; HAR § 3-148-501.)

B. Bid Protest Appeals

Prior to commencement of administrative or court action, the CPO or designee may settle and resolve bid solicitation and award protests. When settlement is not reached, the CPO shall issue a written decision upholding or denying the protest that will be final and conclusive unless the protestor commences administrative review. The protestor must inform the head of the purchasing agency within seven calendar days after issuance of the decision if the protestor will be filing an administrative appeal and must submit its appeal to the Department of Commerce and Consumer Affairs (DCCA) Office of Administrative Hearings. Each request for hearing must be accompanied by both a nonrefundable filing fee plus a bond or cashier's check equivalent to 1 percent of the bid price of the prospective project under review. The bond will be returned only if the protestor prevails in its appeal. (HRS § 103D-701; HAR § 3-126-7(c).) The decision issued on administrative appeal is typically a written decision either on motion or after an evidentiary hearing. Past procurement decisions can be found at https://cca.hawaii.gov/oah/oah_decisions/procurement/.

C. Contract Disputes

The CPO or head of the purchasing agency, if expressly provided for in the contract, is authorized to settle and resolve controversies between an agency and a contractor that arise under a contract between them, prior to commencement of a court action. If the controversy is not resolved, the CPO or designee promptly shall issue a decision in writing that includes information about the contractor's right to judicial review. The CPO or designee shall issue a written decision within 90 calendar days after receipt of a claim under $50,000. For claims exceeding $50,000, the written decision should be issued within 90 days after receipt of the claim; however, if the decision is not issued within that time frame, the CPO or designee shall inform the contractor when a decision will be made. (HRS § 103D-703; HAR § 3-126, subchs. 1 and 3.)

Provisions governing the modification and termination of contracts are located at HRS section 103D-501 and HAR section 3-125.

D. Suspension and Debarment

The causes for debarment or suspension are set forth at HRS section 103D-702(b) and HAR section 3-126-11.01. However, "[t]he existence of a cause for debarment does not necessarily require that a contractor be debarred," and before arriving at a decision, the CPO shall consider "[t]he seriousness of a contractor's acts or omissions and any remedial measure or mitigating factors" such as are provided for at HRS section 103D-702(c). The CPO's decision to debar or suspend shall be final and conclusive, unless the debarred or suspended contractor commences an administrative proceeding. (HRS § 103D-702; HAR § 3-126, subch. 2.)

1. Debarment

The CPO may debar a contractor for cause from consideration for award on all public contracts and from performance on any public contract for a period not more than three years. A written notice of a proposed debarment action must be sent by certified mail and include a statement about the contractor's right to request a review as long as the request is received by the CPO within ten days of the contractor's receipt of the proposed debarment notification. If a review is requested, the CPO shall respond in writing within 15 working days and state the time, place, and nature of the proceedings to be held. The review shall be "as informal as may be reasonable under the circumstances and in accordance with applicable due process completed within sixty days." The CPO's final decision shall inform the contractor of the right to request administrative review. (HRS § 103D-702; HAR § 3-126, subch. 2.)

2. Suspension

The CPO may suspend a contractor from consideration for award on all public contracts if there is probable cause for debarment for a period not exceeding three months. A contractor is suspended upon issuance of the notice of suspension, and such notice shall signal the start of an investigation for debarment. A suspended contractor may submit a written request for review within ten days of receipt of a suspension notice. (HRS § 103D-702; HAR § 3-126, subch. 2.)

V. Administrative and Judicial Review

A. Administrative Review

The several hearing officers of the DCCA review and determine de novo any request from any bidder, offeror, contractor, or governmental body aggrieved by determinations involving contractor responsibility; bid solicitation and award protests; and debarment and suspensions. Requests for administrative review shall be made directly to the DCCA Office of Administrative Hearings within seven calendar days of the CPO's written determination. The request for administrative hearing is required to be accompanied by a filing fee, as well as a bond that must be in the amount of 1 percent of the total bid price of the bidder submitting the bid. The cost of proceeding with an administrative appeal of a procurement officer's decision has no cap.[7] A hearing

7. Filing fees and bond requirements for administrative review of public agency decisions on pending bid protests were imposed by Hawaii's legislature in an attempt to discourage bid protests, due to complaints by public agencies that because of the automatic stay on contract awards imposed upon bid protest submission, bid protests delayed award of projects. It is unclear why or how the imposition of a bond and filing fee upon review of agency decisions on protests would affect the number of bid protests filed, however, much less the delay caused by protests. Although the procurement statutes impose strict deadlines for submitting a protest, requesting administrative hearings, and the terms of such hearings, until 2021 there was no objective time limit for the public agency to act on bid protests, and protests could await agency decisions for months and in some cases more than a year. In 2021 the legislature imposed a 75-day deadline,

shall be held within 21 calendar days of receipt of the request. The party initiating the proceedings bears the burden of production as well as persuasion; the quantum of proof is a preponderance of the evidence. In the event that a bidder does not prevail at the administrative hearing level, its bond will be deposited into the state's general fund. In order for a matter to be heard at the administrative level, the issue in dispute must be equal to 10 percent of the bid price, or the action will be dismissed for lack of jurisdiction. (HRS § 103D-709.)

The DCCA hearing officer shall compile a record of each proceeding that shall include all pleadings, motions, and intermediate rulings; evidence received or considered; proposed findings of fact; and a recording of the proceedings. If the solicitation of award was previously stayed during the initial protest, no action shall be taken on a solicitation or award during the administrative proceeding. The hearing officer decides whether or not the CPO's determinations were "in accordance with the Constitution, statutes, rules, and the terms and conditions of the solicitation or contract," and may order relief depending upon the status of the award at the time of the administrative action. Any party to the administrative proceeding may appeal the hearing officer's decision and order in the circuit court where the controversy has arisen. (HRS §§ 103D-709, 103D-712; HAR § 3-126, subch. 5.)

B. Judicial Review

1. Review of Administrative Decisions

Requests for judicial review of administrative proceedings must be filed in the circuit court applicable to the prospective project within ten calendar days after the issuance of the hearing officer's written decision and order, and the party requesting judicial review immediately shall serve a copy of the application for judicial review upon the administrative review officer. The hearing officer shall transmit the record of proceedings to the circuit court within ten days[8] after an aggrieved party files an application for judicial review. The review shall be scheduled as soon as possible and based on the administrative proceeding record. Newly discovered evidence is only allowed if it is material to the outcome. (HRS § 103D-710; HAR § 3-126.)

The circuit court may affirm or remand for further consideration the hearing officer's decision and order. The court may modify or reverse the decision and order when

> substantial rights may have been prejudiced because the administrative findings, conclusions, decisions, or orders are: (1) In violation of constitutional or statutory provisions; (2) In excess of the statutory authority or jurisdiction

---

subject to certain exceptions, for agencies to make decisions on pending bid protests. While this would seem a logical step towards controlling perceived project delays caused by bid protests, the legislature unaccountably also eliminated the bond amount required to request administrative review of an agency's decision on a protest. Because of the already-in-place time limits for administrative review of agency decisions, it is unclear what benefit this change to the law afforded, other than reducing public scrutiny of public agencies' determinations of how public monies will be spent. Caroline Colpoys, *A Gamble for Hawaiian Contractors: Hawaii Raises the Stakes for Contractors Betting on State Bid Protest Appeals*, McCarter & English (June 11, 2021), https://www.jdsupra.com/legalnews/a-gamble-for-hawaiian-contractors-6152192/.

8. HRS section 103D-710(c) requires that the administrative hearing record be transmitted to the circuit court within ten days, whereas HAR section 3-126-78(c) requires 20 days. The inconsistency is most likely an error and the statute should be controlling.

> of the chief procurement officer . . . ; (3) Made upon unlawful procedure; (4) Affected by other error of law; (5) Clearly erroneous in view of the . . . substantial evidence on the whole record; or (6) Arbitrary, or capricious, or characterized by an abuse of discretion . . . .

(HRS § 103D-710.) The court has 30 days from the filing for judicial review to issue a decision on the appeal, after which the court loses jurisdiction to act on the case. A party dissatisfied with a circuit court decision may file an appeal pursuant to HRS sections 641-1 to 641-3, and the appeal shall receive priority. (HRS §§ 103D-710, 103D-712; HAR § 3-126, subch. 6.)

2. Judicial Action on Contract Disputes

Contract disputes must be filed in circuit court within six months after the issuance of the CPO's or designee's written determination. Contract dispute claims may be filed in circuit court by individuals, governmental bodies, or parties to the contract aggrieved by a state or county CPO's or designee's decision. Once an action is filed in the circuit court, only the attorney general is authorized to settle and resolve the matter. (HRS §§ 103D-711, 103D-712; HAR § 3-126, subch. 7.[9])

VI. Extent of State's Adoption or Adaptation of ABA Model Procurement Code

As mentioned previously, Hawaii's procurement laws are based upon the 1979 ABA MPC. In 1992, the state auditor was tasked with undertaking a study to recommend changes to the procurement code and subsequently suggested Hawaii enact revisions consistent with the 1979 MPC.[10] As a result, chapter 103D was enacted in 1993 with some, but not all, of the MPC's innovations and continues to be revised as needed, with the MPC as a guide.[11] (1993 Hawaii Special Session Laws act 8, at 37–82.)

VII. Cooperative Purchasing

A. Authority

Hawaii's procurement code provides for cooperative purchasing between different agencies and under certain conditions with external procurement entities. The enabling statute for this is HRS section 103D-802, and the conditions of cooperative purchasing are the accompanying administrative rules set forth in HAR chapter 3-128. "Cooperative purchasing" under the code is defined as procurement conducted by a public or external procurement unit with one or more public procurement units, external procurement units, or nonprofit private procurement units. An "external procurement unit" means any buying organization not located in the state, which, if located in the state, would qualify as a public procurement unit. "Local public procurement

9. Currently there are no administrative rules elucidating judicial action on contract disputes beyond that contained in the statutes. HAR section 3-126, subchapter 7 is reserved should rules become necessary.

10. State of Hawaii Office of the Auditor, Report No. 92-29, A Review of Hawaii's Procurement Law: A Report to the Governor and the Legislature of the State of Hawai'i 1, 8 (1992), https://files.hawaii.gov/auditor/Reports/1990-1995/92-29.pdf.

11. 1993 Haw. Spec. Sess. Laws Act 8, at 37–82.

unit" is defined by statute to include any county of the state or public agency of any county, public authority, educational, health, or other institution, and to the extent provided by law, any other entity that expends public funds for the procurement of goods, services, and construction.

Pursuant to HRS section 103D-802, a public procurement unit may either participate in, sponsor, conduct, or administer a cooperative purchasing agreement for the procurement of goods, services, or construction with one or more public procurement units, external procurement units, or nonprofit private procurement units pursuant to the guidelines established by the Procurement Policy Board, and the agreement entered into between the participants.

B. Requirements

HRS section 103D-802 provides that the cooperative purchasing may include, but shall not be limited to, joint or multiparty contracts between public procurement units, and state public procurement units requirements contracts that are made available to local public procurement units. Under the administrative rules, HAR section 3-128, cooperative purchasing must be done under the following conditions. First, there must be prior written approval by the CPO for the applicable agency. (HAR § 3-128-2.) Second, the purchase must be completed in compliance with the procurement code, HRS chapter 103D, except when done by an external procurement unit. The rules specifically prohibit agencies from attempting to "piggyback" on an existing cooperative purchasing agreement. "Piggybacking" is defined as procuring goods, services, or construction using another agency's contract without prior public notice and intent to participate. (HAR § 3-128-2(d).)

All cooperative purchasing agreements shall designate a single agency as the lead for the procurement. (HAR § 3-128-3 (1).) An order for any good or service shall be placed as needed in accordance with the terms and conditions of the purchasing agreement. (HAR § 3-128-3 (2).) Payment, inspection, and acceptance of any good or service, as well as exercise of warranty rights and termination of the cooperative agreement, shall be the exclusive responsibility and obligation of the procurement agency that placed the order. (HAR § 3-128-3 (3)–(6).)

Idaho Procurement Rules and Regulations

Prepared by Frederick J. Hahn, III
Hahn Law Office
Email: FJH@Hahn-Law.net

I. Statutory Reference

A. Procurement/Purchasing Statutes

Idaho purchasing is managed by the Idaho State Division of Purchasing (DOP), a division of the Department of Administration. Information about the DOP can be accessed through the Idaho state website at https://purchasing.idaho.gov/. The physical address for the DOP is 650 W. State Street, Boise, Idaho, 83702, and the telephone number is (208) 327-7465. The statutes relevant to the DOP are located in Idaho Statutes, title 67, chapter 57. Purchasing is governed by Idaho Code Annotated section 67-5714 to section 67-5748. The official Idaho Code can be accessed through the Idaho State Legislature's website found at https://legislature.idaho.gov/statutesrules/idstat/.

A table of contents of the State Procurement Act is set forth below.

§ 67-9201. SHORT TITLE.
§ 67-9202. DECLARATION OF POLICY.
§ 67-9203. DEFINITIONS.
§ 67-9204. DIVISION OF PURCHASING—ADMINISTRATOR.
§ 67-9205. POWERS AND DUTIES OF THE ADMINISTRATOR.
§ 67-9206. DELEGATION OF AUTHORITY.
§ 67-9207. PROCUREMENT TRAINING.
§ 67-9208. SOLICITATIONS.
§ 67-9209. BIDS.
§ 67-9210. AWARD OF CONTRACT.
§ 67-9211. MULTIPLE AWARDS.
§ 67-9212. CONTRACTS SHALL BE IN WRITING.
§ 67-9213. CONTRACTS IN VIOLATION OF PROVISIONS OF THE ACT.
§ 67-9214. ACCEPTANCE OF PROPERTY.
§ 67-9215. PRESERVATION AND DISCLOSURE OF RECORDS—EXCEPTION.
§ 67-9216. OPEN CONTRACTS.

§ 67-9217. DISQUALIFICATION OF VENDORS.
§ 67-9218. PAYMENT OF CONTRACTORS.
§ 67-9219. CONTRACT OVERSIGHT.
§ 67-9220. INVENTORIES.
§ 67-9221. NON-COMPETITIVE AND EMERGENCY PROCUREMENTS.
§ 67-9222. NON-OWNED PROPERTY.
§ 67-9223. EXCHANGE OF STATE PROPERTY.
§ 67-9224. COOPERATIVE AND GROUP DISCOUNT PURCHASING.
§ 67-9225. PROCUREMENT BY STATE INSTITUTIONS OF HIGHER EDUCATION.
§ 67-9226. DISCOUNTS.
§ 67-9227. CONTRACTS WITH FEDERAL GOVERNMENT EXEMPT FROM CERTAIN PROVISIONS.
§ 67-9228. ACQUISITION OF PROPERTY—GENERAL SERVICES ADMINISTRATION FEDERAL SUPPLY SCHEDULE CONTRACTS.
§ 67-9229. APPLICATION OF THE ADMINISTRATIVE PROCEDURES ACT.
§ 67-9230. PROHIBITIONS.
§ 67-9231. PENALTIES.
§ 67-9232. CHALLENGES AND APPEALS.
§ 67-9233. ETHICS IN PROCUREMENT.
§ 67-9234. SEVERABILITY.

B. Other Applicable Statutes

1. Exemptions from the State Procurement Act

a. Group insurance: The director of the Department of Administration is authorized to negotiate and procure group insurance as described in Idaho Statutes title 67, chapter 57, section 61.
b. Risk management: The director of the Department of Administration is authorized to procure risk management insurance as described in Idaho Statutes title 67, chapter 57, section 73.

2. Evidence, Public Writings, section 9-301 *et seq*. As amended and repealed.

3. Highways and Bridges, Appropriations, section 40-701 *et seq*.

4. Highways and Bridges, Contracts-Bids, section 40-901 *et seq*.

5. Crimes and Punishments, Public Funds and Securities, section 18-5701 *et seq*.

6. Ethics in Government, section 74-401 *et seq*.

7. Prohibitions against Contracts with Officers, section 74-501 *et seq*.

8. Purchasing by Political Subdivisions, section 67-2801 *et seq.*

9. Idaho Public Works Licensing, section 54-1905 *et seq.*

II. Regulations

A. Regulations

Regulations are promulgated pursuant to the statutory authority of Idaho Code Annotated section 67-9229 and the Idaho Administrative Procedure Act (IDAPA), Idaho Code Annotated section 67-5201 *et seq.*, which are available online at https://adminrules.idaho.gov/rules/current/38/380501.pdf.

- State of Idaho Standard Contract Terms and Conditions are found at https://purchasing.idaho.gov/wp-content/uploads/Standard-Terms-and-Conditions_May-2021.pdf.
- Solicitation Instructions to Vendors are found at https://purchasing.idaho.gov/wp-content/uploads/2019/08/solicitation_instructions-Jan-2017.pdf.
- Standard Contract Terms and Conditions are found at https://purchasing.idaho.gov/wp-content/uploads/Terms_Conditions/Standard%20Terms%20and%20Conditions%20Jan%202017.pdf.
- Standard Terms and Conditions for Cloud Services are found at https://purchasing.idaho.gov/wp-content/uploads/2019/01/Standard-Ts-and-Cs-for-Cloud-Services-010819.pdf.
- Standard Terms and Conditions for On-Premise Software and Related Services are found at https://purchasing.idaho.gov/wp-content/uploads/2019/01/Standard-Ts-and-Cs-for-OnPrem-Software-010819.pdf.
- Special Contract Terms and Conditions for Telecommunications Services are found at https://purchasing.idaho.gov/wp-content/uploads/Terms_Conditions/special_terms_and_conditions_for_telecommunications.pdf.
- Special Banking Solicitation Instructions to Vendors and Contract Terms and Conditions are found at https://purchasing.idaho.gov/wp-content/uploads/Terms_Conditions/special_terms_and_conditions_for_banking.pdf.
- Idaho State Policy Regarding Contracts to Natural Persons and Verification of Lawful Presence is found at https://purchasing.idaho.gov/wp-content/uploads/Terms_Conditions/verificaton_process.pdf.
- The Idaho DOP Procurement Desk Manual is found at https://purchasing.idaho.gov/wp-content/uploads/2018/12/Desk_manual-correct-links-dec-18.pdf.
- The Idaho Government Contracting/Procurement website is found at https://business.idaho.gov/assistance-resources/contracting/.

B. Policy Directives

Policy directives can be found at the following website: https://purchasing.idaho.gov/governing-laws-and-policies/.

The following policy directives have been promulgated by the DOP since 2010:

- Policy Directive No. 10-02 (July 2010): Universities and colleges—A determination has been made that competitive solicitation procedures may be impractical, disadvantageous, or unreasonable when applied to scientific equipment required for research conducted by State of Idaho university and college research departments that enable specific scientific measurement, readings, tolerances, or performance applicable to the research project.

- Policy Directive No. 11-01 (Jan. 2011): State appellate public defender—A determination has been made that competitive solicitation procedures may be impractical, disadvantageous, or unreasonable when applied to legal and professional services as they relate to client representation (not already exempt as a small purchase) by those state entities within the Department of Self-Governing Agencies.
- Policy Directive No. 11-02 (Mar. 2011): Idaho State Police—A determination has been made that purchase of property under existing state contracts are disadvantageous when applied to property acquired for and used in Idaho State Police undercover investigative work that remains anonymous.
- Policy Directive No. 11-03 (Aug. 2011): Exempts purchases of vaccines from Centers for Disease Control and Prevention (CDC) contracts from competitive bidding. Used by public health agencies only.
- Policy Directive No. 11-04 (Aug. 2011): Exempts legal advertising, public service announcements, and purchase of copyrighted materials primarily available from the publisher from competitive bidding.
- Policy Directive No. 11-05 (Aug. 2011): Establishes a policy and procedure for true and extreme emergency purchasing. Exempts true emergencies that create an immediate and serious threat to public health, welfare, or safety from competitive bidding.
- Policy Directive No. 11-06 (Aug. 2011): Exempts some educational discounts offered to qualifying educational institutions from the bidding process where the property is for the express purpose of educating students. The exemption shall not exceed $100,000.
- Policy Directive No. 11-07 (Aug. 2011): Endowment Fund Investment Board—A determination has been made that competitive solicitation procedures are impractical, disadvantageous, or unreasonable when applied to acquisition of services related to fiduciary responsibilities related to the Idaho Prudent Investor Act, Idaho Code Annotated sections 68-501 to 68-514.
- Policy Directive No. 11-09 (Aug. 2011): Juvenile Corrections—A determination has been made that competitive solicitation procedures are impractical, disadvantageous, or unreasonable when applied to some services used by Juvenile Corrections.
- Policy Directive No. 11-10 (Aug. 2011): Legal services—A determination has been made to exempt from competitive acquisition procedures the acquisition of legal services (not already exempt as a small purchase under Idaho Purchasing Rule 44) by those state entities within the Department of Self-Governing Agencies.
- Policy Directive No. 11-11 (Nov. 2013): Raises the no-bid limit to up to $100,000 for state employee education, training, and related expenses. The new revision adds the cost of funding training or training-related travel for other public employees receiving training.
- Policy Directive No. 13-1 (Sept. 2012): Idaho Department of Correction—A determination has been made that competitive solicitation procedures are impractical, disadvantageous, or unreasonable when applied to payments pertaining to lodging and living expenses that are made by the Department of Correction

on behalf of offenders that are transitioning into the community, and made in accordance with Department of Correction Standard Operating Procedure.

- Policy Directive No. 13-2 (Apr. 2013): Idaho Department of Correction—A determination has been made that competitive solicitation procedures are impractical, disadvantageous, or unreasonable when applied to offender medical insurance purchased by the Idaho Department of Correction for the purpose of providing medical insurance coverage for offenders when traveling to and from job sites and for offenders engaged in community work projects or special projects such as firefighting.
- Policy Directive No. 13-03 (Sept. 2013; revised Dec. 2018): Department of Health and Welfare and Division of Veterans Services—A determination has been made that competitive solicitation procedures may be impractical, disadvantageous, or unreasonable when applied to various divisions within the Department of Health and Welfare and the Division of Veterans Services relating to professional, treatment foster care, and intensive treatment/residential care facilities.
- Policy Directive No. 13-4 (July 2013; second amendment June 2016): Legal services—A determination has been made to exempt from competitive acquisition procedures the acquisition of legal services (not already exempt as a small purchase under Idaho Purchasing Rule 44) by those state entities within the Department of Self-Governing Agencies.
- Policy Directive No. 13-5 (Oct. 2013): Federal Surplus Program—A determination has been made that competitive solicitation procedures are often impractical, disadvantageous, or unreasonable when applied to the acquisition of inbound freight services for the Federal Surplus Property Program (located within the Department of Administration).
- Policy Directive No. 15-01 (Aug. 2015): Youth seasonal work and job training—A determination has been made that competitive solicitation procedures are impractical for limited duration (or seasonal) work and job training opportunities for the youth of Idaho (generally defined as individuals between the ages of 16 and 25) established through a written agreement with a Youth or Conservation Corps (or similar entity).
- Policy Directive No. 15-02 (Aug. 2015): Exempts competitive solicitations for agency memberships in national and other associations and partnerships where the annual agency spend is no more than $50,000.
- Policy Directive No. 15-03 (Aug. 2015): Provides exemption from use of open contracts for purchases of services and commodities from Idaho Correctional Industries where purchases are no more than $10,000.
- Policy Directive No. 15-04 (Aug. 2015): Exempts competitive solicitations for acquisition of extradition services to return parole violators and dual commitment offenders back to the state of Idaho in certain circumstances.
- Policy Directive No. 16-01 (Apr. 2016): Exempts competitive solicitations with respect to services and equipment procured by the Idaho Division of Vocational Rehabilitation relating to prosthetics, tuition, or training for individualized job training or vehicle modifications in an amount of less than $100,000.
- Policy Directive No. 16-02 (May 2016): Exempts competitive solicitations with respect to services of inspectors to perform organic inspections and specialized material reviews in compliance with the U.S. Department of Agriculture and Idaho State Department of Agriculture regulations related to the National Organic Program.

- Policy Directive No. 16-03 (Apr. 2017): Exempts competitive solicitations with respect to instructional services and related facility use for college/university (institution) courses when geographic or other factors result in a limited pool of instructors and/or facilities.
- Policy Directive No. 16-04 (Nov. 2016): Exempts competitive solicitations with respect to investigative case support and/or analysis from individuals who must meet security policy requirements of federal, state, and local agencies to provide services to the Idaho State Police.
- Policy Directive No. 18-01 (Oct. 2018): Exempts competitive solicitations with respect to preventative maintenance and repair of scientific equipment when services are only available from a single supplier.
- Policy Directive No. 19-01 (Jan. 2019): Exempts competitive solicitations with respect to hiring and retaining instructors for the Certified Public Manager Program.
- Policy Directive No. 19-02 (Jan. 2019): Exempts competitive solicitations with respect to software applications, licenses, maintenance, and support agreements for and related to OpenFox Message Switch supplied by Computer Projects of Illinois, Inc. acquired by the Idaho State Police.
- Policy Directive No. 19-03 (Mar. 2019): Exempts competitive solicitations with respect to American Association of State Highway and Transportation Officials software, licensing, maintenance and support services, analytics modules, training, and software development.
- Policy Directive No. 19-04 (Mar. 2019): Exempts competitive solicitations with respect to the Wood Stove Change-Out Program.
- Policy Directive No. 19-05 (May 2019): Exempts competitive solicitations with respect to collection of trash, recycling, and other waste (not including hazardous waste) at state facilities.
- Policy Directive No. 19-06 (June 2019): Exempts competitive solicitations with respect to social media influencers and content creators to be used for marketing/promoting tourism in Idaho.
- Policy Directive No. 19-07 (Sept. 2019): Exempts competitive solicitations with respect to the purchase of temporary staffing services from a rehabilitation agency, when the purchase is made pursuant to Idaho Code Annotated section 67-2319 and IDAPA 38.05.01.042.06 and 38.05.01.046.
- Policy Directive No. 20-01 (Jan. 2020): Exempts competitive solicitations with respect to expenses associated with agency participation in trade shows or other events at which the agency is promoting the state; which expenses include all registration costs, activities, fees, booth construction/set-up (rental, lease, or purchase), and all other costs directly associated with participation in the event, for which there is no other source from which to obtain competitive bids or quotes.
- Policy Directive No. 20-02 (Feb. 2020): Exempts competitive solicitations with respect to repair services for non-licensed heavy equipment (e.g., Class 8 trucks, construction equipment, heavy-duty mowing equipment, etc.), when the ability of a vendor to provide a quote for services requires significant labor (e.g., disassembling the equipment).
- Policy Directive No. 20-03 (Nov. 2020): Exempts competitive solicitations with respect to property acquired for direct resale, which is unique or otherwise impractical to compete. Specifically exempted are liquor, wine, and other

alcoholic and non-alcoholic products acquired by the Idaho State Liquor Division, and souvenirs or unique items acquired for direct sale by the Idaho State Historical Society.

- Policy Directive No. 21-01 (Aug. 2020): Exempts competitive solicitations with respect to access to the exchange for the posting and retrieval of medical client confidential electronic health information, currently provided by the Idaho Health Data Exchange.
- Policy Directive No. 21-02 (Feb. 2021): Exempts competitive solicitations with respect to the acquisition of executive coaching services where the success of the engagement relies on developing a relationship of personal trust.

III. Source Selection

A. Noncompetitive and Emergency Purchases

The administrator of the DOP determines that a particular savings to the state may be obtained through educational discounts, reverse public auctions, or acquisition of federal surplus or excess property. Sole source procurements are subject to posting notice, unless a "life-threatening" or a situation involving immediate detriment to public welfare or property occurs. (Idaho Code Annotated § 67-9221; Division of Purchasing Rules: IDAPA 38.05.01.043 (Emergency Purchases); IDAPA 38.05.01.045 (Sole Source Purchases); IDAPA 35.05.01.044 (Small Purchases).)

B. Small Purchases

Procurements of $10,000 or less are deemed exempt and may be purchased using informal solicitation with the assistance of counsel, but subject to limitations. (IDAPA 35.05.01.044 (Mar. 29, 2017).)

C. Sole Source Purchases

Sole source purchase shall be used only if the required property is reasonably available from a single supplier. A requirement for a particular proprietary property item does not justify a sole source purchase if there is more than one potential supplier that can provide the required property. (IDAPA 38.05.01.045.01. (Mar. 29, 2017).)

D. Formal Sealed Bids or Proposals

Formal sealed bids or proposals are used for purchases exceeding $100,000. (IDAPA 35.05.01.041 (Apr. 7, 2011).) Specifications must be written in accordance with DOP regulations. Solicitation must specify the opening date, time, and location and the contract terms and any evaluation criteria. (IDAPA 35.05.01.051 (Mar. 15, 2002).) Bids or proposals may be submitted manually or electronically. (IDAPA 35.05.01.061 (Apr. 6, 2015).) Award must be made to the lowest responsible and responsive bidder or offeror. (IDAPA 35.05.01.081 (Mar. 15, 2002).) All contracts for public works shall be awarded to the lowest responsible and responsive bidder pursuant to sealed bidding. (Idaho Code Annotated § 67-5711C, except as provided in Idaho Code Annotated § 67-5711B (emergency public works contracting), § 67-5711D (energy savings performance contracts), and § 67-5713 (construction and alteration of state correctional facilities).)

E. Reverse Auctions

Reverse auctions are authorized for noncompetitive and emergency procurements by Idaho Code Annotated section 67-9221, and are thus accounted for under IDAPA 38.05.01.42.03 (Mar. 15, 2002), but the procedures are not specified in the statute or the rules.

IV. Bid Protests and Contract Disputes

A. Bid Protests

1. Deadlines

Specification Protest: Protest must be filed in writing within ten working days to the administrator of the DOP. The protest must specifically state the exact nature of his challenge; describe the location of the challenged portion or clause in the specification document (unless the challenge concerns an omission); explain why any provision should be struck, added, or altered: and contain suggested corrections. (Idaho Code Annotated § 67-9232.) Procedures for the protest determination are set forth at section 67-9232(1)(b)–(d).

Non-responsive Bid: A bidder whose offer is found to be non-responsive has five working days to protest this decision in writing to the director of the Department of Administration. (Idaho Code Annotated § 67-9232(2).)

Award Protest: An aggrieved bidder has five working days to protest an award in writing to the director of the Department of Administration. The protest must set forth in specific terms the reasons why the administrator's decision is thought to be erroneous. (Idaho Code Annotated § 67-9232(3).)

Sole Source Procurement Protest: Within five days from the last date of public notice any vendor who is able to sell or supply the item(s) to be acquired may protest in writing to the administrator of the DOP an intent to conduct a sole source procurement. (Idaho Code Annotated § 67-9232(4).)

2. Standing

Any vendor may file a specification protest. A bidder whose offer was found non-responsive may file a non-responsive protest, while a bidder whose bid was responsive, but lost the award to another bidder, may file an award protest. (See Idaho Code Annotated § 67-9232.)

3. Stay of Procurement

When a complaint is filed pursuant to section 67-9232(2) (non-responsive bids), no bid may be awarded until the final decision is rendered by the director; provided that in all other cases where a determinations officer is appointed by the director, the director shall have the power to allow the acquisition contract to be awarded to the successful bidder prior to or after the decision of the determinations officer if he determines such award to be in the best interests of the state. (Idaho Code Annotated § 67-9232(6).)

4. Hearing

Hearings are allowed only at the discretion of the director of the Department of Administration and only then in the case of award protests. (Idaho Code Annotated § 67-9232(3).)

B. Bid Protest Appeals

1. Deadline

Only decisions made pursuant to a hearing are appealable. (Idaho Code Annotated § 67-9232(7); § 67-5270.) Appeals must be filed within 28 days of a final order. (Idaho Code Annotated § 67-5273.) Challenges or appeals conducted under Idaho Code Annotated section 67-9232(1), (2), (3)(a)(i), or (ii) are not contested cases under the IDAPA. (Idaho Code Annotated § 67-9233(7).) An appeal conducted pursuant to section 67-9232(3)(iii) shall be conducted as a contested case according to the provisions of chapter 52, title 67 of the Idaho Code.

2. Filing

Appeals are normally made to the district court in the county in which the hearing was held, the final agency action was taken, the aggrieved party resides or operates its principal place of business, or the property subject to the agency decision is located. (Idaho Code Annotated § 67-5272.)

3. Stay of Procurement

The filing of the petition for review does not itself stay the effectiveness or enforcement of the agency action. The agency may grant, or the reviewing court may order, a stay upon appropriate terms. (Idaho Code Annotated § 67-5274.)

4. Hearing

Hearings are conducted in accordance with Idaho Code Annotated section 67-5242.

C. Contract Disputes

There are no statutes or regulations that govern a dispute arising between a contractor and the state during the performance of a public contract. Either the contractor or the state is permitted to bring an action in state court for breach of contract.

D. Suspension and Debarment

Vendors may be disqualified for any of the following reasons:

(a) Failure to perform according to the terms of any contract;

(b) Attempts by whatever means to cause specifications to be drawn so as to favor a specific vendor;

(c) Use of the provisions of this chapter to obstruct or unreasonably delay acquisitions by the state;

(d) Perjury in a vendor disqualification hearing;

(e) Knowingly violate the provisions of this chapter; or

(f) Debarment, suspension, or ineligibility from federal contracting of the vendor, its principals, or its affiliates.

(Idaho Code Annotated § 67-9217.)

A vendor shall be notified by registered mail within ten days of disqualification and may, within 30 days of the receipt of such notice, request of the director of the

Department of Administration a hearing before a determinations officer. Any hearing shall be held in accordance with chapter 52, title 67 of the Idaho Code. (Idaho Code Annotated § 67-9217(3).)

In lieu of disqualification, the determinations officer may recommend to the director of the Department of Administration specific conditions to the vendor's continued participation in acquisitions by the state. (Idaho Code Annotated § 67-9217(4).) Disqualification or conditions may be imposed for a period of not less than six months or not more than five years. (Idaho Code Annotated § 67-9217(5).)

V. Administrative and Judicial Review

A. Administrative Review

The administrative review process for bid protests, administrative appeals, stays, debarment, and suspension are set forth above and are subject to the IDAPA. (Idaho Code Annotated § 67-9229.)

B. Judicial Review

Only appeals conducted as contested cases pursuant to Idaho Code Annotated section 67-9232(1), (2), (3)(i), and (ii) shall be subject to the judicial review provisions of chapter 52, title 67 of the Idaho Code. This section shall not impair any contract right or contract remedy, which may exist between the state and a properly licensed contractor or vendor. (Idaho Code Annotated § 67-9229.)

VI. Extent of State's Adoption or Adaptation of ABA Model Procurement Code

The Idaho Code governing the DOP was originally added in 1974. Idaho has partially adopted or partially complies with the American Bar Association's (ABA's) Model Procurement Code for State and Local Governments.

VII. Cooperative Purchasing

A. Authority

Idaho Code Annotated section 67-2807 authorizes political subdivisions of the state and other governmental entities and associations thereof to participate in cooperative purchasing agreements with the approval of such entities' governing boards. Goods or services procured through cooperative agreements or programs are deemed to meet the requirements of state procurement laws. Idaho Code Annotated section 67-4223(12) specifically authorizes the Idaho Department of Parks and Recreation to purchase and lease through cooperative agreements.

Additionally, Idaho Code Annotated section 67-9224 provides for cooperative and group discount purchasing when authorized by the administrator of the DOP and when formalized in writing.

B. Requirements

The IDAPA regulations provide for cooperative purchasing and states:

> The various bid statutes relating to municipal corporations, school districts, and counties may authorize these political subdivisions to utilize any contract entered into by the state. A public agency may use open contracts as authorized by statute and the terms of the open contract; and the state may otherwise cooperate with political subdivisions in the acquisition of property.

(IDAPA 38.05.01.031 (Mar. 15, 2002).)

Cooperative and group discount purchasing must be formalized by a written agreement and based upon criteria applied to all members of the organization (Idaho Code Annotated § 67-9224(2) and (3)), which is maintained on file with the DOP as well as the procuring agency. (Idaho Code Annotated § 67-9224(4).)

Illinois Procurement Rules and Regulations

Prepared by Jeff H. Eckland
Eckland & Blando LLP
Email: jeckland@ecklandblando.com
With assistance from Mark J. Blando, Vince Reuter, and Robert Dube[1]

I. Statutory Reference

The main authority for statewide procurement rests with the Department of Central Management Services. However, as described below, many agencies conduct their own procurements and have issued supplemental rules for procurements.

A. Procurement/Purchasing Statutes

The Illinois Procurement Code is found at Illinois Compiled Statutes chapter 30, act 500.

B. Other Applicable Statutes

The Uniform Commercial Code is found at Illinois Compiled Statutes chapter 810, act 5, and the Court of Claims Act is located at Illinois Compiled Statutes chapter 705, act 505.

II. Regulations

A. General Procurement Rules—Department of Central Management Services

The following is a guide to Illinois general procurement rules, Illinois Administrative Code title 44:

1. Subpart A: General

§ 1.1 (2012). Title

§ 1.3 (2012). Authority

1. Research, drafting, proofing, and citation assistance provided by Kenneth Cooper of Eckland & Blando LLP.

§ 1.5 (2014). Policy
§ 1.8 (2012). Purpose and Implementation of This Part
§ 1.10 (2014). Application
§ 1.15 (2014). Definition of Terms Used in This Part
§ 1.25 (2012). Property Rights

2. Subpart B: Procurement Rules
   § 1.525 (2014). Rules
   § 1.530 (2012). Policies and Procedures

3. Subpart C: Procurement Authority
   § 1.1005 (2014). Exercise of Procurement Authority
   § 1.1040 (2014). Central Procurement Authority of the CPO
   § 1.1060 (2014). Delegation
   § 1.1070 (2012). Toll Highway Authority

4. Subpart D: Publicizing Procurement Actions
   § 1.1501 (2014). Illinois Procurement Bulletin
   § 1.1525 (2014). Bulletin Content
   § 1.1560 (2012). Supplemental Notice
   § 1.1570 (2014). Error in Notice
   § 1.1580 (2012). Direct Solicitation

5. Subpart E: Source Selection and Contract Formation
   § 1.2005 (2014). General Provisions
   § 1.2010 (2014). Competitive Sealed Bidding
   § 1.2012 (2014). Multi-Step Sealed Bidding
   § 1.2015 (2014). Competitive Sealed Proposals
   § 1.2020 (2016). Small Purchases
   § 1.2025 (2014). Sole Economically Feasible Source Procurement
   § 1.2030 (2014). Emergency Procurements
   § 1.2035 (2014). Competitive Selection Procedures for Professional and Artistic Services
   § 1.2036 (2014). Other Methods of Source Selection
   § 1.2037 (2012). Tie Bids and Proposals
   § 1.2039 (2014). Mistakes
   § 1.2040 (2014). Cancellation of Solicitations; Rejection of Bids or Proposals

6. Subpart F: Suppliers, Prequalification, and Responsibility
   § 1.2043 (2014). Suppliers
   § 1.2044 (2014). Vendor List

§ 1.2045 (2014). Prequalification
§ 1.2046 (2014). Responsibility

7. Subpart G: Bid, Proposal, and Performance Security
§ 1.2047 (2012). Security Requirements

8. Subpart H: Specifications and Samples
§ 1.2050 (2014). Specifications and Samples

9. Subpart I: Contracts
§ 1.2055 (2014). Types of Contracts
§ 1.2060 (2014). Duration of Contracts—General

10. Subpart K: Working Conditions
§ 1.2560 (2012). Prevailing Wage
§ 1.2570 (2012). Equal Employment Opportunity; Affirmative Action

11. Subpart M: Construction, Construction-Related Professional Services
§ 1.3005 (2014). Construction and Construction-Related Professional Services

12. Subpart N: Real Property Leases and Capital Improvement Leases
§ 1.4005 (2012). Real Property Leases and Capital Improvement Leases

13. Subpart O: Preferences
§ 1.4505 (2012). Procurement Preferences
§ 1.4510 (2012). Resident Vendor Preference
§ 1.4530 (2014). Correctional Industries
§ 1.4535 (2014). Qualified Not-for-Profit Agencies for Persons with Severe Disabilities
§ 1.4540 (2014). Gas Mileage and Flex-Fuel Requirements
§ 1.4545 (2014). Small Business
§ 1.4570 (2012). Contracting with Businesses Owned and Controlled by Minorities, Females, and Persons with Disabilities
§ 1.4575 (2012). Domestic Products

14. Subpart P: Ethics
§ 1.5013 (2014). Conflicts of Interest Prohibited by the Code
§ 1.5015 (2012). Negotiations for Future Employment
§ 1.5020 (2014). Exemptions
§ 1.5030 (2012). Revolving Door Prohibition

§ 1.5035 (2014). Disclosure of Financial Interests and Potential Conflicts of Interest

§ 1.5037 (2014). Vendor Registration, Certification, and Prohibition on Political Contributions

15. Subpart Q: Concessions

§ 1.5310 (2012). Concessions

16. Subpart R: Cooperative Purchasing

§ 1.5400 (2012). General

§ 1.5420 (2012). Governmental Joint Purchasing Act Contracts

§ 1.5440 (2012). Non-Governmental Joint Purchasing

§ 1.5460 (2012). No Agency Relationship

17. Subpart S: Protests

§ 1.5550 (2014). Protests

18. Subpart W: Miscellaneous Provisions of General Applicability

§ 1.7000 (2012). Severability

§ 1.7010 (2012). Government Furnished Property

§ 1.7015 (2014). Inspections

§ 1.7020 (2012). Records and Audits

§ 1.7030 (2012). No Waiver of Sovereign Immunity

19. Social Policies Applicable to All Contracts

Title 44 Illinois Administrative Code Part 750. Department of Human Rights

B. Supplemental Rules for Other Agencies

Title 44 Illinois Administrative Code Part 500. Office of Auditor General

Title 44 Illinois Administrative Code Parts 610, 1150. Department of Natural Resources

Title 44 Illinois Administrative Code Chapter IX, Parts 625 to 660. Department of Transportation

Title 44 Illinois Administrative Code Chapter XII, Parts 910 to 1030. Capitol Development Board

Title 44 Illinois Administrative Code Part 1110. Department of Education

Title 44 Illinois Administrative Code Chapter XII, Parts 1120 to 1130. Comptroller

Title 44 Illinois Administrative Code Part 1300. Attorney General

Title 44 Illinois Administrative Code Part 1400. Treasurer

Title 44 Illinois Administrative Code Part 1500. Governor

Title 44 Illinois Administrative Code Part 1600. Lieutenant Governor
Title 44 Illinois Administrative Code Part 2000. Secretary of State
Title 44 Illinois Administrative Code Part 2600. State Board of Elections

III. Source Selection

Illinois uses competitive sealed bidding as the preferred procurement method. (30 Illinois Compiled Statutes 500/20-5 (amended 2015) ("[A]ll State contracts shall be awarded by competitive sealed bidding, [unless excepted by law].").) Further, an agency may cancel an invitation for bids (IFB) or a request for proposals (RFP) when in the best interests of the state and in accord with the relevant rules. (30 Illinois Compiled Statutes 500/20-40 (amended 2015).) Also, home rule units are not ordinarily required to engage in competitive bidding. (*American Health Care Providers, Inc. v. County of Cook*, 638 N.E.2d 772, 781 (Ill. App. Ct. 1994).)

A. Competitive Sealed Bidding

Competitive sealed bidding begins with an IFB published at least 14 days prior to the bid opening. (See generally 30 Illinois Compiled Statutes 500/20-10 (2021).) Bids shall be evaluated by criteria included within the IFB and shall be awarded to the lowest responsible and responsive bidder except for when "a State purchasing officer determines it is not in the best interest of the State." (*Id.* 500/20-10(g) (2020).) After bid opening, no changes in the bid price or other provisions "prejudicial to the interest of the State or fair competition shall be permitted." (*Id.* 500/20-10(f) (2020).)

The state may create alternative procedures such as multi-step bidding, where unpriced bids are first submitted to narrow the purchase description and acceptable bidders are then invited to submit prices for the second part. (*Id.* 500/20-10(h) (2020).) Additionally, the state may use a reverse auction process in some circumstances. (*Id.* 500/20-10(j) (2020).)

B. Competitive Sealed Proposals

When a purchasing agency determines in writing that sealed competitive bidding is not practicable or not advantageous to the state, the agency may solicit proposals through an RFP. (*Id.* 500/20-15 (2020).) The RFP shall state the relative importance of price and other criteria. (*Id.*) Further, the proposals shall be submitted in two parts, the first to include price and the second to include all other non-price items. (*Id.*) The agency shall evaluate each part of all proposals independently of the other parts.

Commencing on January 1, 2022, proposals also must include a third part stating a commitment to diversity. (*Id.* 500/20-15(e), (e-5) (effective Jan. 1, 2022).) When scoring the RFP, the purchasing agency will weigh the commitment to diversity as 20 percent of the points assigned to the part of the proposal stating all other non-price items. (*Id.*) In scoring these points, factors include, but are not limited to, whether the respondent contracts "with businesses owned by women, minorities, or persons with disabilities," whether the respondent uses diversity vendors in its supply chain, and the percentage of past revenue "of the respondent that involve[d] businesses owned by women, minorities, or persons with disabilities." (*Id.*)

The agency is permitted to conduct negotiations with offerors who submit responsive proposals that are "reasonably susceptible to being selected" for the purpose of "clarifying and assuring full understanding of[,] and responsiveness to[,] the solicitation requirements." (*Id.* 500/20-15(f) (2020).) These offerors shall be treated equally with respect to an opportunity for discussion and revision to the proposals. (*Id.*) Additionally, revisions after submission but before the award may occur "for the purpose of obtaining best and final offers." (*Id.*)

C. Small Purchases Threshold

"Any individual procurement of supplies or services other than professional or artistic services, not exceeding $100,000 and any procurement of construction not exceeding $100,000 may be made without competitive sealed bidding." (*Id.* 500/20-20 (2017).) Contracts may not be artificially broken up to fall under this threshold.

D. Sole Source Procurements

Sole source procurements are only available when there is only one economically feasible source for an item. (*Id.* 500/20-25 (2020).) Further, a contract following a sole source procurement may not be awarded unless approved by the chief procurement officer (CPO) following a public hearing and upon a written determination by the agency. (*Id.*)

E. Emergency Purchases

Emergency procurements may be made without notice and without competitive bidding (1) where "there exists a threat to the public health or safety"; (2) when an immediate expenditure is necessary to protect state property from further damage or loss; (3) to prevent serious disruption to state services; or (4) to ensure the integrity of state records. (*Id.* 500/20-30(a).) A contract under these provisions may not exceed 90 days, unless an extension is deemed necessary and subject to a public hearing. (*Id.*) Even for emergency purchases, the agency must use as much competition as practicable. (*Id.*) Additionally, commencing on January 1, 2022, purchasing agencies must use best efforts when making emergency purchases to include contractors certified under the Business Enterprise Program. (*Id.* 500/20-30 (effective Jan. 1, 2022).)

F. Types of Contracts Available

Any type of contract that serves the best interest of the state is permitted with the exception that cost-plus-percentage-of-cost contracts are prohibited. (*Id.* 500/20-55.) Further, a cost-reimbursement contract requires a written determination that other types of contracts are impracticable. (*Id.*)

G. Notification of Intended Subcontractors

Contract awardees have obligations to notify the government of the identity of subcontractors with subcontracts expected to exceed $50,000 in value annually. (*Id.* 500/20-120 (amended 2015).) Additionally, contract awardees are required to include the general type of work to be performed by the subcontractors and the expected amount of money each subcontractor will receive. (*Id.* 500/20-120, subdiv. a.) Further, changes to the subcontractor roster need to be passed on to the government. (*Id.*)

IV. Bid Protests and Contract Disputes

A. Bid Protests

The CPO is responsible for creating a bid protest procedure. (*Id.* 500/20-75.) Details about protest rules and procedure can be found at Illinois Administrative Code title 44, section 1.5550 (amended 2014). "Any person who has submitted a bid or proposal may protest a decision to reject the person's bid or proposal or to award to another person." (Illinois Administrative Code tit. 44, § 1.5550(a)(2).)

The aggrieved party must file the protest with the protest review officer identified in the bid. (*Id.* § 1.5550(c).) Significantly, the protest must be received within 14 days of when the protesting party knew, or should have known, of the facts supporting the protest. (*Id.*) Alternatively, if the protest is based upon the solicitation document itself, the protest must be filed with 14 days of the publication of the solicitation. (*Id.*)

The protesting party must disclose their name, address, the relief sought, and identification of the procurement, including whether a contract has been awarded or not. (*Id.*) The written protest should set forth specific reasons for the protest, citing any procurement rules, statutes, or solicitations that have been violated, including a section for the evaluation and award. (*Id.*) The protesting party should include "supporting exhibits, evidence, or documents to substantiate any claims," not to exceed 20 pages in length. (*Id.*) If a protest includes any trade secrets or confidential information, this must be identified by the party submitting the protest. (*Id.*)

When a protest is timely filed, and the award has not been made, the procurement officer shall refrain from awarding the contract until the protest has been resolved, unless a determination has been made that the state requires an immediate award and performance under the contract. (*Id.* § 1.5550(e).) Further, if a determination is made that a solicitation or award was made contrary to law, then the CPO or the state purchasing officer may cancel or make modifications to the contract. (*Id.* § 1.5620(a) (amended 2014).) In cases where a contract is voided, any supplies that were not used or released will be returned and the state will cease payment on the contract. (*Id.* § 1.5620(c).) Also, any claims of lost profits are not available for an unsuccessful bidder. (*Keefe-Shea Joint Venture v. City of Evanston*, 773 N.E.2d 1155 (Ill. App. Ct. 2002).)

B. Bid Protest Appeals

If an action concerning a protest has already begun in court, the Protest Review Office does not have to act on the protest until there has been a final judicial or administrative decision. (Illinois Administrative Code tit. 44, § 1.5550(g) (amended 2014).) Review of a bid protest decision, if the administrative process is complete, may be available in the Court of Claims of Illinois. (See *Walsh v. State*, 60 Ill. Ct. Cl. 238, 241 (2008).) If a party seeks a review of the bidding process in court, normal appellate review for civil claims is available. (See, e.g., *Walsh/II in One Joint Venture III v. Metropolitan Water Reclamation District of Greater Chicago*, 904 N.E.2d 1158 (Ill. App. Ct. 2009).)

C. Contract Disputes

1. Contract Claims

Contract claims against the government must be filed with the Court of Claims of Illinois, which has "exclusive jurisdiction" for all "claims against the State founded upon any contract entered into with the State of Illinois." (705 Illinois Compiled Statutes 505/8(b) (2010) (Court of Claims Act); but see *Vogt v. Bartelsmeyer*, 636 N.E.2d 1185 (Ill. App. Ct. 1994) (circuit court is appropriate forum to enforce settlement agreement with the state).)

The Court of Claims may order equitable remedies. (*Liebman v. Board of State Colleges & Universities*, 398 N.E.2d 305, 308 (Ill. App. Ct. 1979).) But the Court of Claims will decline to issue injunctions in the absence of specific statutory provisions empowering it to do so. (*Garimella v. Board of Trustees of the University of Illinois*, 50 Ill. Ct. Cl. 350, 353 (1996).) While the issue has not been decided by higher courts, the rough consensus is that declaratory judgments, especially statements of a party's rights related to contract or tort claims against the state, may be issued by the Court of Claims of Illinois. However, equitable remedies in the form of injunctions, mandamus, habeas corpus, or punitive damages are not available in this forum.

2. Contract Claims Appeals

While no means of appellate review is granted by statute, "*certiorari* is available to address alleged deprivations of due process by the Court of Claims." (*Reichert v. Court of Claims*, 786 N.E.2d 174, 177 (Ill. 2003) (citation omitted).) However, this process cannot be used to challenge the decision of the Court of Claims on its merits. (*Id.*) Consequently, the court will only review decisions from the Court of Claims if the decision deprived a party of its constitutional right to due process, or the opportunity to be heard at a meaningful time in a meaningful manner. (*Klopfer v. Court of Claims*, 676 N.E.2d 679, 682 (Ill. App. Ct. 1997).)

D. Suspension and Debarment

"The CPO-GS [CPO for General Services] may suspend a vendor from doing business with the State . . . upon a showing the vendor violated the Code or this Part or failed to conform to specifications or terms of delivery." (Illinois Administrative Code tit. 44, § 1.5560(b) (amended 2014).) A vendor's suspension should mirror the seriousness of the offense, but shall not exceed ten years, and "will be effective seven calendar days after receipt of notice unless an objection is filed." (*Id.* § 1.5560(d).)

The CPO may also debar, or permanently suspend, a vendor from engaging in business with the state. (*Id.* § 1.5560(e).) "A debarment may only take place in those instances involving bribery or attempted bribery of a State of Illinois officer or employee, or as otherwise allowed or required by law." (*Id.*) The CPO "shall maintain a master list of all suspensions and debarments," which is considered a public record. (*Id.* § 1.5560(h).)

V. Administrative and Judicial Review

Claims based on executed contracts must be presented to the Court of Claims of Illinois pursuant to statute. (705 Illinois Compiled Statutes 505/8 (2018).) For claims related to the procurement process itself, prior to the award of contracts, avenues for relief are available depending on the procuring authority. For procurements conducted by the Department of Central Management Services, administrative rules provide for a bid protest mechanism. Failure to use these mechanisms is a failure to exhaust administrative remedies. (See generally *Walsh v. State*, 60 Ill. Ct. Cl. 238, 241 (2008).) Otherwise, if no means of administrative review is available pursuant to supplemental procurement rules, the remedy remains filing a complaint in court seeking an injunction to prevent an award. (See, e.g., *Walsh/II in One Joint Venture III v. Metropolitan Water Reclamation District of Greater Chicago*, 904 N.E.2d 1158 (Ill. App. Ct. 2009).) However, seeking injunctive relief requires a prima facie case of injury. (*Keefe-Shea Joint Venture v. City of Evanston*, 773 N.E.2d 1155, 1159 (Ill. App. Ct. 2002).)

VI. Extent of State's Adoption or Adaptation of ABA Model Procurement Code

The Illinois Procurement Code, originally adopted in 1998, is not modeled after the American Bar Association's (ABA's) initial version of the Model Procurement Code for State and Local Governments.

VII. Cooperative Purchasing

A. Authority

Information on Illinois's cooperative purchasing agreement program, denominated the Unified Procurement Program (UPP), can be found on the CPO's website at https://www2.illinois.gov/cpo/general/Pages/UnifiedProcurementProgram.aspx. Under the UPP, which is administered by the CPO-GS, any "governmental unit" (i.e., any state agency, state official, municipality, or public entity created by statute) is authorized to make joint purchases for personal property, supplies, or services through competitive solicitation. (30 Illinois Compiled Statutes 525/1 (definition of governmental unit), 525/2 (2017).) Any nonprofit agency receiving state grants and serving persons with significant disabilities is eligible to join in contracts established by the state. (*Id.*; see 30 Illinois Compiled Statutes 500/45-35 (defining qualified not-for-profit agencies).)

Any joint procurement activity or contract must be approved by the CPO-GS. (Illinois Administrative Code tit. 44, § 1.5400.) The CPO-GS may also permit a state agency to "enter into joint procurement agreements with non-governmental entities," including nonprofit and commercial entities. (*Id.* § 1.5440.) When the appropriate CPO determines that competition is impractical, governmental units may make purchases using the procedure for sole source procurements (30 Illinois Compiled Statutes 500/20-25) or the procedure for emergency purchases (30 Illinois Compiled Statutes 500/20-30). (30 Illinois Compiled Statutes 525/4.)

B. Requirements

Joint purchasing agreements can be found using the state's electronic procurement system, BidBuy, at https://www.bidbuy.illinois.gov/bso/view/login/login.xhtml. The procedure for soliciting joint purchases is subject to the Illinois Procurement Code. (30 Illinois Compiled Statutes 500/1-1 *et seq.*) If the competitive solicitation process is deemed impractical by the applicable CPO (thus authorizing the governmental unit to pursue sole source procurement or an emergency purchase), the respective procedures in the Illinois Procurement Code apply. All purchases must "be awarded to the lowest responsible bidder or highest-ranked offeror, taking into consideration the qualities" of the services and their conformity with the specifications and requirements of the participating governmental units. (30 Illinois Compiled Statutes 525/4.) There is not currently any case law indicating what a bidder must do to challenge a bid awarded through a joint purchasing agreement.

Indiana Procurement Rules and Regulations

Prepared by Barbara A. Duncombe, Esq., Taft Stettinius & Hollister LLP
Email: bduncombe@taftlaw.com
Erin R. Davis, MPA, Esq., Taft Stettinius & Hollister LLP

I. Statutory Reference

Indiana has no consolidated public contracting statute. Different rules may apply to contracting with the state, counties, cities, towns, political subdivisions, and municipal corporations. However, procurement rules must be consistent with state law. (Indiana Code § 5-22-3-3.) Applicable sources include the Indiana Constitution, the Indiana Code (IC), and the Indiana Administrative Code (IAC) for government public contracting in Indiana. Indiana favors competitive bidding. Several sections of the state constitution apply to public contracts. Relevant sections include article 1, section 1, the state's equal protection clause, article 6, governing the duties of state and county officers, and article 10, section 3, governing the spending of appropriations.

A. Procurement/Purchasing Statutes

1. Title 4: State Public Works

IC section 4-13.6 governs state public works solicited after June 30, 1985, where the work is to be performed on property that is leased by the state from another, if the lease grants the state an option to buy the property. (See IC § 4-13.6-2-2.) This article "applies to every expenditure of public funds, regardless of their source, including federal assistance money, by any governmental body for any public works project," according to IC section 4-13.6-2-3. The following, however, are not bound by IC section 4-13.6: the Indiana Commission for Higher Education; state educational institutions; military officers and military and armory boards of the state; the state fair commission; any entity established by the General Assembly as a body corporate and politic having authority and power to issue bonds to be secured and repaid solely by revenues pledged for that purpose (although it may be required to comply with this article if the law creating the entity requires it to do so); and the Indiana Department of Transportation (INDOT), except to the extent that it uses the services provided by the department under this article.

Effective January 1, 2017, contractors must be prequalified prior to performing any work on most public works projects for local units of government and state projects. (IC § 4-13.6-4-2.5.) Project value thresholds apply and vary by the type of entity acquiring the work. Suppliers meeting the definition at IC section 4-13.6-1-20 are exempt. State public works contracts must comply with the following provisions of title 5: IC sections 5-16-3, 5-16-6, 5-16-7 (if the project is at least worth $25,000), 5-16-8, and 5-16-9. Other title 5 provisions explicitly do not apply to public works contracts or professional service contracts. (IC §§ 5-16-1, 5-16-2, 5-16-5, 5-16-5.5.)

2. Title 5, Article 22: The Public Purchasing Statute

The Indiana Department of Administration (IDOA) is the executive purchasing authority. Its duties are listed in IC section 4-13-1-4.[1] (See generally IC § 4-13-1.) Although IDOA is established under title 4, it is authorized to adopt rules to implement and enforce IC section 5-22, related to procurement procedures. The IDOA is separated into various divisions, including the Public Works Division; the State Resource Management Division; the Procurement Division (IDOA is the purchasing agency for all agencies of the executive branch. IC §§ 4-13-1.3-3 and 5-22-4-1.); and the Supplier Diversity Division.

IC section 5-22-1 states that "this Article applies to every expenditure of public funds by a governmental body." For public works projects, title 5 applies to projects that are performed on property owned by the state or other non-title 4 public works. However, this article does not apply to certain *entities*: the Commission for Higher Education; a state educational institution (although IC §§ 5-22-5-9 and 5-22-15 do apply); military officers and military and armory boards of the state; an entity established by the General Assembly as a body corporate and politic (although IC § 5-22-15 does apply); a local hospital authority; a municipality-owned utility; hospitals established under certain parts of IC title 16; a library board; a local housing authority; tax-exempt Indiana nonprofit corporations leasing and operating a city market owned by a political subdivision; a person paying for a purchase or lease with funds other than public funds; a person that has entered into an agreement with a governmental body under IC section 5-23 (Public-Private Agreements); a municipality for the operation of municipal facilities used for sanitation/trash; Department of Financial Institutions established by IC title 28; the insurance commissioner in retaining an examiner for purposes of IC section 27-1-3.1-9; the Department of Natural Resources for the procurement of supplies purchased for resale at properties owned or managed by the Department of Natural Resources; and the Indiana Horse Racing Commission in making an expenditure under IC section 4-31-3-15(b).

According to IC section 5-22-1-3, certain *activities* are also exempt[2] from title 5: contracts between governmental bodies except for contracts authorized under this article; public works projects; collective bargaining agreements for public employees; public employee employment relationships; investment of public funds; contracts between a governmental body and a body corporate and politic; contracts for social services; and contracts with a body corporate and politic.

3. Title 8, Article 23: INDOT

This article governs INDOT contracting and leasing. (IC § 8-23-2-6.) INDOT is the purchasing agency for state transportation projects. (IC § 5-22-4-2.)

---

1. The State Lottery Commission and the State Fair Commission also have authority to enter into contracts. *See* IND. CODE §§ 4-30-8-1, 15-13-2-9.

2. However, these activities are not exempt from IC section 5-22-3-7. *See id.* § 5-22-1-3.

4. Title 36, Article 1, Chapter 12: Local Public Works Projects

This chapter of Indiana law governs all public work performed or contracted for by political subdivisions and their agencies, regardless of whether it is performed on land owned or leased by the political subdivision or agency. (IC § 36-1-12-1.) This chapter does not apply to utility maintenance, extensions, or installations if done by employees of the utility (IC § 36-1-12-1(b)); hospitals organized or operated under certain provisions within title 16, unless the public work is financed in whole or in part with cumulative building fund revenue (IC § 36-1-12-1(c)); and tax-exempt Indiana nonprofit corporations leasing and operating a city market owned by a political subdivision (IC § 36-1-12-1(d)).

A "public work" is defined as "the construction, reconstruction, alteration, or renovation of a public building, airport facility, or other structure that is paid for out of a public fund or out of a special assessment. The term includes the construction, alteration, or repair of a highway, street, alley, bridge, sewer, drain, or other improvement that is paid for out of a public fund or out of a special assessment," including any public work leased by a political subdivision where the lease contains an option to purchase. The term does not include an extension or installation of utility infrastructure. (IC § 36-1-12-2.)

II. Regulations

A. IDOA

The pertinent regulations, enacted by the IDOA, are at title 25 of the IAC. The following articles apply:

1. IAC 25-1.1, State Procurement
2. IAC 25-1.5, Small Business Procurements and Projects
3. IAC 25-2, Public Works Division
4. IAC 25-5, Minority and Women's Business Enterprises

B. INDOT

INDOT administrative regulations are at title 100 of the IAC.

III. Source Selection

A. Title 4 Procurements (State Public Works)

1. Qualifications for State Public Works Projects

"All persons desiring to perform professional services relating to a public works project must apply to the board for qualification" unless the estimated cost of the project is less than $150,000. (IC § 4-13.6-4-2(a), (b).) Subcontractors must also apply for qualification, unless the estimated cost of the contract is less than $150,000. (IC § 4-13.6-4-10(a).) If the estimated cost of the contract is $150,000 or more, the contractor must complete at least 15 percent of the work with its own forces (employees). (IC § 4-13.6-4-10(b).)

2. Bidding Requirements

The division shall use competitive bids for any public works project that is estimated to cost at least $150,000. (IC § 4-13.6-5-2(a).) "Competitive bids are not required for the acquisition of land or for professional services relating to public works projects." (IC § 4-13.6-5-7(a).) A division shall reject a bid under any of the following conditions: the estimated cost of the public works project is $150,000 or more and the contractor is not qualified under chapter 4 of this article; the estimated cost of the public works project is less than $150,000 and the director makes a written determination, based upon information provided under subsections (d) and (e), that the contractor is not qualified to perform the public works contract; the contractor has failed to perform a previous contract with the state satisfactorily and has submitted the bid during a period of suspension imposed by the director (the failure of the contractor to perform a contract satisfactorily must be based upon a written determination by the director); the contractor has not complied with a rule adopted under this article and the rule specifies that failure to comply with it is a ground for rejection of a bid; or the contractor has not complied with any requirement under section 2.5 of this chapter. (See IC § 4-13.6-5-2(g)(1)–(5).) Under certain circumstances, the division must make a written determination before rejecting a bid.

If the public works acquisition is less than $150,000, the division may either use the competitive bidding procedures as identified in IC section 4-13.6-2 or the following procedures: The division "shall invite quotations from at least three contractors known to the division" to perform the type of work to be acquired. (IC § 4-13.6-5-3(b).) If the division does not know three contractors, the division "shall invite quotations from as many contractors as are known to be qualified to perform the work." (IC § 4-13.6-5-3(b).) "Failure to receive three (3) quotations shall not prevent an award from being made." (IC § 4-13.6-5-3(b).) The division shall make award to the lowest responsible and responsive contractor. (IC § 4-13.6-5-3(e).) Under certain circumstances, the division has the option to perform the work itself rather than using a public works contractor to perform the work. (See IC § 4-13.6-5-4.) In cases of emergencies that endanger health, safety, or welfare of the public or necessary governmental operations, the division may award a public works contract under other than competitive bidding procedures as identified in IC section 4-13.6-5-2. (IC § 4-13.6-5-5(a).) The division must make a written determination that an emergency condition exists. (IC § 4-13.6-5-5(a).) Upon a written determination, the division may award a maintenance contract to a contractor under other than competitive bidding procedures as identified in IC section 4-13.6-5-2. (IC § 4-13.6-5-6.) The division may award the contract to the manufacturer of the systems or a person recommended by the manufacturer of the system. The written determination must include the following: a statement that the contractor has knowledge of the system unlikely to be shared by other persons potentially able to bid to provide the maintenance services; and the savings the division might receive by inviting bids does not outweigh the benefit(s) of awarding the contract directly to the manufacturer of the systems or a person recommended by the manufacturer of the system. (IC § 4-13.6-5-6.)

3. Bid Opening and Award of Contracts

The bid openings are open to the public. (IC § 4-13.6-6-1(b).) The division will award the contract to the lowest responsible and responsive bidder. (IC § 4-13.6-6-2.) Award to the lowest responsible and responsive bidder gives the division "wide discretion." (*Bowen Engineering Corp. v. W.P.M. Inc.*, 557 N.E.2d 1358, 1364 (Ind. Ct. App. 1990).) "[A] reviewing court must not substitute its judgment for that of the awarding body, but will reverse only when the challenged determination is clearly arbitrary, illegal, corrupt or fraudulent." (*Id.*) "In the determination of whether a bidder is 'responsible,' the awarding body may properly consider a variety of factors, such as: ability and capacity, capital, character and reputation, competency and efficiency, energy, experience, facilities, faithfulness, fraud or unfairness in previous dealings, honesty, judgment, promptness, quality of previous work, and suitability to the particular task." (*Id.* at 1366.) "[T]he determination of 'responsibleness' is to be made *independently* for each bidder. The Board may not make comparisons of bidders to determine responsibleness. Responsibleness is a minimal requirement of bidders, not a competitive standard among bidders. A bidder can be unresponsible only if the awarding body would not award the contract to the bidder *even if* that bidder had submitted the sole bid." (*Id.*) "[J]udicial review of the decisions of a public agency is limited . . . When the awarding body has been vested with wide discretion, a reviewing court must not substitute its judgment for that of the awarding body, but will reverse only when the challenged determination is clearly arbitrary, illegal, corrupt or fraudulent." (*Id.* at 1364.) The State of Indiana may give preferences to Indiana businesses if the out-of-state bidder is from a state that gives preferences "unfavorable to Indiana businesses." (IC § 4-13.6-6-2.5.) "The division may, in reasonable exercise of discretion, reject all bids." (IC § 4-13.6-6-3.) The division shall award the contract and provide notice to successful offeror within 60 days from the date on which the division opens the bids. (IC § 4-13.6-6-4.)

4. Bonding, Escrow, and Retainages

a. Retainages

If a public works project is estimated to cost $1,000,000 or more, the division shall retain a portion of payments to the contractor (and by the contractor to the subcontractor, if any) for payment to subcontractor and supplies by the contractor. (IC § 4-13.6-7-2(a).) The retainage will be held in an escrow account. (IC § 4-13.6-7-2(b).) The amount of the retainage is discussed in IC section 4-13.6-7-3.

b. Bid Bonds

The division must require a bid bond if the estimated cost is more than $200,000. "The bid bond may equal any percentage of the estimated cost of the . . . project." (IC § 4-13.6-7-5(a).)

c. Payment Bonds

If the estimated cost of the project is more than $200,000, the division shall require a payment bond equal to 100 percent of the total contract price. (IC § 4-13.6-7-6(a).) If the estimated cost of the project is less than or equal to $200,000, the division shall require one of the following: a payment bond in any percentage, but no more than 100 percent of the cost of the project, or withholding a retainage of 10 percent "of the dollar value of all payments made to the contractor until the public work is substantially completed." (IC § 4-13.6-7-6(f).)

d. Performance Bonds

If the estimated cost of the project is at least $200,000, the division shall require a performance bond equal to 100 percent of the total contract price. (IC § 4-13.6-7-7(a).) For those under $200,000, the performance bond is discretionary.

e. *Final Settlement*

The division shall complete final settlement with the contractor within 61 days following the date of substantial completion if the contractor has materially fulfilled its obligations; the division has no outstanding subcontractor claims; and the contractor provided satisfactory evidence showing that it paid all its subcontractors and suppliers in full.

f. *Subcontractor and Supplier Claims*

Subcontractors and suppliers "must file a verified claim with the division within 60 days from the last labor performed, last material furnished, or last service rendered. The claim shall state the amount due and owing to the person and shall give as much detail explaining the claim as possible." (IC § 4-13.6-7-10(a). See *Electrical Specialties, Inc. v. Siemens Building Technologies, Inc.*, 837 N.E.2d 1052, 1057 (Ind. Ct. App. 2005).) The 60-day window is measure against the life of the project, not when the claimant's last work was performed. (*Id.* at 1058.) In other words, a contractor must file its verified claim within 60 days from the day the last labor is performed, material is furnished, or service is rendered by anyone on the project, not when the claimant's last work is performed. For example, if the claimant contractor, Contractor A, completed its work on January 1, 2010, and the last contractor, Contractor B, to work on the project completed its work on April 1, 2010, then the claimant contractor has until May 31, 2010, to file its claim.

g. *Limitation of Actions against Sureties*

"Unless the bond provides a greater period of time, all suits must be brought against a surety on a bond required by this chapter within one (1) year after final settlement with the contractor . . . All suits against the surety after this time are time barred." (IC § 4-13.6-7-11.)

5. Energy Cost Savings Contracts

The State of Indiana promotes energy conservation by implementing an energy savings project. Such projects may include but are not limited to installing or providing for window and door systems, including installing storm windows and storm doors; caulking or weather-stripping; and multi-glazing windows and doors. (See IC § 4-13.6-8.)

6. Use of Energy-Efficient Technology

"To the extent technically and economically feasible, the division shall consider the use of energy efficient technology in the plans and specifications for the public works project." (IC § 4-13.6-9-3.)

B. Title 5 Procurements

1. Contracts with the State

Indiana competitively awards contracts. The IC provides a set of procurement rules that "applies to every expenditure of public funds by a governmental body." (See IC § 5-22-1-1.) However, the INDOT and the Division of Public Works maintain separate purchasing rules for certain goods and services specific to those agencies. (INDOT Vendor Handbook is available at https://secure.in.gov/indot/files

/Procurement_VendorHandbook.pdf; State of Indiana Supplier Resource Center is available at https://www.in.gov/idoa/procurement/supplier-resource-center/.)

2. Public Purchasing

a. Specifications

All purchasing agents shall prepare, issue, revise, maintain, and monitor the use of specifications. A specification must promote overall economy for the purposes intended and encourage competition in satisfying the governmental body's needs. The State of Indiana requires governmental bodies to promote the use of biodegradable, recyclable, and environmentally clean vehicles and fuels. (IC § 5-22-5.)

b. Purchase of Services

Agencies may purchase services using any procedure the governmental body or the purchasing agency of the governmental body considers appropriate. (IC § 5-22-6.) Governmental bodies may use their own rules to purchase services. Without authority, a governmental body cannot control the purchases of another governmental body. (*Township Board of Calumet Township of Lake County v. Elgin*, 850 N.E.2d 1020, 1024 (Ind. Ct. App. 2006).) An agency "may purchase services using any procedure the governmental body or the purchasing agency of the governmental body considers appropriate." (IC § 5-22-6-1. See *Harmony Health Plan of Indiana, Inc. v. Indiana Department of Administration*, 864 N.E.2d 1083, 1091 (Ind. Ct. App. 2007).) For *personal services* acquisitions, agencies are not required to follow the Indiana public purchasing law as codified in title 5 of the IC. (IC § 5-22-6-1; *Trans-Care, Inc. v. Board of Commissioners of County of Vermillion*, 831 N.E.2d 1255, 1259 (Ind. Ct. App. 2005).) An agency may adopt its own procurement rules regarding the purchase of personal services. (*Trans-Care, Inc.*, 831 N.E.2d at 1259.) The acquisitions of personal services are not within the scope of Indiana's public purchasing statutes. (*Id.*)

c. Competitive Bidding for Supplies

Purchasing agents shall use the competitive bidding procedures for supplies, unless another purchasing method is required or authorized. (IC § 5-22-7-1.) An agency must award the contract to the lowest responsible and responsive bidder. (IC § 5-22-7-8. See *Brownsburg Community School Corp. v. Natare Corp.*, 824 N.E.2d 336, 338 (Ind. 2005).)

d. Invitation for Bids

Agencies must use an invitation for bids. An invitation for bids must include the following: (1) a purchase description; (2) all contractual terms and conditions that apply to the purchase; (3) a statement of the evaluation criteria that will be used, including any of the following: (4) the time and place for opening the bids; (5) a statement concerning whether the bid must be accompanied by a certified check or other evidence of financial responsibility that may be imposed in accordance with rules or policies of the governmental body; and (6) a statement concerning the conditions under which a bid may be canceled or rejected. (IC § 5-22-7-2.) Agencies must publish notice of the invitation for bids in a newspaper and/or electronic media. The agency will open the bids publicly with at least one witness. Agencies must accept bids unconditionally without alteration or correction and evaluated based on the requirements provided in the invitation for bids. Award will be made to the lowest responsive and responsible bidder. After bid opening, bidders cannot change prices or other provisions of bids prejudicial to the interest of the governmental body or fair competition. Bidders may offer items that are outside the scope of the original invitation; however, the agency may declare the bidder nonresponsive, permit the bidder to withdraw the proposed additions, or accept the additions if the additions are not prejudicial to the interest of the governmental body or fair competition. (IC § 5-22-7.)

e. *Negotiated Bidding*

Negotiated bidding is only applicable to purchases from the executive branch and only for purchases that are more than $200,000. (IC § 5-22-7.3-10.) The procedures remain the same as for invitation for bids as described above, except that agencies may negotiate terms of the bid after receipt. After the agency has completed negotiations, the agency must publish the bid register not less than seven days after notifying the successful bidder of the award of the contract. Award will be made to the lowest responsive and responsible bidder. (IC § 5-22-7.3.)

f. *Small Purchases*

For purchases under $50,000, agencies may make a purchase under small purchase policies established by the purchasing agency or under rules adopted by the governmental body. (IC § 5-22-8-2.) For purchases for at least $50,000 but not more than $150,000, agencies may purchase supplies under this section by inviting quotes from at least three vendors known to deal in the lines or classes of supplies. The agency must mail the invitation to quote at least seven days before the fixed time for receiving quotes. (IC § 5-22-8-3.) The agency shall award the contract to the lowest responsible and responsive offeror.

g. *Request for Proposals*

A request for proposals is to be used when a governmental body provides by rule or policy that it is "either not practicable or not advantageous to the governmental body to purchase specified types of supplies by competitive sealed bidding; and receiving proposals is the preferred method for purchase of that type of supply." (IC § 5.22-9-8.) A request for proposals must include (1) the factors or criteria that will be used in evaluating the proposals; (2) a statement concerning the relative importance of price and the other evaluation factors; (3) a statement concerning whether the proposal must be accompanied by a certified check or other evidence of financial responsibility, which may be imposed in accordance with rules of the governmental body; and (4) a statement concerning whether discussions may be conducted with responsible offerors, who submit proposals determined to be reasonably susceptible of being selected for award. (See IC § 5-22-9.)

h. *Special Purchasing Methods*

Under certain circumstances, the IC authorizes the purchase of items with limited to no competition. Such instances include emergencies; threats to public health, welfare, or safety; potential for substantial savings; finding only one reasonable source; when other purchasing methods would seriously impair the functioning of the using agency; when an agency has not received a responsive offer; when the purchase was at or below U.S. General Services Administration price, if purchased or transferred from an entity that has a contract with a federal or state agency; when it involves copyrighted material or petroleum products; or when based on an independent appraisal.

i. Small Business Set-Aside Purchases

The IC provides for small business set-asides. The IC provides specific rules that identify the criteria to qualify as a small business. That criterion is based on annual sales and the number of employees. (*Id.*) Before designating a purchase as a small business set-aside, the agency must have a reasonable expectation it will obtain at least two small businesses capable of furnishing the desired supplies or service at a fair and reasonable price. And the agency must award the contract to the lowest responsible and responsive small business that offers a reasonable price. The Indiana Economic Development Corporation may assist agencies to develop, target, and promote specific acquisitions for small businesses. (IC § 5-22-14-9.)

j. Purchasing Preferences

Indiana allows prices preferences for small businesses, Indiana businesses ("Buy Indiana"), and the purchases of recycled and soy-based products. The state also has a preference for the purchase of high calcium foods. The preference may be absolute (e.g., set-aside procurement) or adjusted price. Agencies may require offerors to certify that they qualify for a certain preference. The IC provides specific rules that identify the criteria to qualify for a price preference. There are also price preferences for coal and steel products from Indiana and for supplies manufactured in the United States. (IC § 5-22-15.)

k. Responsive and Responsible Bidders/Offerors

When determining *responsibility*, agencies may consider (1) the ability and capacity of the offeror to provide the supplies or service; (2) the integrity, character, and reputation of the offeror; and (3) the competency and experience of the offeror. (IC § 5-22-16-1.) When determining *responsiveness*, agencies may consider (1) whether the offeror has submitted an offer that conforms in all material respects to the specifications; (2) whether the offeror has submitted an offer that complies specifically with the solicitation and the instructions to offerors; and (3) whether the offeror has complied with all applicable statutes, ordinances, resolutions, or rules pertaining to the award of a public contract. (IC § 5-22-16-2.) An offeror that is a foreign corporation must be registered with the secretary of state to do business in Indiana in order to be considered responsible. Agencies may require offerors to provide evidence of financial responsibility such as in the form of a bond or certified check. Offerors must also file with the purchasing agent an affirmation, made under the penalties for perjury, that states that the offeror has not entered into a combination or an agreement (1) relative to the price to be offered by a person; (2) to prevent a person from making an offer; or (3) to induce a person to refrain from making an offer. (IC § 5-22-16.)

l. Other Procedures Governing Purchasing

Any required public notice of a solicitation must be for at least seven days. An agency may open offers after the time stated in the solicitation if it is in the best interest of the government to delay that opening and the agency announces the delay at the day, time, and place of the originally scheduled opening. (IC § 5-22-18.)

m. Modification and Termination of Contracts

Agencies may include contract clauses that provide that the agency has a unilateral right to make in-scope changes and temporarily to stop work or delay performance.

The price for any modifications will be determined by mutual agreement or unilaterally by the agency with adjustment of profit or fee. (IC § 5-22-20.)

C. Title 8: INDOT

1. Bidder Prequalification

All bidders must be prequalified before they may submit a bid. Generally, this prequalification requires an application verified by the contractor. Unqualified bidders' bids must be disqualified or rejected, even if not discovered until after bids are opened. (IC § 8-23-10-6.) Subcontractors who are engaged in a subcontract valued at over $300,000 must also be qualified. (IC § 8-23-10-4.) Any contractor who makes a false statement regarding its financial worth to INDOT is disqualified from submitting bids for two years following a conviction. (IC § 8-23-10-8.)

2. Emergency Procurements

Whenever a bridge, culvert, roadway, or other physical property in the state highways is no longer usable due to damage, or is unsafe, INDOT must operate with "due diligence" to repair, reopen, and make it safe. (IC § 8-23-11-1.) Therefore, in the event that the government declares an emergency, INDOT may proceed without advertising for bids if it invites three or more bids from persons prequalified and INDOT maintains records of the names of those invited to bid. When the low bid exceeds the engineer's estimate, award may be made only if at least three bids were received and the low bid does not exceed the estimate by more than 10 percent. (IC § 8-23-11-2.) INDOT is required to make a "concentrated effort" to seek bids from racial minority businesses. (IC § 8-23-11-3.)

3. Bidding Procedures

Generally,[3] bid procedures are less specific than other public contracting statutory provisions. The commissioner is required to receive all sealed bids and open them publicly, as designated in the notice. (IC § 8-23-9-1.)

The commissioner may reject all the proposals for cause. (IC § 8-23-9-2.) When the commissioner chooses to reject all the proposals because none were satisfactory, he or she may purchase the necessary materials, employ the necessary labor, and have INDOT perform the work itself. (IC § 8-23-9-5.) When the commissioner chooses to employ this option, the amount of monies expended may not exceed 85 percent of the lowest and best proposals submitted. (IC § 8-23-9-6.)

Award must be made to the lowest and best bidder. The lowest and best bid may not exceed the estimated cost of the project. (IC § 8-23-9-3.) Notwithstanding IC section 8-23-9-3, INDOT may make an award for the construction, improvement, or maintenance of a road when the lowest and best bid exceeds the estimated cost of the project when it is less than $1,000,000; it was one of at least four bids received; it does not exceed the estimated cost by more than 15 percent; the award is in the best interests of the state; and in the event of a bid by a trust, the bid complies with IC section 8-23-9-13. (See IC § 8-23-9-4.) Contracts must be made in the name of the state, signed by the commissioner and the contracting parties, and acknowledged before an

3. The code also contains rules specific to railroad crossings. *See id.* §§ 8-23-9-40 through 8-23-9-47.

officer authorized to administer oaths. The contract must be approved by the attorney general with regard to legality and form. (IC § 8-23-9-21.)

a. Bonds

If the estimated cost of the project exceeds $200,000, a bid guarantee and performance bond are required. (IC § 8-23-9-8(1).) If the estimated cost of the project does not exceed $200,000, then INDOT may require a bid guarantee and performance bond. (IC § 8-23-9-8(2).) The amounts of the bid guarantee must be in an amount equal to 5 percent of the bid price. (IC § 8-23-9-9.) The amount of the performance bond must be set by the commissioner and may not be less than the bidder's proposal or contract price. A performance bond must be conditioned upon the faithful performance of the work. (IC § 8-23-9-9.) The bond is deposited with the commissioner. (IC § 8-23-9-10.) The bond must follow the form put forth in IC section 8-23-9-12. Any person with a claim to payment for having performed labor, provided materials, or other service under the contract must submit a statement of the amount due within one year of performance. (IC § 8-23-9-10.) These persons may not bring a suit against the sureties on a bond until 60 days after this statement is submitted if the amount is not paid in full. (IC § 8-23-9-11.) In any case, such a suit must be brought within 18 months of final acceptance of the work. (*Id.*) The purpose of the federal Miller Act and the payment bond is to protect subcontractors, suppliers, and laborers. (*Electrical Specialties, Inc. v. Siemens Building Technologies, Inc.*, 837 N.E.2d 1052, 1056 (Ind. Ct. App. 2005).) Coverage under a performance bond is generally extended only to the first and second tier subcontracts. A "'subcontractor' is any person or organization entering into a contract with a contractor to furnish labor and materials used in the actual construction of a state highway project. A pure material supplier or laborer is not a subcontractor." (*Alberici Constructors, Inc. v. Ohio Farmers Insurance Co.*, 866 N.E.2d 740, 746–47 (Ind. 2007).) Thus, coverage does not extend "to any entity more remote than a second-tier laborer or material supplier." (*Id.*)

b. Nonperformance

If a contractor, at any time, is failing to commence, perform properly, or complete a contract, the project may be relet or INDOT may complete the work. The cost of completion is payable by the contractor. (IC § 8-23-9-25.) Prior to cancelling any contract for nonperformance, if the contract involves INDOT performing tests on material furnished by the contractor, INDOT must perform those tests in accordance with the usage of trade in the industry. (*Todd Heller, Inc. v. Indiana Department of Transportation*, 819 N.E.2d 140, 149 (Ind. Ct. App. 2004).)

c. Payment and Acceptance

Partial progress payments to contractors are authorized. (IC § 8-23-9-14.) Work must be approved and accepted in increments of not less than one mile, unless otherwise permitted under the contract. After a portion is accepted, the contractor is relieved of all liability for maintenance, reconstruction, or restoration of the section, to the same extent the contractor would be at final acceptance of the entire project. (IC § 8-23-9-16.) After substantial completion, the contractor may draw from the retained percentage withheld by INDOT, in an amount in the best interest of the state by INDOT, by filing a written form request. (IC § 8-23-9-17.) Final payments must be made within 180 days after final acceptance of the contract for any amount that is not in dispute or the subject of a claim. (IC § 8-23-9-18.)

4. Labor Provisions

Contract wages must not be lower than the hourly rate paid for common labor by the department. (IC § 8-23-9-22.) Generally, all contracts must be conditioned on all unskilled laborers employed on a work being residents of the county or counties in which the highway or bridges are being constructed, if available. (IC § 8-23-9-23.)

5. Claims against the Contractor

Detailed procedures for claims against contractors are contained in IC sections 8-23-9-26 through 8-23-9-39. Generally, a person with a claim against a contractor may file an itemized statement of the amount due within 60 days of performance and within 30 days of final acceptance of the project. (IC § 8-23-9-26.)

D. Title 36: Local Public Works

1. Bidding Procedures[4]

Generally, for projects that are at least $150,000 the political subdivision must comply with the requirements of IC section 36-1-12-4(b), pertaining to specifications, notice, and other requirements. The board must make award to the lowest responsible and responsive bidder, or it must reject all bids. (IC § 36-1-12-4(b)(8).) When the award is made to a bidder who was not the lowest bidder, the procuring entity must state in the minutes at the time award is made, the factors that justified the award, and those minutes must be made available to the public for inspection. (IC § 36-1-12-4(b)(9). See generally IC § 36-1-12-4.)

For projects that are under $150,000, if the public work is the routine operation, routine repair, or routine maintenance of existing structures, buildings, or real property, the board may make award pursuant to IC section 5-22. (IC § 36-1-12-4.9.) IC section 36-1-12-4.7 applies to projects estimated to cost at least $50,000 but less than $150,000. The procuring entity shall invite quotes from at least three persons known to deal in the class of work proposed for the project by mailing them a notice stating that plans and specifications are on file in a specified location. The notice must be mailed at least seven days before the time for receiving quotes. Quotes cannot be required prior to the meeting at which they are to be received. That meeting must be open to the public, where the quotes shall be opened and publicly read aloud. (*Id.*) Award must be made to the lowest responsible and responsive quote. (*Id.*) For projects under $50,000, see IC section 36-1-12-5.

4. *See also id.* § 36-1-12-3 (for specific rules pertaining to alternative situations where the board may use its own work force, the project involves rental of equipment with an operator furnished by an owner, the project involves a board of aviation commissioners or an airport authority board, or the project involves municipal and county hospital contracts or artificial division of projects) and § 36-1-12-3-5 (contracts for engineering, architectural, or accounting services). Pursuant to IC section 36-1-12-19, a project must include the materials, labor, equipment, and all other expenses incidental to the performance of the project; a single work may not be divided into more projects to avoid the requirements of this chapter. The term "board" herein indicates the board or officer of a political subdivision or agency with the power to award contracts for public work. *Id.* § 36-1-12-1.2(1).

2. Award and Time to Commence

Generally, the procuring entity must award a contract and provide the awardee with written notice to proceed within 60 days after the date on which bids were opened. (IC § 36-1-12-6(a).) Failure of the procuring entity to execute the contract and to issue notice within the time limit required above, entitles the awardee to reject the contract and withdraw its bid without prejudice;[5] or extend the time to award the contract and provide notice to proceed at an agreed later date. (IC § 36-1-12-6(d).)

3. Bond Requirements

a. Bid Bonds

For projects over $200,000, the procuring entity *must* require a bond or certified check to be filed with each bid, in an amount to be determined by the entity and specified in the notice of the letting. For projects under $200,000, the procuring entity *may* require a bond or certified check to be filed with each bid, in an amount set at not more than 10 percent of the contract price, made payable to the procuring entity. The bond/check amount cannot exceed 10 percent of the contract price, and all bonds/checks must be made payable to the procuring entity. Unsuccessful bidders will have their checks returned to them when an awardee is selected. Checks of awardees are held until delivery of the performance bond. (See IC § 36-1-12-4.5.)

b. Payment Bonds

All contracts for public works must contain a provision for the payment of subcontractors, laborers, material suppliers, and service providers. The procuring entity will withhold the amount from a contract price sufficient to make those payments. Payment bonds are required for contracts estimated to be over $200,000, in an amount equal to the contract price. Such bonds shall be approved by and for the benefit of the procuring entity. For contracts estimated to be worth less than $200,000, the payment bonds *may* be required by the procuring entity and must state that they are for the benefit of the subcontractors, laborers, material suppliers, and service providers.[6] Payment bonds are deposited with the board and must specify that modifications, contract defects, or defects in the procurement process do not discharge the surety. Sureties are not released until one year after the board's final settlement with the contractor. Those with claims under such bonds are required to bring those claims to the board within 60 days in accordance with IC section 36-1-12-13.1(c). An action may not be brought against the surety until 30 days after the claim was filed with the board, at which time if indebtedness is not repaid, the person may bring an action in court.

c. Performance Bonds and Escrow

A board may comply with this provision for projects under $200,000,[7] but compliance is required for all projects over that amount.[8] A contract for public work must contain provisions that provide for retainage of payments in escrow to ensure payment to

5. If this option is selected, the awardee must give notice to the procuring entity in writing within 15 days of the 60 (or 90 or 150) day expiration date.

6. For projects involving the Indiana stadium and convention building authority created by IC section 5-1-17-6, see IC section 36-1-12-13.1(e).

7. For projects under $200,000, see IC section 36-1-12-14(h).

8. If the project is an Indiana stadium or convention building (IC § 5-1-17-6), see IC section 36-1-12-14(i).

subcontractors. (See required terms at IC § 36-1-12-14(b) and (d).) The amount of retainage must be between 6 percent and 10 percent of all work satisfactorily completed until the work is 50 percent completed, after which no retainage may be made, *or* the board may withhold between 3 percent and 5 percent of all work satisfactorily completed until the time the project is substantially completed. A performance bond is required equal to the contract price. (See IC § 36-1-12-14(e) for terms.) Actions against a surety of a performance bond must be brought within one year of the date of the board's final settlement with the contractor.

d. Open Price Provision

When the contract is for a road, street, or bridge, the board may make award subject to the open price provision of IC section 26-1-2-305, part of the Indiana Uniform Commercial Code, which permits the parties to enter into a contract even though the price term is not set. The prices for construction materials may be subject to a price of materials adjustment clause, when the method of adjustment is specified in the contract and the total expenditure does not exceed the total amount of money appropriated by the political subdivision or agency. (IC § 36-1-12-8.)

4. Changes

Specifications may be changed at any time during the course of performance by addendum, if approved by the board, the contractor, and a licensed architect or engineer, if one is assigned to the project. Change orders are only permissible prior to commencement if a declaration is declared by the board. The total of all change orders may not increase the scope of the project by more than 20 percent of the original amount of the contract. Change orders that are required as a result of unforeseen circumstances do not increase the scope of a project. All change orders must be directly related to the original project. When additional materials are required, the cost per unit must be the same as the cost in the original contract. (See IC § 36-1-12-18.)

5. Contractor Requirements and Antidiscrimination

Contracts awarded after June 30, 2015, and under title 36 must conform to IC section 5-16-13 and inconsistent provisions are void. Contractors must comply with certain statutes and other requirements outlined in IC section 5-16-13-11, including E-Verify, non-cash payments, Fair Labor Standards, and the identified labor and safety, unemployment compensation, and drug-free workplace requirements as outlined. Contractors may not engage in discriminatory behavior. (IC § 5-16-6 (antidiscrimination provisions).) Failure to comply with the antidiscrimination provision may be considered a material breach.

6. Completion and Final Payment

For road or street work, the contract must contain a provision for the timely payment of claims made by the contractor, and final payment is required within 120 days of final acceptance and completion. (IC § 36-1-12-17.) For each day over 120 days, interest shall be payable pursuant to subsection (c). Generally, final payments shall be made in accordance with IC section 36-1-12-12. This requires payment to be made to all subcontractors within 60 days of their last labor performed and final payment will not be made to the contractor until such time as all disputes, including those between the board and the contractor, are resolved. (See also § 36-1-12-14(f) regarding payment from retainages held in escrow.)

E. Preferences and Set-Aside Programs

1. Small Business Set-Asides

The IDOA may adopt rules to establish a small business set-aside program for supplies and services. (IC § 4-13.6-2-11; IC § 5-22-14-3.[9]) The policy of the state is that a fair proportion of purchases and contracts for supplies and services be placed with small businesses. (25 IAC 1.5-2-1.)

A small business is one that is independently owned and operated; is not dominant in its industry; and meets the other requirements of the small business set-aside rule. (25 IAC 1.5-1-9.) The affiliates of a business are included in the determination of whether a business is a small business. A small business must meet the following criteria: (1) construction business—average gross annual receipts for the current and three previous fiscal years are $4,000,000 or less; (2) manufacturing business—100 or fewer employees; (3) retail business—average gross sales and receipts for the current and three previous fiscal years are $500,000 or less; (4) service business—sales for the current and three previous fiscal years are $500,000 or less and 25 or fewer employees; and (5) wholesale business—annual sales for its most recently completed fiscal year are $4,000,000 or less. (25 IAC 1.5-3-1.)

The director of the Public Works Divisions may require a procurement or project be performed as a small business project, *provided, however,* that there must be at least two responsible small businesses capable of submitting an offer at a fair and reasonable price. (25 IAC 1.5-3-2.)

The project shall be awarded to the small business submitting the lowest bid if the business is responsive and responsible and the offer is reasonable. (25 IAC 1.5-3-5.) If those criteria are not met, see IAC title 25, rule 1.2-3-5.

Any person may challenge the small business status of a bidder or prospective bidder either before award (25 IAC 1.5-4-1) or after award (25 IAC 1.5-4-2). If a bidder is determined to be other than small, sanctions may be imposed, including debarment for up to two years.

2. Minority Business Enterprise/Woman-Owned Business Enterprise Participation Goals

"Minority business enterprise" (MBE) is defined at IC section 4-13-16.5-1 and IAC title 25, rule 5-2-1. Generally, a minority (Blacks, American Indians, Hispanics, Asian Americans, or other similar groups identified at 13 C.F.R. § 124.103) must own the business and control the management and be active in day-to-day operations. The business also has to have been in continuous existence for at least five years. "Woman-owned business enterprise" (WBE) is defined at IC section 4-13-16.5-1.3 and IAC title 25, rule 5-2-1. Generally, a woman (or women) must be at least 51 percent owner and control the management and daily operations of the business. Indiana law establishes participation goals for MBEs and WBEs. (IC § 4-13-16.5; 25 IAC 5-5-1.) The Governor's Commission on Minority and Women's Business Enterprises establishes the participation goals for state contracts annually. (25 IAC 5-7-3.) The current goals are as follows:

9. It appears that the administrative regulations promulgated by the IDOA at title 25 of the IAC article 1.5 apply to both title 4 and title 5 public purchasing.

	MBE Participation	WBE Participation
Construction	7%	5%
Professional Services	8%	8%
Supplies	4%	9%

The governmental body of a political subdivision may establish MBE/WBE participation goals. (IC § 4-13-16.5.)

MBEs and WBEs must apply for certification pursuant to the provisions of IAC title 25, rule 5-3-2. A basic criterion for certification is that the owner of 51 percent or more of the business is a member of a minority group or is a woman and that he or she controls the business. (See generally 25 IAC 5-3.[10]) Certification may be revoked pursuant to IAC title 25, rule 5-4-1. Denial of an application for certification may be reviewed pursuant to IAC title 25, rule 5-4-2. Where a contractor cannot meet the WBE/MBE participation goal for a project, the contractor may petition the IDOA for a waiver. (See generally 25 IAC 5-7-1.) The contractor must provide a detailed statement and supporting documentation with the contractor's waiver request. (25 IAC 5-7-5.)

3. Construction Projects

IDOA has promulgated separate guides for construction projects[11] and INDOT state-funded construction projects.[12]

4. Veteran-Owned Businesses

Effective January 1, 2013, Indiana enacted a statute, IC section 5-22-14-3.5, creating the Indiana Veteran Owned Small Business Enterprises (IVBE) Program to assist IVBEs. (See IDOA, Indiana Veteran Business Program, https://www.in.gov/idoa/mwbe/indiana-veteran-business-program/.) IVBEs must qualify under the Veterans Small Business Regulations at 38 C.F.R. Part 74 and be verified under the U.S. Department of Veterans Affairs VetBiz registry, available at https://www.vetbiz.va.gov/.

IV. Bid Protests and Contract Disputes

A. Bid Protests

1. Public Works

Indiana has no general bid protest forum or procedure for public works or INDOT. (See Part V.)

10. More thorough guidance on ownership and control determinations are contained in the administrative code at IAC title 25, rules 5-3-4 and 5-3-5, respectively.

11. IDOA, M/WBE Participation Policy for Construction Projects (rev. 2010), https://www.in.gov/idoa/mwbe/files/Microsoft_Word_-MWBE_Construction_Policy_and_Attachments_12-15-10_Rev.pdf.

12. IDOA MBE/WBE and IVOSB Participation Policy for INDOT Construction Projects (Apr. 2021), https://www.in.gov/idoa/mwbe/files/MBE,-WBE,-and-IVOSB-Participation-Policy-for-INDOT-Construction-Projects-4-21.pdf.

2. Title 5

IC section 5-22-7-10(a) provides that "[t]he governmental body may adopt rules or establish policies to allow any of the following: (1) Correction or withdrawal of inadvertently erroneous bids before or after award; or (2) Cancellation of awards or contracts based on a mistake described in subdivision (1)." Except as otherwise provided in a rule or policy, a purchasing agency may only correct/withdraw a bid or cancel an award by written decision. (*Id.*) The IDOA Procurement Division issued a "Procurement Protest Policy," effective August 12, 2021. It is available at https://www.in.gov/idoa/procurement/files/ProcurementProtestPolicy.pdf. Protests must be submitted in writing, stating all grounds for protest with specificity.

a. Time

Protests challenging bid specifications must be received within five business days prior to the proposal or bid due date. Protests challenging contract awards must be received within five business days of "contract award," which is deemed made when IDOA provides the required notification to bidders and offerors under IC sections 5-22-7-8 and 5-22-9-7. For a reverse auction protest, the letter must be received by the department within five business days after the date of the notification of rejection.

b. Standing

Remedies are available to those that directly participated in the solicitation process.

c. Grounds

Bid specifications may be challenged because they are inadequate, unduly restrictive, or ambiguous.

Contract awards may be challenged on the grounds that the award was arbitrary, capricious, or an abuse of discretion; any aspect of the procurement that was conducted was contrary to a constitutional, statutory, or regulatory provision; the award was in excess of statutory jurisdiction, authority, power, privilege, or immunity; the award was made without observance of a procedure required by the solicitation; the award was unsupported by substantial evidence that may include but is not limited to technical or mathematical mistake or error in the evaluation; bids or proposals were not independently arrived at in open competition, may have been collusive, or were submitted in bad faith; or there was unfair or unequal treatment of an offeror with regards to discussions or proposal revisions.

B. Bid Protest Appeals

An appeal of a written decision may be appealed to the commissioner of the IDOA. It must be in writing and may not raise new protest grounds. *Note*: When contracting through agencies other than the IDOA, those agencies may have their own protest processes.

C. Contract Disputes

IDOA policy simply states that IDOA is responsible for ensuring the state and the vendor are in compliance with the contract. IDOA is responsible for managing all post-award actions, including delivery, inspections, acceptance, payment, closing of contracts, and so on. IDOA may place vendors on surveillance or suspension. Vendors on surveillance are permitted to conduct business with the state, although closely monitored. Vendors on suspension may not conduct business with the state.

V. Administrative and Judicial Review

A. Bid Protests

Unsuccessful bidders do not have a cause of action for an injunction under Indiana law if the theory is that the selected bidder was not the lowest responsible, responsive bidder as required by IC section 36-1-9 or title 5, the public purchasing statute. (*City of Fort Wayne v. Pierce Manufacturing, Inc.*, 853 N.E.2d 508 (Ind. Ct. App. 2006) (citing *Shook Heavy & Environmental Construction Group, a Division of Shook, Inc. v. City of Kokomo*, 632 N.E.2d 355, 362 (Ind. 1994)); *All-Star Construction & Excavating, Inc. v. Board of Public Works*, 640 N.E.2d 369 (Ind. 1994).) If the contract was for services, then, because those services are not within the scope of the public purchasing laws, a disappointed bidder has "even less of an argument regarding standing" under the public lawsuit statute, now located at IC chapter 34-13-5. (*Trans-Care, Inc. v. Board of Commissioners of County of Vermillion*, 831 N.E.2d 1255, 1259 (Ind. Ct. App. 2005).)

Disappointed bidders may only challenge a contract award when citizens or taxpayers of the municipality bring a "public lawsuit,"[13] questioning the validity or construction of any public improvement by the municipality, pursuant to IC section 34-13-5-2; or any person or business who is injured by an action, on behalf of the governmental entity and successful bidder, that violates the Indiana Antitrust Act prohibition of collusion or fraud, pursuant to IC section 24-1-2. (See *City of Fort Wayne v. Pierce Manufacturing, Inc.*, 853 N.E.2d 508 (Ind. Ct. App. 2006).)

For title 5 procurements, judicial review of agency "determinations" is available under IC section 5-22-19 (enacted as part of the public purchasing statute). However, disappointed bidders have no right to challenge an award under the public purchasing statute, because this is not a determination. (*Brownsburg Community School Corp. v. Natare Corp.*, 824 N.E.2d 336 (Ind. 2005).)

The court may grant relief when it determines that a person has been substantially prejudiced by a determination of the governmental agency that is arbitrary, capricious, an abuse of discretion, or otherwise not in accordance with law; contrary to constitutional right, power, privilege, or immunity; in excess of statutory jurisdiction, authority, or limitations, or short of statutory right; without observance of procedure required by law; or unsupported by substantial evidence. (IC § 5-22-19-2.) Standing is limited to Indiana taxpayers. (IC § 5-22-19-5.) As relief, the court may set aside a determination and remand to the governmental body for further proceedings. No damages may be awarded. (IC § 5-22-19-4.)

---

13. A public lawsuit is defined by IC section 34-6-2-124 as "any action in which the validity, location, wisdom, feasibility, extent, or character of construction, financing, or leasing of a public improvement by a municipal corporation is questioned directly or indirectly, including but not limited to suits for declaratory judgments or injunctions to declare invalid or to enjoin the construction, financing, or leasing . . . ." In order to bring such a lawsuit, the plaintiff must have exhausted administrative remedies, if available (IC § 34-13-5-11), and must have brought a proper objection at a public hearing when the municipal corporation is required to hold a public hearing (IC § 34-13-5-12). See IC section 34-13-5-10 regarding timing of a public lawsuit (generally ten days from first publication required by law). Cristiani v. Clark Cnty., Ind. Solid Waste Mgmt. Dist., 675 N.E.2d 715 (Ind. Ct. App. 1996).

Indiana explicitly exempts "acquisition, leasing, or disposition of property or procurement of goods or services by contract" from judicial review under the Administrative Orders and Procedures Act (AOPA). (IC § 4-21.5-2-5(11); *Harmony Health Plan of Indiana, Inc. v. Indiana Department of Administration*, 864 N.E.2d 1083 (Ind. Ct. App. 2007) (upholding trial court's dismissal of disappointed bidder's claims for relief under Trial Rule 12(B)(6) for failure to state a claim under AOPA).)

By statute, no bidder or offeror has a property interest in the award of a contract until there is an award and the contract is fully executed. (IC § 4-13-1-19.)

B. Claims

1. Claims against the State

Claims may arise out of express or implied contracts. Claims must be brought within ten years of accrual of the claim, and they shall be tried to the court, not to the jury. (IC § 34-13-1-1.) Appeals of these decisions are made directly to the Indiana Supreme Court. (IC § 34-13-1-5.)

2. Claims against Counties

Such claims may be brought by filing an invoice or bill with the county auditor, who shall present that invoice/bill to the executive. The executive may allow any part of the claim that he or she finds to be valid. (IC § 36-2-6-2. See IC § 36-2-6 for detailed procedures and rules.)

VI. Extent of State's Adoption or Adaptation of ABA Model Procurement Code

Indiana adopted state procurement laws closely modeled after the American Bar Association's (ABA's) Model Procurement Code for State and Local Governments in 1982 in title 4. In 1998, Indiana moved their procurement law to title 5, chapter 22. (IC § 5-22.) Since then, however, there is reason to believe that Indiana has stepped back from fully adopting the Model Procurement Code.

VII. Cooperative Purchasing

A. Authority

Under IC section 36-1-7, the State of Indiana permits cooperative purchasing or interlocal cooperation. The chapter applies to the state, all political subdivisions, all state agencies, public instrumentalities, public corporate bodies, another state and its political subdivisions to the extent authorized by that state, federal agencies, Indiana charter schools, and federally recognized Indian tribes. (IC § 36.1.7.1.)

B. Requirements

One or more governmental entities may enter into a written agreement, pursuant to IC section 36-1-7-3 (state) or IC section 36-1-7-9 (county or municipality) "for the purchase, sale, or exchange of services, supplies, or equipment" without notice of publication of posting required, if the governmental entity piggybacks on a previously competed award by a different government entity that complied with state purchasing law. (IC

§ 36-1-7-12.) The attorney general's approval is required for certain procurements. (IC § 36-1-7-4.) State, municipal, and county agreements must be recorded. (IC § 36-1-7-6; IC § 36-1-7-10.) Political subdivisions may also enter into agreement for sharing powers in order to save money or reduce foreseeable expenses. (IC § 36-1-7-16.)

Iowa Procurement Rules and Regulations

Prepared by Willard L. Boyd III
Nyemaster Goode, P.C.
Email: WLB@nyemaster.com

I. Statutory Reference

A. Procurement/Purchasing Statutes

The Central Procurement Bureau of the Iowa Department of Administrative Services establishes statewide general and individual contracts for commodities and services that are used in high volume by state agencies. Generally, all formal bidding for the purchase of commodities or services needed by agencies that are not otherwise exempt is conducted through the Central Procurement Bureau. The agencies and Iowa Board of Regents' institutions that may purchase commodities and services independent of the Central Procurement Enterprise include the Terrace Hill Commission, Department of Transportation, Iowa State University, University of Iowa, University of Northern Iowa, Iowa Braille and Sight Saving School, Iowa School for the Deaf, Department for the Blind, Iowa Prison Industries, Iowa Lottery, and Iowa Communications Network.

The Iowa Code chapters relating to procurements of goods and services by the State of Iowa and public improvements are as follows: chapter 8 (Department of Management—Budget and Financial Control Act); chapter 8A (Department of Administrative Services); chapter 26 (Public Construction Bidding); chapter 72 (Duties Relating to Public Contracts); chapter 73 (Preferences); chapter 73A (Public Contracts and Bonds); chapter 262 (Board of Regents); chapter 307 (Department of Transportation); and chapter 573 (Labor and Material on Public Improvements). Iowa Code section 8.47 sets forth specific requirements relating to the procurement of services by the State of Iowa. Iowa Code section 8.47 was enacted as part of the Accountable Government Act.

Iowa Code chapter 8F sets forth government accountability and service contract requirements for contracts for services with the State of Iowa with a value in excess of $500,000. The statute sets forth requirements relating to pre-contract certification, annual reporting, and enforcement and review of contractors.

B. Other Applicable Statutes

1. Counties, Municipalities, and Utilities Procurements

Procurements by counties, municipalities, and utilities are governed by other sections of the Iowa Code including Iowa Code chapters 331 (County Home Rule Implementation); 362 (Cities—Definitions and Miscellaneous Provisions), 364 (Powers and Duties of Cities); 384 (City Finance); and 473 (Energy Development and Conservation).

2. Ethics Law

State officials and employees adhere to a high standard of ethics and conduct as set forth by the National Institute of Governmental Purchasing, and must comply with applicable state and federal law in conducting the procurement process. They are to avoid acts that are improper or give the appearance of impropriety. Among other things, no official or employee is to disclose or use confidential information, including the contents of a sealed bid acquired during the course of the official's or employee's state duties, for personal gain or benefit of any person. (See Iowa Administrative Code r. 351-6.9.) Iowa Code section 68B.22 contains prohibitions against public employees and public officials accepting or receiving gifts or a series of gifts from a restricted donor. For purposes of the procurement process, a restricted donor is a person or entity that is seeking to be a party to any one or any combination of sales, purchases, leases, or contracts to, from, or with the agency in which a public employee or public official is employed or holds office.

Lobbyists and lobbyists' clients are generally prohibited from making gifts to legislators and other public officials. Lobbyists are generally prohibited from making campaign contributions to legislators, elected state officials, or candidates for state office during a regular legislative session.

Iowa Code chapter 68B addresses gifts to public officials. Iowa Code sections 68B.2A and 68B.2B address conflicts of interest of public employees and officials. The Iowa Ethics and Campaign Disclosure Board is statutorily charged with the oversight of campaign finance laws in Iowa Code chapter 68A and the ethical conduct of executive branch personnel and executive branch lobbyists under Iowa Code chapter 68B.

Iowa Code chapter 722 prohibits bribery of public officials. Iowa Code chapter 722 makes a felony the offering, promise, or giving of anything of value or any benefit to a public official or employee pursuant to an agreement, arrangement, or understanding that the promise or thing of value or benefit will influence the act, vote, opinion, judgment, decision, or exercise of discretion of that person with respect to that person's official capacity.

3. Open Records

Iowa has a single public records law, Iowa Code chapter 22. Generally, every person has a right to examine and copy a public record and to publish or otherwise disseminate a public record or the information contained in a public record. (See Iowa Code § 22.2(1).) Iowa Code section 22.7 sets forth a list of public records that are to be kept confidential, unless otherwise ordered by a court, by the lawful custodian of the records, or by another person duly authorized to release such information. For purposes of procurements, some of the exceptions include (1) trade secrets that are recognized and protected as such by law; (2) communications not required by law, rule, procedure, or contract that are made to a government body or to any of its employees by identified persons outside of government, to the extent that the government body receiving those communications from such persons outside of government could reasonably believe that those persons would be discouraged from making them to that government body if they were available for general public examination; and (3) tentative, preliminary, draft, speculative, or research material, prior to its completion for the purpose for which it is intended and in a form prior to the form in which it is submitted for use or used in the actual formulation, recommendation, adoption, or execution of any official policy or action by a public official authorized to make such decisions for the governmental body or the government body. (See, e.g., Iowa Code § 22.7(3), (18), and (65).)

Any request for confidential treatment of specific information is to be included in the transmittal letter with the vendor's bid. In addition, the vendor is to enumerate the specific grounds in Iowa Code chapter 22 or other applicable law that support treatment of the material as confidential and explain why disclosure is not in the best interest of the public. The request is to also include the name, address, and telephone number of the person authorized by the vendor to respond to any inquiries by the procuring agency concerning the confidential status of the materials.

The statutes may be accessed through the Iowa General Assembly website at https://www.legis.iowa.gov/law/iowaCode.

II. Regulations

The Iowa Department of Administrative Services' regulations address procurement of goods and services by the State of Iowa. Iowa Administrative Code 11, chapter 117, Procurement of Goods and Services of General Use. Its table of contents is as follows:

Iowa Administrative Code 11, chapter 118 addresses the purchasing standards for service contracts. Its table of contents is as follows:

11-118.1(8A)	Authority and scope.
11-118.2(8A)	Applicability.
11-118.3(8A)	Definitions.
11-118.4(8A)	Intergovernmental agreements.
11-118.5(8A)	Use of competitive selection.
11-118.6(8A)	Reserved.
11-118.7(8A)	Sole source procurements.
11-118.8(8A)	Emergency procurements.
11-118.9(8A)	Informal competitive procedures.
11-118.10(8A)	Reserved.
11-118.11(8A)	Duration of service contracts.
11-118.12(8A)	Additional procedures or requirements.
11-118.13–14(8A)	Reserved.
11-118.15(8A)	Exclusion and limitations.
11-118.16(8A)	Waiver procedure.
11-118.17(8A)	Effective date.

Iowa Administrative Code 11, chapter 119 sets forth the uniform terms and conditions for service contracts. Its table of contents is as follows:

11-119.1(8,8A)	Authority and scope.
11-119.2(8,8A)	Applicability.
11-119.3(8,8A)	Definitions.
11-119.4(8,8A)	Uniform terms and conditions for service contracts.
11-119.5(8,8A)	Special terms and conditions.
11-119.6(8,8A)	Exclusions and limitations.
11-119.7(8,8A)	Effective date.

Iowa Administrative Code 11, chapter 120 sets forth requirements relating to contractual limitation of vendor liability provisions. Its table of contents is as follows:

11-120.1(8A)	Authority and scope.
11-120.2(8A)	Definitions.
11-120.3(8A)	Applicability.
11-120.4(8A)	Authorization of limitation of vendor liability and criteria.
11-120.5(8A)	Prohibited limitation of vendor liability provisions.
11-120.6(8A)	Negotiation of limitation of vendor liability provision.
11-120.7(8A)	Additional requirement.

Iowa Administrative Code 11, chapter 121 sets forth requirements relating to contract compliance and promotion of equal opportunity in all state contracts and services and the provision of leadership in affirmative action to ensure fair and equitable participation within all programs receiving or benefiting from state financial assistance in whole or in part. Its table of contents is as follows:

11-121.1(19B). Policy.

The Iowa Department of Transportation has issued regulations regarding the procurement of equipment, materials, supplies, and services. The table of contents is as follows:

761-20.1(307)	Scope of chapter.
761-20.2(307)	Definitions.
761-20.3(307)	Procurement policy.
761-20.4(307)	Formal advertising procedures and requirements.
761-20.5(307)	Limited solicitation of bids.
761-20.6(307)	Professional and technical services.
761-20.7(307)	Sole source or emergency solicitations.
761-20.8(307)	Conflicts with federal requirements.
761-20.9(307)	Reserved.
761-20.10(307)	Negotiation—architectural, landscape architectural, engineering, and related professional and technical services.

The website for the Iowa Administrative Code is https://www.legis.iowa.gov/law/administrativeRules/agencies.

The website for the Iowa Department of Administrative Services, General Services Enterprise is https://das.iowa.gov/general-services.

III. Source Selection

It is the policy of the State of Iowa to obtain goods and services from the public sector for public purposes to achieve value for the taxpayer through a fair, open, and objective competitive process. Competitive procurements are the primary solicitation type used to procure goods and services greater than the maximum noncompetitive dollar threshold. (See, e.g., Iowa Code § 8A.311; Iowa Administrative Code r. 11-117.3.)

A. Competitive Sealed Bidding

The Department of Administrative Services maintains an approved vendor list for the procurement of goods, services, and construction projects. Any person or entity desiring to conduct business with the state is required to complete the vendor application form and submit it to the Department of Administrative Services General Services Enterprise.

Expenditures of less than $5,000 are deemed "small purchases." For goods and services relating to small purchases, a minimum of three quotations are required to be obtained and award is to be made to the vendor with the lowest compliant bid.

Expenditures for goods and services between $5,000 and $50,000 and expenditures for construction costs less than $25,000 are deemed informal bids or solicitations and require written response to an invitation to bid. Bids are to be opened within 24 hours of the due date. Award is to be made to the lowest compliant bid meeting the agency's specifications.

Purchases of goods and services in excess of $50,000 or construction projects in excess of $25,000 are considered formal bids or solicitations and are to be made through competitive sealed bidding. An award is to be made to the lowest compliant bidder within 30 calendar days of the formal bid opening. If an award is not made in this time period, then all of the bids shall be deemed rejected and prices quoted by a vendor shall not be deemed binding.

B. Competitive Negotiations

When competitive sealed bidding is determined to be not practicable or not advantageous to the state for procurements in excess of $50,000, awards of goods, services, and construction projects may be made through a request for proposals (RFP). Proposal evaluation methods will be set forth in the RFP and rating systems may be used.

Multi-step sealed bidding may be used when it is not practical to initially prepare definitive specifications that will be suitable to permit an award based on price. Such bidding is a combination of the competitive sealed bidding and proposal procedures.

C. Sole Source Procurement

Sole source procurements are made without competition if the goods, services, or construction needed are available from only one source. Sole source procurements are for commodities, services, or construction of $5,000 or more. Permitted justifications for sole source procurements are set forth at Iowa Administrative Code rule 11-118.7. In such procurement, the end user must justify and document the need for such a procurement process.

D. Emergency Procurements

Emergency procurements are permitted in times of an emergency. An emergency includes, without limitation, a condition (1) in which an immediate or emergency need exists for the item or service because of events and circumstances not reasonably foreseeable; (2) that threatens the public health, safety, or welfare; (3) in which there is a need to protect the health, safety, or welfare of persons occupying or visiting a public improvement or property located next to a public improvement; and (4) in which a state agency must act to preserve critical services or programs. For such procurements the state is still required to negotiate a fair and reasonable price.

E. Professional Services

Professional services may be procured through competitive sealed bids, competitive sealed proposals, small purchase process, sole source, and emergency procurements.

F. Cooperative Purchasing

(See Part VII.)

G. Master Agreement

A master agreement is a competitive bid contract for goods or services that establishes prices, terms, and conditions for the purchase of goods or services of general use and may be designed for use by more than one agency. They are effective for a defined period. When purchasing from a master agreement, agencies are able to compare the invoice to the master agreement price list to ensure the vendor is charging the negotiated amount.

H. Multiple Award Contract

A master agreement for a particular item or class of items may be awarded to a single vendor or multiple vendors. A multiple award contract may be used where there is more than one vendor for the same or comparable goods or services or may be necessary for operational purposes. It is effective for a defined period.

IV. Bid Protests and Contract Disputes

A. Bid Protests

Any vendor whose bid or proposal has been timely filed and who claims to be aggrieved by the award of the Department of Administrative Services may appeal the decision by filing a written notice of appeal before the director of the Department of Administrative Services within five days of the date of award, exclusive of Saturdays, Sundays, and legal state holidays. The Department must actually receive the notice of appeal within the specified time frame to be considered timely. The notice of appeal must state the grounds upon which the vendor challenges the Department's award. The appealing party may petition for stay of the award of the contract until the appeal process is completed. The petition must be filed with the notice of appeal.

In Department of Transportation procurements, a written protest must be received by the director of purchasing within seven days after the recommended award has been posted. The protest shall be considered by the authority making the award. It is not a contested case as defined in Iowa Code section 17A.2.

B. Bid Protest Appeals

The vendor appeal is considered a contested case and must follow the procedures set forth in Iowa Administrative Code rule 11-117.20. Upon receipt of a notice of a vendor appeal, the Department of Administrative Services is required to contact the Department of Inspections and Appeals to arrange for a hearing. The Department of Inspections and Appeals is to send a written notice of the date, time, and location of the appeal hearing to the aggrieved vendor or vendors. The presiding officer shall hold a hearing on the vendor appeal within 60 days of the date that the notice of appeal was received. Any discovery requests shall be served simultaneously on the parties at least 30 days prior to the date set forth in the hearing.

The parties are to contact each other about witnesses and exhibits at least ten days prior to the date set for hearing. The parties also are to serve responses to discovery at least 15 days prior to the hearing. Any party appealing the notice of award may petition the state for a stay of the award. A petition for a stay of award may require a bond equal to 120 percent of the contract value.

The proposed decision shall become the final decision of the Department of Administrative Services within 15 days after mailing the proposed decision unless, prior to that time, the protestor submits an appeal of the proposed decision. In the event that an appeal of the proposed decision is filed, the director of the Department must issue a final decision not less than 30 days after the notice of appeal is filed. The director is to notify the parties if the Department deems oral arguments to be necessary.

The Department is to review the proposed decision based on the record and issues raised in the hearing. The Department is not to take any further evidence and is not to consider issues that were not raised at the hearing. The issues for review are to be specified in the party's notice of appeal. The party appealing the proposed decision shall be responsible for transcribing any tape of the proceeding before the presiding officer and filing the transcript as part of the record for review. The party appealing the proposed decision is to bear the cost of the transcription regardless of the method used to transcribe the tape.

Each party in appeal is to have the opportunity to file exceptions to the proposed decision and present briefs in support of or in opposition to the proposed decision. The Department may set a deadline for submission of briefs. When the Department consents, oral arguments may be presented. A party wishing to make an oral argument shall specifically request it. The Department in its sole discretion may schedule oral arguments regarding the appeal. The Department is to notify all parties in advance of the scheduled time and place for oral arguments.

The director of the Department is to issue a final decision by the Department. The decision is to be in writing and is to conform to the requirements of Iowa Code chapter 17A.

Judicial review of the Department of Administrative Services' final decision may be sought in accordance with the Iowa Administrative Procedure Act, Iowa Code chapter 17A.

C. Contract Disputes

The state may, by the terms of the agreement with the vendor, agree to nonbinding voluntary alternative dispute resolution. (See State of Iowa Model Contract, https://das.iowa.gov/sites/default/files/procurement/htm/AppI_ModelContract.htm.)

D. Suspension and Debarment

A contractor or supplier of goods or services to the state or a governmental agency, and the enterprise for which the illegal action was taken, convicted under the Iowa Competition Law, or convicted under the laws of any other state or the federal government for actions that would constitute a violation of the Iowa Competition Law, are prohibited from bidding on a governmental contract for one year from the date of conviction, unless the state or governmental agency accepting bids expressly allows the contractor or supplier to bid after being informed of the conviction. (Iowa Code § 553.18.)

V. Administrative and Judicial Review

A. Administrative Review

Disputes that arise between a vendor and an agency are to be heard by the director of the Department of Administrative Services pursuant to the Iowa Administrative Procedure Act, Iowa Code chapter 17A and implementing regulations.

B. Judicial Review

A determination by the director of the Department of Administrative Services is deemed a final decision for which an appeal may be made to the Iowa district court under the Iowa Administrative Procedures Act, Iowa Code chapter 17A. A determination by the Iowa district court may be appealed to the Iowa Supreme Court.

The website for the Iowa Judicial Branch that contains the decisions of the Iowa Supreme Court and Iowa Court of Appeals is https://www.iowacourts.gov.

VI. Extent of State's Adoption or Adaptation of ABA Model Procurement Code

Iowa has not adopted the American Bar Association's (ABA's) Model Procurement Code.

VII. Cooperative Purchasing

A. Authority

Cooperative purchasing is permitted under the Department of Administrative Services' regulations. (See Iowa Administrative Code r. 11-117.5(4) (Procurement Based on Competition Managed by Other Governmental Entities).) Other state agencies also have authority to pursue cooperative purchasing. (See, e.g., Iowa Code § 262.9B (Board of Regents—Cooperative Purchasing).)

The Central Procurement Bureau of the Department of Administrative Services is encouraged to exchange price information, vendor lists, bidder histories, and standard specifications with other governmental agencies and to enter into a purchasing consortium if the Bureau believes such a consortium is in the best interests of the state, and that the agreement was awarded in a fair and competitive manner. Cooperative purchasing benefits states as well as cities, counties, public schools, institutions of higher education, and other eligible entities. The Bureau may develop master agreements from purchasing contracts established by state agencies or other governmental entities if it is in the best interest of the state. Agencies cannot establish master purchasing agreements. (See State of Iowa Department of Administrative Services Central Procurement Policy and Procedures Manual, https://das.iowa.gov/procurement.)

B. Requirements

The Department of Administrative Services is to notify the other governmental entity and the requesting agency of its intent to use a contract, agreement, or purchase order prior to procuring the good or service in this manner. The Department may purchase goods or services from contracts let by other governmental entities provided that the vendor is in agreement and the terms and conditions of the purchase do not adversely impact the governmental entity that was the original signatory to the contract. (Iowa Administrative Code r. 11-117.5(4)(b).)

Kansas Procurement Rules and Regulations

Prepared by Brian E. Sobczyk
Stinson LLP
Email: Brian.Sobczyk@Stinson.com

I. Statutory Reference

A. Procurement/Purchasing Statutes

The agency responsible for procurement in Kansas is the Kansas Department of Administration, Office of Procurement and Contracts (formerly the Division for Purchases). The Office is headed by the director of procurement and contracts (the "director") (formerly the director of purchases). The Office of Procurement and Contracts website is https://admin.ks.gov/offices/procurement-contracts.

The statutory provisions governing procurement in Kansas have not been consolidated into a single code. The governing statutes are generally contained in chapter 75, State Departments; Public Officers and Employees, of the Kansas Statutes Annotated (KSA), in the following articles:

Article 12. Architectural Services
Article 30. General Provisions
Article 37. Department of Administration
Article 69. Contracts for Public Improvement Projects

In particular, statutes governing the Office of Procurement and Contracts are found at KSA sections 75-3737a to 75-3744a. The KSA are publicly available at http://www.kslegislature.org/li_2016/b2015_16/statute/.

B. Other Applicable Statutes

- Kansas Administrative Procedure Act (KAPA), KSA section 77-501 *et seq*.
- Kansas Judicial Review Act (KJRA), KSA section 77-601 *et seq*.

II. Regulations

- Kansas Administrative Regulations governing the Department of Administration are available at Kansas Administrative Regulations section 1-1-1 *et seq.*
- Procurement Informational Circulars are available online at https://admin.ks.gov/offices/procurement-contracts/procurement-resources/procurement-informational-circulars.

III. Source Selection

A. Vendor Registration

Any prospective or current vendor in Kansas must register and create a vendor profile with the PeopleSoft Financial Management System (SMART) in order to respond to any bid event. Information and instructions regarding registration are available at https://admin.ks.gov/offices/procurement-contracts/bidding--contracts/bidder-registration.

To bid on events, vendors must be invited in SMART by the procurement officer before the bidding closes.

B. Competitive Bids

Generally, all contracts for construction and repairs, and all purchases of and contracts for supplies, materials, equipment, and contractual services to be acquired for state agencies, must be based on competitive bids. (KSA § 75-3739.) Kansas provides for exceptions to the general rule, however, and competitive bids are not required in the following instances:

> (1) For contractual services, supplies, materials, or equipment when, in the judgment of the director of purchases, no competition exists;
>
> (2) when, in the judgment of the director of purchases, chemicals and other material or equipment for use in laboratories or experimental studies by state agencies are best purchased without competition, or where rates are fixed by law or ordinance;
>
> (3) when, in the judgment of the director of purchases, an agency emergency requires immediate delivery of supplies, materials, or equipment, or immediate performance of services;
>
> (4) when any statute authorizes another procedure or provides an exemption from the provisions of this section;
>
> (5) when compatibility with existing contractual services, supplies, materials or equipment is the overriding consideration;
>
> (6) when a used item becomes available and is subject to immediate sale; or
>
> (7) when, in the judgment of the director of purchases and the head of the acquiring state agency, not seeking competitive bids is in the best interest of the state.

(KSA § 75-3739(a).)

For contracts in excess of $100,000 that are authorized to be let without competitive bids, except for contracts entered under instances (3), (4), and (6) above and contracts entered between Kansas state agencies and certain other state or federal agencies, the director must first post an online notice of the proposed purchase or contract at least seven days before the purchase or contract is awarded. (*Id.*) A person or entity interested in supplying the goods or services under such a contract may submit a written protest of the award during the seven-day notice period. (*Id.*) If the director is satisfied as to the validity of the protest and existence of competition, the director shall then proceed with competitive procurement. (*Id.*)

C. Sealed Bids

If the amount of a purchase is estimated to exceed $50,000, sealed bids must be solicited by notice published once in the *Kansas Register* not less than ten days before the date stated in the notice for the opening of the bids. (KSA § 75-3739(b)(1).) The director may waive this notice requirement if the director determines a more timely procurement is in the best interest of the state. (*Id.*) Additionally, the director must also solicit bids by mailing notices to prospective bidders and by posting the notice on a public bulletin board for at least ten business days before the date stated for the opening of the bids unless otherwise provided by law. (*Id.*) All bids must be sealed when received and must be opened in public at the hour stated in the notice. (*Id.*)

For purchases estimated to exceed approximately $25,000, but not more than $50,000, the purchases must be made after receipt of sealed bids following at least three days' notice posted on a public bulletin board. (KSA § 75-3739(c).) Purchases estimated to be more than $5,000, but less than $25,000, may be made after the receipt of three or more bid solicitations by telephone, telephone facsimile, or sealed bid, following at least three days' notice. (KSA § 75-3739(d).)

References to "sealed bids," "bulletin boards," and "mail" are deemed to include electronic bids, electronic bulletin boards, and electronic mail when such electronic submissions or services are utilized in accordance with procedures prescribed by the director. (KSA § 75-3739(n).)

D. Reverse Auctioning

With limited exceptions, the director may utilize reverse auctioning electronic procurement processes for the purchase of selected goods or materials. (KSA § 75-3739a(a).) Reverse auctioning, as defined by Kansas statute, is a procurement process where bidders are invited to bid on specific goods through real-time electronic bidding, during which bid prices are revealed to other bidders and bidders may modify their bid prices. (KSA § 75-3739a(d).) Contracts are awarded to the lowest responsible and responsive bidder. (*Id.*) Statutes relating to advertisements in the *Kansas Register* and procedures for sealed bidding do not apply to purchases made through the reverse auctioning electronic procurement process. (KSA § 75-3739a(b).)

Reverse auctioning may not, however, be utilized to procure any services, including, without limitation, services for construction projects. (KSA § 75-3739a(c).)

E. Negotiation

Upon request of the chief administrative officer of a state agency and subject to the approval of the secretary of administration, the director may convene procurement negotiating committees for the purpose of obtaining services or technical products. (KSA § 75-37,102(a).) A negotiating committee is authorized to negotiate contracts with qualified parties to provide services or technical products needed by a state agency. (KSA § 75-37,102(c).) The committee may negotiate with one or more firms submitting bids or proposals and select from among those firms the party with whom to contract. (KSA § 75-37,102(d).) In the event a committee selects a bid that is not the lowest on a given contract, the rationale for the selection must be explained in the director's quarterly report to the legislature. (KSA § 75-37,102(e).)

F. Purchases under Other Prescribed Conditions and Procedures

With the approval of the secretary of administration, the director may delegate authority to any state agency to make purchases of less than $25,000 under prescribed conditions and procedures. (KSA § 75-3739(e).) Purchases estimated to be less than $5,000 may be made under conditions and procedures prescribed by the director. (KSA § 75-3739(d).) The director may also delegate authority to any state agency to make purchases under prescribed conditions and procedures when the acquisition is funded, in whole or in part, from a grant. (KSA § 75-3739(j).)

G. Specifications

Contracts and purchases must be based on specifications approved by the director. (KSA § 75-3739(f).) When applicable and feasible, such specifications must include either energy efficiency standards or appropriate life-cycle cost formulas, or both, for all supplies, materials, equipment, and contractual services to be purchased by the state. (*Id.*) Contracts and purchases may be rejected by the director if a product is manufactured or assembled outside of the United States. (*Id.*) Agencies must not fix specifications in a manner that excludes any responsible bidder that can offer comparable supplies, materials, equipment, or services. (*Id.*)

H. Contract Award

In general, all contracts and purchases made by or under the supervision of the director or any state agency for which competitive bids are required shall be awarded to the lowest responsible bidder, taking into consideration conformity with the specifications, terms of delivery, and other conditions imposed in the call for bids. (KSA § 75-3740(a).)

Preferences are afforded to "certified businesses" (see KSA § 75-3740(g)(1)) and to disabled veteran businesses (see KSA § 75-3740(g)(6)). Contracts shall be awarded to a certified business or disabled veteran business that is also a responsible bidder, if the total bid cost of the bid submitted by the business is not more than 10 percent higher than the lowest competitive bid. (KSA § 75-3740(b).) Such contracts are subject to certain conditions that must be met by the qualifying business. (*Id.*)

A preference is also afforded to local companies. If the bid amount from the lowest responsible bidder from within the state is identical to the bid amount from the lowest responsible bidder from without the state, the contract shall be awarded to the local bidder. (KSA § 75-3740(c)(2).)

I. Attorney General to Approve Certain Contracts

Whenever the secretary of administration or any division head of the Department of Administration requires, certain specified contracts and leases of any state agency shall be approved as to form or execution by the attorney general. (KSA § 75-3743.) A copy of every contract or lease extending for a term longer than one year shall be filed with the director of accounts and reports. (*Id.*) All orders or requisitions for supplies, materials, equipment, and contractual services shall be on forms prescribed by the director of accounts and reports. (*Id.*)

J. Prequalification of State Contractors

State agencies, in cooperation with the director, are authorized to develop a list of prequalified vendors of particular goods and services and a set of standards that vendors must meet in order to be qualified. (KSA § 75-37,104.) Any prequalification procedure must be in writing and published sufficiently in advance to permit vendors to comply with the process. (*Id.*) Additionally, state agencies may require that any prequalified vendor has sufficient administrative and accounting controls to insure compliance with any contractual requirements. (*Id.*) Solicitation mailing lists of potential contractors must include prequalified firms. (*Id.*)

K. Professional and Consultant Services; Alternative Delivery Methods

State procurement for professional and consultant services generally requires different procedures than those noted above. Such contracts generally require negotiation pursuant to KSA section 75-37,102, section 75-37,132, or section 75-430a. Notably, all contracts for architectural, engineering, construction management, or ancillary technical services must be entered into in accordance with the provisions of KSA sections 75-430a, 75-1250 through 75-1266, and 75-5801 through 75-5807.

Additionally, certain Kansas construction projects may be subject to the Kansas Alternative Project Delivery Building Construction Procurement Act, KSA section 75-37,141 *et seq*. Projects that may be governed by the act include projects utilizing construction management at-risk or building design-build procurement processes. (KSA §§ 75-37,144, 75-37,145.)

Care should be taken to consult the relevant statutes and regulations applicable to the project or services when engaging in any Kansas construction project or entering into a contract for professional or consultant services.

IV. Bid Protests and Contract Disputes

A. Bid Protests

As discussed above, for certain contracts in excess of $100,000 that are authorized to be let without competitive bids, the director must first post an online notice of the proposed purchase or contract at least seven days before the purchase or contract is awarded. (KSA § 75-3739(a).) A person or entity interested in supplying the goods or services under such a contract may submit a written protest of the award during the seven-day notice period. (*Id.*) If the director is satisfied as to the validity of the protest and existence of competition, the director shall then proceed with competitive procurement. (*Id.*)

There are no uniform rules or procedures that specifically govern bid protests relating to other contracts. Generally, the director is granted substantial discretion to decide as to the lowest responsible bidder, including the discretion to reject "[a]ny or all bids." (KSA § 75-3740(c), (d).) Kansas courts have addressed bid disputes, but those decisions are beyond the scope of this chapter.

B. Bid Protest Appeals

There are no detailed rules or procedures specifically applicable to bid protest appeals. However, since bid protest appeals relate to "agency action," a petition for judicial review may be made to the district court, or directly to the court of appeals if a statute so provides, in accordance with the KJRA, KSA section 77-601 *et seq*. This law provides for the filing of a petition for judicial review of an agency action after the exhaustion of all administrative remedies available. The procedures governing petition for judicial review are outlined in Section V.B below.

C. Contract Claims

The terms of the contract, including claim notice and procedure provisions, are relevant in determining what to do when a contract dispute arises and should be studied. As a general rule, contracts are enforceable in Kansas provided they are neither illegal nor contrary to public policy. (*National Bank of Andover v. Kansas Bankers Surety Co.*, 225 P.3d 707, 715 (Kan. 2010).) Contracting parties are, of course, entitled to institute legal action in a court of competent jurisdiction for breach of contract. All agency actions are subject to judicial review under the KJRA. Thus, contract claims and contract appeals involving the decision of an agency may generally be filed in district court, unless otherwise provided by law. Further, pursuant to the KJRA, decisions on petitions for judicial review are reviewable by the appellate courts as in other civil cases.

D. Suspension and Debarment

The secretary of administration has authority to debar a contractor for cause from consideration for award of contracts. (KSA § 75-37,103(a).) The contractor must be provided reasonable notice and opportunity to be heard. (*Id.*) Any debarment must not exceed a period of three years. (*Id.*) The secretary also has authority to suspend a contractor from consideration for award of contracts on probable cause to believe the contractor has engaged in any activity that might lead to debarment. (*Id.*) Any suspension must not exceed a period of three months unless an indictment has been issued for an offense that would be a cause for debarment, in which case the suspension must remain in effect until after the trial of the suspended person. (*Id.*) Causes for debarment include (1) conviction of a criminal offense as an incident to obtaining or attempting to obtain a public or private contract, or in the performance of such contract; (2) conviction for embezzlement, theft, forgery, bribery, falsification or destruction of records, receiving stolen property, or any other offense indicating a lack of business integrity or business honesty that currently, seriously, and directly affects responsibility as a state contractor; (3) conviction under antitrust statutes; (4) failure without good cause to perform in accordance with the terms of the contract; or (5) any other cause the secretary determines to be so serious and compelling as to affect responsibility as a state contractor. (KSA § 75-37,103(b).)

V. Administrative and Judicial Review

A. Administrative Review

The Office of Administrative Hearings (OAH) employs administrative law judges and other support personnel to conduct proceedings for various departments, along with many other state agencies. Hearings are conducted pursuant to the KAPA, KSA section 77-501 *et seq.*, and other state statutes. The website of the OAH is https://oah.ks.gov/.

B. Judicial Review

1. Jurisdiction and Venue

The district court has jurisdiction to conduct judicial review of agency action except when a statute specifically provides for review by appeal directly to the court of appeals, or as otherwise provided by law. (KSA § 77-609.) Unless otherwise specifically provided by statute, venue for a review action lies in the county in which the order or agency action is entered or is effective or the rule and regulation is promulgated. (*Id.*)

2. Initiation of Action: Form of Action

Judicial review is initiated by filing a petition for judicial review in the appropriate court and payment of the docket fee. (KSA § 77-610.)

3. Standing

The following persons have standing to obtain judicial review of agency actions: (1) a person to whom the agency action is specifically directed; (2) a person who was a party to the agency proceedings that led to the agency action; (3) if the challenged agency action is a rule and regulation, a person subject to that rule; or (4) a person eligible for standing under another provision of law. (KSA § 77-611.)

4. Nonfinal Agency Actions

Interlocutory review of nonfinal agency actions is available only if (1) it appears likely that the person will qualify for judicial review of the related final agency action and (2) postponement of judicial review would result in an inadequate remedy or irreparable harm disproportionate to the public benefit derived from postponement. (KSA § 77-608.)

5. Exhaustion of Administrative Remedies

Generally, petitions for judicial review of agency actions may only be filed after exhausting all administrative remedies available within the agency whose action is being challenged and within any other agency authorized to exercise administrative review. (KSA § 77-612.) Limited exceptions apply to the requirement of exhausting all administrative remedies, including when administrative remedies are inadequate or would result in irreparable harm. (*Id.*)

6. Time for Filing Petition and Service

A petition for judicial review of a rule and regulation may be filed at any time, unless otherwise provided by law. (KSA § 77-613.) If reconsideration of an agency action has not been requested and is not a prerequisite for seeking judicial review, a petition for judicial review of a final order must be filed within 30 days after service of the order. (*Id.*) If reconsideration has been requested or is a prerequisite for seeking judicial review, a petition for judicial review of a final order shall be filed (1) within 30 days after service of the order rendered upon reconsideration, unless a further petition for reconsideration is required, or (2) within 30 days after service of an order denying the request for reconsideration. (*Id.*) A petition for judicial review must be filed with the clerk of the court. (KSA § 77-614(a).) Within 30 days after service on the agency or notice to other parties, a party to judicial review proceedings may file an answer or other responsive pleading. (KSA § 77-614(d).)

7. Stay and Temporary Remedies

Unless precluded by law, the agency may grant a stay on appropriate terms or other temporary remedies during the pendency of judicial review. (KSA § 77-616(a).) A party may also file a motion in the reviewing court, during the pendency of judicial review, seeking interlocutory review of the agency's action on an application for stay or other temporary remedies. (KSA § 77-616(b).)

8. Relief on Final Disposition

In an action for judicial review, a court may award damages or compensation only to the extent expressly authorized by another provision of law. (KSA § 77-622(a).) The court may grant other appropriate relief, whether mandatory, injunctive, or declaratory; preliminary or final; temporary or permanent; equitable or legal. (KSA § 77-622(b).) The court may also grant necessary ancillary relief to redress the effects of official action wrongfully taken or withheld. (KSA § 77-622(c).) If the court sets aside or modifies agency action or remands the matter to the agency for further proceedings, the court may make any interlocutory order it finds necessary to preserve the interests of the parties and the public pending further proceedings or agency action. (KSA § 77-622(d).)

9. Review by Higher Court

Decisions on petitions for judicial review of agency action are reviewable by the appellate courts as in other civil cases. (KSA § 77-623.)

VI. Extent of State's Adoption or Adaptation of ABA Model Procurement Code

Kansas has not adopted the 1979 or 2000 version of the American Bar Association's (ABA's) Model Procurement Code.

VII. Cooperative Purchasing

A. Authority

The director may authorize state agencies to contract for services and materials with other state agencies, or with federal agencies, political subdivisions of Kansas, agencies of other states, or subdivisions or private nonprofit educational institutions, without competitive bids. (KSA § 75-3739(h).) The director may also participate in, sponsor, conduct, or administer a cooperative purchasing agreement or consortium for purchases of supplies, materials, equipment, and contractual services with federal agencies or agencies of other states or local units of government. (KSA § 75-3739(i).)

B. Requirements

Such cooperative purchasing agreements are not subject to the competitive bidding provisions set forth in KSA sections 75-3739 through 75-3740a. (*Id.*)

Kentucky Procurement Rules and Regulations

Prepared by Amanda S. Johnson, Erin R. Davis, and Christina Heidecker[1]
Taft Stettinius & Hollister, LLP
Email: asjohnson@taftlaw.com and edavis@taftlaw.com

I. Statutory Reference

A. Procurement/Purchasing Statutes

The basic procurement legislation in the Commonwealth of Kentucky was based on the American Bar Association (ABA) Model Procurement Code for State and Local Governments. Kentucky was the first state to adopt the code in 1978, and it is found at chapter 45A of the Kentucky Revised Statutes (KRS) (Kentucky Model Procurement Code (KMPC)) at https://apps.legislature.ky.gov/law/statutes/chapter.aspx?id=37250. This site provides a direct link to all sections of chapter 45A and other applicable statutes on procurement.

KRS chapter 13B sets forth the procedures and policies for the conduct of administrative hearings in the following statutes:

§ 13B.005. Short title for KRS 13B.005 to 13B.170.
§ 13B.010. Definitions for chapter.
§ 13B.020. Application of chapter—Exemptions.
§ 13B.030. Powers of agency head—Hearing officers.
§ 13B.040. Qualifications of hearing officer.
§ 13B.050. Notice of administrative hearing.
§ 13B.060. Petition for intervention.
§ 13B.070. Prehearing conference—Mediation and informal settlement procedures.
§ 13B.080. Conduct of hearing.
§ 13B.090. Findings of fact—Evidence—Recording of hearing—Burdens of proof.
§ 13B.100. Recommended order.
§ 13B.120. Final order.
§ 13B.125. Emergency action—Hearing—Appeal.

1. The Kentucky chapter in the prior edition was prepared by Larry Ethridge, Esq.

§ 13B.130. Official record of hearing.
§ 13B.140. Judicial review of final order.
§ 13B.150. Conduct of judicial review.
§ 13B.160. Judicial appeal.
§ 13B.170. Administrative regulations.

Use the following link for the full text of each section listed above: https://apps.legislature.ky.gov/law/statutes/chapter.aspx?id=37085.

II. Regulations

The basic procurement regulations for the KMPC are found at title 200, chapter 5 of the Kentucky Administrative Regulations (KAR), and the regulations can be found at https://apps.legislature.ky.gov/law/kar/titles/200/005.

III. Source Selection

A. Competitive Sealed Bidding

Contracts exceeding the amount provided by KRS section 45A.100 (small purchases) and related regulations shall be awarded by competitive sealed bidding under KRS section 45A.080, unless it is determined in writing by a purchasing officer that use of this source selection method is not practicable. Factors to be considered in determining whether competitive sealed bidding is not practicable include whether specifications can be prepared that permit award on the basis of best value; and, the available sources, the time and place of performance, and other relevant circumstances as are appropriate for the use of competitive sealed bidding. In competitive sealed bidding, the invitation for bids must state that awards will be made on the basis of "best value." Adequate public notice of the invitation for bids is to be given in a sufficient time prior to the date set forth for the opening of bids, usually seven days prior to the date set for bid opening. This notice may be posted on the internet or published in a newspaper or newspapers of general circulation in the state as determined by the secretary of the Finance and Administration Cabinet. The notice is also posted on the Finance and Administration Cabinet's website. Bids are to be opened publicly at the time and place designated in the invitation, and each bid shall be recorded on a bid tabulation summary sheet (listing the bidder's name, description of products or services, and the price of the bid) and open to public inspection. The contract is awarded by written notice to the responsive and responsible bidder whose bid offers the "best value" (as that term is defined in KRS section 45A.070(1)). Regulations concerning competitive sealed bidding are found at KAR title 200, rule 5:306, and at KAR title 200, rule 5:375 for multi-step sealed bidding.

B. Competitive Negotiation

Competitive negotiation can be used when (1) a purchasing officer determines in writing that the use of competitive sealed bidding is not practicable; (2) a purchasing officer determines that the bids received through competitive sealed bidding are either unreasonable as to all or part of the requirements, or were not independently reached in open competition, and for which each bidder has been notified of the intention to negotiate and is given a reasonable opportunity to do so; or (3) all competitive sealed bids exceed available funds.

Adequate public notice of the request for proposals shall be given in the same manner and circumstances as an invitation for bids. The request for proposals must indicate the relative importance of price and all other evaluation factors. Awards under competitive negotiation are made to the responsible offeror whose proposal is determined to be the most advantageous to the commonwealth, taking into consideration price and the evaluation factors set forth in the request for proposals. (See also 200 KAR 5:307.) Written or oral discussions are required to be conducted with all responsible offerors who submit proposals determined to be reasonably susceptible of being selected for award unless they qualify as an exception under KRS section 45A.085(7). Such discussions shall not disclose any information derived from the proposals submitted by other offerors.

C. Noncompetitive Negotiation

A contract may be made by noncompetitive negotiation under KRS section 45A.095 for sole source purchases, when competition is not feasible as determined by the purchasing officer in writing prior to award, emergencies, or sponsorships, naming rights, or other advertising products. Such determinations must be made under administrative regulations promulgated by the secretary of the Finance and Administration Cabinet. (See 200 KAR 5:309.) A sole source procurement occurs when there is only one known capable supplier of a commodity or service, occasioned by the unique nature of the requirement, the supplier, or market conditions. However, every effort should be made to effect a competitively established price for all purchases made by the commonwealth under this section.

D. Small Purchases by State Governmental Bodies

Procurements made under KRS section 45A.100 require the amount involved to be less than $10,000 per project for construction and $1,000 for purchases of supplies and equipment by any state governmental body, or up to $40,000 per project for construction or purchases by the Finance and Administration Cabinet, state institutions of higher education, and the legislative branch. The secretary of the Finance and Administration Cabinet may delegate small purchase authority in excess of these amounts to requesting agencies. For advertising requirements for local government procurements, see KRS section 424.260. Procurement requirements shall not be artificially divided to constitute small purchases.

E. Cancellation of Invitations for Bids or Requests for Proposals

An invitation for bids, a request for proposals, or other solicitations may be canceled, or all bids or proposals may be rejected, if it is determined in writing that such action is taken in the best interest of the commonwealth and is approved by the purchasing officer. (See KRS § 45A.105.)

F. Responsibility of Bidders and Offerors

A written determination of responsibility of a bidder or offeror under KRS section 45A.110 is made in accordance with administrative regulations promulgated by the secretary of the Finance and Administration Cabinet. A reasonable inquiry to determine the responsibility of a bidder or offeror may be conducted and the failure of a party to promptly supply information in connection with such an inquiry may be grounds for a determination of non-responsibility. The information provided to the agency in the course of this inquiry may not be released without the bidder's or offeror's prior written consent. (See also 200 KAR 5:314.)

G. Prequalification of Suppliers

The secretary of the Finance and Administration Cabinet may provide for prequalification of suppliers as responsible prospective contractors for particular types of supplies, services, and construction pursuant to KRS section 45A.115.

H. Specifications

The Finance and Administration Cabinet has responsibility for issuing and maintaining all standard specifications for supplies, services, and construction required by the commonwealth under KRS section 45A.170. Among its duties, the Cabinet must (1) revise all standard specifications to conform to all technical and scientific advances pertaining to the supplies, services, and construction described in those specifications and to reflect changes in the commonwealth's requirements; (2) establish guidelines for drafting specifications; and (3) ensure that every invitation for bids or request for proposals provides that an item equal to that named or described in the specifications may be furnished. All specifications must be drafted so as to maximize completion to the extent practicable.

I. Bid Bonds

Bid security is required for all competitive sealed bids for construction contracts when the price is estimated to exceed $40,000 under KRS section 45A.185. Such security shall be a bond provided by a surety company authorized to do business in the commonwealth, or the equivalent in cash, in a form satisfactory to the commonwealth. (See also 200 KAR 5:305 regarding performance bonds.) Bonds may also be required on construction contracts under $40,000 when circumstances warrant. Bidders' security shall be in an amount equal to at least 5 percent of the amount of the bid, and noncompliance will result in rejection of the bid. These bonds may be forfeited if it is determined by the purchasing official that the contractor is in breach of the terms and conditions of the contract.

IV. Bid Protests and Contract Disputes

A. Bid Protests

The secretary of the Finance and Administration Cabinet or a designee has authority to determine protests and other controversies of actual or prospective bidders or offerors in connection with the solicitation or selection for award of a contract under KRS section 45A.285. Any actual or prospective bidder, offeror, or contractor who is aggrieved in connection with the solicitation or selection for award of a contract may file a protest with the secretary of the Finance and Administration Cabinet. A protest or notice of other controversy must be filed promptly and in any event within two calendar weeks after such aggrieved person knows or should have known of the facts giving rise to the protest. (See 200 KAR 5:380 for the computation of filing time under various circumstances.) All protests or notices of other controversies must be in writing, and the secretary must promptly issue a written decision stating the reasons for the action taken. A copy of that decision shall be mailed or otherwise furnished to the aggrieved party. The decision by the secretary is final and conclusive unless it is clearly erroneous, arbitrary, capricious, or contrary to law. In the event of a timely filed protest, the commonwealth cannot proceed with the solicitation or award unless the secretary or a designee makes a written and adequately supported determination that continuation of the procurement is necessary to protect substantial interests of the commonwealth. (KRS § 45A.290.)

B. Bid Protest Appeals

An application for judicial review can be made in Franklin Circuit Court when the secretary's decision regarding a bid protest is clearly erroneous, arbitrary, capricious, or contrary to law. (*Laboratory Corp. of America Holdings v. Randolph*, 184 S.W.3d 68 (Ky. Ct. App. 2005); *Pendleton Brothers Vending, Inc. v. Commonwealth Finance & Administration Cabinet*, 758 S.W.2d 25, 28–29 (Ky. 1988).)

C. Contract Disputes

1. Contract Claims

Prior to the institution of any action in court concerning a contract, claim, or controversy, the secretary of the Finance and Administration Cabinet has authority to settle, compromise, pay, or otherwise adjust the claim by or against, or controversy with a contractor relating to a contract entered into by the secretary on behalf of the commonwealth or any state agency. (KRS § 45A.230.) If such claim or controversy between the commonwealth and a contractor is not resolved by mutual agreement, the secretary or a designee must promptly issue a decision in writing. (KRS § 45A.235.) Any such decision is final and conclusive unless fraudulent, or the contractor sues in an action for damages under KRS section 45A.245. If the secretary does not issue a written decision within 120 days after written request for a final decision, or within such longer period as might be established by the parties to the contract, the contractor may proceed as if an adverse decision had been received. Any person, firm, or corporation having a lawfully authorized written contract with the commonwealth may bring an action against the commonwealth on the contract, including but not limited to actions either for breach of contract or for enforcement of the contract or for both. (KRS § 45A.245.) Any such action must be brought in the Franklin Circuit Court and is tried by the court sitting without a jury. All defenses in law or equity, except the defense of governmental immunity, are preserved to the commonwealth. Damages are limited to an amount that does not exceed the amount of the original contract. Any claim arising from a construction contract executed and administered by the Transportation Cabinet must be commenced in Franklin Circuit Court within one year from the time the commonwealth has determined final pay quantities and issued a final pay estimate to the contracting party notifying it of the final determination, or from the receipt of a final adverse decision from the commonwealth, whichever occurs later. (KRS § 45A.260.) Any other claim must be commenced in the Franklin Circuit Court within one year from the date of completion specified in the contract.

2. Contract Claims Appeals

Contract claim appeals may be taken to the court of appeals from the Franklin Circuit Court under the same conditions and under the same practice as appeals are taken from judgments in civil causes rendered by circuit courts. (KRS § 45A.255.)

D. Suspension and Debarment

Penalties for violation of the various provisions of the KMPC are set forth at KRS section 45A.990. Regulations concerning disciplinary action for failure to perform and debarment are found at KAR title 200, rule 5:315.

V. Administrative and Judicial Review

A. Administrative Review

An agency head may exercise all powers conferred on an agency relating to the conduct of administrative hearings, and may delegate conferred powers to a hearing officer or a member of a collegial body that serves as an agency head, or he or she may delegate conferred powers to a hearing officer to conduct an administrative hearing before a hearing panel. (KRS § 13B.030.) An agency head may not, however, delegate the power to issue a final order unless specifically authorized by statute, or unless disqualified.

B. Judicial Review

All final orders of an agency are subject to judicial review. A party may institute an appeal by filing a petition in the circuit court of venue, as provided in the agency's enabling statutes, within 30 days after the final order of the agency is mailed or delivered by personal service. (KRS § 13B.140.) If venue for such an appeal is not stated in the enabling statutes, a party may appeal to the Franklin Circuit Court or the circuit court of the county in which the appealing party resides or operates a place of business. Copies of the petition must be served by the petitioner upon the agency and all parties of record, which petition shall include the names and addresses of all parties to the proceeding and the agency involved, and a statement of the grounds on which the review is requested. The petition must be accompanied by a copy of the final order. A party may file a petition for judicial review only after the party has exhausted all administrative remedies available within the agency whose action is being challenged, and within any other agency authorized to exercise administrative reviews.

Within 20 days after the service of the petition, or within further time allowed by the court, the agency must transmit to the reviewing court the original or a certified copy of the office record of the proceeding under review. By stipulation of all parties to the review proceedings, the record may be shortened. A petition for judicial review does not automatically stay a final order pending the outcome of the review, unless (1) an automatic stay is provided by statute upon appeal or at any point in the administrative proceedings; (2) a stay is permitted by the agency and granted upon request; or (3) a stay is ordered by the circuit court of proper jurisdiction upon petition.

Reviews of final orders are conducted by the court without a jury and are confined to the record, unless there are allegations of fraud or misconduct involving a party administering the process. The court, upon request, may hear oral arguments and receive written briefs. The court may affirm or reverse the final order in whole or in part, or remand the case for further proceedings if it finds the agency's final order is (1) in violation of constitutional or statutory provisions; (2) in excess of the statutory authority of the agency; (3) without support of substantial evidence on the whole record; (4) arbitrary, capricious, or characterized by abuse of discretion; (5) based on an ex parte communication that substantially prejudiced the rights of any party and likely affected the outcome of the hearing; or (6) prejudiced by a failure of the person conducting a proceeding to be disqualified. (*Laboratory Corp. of America Holdings v. Randolph*, 184 S.W.3d 68 (Ky. Ct. App. 2005).)

VI. Extent of State's Adoption or Adaptation of ABA Model Procurement Code

As noted above, Kentucky was the first state to adopt the ABA Model Procurement Code for State and Local Governments in 1978. Since then, the Kentucky Legislature has regularly amended the Kentucky Procurement Code so that it is consistent with the ABA Model Procurement Code.

VII. Cooperative Purchasing

A. Authority

Since 2003, Kentucky has permitted cooperative purchasing. Essentially any public purchasing unit (meaning state or local government entities) may "participate in, sponsor, conduct, or administer a cooperative purchasing agreement for the acquisition of any supplies, services, or construction with any other public purchasing unit or foreign purchasing activity, in accordance with an agreement entered into between the participants." (KRS § 45A.300.)

B. Requirements

In general, there are few limitations so long as the procurement meets the requirements of KRS section 45A.045(5) and KRS sections 45A.070 to 45A.165. Public purchasing units may piggyback on other procurements regardless of whether performed by other commonwealth governments or by government entities in other states. Notably, school districts are limited to purchases under $2,500, and using the exact same specifications as the procuring agency did.

Cooperative purchasing prices, much like federal General Services Administration schedules, represent the ceiling pricing, and contractors may offer temporary discounts on their services, supplies, and equipment. (KRS § 45A.300(6).)

Louisiana Procurement Rules and Regulations

Prepared by Gerard E. Wimberly, Jr., Angelina Christina, and Elizabeth S. Horn
Akerman LLP
Email: gerard.wimberly@akerman.com, angelina.christina@akerman.com, elizabeth.horn@akerman.com
and
Melissa Harris
Kahn, Swick & Foti, LLC
Email: melissa.harris@ksfcounsel.com

I. Statutory Reference

A. Procurement/Purchasing Statutes

The Louisiana Procurement Code[1] is codified at title 39, chapter 17 of the Louisiana Revised Statutes (RS), sections 39:1551–:1755, and is divided into the following nine parts:

Part 1. General Provisions (RS §§ 39:1551–:1558)
Part 2. Purchasing Organization (RS §§ 39:1561–:1590)
Part 3. Source Selection and Contract Formation (RS §§ 39:1593–:1648)
Part 4. Specifications (RS §§ 39:1651–:1658)
Part 5. Modification and Termination of Contracts for Supplies, Services, and Major Repairs (RS §§ 39:1661–:1662)
Part 6. Legal and Contractual Remedies (RS §§ 39:1671–:1697)
Part 7. Intergovernmental Relations (RS §§ 39:1702–:1716)
Part 8. Assistance to Small and Disadvantaged Businesses and Women Owned Businesses (RS §§ 39:1731–:1736)
Part 9. Telecommunications Procurement (RS §§ 39:1751–:1755)

The Procurement Code applies to the procurement of supplies, services, major repairs, and personal, professional, consulting, or social services, as well as the lease of certain equipment and real property by state executive departments and agencies.

1. This summary covers acquisitions governed by the Louisiana Procurement Code. Only limited information is provided for other acquisitions.

Various exceptions are set forth in the statutes, including, inter alia, certain professional and consulting service contracts for the Department of Transportation and Development, and services performed by architects, engineers, or landscape architects. (RS § 39:1554.)

Political subdivisions of the state are authorized, but are not required, to adopt the Procurement Code. (RS § 39:1554(E)(1).) Those that do not choose to do so are governed by the Public Bid Law, RS sections 38:2181–:2320.11.

With certain exceptions, all state procurement activities are now handled by the Office of State Procurement (OSP), located online at https://www.doa.la.gov/doa/osp/.[2]

B. Other Applicable Statutes

1. Public Bid Law

The Public Bid Law, RS sections 38:2181–:2320.11, applies to contracts awarded by public entities for the making of public works, including the construction, alteration, improvement, or repair of any public facility or real property. (RS § 38:2211.) It also applies to other procurements by political subdivisions who have not adopted the Procurement Code. (RS § 39:1554(E)(1).)

2. State Lease-Purchase Act

RS sections 39:1761–:1771 govern the acquisition of essential equipment by the state under equipment-lease-purchase contracts.

3. Telecommunications Procurement

RS sections 39:1751–:1755 govern the procurement of all telecommunications systems and services by state agencies.

4. Contracting Initiatives

Louisiana has the following initiatives designed to encourage participation in state contracting and procurement by historically disadvantaged businesses:

The Louisiana Small Business Procurement Act, RS sections 39:1731–:1736, establishes a set-aside program for small businesses, disadvantaged businesses, and women-owned businesses. The Initiative for Small Entrepreneurships, also known as the "Hudson Initiative," RS sections 39:2001–:2008, requires the commissioner of administration (the "commissioner") to set annual goals for contracting with entities that have been certified by the Department of Economic Development as small entrepreneurships. And the Initiative for Veteran and Service-Connected Disabled Veteran-Owned Small Entrepreneurships, RS sections 39:2172–:2179, requires the commissioner

2. Act 864 of the 2014 Regular Legislative Session merged the Professional, Personal, Consulting, and Social Services Procurement Code (formerly chapter 16 of title 39, RS §§ 39:1481–:1526) into the Procurement Code and placed all authority for state procurement in the OSP, a new centralized purchasing agency, as of January 1, 2015. Prior to that, the Office of Contractual Review handled procurement of professional, personal, consulting, and social services contracts, and the Office of State Purchasing handled other procurements.

to set annual goals for veteran and service-connected disabled veteran-owned small entrepreneurship participation in state procurements and public contracts.

5. Retention and Employment of Attorneys

The procurement of legal services, including the retention and employment of attorneys, by parishes and all state boards and commissions is governed by RS sections 42:261–:264.

6. Licensing

Louisiana's licensing laws are set forth in title 37 of the RS.

7. Public Records Law

The Louisiana Public Records Law, RS section 44:1 *et seq.*, generally provides for a broad right of public access to, inter alia, all documents relating to any state business transactions or concerning the payment of any money under state law, including procurement-related documents.

In addition, the Procurement Code expressly provides that procurement information is a public record under the Public Records Law and shall be available to the public as provided in that statute. (RS § 39:1557.) Further, the Procurement Code provides that required annual reports of procurement actions related to professional, personal, consulting, and social services contracts shall be retained as public records. (RS § 39:1569.) In addition, it is explicitly stated in the regulations that specifications and any written determination or other document generated or used in the development of a specification, as well as any reasons for cancellation of a solicitation, shall be available for public inspection. (Louisiana Administrative Code tit. 34, pt. V, § 103; Louisiana Administrative Code tit. 34, pt. V, § 1307(D).)

Note that under the Public Records Law, proprietary information or trade secrets are exempt from disclosure. (RS § 44:3.2.) This protection could come into play with respect to public records requests for bid proposals or other procurement-related materials.

8. Ethics

The Code of Governmental Ethics is codified at chapter 15, title 42, of the RS at sections 42:1101–:1170, and is enforced by the Louisiana Board of Ethics. The following list identifies those provisions of particular relevance to procurement:

§ 42:1102. Definitions
§ 42:1111. Payment from nonpublic sources
§ 42:1112. Participation in certain transactions involving the governmental entity
§ 42:1113. Prohibited contractual arrangements; exceptions; reports
§ 42:1114.3. Disaster or emergency contracts; prohibition; disclosure
§ 42:1152. Rescission of action of a governmental entity
§ 42:1153. Penalties
§ 42:1154. Civil penalties for illegal payments
§ 42:1155. Penalties for illegal gain; forfeiture of gifts, payments
§ 42:1156. Finding of possible criminal violation

9. Prohibitions in Public Government Contracts and Procurement

Chapters 24 and 25 of title 39 of the RS set forth various prohibitions regarding contracting and procurement. These include prohibitions of bids from or contracts with unlicensed dealers and authorization for public entities to reject low bids from or not award contracts to businesses in which an individual with an ownership interest of 5 percent or more has been convicted of (or entered a plea of not guilty or nolo contendere to) a felony committed in the solicitation or execution of a contract or bid under any Louisiana state procurement laws. (RS §§ 39:2181–:2192.)

II. Regulations

Regulations promulgated by OSP with respect to procurement appear in title 34 of the Louisiana Administrative Code (LAC). The following is the table of contents for part V, Procurement:

OSP also maintains the following manuals, which provide additional guidance with respect to procurement:

- Procurement Handbook (Nov. 2016) (available at https://www.doa.la.gov/media/wlflseyg/procurementhandbook.pdf)
- Vendor Guide: How to Do Business with the State of Louisiana (Apr. 2022) (available at https://www.doa.la.gov/media/z0xfhsov/vendor-guide-final.pdf)
- Request for Proposals Manual (Oct. 2014) (available at https://www.doa.la.gov/doa/osp/agency-resources/osp-purchasing/complex-services-rfp/)

III. Source Selection

Unless otherwise authorized by law, all state contracts must be awarded by one of the following methods of procurement:

A. Competitive Sealed Bidding

1. Applicability

Competitive sealed bidding is generally required by the Procurement Code for contract awards of $25,000 or more; the governor has the power, via executive order, to establish the amounts for which competitive sealed bidding is required. (RS § 39:1594(A); RS § 39:1596; LAC tit. 34, pt. V, § 301(A)(1).) However, contracts for professional or personal services, as well as for consulting services with a total maximum compensation of less than $75,000 for a 12-month period, may be awarded without the necessity of competitive bidding or competitive negotiation. (RS § 39:1617; RS § 39:1620; RS § 39:1621(A); LAC tit. 34, pt. V, § 2542(A).) Further, contracts for consulting services with a total maximum compensation of $75,000 or more for a 12-month period, and social services contracts for $250,000 or more, must be awarded pursuant to a competitive sealed proposals process. (RS § 39:1621(B); LAC tit. 34, pt. V, § 2521(H), (J).)

2. Invitations to Bid

Competitive sealed bidding begins with the issuance of an invitation for bids (ITB) containing a general description of the supplies, services, or major repairs to be procured and all applicable contractual terms and conditions. (RS § 39:1594(B).) ITBs must be on the state's standard forms and must state (1) the date and time when bids will be received, opened, and publicly read; (2) the names and locations of the agencies for which the purchases are to be made; (3) where and how specifications and bid forms may be obtained; (4) the purchase description, evaluation factors, delivery or performance schedule, inspection, and acceptance requirements; (5) the contract terms and conditions; and (6) any special conditions. (LAC tit. 34, pt. V, § 301.)

Addenda modifying ITBs shall not be issued within three business days prior to the opening of bids. If an addendum must be issued within this three-day period, the opening of bids shall be extended one week, without the requirement of re-advertising. Addenda shall be sent to all prospective bidders known to have received an ITB. (LAC tit. 35, pt. V, § 305(A).)

Bidders must be given a reasonable time to prepare their bids. For bids over $25,000, a minimum of ten days should be provided unless the chief procurement officer (CPO) deems a shorter time necessary. (LAC tit. 34, pt. V, § 303(A).)

3. Notice

Adequate public notice must be given of the ITB at least ten days prior to bid opening (20 days for bids for housing of state agencies and certain other state agency activities) by providing notices of solicitation in writing to potential vendors. Advertising of the ITB is required if the amount of the purchase is $25,000 or more. (RS § 39:1594(C).)

4. Bid Requirements

Written bids will not be considered unless they are submitted on, and in accordance with, the provided forms. (LAC tit. 34, pt. V, § 307.A.) As well, written bids must be properly signed and must be received at the address specified in the ITB prior to bid opening time. (*Id.*) Bids that are unsigned or filled out in pencil will not be accepted. (*Id.*)

Prior to the opening of bids, bids may be modified or withdrawn by written notice. (LAC tit. 34, pt. V, § 315(A), (B); RS § 39:1594(G).) A request for the withdrawal of a bid will be granted if it is received prior to the opening of bids. (LAC tit. 34, pt. V, § 315(B).) After the opening of bids, a request to withdraw must be made within three business days after bid opening. (LAC tit. 34, pt. V, § 321(A); RS § 39:1594(G).) In the event of errors that are patent or are supported by clear and convincing evidence, bids may be corrected or withdrawn as long as other bidders are not prejudiced. (RS § 39:1594(G); LAC tit. 34, pt. V, § 321(A).)

Depending on what is in the best interest of the state, the CPO may waive, or allow a bidder to correct, minor informalities.[3] (LAC tit. 34, pt. V, § 321(B).) Informalities are matters of form rather than substance that are evident from the bid document, or insignificant mistakes that can be waived or corrected without prejudice to other bidders (i.e., without significant effect on price, quantity, quality, delivery, or contractual conditions). Examples include, but are not limited to, failure to (1) return the required number of signed bids; (2) sign the bid (but only if the unsigned bid is accompanied by other signed material indicating the bidder's intent to be bound); (3) sign or initial write-overs, or corrections in bids; (4) get an agency's certification that a mandatory jobsite visit was made; and (5) return nonmandatory pages of the bid proposal. (*Id.*)

If the mistake and the intended bid are clearly evident on the face of the bid document, the bid may not be withdrawn but shall be corrected to the intended bid. (LAC tit. 34, pt. V, § 321(C).) Some examples of mistakes that may be clearly evident on the face of the bid document are typographical errors, errors in extending unit prices, unit prices placed in the extended amount column, and failure to return an addendum provided there is evidence that the addendum was received. (*Id.*)

---

3. By contrast, under the Public Bid Law, no bidding requirements may be waived. La. Rev. Stat. § 38:2212(B)(1).

Bid samples or descriptive literature may be required when necessary to evaluate required characteristics of the items bid. (LAC tit. 34, pt. V, § 307(B)(3).) The ITB shall state whether bid samples or descriptive literature should be submitted. (LAC tit. 34, pt. V, § 307(B)(4).) When required, samples must be received not later than the time set or specified for bid opening. (LAC tit. 34, pt. V, § 307(B)(5).) Failure to submit samples within the time allowed will result in disqualification or non-consideration of a bid. (*Id.*)

5. Pre-Bid Conferences

Pre-bid conferences may be conducted to explain the procurement requirements. (LAC tit. 34, pt. V, § 311(A).) Pre-bid conferences shall be announced to all prospective bidders known to have received an ITB, and shall be advertised and/or electronically posted if the contract is over $25,000 and attendance is mandatory. (*Id.*) The conference should be held long enough after the ITB has been issued to allow bidders to become familiar with it, but sufficiently before bid opening to allow consideration of the conference results in preparation of bids. (*Id.*) Nothing stated at the pre-bid conference shall change the ITB unless a change is made by a written addendum. (*Id.*)

6. Opening and Evaluation of Bids

Bids must be publicly opened at the appointed date, time, and place, in the presence of one or more witnesses, must be recorded, and are subject to public inspection. (RS § 39:1594(E); LAC tit. 34, pt. V, § 319(B)(1), (2).) Bids shall be evaluated based on the requirements and evaluation criteria set forth in the ITB; no criteria that are not set forth in the ITB shall be used. (RS § 39:1594(D)(1); LAC tit. 34, pt. V, § 327(A).)

7. Contract Awards

Award must be made with "reasonable promptness" to the lowest responsive and responsible bidder whose bid meets the requirements and criteria set forth in the ITB. (RS § 39:1594(H); LAC tit. 34, pt. V, § 327(A).) Award shall be made by unconditional acceptance of a bid without alteration or correction except as otherwise authorized. (RS § 39:1594(H).)

Awards shall be made in any manner that will discourage tie bids, including consideration of factors such as resident business, proximity, past performance, delivery, and completeness of bid proposal. (LAC tit. 34, pt. V, § 329(C).) Where there is a tie bid, Louisiana businesses receive a preference as long as there will be no loss in quality. (LAC tit. 34, pt. V § 329(B)(1), (C).)

Conditional bids are subject to rejection in whole or in part. (LAC tit. 34, pt. V, § 307(C).) A conditional bid may be accepted if the condition is not a substantial deviation from the ITB. (*Id.*)

Notice of award shall be sent to the successful bidder and made part of the procurement file. (LAC tit. 34, pt. V, § 335(A).) For procurements over $25,000, notice shall also be sent to unsuccessful bidders if they provided a self-addressed stamped envelope requesting this information. (*Id.*)

B. Competitive Sealed Proposals (Requests for Proposals)

1. Applicability

A competitive request for proposals (RFP) process may be utilized for the procurement of either (1) supplies, services, or major repairs; or (2) medical and laboratory supplies and medical equipment required for the purpose of diagnosis or direct treatment of a patient by a health care provider in a hospital or clinic setting (though a group purchasing contract), as long as the commissioner determines the total cost to be less than the state procurement prices and in the best interest of the state. (RS § 39:1595(A)(1).) In addition, the RFP process is required for consulting services contracts with a total maximum compensation of $75,000 or more for a 12-month period, and social services contracts for $250,000 or more. (RS § 39:1621(B); LAC tit. 34, pt. V, § 2521(H), (J).)

To use the RFP process, the commissioner's approval and the state CPO's written determination that the best interests of the state would be served by this method are required. (RS § 39:1595(A)(1).) However, these requirements do not apply to an RFP for professional, personal, consulting, or social services. (RS § 39:1595(A)(1)(c).)

2. Notice

The agency must give adequate public notice of the RFP by advertising in the state's official journal at least 30 days before the last day that proposals will be accepted. (RS § 39:1595(A)(2).) In addition, the agency shall mail written notice to firms who are known to be in a position to furnish the required services at least 30 days before the last day that proposals will be accepted. (*Id.*) Further, all RFPs must be advertised through a centralized electronic interactive environment administered by the Division of Administration; the advertisement shall establish the specific date, time, and place by which the RFPs must be received. (RS § 39:1595(B)(4).) Certain additional public notices are required depending on the type of contract. (RS § 39:1595(B)(1)–(3).)

3. RFP Requirements

All RFPs must indicate the relative importance of price and other evaluation factors; clearly define the tasks to be performed under the contract and the desired results; state the criteria, selection, methodology, and weight to be applied to each significant evaluation criterion to be used in evaluating the proposals' responsiveness to the RFP; and, except for consulting, social, and professional services RFPs, clearly state the technological or other outcome desired from the procurement of the supplies, services, or major repairs. (RS § 39:1595(B)(5).) RFPs must also specifically define the task and desired results of the project; identify agency liaison personnel and resources available to the contractor; state the approximate time when the contractor can begin the work as well as an estimate of the time necessary to accomplish the work (if available); specify the time frames within which the work must be started and completed; and specify applicable procedures concerning billing, documentation requirements, progress reports, and final reports. (LAC tit. 34, pt. V, § 2545(A)(1).)

Additional information that RFPs must require potential contractors to include in their proposals is listed in the regulations. (LAC tit. 34, pt. V, § 2545(A)(1)(g).)

4. Written or Oral Discussions

Written or oral discussions shall be conducted with all responsible proposers whose proposals are determined in writing to be reasonably susceptible of being selected for award. Discussions shall not disclose any information derived from proposals submitted by competing proposers. (RS § 39:1595(B)(7).)

Discussions need not be conducted if (1) prices are fixed by law or regulation; (2) time of delivery or performance will not permit discussions; or (3) it can be clearly demonstrated that acceptance of an initial offer without discussion would result in fair and reasonable prices, and the RFP states that award may be made on the basis of initial offers. (*Id.*)

5. Contract Award/Approval

Final selection of a contractor shall be made in accordance with the RFP's selection criteria. (LAC tit. 34, pt. V, § 2545(A)(2).) Contract award shall be made to the responsible proposer whose proposal is determined in writing by the agency to be the most advantageous to the state, taking into consideration price and the evaluation factors set forth in the RFP. (RS § 39:1595(B)(8)(a).)

No contract may be enforced against the state until OSP has approved it. (RS § 39:1595(B)(11)(b)(i).) When a final selection has been made and prior to notice of award, the contract file, including the RFP, along with a selection memorandum justifying the final selection, shall be sent to OSP for final approval. (LAC tit. 34, pt. V, § 2545(A)(2).) The selection memorandum shall include, but not be limited to (1) a list of criteria used along with the weight assigned each criteria; (2) scores of each proposal considered in each of the categories listed above, along with overall scores of each proposal considered; and (3) a narrative justifying selection. (*Id.*) After final negotiation and execution, the contract shall be sent to OSP for final review and approval. (LAC tit. 34, pt. V, § 2545(A)(3).)

C. Small Purchases

Purchases not exceeding $30,000 may be made in accordance with the small purchase procedures set forth in Executive Order No. JBE 2020-21. (The executive order is available at https://gov.louisiana.gov/assets/ExecutiveOrders/2020/JBE-2020-21-Small-Purchases-Amending-JBE-2017-18.pdf; see also RS § 39:1596; LAC tit. 34, pt. V, § 701(A).) The dollar amount of the procurement determines the specific procedures that must be followed.

D. Reverse Auctions

1. Applicability

Reverse auctions may be utilized for the acquisition of materials, supplies, services, products, or equipment where the CPO finds that the best interests of the state would be served. (RS § 39:1600(D).)

2. Notice

Adequate public notice of a reverse auction must be given. (RS § 39:1600(D)(3).) The notice or advertisement notice shall conform to the requirements for public notice of sealed bidding or small purchases as applicable, pursuant respectively to RS section 39:1594 or section 39:1596. (*Id.*)

It is the responsibility of the bidder to obtain any solicitation amendment(s) if the solicitation and addenda are posted on the Louisiana Procurement and Contract Network (LaPAC). (LAC tit. 34, pt. V, § 505(B).)

3. Vendor Registration and Qualification

Prior to the use of a reverse auction, the CPO may require vendors to register before the opening date and time and agree to any terms and conditions and other requirements of the solicitation. (LAC tit. 34, pt. V, § 503(B)(1).) The CPO may also require in the solicitation language that only bidders who are prequalified be allowed to submit bids. (LAC tit. 34, pt. V, § 503(B)(2).)

4. The Bidding Process and Requirements

The solicitation shall designate an opening and closing date and time. (LAC tit. 34, pt. V, § 503(B)(3).) The closing date and time may be fixed or remain open depending on the nature of the item being bid. (*Id.*) At the opening date and time, the agency shall begin accepting online bids and continue accepting bids until the bid is officially closed. (LAC tit. 34, pt. V, § 503(B)(4).) Registered bidders shall be allowed to lower the price of their bid below the lowest bid posted on the internet until the closing date and time. (*Id.*) Bidders' identities shall not be revealed during the bidding process; only the successively lower prices, ranks, scores, and related bid details shall be revealed. (LAC tit. 34, pt. V, § 503(B)(5).)

All bids shall be posted electronically and updated on a real-time basis. (LAC tit. 34, pt. V, § 503(B)(6).) In the event that multiple bidders submit identical prices for the same goods or services, the bid received first will be considered to be the lowest. Any other identical bids received later will be considered in the order received. (LAC tit. 34, pt. V, § 511(A).) Bidders may submit multiple prices during the event. (LAC tit. 34, pt. V, § 507(A).) The lowest price offered will become the price portion of the bid response. (*Id.*)

The awarding authority may reject any bid, in whole or in part, if (1) bids are not in compliance with the requirements, specifications, terms, or conditions as stated in the reverse auction; (2) the price of the lowest responsive and responsible bid exceeds the amount budgeted for the procurement; or (3) it is determined that awarding any item is not in the best interest of the agency/department. (LAC tit. 34, pt. V, § 513(A).)

After the auction is over, the event record will be available to the public. (LAC tit. 34, pt. V, § 515(A).)

E. Sole Source Contracts

The CPO may authorize sole source procurements when he or she determines in writing that there is only one source for the required supply, service, or major repair item, and when such procurement is in the best interest of the state. (RS § 39:1597; LAC tit. 34, pt. V, § 905(A)(1).) This determination shall be final and conclusive unless clearly erroneous, arbitrary, capricious, or contrary to law. (RS § 39:1630).

A requirement for a particular proprietary item does not justify a sole source procurement if there is more than one potential bidder or offeror for that item. (LAC tit. 34, pt. V, § 905(A)(2).) Examples of circumstances that could necessitate sole source procurement include where the compatibility of equipment, accessories, or replacement parts is the paramount consideration and where a sole supplier's item is needed for trial use or testing. (*Id.*) Other examples are listed in the regulations. (*Id.*)

F. Emergency Contracts

1. Applicability

Emergency procurements are authorized where there exists an imminent threat to the public health, welfare, safety, or public property under emergency conditions creating an immediate and serious need for supplies, services, or major repairs that cannot be met through normal procurement methods and the lack of which would seriously threaten the functioning of state government, the preservation or protection of property, or the health or safety of any person. (RS § 39:1598; LAC tit. 34, pt. V, § 1103(A).) Emergency conditions may arise by floods, epidemics, riots, equipment failures, or such other reason as may be proclaimed by the CPO. (LAC tit. 34, pt. V, § 1103(A).)

Emergency procurements may also be made if emergency conditions exist as a result of an unsuccessful attempt to use competitive sealed bidding, such as where bids received pursuant to an ITB are unreasonable, noncompetitive, or the low bid exceeds available funds, and time or other circumstances will not permit the delay required to re-solicit competitive sealed bids. (LAC tit. 34, pt. V, § 1109(B).)

2. Procedures

The procurement method shall be selected with a goal of assuring that the required supplies, services, or major repair items are procured in time to meet the emergency. (LAC tit. 34, pt. V, § 1109(A).) Nevertheless, such competition as is practicable should be obtained. Every effort shall be made to obtain quotations from three or more vendors when supplies, services, or major repairs are to be purchased on an emergency basis. (*Id.*) Emergency procurement shall be limited to only those supplies, services, or major repair items necessary to meet the emergency. (LAC tit. 34, pt. V, § 1105(A).)

The CPO shall make a written determination of the basis of the emergency, the steps taken prior to selecting a particular contractor, and the basis for the final selection. (RS § 39:1598(C).) The written determination shall be included in the contract file, either prior to contracting or as soon thereafter as practicable. (*Id.*) This determination shall be final and conclusive unless clearly erroneous, arbitrary, capricious, or contrary to law. (RS § 39:1630).

The Division of Administration has published a handbook summarizing the rules and procedures governing emergency procurements, "Helpful Information about Louisiana Emergency Procurement" (rev. Sept. 2020). It is available at https://www.doa.la.gov/media/j4enytfo/emergencyprocurement.pdf.

G. Other Procurement Methods

1. Unstable Market Conditions

Procurements may be made under this section for contracts under $50,000 when it is determined by the CPO that market conditions are unstable and the competitive bid process is not conducive to the best pricing for products, supplies, and other materials. (RS § 39:1600(A).) Written responses must be solicited from at least three bona fide bidders. (*Id.*)

2. Group Purchasing

The Louisiana State University (LSU) Health Sciences Center is authorized to contract with a group purchasing organization (GPO) through a competitive RFP process for medical and laboratory supplies and medical equipment in a hospital or clinic setting. (RS § 39:1600(B)(1).) Prior to award, the proposed contract shall be approved by the commissioner, provided that LSU Health Sciences Center makes a written determination that prices from the GPO are fair market prices and that the contract is in the best interest of the state. (RS § 39:1600(B)(2).)

No later than 60 days after an agency submits a proposed contract to the commissioner for approval, the commissioner shall notify the agency in writing as to whether the proposed contract has been approved or rejected. (RS § 39:1600(B)(3).) If the commissioner does not timely notify the agency of his or her decision, the request shall be deemed approved. (*Id.*) The commissioner shall not unreasonably withhold approval. (*Id.*)

3. Used Equipment

Any agency may procure used equipment where it can demonstrate to the satisfaction of the CPO that the procurement is cost effective to the state. (RS § 39:1600(C)(1).) The head of the agency shall certify in writing all of the following: (1) the price for which the used equipment may be obtained; (2) the plan and cost for maintenance and repair of the equipment; (3) the savings that will accrue to the state because of the purchase; and (4) the fact that following the procedures set out in the Procurement Code will result in loss of the opportunity to purchase the equipment. (RS § 39:1600(C)(2)(b).)

H. Responsibility

Before awarding a contract, the procurement officer must be satisfied that the prospective contractor is responsible. (LAC tit. 34, pt. V, § 1509(A).) A responsible bidder is one who has the capability in all respects to perform fully the contract requirements, and the integrity and reliability that will assure good faith performance. (LAC tit. 34, pt. V, § 1501.)

Factors to be considered in making a responsibility determination include, but are not limited to, whether a prospective contractor (1) has adequate financial, material, equipment, facility, and personnel resources and expertise, or the ability to obtain them, necessary to meet all contractual requirements; (2) has the necessary experience, organizations, technical qualifications, skills, and facilities, or the ability to obtain them; (3) is able to comply with the proposed time of delivery or performance schedule; (4) has a satisfactory record of integrity, judgment, and performance; and (5) is otherwise qualified and eligible to receive an award under applicable laws and regulations. (LAC tit. 34, pt. V, § 1505(A); LAC tit. 34, pt. V, § 2536(A).)

The prospective contractor shall supply information requested by the procurement officer concerning its responsibility. If the contractor fails to supply the requested information, the procurement officer shall base the determination of responsibility upon any available information or may find the prospective contractor nonresponsible if such failure is unreasonable. (RS § 39:1606(A); LAC tit. 34, pt. V, § 1505(B).)

A responsibility determination is final and conclusive unless clearly erroneous, arbitrary, capricious, or contrary to law. (RS § 39:1630.)

If a bidder or offeror on a contract of $5,000 or more is found to be nonresponsible, a written determination of nonresponsibility setting forth the basis of the finding shall be prepared by the CPO. Whenever the CPO proposes to disqualify the lowest bidder on bids of $5,000 or more, the CPO shall (1) give written notice of the proposed disqualification to such bidder and include in the written notice all reasons for the proposed disqualification, and (2) give such bidder a reasonable opportunity to be heard at an informal hearing. (RS § 39:1606(B); LAC tit. 34, pt. V, § 1511(B).)

IV. Bid Protests and Contract Disputes

A. Bid Protests

Any person who is aggrieved in connection with the solicitation or award of a contract may protest to the CPO. (RS § 39:1671(A).) Protests with respect to a solicitation shall be submitted in writing at least two days prior to the opening of bids on all matters except with respect to housing of state agencies, for which protests shall be submitted at least ten days prior to the opening of bids. (*Id.*) Protests with respect to a contract award shall be submitted in writing within 14 days after contract award. (*Id.*)

The CPO is authorized to settle and resolve the protest prior to the commencement of a court action. (RS § 39:1671(B).) If the protest is not resolved by mutual agreement, the CPO shall, within 14 days, issue a written decision stating the reasons for the action taken and informing the protesting party of its right to administrative and judicial review. (RS § 39:1671(C).) The written decision shall be mailed or otherwise provided immediately to the protesting party and any party that has intervened. (RS § 39:1671(D).) This decision shall be final and conclusive unless it is fraudulent or an administrative appeal has been timely filed. (RS § 39:1671(E).)

If it is determined prior to award that a solicitation or proposed contract award is in violation of law, then the solicitation or proposed award shall be cancelled. (RS § 39:1677.) If it is determined after an award that a solicitation or contract award is in violation of law, and the person awarded the contract has not acted fraudulently or in bad faith, then (1) the contract may be ratified and affirmed, provided it is determined in writing by the commissioner that doing so is in the best interests of the state and the violation had no significant effect on the outcome of the contract award, or (2) the contract may be terminated and the person awarded the contract compensated for the actual expenses reasonably incurred prior to termination. (RS § 39:1678(1).) If the person awarded the contract has acted fraudulently or in bad faith, the contract shall be declared null and void. (RS § 39:1678(2).)

Where a protest is timely filed, the state shall not proceed further with the solicitation or award of the contract unless the CPO makes a written determination that the awarding of the contract is necessary without delay to protect the substantial interests of the state. Upon such determination, no court shall enjoin progress under the award except after notice and hearing. (RS § 39:1671(F)).

B. Bid Protest Appeals

Appeals of protest decisions must be filed with the commissioner within seven days of receipt of the CPO's decision. (RS § 39:1683(B).) The commissioner must issue a written decision within 14 days whether the solicitation or award was in accordance with the constitution, statutes, regulations, and the terms and conditions of the solicitation. (RS § 39:1693(C).) The decision is final and conclusive unless it is fraudulent or the person adversely affected has timely appealed to the court in accordance with RS section 39:1691(A). (RS § 39:1683(E).)

C. Contract Disputes

1. Proceedings before the CPO or Commissioner

Any contractor who seeks a remedy with regard to any claim arising under a contract with the state, including relating to breach of contract, mistake, misrepresentation, or any other cause of contract modification or rescission, shall file a complaint with the CPO. (RS § 39:1673(A).) However, for professional, personal, consulting, and social services contracts, such complaints shall be raised with the commissioner. (RS § 39:1672.3.)

Prior to the institution of any court action, the CPO (or the commissioner, in the case of professional, personal, consulting, and social services contracts) is authorized to settle and resolve the controversy, with the approval of the attorney general. (RS § 39:1673(B); RS § 39:1672.2.) If the controversy is not resolved by mutual agreement, the CPO (or the commissioner) shall promptly issue a written decision that shall state the reasons for the action taken and inform the contractor of its right to appeal. (RS § 39:1673(C); RS § 39:1672.3.)

The decision shall be final and conclusive unless it is fraudulent or the contractor has timely appealed administratively to the commissioner (or, in the case of professional, personal, consulting, and social services contracts, has instituted a judicial action). (RS § 39:1673(E); RS § 39:1672.3.)

If the commissioner does not issue a written decision within 120 days after written request for a final decision, or the CPO does not issue a written decision within 60 days after written request, then the contractor may proceed as if an adverse decision had been received. (RS § 39:1673(F); RS § 39:1672.3.) The parties may agree in writing to a longer period in which to issue a final decision after written request. (RS § 39:1673(F); RS § 39:1672.3.)

2. Administrative Appeals

For professional, personal, consulting, and social services contracts, there is no administrative appeal process; the commissioner makes the initial administrative decision, and from there the aggrieved contractor may proceed to court. (RS § 39:1672.3.)

For other contracts, an administrative appeal shall be filed with the commissioner within 14 days of the receipt of the CPO's decision. (RS § 39:1685(B).) The commissioner shall issue a decision within 14 days. (RS § 39:1685(C).) The decision shall be final and conclusive unless the decision is fraudulent or the contractor has timely appealed to the court. (RS § 39:1685(E).) Any prior determination by the CPO shall not be final or conclusive. (RS § 39:1685(C).)

D. Suspension and Debarment

1. Proceedings before the CPO

After providing reasonable notice and an opportunity to be heard, the CPO can suspend or debar a person for cause from consideration for award of contracts, provided that doing so is in the best interests of the state. (RS § 39:1672(B); LAC tit. 34, pt. V, § 2539(A).) The CPO may suspend a person if there is probable cause to believe that he or she has engaged in any activity that might lead to debarment. (RS § 39:1672(B).) The suspension shall not exceed six months. (*Id.*)

Causes for debarment include (1) conviction for a criminal offense as an incident to obtaining, attempting to obtain, or performing under a public or private contract or subcontract; (2) conviction under state or federal statutes of embezzlement, theft, forgery, bribery, falsification or destruction of records, receipt of stolen property, or any other offense indicating a lack of business integrity or honesty that currently, seriously, and directly affects responsibility; (3) conviction under state or federal antitrust statutes arising out of the submission of bids or proposals; (4) violation of contract provisions of a character so serious as to justify debarment action, which includes deliberate failure without good cause to perform in accordance with the contractual specifications or time limit and a recent record of failure to perform or of unsatisfactory performance in accordance with the terms of one or more contracts (although if the failure to perform or unsatisfactory performance is caused by acts beyond the control of the contractor, this shall not be a basis for debarment); (5) any other cause so serious and compelling as to affect responsibility, including debarment by another governmental entity; and (6) violation of the ethical standards set forth in the Code of Governmental Ethics. (RS § 39:1672(C).)

The CPO shall issue a written decision to debar or suspend, which shall contain reasons for the action taken and inform the person involved of his or her right to administrative and judicial review. (RS § 39:1672(D).) The decision is final unless it is fraudulent or the debarred or suspended person has timely appealed administratively to the commissioner. (RS § 39:1672(F).)

2. Administrative Appeals

An administrative appeal must be filed within 14 days of receipt of the CPO's decision. (RS § 39:1684(B).) After an appeal is filed, the commissioner shall decide within 14 days whether the debarment or suspension was in accordance with the constitution, statutes, regulations, and best interests of the state, and was fair. (RS § 39:1684(C).) Any prior determination by the CPO shall not be final or conclusive. (*Id.*)

If the commissioner finds that the CPO erred, he or she may reinstate the individual or business. If the commissioner affirms the decision of the CPO, that decision is final and conclusive unless it is fraudulent or the debarred or suspended person has timely appealed to the court. (RS § 39:1672(F).)

Upon request of a debarred individual or business, the CPO shall review their file on an annual basis, and may reinstate the contractor for future consideration if the circumstances warrant reinstatement and it would be in the best interest of the state. (LAC tit. 34, pt. V, § 2539(B).)

V. Administrative and Judicial Review

A. Administrative Review

Administrative review of bid protests, contracts claims, and suspensions and debarment proceedings have been detailed above. No party may seek court review without exhausting their administrative remedies before the pertinent agency and/or the commissioner.

B. Judicial Review

The 19th Judicial District Court shall have exclusive venue over suspension and debarment actions, bid protest appeals, and actions under contracts or for breach of contract. (RS § 39:1691(A), (B), (C).) Such actions include those for declaratory, injunctive, or other equitable relief and, in the case of bid protests, actions for monetary damages. (*Id.*)

Actions on bid protests must be filed within 14 days after receipt of the commissioner's decision. (RS § 39:1692(A); RS § 39:1691(A).) Actions under contracts, as well as actions challenging debarments or suspensions, must be commenced within 60 days after receipt of the decision of the commissioner. (RS § 39:1692(B), (C); RS § 39:1691(B), (C).)

No breach of contract action may be brought by a contractor based on any contract or any act of any state officer that the officer is not authorized to make or do, unless the contractor, acting in good faith and without actual or constructive knowledge of the lack of authorization, has commenced performance under the contract. (RS § 39:1672.4(B).) In that event, the court may (1) cancel the contract and reimburse the contractor only for the actual expenses incurred for work already performed, or (2) allow the performance of the contract to continue, where the best interests of the state require. (*Id.*)

In judicial proceedings, factual or legal determination by employees or agents of the state shall have no finality and shall not be conclusive, notwithstanding any contract provision, regulation, or rule of law to the contrary, except to the extent otherwise provided in the Procurement Code. (RS § 39:1691(D).)

For the most part the district court will function as an appellate court in reviewing a decision of the commissioner. In doing so, the court will generally limit its review to the administrative record. (*Metro Riverboat Associates, Inc. v. Louisiana Gaming Control Board*, 2001-0185, p. 7 (La. 10/16/01); 797 So. 2d 656, 661.) An agency is afforded a great deal of discretion and its decision will be upheld unless it was made in violation of the law or the agency's authority, is irrational, or is arbitrary and capricious. (RS § 49:964(F); *Haughton Elevator Division v. State*, 367 So. 2d 1161, 1165 (La. 1979); *Bowers v. Firefighters' Retirement System*, 2008-1268, p. 4 (La. 3/17/09); 6 So. 3d 173, 176.)

Any party may appeal a decision of the 19th Judicial District Court to the court of appeal, First Circuit, or the Supreme Court of Louisiana, as otherwise permitted in civil cases. (RS § 39:1691(E).)

C. Damages

If a bid protest is sustained, the bidder or offeror shall be entitled to its reasonable costs incurred in connection with the solicitation, including bid preparation costs other than attorney's fees. (RS § 39:1678.1(A).) On a contract claim, a contractor may only recover the actual expenses reasonably incurred in performance of the contract. (RS § 39:1678.1(B).)

In no event shall damages include attorney's fees or any incidental, indirect, special, or consequential damages, including but not limited to loss of use, revenue, or profit, whether reasonably certain or not. (RS § 39:1678.1(E).)

Any administrative determination of recoverable costs or expenses is subject to the written concurrence of the attorney general. (RS § 39:1678.1(D).)

VI. Extent of State's Adoption or Adaptation of ABA Model Procurement Code

The Louisiana Procurement Code, originally adopted in 1980, is closely modeled after the American Bar Association's (ABA's) initial version of the Model Procurement Code for State and Local Governments.

VII. Cooperative Purchasing

A. Authority

Any public procurement unit may participate in a cooperative purchasing agreement for the acquisition or use of any supplies, services, major repairs, facilities, or construction with one or more public procurement units or external procurement activities or one or more private procurement units in accordance with an agreement entered into between the participants. (RS § 39:1702(A)(1); RS § 39:1704; RS § 39:1705.)

Any public procurement unit may procure materials, supplies, and equipment from federal General Services Administration (GSA) supply schedules in accordance with rules and regulations. (RS § 39:1702(A)(2).) Such purchases need not comply with competitive bidding requirements; however, such materials, supplies, or equipment shall not be purchased at a price higher than the price of the same item listed on any available state purchasing contract. (*Id.*) Any public procurement unit may procure materials, supplies, equipment, and services related to homeland security from GSA supply schedules. (RS § 39:1702(A)(3).)

B. Requirements

Public procurement units may not enter into a cooperative purchasing agreement for the purpose of circumventing the Louisiana Procurement Code. (RS § 39:1708.)

To the extent possible, the CPO shall collect information concerning the type, cost, quality, and quantity of commonly used supplies, services, major repairs, or construction being procured or used by state public procurement units. (RS § 39:1709.) Although not required, the CPO may also collect such information from local public procurement units. (*Id.*)

Maine Procurement Rules and Regulations

Prepared by A. Robert Ruesch
Verrill, LLP
Email: rruesch@verrill-law.com

I. Statutory Reference[1]

A. Procurement/Purchasing Statutes

1. Construction

The State of Maine's procurement of construction and design services is handled through the Bureau of General Services (BGS), a division of the Department of Administrative and Financial Services. The state has a statutory framework to address prequalification of contractors on public projects. Key statutes include Maine Revised Statutes Annotated (MRSA) title 5, section 1741 *et seq*. The following is a table of contents for these statutes:

§ 1741.	Definitions
§ 1742.	Powers and Duties
§ 1742-B.	Municipal Building Ordinances
§ 1742-C.	Institutions of Higher Education
§ 1742-D.	Bureau of General Services; Real Property Leases
§ 1742-E.	Bureau of General Services; Asbestos, Lead, and Indoor Air Quality Assessment and Mitigation Services
§ 1743.	Public Improvement Construction Contracts
§ 1743-A.	Competitive Bids; Advertisement
§ 1743-B.	Design of Buildings
§ 1743-C.	Information to Bidders on Public Improvement Projects
§ 1745.	Advertisement for Sealed Proposals; Bonds
§ 1746.	Retention of Part of Contract Price
§ 1747.	Questionnaire as Prebid Qualification
§ 1748.	Procedure if Answers Unsatisfactory

1. All statutes can be accessed through the Maine Legislature website at http://www.mainelegislature.org/legis/statutes/search.htm or through Westlaw and LexisNexis.

§ 1749.	Procedure for Contractor
§ 1751.	Employment of a Clerk-of-the-Works
§ 1752.	Centrally Leased Space and Food Vending
§ 1753.	Employment of Owner's Representative

2. Procurement of Goods, Services, Supplies, and Equipment

The Division of Procurement Services (DPS), a division of the Department of Administrative and Financial Services, has the primary responsibility for the procurement of materials, supplies, equipment, and services for the State of Maine. DPS has responsibility to make purchases on behalf of all departments and agencies of the state government. DPS has the authority to adopt and enforce specifications that apply to services, supplies, materials, and equipment purchased for the use of the state or any department or agency. DPS also has control over the awarding of state building construction and improvement projects and school building contracts.

The commissioner of the Maine Department of Transportation (DOT) has authority over procurement of transportation-related contracts generally related to roads, bridges, and highway construction and improvements.

Maine's primary legislation concerning the power and authority for public procurement of materials, supplies, equipment, and services is found at MRSA title 5, sections 1811–1826-C. Following is the table of contents for those statutory provisions:

§ 1811.	Powers and Duties
§ 1812.	Scope of Purchasing Authority
§ 1812-A.	Report on Purchase of Recycled Products
§ 1812-B.	Purchasing of Paper and Paper Products
§ 1812-C.	Use of Composted and Recycled Organic Materials and Reclaimed Soil and Residuals
§ 1812-D.	Coordination of Procurement Information and Policies
§ 1812-E.	Purchasing of Vehicles; Fuel Efficiency
§ 1812-F.	Water Conservation Devices; Purchase and Installation
§ 1812-G.	Payment for Hotel Rooms
§ 1813.	Rules and Regulations
§ 1815.	Requisitions Required
§ 1816-A.	Personal Services Contracting
§ 1817.	Printing of Laws
§ 1818.	Deliveries
§ 1819.	Unlawful Purchases
§ 1820.	Motor Vehicles Sold by State
§ 1821.	Purpose
§ 1825.	Prohibitions

Maine law, MRSA title 5, sections 1825-A–1825-J, requires that public procurement of certain materials, supplies, equipment, and services be governed by a competitive bidding process. Following is the table of contents for those statutory provisions:

§ 1825-A.	Definitions
§ 1825-B.	Bids, Awards, and Contracts

§ 1825-C.	Rulemaking
§ 1825-D.	Public Notice and Review of Bids
§ 1825-E.	Appeal Procedures
§ 1825-F.	Final Agency Action
§ 1825-G.	Failure to Act
§ 1825-H.	Deadline for Adoption of Rules
§ 1825-I.	Consultants
§ 1825-J.	Reports

Maine's legislation governing state purchasing code of conduct for suppliers of apparel, footwear, or textiles is found at MRSA title 5, sections 1825-K–1825-T. Following is the table of contents for those statutory provisions:

§ 1825-K.	Application of State Purchasing Code of Conduct to Certain Bidders Seeking Contracts as Part of Competitive Bid Process; Affidavit Required
§ 1825-L.	State Purchasing Code of Conduct
§ 1825-M.	Exception
§ 1825-N.	Support to Suppliers of Goods and Services
§ 1825-O.	Rulemaking
§ 1825-P.	Report
§ 1825-Q.	Complaints of Noncompliance with Code of Conduct; Investigations of Complaints
§ 1825-R.	Determinations of Noncompliance with Code of Conduct
§ 1825-S.	Consequences of Noncompliance with Code of Conduct

Maine's legislation regarding transportation related to the DOT's procurement and letting of all contracts for transportation-related services is found at MRSA title 23, sections 4206, 4241–4244.

MRSA title 30-A, section 124 provides that any contract for construction, renovation, or improvement of county buildings or facilities involving a total cost of $2,500 or more must be awarded by a system of competitive bidding.

B. Other Applicable Statutes

The following statutes relate to public procurement in Maine:

1. MRSA title 5, section 1587 applies to leases and/or purchase of buildings or equipment above $2,000 ($40,000 for telecommunications-related equipment).
2. MRSA title 5, sections 1766 and 1767 apply to contracts for energy services and third-party financing.
3. MRSA title 20-A, section 15915 applies to contracts for energy services and third-party financing by a school administrative unit.
4. MRSA title 5, sections 11001–11008 provide the rights to and rules governing appeals of public procurement decisions. Following is the table of contents for that statute:

§ 11001.	Right to Review
§ 11002.	Commencement of Action
§ 11003.	Service

§ 11004. Stay
§ 11005. Responsive Pleading; Filing of the Record
§ 11006. Power of Court to Correct or Modify Record
§ 11007. Manner and Scope of Review
§ 11008. Appeal to Law Court

5. MRSA title 30-A, section 903 applies to county authority to enter into an agreement with a private party, such as an energy service or third-party financing company, for the design, installation, operation, maintenance, and financing of energy conservation improvements at county facilities.
6. MRSA title 30-A, section 5656 establishes requirements for each municipality to review its procurement procedures and specifications to identify procedures and specifications that explicitly discriminate against goods, supplies, equipment, materials, and printing with recycled content.
7. MRSA title 30-A, section 3001 establishes broad local[2] authority for any municipality, by the adoption, amendment, or repeal of ordinances or bylaws, to exercise any power or function that the legislature has power to confer upon it, which is not denied either expressly or by clear implication, and to exercise any power or function granted to the municipality by the Constitution of Maine, general law, or charter.
8. MRSA title 5, section 1831 requires that every department or agency of the state purchasing services or awarding grants or contracts that are not subject to the authority of the Department of Administration or the Maine Turnpike Authority, as defined in MRSA title 5, section 1741 *et seq.* and section 1811 *et seq.*, establish a procedure by which these services are purchased, or by which grants or contracts are awarded. This procedure must be adopted in accordance with chapter 375 of the Maine Administrative Procedure Act (MRSA tit. 5, § 8001 *et seq.*), and must be approved by the state purchasing agent prior to their adoption. Thus, in addition to the main statutes as herein outlined, there are department or agency-related rules that must meet the standards of public notice, administrative review, and rights to appeal as set forth in MRSA title 5, section 1825-A *et seq.*

The following government orders, guidance, and policy relate to procurement:

- Competitive bidding (MRSA tit. 5, § 1825-B), http://www.mainelegislature.org/legis/statutes/5/title5sec1825-B.html
- Sweat-free clothing code of conduct (MRSA tit. 5, § 1825-L), http://www.mainelegislature.org/legis/statutes/5/title5sec1825-L.html
- Purchasing of paper and paper products (MRSA tit. 5, § 1812-B), http://www.mainelegislature.org/legis/statutes/5/title5sec1812-B.html
- DPS Policy on the Purchasing of Paper and Paper Products
- Work centers and rehabilitation facilities (MRSA tit. 5, § 1826-C), http://www.mainelegislature.org/legis/statutes/5/title5sec1826-C.html
- Lease-purchase agreements (MRSA tit. 5, § 1587), http://www.mainelegislature.org/legis/statutes/5/title5sec1587.html

2. *See generally* Ryan Almy, State v. Brown: *A Test for Local Food Ordinances*, 65 ME. L. REV. 789, 795 (2013) ("Maine is a 'home rule' state, and grants its municipalities a plenary power to exercise, by ordinance or otherwise, any constitutionally granted power or function not expressly or implicitly denied by the Legislature.").

II. Regulations

18-554 Code of Maine Rules (CMR) chapter 1, sections 1–4 provide DPS procedures for the procurement of professional architectural and engineering services for projects that exceed $25,000. (Statutory authority: MRSA tit. 5, § 1742(6).)

18-554 CMR chapter 8, sections 1–5 govern the implementation of DPS's authority to establish procedures, in addition to those established by statute, for procuring and awarding construction contracts using alternative project delivery methods such as construction manager or design-build contracts. (Statutory authority: MRSA tit. 5, § 1743.)

18-554 CMR chapter 11, sections 1–2, 21–22, and 31 apply only to DPS's single-source procurement of professionals for services involving expenditures not exceeding $25,000. (Statutory authority: MRSA tit. 5, § 1742(6).)

18-554 CMR chapter 101 prohibits any department, agency, commission, or institution of state government from purchasing products made by any manufacturer or their affiliates determined not to be a responsible bidder and further specifies that the manufacturer or their affiliates in historic and continuing violation of labor laws are not responsible bidders. (Statutory authority: MRSA tit. 5, § 1813(8), in conjunction with MRSA tit. 5, § 1825-B(7).)

18-554 CMR chapter 110, sections 1–3 provide DPS regulations regarding rules, procedures, and the award of grants and contracts. (Statutory authority: MRSA tit. 5, § 1825-C.)

18-554 CMR chapter 120, sections 1–4 provide the procedures and criteria to be used in the appeal of contract or grant awards, outlines the appointment of an appeal committee, describes procedures to be used in hearing an appeal, and details how appellants will be notified of final agency action. (Statutory authority: MRSA tit. 5, §§ 1825-C, -D, -E, -F.)

18-554 CMR chapter 130, sections 1–7 supplement the state purchasing code of conduct, as set forth in MRSA title 5, section 1825-K *et seq.*, and applies to competitive bids for sale of apparel, footwear, or textiles pursuant to MRSA title 5, C. 155, sub-c. I-A. Additionally, as set forth in MRSA title 5, section 1825-B, it establishes a fee for vendors for developing a consortium to monitor and investigate alleged violations of the code of conduct. (Statutory authority: MRSA tit. 5, §§ 1825-O, 1825-B.)

18-554 CMR chapter 150, sections 1–4 define the way contractors and subcontractors are to provide specified records to DPS and identify the types of information in such records that may be made publicly available. This regulation is applicable to public improvements for which proposals, plans, specifications, contracts, inspections, or renovations are subject to the approval of DPS, except for such improvements made by school administrative units, including construction, repair, or renovation of school buildings. (Statutory authority: MRSA tit. 26, §§ 1311, 1312.)

18-554 CMR chapter 155, part one, sections 1–2, part two, sections 1–2, and part three, sections 1–2 provide BGS's rules governing the equitable selection of contractor personal services. (Statutory authority: MRSA tit. 5, §§ 1816-A, 1825-B.)

17-229 CMR chapter 105, sections 105.01–.11 set forth the rules used by the DOT to suspend a contractor's right to bid on construction contracts. (Statutory authority: MRSA tit. 23, §§ 52, 4206(5).)

17-229 CMR chapter 102, sections 102.01–.07 set forth the rules used by the DOT for considering debarment of contractors. (Statutory authority: MRSA tit. 23, §§ 4204, 4206.)

III. Source Selection

A. Purchases by Competitive Bidding—Goods

The director of DPS must purchase all goods and services for the state or any department or agency of the state in a manner that best secures the greatest possible economy consistent with the required grade or quality of the goods or services. Purchases of goods or services by the state or any department or agency of the state must be made by competitive bidding unless waived as set forth below. Except as otherwise provided by state law, all contracts and grants are to be awarded to the best-value bidder, taking into consideration the quality of the goods or services to be supplied, their conformity with the specifications, the purposes for which they are required, the date of delivery, and the best interest of the state. If the bidder that was initially awarded the order, grant, or contract does not perform, the director of DPS may cancel the contract or grant and award a new contract or grant to the second-best-value bidder. The order, contract, or grant may not be awarded to a bidder who was not in compliance at the time the initial bid was submitted. (MRSA tit. 5, § 1825-B(7).)

Competitive bidding requires the state to transmit a written proposal or invitation to bid to at least three responsible suppliers. If the state finds that three responsible bidders are not available, the state may make exceptions as are in the best interests of the state. (MRSA tit. 5, § 1825-A(3).)

Under MRSA title 5, section 1825-B(2), the requirement of competitive bidding may be waived by the director of DPS when:

> (A) The procurement of goods or services by the State for county commissioners . . . involves the expenditure of $2,500 or less, and the interests of the State would best be served;
>
> (B) The Director of the Bureau of General Services is authorized by the Governor or the Governor's designee to make purchases without competitive bidding because in the opinion of the Governor or the Governor's designee [expressed in a written approval] an emergency exists that requires the immediate procurement of goods or services (See Executive Order No. 26, FY 11/12.);
>
> (C) After reasonable investigation by the Director of the Bureau of General Services, it appears that any required unit or item of supply, or brand of that unit or item, is procurable by the State from only one source;
>
> (D) It appears to be in the best interest of the State to negotiate for the procurement of petroleum products;
>
> (E) The purchase is part of a cooperative project between the State and the University of Maine System, the Maine Community College System . . . involving
>
> > (1) An activity assisting a state agency and enhancing the ability of the university system, community college system, Maine Maritime Academy or a private, nonprofit, regionally accredited institution of higher education with a main campus in this State to fulfill its mission of teaching, research and public service; and
> >
> > (2) A sharing of project responsibilities and, when appropriate, costs;

(F) The procurement of goods or services involves expenditures of $10,000 or less, in which case the Director of the Bureau of General Services may accept oral proposals or bids; or

(G) The procurement of goods or services involves expenditures of $10,000 or less, and procurement from a single source is the most economical, effective and appropriate means of fulfilling a demonstrated need.

1. Registry of Suppliers

DPS maintains a list of suppliers. Suppliers desiring to have their names entered on the registry of suppliers may submit a request to the director of DPS in writing. The name of any supplier entered in the registry who fails to submit a bid on three consecutive proposals or invitations to bid may be removed from the registry at the discretion of the director. (MRSA tit. 5, § 1825-B(4).)

2. Request for Proposals

A Contract Review Committee, established by Executive Order No. 7, FY 10/11, reviews agency documents and actions related to contracts for special services. All contracts issued under the review of the Contract Review Committee that do not qualify as sole source or emergency procurements must be competitively bid using a request for proposals (RFP). The RFP must contain at a minimum a clear definition of the project, the evaluation criteria and relative scoring weights to be applied, the proposal opening date and time, and agency contact person. Cost of the contract must be included in the evaluation criteria and must receive a minimum of 25 percent of the total weight of all criteria. All proposals are opened publicly at the Division of Purchases' main office. Proposals received at the Division of Purchases' main office after the advertised opening time are to be rejected, unless the advertised opening date and time have been extended by the director of the Division of Purchases due to circumstances requiring such an extension of time. RFPs must be submitted to the Contract Review Committee for review prior to release. RFPs are advertised for a minimum of three consecutive days in the *Kennebec Journal* of Augusta, allowing a minimum of 15 calendar days from the final day of advertising to the proposal opening date. Pre-bidders conferences are allowed, but are not required. No alterations or changes to any requirement or specification within the original RFP can be made without notifying all bidders in writing a minimum of seven calendar days before the opening date. (18-554 CMR ch. 110, §§ 1–5.)

3. Alternate Bids

When under section 1825-B(5) an article or material is identified by the bid invitation or specification by using a trade name and catalog number of a manufacturer or vendor, the term "or approved equal," if not inserted with the identification, is implied. There is an express statutory "presumption that any reference to a particular manufacturer's product either by trade name or by limited description has been made solely for the purpose of more clearly indicating the minimum standard of quality desired." Consideration must be given to proposals submitted on approved equal alternate commodities to the extent that such action serves the best interest of the state. The bidder submitting a proposal based on an "equal" commodity must furnish complete identification, descriptive literature, or data with respect to the alternate commodity. Lack of such information on the bid is to be construed to mean that the bidder proposes to furnish the exact commodity described.

4. Tie Bids

Under section 1825-B(8), contracts or purchases may be awarded to or made from in-state bidders or to bidders offering commodities produced or manufactured in the state if the price, quality, availability, and other factors are equivalent.

5. Determination of Best-Value Bidder

In determining the best-value bidder, a percent increase may be added on the bid of a nonresident bidder equal to the percent, if any, of the preference given to that bidder in the state in which the bidder resides. The director of DPS must prepare and publish a list of states with local preferences or any department or agency of the state may rely on that list in determining the best-value bidder without incurring any liability to any bidder. (MRSA tit. 5, § 1825-B(9), (10).)

6. Vendor's Fee

The state purchasing agent may collect a fee in an amount equal to 1 percent of the bid from a supplier of apparel, footwear, or textiles with a winning bid under section 1825-B(12). The fee is then applied to the costs of implementing and administering the state purchasing code of conduct, including developing a consortium to monitor and investigate alleged violations of the code of conduct.

7. Condition of Doing Business with the State

Under section 1825-B(14), any purchase by the state of $100,000 or more of tangible personal property, except for public utility purchases or emergency purchases, may be made only from a person who is registered as a seller under MRSA title 36, section 1754-B (which governs Maine's sales and use tax requirements). As a condition of doing business with the state the seller must collect, report, and remit taxes. The state is prohibited from doing business with a person who is not registered as a seller and is not in compliance with the requirement to collect, report, and remit taxes. After notification of the award, the seller must provide the state purchasing agent with a valid retailer certificate issued by the state tax assessor within seven business days. If the seller fails to provide the registration certificate within seven business days, the state purchasing agent may cancel the award and make a new award. The state purchasing agent must provide the state tax assessor with a copy of all contracts awarded. The state tax assessor is required to notify the state purchasing agent if at any time during the term of the contract the person is no longer registered or is not collecting, reporting, and remitting taxes in compliance with these requirements. Until the noncompliance is corrected, the state purchasing agent may withhold any payments to the person.

8. Unlawful Purchases

Whenever any department or agency of the state government contracts for the purchase of services, supplies, materials, or equipment contrary to statute, rules, or regulations, such contract is void and has no effect. In such a case, the head of such department or agency is personally liable for the costs. If such services, supplies, materials, or equipment are so unlawfully purchased and paid for out of state monies, the amount may be recovered in the name of the state in an appropriate action. (MRSA tit. 5, § 1819.)

9. Performance Bonds

The state must maintain a record of all bids. The director of BGS may also require a bond for the proper performance of each successful bidder. (MRSA tit. 5, § 1825-B(6).)

10. Public Notice and Review of Bids; Changes to Bid Initiation

The state purchasing agent is required to make the public aware of contracts and/or grants for which bids are being requested and the procedure to be used in reviewing bids. (MRSA tit. 5, § 1825-D.) The state must notify all bidders in writing in the event of any significant change in the content, nature, or requirements of any proposal or invitation and allow bidders sufficient time to reflect such changes in their bids.

11. State Purchasing Code of Conduct

All bidders seeking contracts and/or grants to supply the state must sign an affidavit affirming, to the best of its knowledge, that suppliers at the point of assembly comply with workplace laws of the vendor's or supplier's site of assembly and with treaty obligations that are shared by the United States and the country in which the goods are assembled. Any contract or grant with the state requires the contracting party to comply with all applicable wage, health, labor, environmental, and safety laws; legal guarantees of freedom of association; building and fire codes; and laws relating to discrimination in hiring, promotion, or compensation on the basis of race, disability, national origin, gender, sexual orientation, or affiliation with any political, nongovernmental, or civic group except when federal law precludes the state from attaching the procurement conditions. (MRSA tit. 5, § 1825-L.)

B. Personal Services Contracting

Personal services contracting is permissible under MRSA title 5, section 1816-A when any one of the following is met:

> A. The services contracted are not currently available within a state agency, can not be performed satisfactorily by civil service employees or are of such a highly specialized or technical nature that the necessary expert knowledge, experience or ability is not available through the civil service system.
>
> B. The services are incidental to a contract for the purchase or lease of real or personal property. [Such incidental services] include, but are not limited to, agreements to service or maintain office equipment or computers that are leased or rented.
>
> C. The legislative, administrative or legal goals and purposes can not be accomplished by using persons selected pursuant to the civil service system. Contracts are permissible under this criterion to protect against a conflict of interest or to ensure independent and unbiased findings when there is a clear need for a different outside perspective.
>
> D. A state agency needs private counsel because a conflict of interest on the part of the Department of the Attorney General prevents it from representing the agency without compromising the agency's position . . . .

E. The contractor provides equipment, materials, facilities or support services that the State cannot feasibly provide in the location where the services are to be performed.

F. The contractor conducts training courses for which appropriately qualified civil service instructors are not and can not be made available.

G. The services are of such an urgent, temporary or occasional nature that the delay incumbent in implementation under civil service would frustrate the purpose.

H. The contracting agency demonstrates a quantifiable improvement in services that can not be reasonably duplicated within existing resources.

Personal services contracting is permissible to achieve actual cost savings when all the following conditions are met. The contracting agency must clearly demonstrate that the proposed contract would result in actual overall cost savings to the state as long as, in comparing costs:

(1) The State's costs of providing the same service as proposed by a contractor are included. These costs must include the salaries and benefits of additional staff that would be needed and the cost of additional space, equipment and materials needed to perform the service; and

(2) Any continuing state costs directly associated with a contractor providing a contracted function are included. These continuing state costs include, but are not limited to, those costs for inspection, supervision, monitoring and any pro rata share of existing costs or expenses, including administrative salaries and benefits, rent, equipment costs, utilities and materials.

(MRSA tit. 5, § 1816-A.) Additional considerations include:

- The contract does not adversely affect the state's affirmative action efforts.
- The contract is awarded in accordance with section 1825-B.
- The contract includes specific provisions pertaining to the qualifications of the staff that is to perform the work under the contract, as well as a statement that the contractor's hiring practices meet applicable affirmative action and antidiscrimination standards.
- The potential for future economic risk to the state from potential rate increases or work interruptions by the contractor is minimal.
- The contract is with a firm or a licensed, registered, or otherwise professionally qualified individual. For the purposes of this section, "firm" means a corporation, partnership, nonprofit organization, or sole proprietorship.
- The potential economic advantage of contracting is not outweighed by the public's interest in having a particular function performed directly by state government.
- The contract does not contain standards of performance or employee qualifications lower than existing state standards or minimum qualifications.
- An equivalent basis for cost comparison between state employee and private contractor provision of services is calculated, as established by rules adopted by the state purchasing agent pursuant to section 1825-B, subsection 11, and it is determined that the private contractor provides the best value.

(MRSA tit. 5, § 1816-A(2)(B)–(I).)

IV. Bid Protests and Contract Disputes

A. Bid Protests

Under MRSA title 5, section 1825-E, the director of BGS is required to ensure that every department or agency of state government affords aggrieved persons an opportunity to appeal an award decision.

1. Stay

An aggrieved bidder may request a stay of the state's award decision under section 1825-E(1). Such a request must be made to the director of BGS in writing within ten days of notification of the award and must state the nature of the grievance. The director must issue a stay of an award decision, pending appeal, upon a showing of irreparable injury to the petitioner, a reasonable likelihood of success on the merits, and no substantial harm to adverse parties or to the general public. The director must notify the petitioner in writing of the director's decision regarding the issuance of a stay within seven days of receipt of the request. Failure of the petitioner to obtain a stay does not affect the petitioner's right to a hearing of appeal.

B. Bid Protest Appeals

Persons aggrieved by an agency award decision may request a hearing of appeal to the director of BGS in writing within 15 days of notification of the award. The director shall grant a hearing of appeal unless the director determines that (1) the petitioner is not an aggrieved person as defined in section 1825-A(1); (2) a prior request by the same petitioner relating to the same award has been granted; (3) the request was made more than 15 days after notice of the award; or (4) the request is capricious, frivolous, or without merit. A hearing is not required if no award was granted in the first place. An "aggrieved person" is any person who bids on a contract or grant and who is adversely affected, financially, professionally, or personally, by that award decision. (MRSA tit. 5, § 1825-A(1).)

The director must notify the petitioner in writing of the director's decision regarding a request for a hearing of appeal within 15 days of receipt of the request. If a request for a hearing is granted, notification must be made at least ten days before the hearing date and must include the date and location of the hearing and the names of the appeal committee members.

1. Appeal Committee

A committee of three members shall hear a petitioner's appeal within 60 days of receipt of the request for an appeal. The commissioner of Administrative and Financial Services appoints two members of an appeal committee. Persons who have any direct or indirect personal, professional, or financial conflict of interest in the appeal or employees of any department affected by the contract or grant may not serve on the appeal committee. The third member of the committee is the director of BGS or the director's designee.

Members of an appeal committee meet at the appointed time and place in the presence of the petitioner and such individuals as the petitioner determines necessary for a full and fair hearing. The petitioner may present to the appeal committee any materials the petitioner considers relevant to the appeal. The appeal committee must keep a written record of each hearing and submit its decision and the reasons for its decision to the director of BGS in writing no later than 15 days following the hearing of appeal. The appeal committee may decide either to validate the award decision under appeal, or invalidate the award decision under appeal. The committee may not modify the award under appeal, or make a new award. Contracts or grants found invalid by an appeal committee become immediately void and of no legal effect. (MRSA tit. 5, § 1825-E(3).)

2. Final Agency Action

Decisions made by an appeal committee constitute final agency action on the petitioner's appeal for the purposes of judicial review. The state purchasing agent is required to notify a petitioner of a final agency action made in writing within seven days of the final agency action. Notification of final agency action must include a brief summary of the nature of the petitioner's appeal; notification of the decision of the appeal committee; an explanation of the reasons for the decision; and an explanation of the petitioner's right to judicial review of a final agency action. (MRSA tit. 5, § 1825-F.)

C. Contract Claims

Contract claims must be raised and resolved in accordance with the dispute resolution provisions clause set forth in the contract. Absent dispute resolution requirements in the contract, parties have recourse in Maine's superior or district courts or federal court as the facts and circumstances may allow.

D. Suspension and Debarment

In certain instances, the state reserves its right to debar contractors for violations of law. The Department of Labor may debar contractors from participation in state contracts for two years for serious, willful, or repeated violations of federal Occupational Safety and Health Administration (OSHA) standards. (MRSA tit. 26, § 1402.) In addition, under MRSA title 38, section 349-B, the commissioner of the Maine Department of Environmental Protection (DEP) may debar contractors, developers, or others from participating in contracts with the DEP for repeated violation of permits or licenses issued by the DEP.

Contractors doing business with the state must also comply with the state tax requirements regarding reporting and remitting taxes in accordance with MRSA title 36, section 1751 *et seq*. Noncompliance with state tax obligations can result in the state withholding payments. Companies doing business with the state in regard to contracts for textiles, footwear, and apparel must honor the state's code of conduct under MRSA title 5, section 1825-L. Failure to comply with the state's code of conduct can result in termination of the contract under MRSA title 5, section 1825-S(2).

In addition to these statutes, the Maine DOT and BGS have authority through their prequalification process to eliminate contractors who have failed to satisfy prequalification criteria identified in their requirements. (See MRSA tit. 5, §§ 1747–1749.) The Maine DOT prequalification requirements are set forth in its standard specifications.

V. Administrative and Judicial Review

A. Administrative Review

The administrative review process is set forth above.

B. Judicial Review

Any person who is aggrieved by final agency action is entitled to judicial review in the superior court under the Maine Administrative Procedure Act, MRSA title 5, section 11001 *et seq*. Preliminary, procedural, intermediate, or other nonfinal agency action is independently reviewable only if review of the final agency action would not provide an adequate remedy. The relief available in the superior court includes an order requiring the agency to make a decision within a time certain. (MRSA tit. 5, § 11001.) Maine's Rules of Court 80B and 80C also govern procedural aspects for judicial review.

1. Commencement of Proceedings

Proceedings for judicial review of final agency action or the failure or refusal of an agency to act are instituted by filing a petition for review in the superior court for the county where one or more of the petitioners reside or have their principal place of business; the agency has its principal office; or the activity or property that is the subject of the proceeding is located. The court may grant a change of venue for good cause shown. (MRSA tit. 5, § 11002.)

2. Contents of Petition

The petition for review must specify the persons seeking review, the manner in which they are aggrieved, and the final agency action or agency inaction that they wish reviewed. It must also contain a concise statement as to the nature of the action or inaction to be reviewed, the grounds upon which relief is sought, and a demand for relief, which may be in the alternative. (MRSA tit. 5, § 11002.)

3. Deadline to File Petition

The petition for review must be filed within 30 days after receipt of notice if taken by a party to the proceeding of which review is sought. Any other person aggrieved has 40 days from the date the decision was rendered to petition for review. If the review sought is from an agency's failure or refusal to act, the petition for review must be filed within six months of the expiration of the time within which the action should reasonably have occurred. (MRSA tit. 5, § 11002.)

4. Service

The petition for review must be served by certified mail, return receipt requested, upon the agency, all parties to the agency proceeding, and the attorney general. (MRSA tit. 5, § 11003.)

5. Stay by the Court

The filing of a petition for review in superior court does not operate as a stay of the final agency action pending judicial review. Application for a stay of an agency decision may ordinarily be made first to the agency, which may issue a stay upon a showing of irreparable injury to the petitioner, a strong likelihood of success on the merits, and no substantial harm to adverse parties or the general public. A motion for stay of an agency decision may be made to the superior court, but the motion must show that application to the agency for the relief sought is not practicable, or that application has been made to the agency and denied. In addition, the motion must show the reasons for the relief requested and the facts relied upon. These facts, if subject to dispute, must be supported by affidavits. Reasonable notice of the motion is to be given to all parties to the agency proceeding. The court may condition relief under this rule upon the posting of a bond or other appropriate security. However, no bond or security is required of the state or any state agency or any official. (MRSA tit. 5, § 11004.)

6. Responsive Pleading

No responsive pleading needs to be filed unless required by order of the reviewing court. The agency is required to file in the reviewing court within 30 days after the petition for review is filed, or within such shorter or longer time as the court may allow on motion. Within 20 days after the petition for review is filed, all parties to the agency proceeding who wish to participate in the review must file a written appearance stating a position with respect to affirmance, reversal, or modification of the decision under review. (MRSA tit. 5, § 11005.)

7. Manner and Scope of Review

The court is not to substitute its judgment for that of the agency on questions of fact. The court may affirm the decision of the agency; remand the case for further proceedings, findings of fact, or conclusions of law; or direct the agency to hold such proceedings or take such action as the court deems necessary. The court may also reverse or modify the decision if the administrative findings, inferences, conclusions, or decisions are in violation of constitutional or statutory provisions; in excess of the statutory authority of the agency; made upon unlawful procedure; affected by bias or error of law; unsupported by substantial evidence on the whole record; or arbitrary or capricious or characterized by abuse of discretion. (MRSA tit. 5, § 11007.)

8. Appeal to Supreme Judicial Court

Any party to the review proceeding in the superior court may obtain review by appeal to the Maine Supreme Judicial Court. In this case the appeal will be taken as in other civil cases. The Supreme Judicial Court has the power to make and amend rules of pleading, practice, and procedure, for the purposes of securing a simple, speedy, and effective judicial review. (MRSA tit. 5, § 11008.)

C. Judicial Decisions

1. De-Appropriation of Funds

There are several relevant cases. In *SC Testing Technology, Inc. v. Department of Environmental Protection*, 688 A.2d 421 (Me. 1996), Maine's Supreme Judicial Court upheld a summary judgment ruling in favor of the state when the DEP canceled a contract for construction and operation of automobile emissions control inspection facilities. In this case DEP, following an RFP process, awarded a contract for automobile emissions testing to the claimant. The claimant undertook construction of various automobile emissions testing centers in southern Maine. In response to a public outcry about the automobile emissions testing program, the state cancelled the contract. The trial court rejected the claimant's lawsuit for compensation in connection with its efforts to construct and operate the emissions testing system on the basis of a note in the state's RFP, which provided: "In the event the Maine Legislature repeals all or part of the program, the Department and the State shall bear no responsibility to compensate the Contractor." In reaching this conclusion, the court held that the language in the RFP was incorporated into the final contract between the claimant and the state. The court also relied on general law that "when a party enters into a contract with a State agency, it does so with the understanding that the Legislature may at some time in the future take action that nullifies the subject matter of the contract and, necessarily, the respective performance obligations of the parties." (*SC Testing Technology, Inc.*, 688 A.2d at 424.)

Also of note in regard to the ability of the legislature to de-appropriate funding for a project is *KHK Associates v. Department of Human Services*, 632 A.2d 138 (Me. 1993). In this case, KHK was awarded a contract to lease a building to the Department of Human Services for ten years. Relying upon the lease, KHK constructed a building to the Department's specifications. During the first year of the lease, the legislature, in response to budgetary constraints, reduced the appropriation for the building's lease and required renegotiation of the lease. KHK and the Department did not successfully renegotiate the lease. The Department terminated the lease agreement. KHK sued for breach of the lease. The court found for the Department on the basis of the lease provision stating that the Department's performance was "subject to available budgetary appropriations." (*KHK Associates*, 632 A.2d at 140.) The court premised its ruling on article V, paragraph 3, section 4 of the Maine Constitution, which requires that state contracts be subject to funding by the legislature.

2. Agency Discretion

In order to overturn a bid award, the bid protestor has the burden to establish that the government's decision in awarding the contract or grant was arbitrary and capricious. (*Help-U-Sell, Inc. v. Maine Real Estate Commission*, 611 A.2d 981, 984 (Me. 1992).) Arbitrary and capricious conduct by an administrative agency means willful and unreasoning action, without consideration of facts or circumstances. The burden of proof rests with a party seeking to overturn an administrative decision. Where there is room for two opinions, action is not arbitrary or capricious when exercised honestly and upon due consideration, even though it may be believed that an erroneous conclusion has been reached.

Municipalities have considerable discretion when it comes to deciding what constitutes their best interest in awarding a contract or grant, and, as a general rule, courts will interfere only if there is fraud, favoritism, or corruption. Disappointed bidders do not have a property interest unless the applicable law or regulation mandated that the contracting body accept the bid and gave it no discretion whatsoever to reject the bid. (*Dineen v. Town of Kittery*, 639 A.2d 101 (Me. 1994).)

VI. Extent of State's Adoption or Adaptation of ABA Model Procurement Code

Maine has not adopted the American Bar Association's (ABA's) Model Procurement Code. (See National Association of State Procurement Officials (NASPO), 2020 Survey of State Procurement Practices, https://www.naspo.org/research-innovation/publications/survey-state-procurement-practices/.)

VII. Cooperative Purchasing

A. Authority

BGS is authorized to undertake cooperative purchasing pursuant to MRSA title 5, section 1811(8). The statute provides that BGS has authority

> [t]o permit any political subdivision or school administrative district in the State or nonprofit free health care clinic that provides free primary or preventative services to make purchases of foodstuffs, materials, equipment and supplies through the Bureau of General Services, subject to such procedures, rules and regulations as may be prescribed by the director. This subsection applies to a municipality notwithstanding any provision in its municipal charter to the contrary . . . .

(MRSA tit. 5, § 1811(8).)

B. Requirements

Maine, through DPS, is a member of NASPO for the purpose of cooperative purchasing with other states who have similar procurement processes. Through NASPO's ValuePoint cooperative, DPS can directly participate in a procurement process. A multi-state team of procurement and subject matter experts cooperate in the creation of the solicitation, which is conducted by a lead state, in full compliance with that state's laws and procedures, including public notice requirements.

The following links provide more information regarding NASPO and the contracts that Maine is currently participating in: https://www.maine.gov/dafs/bbm/procurementservices/reports/multi-state-cooperative-purchasing and https://www.naspovaluepoint.org/.

Maryland Procurement Rules and Regulations

Prepared by C. Scott Maravilla[1]
Federal Aviation Administration
Email: cmaravilla@hotmail.com

I. Statutory Reference

A. Procurement/Purchasing Statutes

Laws governing Maryland state procurement as well as some aspects of local and county procurement can be found in division II of the State Finance and Procurement Article of the Maryland Code, titles 11 through 19 (also known as "General Procurement Law"). Division II is organized in the following titles:

Title 11	Definitions; General Provisions
Title 12	Organization and Supervision of State Procurement
Title 13	Source Selection—State Procurement Contracts
Title 14	Preferences
Title 15	Procurement Contract Administration and Dispute Resolution
Title 16	Suspension and Debarment of Contractors
Title 17	Special Provisions—State and Local Subdivisions
Title 18	Living Wage
Title 19	Commercial Nondiscrimination Policy

Division II identifies the institutional structures that implement procurement. Pursuant to article XII of the Maryland Constitution and the Maryland Code, Maryland state procurement is under the control and supervision of the Board of Public Works, a body composed of the governor, the state treasurer, and the comptroller. (See Annotated Code of Maryland, State Finance and Procurement § 12-101.) The Board has plenary authority over all procurement, with various exceptions. It controls the award of most contracts and the approval of most change orders.

Three major developments impacted Maryland procurement. First, a 1976 statute waived the doctrine of sovereign immunity in written contracts. (See Annotated Code of Maryland, State Finance and Procurement § 12-201.) Second, the Maryland Code introduced standard clauses and methods of source selection. (See Annotated Code of Maryland, State Finance and Procurement §§ 13-217–13-219.) Third, Maryland established the Maryland State Board of Contract Appeals (MSBCA). The MSBCA has

1. Prior editions prepared by Erica J. Geibel and Scott Livingston.

jurisdiction to handle bid protests and claims arising out of contracts. (See Annotated Code of Maryland, State Finance and Procurement § 15-201 *et seq.*)

B. Other Applicable Statutes

1. Lobbying

Maryland law requires individuals attempting to influence executive action on a procurement contract exceeding $100,000, including attorneys, to register as an "executive lobbyist." (See Annotated Code of Maryland, General Provisions § 5-702.) On October 1, 2014, the Maryland State Ethics Commission issued guidance to procurement agencies, vendors, and lobbyists reviewing the Public Ethics Law addressing lobbying registration requirements applicable to procurement and business grants. The statutory references cited in the guidance are located in the Maryland Code, General Provisions Article, title 5, subtitle 7.

2. Pay-to-Play

Maryland law requires public contractors to file campaign contribution disclosure reports with the State Board of Elections. (Annotated Code of Maryland, Election Law § 14-101 *et seq.*)

3. Maryland Department of Transportation Minority Business Enterprise/Disadvantaged Business Enterprise Program

The Code of Maryland Regulations (COMAR) incorporates by reference the Maryland Minority Business Enterprise Program Manual to govern the Maryland Department of Transportation (MDOT) Minority Business Enterprise/Disadvantaged Business Enterprise (MBE/DBE) Program. (See COMAR 11.01.10.01.)

4. Video Lottery Facility Location Commission

The Video Lottery Facility Location Commission (VLFLC) is responsible for awarding video lottery operation licenses to qualified applicants through a competitive procurement process. Laws governing the structure and duties of the VLFLC can be found in Annotated Code of Maryland, State Government, section 9-1A-36.

5. University System of Maryland

The University System of Maryland, Morgan State University, and St. Mary's College of Maryland are not governed by the procurement laws set forth in the Maryland Code or COMAR. Rather, the University of Maryland System has published procurement regulations at section VIII-3.00 of the System's Policies and Procedures that are nearly identical to the procurement regulations governing other executive agencies. (Section VIII-3.00 may be found at https://www.usmd.edu/regents/bylaws/SectionVIII/VIII300.pdf.)

6. The Board of Public Works Procurement Advisories

The Board of Public Works issues advisories, which can be found on the Board's web page, https://bpw.maryland.gov/Pages/advisories.aspx. The website explains that the advisories provide "clarification for State Agencies on items important to Board oversite and functions." The advisories are meant to act as guidance for agencies to help "decipher requirements in procurement, reporting, definitions, [and] Agenda submissions."

7. Governor's Office of Performance Improvement

The Governor's Office of Performance Improvement (which originated as the Governor's StateStat Office) is a performance measurement and management tool. (See Annotated Code of Maryland, State Finance and Procurement § 3-1001 *et seq.*) The Office strives to increase the responsiveness and level of customer service of state agencies and departments; regularly review procedures, rules, and regulations of state agencies and departments to increase their efficiency and effectiveness; and promote business process improvement strategies to make government more efficient and responsive to taxpayers. Additional information can found on the website at https://gopi.maryland.gov/.

II. Regulations

COMAR title 21, State Procurement Regulations, governs procurement. (See COMAR 21.01.01.01 *et seq.*) Title 21 is organized in the following subtitles:

Subtitle 01. General Provisions
Subtitle 02. State Procurement Organization
Subtitle 03. State Procurement Regulations and Contracts
Subtitle 04. Specifications
Subtitle 05. Procurement Methods and Project Delivery Methods
Subtitle 06. Contract Formation and Award
Subtitle 07. Contract Terms and Conditions
Subtitle 08. Suspension and Debarment
Subtitle 09. Contract Cost Principles and Procedures
Subtitle 10. Administrative and Civil Remedies
Subtitle 11. Socioeconomic Policies
Subtitle 12. Procurement of Architectural Services and Engineering Services
Subtitle 13. Procurement Reporting Requirements
Subtitle 14. Procurement of Human, Social, Cultural, and Educational Services

III. Source Selection

A. Methods of Source Selection

Division II of the State Finance and Procurement Article of the Maryland Code, title 13, Source Selection—State Procurement Contracts, identifies the methods of source selection. In general, Maryland law requires procurement by competitive sealed bids, but does allow the use of other methods including competitive sealed proposals. (Annotated Code of Maryland, State Finance and Procurement § 13-102.) Maryland also employs multi-step sealed bidding, where bidders first submit unpriced technical offers or samples for review, after which price bids will be opened on all acceptable offers or samples. (COMAR 21.05.02.17.) Maryland limits the use of sole source procurement. In general, a procurement officer must determine that there is only one available source for the subject of a procurement contract to award the procurement without competition. (Annotated Code of Maryland, State Finance and Procurement § 13-107.)

Per competitive sealed bid procedures, a procurement officer drafts the specifications, publishes the solicitation, and awards the contract to the responsible bidder or offeror submitting either (1) the lowest bid price; (2) if the invitation for bids so provides, the lowest evaluated bid price; or, in some cases, (3) the bid most favorable to the state. (See Annotated Code of Maryland, State Finance and Procurement § 13-103.)

Competitive sealed proposal procedures require a procurement officer to seek proposals by issuing a request for proposals. The request for proposals is required to include the scope of the contract; the factors, including price, that will be used in evaluating proposals; and the relative importance of each factor. (Annotated Code of Maryland, State Finance and Procurement § 13-104(b).) The procurement officer will award the contract to the responsible offeror whose submission is most advantageous to the state considering the evaluation factors in the request for proposals. (Annotated Code of Maryland, State Finance and Procurement § 13-104(f).)

Under the competitive sealed proposals process, the procurement officer may make a determination that a proposal is "not reasonably susceptible of being selected for award." (COMAR 21.05.03.03B.) If a proposal is so determined, the proposal is effectively rejected and will be excluded from the remainder of the procurement.

In making a determination of the most advantageous offer under competitive negotiation, often an evaluation committee will make an initial recommendation for award to the procurement officer after reviewing proposals. (COMAR 21.05.03.03A(6).) The procurement officer makes the final decision as to award of the contract. (*Id.*) The agency may choose to hold discussions with offerors deemed reasonably susceptible for award, but discussions are not required. (Annotated Code of Maryland, State Finance and Procurement § 13-104; COMAR 21.05.03.03C.)

When a contract is to be awarded on some basis other than price alone, unsuccessful offerors may submit a written request for a debriefing from the procurement officer, which must occur prior to the contract award being presented for approval by the agency head or Board of Public Works. (COMAR 21.05.03.06.) The debriefing focuses on the deficiencies found in the disappointed offeror's proposal, and may lead to grounds for protest of award.

B. Procurement Preferences

Division II of the State Finance and Procurement Article of the Maryland Code, title 14, Procurement of Human, Social, Cultural, and Educational Services, provides a number of procurement preferences for certain sources of supply and services. Most notably, Maryland requires that agencies provide maximum contracting opportunities to certified MBEs, as both prime contractors and subcontractors. (See COMAR 21.11.03.01; Annotated Code of Maryland, State Finance and Procurement § 14-302.) In 2012, the Maryland General Assembly extended the MBE Program for four years and, in doing so, made several changes to the existing law. The MBE goals are now established on a biennial basis and are reevaluated every two years. If new goals are not established, the prior year's goals will apply. The 2015 regulations require procurement agencies to try to award 29 percent of the agency's total contract dollars to MBEs. (COMAR 21.11.03.01.)

Pursuant to COMAR 21.11.03.09, offerors must accurately complete and submit an MBE utilization and fair solicitation affidavit and an MBE participation schedule with their bid or proposal, listing the offeror's specific commitment to MBE subcontractors. Maryland agencies, most notably MDOT and the Department of General Services, consider the content of the MBE participation schedule to be a matter of responsiveness, including the description of work to be performed by each certified MBE listed.

Maryland has two small business procurement programs—the Small Business Preference Program and the Small Business Reserve Program. Maryland's Small Business Preference Program applies to certain procurements designated by agencies as available for the preference. (COMAR 21.11.01.05.) These procurements may include a preference of up to 5 percent for small businesses; 7 percent for certified veteran-owned small businesses; and 8 percent for certified disabled veteran-owned businesses. (COMAR 21.11.01.05B(2)(a).) The Small Business Reserve Program's goal is to provide small businesses with the opportunity to participate as prime contractors on state contracts by limiting competition to other small business and precluding larger, more established companies from competing. (See COMAR 21.11.01.06.)

While Maryland does not apply residency preferences, it does recognize reciprocal preferences. (COMAR 21.05.01.04.) For example, Maryland will apply a reciprocal 1 percent preference for resident bidders against Indiana competitors for construction work over $1,000,000, due to Indiana's resident preference.

IV. Bid Protests and Contract Disputes

A. Bid Protests

Regulations governing protests can be found in COMAR, title 21, subtitle 10, Administrative and Civil Remedies. Protests based on alleged improprieties in a solicitation (e.g., unduly restrictive specifications) must be filed with the procurement officer prior to bid opening or the deadline for submission of initial proposals. (COMAR 21.10.02.03A.)

Protests regarding contract formation must be filed with the procurement officer within seven days after the basis of the protest is known or should have been known to the protestor, whichever is earlier. (COMAR 21.10.02.03B.) Generally, in a competitive sealed bidding procurement, this will likely be seven days after bid opening. In the case of competitive sealed proposals, this time period may begin with the notice of intent to award, or with the debriefing.

B. Bid Protest Appeals

After a final determination from the procurement officer, aggrieved protestors or interested parties may appeal to the MSBCA within ten days of receipt of final agency action. (COMAR 21.10.02.10A.) Maryland agencies may not award a contract and a contract may not be executed during the pendency of a protest or appeal unless the Board of Public Works or delegated agency determines that award is necessary to protect substantial state interests. (COMAR 21.10.02.11.)

Before 2011, the bid protest procedure was not available to challenge an act or omission by the procurement officer concerning the MBE regulations. In 2011, the Court of Special Appeals of Maryland found the regulation to be invalid as ultra vires, because it conflicted with statutes granting contractors aggrieved by agency MBE decisions the right to submit bid protests. (*Salisbury University v. Joseph M. Zimmer, Inc.*, 20 A.3d 838 (Md. Ct. Spec. App. 2011); Annotated Code of Maryland, State Finance and Procurement §§ 15-215, 15-217.)

C. MSBCA

The MSBCA was formed in 1980 out of the Department of Transportation Board of Contract Appeals. The MSBCA is composed of three members with staggering five-year terms. The Board has jurisdiction over protests, contract claims, and final decisions of procurement officers involving the state and its contractors. Decisions of the Board are subject to appeal to the circuit courts of Maryland. All registered business entities that appear before the MSBCA must be represented by counsel. The MSBCA's rules of procedure are found in COMAR title 21, subtitle 10.

1. Protests

An interested party may file a protest in writing with the MSBCA of an award or pending award of a contract. For pre-award protests based on improprieties in the solicitation, a protest must "be filed before bid opening or the closing date for receipt of initial proposals." Otherwise, protests are required to be filed within "7 days after the basis for protest is known or should have been known."

The procurement officer has authority to negotiate with the protester or other interested parties to attempt to resolve the matter. If a settlement is reached, the resulting agreement must be approved by the reviewing authority and the attorney general of Maryland. Maryland also requires protesters to initially try to resolve matters with the agency. An appeal from a final agency action must be filed with ten days of receipt of the notice. A contract may still be awarded pending review by the MSBCA under certain circumstances. These include where the Board of Public Works or the head of an agency finds it "necessary to protect substantial State interests."

2. Contract Claims

Under COMAR, a contractor is required to file a written notice of its claim with the procurement officer "within 30 days after the basis for the claim is known or should have been known." The procurement officer may under "satisfactory" conditions extend the time for filing of the claim. What constitutes satisfactory is at the procurement officer's discretion. If the claim is not filed within the provided timelines, it will be dismissed.

A claim must be in writing and provide (1) an explanation of the claim, including reference to all contract provisions upon which it is based; (2) the amount of the claim; (3) the facts upon which the claim is based; (4) all pertinent data and correspondence that the contractor relies upon to substantiate the claim; and (5) a certification by a senior official, officer, or general partner of the contractor or the subcontractor, as applicable, that, to the best of the person's knowledge and belief, the claim is made in good faith, supporting data is accurate and complete, and the amount requested accurately reflects the contract adjustment for which the person believes the procurement agency is liable.

After the filing of a claim, the procurement officer investigates the allegations, may seek information from the claimant, and consults with the attorney general. There are corresponding procedures for review and investigation of government claims. Appeals to the MSBCA from a procurement officer's final decision must be filed within 30 days of receipt.

D. Contract Disputes

Maryland regulation mandates a disputes clause in each construction contract that requires a contractor to file a written notice of claim in writing with the procurement officer within 30 days after the contractor knew or should have known of the basis for the claim. (COMAR 21.07.02.05-1.) Within 90 days after filing the notice, a contractor must file a written claim detailing the facts supporting the claim. Within 180 days of the claim, the procurement officer will deliver a written decision on the claim to the contractor. An appeal of the procurement officer's decision may be made to the MSBCA. (See COMAR 21.10.06.)

V. Administrative and Judicial Review

A. Administrative Review

The MSBCA was formed in 1980 and, with expanded jurisdiction, replaced the Department of Transportation Board of Contract Appeals. Roughly three-quarters of the MSBCA's decisions involve bid protest appeals. The MSBCA is an administrative agency providing quasi-judicial rulings. The proceedings are on the record and witnesses are subject to cross-examination. In all instances, the MSBCA's decision may be appealed for judicial review as a "contested case" under the Maryland Administrative Procedure Act. (See Annotated Code of Maryland, State Government § 10-201 *et seq.*) The entire bid protest process from initial filing through MSBCA decision generally takes between three to four months, depending on the complexity of the case and any need for discovery during the appeal.

Although disappointed bidders often believe state officials are biased against them, the MSBCA rarely overrules the procurement agency's decision to award a contract on this basis. In *In the Appeals of Yellow Transportation*, Nos. MSBCA 2374, 2380, 2381, 2381 & 2389 (Apr. 9, 2004), government officials committed numerous violations of the procurement regulations, including improper communications between the technical committee members and a preferred vendor. The appeal hearing lasted 22 days, included 21 witnesses, and was the longest bid protest appeal in state history. The bias on the part of the evaluation committee was only uncovered during the appeal's discovery process in the form of email communications, which the MSBCA determined to be "substantive hard facts and evidence of the existence of bias." (*Id.* at 18; *compare In the Appeals of Benton & Associates*, Nos. MSBCA 2196 & 2201, 5 MSBCA ¶ 487 (Nov. 1, 2000) (the Board did not find actual bias where member of evaluation committee served concurrently on a board or commission with an offeror who had oversight on that board of the evaluation committee member).)

B. Judicial Review

Pursuant to Maryland's Administrative Procedure Act, subtitle 2 of the State Government Article, a decision of the MSBCA is a "contested case," which is subject to a petition for judicial review in circuit court. (See Annotated Code of Maryland, State Government § 10-222.) Since 1981, there have been relatively few procurement-related opinions of the Court of Appeals of Maryland, the highest court in the state.

Opinions by the MSBCA provide detailed precedent for the resolution of bid protests and claims, especially at the administrative agency level. Federal case law and decisions of the General Accountability Office and various federal Boards of Contract Appeals are considered persuasive precedent by the MSBCA, since Maryland's procurement law is generally derived from federal provisions.

VI. Extent of State's Adoption or Adaptation of ABA Model Procurement Code

The Maryland procurement regulations generally reflect the American Bar Association's (ABA's) Model Procurement Code, which, in turn, corresponds loosely to federal procurement.

VII. Cooperative Purchasing

A. Authority

Maryland law provides for cooperative purchasing among state and local entities for the "joint administration of programs." (Annotated Code of Maryland, State Finance and Procurement § 13-110.)

B. Requirements

The government entities electing to use cooperative purchasing must first execute an intergovernmental cooperative purchasing agreement. The agreement is a contract between at least a government entity and a contractor, and available for use by other governmental units, who need not be original parties to the contract. The agreement is "intended to promote efficiency." It also provides for piggybacking on awarded contracts with the federal government and other states, so long as they are on the same terms and conditions and identical prices.

Before the local government entity may enter into an intergovernmental cooperative purchasing agreement, the statute requires a written determination from a procurement officer that the agreement will, among others, promote efficiency, cost savings, and "is in the best interests of the State." The statute also requires that the procurement officer's determination be posted on the agency's website. If the primary procurement officer consents, the resulting contract must be awarded consistent with Maryland procurement law as if the entity were the sole purchaser, and "all procedures under this Division II, including procedures governing contract claims and protests" apply. Protests and contract claims arising under the agreement will be subject to the terms of the agreement.

Massachusetts Procurement Rules and Regulations

Prepared by Brian J. O'Rourke[1]
Verrill Dana LLP
Email: borourke@verrill-law.com

I. Statutory Reference

A. Procurement/Purchasing Statutes

1. Uniform Procurement Act

Chapter 30B of the Massachusetts General Laws (MGL), the "Uniform Procurement Act," establishes uniform procedures for local governments to use when contracting for supplies, services, and real property. Approximately 1,500 local governmental jurisdictions in Massachusetts (including cities, towns, counties, districts, regional school districts, Horace Mann charter schools, and local authorities, including housing and redevelopment authorities) follow the chapter 30B procedures to award contracts worth billions of dollars each year. (See The Chapter 30B Manual: Procuring Supplies, Services, and Real Property, issued by the Commonwealth of Massachusetts, Office of the Inspector General (Nov. 2016) ("Procurement Manual"), https://www.mass.gov/doc/the-chapter-30b-manual-procuring-supplies-services-and-real-property-legal-requirements/download.)

Chapter 30B establishes procedures to follow for most agreements for supplies and services, dispositions of surplus supplies, and real property acquisitions and dispositions by local governmental bodies. A "governmental body" is defined in the law as a city, town, district, regional school district, county, or agency, board, commission, authority, department, or instrumentality of a city, town, district, regional school district, or county. Chapter 30B does not apply to state agencies, counties that were abolished by MGL chapter 34B, county sheriffs, state colleges and universities, or commonwealth charter schools. Moreover, chapter 30B does not apply to contracts governed by specific provisions of other statutes, such as the public construction bid laws, the designer selection law, or the law governing takings by eminent domain. (Procurement Manual ch. 1.)

1. The author acknowledges the work on the prior editions performed by Kimberly C. Welch, Meridian Law Group.

B. Other Applicable Statutes

(Includes Executive Orders.)

1. Conduct of Public Officials and Employees (MGL ch. 268A)

This chapter can be found at https://www.malegislature.gov/Laws/GeneralLaws/PartIV/TitleI/Chapter268A.

2. Lobbying

a. Lobbying Laws (MGL ch. 3, §§ 39–50)
b. Secretary of the Commonwealth "Lobbying FAQs," https://www.sec.state.ma.us/lob/lobfaq/lobfaq.htm

3. Small Business Purchasing Program

a. Executive Order No. 523, Establishing the Massachusetts Small Business Purchasing Program (June 29, 2010), https://www.mass.gov/doc/executive-order-523-mass-register-1161/download
b. Small Business Purchasing Program (information page), https://www.mass.gov/service-details/learn-about-the-small-business-purchasing-program-sbpp
c. Small Business Purchasing Program Registration Page, https://www.mass.gov/how-to/register-for-the-small-business-purchasing-program-sbpp

4. Environmental Purchasing Policy

a. Executive Order No. 515, Establishing an Environmental Purchasing Policy (Oct. 27, 2009), https://www.mass.gov/doc/executive-order-515-mass-register-1143/download
b. Environmentally Preferable Products Procurement Program (information page), https://www.mass.gov/environmentally-preferable-products-epp-procurement-programs
c. Environmentally Preferable Products and Services Guide (updated Aug. 12, 2021), https://www.mass.gov/handbook/environmentally-preferable-products-and-services-guide
d. Executive Order No. 484, Leading by Example—Clean Energy and Efficient Buildings (supersedes Executive Order No. 438) (Apr. 18, 2007), https://www.mass.gov/doc/executive-order-484-mass-register-1077/download

5. Public Construction Laws

a. MGL chapter 30, section 39M (non-building construction)
b. MGL chapters 149 and 149A (building construction)

6. Designer Selection Laws

a. MGL chapter 7C, sections 44–57 (selection of designers, building projects)
b. MGL chapter 7C, section 58 (selection of designers, non-building construction)

II. Regulations

Code of Massachusetts Regulations (CMR) title 801, 21.00—Procurement of Commodities or Services, Including Human and Social Services, shall apply to all procurements of commodities or services, or both, by any executive office, department, agency, office, division, board, commission, or institution within the executive branch. CMR title 801, 21.00 does not apply to the legislative branch, judicial branch, constitutional offices, elected offices, public institutions of higher education, the military division, and independent public authorities, although the use of CMR title 801, 21.00 by these entities is encouraged. The Executive Office for Administration and Finance or the Operational Services Division (OSD) will interpret CMR title 801, 21.00 and may take whatever actions necessary to carry out the purposes of CMR title 801, 21.00. No department shall incur any obligation for, or authorize payments for, any commodities or services except in accordance with CMR title 801, 21.00. (See also 808 CMR 1—Compliance, Reporting, and Auditing for Human and Social Services.)

III. Source Selection

All acquisitions of commodities or services, or both, must be competitively procured unless the acquisition qualifies as an exception under CMR title 801, 21.05. Competitive procurement standards are set forth at CMR title 801, 21.06. A request for response (RFR) shall be used to solicit and select responses from qualified bidders under a competitive procurement. The goal of all RFRs shall be to obtain the best value of commodities or services, or both, for the state. An RFR may include attributes of any of the methods of competitive procurement formerly referred to as a request for proposals, request for qualifications or quotes, invitation for bids, or good business practices. (801 CMR 21.06(4)(a).)

"Best value" means "[t]he result of common sense Procurement decision-making consistent with the State's Procurement Principles, which are to balance and support the achievement of: required outcomes, best quality economic value, timely performance, minimizing the burdens on administrative resources, expediting simple or routine purchases, flexibility in developing alternative Procurement and business relationships, encouraging competition, encouraging the continuing participation of quality Contractors and supporting State and Department Procurement planning and implementation." (801 CMR 21.02.)

Competitive sealed bidding procedures are addressed at Uniform Procurement Act section 5, https://malegislature.gov/laws/generallaws/parti/titleiii/chapter30b/section5. These are applicable to award of procurement contracts over $50,000. For procurements between $10,000 and $50,000 see Uniform Procurement Act section 4. Exceptions to the requirements of section 5 are found at sections 6, 6A, and 8 of the Uniform Procurement Act. Awards under section 5 shall be made to the "lowest responsible and responsive bidder."

Sole source procurements are addressed at Uniform Procurement Act section 7, https://malegislature.gov/Laws/GeneralLaws/PartI/TitleIII/Chapter30B/Section7.

IV. Bid Protests and Contract Disputes

A. Bid Protests

There are no statutory provisions or regulations establishing an administrative procedure for bid protests under MGL chapter 30B. However, the Office of Inspector

General (OIG) notes that under Massachusetts law "any bidder or proposer competing for a public contract can challenge the award of that contract in court on the grounds that the awarding authority did not comply with public bid laws." (Procurement Manual ch. 10 (citing *Quincy Ornamental Iron Works, Inc. v. Findlen*, 353 Mass. 85 (1967)).)

Vendors may bring bid protests to the local jurisdiction or directly to superior court. There is no requirement to exhaust administrative remedies with the inspector general before filing a complaint in superior court. (Procurement Manual ch. 10.) OIG includes guidance for contracting officials to avoid bid protests. (Procurement Manual ch. 10, Ten Tips for Avoiding Bid Protests.)

An RFR may contain the opportunity for non-successful bidders to request a debriefing to be conducted after contract execution with selected bidder(s). Debriefings are designed to identify the weak areas of a bidder's response and suggest improvements for future procurements. Comparisons with other responses will not be made during a debriefing. If an RFR is silent as to an opportunity for a debriefing, the procuring department shall have the option to grant or deny a debriefing and may limit the number of debriefings granted. (801 CMR 21.06(14).) Decisions made pursuant to the provisions of CMR title 801, 21.00 are not subject to the provisions of MGL chapter 30A, sections 10 and 11 (State Administrative Procedure, Adjudicatory Proceedings; Appeals and Adjudicatory Proceedings; Additional Requirements). Note that the OSD includes on its website a guide entitled "How to Conduct a Procurement Debriefing" at https://www.mass.gov/doc/how-to-conduct-a-procurement-debriefing/download.

B. Bid Protest Appeals

Since there is no formal administrative procedure for bid protests, any protester with standing to bring a complaint to superior court may do so in the first instance, without resort to the OIG. By the same token, if a disputed award is not resolved by the issuance of an OIG opinion, the protestor may bring the complaint to superior court, where the matter will proceed de novo.

MGL chapter 30B expressly incorporates a rule previously established in a series of Massachusetts decisions interpreting other bidding statutes: any contract entered into in violation of the statute is invalid and payment to the vendor under such an invalid contract is prohibited. (MGL ch. 30B, § 17(b). See also *Majestic Radiator Enclosure Co., Inc. v. County Commissioners of Middlesex*, 397 Mass. 1002 (1986).) A civil action to enjoin the award and performance of a contract is the primary enforcement mechanism for MGL chapter 30B and other public bidding statutes. Under Massachusetts law, any aggrieved bidder has standing to bring a civil action challenging the award of a contract in violation of a public procurement law. The protesting bidder need not show that "but for" the awarding authority's failure to comply with the statute, the bidder would have been awarded the contract; the challenging party need only show that it possessed the potential to obtain the contract by virtue of having submitted a bid. (*Quincy Ornamental Iron Works, Inc. v. Findlen*, 353 Mass. 85, 87–88 (1967) (Bid Protests Article/OIG).)

C. Contract Disputes

1. Contract Claims

The Commonwealth Terms and Conditions include the following clause:

> Any actions arising out of a Contract shall be governed by the laws of Massachusetts, and shall be brought and maintained in a State or federal court in

> Massachusetts which shall have exclusive jurisdiction thereof. The Department, with the approval of the Attorney General's Office, and the Contractor may agree to voluntary mediation through the Massachusetts Office of Dispute Resolution (MODR) of any Contract dispute and will share the costs of such mediation. No legal or equitable rights of the parties shall be limited by this Section.

(Commonwealth Terms and Conditions, section 14, https://www.mass.gov/doc/exhibit-f-1-commonwealth-terms-and-conditions-0/download.)

The OSD statutory authority, regulations, executive orders, and policies, with links to relevant references, policies, and procedures, are available at https://www.mass.gov/service-details/osd-statutory-authority-regulations-executive-orders-and-policies. This website is a useful source for OSD forms and policy guidance.

2. Contract Claims Appeals

The commonwealth has waived sovereign immunity for claims brought in state court but not in federal court. (*McGuigan v. Conte*, 629 F. Supp. 2d 76, 83 (D. Mass. 2009).) Claims against the commonwealth are enforced in superior court. (MGL ch. 258, § 12.) Claims against the commonwealth must be brought within three years after the cause of action accrues. (MGL ch. 260, § 3A.)

D. Suspension and Debarment

The secretary of administration shall establish and maintain a consolidated list of contractors to whom public contracts shall not be awarded and from whom offers, bids, or proposals shall not be solicited. (MGL ch. 29, § 29F(b).) Causes for debarment and the debarment process are identified at MGC chapter 29, section 29F(c).

Pursuant to CMR title 801, 21.06(10), a "Procuring Department shall disqualify any response that the Department determines to be unresponsive, including, but not limited to: . . . (d) Responses submitted by a Bidder, or which identify a subcontractor, currently subject to any State or federal debarment order or determination." If the identified subcontractor is replaceable without a material effect on the bidder's response, the bidder may be given the opportunity to select another subcontractor prior to execution of the contract. (801 CMR 21.06(10).)

Various lists of debarred or suspended contractors can be found from links located at https://www.mass.gov/debarred-suspended-or-decertified-contractors.

V. Administrative and Judicial Review

A. Administrative Review

No formal administrative review process is prescribed by law. (See guidance above under Part IV of this summary.)

B. Judicial Review

Since there is no formal administrative procedure for bid protests, any protester with standing to bring a complaint to superior court may do so in the first instance, without resort to the OIG. By the same token, if a disputed award is not resolved by the issuance of an OIG opinion, the protestor may bring the complaint to superior court, where the matter will proceed de novo.

MGL chapter 30B expressly incorporates a rule previously established in a series of Massachusetts decisions interpreting other bidding statutes: any contract entered into in violation of the statute is invalid and payment to the vendor under such an invalid contract is prohibited. (MGL ch. 30B, § 17. See also *Majestic Radiator Enclosure Co., Inc. v. County Commissioners of Middlesex*, 397 Mass. 1002 (1986).) A civil action to enjoin the award and performance of a contract is the primary enforcement mechanism for MGL chapter 30B and other public bidding statutes. Under Massachusetts law, any aggrieved bidder has standing to bring a civil action challenging the award of a contract in violation of a public procurement law. The protesting bidder need not show that "but for" the awarding authority's failure to comply with the statute, the bidder would have been awarded the contract; the challenging party need only show that it possessed the potential to obtain the contract by virtue of having submitted a bid. (*Quincy Ornamental Iron Works, Inc. v. Findlen*, 353 Mass. 85, 87–88 (1967) (Bid Protests Article/OIG).)

The commonwealth has waived sovereign immunity for claims brought in state court but not in federal court. (*McGuigan v. Conte*, 629 F. Supp. 2d 76, 83 (D. Mass. 2009).) Claims against the commonwealth are enforced in superior court. (MGL ch. 258, § 12.) Claims against the commonwealth must be brought within three years after the cause of action accrues. (MGL ch. 260, § 3A.)

VI. Extent of State's Adoption or Adaptation of ABA Model Procurement Code

In 1990, Massachusetts adapted the American Bar Association's (ABA's) Model Procurement Code to reflect Massachusetts practice and case law. (See Procurement Manual ch. 1.)

VII. Cooperative Purchasing

A. Authority

Pursuant to MGL chapter 30B, section 22 local jurisdictions may purchase supplies from contracts that have already been procured by an in-state or out-of-state public procurement unit. Specifically, MGL chapter 30B, section 22 provides:

> A public procurement unit may participate in, sponsor, conduct or administer a cooperative purchasing agreement for the procurement of supplies with public procurement units or external procurement activities in accordance with an agreement entered into between the participants. The public procurement unit conducting the procurement of supplies shall do so in a manner that constitutes a full and open competition.

A local jurisdiction may not use a cooperative purchasing agreement to procure services, unless those services are "incidental to the delivery, conveyance and installation of" supplies procured. (See MGL ch. 30B, § 2 (definition of "supplies").)

Parties should also be aware of the differences between cooperative purchasing and collaborative procurement where two or more local jurisdictions join together to procure supplies or services as a group. Collaborative purchasing is also allowed under MGL chapter 30B, section 1(c). Massachusetts law requires both the lead jurisdiction to comply fully with chapter 30B, and also that each participating jurisdiction accept sole responsibility for payment for its purchases and compliance with contract terms. A local jurisdiction must be a member of the purchasing group prior to contract solicitation.

B. Requirements

Cooperative purchase agreements are required to be procured using full and open competition. The Procurement Manual recommends parties ask whether the awarding authority completed the following five steps: (1) advertised a procurement solicitation in a relevant publication; (2) used specific purchase descriptions in the solicitation; (3) provided for renewed competition; (4) used a clear rule for award or determination of best value in its solicitation; and (5) used an appropriate comparative evaluation process for choosing vendors.

Massachusetts OIG recommends the following best practices regarding cooperative purchasing:

Verify Eligibility and Competition: Before purchasing supplies through a cooperative purchasing agreement, confirm that the public purchasing unit offering the contract used a competitive process and that the contract is open to Massachusetts jurisdictions.

Understand Contract Pricing: Vendors generally offer their best prices when they have an actual quantity or a reliable estimate on which to bid. In cooperative purchasing, jurisdictions purchase supplies from a previously awarded contract. This contract may not yield the lowest price available given the bidding parameters.

Conduct Market Research: Multiple contracts may offer the supplies your jurisdiction needs, including out-of-state contracts, Massachusetts statewide contracts, and other in-state contracts. Choose the contract that offers what your jurisdiction needs at the best price. If prices on existing contracts are too high, consider conducting a new procurement using a competitive process under chapter 30B to obtain a lower price.

Verify the Terms and Conditions in the Contract, Including Delivery Terms: Verify whether the contract includes shipping, warranty, or other costs.

Understand Dispute Resolution Procedures before Using a Cooperative Purchasing Agreement: For example, how are disputes related to contract performance resolved? If a product is defective, where and how can the jurisdiction seek a remedy?

Michigan Procurement Rules and Regulations

Prepared by Jeff H. Eckland
Eckland & Blando LLP
Email: jeckland@ecklandblando.com
With assistance from Mark J. Blando, Vince Reuter, and Robert Dube

I. Statutory Reference

Effective March 21, 2010, the Department of Technology, Management, and Budget (DTMB) holds the authority to make all discretionary decisions concerning "solicitation, award, amendment, cancellation, and appeal of state contracts," unless otherwise expressly stated by law. (Michigan Compiled Laws § 18.1261(1), (2) (2020).) The DTMB draws its principal authority from the Management and Budget Act 431 of 1984. (*Id.*) Contracting authority previously resided within the state's Department of Management and Budget (DMB), which has since been abolished. Any and all references to the DMB contained within the Management and Budget Act now refer to the DTMB, although various references to the DMB remain in the act. (*Id.* § 18.441(II)(A), (B) (2009).) This outline will refer to the department as the DTMB for the sake of clarity.

The DTMB may delegate its procurement authority to other state agencies "within dollar limitations and for designated types of procurements," as long as the department approves the agency's procurement policies and procedures as adequate to ensure that goods and services are purchased "at fair and reasonable prices." (*Id.* § 18.1261(3)(f)–(4).) The DTMB may withdraw its delegated authority upon its finding that a state agency is not in compliance with established departmental procurement directives. (*Id.* § 18.1261(4).)

The DTMB is charged with providing "standard specifications and standards of performance" applicable to all state purchases. (*Id.* § 18.1261(6).) Unless a specified exception applies, the DTMB and other state agencies with delegated contracting authority must use competitive solicitation for all purchases. (*Id.* § 18.1261(3).)

All procurement opportunities are advertised on the state's "Bid4Michigan" contracting portal, located at http://www.bid4michigan.com/.[1] The DTMB's detailed guide to the elements of a quality proposal, called "Contracting 201," is available on its website at https://www.michigan.gov/dtmb/-/media/Project/Websites/dtmb/Procurement/documents/training/Contracting_201.pdf?rev=d252e16e948a4f09ae360e364769dba8&hash=BF3B380E14F52DAFA661B71923B0E616.

1. The State of Michigan appears to frequently update its web addresses such that the links provided in this chapter might be out of date within several years of publication.

Michigan is not a Model Procurement Code state. Michigan law governing the procurement of government contracts is located in several different chapters of the Michigan Compiled Laws, and depends on whether the DTMB has delegated its procurement authority for certain purchases to a particular state agency.

Michigan's Compiled Laws can be found by searching the state legislature's website at http://www.legislature.mi.gov/(S(02dzna00rrmyt4ht1htnxnfk))/mileg.aspx?page=home.

A. Procurement/Purchasing Statutes

The following are the relevant portions of the Michigan Compiled Laws.

1. DMB

ch. 18. Department of Management and Budget

2. Department of Transportation

ch. 15. Department of Transportation

§ 247.659b. Contracts to Construct or Repair Roads or Bridges; Departmental Duties

§ 247.661c. Contracts for Department Projects Awarded by Competitive Bidding; Report of Findings; Exception

B. Other Applicable Statutes

The following are the relevant portions of the Michigan Compiled Laws, unless noted otherwise.

Uniform Commercial Code

ch. 440, art. 2. Sales

Administrative Law

§ 600.631. Appeals from State Agency Decisions

Legislative Lobbying

§ 4.417. Registration of Lobbyists; Offenses and Penalties; Notice of Termination

Construction and Engineering Contracts

§ 224.19. County Road Commissioners; Roads and Bridges; Borrowing Power; Validation of Bonds; County Highway Engineer; Duties; Gravel; Actions for Injuries to Road; Bids; Review of Plans

§ 280.221. Bids for Petitioned Projects or Nonpetitioned Maintenance Work; Procedure

§ 124.417. Competitive Bids, Necessity, Procedure; Written Price Quotations; Procurement Procedures; Waiver

§ 331.158. Approval of Building Plans; Bids, Advertisement

§ 41.278. Contracts for Construction; Effect of Delinquent Taxes; Bids, Procedure for Letting; Commencement of Construction

§ 108.50. Board of Public Works; Letting Contracts, Conditions

§ 380.1267.	Construction Contracts; Competitive Bidding Requirements and Procedure; Adoption of Policy Giving Preference to Michigan-based Businesses; Applicability
§ 18.1241.	Contracts for Construction, Repair, Remodeling, or Demolition of Facilities; Bidding Procedure; Award and Expenditure; Director as Agent; Preference to Qualified Disabled Veteran; Award to Responsive and Responsible Best Value Bidder
§ 247.807.	Powers and Duties of Commission

Elliot-Larsen Civil Rights Act
Michigan Compiled Laws sections 37.2101–.2804, referred to as the "Elliot-Larsen Civil Rights Act," provide for equal opportunity in obtaining employment regardless of religion, race, color, national origin, age, sex, height, weight, or marital status. As such, the DTMB is not allowed to award contracts to vendors who are not in compliance with this law.

Michigan Constitution
- art. 4, § 10. Legislators and State Officers, Government Contracts, Conflicts of Interest
- art. 6, § 28. Administrative Action, Review

Executive Orders of the state governor allow the governor to restructure state agencies, reassign functions among executive branch agencies, and establish advisory bodies, task forces, and commissions. Full-text, searchable versions of Executive Orders by the current governor of Michigan are located on the governor's website at https://www.michigan.gov/whitmer/news/state-orders-and-directives. Executive Orders by former governors of Michigan are located at https://www.michigan.gov/formergovernors/recent/snyder/exec-orders. Executive Directives establishing executive policy, guidelines, and rules for various state departments are also located on the current governor's website at https://www.michigan.gov/whitmer/news/state-orders-and-directives.

Opinions by the state attorney general are located at https://www.michigan.gov/ag/opinions. Michigan courts are not required to follow the opinions of the Michigan attorney general, but often cite to them as persuasive authority. (*Frey v. Department of Management & Budget*, 414 N.W.2d 873 (Mich. 1987).)

II. Regulations

Michigan's Administrative Procedures Act, which grants the authority to promulgate state regulations, is found at Michigan Compiled Laws sections 24.201–.328. Current and archived versions of the *Michigan Register* are located on the Department of Licensing and Regulatory Affairs (LARA) website at https://www.michigan.gov/lara/bureau-list/moahr/admin-rules/Publications/Michigan-Register. Michigan's Administrative Code is located on LARA's website at https://ars.apps.lara.state.mi.us/AdminCode/DeptBureauAdminCode?Department=Licensing%20and%20Regulatory%20Affairs&Bureau=Bureau%20of%20Construction%20Codes. The code can be searched by department or by numeric range.

The DTMB has specific regulations that are located on its own website at https://www.michigan.gov/dtmb/policies/adminguide. Currently, the following list of DTMB regulations pertain to procurement:

Michigan Administrative Code r. 18.501-09. Real Estate Services
Michigan Administrative Code r. 24.61-69. State Printing—Prevailing Wage Rates

Michigan Department of Transportation (MDOT)-specific regulations are located on MDOT's website at https://www.michigan.gov/mdot/travel/mobility/pub-transit/laws-and-regulations.

III. Source Selection

A. Procurement Policy and Selected Regulatory Definitions

1. State Preference for Competitive Bidding and for Michigan Firms

Public contracting shall be done, whenever possible, by the competitive solicitation process; contracts may be let by other methods only after the DTMB determines that competitive bidding is not appropriate. (Michigan Compiled Laws § 18.1261(1) (2020).)

The DTMB is required to give preference to products manufactured or services offered by Michigan-based firms or facilities, to the extent consistent with federal laws. (*Id.*) Section 18.1268 of the Michigan Compiled Laws sets forth the criteria by which a company may be classified as a "Michigan business." (*Id.* § 18.1268(1) (2007).) A bidder is considered a Michigan business if it is able to certify that it has done any of the following activities during the past 12 months before the bid deadline: (1) filed a Michigan business tax return "showing a portion or all of the income tax base allocated or apportioned to the state of Michigan" (*Id.* § 18.1268(1)(a).); or (2) "[f]iled a Michigan income tax return showing income generated in or attributed to the state of Michigan" (*Id.* § 18.1268(1)(b).); or (3) "[w]ithheld Michigan income tax from compensation paid to the bidder's owners and remitted the tax to the [D]epartment of [T]reasury." (*Id.* § 18.1268(1)(c).) The filing or withholding must "indicate a significant business presence in the State." (*Id.* § 18.1268(2).)

A bidder certifying that it meets the criteria above must also authorize the Treasury Department to verify its claim. (*Id.* § 18.1268(3).) Only bidders certified as Michigan businesses qualify for the Michigan-based company preference. (*Id.* § 18.1268(4).) A bidder waives any claim to a preference under Michigan law if the bidder has not certified itself as a Michigan business and has authorized Treasury Department verification. (*Id.* § 18.1268(7).)

2. Prohibition of Sole Source Contracts

In the interest of promoting competition for bids and reducing expenditures on state contracts, Executive Directive No. 2005-3 prohibits the use of no-bid contracts except if certain emergency conditions apply: (1) the procurement of goods or services is necessary for the imminent protection of, or to mitigate an imminent threat to, public safety, as determined by the DTMB; (2) the procurement of goods or services is necessary to protect life or property; (3) the procurement of goods or services is in response to a declared state of emergency; or (4) the procurement of goods or services is within a department's purchasing authority, the value of the procurement is less than $25,000, and the department's policies regarding procurement are designed to award contracts in a fair and reasonable manner and are approved by the DTMB. (Michigan Executive Directive No. 2005-3 (Apr. 30, 2005), https://www.michigan.gov/formergovernors/recent/granholm/executive-directives/2005/executive-directive-no--2005-3.)

3. Vendor Registration

In order to receive bids, vendors must first register with the SIGMA Vendor Self-Service (SIGMA VSS) system. The DTMB's State Budget Office has put together a detailed guide on its website with step-by-step instructions on the vendor registration process at https://www.michigan.gov/dtmb/procurement/contractconnect/how-to-register.

Those vendors wishing to certify themselves as Michigan-based companies also need to complete and submit a certification form along with their vendor registration. A blank copy of this form is located at https://www.michigan.gov/documents/dtmb/Certification_Forms_PSC_442633_7.doc.

4. Limitation of Solicitation to Prequalified Vendors

The state has the right to limit a solicitation to "prequalified vendors to meet statutory or licensing requirements applicable to the solicitation or when the time necessary to verify vendor qualifications would jeopardize the timely award of contracts." (Michigan Compiled Laws § 18.1262 (1988).)

5. Preference for Disabled-Veteran Contractors

The DTMB must give a preference of up to 10 percent of the amount of the contract to disabled veteran contractors that meet the contract's solicitation specifications. (*Id.* § 18.1261(8).) A contractor qualifies as a disabled veteran firm if it is 51 percent or more owned by one or more service-disabled veterans. (*Id.* § 18.1261(15)(e).) If the disabled veteran contractor's proposal is the low bid, including the 10 percent reduction in contract price permitted by Michigan Compiled Laws section 18.1261(8), the contract shall be awarded to the disabled veteran. It is the goal of the DTMB to award 5 percent of all state contracts to disabled veterans or to contractors that subcontract with disabled veterans. (*Id.* § 18.1261(9).)

6. Preference for Disabled Contractors

Under the Business Opportunity Act for Persons with Disabilities of 1988, the DTMB's goal is to award "not less than 3 percent of its total expenditures for construction, goods, and services to businesses owned by individuals with disabilities." (*Id.* § 450.793(1) (2005).) To qualify as a business owned by individuals with disabilities, a disabled person must own more than 50 percent of the voting shares or interest, more than 50 percent of net profits or losses must accrue to the disabled owner, and more than 50 percent of the businesses' employees must be state residents. (*Id.* § 450.792(a)(i)–(iii).)

7. Environmental/Recycled Material Preferences

At least 20 percent of all supplies, materials, and equipment procured in Michigan are required to be made from recycled materials, if there is a readily identifiable source of materials and if the cost does not exceed 110 percent of the cost of supplies, materials, and equipment not containing recycled materials. (*Id.* § 18.1261a(1) (1989).) "Recycled materials" includes

> recycled paper products, structural materials made from recycled plastics, rerefined lubricating oils, reclaimed solvents, recycled asphalt and concrete, recycled glass products, retreaded tires, and ferrous and nonferrous metals containing recycled scrap metals, that contain 1 or more of the following in

> a percentage as determined by the department [DTMB] as provided by law: (a) waste materials generated by a business or consumer; (b) materials that have served their intended purposes; and (c) materials that have been separated from solid waste for purposes of collection, recycling, and disposition.

(*Id.* § 18.1261a(6)(a)–(c).)

In addition, at least 50 percent of the paper products purchased by the state must be made with recycled paper if the cost of procurement is not greater that 110 percent of the cost of non-recycled paper products. (*Id.* § 18.1261b(1) (1989).) To meet the state's requirements, a paper product must not contain less than 50 percent recycled paper product. (*Id.* § 18.1261b(5)(a).)

Since October 2006, the DTMB has given a preference to "wood and paper products that are derived from sustainably managed forests or procurement systems." (*Id.* § 18.1261c(1) (2005).) "Sustainably managed forests or procurement systems" must be certified by one of the independent third parties listed in Michigan Compiled Laws section 18.1261c(3)(a)–(h).

8. Debarring/Penalizing Contractors

If a vendor or contractor does not perform responsibly, *or* if an owner or officer of 25 percent or more of the vendor's or contractor's firm has "demonstrated a lack of integrity that could jeopardize the state's interest," the DTMB may debar the vendor/contractor from participating in the bid process and from contract award. (*Id.* § 18.1264 (1988).)

9. Bid Submission

The DTMB's website provides a detailed PowerPoint on preparing responses to solicitations, located at https://www.michigan.gov/documents/dtmb/contracting-101_645983_7.pdf. The website formerly stated that a bidder should take the following actions when preparing and submitting bids to the DTMB:

1. Thoroughly read and understand the solicitation and its accompanying documents. Unless the solicitation specifies otherwise, a bidder may contact the buyer listed on the solicitation for clarification of unclear material.
2. Note any exceptions to bid specifications.
3. Have an officer or authorized agent sign the response, in ink,
4. Submit the response and all other required information by the deadline, making sure to follow all provided submission instructions.

In addition, the website provided that submission of sealed bids must comply with the sealed bid envelope identification instructions provided in the solicitation. However, this information can no longer be found on the website so it is unclear how operative these instructions remain.

10. Bidder's Responsibility to Notify Agency of Faulty Bidding Requirements

Per DTMB policy, a bidder who learns of faulty bidding requirements must inform the agency.

11. Bid Withdrawal

Bidders may withdraw their bids at any time before the bid opening. However, all bids become state property upon submission and, as such, DTMB will not honor requests to return bids. If a bidder requests to withdraw a bid that has been recommended for award, the state has discretion to act within the state's best interest in deciding to withdraw.

B. MDOT

MDOT's website, located at https://www.michigan.gov/mdot/business/contractors, contains useful information regarding its bidding process. All solicitations calling for the expenditure of $100,000 or more must be let through a competitive bidding process "unless the department finds that under the circumstances relating to those projects, some other method is in the public interest." (Michigan Compiled Laws § 247.661c (2015).)

MDOT is transitioning to an exclusively electronic bidding system, and all solicitations posted online must be bid on electronically. Vendors must register to use the electronic bidding process, and the agency recommends setting aside at least five days to complete the vendor registration process.

Project proposals and solicitations are listed on MDOT's e-proposal website, called MILogin, at https://milogintp.michigan.gov/eai/tplogin/authenticate?URL=/. To view project proposals, vendors must register a username and password on the MILogin website. Printed proposal plans are available for purchase through select vendors.

A landing page containing various contractor-focused program guides and FAQs can be found at https://www.michigan.gov/mdot/business/contractors.

IV. Bid Protests and Contract Disputes

A. Bid Protests

Bid protests must be received by the date and time identified in the notice of recommendation issued in the Buy4Michigan portal. The protest must be directed to the chief procurement officer, DTMB, First Floor NE, Constitution Hall, P.O. Box 30026, Lansing, Michigan, 48909, or by email to BidProtest-DTMB@michigan.gov. The protest should set forth the facts of the alleged error in the procurement process, the invitation to bid (ITB) or request for proposal (RFP) number, and the protestor's desired remedy. All information the protestor thinks may be relevant should be included in this initial submission, as the chief procurement officer is not required to take into account any information submitted after the protest deadline.

Upon receiving the protest, the chief procurement officer will either issue a written decision or will schedule an informal meeting to elicit additional information. The decision of the chief procurement officer is final. Under most circumstances, the contract award will be delayed pending the chief procurement officer's decision. However, if the delay of award will impact public health, safety, or jeopardize state property, the chief procurement officer may proceed with the contract award.

The DTMB's website, located at https://www.michigan.gov/dtmb/procurement/contractconnect/programs-and-policies/Policies/bidder-protests, lists the following issues as not subject to protest:

- Failure of a bidder to properly follow solicitation submission instructions.
- Failure of a bidder to submit the bid to Central Procurement by the due date and time, in the format required (online vs. hard copy), and through the forum required (i.e., e-procurement system).
- Failure of a bidder to provide mandatory samples, descriptive literature, or other required documents by the date and time specified.

- Failure of a bidder to provide a required bid deposit or performance bond by the date and time specified.
- Failure of a bidder to submit a protest within the time stipulated in the solicitation (RFP, ITB, etc.) or as determined by the Chief Procurement Officer.

However, the website further specifies that, "if there are no responsive responses, the requirements may be put aside at the discretion of the Chief Procurement Officer." (*Id.*)

1. Standing for Bid Protests

Under Michigan law, standing is dependent upon the protestor having contractual rights in the bidding process; it is insufficient to allege standing based upon the fact that the protestor participated in the bidding process and is disappointed in the award. (*Talbot Paving Co. v. Detroit*, 109 Mich. 657, 660 (1896); see also *City Communications Inc. v. Detroit*, 650 F. Supp. 1570, 1581 (E.D. Mich. 1987) ("[T]he law of Michigan gives no rights to an unsuccessful bidder . . . only the public, and not the bidder, has standing to challenge the bidding process."); *Malan Construction Corp. v. Board of County Road Commissioners*, 187 F. Supp. 937, 939 (E.D. Mich. 1960) ("Competitive bidding is not intended to benefit bidders . . . . [t]he incidental benefit received by bidders from competitive bidding does not allow an unsuccessful bidder to bring a private action."); *WDG Investment Co., LLC v. Michigan Department of Management & Budget*, No. 229950, 2002 WL 31424731 (Mich. Ct. App. Oct. 25, 2002) ("one who is unsuccessful in bidding on a public contract does not have standing to challenge the result or the bidding process itself").) Standing can be established by demonstrating that the protestor had a contractual right to the contract (i.e., a claim of entitlement to the benefit of the contract), or by alleging that the state and/or local rules limited the award of the contract to the protestor (e.g., mandating that the contract be awarded to the low bid). (*United of Omaha Life Insurance Co. v. Solomon*, 960 F.2d 31, 34 (6th Cir. 1992).)

2. Bid Protest Remedies

Michigan courts recognize injunctions as one form of remedy that may potentially be sought in a bid protest. (See *L.R. Mullins Contracting Co. v. State*, No. 255562, 2005 WL 3050631 (Mich. Ct. App. Nov. 15, 2005).) However, the courts do not permit damages or lost profits as a remedy in bid protest actions. (*Id.* ("a disappointed bidder cannot maintain an action for damages, such as lost profits.") (citing *Talbot Paving Co. v. Detroit*, 109 Mich. 657, 660 (1896)).) Further, the courts refuse to recognize any remedy in response to protests to the fairness and legality of an ITB if the protestor submitted a proposal and competed for the contract. (*Detroit Free Press Co. v. Board of State Auditors*, 47 Mich. 135, 144 (1881) ("If the proposition for bids was unfair and illegal, a proper remedy might have been found in advance; but a party who participates and competes for the contract is too late afterwards to complain on his own account.").)

B. Bid Protest Appeals

Protestors may appeal an adverse decision by the chief procurement officer to Michigan's district courts. (Michigan Constitution art. 6, § 28.) Appeals from trial court decisions involving bid protests follow normal civil appellate practice.

V. Extent of State's Adoption or Adaptation of ABA Model Procurement Code

Michigan is not a Model Procurement Code state. Michigan law governing the procurement of government contracts is located in several different chapters of the Michigan Compiled Laws, and depends on whether the DTMB has delegated its procurement authority for certain purchases to a particular state agency.

VI. Cooperative Purchasing

A. Authority

Michigan does not have a single cooperative purchasing agreement statute; instead, it authorizes cooperative purchasing agreements in several locations. First, Michigan Compiled Laws section 18.1261(7) provides that the DTMB "may enter into a cooperative purchasing agreement with 1 or more other states or public entities for the purchase of goods, including, but not limited to, recycled goods, and services necessary for state programs." Under Michigan Compiled Laws chapter 141, a Board of County Sinking Fund Commissioners is created, which has the authority to allow counties to "enter into a cooperative purchasing agreement with the federal government, [Michigan], or other public entities for the purchase of goods or services necessary for the authority. (Michigan Compiled Laws § 141.1361(6).) This section specifically permits counties to forgo using the competitive bidding process in favor of a cooperative purchasing agreement. (*Id.* § 141.1361(6)(f).) Further, regional authorities may also enter into a cooperative purchasing agreement with Michigan or another public entity. (*Id.* § 259.142(7) (2015).)

B. Requirements

Michigan has not issued pertinent guidance on how a contractor can qualify for a contract under a cooperative purchasing agreement, but the DTMB does have examples of cooperative purchasing agreements available at https://search.michigan.gov/AppBuilder/search?ctx=DTMB&q=cooperative%20purchasing%20agreement.

Further, there is not yet any case law interpreting any of the pertinent statutes' cooperative purchasing agreement sections, so it remains unclear what rights and remedies are available to a disappointed bidder who would like to lodge a bid protest on a cooperative purchasing agreement contract.

Minnesota Procurement Rules and Regulations

Prepared by Jeff H. Eckland
Eckland & Blando LLP
Email: jeckland@ecklandblando.com
With assistance from Mark J. Blando, Vince Reuter, and Robert Dube[1]

I. Statutory Reference

The Minnesota Department of Administration has the authority to contract on behalf of the state, unless otherwise expressly stated by law. (Minnesota Statutes § 16C.03, subdiv. 3 (2014).) Contracting duties may be delegated to any government agency as long as the commissioner for the Department of Administration retains supervisory oversight. (*Id.* subdiv. 16.) Additionally, state agencies may add to the regulatory framework with specific regulations and procedures. (*Id.* subdivs. 2, 8.)

The official Minnesota Code can be found on the Minnesota Legislature's website, maintained by the Office of the Revisor of Statutes, at https://www.revisor.mn.gov/pubs.

A. Procurement/Purchasing Statutes

In Minnesota, the subject matter of the contract determines which agency's procurement rules will govern. For example, purchases of goods and general services, as well as general construction contracts, are conducted through the Materials Management Division (MMD) of the Department of Administration, while contracts for professional or technical services are let through specific agencies. The Department of Transportation (MnDOT) oversees contracts for road construction.
Below is a list of relevant sections of the Minnesota Statutes.

1. General State Procurement Statutes (Including MMD)

ch. 16C (2019). State Procurement

1. Research, drafting, proofing, and citation assistance provided by Kenneth Cooper of Eckland & Blando LLP.

2. Other Competitive Bidding Statutes

§§ 161.315–.391 (2019).	Department of Transportation
§§ 471.345–.346 (2019).	"Municipalities" (defined at Minnesota Statutes § 471.345, subdiv. 1 (2019))

3. Other Professional and Technical Services Statutes

§ 15.061 (1998).	Professional or Technical Services
§ 16C.08 (2014).	Professional or Technical Services

B. Other Applicable Statutes

Below is a list of relevant sections of the Minnesota Statutes, except where otherwise noted.

1. Minnesota Constitution Provisions

arts. I, XI.	State shall not impair contracts; state may contract, and so on

2. Agency Authority

ch. 16A (2020).	Department of Management and Budget
ch. 16B (2020).	Department of Administration
§ 471.59 (2015).	Joint Exercise of Powers

3. Causes of Action

§ 3.736 (2017).	Tort Claims
§ 3.751 (2002).	Contract Claims (waiver of immunity, etc.)
ch. 337 (2019).	Building and Construction Contracts
§ 270C.65 (2005).	Right of Setoff (withhold payment to resolve tax liability)

4. Minnesota Uniform Commercial Code

ch. 336 (2013).	Uniform Commercial Code

5. Other Governmental Units

§§ 471.345–.346 (1974).	Uniform Municipal Contracting Law
ch. 383A.	Ramsey County
ch. 383B.	Hennepin County
ch. 383C.	St. Louis County
ch. 383D.	Dakota County
ch. 383E.	Anoka County
ch. 137F (2014).	Minnesota State Colleges and Universities

6. Record Keeping

ch.13.	Government Data Practices
§ 138.163 (1971).	Preservation and Disposal of Public Records
§ 138.17 (2006).	Government Records; Administration

7. Other Contracting Requirements

§ 16A.1245 (1990).	Prompt Payment to Subcontractors
§ 471.425 (1995).	Prompt Payment of Local Government Bills (Municipal Subcontractor Payment)
§ 337.10 (2019).	Building and Construction Contracts; Prohibited Provisions
§ 176.181 (2020).	Insurance
§§ 177.41–.45 (2019).	Prevailing Wage
§ 181.59 (1984).	Discrimination on Account of Race, Creed, or Color Prohibited in Contract
§ 221.171(2) (2018).	Permit Carrier Compensation Exemption
§ 363A.36 (2020).	Certificates of Compliance for Public Contracts

8. Lobbying Laws

ch. 10A.	Campaign Finance and Public Disclosure
§ 10A.025 (2018).	Filing Requirements
§ 10A.071 (2017).	Certain Gifts by Lobbyists and Principals Prohibited

9. Ethics and Anti-Bribery Statutes

a. General

§ 43A.38 (2009).	Code of Ethics for Executive Branch Employees
§ 16C.04 (2014).	Ethical Practices and Conflicts of Interests
§ 10A.07 (2018).	Conflicts of Interest

b. Specific Offices

Contracts may be voided if a public official has a personal or pecuniary interest in such contract:

City Officials—Minnesota Statutes § 412.311 (2015) (council members)

County Officials—Minnesota Statutes §§ 382.18 (county officials); 383A.201 (Ramsey County officials); 383B.151 (Hennepin County officials) (2015)

Local Government Officials—Minnesota Statutes §§ 469.009 (local government officials); 469.098 (local government officials); 473.706 (metropolitan government officials) (2015)

School Officials—– Minnesota Statutes § 471.88 (2015) (school officials and exceptions)

c. Criminal Penalties

§ 15.43 (1996).	Acceptance of Advantage by State Employee; Penalty
§§ 325D.53, 325D.56 (1990).	Prohibited Contracts, Combinations, and Conspiracies
§ 471.87 (2015).	Public Officers, Interest in Contract; Penalty
§ 609.42 (1986).	Bribery
§ 609.43 (1986).	Misconduct of Public Officer or Employee
§ 609.456 (2013).	Reporting to State Auditor and Legislative Auditor Required
§ 609.86 (2004).	Commercial Bribery

10. Minnesota False Claims Act

On May 16, 2009, Minnesota joined 25 other states in passing a state version of the federal False Claims Act, which became effective on July 1, 2010. (Minnesota Statutes §§ 15C.01–.16 (2019).)

Opinions of the Minnesota attorney general may be found online at https://www.ag.state.mn.us/office/Opinions/Default.asp.

II. Regulations

The Minnesota Administrative Rules are available online at https://www.revisor.mn.gov/rules/. Included below is a relevant list of Minnesota Rules.

A. Bidding and Contracts

ch. 1230.	Department of Administration, State Contracts
1230.0100.	Scope
1230.0150.	Definitions
1230.0300.	Soliciting Responses
1230.0400.	Advertised Solicitations
1230.0500.	Security
1230.0600.	Responder Errors
1230.0700.	Receipt and Opening of Responses
1230.0750.	Organizational Conflicts of Interest
1230.0800.	Award of Contracts
1230.0900.	Tied Bids
1230.1000.	Contract Performance
1230.1100.	Failure to Perform
1230.1150.	Authority to Debar or Suspend Vendors
1230.1175.	Reinstatement and Probation
1230.1180.	Termination of Debarment or Award during Debarment

B. Small Business Procurement Program

C. Debarment and Suspension

III. Source Selection

A. Regulatory Sources and Statutory Definitions

1. Types of Contracts Determine the Procedures and Rules Used

Technical and professional contracts are let through the agency requesting the services. All other goods and services contracts are administered by the Department of Administration's MMD. Construction contracts go through either MMD (for "vertical" construction contracts (i.e., buildings and the like)) or MnDOT (for "horizontal" construction contracts (i.e., roads, bridges, etc.)).

2. Selected Statutory Definitions

The following definitions appear in Minnesota Statutes section 16C.02 (2015).

Formal solicitation "means a solicitation which requires a sealed response." (*Id.* subdiv. 7.)

Informal solicitation "means a solicitation which does not require a sealed response." (*Id.* subdiv. 9.)

Request for bid (RFB) "means a solicitation in which the terms, conditions, and specifications are described and responses are not subject to negotiation." (*Id.* subdiv. 11.)

Request for proposal (RFP) "means a solicitation in which it is not advantageous to set forth all the actual, detailed requirements at the time of solicitation and responses are negotiated to achieve best value for the state." (*Id.* subdiv. 12.)

Single source "means an acquisition where, after a search, only one supplier is determined to be reasonably available for the required product, service, or construction item." (*Id.* subdiv. 18.)

Solicitation "means the process used to communicate procurement requirements and to request responses from interested vendors. A solicitation may be, but is not limited to, a request for bid and request for proposal." (*Id.* subdiv. 19.)

B. Competitive Bids

1. Publication Requirement

Notices of solicitations for acquisitions with an estimated value of greater than $25,000 (or $100,000 for an MnDOT acquisition) must be publicized. (*Id.* § 16C.06, subdiv. 1 (2015).)

2. Formal versus Informal Solicitation

Formal solicitation must be used for acquisitions estimated to be at, or greater than, $50,000 (or $100,000 for MnDOT). (*Id.* subdiv. 2(a).) Informal solicitation may be used for acquisitions estimated to be less than $50,000 (or $100,000 for MnDOT). (*Id.* subdiv. 2(b).)

3. Simplified Acquisitions

Solicitations are not required for acquisitions of goods, services, construction, and utilities in an amount of $5,000 or less. (*Id.* § 16C.10, subdiv. 6 (2015).) Building, construction, and repair contracts estimated at less than $50,000 may use informal bids. (*Id.* § 16C.26, subdiv. 4 (2015).)

4. Exceptions to Solicitation Process

Exceptions to the solicitation process can be found in Minnesota Statutes sections 16C.10-11 and 471.345 (2015). These exceptions include, inter alia, single source acquisitions, emergency acquisitions, acquisitions made pursuant to federal agency price schedules, cooperative agreements with another governmental unit, and cooperative purchasing ventures. (*Id.* § 16C.10 (2015).)

Minnesota's Cooperative Purchasing Venture (CPV) permits state agencies and municipalities to bypass a competitive solicitation process by instead purchasing through the state's CPV. (*Id.* §§ 16C.10, 471.345 (2015); see also *id.* § 471.59 (2015).) The CPV, a contract vehicle similar to a purchasing alliance or cooperative agreement, permits the state to enter into a cooperative purchasing agreement for the provision of goods, services, and utilities with other states or governmental units and to make the terms of these contracts available to Minnesota state agencies and municipalities. These governmental units may then purchase off of the contract listed on the CPV rather than engage in the competitive solicitation process that would otherwise be required by Minnesota Statutes sections 16C.06 and 471.345 (2015).

C. Negotiations

The state may negotiate contracts outside of the competitive bidding process and is generally encouraged to contract with small, targeted group businesses (under section 16C.16) in this situation. (*Id.* § 16C.06, subdiv. 11. (2017).)

1. Architecture, Surveying, Geological, and Engineering Contracts

The commissioner may decide to use "qualification-based selection" procedures for professionals that meet the statutory definition in Minnesota Statutes section 16C.087, subdivision 2 (2015). Under this process, certain professionals are placed in rank order by an agency based on their qualifications. The agency may then solicit pricing information, in rank order, and negotiate the terms of a contract.

2. Design-Build, Construction Manager at Risk, and Job Order Contracts

The state may, in some circumstances for the following contracts, initiate the contracting process by issuing a request for qualifications (RFQ) before the negotiation process. A design-build contract is one where a builder provides architectural services as well as construction services. (*Id.* § 16C.32, subdiv. 1(9) (2015); see also *id.* § 16C.33 (2015) (requirements and procedures).) A construction manager at risk contract is a contract between the state and a construction manager that includes a maximum price for the construction project. (*Id.* § 16C.32, subdiv. 1(8) (2015); see also *id.* § 16C.34 (2015) (requirements and procedures).) Job order contracting is a supply method where state officials select bids from a registry of prescreened contractors who have already signed a master contract. (*Id.* § 16C.32, subdiv. 1(16) (2015); *see also id.* § 16C.35 (2015) (requirements and procedures). See Section III.F for more details on the types of contracts.)

D. Reverse Auctions

Reverse auctions are not frequently used but are permitted at the discretion of the commissioner. (Minnesota Statutes § 16C.10, subdiv. 7 (2016); *id.* § 16C.03, subdiv. 3 (2015).)

E. Other Procurement Issues

1. Electronic Vendor Registration

Vendors are encouraged to register with the state. Registered vendors may be sent invitations to bid. For specific registration requirements, visit the Department of Administration's website at https://www.mmd.admin.state.mn.us/mn02000.htm.

2. Newsletter of State Procurement Office

Monthly procurement updates from the Department of Administration can be found at https://www.mmd.admin.state.mn.us/MonthlyProcurementUpdates.htm.

3. Bid Rules/Procedures

a. State Rules

Data contained in a bid becomes public when the evaluation process is completed, which occurs before the contract is executed. (Minnesota Statutes § 13.591, subdiv. 3(a) (2015).) The evaluation process conducted by the MMD often takes a week; however, a bidder may call the department's helpline and find out if the contract award information has been made public. In addition to the website, a bid book can be found in room 112 of the Department of Administration building.

b. MnDOT Bidding

MnDOT publishes its own guide to bidding, published online at http://www.dot.state.mn.us/bidlet.

F. Types of Contracts

1. Design-Build Contract

A design-build contract is a contract to furnish "architectural, engineering, and related design services as well as the labor, materials, supplies, equipment, and construction services for a project." (Minnesota Statutes § 16C.32, subdiv. 1(9) (2015).) "Each design-builder must be, employ," or otherwise associate itself with a firm or person who is licensed in Minnesota to provide the necessary design services for the project. (*Id.* subdiv. 2(a).) The government will issue an RFQ or RFP using either a qualifications-based selection process or a design-and-price-based selection process. (*Id.* subdiv. 3.)

a. Qualifications-Based Selection Process

Upon request from a government agency, the Board shall review qualifications submitted by potential design-builders and evaluate the qualifications according to the published criteria. (*Id.* subdiv. 5.) The Board shall then narrow the list to three to five potential design-builders. (*Id.* subdiv. 5(b).) If there are fewer than three qualified participants, the Board may re-solicit the project with changed requirements, or continue the process as a design-only contract and engage in competitive bidding for the build portion. (*Id.*) The Board then conducts formal interviews to determine the highest scoring design-builder, and forwards the selection to the commissioner of administration so that a contract may be negotiated in accordance with Minnesota Statutes section 16C.33, subdivision 6 (2015). Among other requirements, the selected design-builder must enter into a contract with a guaranteed maximum price. (*Id.* subdiv. 6(f).)

b. Design-and-Price-Based Selection Process

The design-and-price-based selection process also begins with an RFQ and evaluation of the qualifications of potential design-builders. (*Id.* subdiv. 7.) However, instead of immediately negotiating with the top candidate, the agency will then issue an RFP to the three top scoring candidates. (*Id.*) The evaluation board will then interview the potential design-builders and evaluate the proposals for the "best value." (*Id.* subdivs. 7, 8.) After selection, the design-builder and the commissioner will negotiate a fixed price contract. (*Id.* subdiv. 8.)

2. Construction Manager at Risk

A construction manager at risk refers to "a person selected by the commissioner to act as a construction manager to manage the construction process, which includes, but is not limited to, responsibility for the price, schedule, and workmanship of the construction." (*Id.* § 16C.32, subdiv. 1(7) (2015).) These contracts include "guaranteed maximum price, construction schedule, and workmanship of the construction performed." (*Id.* subdiv. 1(8).)

A selection committee will review the submitted qualifications and request proposals from three to five of the highest-rated potential contractors. (*Id.* § 16C.34.) After formal interviews, the committee will select one contractor for contract negotiations with the purpose of entering into a guaranteed maximum price contract. (*Id.* subdiv. 3.)

3. Job Order Contracting

Job order contracting is a "project delivery method that requests a limited number of bids from a list of qualified contractors, selected from a registry of qualified contractors who have been prescreened and who have entered into master contracts with the commissioner, as provided in section 16C.35." (*Id.* § 16C.32, subdiv. 1(16).) Job order contracts are available to the commissioner for projects with costs under $250,000. (*Id.* § 16C.35.) The commissioner issues an RFQ and signs master contracts with all qualified contractors. (*Id.*) When jobs arise, the commissioner requests bids from the prescreened qualified contractors and awards the job to the lowest bidder. (*Id.*)

4. Professional or Technical Services Contract

Professional or technical services are those services that are intellectual in character and result in the writing of a report or the completion of a task. (*Id.* § 16C.08, subdiv. 1.) Tasks include consultation, analysis, planning, programming, prediction, or recommendations. (*Id.*) These contracts do not include the provision of supplies or materials unless the commissioner of administration approves, or if the supplies are incidental to the professional services. (*Id.*) These contracts may be made directly with the various state agencies.

Master professional/technical contracts (master P/T contracts) are similar to the federal indefinite delivery-indefinite quantity (IDIQ) contracts. Master P/T contracts provide a framework for obtaining the services of multiple contractors. This type of contract may be used for generally identifiable tasks for which no reasonable determination of actual need can be made. A master P/T contract is unencumbered; thus, the duty to perform the contract does not begin until a subsequent work order contract is executed. The state publishes a Professional/Technical Services Contract Manual on its website at https://www.mmd.admin.state.mn.us/mn05001.htm.

5. Service Contract

A general service contract is used for any services not covered by a professional or technical services contract. (Minnesota Statutes § 16C.02, subdiv. 7(a) (2015).) Service contracts must be made with the commissioner of administration unless specifically authorized by statute or otherwise delegated by law.

G. Targeted Group/Economically Disadvantaged (TG/ED) Small Business Program

MMD operates a program for TG/ED small businesses. (See Minnesota Rules 1230.0150, 1230.1400–.1910 (2015).)

1. Must Be a Minnesota-Based "Small Business"

A business must be a Minnesota-based small business, defined by gross annual sales, in order to participate in this program. The size limit can range from $1 million to $10 million or more in annual gross sales depending on the industry. The size requirements, in annual gross sales, for the "Small Business" classification in various industries can be found at https://www.mmd.admin.state.mn.us/sicsize.asp.

2. Must Be Certified by the Administration Department

Additionally, a business needs a certification from the commissioner of administration that the business meets the requirements of a TG or ED small business. (See generally Minnesota Rule 1230.1600.) A certification from MMD allows a business to participate in several similar programs operated by MnDOT and other metropolitan agencies.

a. Eligibility for TG Certification

To be certified as a TG small business, the business must be at least 51 percent owned by a woman, racial minority, or person with a substantial physical disability. In addition, the qualifying owner must also have operational control of the business. With the TG certification, a small business may be eligible for up to a 6 percent preference in selling products or services or bidding on construction projects. Further information regarding eligibility for designation as a TG can be found at https://www.mmd.admin.state.mn.us/tgeligibility.htm.

b. Eligibility for ED Certification

To be certified as an ED small business, the business must be located in an "Economically Disadvantaged Area" in Minnesota. A list of these areas is located on the Minnesota Department of Administration's website at https://www.mmd.admin.state.mn.us/lsalist.htm. With ED certification, small businesses may be eligible for up to a 6 percent preference in selling their products or services, and may be eligible for up to a 4 percent preference on bidding for construction projects.

Once certified, TG and ED vendors are added to the state's bid list, and are listed in the Directory of Certified TG/ED Vendors.

IV. Bid Protests and Contract Disputes

Minnesota does not use a separate, formal bid protest mechanism. In order to prevent a contract from being erroneously let, one must file a motion for an injunction in

Ramsey County or the county where the cause of action arose. (Minnesota Statutes § 3.751, subdiv. 3 (2015).) Otherwise, available relief will be limited.

A. Informal Review Process

Although there is no formal administrative review of bids, state agencies encourage bidders to use an informal review process. First, a disappointed bidder should contact the "authorized representative" identified in the RFB or RFP. After this initial contact, a written statement should be sent that identifies the grounds for the complaint.

An informal appeal may be taken to the authorized representative's superiors within the agency. If the RFB or RFP was issued by an agency other than the Department of Administration, then an appeal of the informal protest decision may be made to the MMD.

B. Bid Protests

Disappointed bidders may challenge public bidding actions in their own name. (*Carl Bolander & Sons Co. v. City of Minneapolis*, 451 N.W.2d 204, 206 (Minn. 1990).) A district court may set aside a governmental decision only if it is "arbitrary, capricious, and unreasonable under all the facts and circumstances" or where the procedures employed are so flawed as to "emasculate the safeguards of competitive bidding." (See *R.E. Short Co. v. City of Minneapolis*, 269 N.W.2d 331, 337–38 (Minn. 1978); *Griswold v. City of Ramsey*, 65 N.W.2d 647, 652 (Minn. 1954).) The "paramount purpose of the statutory bidding process is to protect the public interest by requiring contracts to be let to the lowest responsible bidder." (*J.L. Manta, Inc. v. Braun*, 393 N.W.2d 490, 491 (Minn. 1986) (citing *Foley Brothers, Inc. v. Marshall*, 123 N.W.2d 387, 391 (Minn. 1963)).)

1. Bid Protest Rules May Be in the RFB Itself

For some RFBs, the state will provide a bid protest procedure. These procedures may include a very short window for filing a protest, ten days for example, and should be noted when submitting a bid. Failure to follow the procedures delineated in the RFB may result in waiver of a claim.

2. Award of Solicitation

Generally, the state must award a contract to the contractor that provides the "best value." (See Minnesota Statutes § 16C.28, subdiv. 1 (2021) (requiring that the award be made to the contractor "offering the best value applying the weighted selection criteria").) For building and construction contracts that require competitive bidding, the state may award the contract to either the "lowest responsible bidder" or the vendor offering the best value. (*Id.* subdiv. 1 (2015); see also Minnesota Rule 1230.0150, subdiv. 20 (2015) (defining "responsible vendor").)

Some discretion to determine the lowest bidder exists for government sub-units, but "their judgment must be based upon some reasonable ground before a low bid can be rejected." (*Foley Brothers, Inc. v. Marshall*, 123 N.W.2d 387, 390 (Minn. 1963) (citing *Otter Tail Power Co. v. Elbow Lake*, 49 N.W.2d 197, 201 (Minn. 1951)).)

3. Rejection of Bids

A bid should be rejected if it materially deviates from the bid invitation on price, quality, quantity, time, manner of performance, or "other things that go into the actual determination of the amount of the bid." (*Foley Brothers, Inc. v. Marshall*, 123 N.W.2d 387, 390 (Minn. 1963).) "A proposal containing immaterial variances or minor technical defects, however, should not be rejected if the defect does not affect the substance of the bid." *Transit Team, Inc. v. Metropolitan Council*, 679 N.W.2d 390, 397 (Minn. Ct. App. 2004) (citation omitted).) A variance is considered substantial when it "gives a bidder a substantial advantage or benefit not enjoyed by other bidders." (*Telephone Associates, Inc. v. St. Louis County Board*, 364 N.W.2d 378, 382 (Minn. 1985) (citation omitted); *Byrd v. Independent School District No. 194*, 495 N.W.2d 226 (Minn. Ct. App. 1993), *review denied*.)

Minor irregularities in a solicitation may be waived. (Minnesota Rule 1230.0700, subpt. 4; *J.L. Manta, Inc. v. Braun*, 393 N.W.2d 490, 491 (Minn. 1986); see, e.g., *Foley Brothers, Inc. v. Marshall*, 123 N.W.2d 387, 391 (Minn. 1963) (filing a certificate of non-collusion rather than an affidavit); *Nielsen v. City of St. Paul*, 88 N.W.2d 853, 860 (Minn. 1958) (submitting a bid a short time after the time set by the specifications); but see *Rexton, Inc. v. State*, 521 N.W.2d 51, 53 (Minn. Ct. App. 1994) (state agency did not have discretion to accept bid that was one minute late because of Rule 1230.0700, subpt. 1 (1993)).) Even if considered minor, alterations and erasures on the bid form must be made in ink. (Minnesota Statutes § 16C.28, subdiv. 2 (2015).)

The government may reject all bids and re-advertise a contract only for sufficient cause. (*J.L. Manta, Inc. v. Braun*, 393 N.W.2d 490, 494 (Minn. 1986); Minnesota Rule 1230.0700 (2015).) The express reservation of the right to reject all bids, coupled with the expectation that the next round will produce lower bids, is sufficient cause to reject all bids. (*Ryan v. City of Coon Rapids*, 462 N.W.2d 420, 422 (Minn. Ct. App. 1990).) Officials who reject all bids have not acted in an arbitrary and capricious manner if the contractors were given an equal opportunity to bid and if the process gave the taxpayers the best bargain for the money. (*Schwandt Sanitation v. Paynesville*, 423 N.W.2d 59, 65 (Minn. Ct. App. 1988).)

4. Relief Available for Bid Protests

a. *Injunctive Relief*

A court may enjoin an improper award after reviewing the public agency action but need not directly award the contract to the disappointed bidder. (*J.L. Manta, Inc. v. Braun*, 393 N.W.2d 490, 493–94 (Minn. 1986).) A court must consider five factors when determining whether to issue an injunction preventing an award. (*Dahlberg Brothers v. Ford Motor Co.*, 137 N.W.2d 314, 321–22 (Minn. 1965).) These factors are the (1) pre-existing relationship of the parties; (2) relative hardships suffered by each party if the injunction is or is not issued; (3) likelihood of success on the merits; (4) public policy concerns; and (5) the administrative burdens of judicial supervision. (*Id.*) Applying the factors to a bid protest scenario, an award of a bid can lead to the irreparable injury of unrecoverable lost profits. (*Queen City Construction, Inc. v. City of Rochester*, 604 N.W.2d 368, 372 (Minn. Ct. App. 1999) (Once a contract is let, a contractor's "remedies are limited to recovery of the amount it spent preparing the bid."), *review denied*; (*cf.* Minnesota Statutes § 471.345, subdiv. 14 (2015).)

b. *Monetary Compensation*

Damages for lost profits are not awarded because government contracts benefit the public only. (*Telephone Associates, Inc. v. St. Louis County Board*, 364 N.W.2d 378, 382–83 (Minn. 1985) (denying recovery of lost profits under the rationale that public contracts benefit the public and do not directly benefit the contractor); see also *Carl*

Bolander & Sons Co. v. City of Minneapolis, 451 N.W.2d 204, 206 (Minn. 1990) (citing *Telephone Associates, Inc.* in finding that petitioner was entitled to promissory estoppel costs).) With regard to municipalities and other political subdivisions, only the costs of the actual bid preparation are available. (Minnesota Statutes § 471.345, subdiv. 14 (2015).)

However, there is support for the recovery of the cost of bid preparation and reasonable attorneys' fees if a bid protest *against the state* is successful, as long as the disappointed bidder proceeds diligently. In *Telephone Associates, Inc.*, the Minnesota Supreme Court awarded attorneys' fees and bid costs for a successful protest against a county, including fees and expenses incurred in the challenge before a municipal board. (364 N.W.2d 378, 383 (Minn. 1985).) This holding has not been directly overruled, but has been superseded by statute with regards to municipalities. (Minnesota Statutes § 471.345, subdiv. 14 (2015).) Thus, recovery for fees and costs in a successful protest against the state may be possible.

C. Bid Protest Appeals

Appeals from trial court decisions involving bid protests follow normal civil appellate practice.

D. Contract Disputes

1. Contract Claims

a. Execution of Contract with the State

A state contract or lease is not enforceable until (1) it has been executed by the head of the agency or a delegate that is a party to the contract; (2) it has been approved by the commissioner or delegate; and (3) the accounting system shows an allotment or encumbrance balance for the full amount of the contract liability. (*Id.* § 16C.05, subdiv. 2(a).) Due to these statutory restrictions, no work may begin on a contract until the contract is encumbered, nor can the government indemnify a vendor.

b. Waiver of Sovereign Immunity

Minnesota waives its sovereign immunity for controversies arising out of contracts created under article XI of the Minnesota Constitution. (Minnesota Statutes § 3.751, subdiv. 1; see also *McDonough v. City of Rosemount*, 503 N.W.2d 493, 497 (Minn. Ct. App. 1993) ("Generally sovereign immunity does not apply to contractual obligations."), *review denied*; 10A Eugene McQuillan, *The Law of Municipal Corporations* § 29.119 (3d ed. rev. vol. 1990) (stating that governmental immunity does not apply to contract actions).)

c. Cause of Action

Only a party to a contract may pursue a claim. (Minnesota Statutes § 3.751, subdiv. 1 (2015).) The civil action must be filed within 90 days after the plaintiff has received a "final estimate" from the state, or, at plaintiff's election, within six months after the work under the contract was completed. (*Id.* subdiv. 2.) The action will commence by filing a complaint in the district court where the cause of action arose, or alternatively in Ramsey County, and serving a copy upon the attorney general. (*Id.* subdiv. 3.) The breach of contract claim then continues in the manner of other civil actions. Additionally, a prime contractor can pursue a claim against the state for damages incurred by a subcontractor caused by the state's delay. (*St. Paul Dredging Co. v. State*, 107 N.W.2d 717, 723–24 (Minn. 1961).)

d. Relief Available

Minnesota statutes do not modify the relief available for breaches of contract. Generally, attorneys' fees may not be awarded without a specific contractual basis or statutory authority. (*Cherne Industrial, Inc. v. Grounds & Associates, Inc.*, 278 N.W.2d 81, 96 (Minn. 1979).)

2. Contract Claims Appeals

An appeal from a final judgment or order may be taken as in other civil cases. (Minnesota Statutes § 3.751, subdiv. 4 (2015).)

E. Suspension and Debarment

A business must be debarred upon its, or a principal's, conviction for a "contract crime" or violating antitrust laws in any jurisdiction. (Minnesota Rule 1230.3200 (2015); *see also* Minnesota Statutes § 161.315, subdiv. 2(b) (2015) (definition of "contract crime").) Additionally, an employee's or an agent's conviction may be imputed to the business if the business knows of, or ratifies, the action. (Minnesota Rule 1230.3300 (2015).)

Actual debarment takes place only after a contested case hearing conducted in accordance with the administrative procedures found in Minnesota Statutes chapter 14 (2015). (Minnesota Rule 1230.3400 (2015).) However, when the commissioner of transportation learns of a conviction for a contract crime, the commissioner will suspend any business with the contractor and administrative proceedings must begin within ten days of the mailing of the suspension order. (*Id.* 1230.4200.)

Not only does a bidder not have an interest in the status of another bidder, but a suspension or debarment may be negotiated away. (*Mankato Aglime & Rock Co., Inc. v. City of Mankato*, 434 N.W.2d 490, 494 (Minn. Ct. App. 1989) (court disallowed a disappointed bidder's challenge to MnDOT's settlement agreement that revoked the suspension of an ultimately successful bidder).)

V. Administrative and Judicial Review

A. Administrative Review

There is no formal administrative process for disputes involving contracts and bids. As stated in Part IV, an informal appeal of a bid decision may be made to the procurement contact listed in the bid. If this contact is unsatisfactory to the disappointed bidder, then the bidder may seek redress from the procurement contact's superiors. The Department of Administration encourages these informal appeals procedures in order to resolve conflicts, and ensure proper contract administration as quickly and efficiently as possible.

B. Judicial Review

In lieu of this informal process, a bidder may immediately seek relief in the district courts.

VI. Extent of State's Adoption or Adaptation of ABA Model Procurement Code

As of 2021, Minnesota has not adopted the American Bar Association's (ABA's) Model Procurement Code and no express efforts to do so have been made by the state legislature.

VII. Cooperative Purchasing

A. Authority

Minnesota has adopted the use of cooperative purchasing agreements. (Minnesota Statutes § 16C.10(4); see also *id.* § 471.345, subdiv. 15(a) (2019).) Under Minnesota Statutes section 471.59, municipalities (e.g., cities, towns, school districts, and political subdivisions of other states) are entitled to jointly issue a solicitation for a competitive bid for a specific product or service. Further, municipalities are authorized to make purchases through cooperative agreements without duplicating the bid process or traditional competitive bidding efforts. (*Id.* § 471.345, subdiv. 15 (specifically authorizing a municipality to purchase through a national municipal association's purchasing alliance or cooperative created by a joint powers agreement).) Finally, the Office of the State Auditor has affirmed that state and local government officials may contract through a cooperative purchasing agreement without resort to traditional means of competitive solicitation. (See *Best Practices Review: Contracting and Procurement in the Public Sector* 17 (Nov. 15, 2005).)

B. Requirements

Minnesota has not issued pertinent guidance on how a contractor can qualify for a contract under a cooperative purchasing agreement. However, for a contract in excess of $25,000, a municipality "must consider the availability, price, and quality of supplies, materials, or equipment available through the state's cooperative purchasing venture before purchasing through another source." (Minnesota Statutes § 471.345, subdiv. 15(a) (2019).) There is not yet case law interpreting this provision, so it remains an open question as to whether a municipality's failure to "consider" a cooperative purchasing venture under subdivision 15(a) would entitle a contractor to lodge a bid protest.

Mississippi Procurement Rules and Regulations

Prepared by Adam Stone, Kaytie M. Pickett, and Amber L. Kipfmiller
Jones Walker LLP
Email: astone@joneswalker.com, kpickett@joneswalker.com, and akipfmiller@joneswalker.com

I. Statutory Reference

Mississippi's procurement laws are generally found in the Public Purchases volume of the Code, volume 31 (Mississippi Code titles 29 and 31, primarily sections 29-17-1 through 31-31-41). Volumes 23 through 25 of the Code contain statutes relating to regulation of trade, commerce, and investments, including the Uniform Commercial Code. The following statutes are of particular importance:

A. Public Construction Contracts

Mississippi Code Annotated § 31-3-21

B. Public Works Contracts

Mississippi Code Annotated § 31-5-3 *et seq.*

C. Public Purchases

Mississippi Code Annotated § 31-7-1 *et seq.*

D. Public Leases of Buildings, Facilities, and Equipment

Mississippi Code Annotated § 31-8-1 *et seq.*

E. Surplus Property

Mississippi Code Annotated § 31-9-1 *et seq.*

F. Counties Utility Services

Mississippi Code Annotated § 19-5-185

G. Education Transportation and Textbooks

Mississippi Code Annotated § 37-41-101
Mississippi Code Annotated § 37-43-25

H. Correctional System Operation and Management

Mississippi Code Annotated § 47-5-105

I. Airport Authorities

Mississippi Code Annotated § 61-3-37

J. Highways, Roads, and Bridges

Mississippi Code Annotated § 65-19-31

K. Public Utilities

Mississippi Code Annotated § 77-3-16

II. Regulations

Mississippi has different procurement rules and regulations depending on the type of contract (construction, purchase, or service) and the agencies involved. Service contracts fall within the purview of the Public Procurement Review Board (PPRB) under the Department of Finance and Administration (DFA). Contracts for the purchase of commodities and equipment are also regulated by the DFA but have their own regulations promulgated by the Mississippi Bureau of Purchasing and Contracting. Construction contracts similarly fall under the DFA but have their own regulations promulgated by the Mississippi Bureau of Building, Grounds, and Real Property Management. The following regulations are of particular importance:

A. Procuring Agency Regulations

These regulations can be found at https://www.sos.ms.gov/content/documents/reg_enf/admin/Index%20to%20Titles.pdf.

B. Service Contracts: PPRB

These contracts are under the DFA and the regulations ("PPRB Rules and Regulations") are located at https://www.dfa.ms.gov/media/9413/pprb-opscr-rules-and-regulations-efficetive-01182020.pdf.

C. Purchase/Lease/Rental of Commodities and Equipment: Mississippi Bureau of Purchasing and Contracting

This form of contracting is under the DFA, and details can be found in the Mississippi Procurement Manual at https://www.dfa.ms.gov/media/6014/procurement-manual.pdf.

D. Construction Contracts: Mississippi Bureau of Building, Grounds, and Real Property Management

Regulations for this form of contracting can be found in the BOB Manual at https://www.dfa.ms.gov/media/6241/01-engineering-construction-bob-procedure-manual.pdf.

III. Source Selection

A. Purchase/Lease/Rental of Commodities or Equipment

Unless subject to a specific exception, all agencies and governing authorities shall purchase their equipment; commodities and printing; contract for garbage collection or disposal; contract for solid waste collection or disposal; contract for sewage collection or disposal; contract for public construction; and contract for rentals as provided in Mississippi Code Annotated section 31-7-13 (effective July 1, 2021). Generally, those requirements are:

1. Contracts Not over $5,000

- No bids required

2. Contracts over $5,000 but Not over $50,000

- Two quote bids required
- Awarding body must document best bid (Mississippi Code Annotated § 31-7-13(d).)

3. Contracts over $50,000

- Advertise for bids
- Award to the "lowest and best bidder"
- If not awarded to the lowest bidder, must document why

B. Service Contracts

In Mississippi, service contracts are regulated by PPRB. PPRB's regulations contain the procedures for requests for proposals or bids for service contracts. Generally, those requirements are:

1. Contracts under $75,000

- Does not require approval of PPRB
- Must follow procedures for small purchases (section 3-205 of PPRB's Rules and Regulations)

2. Contracts over $75,000

- Requires approval of PPRB

3. Exempt Contracts

The following contracts are exempt from the purview of PPRB: accountant, actuary, engineer, architect, attorney, utility rate expert services, auditor, and those contracts exempt under section 3-101.02 of PPRB's Rules and Regulations (citing Mississippi Code Annotated § 27-104-7).

IV. Bid Protests and Contract Disputes

A. Bid Protests

In Mississippi, a public owner must award a construction project to the "lowest and best" bidder. (*Parker v. Crawford*, 68 So. 2d 281, 285 (Miss. 1953).) The Mississippi Supreme Court has long held that the lowest responsible bidder is not necessarily synonymous with the lowest bidder. (*M.T. Reed Construction Co. v. Jackson Municipal Airport Authority*, 227 So. 2d 466, 469 (Miss. 1969); *Cooper v. Townsend*, 108 So. 273 (Miss. 1926).) In reviewing decisions not to award jobs to the lowest bidder, Mississippi courts give the awarding body broad discretion. (*Walley v. Board of Trustees of Richton Municipal School District*, 241 So. 2d 644, 646 (Miss. 1970) (holding if discretion honestly exercised award should be upheld).)

The Mississippi Code requires that an awarding body place on its minutes "detailed calculations and [a] narrative summary showing that the accepted bid was determined to be the lowest and best bid" should the low bid not be accepted. (Mississippi Code Annotated § 31-7-13(d)(i) (effective July 1, 2021).) The Mississippi Supreme Court has held that the statutory scheme regarding bidding is not to be taken lightly and should be followed. (*Richardson v. Canton Farm Equipment*, 608 So. 2d 1240 (Miss. 1992).)

However, any error in the bid-letting process does not automatically void the resulting contract. (*Huey Stockstill, Inc. v. Hales*, 730 So. 2d 539, 543 (Miss. 1998).) In *Hales*, there were close and possibly inappropriate ties between the awarding body and the low bidding contractor. (*Id.* at 541.) Because of these ties, and concerns about the appearance of impropriety, the county ultimately decided not to award the job to the lowest bidder. (*Id.*) In so doing, the county at first failed to make a note of the reasoning in the minutes. (*Id.*) Realizing its error, the county subsequently amended its minutes to reflect its reasoning. (*Id.*) The Mississippi Supreme Court held that because the decision of the awarding body was not arbitrary and capricious, and the reasoning was explained in the minutes, it was acceptable for the owner to award the contract to the second lowest bidder. (*Id.* at 542.)

The court in *Hales* also held that the failure to initially comply with the statute was a "technical defect" that did not void the contract. (*Id.* at 543.) When a bid defect is "technical" or a "mere technicality," the job can still be awarded to that bidder. These defects may be waived by the awarding body; defects creating a material change in time, price, or work may not be waived.

Obviously, the definition of a "mere technicality" is all important. In defining a "technicality," the Mississippi Supreme Court holds that if the defect effected "a material change in time, price, or work" the defect is not a technicality. (*Landmark Structures, Inc. v. City Council for the City of Meridian*, 826 So. 2d 746, 747 (Miss. 2002).) A defect is also not technical if it gives the bidder a competitive advantage over other bidders. (*Id.*)

The Mississippi Administrative Procedures Law designates the Office of the Secretary of State as the official registrar for the rules of all state agencies. Each state agency proposes its own rules and regulations, seeks public comment on the proposed changes, and ultimately adopts the final rules or regulations.

Section 7-112.01 of PPRB's Rules and Regulations sets forth the process for protesting a *state agency bid* in Mississippi. Note, however, that the process for protesting a decision by a county or municipality is statutorily governed, as discussed in Section V.B below, and the Mississippi Procurement Manual and PPRB's Rules and Regulations do not apply.

Protestors of an agency bid should seek resolution of their complaints initially with the office that issued the solicitation. Any actual or prospective bidder who is aggrieved in connection with the solicitation or award of a contract may protest to the chief procurement officer and copy the DFA director of the Office of Personal Service Contract Review (OPSCR). The protest must be submitted in writing within seven calendar days of the notice of intent to award or within seven calendar days of the solicitation.

A protest is considered filed when received by the chief procurement officer. Protests filed after the seven-day period will not be considered. The chief procurement officer must then submit a copy of the protest to OPSCR within three business days of receipt of the written protest. OPSCR then forwards a copy of the protest to the special assistant attorney general.

To file a protest directly to PPRB, the aggrieved party must file a protest with OPSCR within seven calendar days after the aggrieved party knew or should have known of the facts and circumstances upon which the protest is based, but in no event later than within seven days of the solicitation posting or award.

To expedite handling of protests, the envelope should be labeled "Protest." The written protest must include at a minimum the following:

1. The name and address of the protestor
2. Appropriate identification of the procurement and, if a contract has been awarded, its number
3. A statement of reasons for the protest
4. Supporting exhibits, evidence, or documents to substantiate any claims unless not available within the filing time, in which case the expected availability date must be indicated

If the protest is not resolved by mutual agreement, the agency head must promptly issue a decision in writing. The decision shall (1) state the reasons for the action taken; and (2) inform the protestor of the right to administrative review. A copy of the decision will then be mailed or otherwise furnished in writing immediately to the protestor and any other interested party.

A decision on a protest will be made by the agency head or PPRB as expeditiously as possible after receiving all relevant, requested information. If a protest is sustained, the available remedies include, but are not limited to, cancellation or revision of the solicitation in accordance with section 5-204 (Remedies Prior to an Award) or cancellation of the contract in accordance with section 5-205 (Remedies after an Award) of PPRB's Rules and Regulations.

A decision is considered final and conclusive, unless fraudulent, or any person adversely affected by the decision appeals administratively to PPRB. The agency head will refuse to decide any protest when a matter involved is the subject of a proceeding before PPRB or has been decided on the merits by PPRB. If an action concerning the protest has commenced in court, the agency head or PPRB must not act on the protest. This section does not apply where PPRB or a court requests, expects, or otherwise expresses interest in the decision of the agency head or PPRB.

On any direct protest, PPRB must decide whether the solicitation or award was in accordance with the Mississippi Constitution, statutes, rules and regulations, and the terms and conditions of the solicitation. The proceeding is de novo. Any prior determinations by administrative officials are not considered final or conclusive. A determination of an issue of fact by PPRB is considered final and conclusive unless arbitrary, capricious, fraudulent, or clearly erroneous.

In the event of a timely protest, the agency must not proceed further with the solicitation or with the award of the contract until PPRB approves the determination that continuation of the solicitation or award of the contract without delay is necessary to protect substantial interests of the state.

Any person adversely affected by the protest decision of an agency head may appeal administratively to PPRB within seven calendar days of receipt of a protest decision.

B. Contract Disputes

How a contract claim is handled in Mississippi varies with every agency. Those dealing with such claims have to review the procedures of the particular agency they are dealing with to determine the procedure.

C. Suspension and Debarment

1. PPRB

PPRB has the authority to debar or suspend a person from consideration for award of contracts. The debarment and suspension processes are found in section 5-101 of PPRB's Rules and Regulations.

After reasonable notice and an opportunity to be heard, a person can be debarred or suspended for (1) conviction for commission of a criminal offense as an incident to obtaining or attempting to obtain a public or private contract or subcontract, or in the performance of such contract or subcontract; (2) conviction under state or federal statutes of embezzlement, theft, forgery, bribery, falsification or destruction of records, receiving stolen property, or any other offense indicating a lack of business integrity or business honesty that currently, seriously, and directly affects responsibility as a Mississippi contractor; (3) conviction under state or federal antitrust statutes arising out of the submission of bids, proposals, or qualifications; (4) violation of contract provisions, as set forth below, of a character that is regarded by PPRB to be so serious as to justify debarment action, including (i) deliberate failure without good cause to perform in accordance with the specifications or within the time limit provided in the contract, or (ii) a recent record of failure to perform or of unsatisfactory performance in accordance with the terms of one or more contracts, provided that failure to perform or unsatisfactory performance caused by acts beyond the control of the contractor shall not be considered to be a basis for debarment; (5) any other cause PPRB determines to be so serious and compelling as to affect responsibility as a Mississippi contractor, including debarment by another governmental entity for any cause listed herein; and (6) violation of the ethical standards set forth in chapter 6 (Ethics in Contracting for Personal and Professional Services) of the PPRB's Rules and Regulations.

2. Mississippi Board of Contractors

Contractors working in Mississippi are regulated by the Mississippi Board of Contractors. The statutes governing the Mississippi Board of Contractors are found at Mississippi Code Annotated section 31-3-1 *et seq*. The Board further regulates commercial construction pursuant to its internal regulations that can be found at http://www.

msboc.us/wp-content/uploads/2015/10/COMMERCIAL-LAWS-AND-RULES-REVISED-2015.pdf.

Residential contractors are regulated under a separate set of rules that can be found at https://www.msboc.us/wp-content/uploads/2022/02/RESIDENTIAL-LAWS-AND-RULES-REVISED-2022.pdf.

The Board has broad authority in Mississippi to regulate contractors and can, after a hearing, revoke a contractor's certificate of responsibility. Under the regulations set forth above, the Board has the authority to hear all complaints, issue monetary fines, suspend licenses, and revoke licenses.

V. Administrative and Judicial Review

A. Administrative Review

The administrative review process is set forth above.

B. Judicial Review

1. Appeals from Decisions of Counties and Municipalities

Appeals from a judgment or decision of a county or municipality are governed by Mississippi Code Annotated section 11-51-75. A person aggrieved by a judgment or decision of a board of supervisors or a municipal authority may appeal within ten days from the date of adjournment at which session the board of supervisors or municipal authorities rendered the judgment or decision being appealed.

2. Appeals from Decision of Agency

There is no uniform statutory procedure for appealing the decision of an administrative body in Mississippi. There are statutory procedures, like the one for counties and cities set forth above, and there is a catch-all process for agencies that do not have their own procedure. Accordingly, it is important that anyone aggrieved by the decision of an administrative body research the Mississippi Code to determine if there is a statutory process for appeal.

There is no statute governing an appeal from the DFA. However, section 5-201 of PPRB's Rules and Regulations and section 6.208 of the Mississippi Procurement Manual provide that any person receiving an adverse decision, the state, or both may appeal from a decision by PPRB to the designated court or courts of Mississippi. But no appeal may be made by the state unless recommended by PPRB or the head of the agency involved.

Where no right to appeal exists in the relevant statutes, limited judicial review via writ of certiorari is available. (*Gill v. Mississippi Department of Wildlife Conservation*, 574 So. 2d 586, 590 (Miss. 1991).) But the appeal must be from a decision that was judicial or quasi-judicial in nature. (*Mississippi Transportation Commission v. Engineering Associates*, 39 So. 3d 1, 3 (Miss. 2010).) Pursuant to Uniform Circuit and County Court Rule 5.04, a notice of appeal must be filed within 30 days of the entry of the order or judgment being appealed.

When handling an appeal from an administrative agency, a court will only entertain an appeal to determine if the order or judgment of the lower authority (1) was supported by substantial evidence; (2) was arbitrary or capricious; (3) was beyond the power of the lower authority to make; or (4) violated some statutory or constitutional right of the complaining party. (Uniform Circuit and County Court Rule 5.03.)

VI. Extent of Mississippi's Adoption or Adaptation of ABA Model Procurement Code

Mississippi has not adopted the American Bar Association (ABA) Model Procurement Code.

VII. Cooperative Purchasing

A. Authority

The DFA's Office of Purchasing, Travel, and Fleet Management (OPTFM) maintains agency and cooperative contracts. OPTFM has the authority to require that agencies purchase from these contracts and grant exemptions from that requirement if it is determined to be in the best interest of the agency and would be an economically feasible transaction. Cooperative purchasing agreements are defined as follows:

> Purchases made by certified purchasing offices of state agencies or governing authorities under cooperative purchasing agreements previously approved by the Office of Purchasing and Travel and established by or for any municipality, county, parish or state government or the federal government, provided that the notification to potential contractors includes a clause that sets forth the availability of the cooperative purchasing agreement to other governmental entities. Such purchases shall only be made if the use of the cooperative purchasing agreements is determined to be in the best interest of the government entity.

(Mississippi Code Annotated § 31-7-13(m)(xxix).)

State agencies should note that this authority does not allow them to purchase outside the terms of the statewide competitive bid contracts unless the contract document specifically says that state agencies may use the contract or choose to purchase from a qualified cooperative purchasing agreement. The current state contracts provide the assurance that all state agencies will purchase from the contract and it would be unfair to those vendors to remove that volume without proper notification. Future contract invitations may include a clause that notifies vendors of the availability of cooperative agreements and at that time agencies would have the option.

A qualified cooperative purchasing agreement is one that has been submitted to and approved by OPTFM after careful consideration of the process used to establish the contract, the products covered, and the available prices. Vendors will not be allowed to submit contracts to OPTFM for approval. OPTFM will only consider contracts submitted by certified purchasing offices. (See sections 1.107(e) and 2.104 of the Mississippi Procurement Manual (defining "Certified Purchasing Office").)

In practical terms, this means that a vendor may approach the certified purchasing office of any city, county, or state agencies. If the certified purchasing office feels that the products/prices available under the cooperative agreement would be advantageous, they would then submit a request to OPTFM, advising OPTFM of the name of the contract, the vendor, copies of applicable websites/price lists, and so on. OPTFM will review the documents and may contact the originating purchasing entity for additional information prior to making a decision concerning the acceptability of the contract. Upon approval or disapproval, OPTFM will notify the certified purchasing offices and maintain a list of all approved contracts. Once approved, all certified purchasing offices may purchase off of the approved cooperative contract.

State agencies with certified purchasing offices are ordinarily exempt from bidding requirements when they purchase from a qualified cooperative contract. The exception would be that if a commodity is covered by a competitively bid contract, the state agencies will be required to purchase from that contract unless the contract specifically allows purchases made from cooperative contracts. Cities and counties (governing authorities) with certified purchasing offices will be exempt from bidding requirements when purchasing from a qualified cooperative contract.

Governing authorities with certified purchasing offices may use the following procedure: Purchases may be made from the bidder offering the best value. In determining the best value, bid, freight, and shipping charges must be included. Life-cycle costing, total cost bids, warranties, guaranteed buy-back provisions, documented previous experience, training costs, and other relevant provisions, including but not limited to a bidder having an office and inventory located within the jurisdiction of the governing authority, may be included in the best value calculation. (See section 2.104 of the Mississippi Procurement Manual.)

B. Requirements

1. Statewide Cooperative Contracts

Statewide cooperative contracts are established on the basis of reviewing and selecting solicited contracts from written specifications and sealed competitive bids or by those on a multiple award scheduled by consortiums that show a demonstrative cost savings. These contracts are usually awarded to the vendor that has submitted the lowest bid that meets specifications. All state agencies are allowed to purchase from cooperative contracts approved by OPTFM management. Governing authorities may purchase from other than the awarded vendor provided they purchase an identical item at or below contract price. Governing authorities may also ignore the contract and follow the procedures for an open market purchase. (See section 2.103.01.3 of the Mississippi Procurement Manual (citing Mississippi Code Annotated §§ 31-7-13 and 31-7-59).)

Any agreements between the state and a local public procurement unit that provide that certain open-ended procurement contracts (requirement contracts) must be available to the local public procurement unit must also provide for the following: (1) the state must conduct the procurements in compliance with the Mississippi Procurement Manual and applicable statutes; (2) when the governing authority elects to procure any commodity under the state contract, all of its purchases for such commodities must be obtained by placing purchase orders against the appropriate state contract in accordance with the terms and conditions of such contract; (3) payment for supplies or services ordered by the local public procurement unit under state contracts is the exclusive obligation of such jurisdiction; (4) inspection and acceptance of supplies or services ordered by the local public procurement unit under state contracts are the exclusive obligation of such jurisdiction; (5) the state may terminate the cooperative agreement for failure of the local public procurement unit to comply with the terms of the contract or pay a contractor to whom the state has awarded a contract; (6) the exercise of any warranty rights attaching to commodities received by the local public procurement unit under state contracts is the exclusive obligation of such jurisdiction; (7) failure of a local public procurement unit that is procuring commodities under a state contract to secure performance from the contractor in accordance with the terms and conditions of its purchase order will not necessarily require the state or any other local public procurement unit to consider the default or to discontinue procuring under the contract; and (8) any transactions shall be in compliance with applicable sections of Mississippi Code Annotated section 31-7. (See section 7.103.01 of the Mississippi Procurement Manual.)

2. Multi-State Cooperative Contracts

OPTFM may enter into multi-state contracts that allow state agencies and governing authorities to purchase commodities and equipment at prices established by the contract. (See section 7.105 of the Mississippi Procurement Manual.)

Missouri Procurement Rules and Regulations

Prepared by Diana C. (Farr) Carter
Brydon, Swearengen & England P.C.
Updated by Melissa J. Copeland
Schmidt & Copeland, LLC
Email: missy@schmidtcopeland.com

I. Statutory Reference

A. Procurement/Purchasing Statutes

Purchasing and procurement of supplies, equipment, and services required by the Missouri state government is governed by chapter 34 of the Revised Statutes of Missouri (RSMo) and is managed, in general, by the Missouri Office of Administration's Division of Purchasing (DP). The DP vendor manual is available at https://oa.mo.gov/sites/default/files/vendormanual.pdf.

The official Missouri Code may be accessed through the Missouri General Assembly's website: https://www.mo.gov/government/legislative-branch/. The table of contents for RSMo chapter 34 is set forth below.

§ 34.010.	Definitions.
§ 34.030.	Commissioner to purchase all supplies and lands—requirements for certain land purchases.
§ 34.031.	Recycled products, preference for products made from solid waste—elimination of purchase of products made from polystyrene foam—commissioner of administration, duties—report.
§ 34.032.	Recycled paper to be used, when—recyclable products to be collected by all state agencies—sale proceeds to fund utilicare.
§ 34.040.	Purchases to be made on competitive bids, when, how—standard specifications, when—exception—failure to pay taxes, effect of—reverse auctions, when—rulemaking authority.
§ 34.042.	Competitive bidding may be waived for competitive proposals, when—procedure—contract to be let to the lowest and best offeror.
§ 34.043.	Competitive bidding—waiver of permitted, when.
§ 34.044.	One source of supplies, waiver of competitive bids and proposals—rescission of waiver, when—single source exists, when—advertising waived, when.

§ 34.045.	Emergency procurement, waiver of competitive bids or proposals.
§ 34.046.	Contract directly with other governmental entities for purchase of supplies.
§ 34.047.	Information technology purchases, online bidding/vendor registration system to be used for notice, when.
§ 34.048.	General Services Administration vendors, purchase of supplies authorized.
§ 34.050.	Regulations for purchase of supplies—rules generally, promulgation, procedure.
§ 34.055.	State to pay late charges for supplies and services, when, rate—vendor to apply, exception—energy assistance program for persons of low income, recipients exempt from interest charges.
§ 34.057.	Public works contracts—prompt payment by public owner to contractor, engineer, architect, or surveyor—prompt payment by contractor to subcontractor—progress payments—retainage—late payment charges—withholding of payments.
§ 34.058.	Public works contract, defined—certain contract clauses against public policy—exceptions.
§ 34.059.	Surety bonds required for public works contracts or construction, public entity cannot require they be obtained from particular insurance or surety company.
§ 34.060.	Requests for bids on supplies and materials to be in general terms—to recite preference for Missouri products.
§ 34.070.	Preference to Missouri products and firms.
§ 34.071.	Commodities defined.
§ 34.073.	Missouri businesses, performance of jobs or services, preference, when.
§ 34.074.	Disabled veterans, state and political subdivision contracts, preference to be given, when—rulemaking authority.
§ 34.076.	Out-of-state contractors or products for public works, requirements, exceptions.
§ 34.080.	Institutions to use coal from Missouri or adjoining states, when—institution defined.
§ 34.090.	Laws requiring purchase from state institutions to be given effect.
§ 34.100.	Direct purchases and emergency purchases, when authorized, procedure.
§ 34.110.	Acceptance of gifts to state—purchase of surplus war materials.
§ 34.115.	Return of gifts made to state to donor, when, how—donation of motor vehicles to assist military veterans, return of title, when.
§ 34.120.	Departments to report supplies on hand, records of purchase.
§ 34.125.	Departments to keep inventories of nonexpendable property.
§ 34.140.	Inventory of removable equipment, when—transfer of supplies between departments, when—distribution to certain donees, definitions, procedure—sale by auction, sealed bid—sidearms and badges, who may purchase, when.
§ 34.150.	Violation by any department renders contract void—liability of head of department.
§ 34.160.	Commissioner not to be interested in concern making bids for furnishing supplies or printing—penalty for violation.
§ 34.165.	Commissioner to give bidding preference to the blind, when—authority to make rules—auditor may examine records, when.

STATE PRINTING	
§ 34.170.	Commissioner to purchase all state printing—exceptions.
§ 34.175.	Soybean-based ink to be used for state printing, when—logo requirement—effective when.
§ 34.180.	To determine form of printed matter—exceptions.
§ 34.190.	Determine size and number of reports to be printed.
§ 34.192.	Reports, method of preparation—minimization of volume of printed material produced.
FAIRNESS IN PUBLIC CONSTRUCTION	
§ 34.203.	Citation of law.
§ 34.206.	Purpose statement.
§ 34.209.	Requirements for certain contracts for construction, repair, remodeling, or demolition of facilities.
§ 34.212.	Grants, tax abatements or tax credits, and cooperative agreements for construction projects prohibited, when.
§ 34.217.	Nonseverability clause.
§ 34.218.	Violations, remedies—investigation of complaints.
DOMESTIC PRODUCT PROCUREMENT ACT (BUY AMERICAN)	
§ 34.350.	Missouri Domestic Products Procurement Act—law, how cited—definitions.
§ 34.353.	All public agencies and political subdivisions to purchase or lease only goods or commodities produced in the United States, exceptions, procedure.
§ 34.355.	Vendor to furnish proof of compliance—misrepresentation of facts, penalty.
§ 34.359.	Treaties and law of the United States to supersede.
§ 34.363.	Listing of Missouri products, Office of Administration to compile and provide access—state agencies to make good faith search for Missouri companies to provide products and services.
MISSOURI CALCIUM INITIATIVE	
§ 34.375.	Purchasing agents for governmental agencies to give preference to food and beverages containing higher levels of calcium, exceptions.
	TRANSPARENCY IN PRIVATE ATTORNEY CONTRACTS ACT
§ 34.376.	Citation of act—definitions.
§ 34.378.	Contingent fee contracts, limitations—written proposals, when—standard addendum—posting of contracts on website—record-keeping requirements—fees, limitation on—report, contents.
§ 34.380.	Contractual authority not expanded.
	ANTI-DISCRIMINATION AGAINST ISRAEL ACT
§ 34.600.	Citation of law—public entity contracts, no boycott of goods or services from Israel—definitions—violation, voiding of contract—rulemaking authority.

B. Other Applicable Statutes

The DP is not responsible for bidding and awarding capital improvements contracts. Bidding for design, construction, renovation, and repair of state facilities is governed by RSMo chapter 8 and is the responsibility of the Office of Administration, Division of Facilities Management, Design, and Construction. (See https://oa.mo.gov/facilities.)

Missouri's effort to conserve natural resources through recycling and the procurement of recycled products is coordinated through the Recycling Program. (Information on this program is available at https://oa.mo.gov/general-services/missouri-state-recycling-program.)

The Office of Equal Opportunity works with the DP and provides certification and assistance services to minority- and women-owned businesses (MBEs and WBEs). (Information may be found at https://oeo.mo.gov. See also Minority and Women Business Enterprises, RSMo §§ 37.020–37.023.)

Ethics rules for certain elected and appointed public officials and employees and others are found at RSMo sections 105.450–105.496.

The State Lottery Law is at RSMo sections 313.200–313.350.

Statutes pertaining to the State Transportation Department can be found at RSMo chapter 226.

RSMo chapters 172, 174, 175, and 178 pertain to Missouri colleges and universities.

Pursuant to RSMo section 34.040(7), state agencies shall not contract for goods or services with a vendor if the vendor or an affiliate makes sales at retail but fails to collect and properly pay the tax as provided in RSMo chapter 144.

Also note that RSMo chapter 34 contains certain preferences, including:

- Domestic Product Procurement Act ("Buy American Act") (RSMo §§ 34.350–34.359)
- Buy Missouri preferences (RSMo §§ 34.070–34.073)
- Missouri service-disabled veteran business preference (RSMo § 34.074)
- Missouri Calcium Initiative (RSMo § 34.375)
- Recycled product preference (RSMo § 34.031)
- Organizations for the blind and sheltered workshops (RSMo § 34.165)

II. Regulations

The Missouri purchasing regulations are promulgated pursuant to the statutory authority of RSMo section 34.050 and are found in the Missouri Code of State Regulations (CSR) at title 1, section 40-1.050 *et seq*. The regulations are available online at https://www.sos.mo.gov/cmsimages/adrules/csr/current/1csr/1c40-1.pdf. The CSR title 1 table of contents for the purchasing regulations is set forth below.

Executive Order No. 05-30 addresses targets for the percentage of goods and services to be procured from certified MBEs and WBEs.

Executive Order No. 04-09 requires each vendor submitting a bid to provide certification of the location where the contracted services are to be performed and whether the vendor contemplates any of the work necessary to provide the contracted services being provided offshore.

III. Source Selection

All purchases over $3,000 are subject to competitive procurement requirements. For all purchases of $25,000 or more, a formal, sealed, and advertised procurement method is required. Other methods may be used as deemed in the best interest of the state of Missouri, but the DP uses three basic types of procurement methods:

Invitation for Bid (IFB): An IFB is a formal request for sealed bids. The document contains standard technical specifications and a formal bid opening date and time with which the bidder must comply in order to be considered for award. Subjective evaluation criteria may be used.

Request for Proposal (RFP): An RFP is used for complex requirements that preclude the use of specific specifications or requirements. An RFP contains functional specifications for which the offeror must respond with a sealed proposal. A formal proposal opening date and time is specified. Subjective evaluation criteria may be used to select a contractor, and negotiations may be conducted with those offerors who submit potentially acceptable proposals.

Single Feasible Source: This method is used when the goods or services are proprietary and only available from the manufacturer or a single distributor. This method may also be used to take advantage of special, limited-time discounts from a single distributor when, based on past procurement experience, it is determined that only one distributor services the region in which the supplies are needed.

State agencies subject to the requirements of RSMo chapter 34 have been delegated the authority to make most purchases of less than $25,000 without involving the DP, subject to compliance with Missouri law and the rules, regulations, and procedures promulgated by the DP.

Universities and colleges subject to the requirements of RSMo chapter 34 have been delegated the authority to make most purchases without involving the DP, subject to compliance with Missouri law and the rules, regulations, and procedures promulgated by the DP.

RSMo sections 34.042–34.045 contain certain exemptions, including authorizing the commissioner of administration to waive the requirement of competitive bids or proposals in certain emergency procurement situations.

All solicitation requests are available on Missouri's online bidding/vendor registration website: https://missouribuys.mo.gov/bidboard. Contract awards are made to the lowest and best bidder in accordance with the evaluation criteria published in the solicitation document. Award results are available on Missouri's online bidding/vendor registration website.

IV. Bid Protests and Contract Disputes

A. Bid Protests

Pursuant to CSR title 1, section 40-1.050(12), a bid or proposal award protest must be submitted in writing and must be received by the DP within ten business days after the date of award. If the tenth day falls on a Saturday, Sunday, or state holiday, the period shall extend to the next state business day. A protest submitted after the ten-business-day period shall not be considered.

The written protest should include the following information: (1) name, address, and phone number of the protester; (2) signature of the protester or the protester's representative; (3) solicitation number; (4) detailed statement describing the grounds for the protest; and (5) supporting exhibits, evidence, or documents to substantiate the claim. A protest that fails to contain the information listed above may be denied solely on that basis. All protests filed in a timely manner will be reviewed by the director or designee. The director or designee will only issue a determination on the issues asserted in the protest. A protest that is untimely or fails to establish standing to protest will be summarily denied. In other cases, the determination will contain findings of fact, an analysis of the protest, and a conclusion that the protest will either be sustained or denied. If the protest is sustained, remedies include canceling the award. If the protest is denied, no further action will be taken by the division.

B. Bid Protest Appeals

The statutes and regulations governing the purchasing and procurement of supplies, equipment, and services required by the Missouri state government do not address appeals to the courts of Missouri. Remedies such as a writ of mandamus or injunctive relief are generally available under Missouri law.

The U.S. Court of Appeals for the Eighth Circuit has held that an unsuccessful bidder has standing to challenge a contract award under Missouri law when "the bidding procedure did not permit all bidders to compete on equal terms." (*Metropolitan Express Services, Inc. v. City of Kansas City*, 23 F.3d 1367 (8th Cir. 1994).)

C. Contract Disputes

RSMo sections 34.055 and 34.057 address payments to contractors, and section 34.057(6) provides possible reasons for the owner to withhold payment from a contractor, subcontractor, or supplier.

The statutes and regulations governing the purchasing and procurement of supplies, equipment, and services required by the Missouri state government do not otherwise address disputes arising between a contractor and the state during the performance of a public contract. The DP Vendor Manual provides that once a contract is awarded, the contractor will begin to work directly with the personnel for the state agency for whom the supplies, equipment, and/or services were purchased.

Asamoah-Boadu v. State, 328 S.W.3d 790 (Mo. Ct. App. 2010), is an example of a breach of contract case involving the Office of Administration.

D. Suspension and Debarment

A vendor suspension is an exclusion from bidding and/or contracting with the state for a set, temporary period of time, while a vendor debarment is an exclusion from contracting with the state for an indefinite period of time.

Pursuant to CSR title 1, section 40-1.060(6), a vendor may be suspended for cause. The vendor is to be mailed a formal notice of suspension outlining the reasons for, the specific conditions of, and the effective period of the suspension. Upon completion of the suspension period, it is the responsibility of the vendor to request reinstatement, if desired. A request for reinstatement is to be made in writing.

Suspension of a vendor may be for a period up to 180 days for the first violation, and not more than a year for subsequent violations. A vendor may appeal a suspension by submitting a written request to the director or commissioner within 14 calendar days after receipt of the formal notice. The vendor must provide specific evidence and reasons why suspension is not necessary. On the basis of such information, the suspension may be modified, rescinded, or affirmed. The decision is to be final and mailed to all parties.

Pursuant to CSR title 1, section 40-1.060(7), a vendor may be debarred whenever, in the director's sole discretion, it is in the best interests of the state to do so. A vendor may be debarred for a single incident of serious misconduct or after multiple less serious incidents. The director is to notify the vendor of the reason(s) for debarment and any action the vendor must take in order to be found eligible to contract again.

A vendor may appeal the debarment by requesting that the determination be reviewed by the commissioner of administration or a designee. Any requests for review must be in writing and filed with the commissioner within 14 calendar days after the date of receipt of the notice of debarment. The request must set forth specific evidence and reasons why debarment should be reversed. The commissioner's determination is to be final and mailed to all parties.

CSR title 1, section 40-1.060(8) contains a nonexclusive list of potential actions that are sufficient cause for suspension or debarment.

V. Administrative and Judicial Review

A. Administrative Review

The administrative review processes applicable to bid award protests and suspension and debarment proceedings are set forth above. CSR title 1, section 40-1.050(12) addresses bid protests. CSR title 1, section 40-1.060(6) and (7) address review of suspensions and debarments.

B. Judicial Review

RSMo section 536.150.1 provides, in part, that

> [w]hen any administrative officer or body existing under the constitution or by statute or by municipal charter or ordinance shall have rendered a decision which is not subject to administrative review, determining the legal rights, duties or privileges of any person, including the denial or revocation of a license, and there is no other provision for judicial inquiry into or review of such decision, such decision may be reviewed by suit for injunction, certiorari, mandamus, prohibition or other appropriate action.

The statute further provides that, in any such review proceeding, the court may hear evidence and determine whether the decision is "unconstitutional, unlawful, unreasonable, arbitrary, or capricious or involves an abuse of discretion." The reviewing court shall

> render judgment accordingly, and may order the administrative officer or body to take such further action as it may be proper to require; but the court shall not substitute its discretion for discretion legally vested in such administrative officer or body, and in cases where the granting or withholding of a privilege is committed by law to the sole discretion of such administrative officer or body, such discretion lawfully exercised shall not be disturbed.

RSMo section 536.100 provides, in part, that "[a]ny person who has exhausted all administrative remedies provided by law and who is aggrieved by a final decision in a contested case, whether such decision is affirmative or negative in form, shall be entitled to judicial review thereof, as provided in sections 536.100 to 536.140. . . ."

The U.S. Court of Appeals for the Eighth Circuit has held that an unsuccessful bidder has standing to challenge a contract award under Missouri law when "the bidding procedure did not permit all bidders to compete on equal terms." (*Metropolitan Express Services, Inc. v. City of Kansas City*, 23 F.3d 1367 (8th Cir.). See also *Public Communications Services v. Simmons*, 409 S.W.3d 538 (Mo. Ct. App. 2013).) The *Simmons* decision also addresses the procedure for judicial review of a noncontested administrative decision.

The Missouri Supreme Court established the right of a taxpayer to bring an action to enjoin the illegal expenditure of public funds under contracts entered into by public officials when the taxpayer is able to demonstrate "a direct expenditure of funds generated through taxation." (*Eastern Missouri Laborers District Council v. St. Louis County*, 781 S.W.2d 43 (Mo. 1989) (en banc). See also *State ex rel. Stricker v. Hanson*, 858 S.W.2d 771 (Mo. Ct. App. 1993).) The *Stricker* decision also addresses the requirements for the Office of Administration to enter into a valid contract, the statutory procedures for awarding state contracts, and the requirements for a "responsive bid."

State ex rel. Deere & Co. v. Missouri State Highway & Transportation Commission, 873 S.W.2d 921 (Mo. Ct. App. 1994), is an example of an injunction and mandamus case involving the Office of Administration.

The website for the Missouri judicial branch is https://www.courts.mo.gov/.

VI. Extent of State's Adoption or Adaptation of ABA Model Procurement Code

Missouri has not adopted the American Bar Association's (ABA's) Model Procurement Act.

VII. Cooperative Purchasing

The Cooperative Procurement Program provides services for political subdivisions and quasi-governmental entities of the state and allows certain qualified entities to purchase supplies and services from contracts established by the DP. Information about this program is available at https://oa.mo.gov/purchasing/cooperative-procurement-program.

A. Authority

"The commissioner of administration may contract directly with other governmental entities for the purchase of supplies. The commissioner of administration may also participate in, sponsor, conduct or administer a cooperative purchasing agreement whereby supplies are procured in accordance with a contract established by another governmental entity provided that such contract was established in accordance with the laws and regulations applicable to the establishing governmental entity." (RSMo § 34.046.) "The commissioner of administration may provide cooperative purchasing services to quasi-public governmental bodies, as defined in section 610.010, in the same manner as those services are provided to political subdivisions pursuant to section 67.360. However, this section shall not authorize the cooperative purchasing of investment and banking services." (RSMo § 37.012.) "Quasi-public governmental bodies" are defined as

> any person, corporation or partnership organized or authorized to do business in this state pursuant to the provisions of chapter 352, 353, or 355, or unincorporated association which either: a. Has as its primary purpose to enter into contracts with public governmental bodies, or to engage primarily in activities carried out pursuant to an agreement or agreements with public governmental bodies; or b. Performs a public function as evidenced by a statutorily based capacity to confer or otherwise advance, through approval, recommendation or other means, the allocation or issuance of tax credits, tax abatement, public debt, tax-exempt debt, rights of eminent domain, or the contracting of leaseback agreements on structures whose annualized payments commit public tax revenues; or any association that directly accepts the appropriation of money from a public governmental body, but only to the extent that a meeting, record, or vote relates to such appropriation.

(RSMo § 610.010.)

B. Requirements

To participate in the state's Cooperative Procurement Program, any entity eligible to participate in the program must complete and submit a Cooperative Procurement Program membership application. The cooperative contracts can only be used for public use, not personal use or consumption unless the contract specifically provides otherwise. Using entities should be prepared to report about their cooperative contracts usage if requested by the DP.

Montana Procurement Rules and Regulations

Prepared by Meghan Holmlund[1]
Chief Procurement Officer, Montana Department of Administration
Email: mholmlund@mt.gov

I. Statutory Reference

Montana purchasing is managed by the Department of Administration. The purpose of the Montana Procurement Act is to simplify, clarify, and modernize the law governing procurement by the State of Montana, specifically to make it more consistent among the various jurisdictions, to ensure fair and equitable treatment of all who deal with the Montana procurement system, and to provide the exclusive remedies for unlawful bid solicitations or contract awards.

A. Procurement/Purchasing Statutes

The table of contents of the Montana Code governing procurement follows:

Title 18. Public Contracts
Chapter 4. Montana Procurement Act

PART 1—GENERAL PROVISIONS

§ 18-4-101.	Repealed
§ 18-4-102.	Repealed
§ 18-4-103.	Repealed
§ 18-4-104.	Renumbered as 18-4-133 (Purchases exempt from general requirements)
§ 18-4-105.	Renumbered as 18-4-141 (Contract transfers and collusion prohibited—violations and penalty
§ 18-4-106.	Reserved through 18-4-110
§ 18-4-112.	Reserved through 18-4-120
§ 18-4-121.	Short title
§ 18-4-122.	Purpose—underlying purposes and policies
§ 18-4-123.	Definitions

1. Prior editions prepared by Edward C. Gassman, Gassman Law Firm, LLC.

§ 18-4-303-02.	Adequate public notice
§ 18-4-303-03.	Bid opened publicly
§ 18-4-303-04.	Records of bid amounts
§ 18-4-303-05.	Public inspection
§ 18-4-303-06.	Bids are unconditionally accepted
§ 18-4-303-07.	Correction or withdrawal
§ 18-4-303-08.	Award
§ 18-4-303-09.	Purchase description
§ 18-4-304.	Competitive sealed proposals
§ 18-4-305.	Small purchases and limited solicitations
§ 18-4-306.	Sole source procurement—records
§ 18-4-307.	Cancellation of invitations for bids or requests for proposals
§ 18-4-308.	Non-responsibility of bidders and offerors
§ 18-4-309.	Prequalification of suppliers
§ 18-4-310.	Types of contracts
§ 18-4-311.	Approval of accounting system
§ 18-4-312.	Bid and contract performance security
§ 18-4-313.	Contracts—terms, extensions, and time limits
§ 18-4-314.	Reporting of anticompetitive practices

PART 4—COOPERATIVE PURCHASING

§ 18-4-401.	Definitions
§ 18-4-402.	Cooperative purchasing authorized
§ 18-4-403.	Sale, acquisition, or use of supplies by a public procurement unit
§ 18-4-404.	Cooperative use of supplies and services
§ 18-4-405.	Joint use of facilities
§ 18-4-406.	Information and services—fees
§ 18-4-407.	Review of procurement requirements

B. Other Applicable Statutes

Title 18. Public Contracts

Chapter 1.	Public Contracts Generally
Chapter 2.	Construction Contracts
Chapter 5.	Special Purchasing Conditions
Chapter 8.	Procurement of Services
Chapter 11.	State-Tribal Cooperative Agreements

II. Regulations

The following Department of Administration Rules are the primary ones supplementing title 18 statutory references. Those interested in conducting procurement with the State of Montana will find review of the applicable administrative rules helpful.

RULE	TITLE
Subchapter 1—Special Purchasing Activities	
2.5.101.	Definitions
2.5.102.	Requisition Time Schedule
2.5.103.	Requisitioning Procedures (Preparation and Submission)
2.5.104.	Agency Purchasing Authority
2.5.105.	Term Contracts
2.5.106.	Bid List
2.5.107.	Bid Preparation
2.5.108.	Solicitation of Bids
2.5.109.	Awarding of Contracts
2.5.110.	Records of Bids
2.5.111.	Quality Control—Receipt and Inspection
2.5.112.	Nonperformance by Vendor
2.5.113.	Nonperformance by State
2.5.114.	Joint Governmental Purchase
2.5.115.	Negotiated Rehabilitation Contracts
2.5.116.	Referenced Forms
2.5.117.	Transfer of Contracts or Collusion—Additional Penalties
2.5.118.	Montana Small Business Purchasing Act
2.5.119.	Student Association Procurement Exemption
2.5.120.	The State Employees' Charitable Giving Campaign
Subchapter 2—Regulation of Procurement Activities	
2.5.201.	Definitions
2.5.202.	Department of Administration Responsibilities
Subchapter 3—Procedures for Using Agencies	
2.5.301.	Delegation of Purchasing Authority
2.5.302.	Requisitions from the Agencies to the Division
2.5.303.	Enforcing the Contract
2.5.304.	Contract Renewal
2.5.305.	Completion Notification for Contracts with Performance Security
Subchapter 4—Information for Vendors, Offerors, Bidders, and Contractors	
2.5.401.	Vendor List
2.5.402.	Suspension or Debarment from Contract Eligibility
2.5.403.	Bidding Preferences
2.5.404.	Bid and Proposal Preparation
2.5.405.	Blind Vendors' Bidding Preference
2.5.406.	Bidder, Offeror, or Contractor Protest
2.5.407.	Determination of Responsiveness/Standards of Responsibility
2.5.408.	Reciprocal Preference

Subchapter 5—General Bid and Proposal Provisions

2.5.501.	Specifications
2.5.502.	Bid, Proposal, and Contract Performance Security
2.5.503.	Public Notice
2.5.504.	Cost Principles
2.5.505.	Mistakes and Minor Variations in Bids and Offers
2.5.506.	Anticompetitive Practices
2.5.507.	Prequalification of Vendors
2.5.508.	Requests for Information
2.5.509.	Late Bids or Proposals

Subchapter 6—Types of Bids

2.5.601.	Competitive Sealed Bids
2.5.602.	Competitive Sealed Proposals
2.5.603.	Small Purchases or Limited Solicitations of Supplies and Services
2.5.604.	Sole Source Procurement
2.5.605.	Exigency Procurements
2.5.606.	Procurement of Used Equipment
2.5.607.	Procurement from Sheltered Workshops or Work Activity Centers
2.5.608.	Direct Negotiation
2.5.609.	Alternative Procurement Methods
2.5.610.	Cooperative Purchasing

Subchapter 7—Surplus Property

2.5.701.	Authority to Dispose of Supplies
2.5.702.	Disposition of Surplus Supplies

Subchapter 8—Federal Surplus Property Program

2.5.801.	Adoption of State Plan of Operation—Federal Surplus Property

Additionally:

2.12.204.	Review and Approval Process for Procurement, Development, and Oversight of Information Technology Resources and Software and Management Systems

III. Source Selection

Under the Montana Procurement Act, all specifications shall encourage competition in meeting the state's needs and may not be unduly restrictive. (Montana Code § 18-4-234.)

A. Methods of Source Selection—Authorization for Alternative Procurement Methods

The state may authorize the procurement by an alternative procurement method, providing the process to request same is followed. The state may also reject all bids if there is a supplier whose publicly advertised or established catalog price for the same material is less than the lowest responsible and responsive bidder or offeror or improves upon the conditions for the best proposal received. (Montana Code § 18-4-302.)

B. Competitive Sealed Bidding

Invitations for bids will be issued and will include the description and conditions applicable to the procurement. There will be adequate public notice. Bids will be opened publicly per the invitation and every bidder or agent has the right to be present, as does the public. Bids, once opened, are recorded and available to the public. Bids will be unconditionally accepted without change or correction, and after opening, changes in bid prices or other provisions prejudicial to the interest of the state or fair competition may not be permitted. Decisions to permit the correction or withdrawal of bids or to cancel awards or contracts based on bid mistakes must be supported by a written determination made by the department. An invitation for bids requesting the submission of unpriced offers may be issued, to be followed by an invitation for bids limited to those bidders whose offers qualified under the criteria of the first solicitation. In case of a tie bid, preference is to be given to the bidder offering American-made products or supplies. (Montana Code § 18-4-303.)

C. Competitive Sealed Proposals

Proposals must be solicited through a request for proposal, with adequate public notice, and opened at the time and place designated with review by the procurement officer for release. Proposal documents may be open to the public, subject to the limitations of the Uniform Trade Secrets Act, title 30, chapter 14, part 4; matters involving individual safety; and other constitutional protections. The department may discuss a proposal with an offeror in order to clarify or revise the proposal. (Montana Code § 18-4-304.)

D. Small Purchases and Limited Solicitation

Any procurement not exceeding the amount specified by rule may follow the procedures established by the department for such purchases. Procurement requirements may not be artificially divided to satisfy this procedure. (Montana Code § 18-4-305.)

E. Sole Source Procurement

Contracts may be awarded without competition, per procedures adopted, when there is only one source for the supply or service item, there is only one source acceptable or suitable for the supply or service item, or the supply or service item must be compatible with current supplies or services. (Montana Code § 18-4-306.)

F. Cancellation of Invitations for Bids or Requests for Proposals

The state may cancel an invitation for bids, a request for proposal, or other solicitation, and any or all bids may be rejected in whole or in part when it is in the best interests of the state. (Montana Code § 18-4-307.)

G. Types of Contracts

Any type of contract that will promote the best interests of the state may be used. (Montana Code § 18-4-310.)

H. Contracts—Terms, Extensions, and Time Limits

With some exceptions, a contract, lease, or rental agreement for supplies or services may not exceed seven years, including any extensions or renewals. (Montana Code § 18-4-313.)

IV. Bid Protests and Contract Disputes

Collusion or secret agreements between vendors to the disadvantage of the state are prohibited. The state may declare the contract void. If any collusion or other anticompetitive practices are suspected, a notice with the relevant facts shall be transmitted to the attorney general by the department. (Montana Code §§ 18-4-141, 18-4-314.)

A. Bid Protests

Except for small purchases or limited solicitations, a bidder, offeror, or contractor who feels aggrieved by the solicitation or award of a contract may protest to the department in writing no later than 14 days after the execution of the contract. If the protest is not mutually resolved, the department must issue a decision in writing within 30 days of receipt of the protest. (Montana Code § 18-4-242.)

B. Bid Protest Appeals

After the department's determination, the aggrieved party may, within 14 days after the date of the decision, request a contested case hearing provided for in the Montana Administrative Procedure Act. (Montana Code § 18-4-242.)

C. Contract Disputes

A contractor, before proceeding to bring an action in court, shall resort to the procedure within the time specified in the contract or, if a time is not specified, within 90 days after the question or dispute has arisen. (Montana Code § 18-1-402.)

D. Suspension and Debarment

The department may remove a vendor for cause, or temporarily suspend a vendor, from consideration for award of contracts by the state. Suspension comes when there is probable cause to believe that the activities of the vendor will lead to removal or there is an indictment for an offense that would lead to removal. The suspension, at the request of the attorney general, will be in effect at a minimum until after the trial. Some causes for removal or suspension include violation of contract provisions, deliberate failure without good cause to perform per the specifications or within the time limit provided, recent record of failure to perform on one or more contracts, or any cause determined to be so serious or compelling, including removal by another government entity. (Montana Code § 18-4-241.)

V. Administrative and Judicial Review

The state is not required to delay, halt, or modify the procurement process pending the result of a protest, contested case proceeding, or judicial review. (Montana Code § 18-4-242.)

A. Administrative Review

The department is responsible for the review of contested bid solicitations and contract awards. In a protest or contested case proceeding, the department may do the following: if a solicitation or award is determined to be in violation of the law, the solicitation or award may be cancelled, or revised to comply with the law. If, after the solicitation or award of a contract, it is determined that the solicitation or award of the contract is in violation of the law, and the awarded person did not act fraudulently or in bad faith, the department may ratify and affirm the contract if the determination is that it is in the best interests of the state; or terminate the contract with compensation for the person awarded the contract. If the department determines the awarded person did act fraudulently or in bad faith, the contract may be declared void, or be ratified and affirmed if that action is in the best interests of the state, without prejudice to the state's rights to appropriate damages. (Montana Code § 18-4-242.)

B. Judicial Review

The specific method of judicial review of a solicitation or award by the department is by a petition for judicial review pursuant to section 2-4-702. The court may, in an appropriate case, order a remedy as provided within section 18-4-242. There is no right, except as provided above, under any legal theory to damages or expenses for a solicitation or award of a contract in violation of the law. (Montana Code § 18-4-242.)

VI. Extent of State's Adoption or Adaptation of ABA Model Procurement Code

The Montana Procurement Act resides in title 18, chapter 4. Montana has not adopted the American Bar Association (ABA) Model Procurement Code. However, in those rules and administrative procedures that Montana has adopted, they are generally similar in nature and requirements to those of the ABA Model Procurement Code.

VII. Cooperative Purchasing

A. Authority

The department may participate in, sponsor, conduct, or administer a cooperative purchasing agreement for the procurement of any supplies or services with one or more public procurement units in accordance with an agreement entered into between the participants. (Montana Code § 18-4-402.) A "public procurement unit" means a local or state public procurement unit of this or any other state, including an agency of the United States, or a tribal procurement unit. (Montana Code § 18-4-401(3).)

B. Requirements

Cooperative purchasing may include purchasing through federal supply schedules of the U.S. General Services Administration, joint or multiparty contracts between public procurement units, open-ended state public procurement unit contracts that are made available to local public procurement units, and competitive contracts established by for-profit, not-for-profit, or nonprofit cooperative entities. (Montana Code § 18-4-402.)

Nebraska Procurement Rules and Regulations

Prepared by William T. Foley and Blake S. Schneiderwind
Erickson | Sederstrom, P.C., L.L.O.
Email: wfoley@eslaw.com, schneiderwind@eslaw.com

I. Statutory Reference

A. Procurement/Purchasing Statutes

The Nebraska Revised Statutes (the Nebraska Statutes) may be accessed through the Nebraska Unicameral Legislature website at https://nebraskalegislature.gov/laws/browse-statutes.php.

Nebraska Statutes section 81-153 *et seq*. set out specific requirements relating to the procurement of goods by the State of Nebraska. Nebraska Statutes sections 73-501 through 73-509 set out specific requirements relating to the procurement of services by the state. These include:

§ 73-501. Purposes of sections.
§ 73-502. Terms, defined.
§ 73-503. Documentation; requirements.
§ 73-504. Competitive bidding requirements.
§ 73-505. State agency directors; duties.
§ 73-506. State agency contracts for services; requirements.
§ 73-507. Exceptions.
§ 73-508. Preapproval; required; when.
§ 73-509. Pre-process; required; when; procedure.

Other chapters of the Nebraska Statutes relating to procurements of goods and services by specific entities or groups include chapter 39 (Highways and Bridges); chapter 73 (Public Lettings and Contracts); chapter 81 (State Administrative Departments); and chapter 84 (State Officers). Nebraska Statutes section 72-803 relates to public buildings construction and repair procurement and section 81-1715 relates to procuring professional services related to architecture, professional engineering, landscape architecture, or registered land surveying.

This outline reflects changes made since the previous version of this publication, which includes 2017 legislation revising threshold values for the basic methods of procurement described in Section III. The information contained herein reflects current legislation and regulations effective as of 2020 and does not reflect any pending legislation or amendments to regulations for the current legislative year. While there is legislation pending regarding certain content herein, it does not appear to be significant.

This outline is not intended to be comprehensive, but does provide basic procurement rules and regulations for the competitive bidding process in Nebraska.

B. Other Applicable Statutes

Procurements by counties, municipalities, and utilities are governed by other sections of the Nebraska Statutes, including chapter 13 (Cities, Counties, and Other Political Subdivisions); chapters 14–17 (classes of cities—powers); chapters 18–19 (laws applicable to cities and villages); chapter 22 (Counties); chapter 23 (County Government and Officers); chapter 66 (Oils, Fuels, and Energy); and chapter 70 (Power Districts and Corporations); as well as Nebraska Constitution article XI, section 5 (Home Rule).

The Department of Administrative Services, Materiel Division performs many of the procurement processes for the State of Nebraska. Materiel Division members and employees are prohibited from accepting gifts or anything of value from a vendor or potential vendor. (Nebraska Statutes § 81-161.05.) A violation of this statute is a class IV felony and results in the loss of the member's office or position. Bribery of public officials is prohibited and violation of the statute can result in a class III misdemeanor. (Nebraska Statutes §§ 49-1492 and 49-14,101.)

The Nebraska Political Accountability and Disclosure Act addresses many issues relating to lobbyists, public officials, and potential conflicts of interest. (See Nebraska Statutes § 49-1401 *et seq.*) Lobbyists and lobbyists' clients are generally prohibited from making gifts (greater than $50) to legislators and other public officials. (Nebraska Statutes § 49-1490.) Campaign contributions are similarly regulated, at Nebraska Statutes section 49-1415, as are conflicts of interest for members of the legislature, at Nebraska Statutes section 49-1499.

II. Regulations

The Nebraska Administrative Code (NAC) can be accessed at the secretary of state's website: https://sos.nebraska.gov/regulations/rules-and-regulations-division.

The Nebraska Administrative Services Materiel Division—State Purchasing Bureau's website can be found at https://das.nebraska.gov/materiel/purchasing.html.

The Nebraska Department of Administrative Services' regulations address procurement of goods by the State of Nebraska. Within the Department of Administrative Services the Materiel Division regulates procurement. The State Purchasing Bureau, mentioned frequently throughout the rules and regulations, is a branch of the Materiel Division.

The table of contents for the Department of Administrative Services' regulations relevant to title 9, Procurement, includes:

Ch. 1. State Purchasing Bureau Bidders List
- 001. Inclusion on Bidders List
- 002. Removal from Bidders List

Ch. 2. Method of Procurement
- 001. Method of Procurement

Ch. 3. Standard Conditions and Terms of Competitive Bid Solicitation and Offer

001. Standard Conditions and Terms of Competitive Bid Solicitation and Offer

Ch. 4. Awarding of Contract

001. Lowest Responsible Bidder
002. Method of Award
003. Tie Bids and Preference
004. Bid Rejection
005. Grievances
006. Notification of Award

Ch. 5. Execution of Contract

001. Packing
002. Delivery Acceptance
003. Performance and Default
004. Assignment of Purchase Order
005. Acts of Subcontractors
006. Nondiscrimination
007. Strikes, Lockouts, or Acts of God
008. Cancellation of Purchase Order

The Nebraska Department of Transportation also addresses procurement in NAC title 409, Construction Division. Its table of contents includes:

Ch. 1. Contracts, Proposal Forms, and Qualifications of Bidders for State Highway Work—English (Metric) System Measurements

001. Abbreviations and Definitions Used on Contracts and Proposal Forms
002. Requirements for Bidders on Contracts Awarded by the Department
003. Bids
004. Disqualification of Bidders and Debarment Policy and Procedures
005. Requirements for Contract Award, Cancellation, and Execution

The NAC addresses purchasing standards in several other locations:

Department of Environmental Quality: title 131, Wastewater Treatment Facilities Construction Assistance, chapter 3, General Requirements for CWSRF and DWSRF Projects, section 001, Contract Award and Construction Activities.

Health and Human Services, Commission for the Blind and Visually Impaired: title 192, Nebraska Commission for the Blind and Visually Impaired, chapter 1, Scope of Services for the Blind and Cost Containment, section 005, Procurement of Goods and Services.

Department of Revenue, title 370, Lottery Regulations, chapter 300, Procurement

- Section 301—General
- Section 302—Competitive Bidding
- Section 303—Bids or Proposals
- Section 304—Financial Security
- Section 305—Evaluation of Bids or Proposals
- Section 306—Awarding of Contracts and Rejection of Bids or Proposals

- Section 307—Contract Remedies
- Section 308—Prospective Bidder Selection
- Section 309—Disclosure Form for Lottery Vendors

III. Source Selection

The Department of Administrative Services, Materiel Division maintains a bidders list for the purchase of goods. A vendor does not need to be on the list to bid for any particular item; however, those on the list receive periodic invitations to bid. Any person or entity wishing to be placed on the list may submit an "Application for Inclusion on Bid List" form to the State Purchasing Bureau. (See 9 NAC § 1; Nebraska Statutes §§ 39-1349, 73-101, 73-504, 81-154, 81-161, and 81-1118.) As a practical matter, a successful bidding vendor must complete the same application paperwork required for inclusion on the bidders list prior to contract award.

The basic methods of procurement include:

A. Competitive Sealed Bidding

Competitive formal sealed bids are required for goods purchases exceeding $50,000. (Nebraska Statutes § 81-1118(5)(a).) Price quotations are received by means of an "invitation to bid" form (a/k/a a "quotation request" form). A minimum of 15 days must pass between advertising for formal sealed bids and the opening of the bids. Bids must be opened publicly. Award is to be made to the lowest responsible bidder who meets the specifications set forth in the invitation to bid. All bids may be rejected; in which case, if the proposed purchase is not abandoned, new bids shall be solicited. All contracts for the construction or repair of roads or bridges must use competitive formal sealed bidding.

The Materiel Division may negotiate purchases and contracts when conditions exist to defeat the purpose and principles of public competitive bidding. (Nebraska Statutes § 81-153(9).)

B. Competitive Informal Bids

For purchases of goods totaling $25,000 to $50,000, competitive informal bids are used. (Nebraska Statutes § 81-1118(5)(b).) Price quotations may be secured and documented in a manner determined to be the most appropriate for the goods involved. An award is to be made to the lowest responsible bidder that meets the specifications set forth in the invitation to bid.

C. Unrestricted Open Market Purchase

For miscellaneous needs under $25,000, unrestricted open market purchases through the Materiel Division are used. (Nebraska Statutes § 81-1118(5)(c).) The State Purchasing Bureau may authorize an agency to purchase directly form a vendor rather than utilizing the Materiel Division if the nature of the items needed, the quantity desired, the anticipated price involved, the location of the requesting agency, the time limitations, or other circumstances indicate that the interests of the state will be served by permitting such a purchase. (See 9 NAC § 2-001.04.)

D. Federal General Services Administration Contracts

The Materiel Division may acquire goods and services through federal General Services Administration contracts without the use of competitive bidding. (See Nebraska Statutes §§ 23-3109, 73-507, and 81-153(7).) The Materiel Division shall provide a written rationale when utilizing this exception to competitive bidding that shall be kept on file.

E. Multi-State Purchasing Contracts

The Materiel Division may acquire goods and services at a price competitively bid by another state or group of states, a group of states and any political subdivision of any other state, or a cooperative purchasing organization on behalf of a group of states without the use of competitive bidding. (See Nebraska Statutes §§ 73-507 and 81-153.) The Materiel Division shall provide a written rationale when utilizing this exception to competitive bidding that shall be kept on file.

F. Sole Source Procurement

All proposals for sole source contracts for goods and services are contemplated by the Code. Contracts for services in excess of $50,000 must be pre-approved by the Materiel Division, except in emergencies. Factors in determining whether a vendor is the sole source of a service include the uniqueness of the service of sole availability at the location required. (See Nebraska Statutes §§ 73-502, 73-507(1)(a), and 73-508.)

G. Emergency Procurement

In case of an emergency, contract approval by the state agency director or his or her designee is required. Emergency direct purchases of $50,000 or more may be approved if the need affects the security or life safety of the citizens of the state of Nebraska. A copy of the contract and agency justification must be provided to the director of Administrative Services within three business days after contract approval. (See 9 NAC § 2-001.04; Nebraska Statutes §§ 39-1343, 73-502, 73-507(1)(a), and 73-508.)

H. Professional Services

Contracts for professional legal services and services of expert witnesses, hearing officers, or administrative law judges retained by state agencies for administrative court proceedings and contracts of $15,000,000 or less with direct providers of medical, behavioral, developmental health services, child care, or child welfare services to an individual are not subject to the generally applicable competitive bidding requirements. (Nebraska Statutes § 73-507.)

I. Other Exceptions

The following types of contracts are not subject to the generally applicable competitive bidding requirements: (1) contracts for services subject to the Nebraska Consultants' Competitive Negotiation Act (See Nebraska Statutes § 81-1701 *et. seq.*); (2) contracts for services subject to federal law, regulation, or policy or state statute, under which a state agency is required to use a different selection process or to contract with an identified contractor or type of contractor; (3) contracts involving state or federal financial assistance passed through by a state agency to a political subdivision; (4) agreements for services to be performed for a state agency by another state or local government agency or contracts made by a state agency with a local government agency for the direct provision of services to the public; (5) agreements for services between a state agency and the University of Nebraska, the Nebraska state colleges, the courts, the legislature, or other officers or state agencies established by the Constitution of Nebraska; (6) Department of Insurance contracts for financial or actuarial examination, for rehabilitation, conservation, reorganization, or liquidation of licensees, and for professional services related to residual pools or excess funds under the agency's control; (7) Department of Transportation contracts for all road and bridge projects; (8) Nebraska Investment Council contracts; and (9) certain contracts regarding oil pipelines under Nebraska Statutes section 57-1503. (See Nebraska Statutes § 73-507.)

IV. Bid Protests and Contract Disputes

A. Bid Protests

Any vendor grievances related to an action or determination of the State Purchasing Bureau shall be expressed in writing to the administrator of the Materiel Division. (See 9 NAC § 4-005.) While title 9 of the NAC does not specifically state a time frame for filing a grievance, the Materiel Division has initiated a policy that requires grievances to be received within ten business days of posting the award for a commodity or intent to award for a service for the grievance to be considered valid. The letter should state the bid number, specific issues that are disputed, and provide a point of contact and mailing address for the aggrieved party.

A response will be made in writing to the point of contact specified in the vendor grievance letter within ten business days of receipt of the grievance by the Materiel Division administrator.

B. Bid Protest Appeals

At the time a grievance is filed with the Materiel Division administrator or, if the response from the Materiel Division administrator has not satisfied the grievance of the vendor, the vendor may make a written request for a meeting with the Materiel Division administrator and the director of the Department of Administrative Services. This meeting request must be received within ten business days of the date of the Materiel Division administrator's response. A meeting will be scheduled and held with the vendor, the Materiel Division administrator, and the director of Administrative Services (or the director's designee) to discuss the issues in the grievance. A final decision of the director of the Department of Administrative Services will be sent to the vendor.

C. Contract Disputes

Contract claims must be filed with the risk manager in the manner prescribed by the State Claims Board. Contract claims must be filed within two years of when the claim accrued. Each claim must include (1) a copy of the contract allegedly breached; (2) the manner in which the contract was allegedly breached; and (3) the damages incurred as a result of the alleged breach. The risk manager will advise the attorney general and the contracting agency and an investigation shall be made. The claimant and the contracting agency may agree to give the State Claims Board authority to consider, ascertain, adjust, compromise, settle, determine, or allow any contract claim. They may also agree to submit the claim to the State Claims Board to resolve. If either party objects in writing within 90 days to submission of the dispute to the State Claims Board, the Board will have no further jurisdiction and the claimant may initiate an action in the district court of Lancaster County. (See Nebraska Statutes §§ 81-8,295–81-8,306.)

D. Suspension and Debarment

A vendor may be removed from the bidder list or suspended for unsatisfactory performance. Unsatisfactory performance includes failure to respond to three consecutive bid invitations, late delivery, failure to deliver, unauthorized substitution of goods, defective products, service deficiencies, or billing errors. (See 9 NAC § 1-002.)

V. Administrative and Judicial Review

A. Administrative Review

Administrative review is not available in Nebraska. Resolution of disputes and contract claims are described in Section IV.

B. Judicial Review

Judicial review of contract disputes mentioned in Section IV.C is available in the district court of Lancaster County. The Nebraska judicial branch's website is https://supremecourt.nebraska.gov/.

VI. Extent of State's Adoption or Adaptation of ABA Model Procurement Code

Nebraska has not adopted or applied the American Bar Association (ABA) Model Procurement Code.

VII. Cooperative Purchasing

A. Authority

The Nebraska Joint Public Agency Act provides that any power, privilege, or authority that a public agency of the state of Nebraska is allowed to exercise may be exercised jointly with any other public agency of the state of Nebraska or any other state or the United States. (Nebraska Statutes § 13-2505.) A "public agency" includes any county, village, school district, or agency of the state government or the United States, any drainage district, sanitary and improvement district, or other municipal corporation or political subdivision of the state of Nebraska, and any political subdivision of another state. (Nebraska Statutes § 13-2503.)

B. Requirements

Nebraska law does not require competitive bidding by counties when the price has been established by a cooperative purchasing agreement where the supplies, equipment, or services are procured in accordance with a contract established by another governmental agency or group of governmental entities if the contract was established in accordance with the laws and regulations applicable to the establishing governmental entity or, if a group, the lead governmental entity. (Nebraska Statutes § 23-3109.)

Further, the Materiel Division may allow the purchase of goods without competitive bidding when a contract has been competitively bid by another state or group of states, a group of states and any political subdivision, or any other state, or a cooperative purchasing organization on behalf of a group of states. (Nebraska Statutes § 81-153(7).)

If an agency desires to purchase goods through a cooperative contract, the agency must make a request to the State Purchasing Bureau who will determine if the use of the cooperative contract is appropriate and, if so, process the purchase.

Nevada Procurement Rules and Regulations

Prepared by Michael B. Brown
Stoel Rives LLP
Email: michael.brown@stoel.com
With assistance from Max S. Fujii

I. Statutory Reference

A. Procurement/Purchasing Statutes

The sections of the Nevada Revised Statutes Annotated related to procurement/purchasing are listed below.

§ 281A.430.	Purchase of Goods or Services by Local Government from Member of Governing Body under Certain Conditions
§§ 287.500 through 287.530.	Contracts for Prepaid Professional Services
§§ 332.005 through 332.830.	Purchasing: Local Governments
§§ 333.010 through 333.820.	Purchasing: State
§§ 333A.010 through 333A.150.	State Performance Contracts for Operating Cost-Savings Measures
§§ 334.010 through 334.080.	Purchasing: Generally

General information about doing business with the state is available on the Nevada state website at https://nv.gov/. The Department of Administration offers information on its website at https://admin.nv.gov/. The statutorily created Purchasing Division is responsible for the timely procurement of needed supplies, equipment, and services for state agencies and may be used by other government entities within the state. Information is available through the division's website at https://purchasing.nv.gov/.

The state of Nevada's Board of Examiners (BOE) is composed of the governor, the attorney general, and the secretary of state, who meet once a month and have final approval on contracts entered into on behalf of the state. The Budget Division reviews these contracts prior to BOE submission and requires a 17-working-day lead time prior to a BOE meeting. All contracts must have the vendor's signature, the attorney general's representative signature, and any necessary agency signatures before their submittal to the Budget Division.

The table of contents of chapter 332 of the Nevada Revised Statutes (NRS) governing state purchasing, which can also be found at https://www.leg.state.nv.us/nrs/nrs-332.html, is set forth below:

CHAPTER 332—PURCHASING: LOCAL GOVERNMENTS

GENERAL PROVISIONS

PROCEDURES FOR LOCAL GOVERNMENT PURCHASING

PROCEDURES FOR SOLICITATIONS

EXCEPTIONS TO REQUIREMENTS FOR COMPETITIVE SOLICITATIONS

GENERAL POWERS AND DUTIES OF LOCAL GOVERNMENTS

PERFORMANCE CONTRACTS FOR OPERATING COST-SAVINGS MEASURES

The table of contents of chapter 333 of the NRS governing state purchasing, which can also be found at https://www.leg.state.nv.us/nrs/nrs-333.html, is set forth below:

CHAPTER 333—PURCHASING: STATE

GENERAL PROVISIONS

ADMINISTRATION

§ 333.030. Administration of chapter.
§ 333.060. Qualifications of Administrator of Purchasing Division.
§ 333.100. Assistants: Number; qualifications.
§ 333.110. Offices of Purchasing Division.
§ 333.120. State Purchasing Fund: Creation; amount; use.
§ 333.125. Temporary transfers from State General Fund to State Purchasing Fund.

GENERAL POWERS AND DUTIES OF ADMINISTRATOR OF PURCHASING DIVISION

§ 333.130. Supervision of administrative and technical activities of Purchasing Division; regulations.
§ 333.135. Regulations establishing procedures for awarding contracts.
§ 333.140. Policy of securing best value.
§ 333.150. Purchases or contracts for rental or lease for using agencies.
§ 333.155. Regulations concerning purchase of new equipment: Consideration of renting equipment and contracting for service to maintain equipment.
§ 333.160. Methods of supplying needs of using agencies.
§ 333.162. Methods of obtaining a contract; regulations.
§ 333.165. Contracts for services: Duty of Administrator to act on behalf of using agency; authority of using agency to contract; requests for assistance by using agency.
§ 333.175. Administrator may exempt purchases by Department of Corrections from Offenders' Store Fund from provisions of chapter.
§ 333.177. Duty of Purchasing Division to report to Office of Economic Development concerning local emerging small businesses.
§ 333.180. Collection, classification, and maintenance of information concerning commodities and suppliers.
§ 333.182. Program to certify vendors that pay employees equal pay for equal work without regard to gender: Establishment; Regulations.
§ 333.184. Program to certify vendors that pay employees equal pay for equal work without regard to gender: Use of certification by Purchasing Division and vendor.
§ 333.186. Program to certify vendors that pay employees equal pay for equal work without regard to gender: Penalties for fraudulent acts in self-certifying; Review of decision.
§ 333.188. Program to certify vendors that pay employees equal pay for equal work without regard to gender: Annual report to Governor and Legislature.
§ 333.190. Inspection of purchased commodities; material or service found to be defective or not as specified; receiving reports.

PROCEDURES FOR STATE PURCHASING

RECYCLED PRODUCTS AND ENERGY-EFFICIENT DEVICES

PURCHASING FOR LEGISLATIVE AND JUDICIAL DEPARTMENTS, CIVIL AIR PATROL, NEVADA SYSTEM OF HIGHER EDUCATION, LOCAL GOVERNMENTS, AND DISTRICTS

PURCHASING THROUGH SOLICITATIONS OR AGREEMENTS OF OTHER GOVERNMENTAL ENTITIES; FEDERAL SURPLUS PROPERTY

INDEPENDENT CONTRACTORS

PROHIBITIONS AND PENALTIES

The table of contents of chapter 333A of the NRS governing state performance contracts for operating cost-savings measures, which can also be found at https://www.leg.state.nv.us/nrs/nrs-333a.html, is set forth below:

CHAPTER 333A—STATE PERFORMANCE CONTRACTS FOROPERATING COST-SAVINGS MEASURES

The table of contents of chapter 334 of the NRS governing purchasing generally, which can also be found at https://www.leg.state.nv.us/nrs/NRS-334.html, is set forth below:

CHAPTER 334—PURCHASING: GENERALLY

B. Other Applicable Statutes

1. Required Disclosures for Certain Candidates and Elected Public Officers

NRS section 281.561 mandates an annual financial disclosure statement (FDS) by certain candidates for the office of legislator and certain elected public officers entitled to receive annual compensation of $6,000 or more.

2. Required Disclosures for Appointed Public Officers

NRS section 281.559 mandates an annual FDS by a public officer who was appointed to office and entitled to receive annual compensation of $6,000 or more.

3. Acknowledgment of Statutory Ethical Standards

NRS section 281A.500.1 requires every public officer to acknowledge that he or she has received, has read, and understands the statutory ethical standards.

4. Agency Representation Disclosure

NRS section 281A.410.3 precludes a member of a legislative body from representing or counseling a private person for compensation before another local agency if the territorial jurisdiction of the other local agency includes any part of the county in which the member serves. The Commission may relieve the member from the strict application of this prohibition if certain conditions and findings are made.

5. Ethics in Government: Prohibitions

NRS section 281A.400 prohibits government employees from accepting gifts, services, favors, employment, economic opportunities, and so on, which would improperly influence them. It also proscribes using a public office to secure unwarranted privileges, preferences, exemptions, or advantages. Participating as an agent of government in the negotiation or execution of contracts with a business in which the person has a pecuniary interest is also prohibited, as is accepting a salary or other compensation from a private source for performing public duties. A government employee is barred from using confidential information to further a significant pecuniary interest or that of others and from suppressing governmental reports or documents that might tend to unfavorably affect a significant pecuniary interest. NRS section 281A.430 regulates when a member of a local legislative body may sell goods or services to his or her local agency as the sole source of supply within the area served by the local agency and prohibits such a member from selling goods or services to his or her local agency unless certain conditions are met. It also allows the Commission to provide the member with relief from strict application of the prohibition.

6. Additional Requirements, Ethical Standards, Remedies, and Penalties

NRS sections 281A.500–.550 provide additional requirements, ethical standards, remedies, and penalties.

Criminal statutes governing public officers include (1) anti-nepotism provisions (NRS § 281.210); (2) prohibited contracts (NRS § 281.221); and (3) no personal profits from public office (NRS § 281.230).

II. Regulations

Pursuant to NRS section 333.130, the chief serves as the executive head of the Purchasing Division. The chief directs and supervises the division's administrative and technical activities and may adopt regulations necessary for the administration of state purchasing. Pursuant to NRS section 333.140, the chief must secure the best value for supplies, materials, equipment, and services.

The table of contents of chapter 333 of the Nevada Administrative Code (NAC) governing state purchasing, which can also be found at https://www.leg.state.nv.us/nac/nac-333.html, is set forth below:

CHAPTER 333—PURCHASING: STATE

GENERAL PROVISIONS

§ 333.010. Definitions.
§ 333.020. "Administrator" defined.
§ 333.030. "Division" defined.
§ 333.040. "Using agency" defined.
§ 333.050. Methods for obtaining contract.

ACQUISITION AND DISPOSAL OF PERSONAL PROPERTY

PROCEDURES FOR AWARDING CONTRACTS

APPEAL FROM UNSUCCESSFUL BID OR PROPOSAL

DECLARATORY ORDERS AND ADVISORY OPINIONS

III. Source Selection

The general methods of procurement include the following:

A. Small Purchases

For contracts of $50,000 or less, there is no need for competitive bidding. (NRS § 333.300.) For a public work procurement of $100,000 or less, local government shall award a contract to a contractor or perform the work itself. (NRS § 338.1442.) For public work of $100,000 or less, NRS section 338.13862 allows informal solicitations, which require three bids for contracts between $25,000 and $100,000, and a bid from at least one contractor for contracts of $25,000 or less. (NRS § 338.1386; NRS § 338.13862; NRS § 338.1444.)

B. Competitive Bidding

Statutory competition requirements are fulfilled when contracts that exceed $50,000 are purchased by formal contract after competitive bidding. (NRS § 333.300.) More information is provided below, in Section VII, regarding competitive bidding in cooperative purchasing.

C. Preference for Bid by Nevada-Based Business

Under certain circumstances, a Nevada-based business, as used in NRS sections 333.3351 to 333.3356, shall be given preference for bids and proposals for state purchasing contracts.

D. Sole Source Procurement

For local governments, there is a long list of contracts that are specifically not adapted to award by competitive bidding, including items that may only be contracted from a sole source. (NRS § 332.115.) The chief of the Purchasing Division has approval authority. (NRS § 333.300.) The General Services Administration also has approval authority. (NRS § 332.115.) The chief of the Purchasing Division gives reasonable notice of all purchases by advertising or by written notice to persons in classes of commodities involved. (NRS § 333.300.)

E. Emergency Procurement

Emergency procurement is used when it is in the best interest of the state as determined by the governor or by the chief of the Purchasing Division of the Department of Administration. The chief may authorize an emergency purchase for any amount. If the chief authorizes an emergency purchase, he or she will provide the using agency with written authorization for the emergency purchase, including, without limitation, a description of the justification for authorizing the emergency purchase. The chief will provide a separate written authorization for each order relating to the emergency purchase.

IV. Bid Protests and Contract Disputes

A. Bid Protests

1. Standing

At the local level, any person who submits a bid on an advertised contract may, after bids are opened and within the period specified by the governing body or authorized representative, file with the governing body or authorized representative a notice of protest regarding award of the contract. (See NRS § 332.068.)

2. Form and Filing

A notice of protest must include a written statement setting forth the reasons the person filing the notice believes the applicable provisions of law were violated. A person filing a notice of protest may be required to post a bond with a good and solvent surety authorized to do business in the state or submit other security, in a form approved by the governing body that shall hold the bond or other security until a determination is made on the protest.

3. Stay of Procurement

Proper notice of protest operates as a stay of action related to award until the governing body determines the protest. (NRS § 332.068.) Notice of appeal operates as a stay of action related to the contract until determination is made by a hearing officer on appeal. (NRS § 333.370.)

4. Decision

Within 20 days after receipt of notice of appeal, a hearing officer of the Hearings Division shall hold a contested hearing on appeal. (NRS § 333.370.)

B. Bid Protest Appeals

1. Standing

For state-level purchases, a person who makes an unsuccessful bid or proposal may file a notice of appeal with the Purchasing Division and the Hearings Division of the Department of Administration within ten days after the date of the award and notice of the award has been posted in at least three public buildings, including the location of the using agency; there will be no judicial intervention until the hearing officer has determined the appeal. (NRS § 333.370.)

2. Form and Filing

A person filing a notice of protest may be required by the governing body or its authorized representative, at the time the notice of protest is filed, to post a bond with a good and solvent surety authorized to do business in the state or submit other security, in a form approved by the chief by regulation, to the Purchasing Division, which shall hold the bond or other security until a determination is made on the protest. If the total value of a successful bid cannot be determined, it must be in an amount equal to 25 percent of the estimated total value of the contract. (NRS § 333.370.)

3. Decision

If the protest is upheld, the bond posted or other security submitted with the notice of protest must be returned to the person who posted the bond or submitted the security. If the protest is rejected, a claim may be made against the bond or other security by the governing body or its authorized representative in an amount equal to the expenses incurred by the governing body or its authorized representative because of the unsuccessful protest. Any money remaining after the claim has been satisfied must be returned to the person who posted the bond or submitted the security. (NRS § 333.370.)

C. Contract Disputes

A person who has entered into a contract with the Purchasing Division or another agency of the state and who does not perform according to the terms of the contract is liable for, in addition to any other applicable damages for breach of contract, a penalty of not more than 5 percent of the total value of the bid or contract. The penalty must be recovered in a civil action in any court of competent jurisdiction. In addition to recovering the penalty and any other applicable damages, acceptance of a bid from the person may be refused or an award of a contract to the person may be refused, or both, for not more than two years. (NRS § 333.365.)

If an action to recover the penalty prescribed by NRS section 333.365.1 is not brought, the following may occur: (1) refusal to accept a bid from the person, refusal to award a contract to the person, or both, for not more than two years; and (2) an administrative penalty, in an amount not to exceed 5 percent of the total value of the bid or contract may be imposed. Notice by mail is required for this penalty. (NRS § 333.365.)

A penalty imposed pursuant to subsection 1 or 2 of section 333.365 must be paid within 30 days and may be satisfied by deduction from any payment due the person, or claimed against a bond or check previously issued to the person. (NRS § 333.365.)

D. Suspension and Debarment

The Purchasing Division maintains a listing of suspended or debarred vendors that is available to officials of the Nevada state agencies. The information is a matter of public record, and any questions concerning vendor status should be referred to the Purchasing Division.

V. Administrative and Judicial Review

A. Administrative Review

Pursuant to NRS section 333.370, an individual or company who makes an unsuccessful bid or proposal may file a notice of appeal with the Purchasing Division and Hearings Division of the Department of Administration. This notice must be filed within the time frame identified in the notification of award letter. A bond or other approved security equal to 25 percent of the total value of the contract, issued by a company authorized to do business in the state of Nevada, must accompany the notice of appeal submitted to the Purchasing Division.

The statute governing appeals by persons who made an unsuccessful bid or proposal (NRS § 333.370) is available at https://www.leg.state.nv.us/NRS/NRS-333.html#NRS333Sec370.

The statute governing the procedures for award or withdrawal of a contract (NAC § 333.170) is available at https://www.leg.state.nv.us/nac/NAC-333.html#NAC333Sec170.

B. Judicial Review

For local government purchasing, a person who submits an unsuccessful bid may not seek any type of judicial intervention until the governing body or its authorized representative has made a determination on the protest and awarded the contract. (NRS § 332.068.)

For state purchases, a person who makes an unsuccessful bid or proposal may not seek any type of judicial intervention until the hearing officer has made a determination on the appeal. (NRS § 333.370.)

VI. Extent of State's Adoption or Adaptation of ABA Model Procurement Code

Nevada has not adopted the American Bar Association's (ABA's) Model Procurement Code for State and Local Governments.

VII. Cooperative Purchasing

A. Authority

Cooperative purchasing is authorized under Nevada law. (NRS § 332.195.) Specifically, a governing body or its authorized representative may join or use the contracts solicited by other local governments located within or outside Nevada, the state of Nevada or other states, or cooperative purchasing organizations. (NRS § 332.195(1)(a)–(c).) A local government in Nevada includes every political subdivision that has the right to levy or receive money from taxes including counties, cities, towns, school districts, and other districts. (NRS § 332.015(1).)

B. Requirements

1. Solicitation

Based on the plain language of the statute, a governing body or its authorized representative may enter into a contract *pursuant to a solicitation by* a local governmental entity located within or outside Nevada, the state of Nevada or another state, or a cooperative purchasing organization. (NRS § 332.195(1)(a)–(c).)

2. Authorization

A governing body may join a contract of another governmental entity or state only when it is authorized by the contracting vendor. (NRS § 332.195(1)(a)–(b).) This authorization is apparently not required when joining a contract pursuant to a solicitation by a cooperative purchasing organization. (NRS § 332.195(1)(c).)

3. Competitive Bidding and Exceptions

Unless an express exception applies, a local government may not join or use a contract of another governmental entity without the contract having been competitively bid at some point in time. (Nev. Op. Att'y Gen. Opinion No. 2008-09 (2008), 2008 WL 6533028.)

Thus, the solicitation requirements set forth in NRS sections 332.043–332.105 apply. These include (1) required solicitation contents (NRS §§ 332.043–.047); (2) limitation on disclosure of proprietary information and negotiable provisions (NRS § 332.061); (3) procedure for contracts between $50,000 and $100,000 (NRS §§ 332.063–.075); and (4) maintenance of records, assignment of contracts, and bonds (NRS §§ 332.091–.105).

The exceptions to competitive bids are set forth in NRS sections 332.112–.148. These include (1) emergency contracts (NRS § 332.112); (2) certain nonprofit organizations whose primary purpose is training disabled persons (NRS § 332.117); (3) contracts with carriers, soliciting, or obtaining materials on a voluntary basis from the Purchasing Division of the Department of Administration (NRS § 332.135); (4) purchases at any public auction, closeout sale, bankruptcy sale, sale of merchandise left after an exhibition, or other similar sale (NRS § 332.146); and (5) where there has been a failure to receive responses (NRS § 332.148). Further, NRS section 332.115 includes numerous exceptions. These exceptions include:

(a) Items which may only be contracted from a sole source;
(b) Professional services;
(c) Additions to and repairs and maintenance of equipment which may be more efficiently added to, repaired or maintained by a certain person;
(d) Equipment which, by reason of the training of the personnel or of an inventory of replacement parts maintained by the local government[,] is compatible with existing equipment;
(e) Perishable goods;
(f) Insurance;
(g) Hardware and associated peripheral equipment and devices for computers;
(h) Software for computers;
(i) Maintenance and support for:
    (1) Hardware and associated peripheral equipment and devices for computers; and
    (2) Software for computers;
(j) Equipment containing hardware or software for computers;
(k) Books, instructional materials, library materials and subscriptions;
(l) Motor vehicle fuel purchased by a local law enforcement agency for use in an undercover investigation;
(m) Motor vehicle fuel for use in a vehicle operated by a local law enforcement agency or local fire department if such fuel is not available within the vehicle's assigned service area from a fueling station owned by the State of Nevada or a local government;
(n) Purchases made with money in a store fund for prisoners in a jail or local detention facility for the provision and maintenance of a canteen for the prisoners;
(o) Supplies, materials, equipment or services that are available pursuant to an agreement with a vendor that has entered into an agreement with the General Services Administration or another federal governmental agency located within or outside this State;
(p) Items for resale through a retail outlet operated in this State by a local government or the State of Nevada;
(q) Commercial advertising within a recreational facility operated by a county fair and recreation board;
(r) Goods or services purchased from organizations or agencies whose primary purpose is the training and employment of persons with disabilities; and
(s) The design of, and equipment and services associated with, systems of communication.

Another exception is the purchase of forensic equipment when certain requirements are met. (NRS § 332.115(2)(a)–(c).) Additionally, the purchase of personal safety equipment for use by a response agency or any other local governmental agency does not require competitive bidding where certain requirements are met. (NRS § 332.115(3)(a)–(b).) Finally, the purchase of goods commonly used by a hospital do not require competitive bidding. (NRS § 332.115(4).)

4. Not Applicable Where Contractor's License Required

A governing body or its authorized representative shall not enter into a contract pursuant to NRS section 332.195 if a contractor's license issued pursuant to chapter 624 of the NRS is required for any portion of the work to be performed under the contract.

5. The Soliciting Entity Is Not Liable for the Governing Body's Contractual Obligations

The soliciting governmental entity, state, or cooperative purchasing organization is not liable for the obligations of the local government that enters into a contract in response to the solicitation. (NRS § 332.195(1)(a)–(c).)

New Hampshire Procurement Rules and Regulations

Prepared by Richard Parsons
Rath, Young & Pignatelli, P.C.
Email: rmp@rypgranite.com

I. Statutory Reference

A. Procurement/Purchasing Statutes

The Department of Administrative Services is an agency under the executive direction of the commissioner of administrative services. The commissioner of administrative services serves as the chief fiscal planning and control officer of New Hampshire. The Department of Administrative Services website is https://www.das.nh.gov/. Within the department, the Bureau of Purchase and Property has the prime responsibility to purchase goods and services for all state agencies and institutions unless they are specifically exempted by law. The Bureau of Purchase and Property website is https://www.das.nh.gov/purchasing/purchasing.aspx. The governor and Executive Council of the State of New Hampshire has the authority and responsibility to approve all state departments' and agencies' receipt and expenditures of state and federal funds, budgetary transfers within the department, and all personal service contracts with a value of $10,000 and all contracts with a value of more than $10,000 unless otherwise stated by statute. Additionally, multiagency service contracts established through the Department of Administrative Services are not subject to Executive Council approval. The Executive Council website is https://www.nh.gov/council/about-us/index.htm.

The New Hampshire Revised Statutes (RSA) may be accessed through the New Hampshire General Court website at http://www.gencourt.state.nh.us/rsa/html/nhtoc.htm.

Pertinent sections of the RSA include the following:

Chapter 4.	Powers of the Governor and Council in Certain Cases
Chapter 21-I.	Department of Administrative Services
§ 28:8.	Competitive Bidding on Purchases (county purchases)
§§ 31:59-a to -d.	Town Central Purchasing Department (town purchasing)
§ 48:17.	City Purchasing Departments (city purchasing)
Chapter 53-A.	Agreements between Government Units (cooperative purchasing)

B. Other Applicable Statutes

1. Bribery, Gifts, and Gratuities

a. RSA chapter 21-G, Organization of Executive Branch, sections 21-G:21 through :35 (Code of Ethics)
b. RSA chapter 640, Corrupt Practices (part of the Criminal Code)

2. Lobbyists

a. RSA chapter 15

II. Regulations

New Hampshire Administrative Rules chapter Adm 600 (Plant and Property Management Rules) includes the following parts:

Part Adm 601. General Provisions
Part Adm 602. Definitions
Part Adm 603. Vendor Code Number Requirements
Part Adm 604. Bidding Requirements
Part Adm 605. Additional Rules regarding Other Purchasing Vendors
Part Adm 606. Selection, Post-selection, and Other Purchasing Procedures
Part Adm 607. Purchasing Requirements for State Agencies
Part Adm 608. Agency Requirements for Plant and Property Maintenance
Part Adm 609. Pre-adjudicative Proceeding Procedures in Cases Involving the Division of Procurement and Support Services, Bureau of Purchase and Property
Part Adm 610. Agency Leases
Part Adm 611. State Surplus Management
Part Adm 612. Federal Surplus Food Distribution Program
Part Adm 613. Federal Surplus Property Program

III. Source Selection

The Department of Administrative Services, Bureau of Purchase and Property maintains an online vendor registry. A vendor can place a bid without being a registered vendor; however, contracts will only be awarded to vendors currently registered and in good standing with the Office of the Secretary of State. The general methods of procurement include the following:

A. Competitive Bidding

1. Multiagency Contracts

New Hampshire Administrative Rules chapter Adm 604 implements RSA chapter 21-I, Department of Administrative Services. Except where competitive bidding has been employed, no purchase involving an expenditure of more than $10,000 or purchase in an approved class may be made by the director without the approval of the commissioner. (New Hampshire Administrative Rules Adm 601.03(c).) Procedural requirements for bids, quotations, and proposals are set forth at New Hampshire Administrative Rules Adm 604.02.

2. Major Projects

RSA sections 21-I:79 and 21-I:80 require competitive bidding for public works design and construction. RSA section 21-I:79 allows contracts under $25,000 to be awarded to independent contractors through competitive bidding administered by the using agency with the approval of the governor and council. RSA section 21-I:80 requires each state project with estimated costs greater than $25,000 to be awarded to the lowest qualified bidder who meets the project specifications through competitive bidding. Exemptions exist for the major project competitive bidding requirements. (See RSA § 21-I:80.)

3. Competition Thresholds for Cities and Counties

A city council must solicit competition for purchases over $100, subject to exceptions as the councils may approve. (RSA § 48:17.) County purchases of equipment or materials over $5,000 must be made by competitive bidding. (RSA § 28:8.) Hillsborough County extends the requirement for competitive bidding of purchases over $5,000 to materials, equipment, supplies, services, insurance, building repairs, or any other item. (RSA § 28:8-e.) Rockingham County extends the requirement for competitive bidding of purchases over $5,000 to equipment, materials, services, or leases. (RSA § 28:8-f.) There is no state law requiring competitive bidding for town contracts, unless a public official is a seller or contractor, in which case competitive bidding is required. (See RSA § 95:1.)

B. Sole Source Procurement

New Hampshire Administrative Rules Adm 607.03 (Sole Source Requests) implements RSA section 21-I:11(I), which requires competitive bidding unless an exception applies. Exceptions include (1) the best interests of the state would be served and the purchase involves an expenditure of less than $10,000 or is a purchase in an approved class; (2) when, after reasonable investigation, it appears that the item is procurable by the state from only one source; (3) when, after reasonable investigation, it appears that the item has a fixed market price at all sources available to the state; or (4) when, in the opinion of the governor, an emergency exists that requires the immediate purchase of supplies. Also, where the rates filed with and approved by the insurance commissioner are uniform, the purchase of state insurance and public state official and employee bonds are excluded from competitive bidding as to price.

Exemptions for certain agencies and purchases are made from the provisions of chapter 21-I. (See RSA § 21-I:18.) There are also certain exemptions for purchases for public works design and construction. (See RSA § 21-I:80.) Exemptions also exist for bidding requirements for transportation projects. (See RSA § 228:4.)

IV. Bid Protests and Contract Disputes

A. Bid Protests

1. Pre-Adjudicative Proceeding Procedures

Any person or association that requests a debriefing within three days of the notice of award (as required by New Hampshire Administrative Rules Adm 609.01) may file a request for informal resolution. (New Hampshire Administrative Rules Adm 609.02.)

2. Form and Filing

A request for informal resolution shall be submitted to the administrator of the division's purchase and property function established under RSA section 21-I:12(I) within 15 days of review of the notice of award or decision. The request for informal resolution shall briefly describe the nature of the grievance and identify the persons, associations, and agencies involved. (New Hampshire Administrative Rules Adm 609.02.)

3. Stay of Procurement

A stay of procurement is not provided in the rules.

4. Decision

Within 15 days of the administrator's receipt of the request for informal review, the administrator shall investigate the matter and inform the person or association who initiated the inquiry, in hard copy, facsimile, or electronic writing, either that (1) corrective action has been taken, describing the nature of the action taken and notifying all persons involved of the corrective action taken; (2) additional informal telephone communication with the person or association will be scheduled to discuss the problem and attempt to reach a mutually agreeable resolution, together with the time and date that the communication will occur; or (3) a further informal meeting will be scheduled to discuss the problem and attempt to reach a mutually agreeable resolution, together with the date, time, and place of the meeting. If the administrator decides to hold an informal meeting, it will be held within 15 days of the administrator's notification. The administrator shall issue his or her conclusions, orally or in writing, within ten days of the informal meeting or informal telephone communication described above. (New Hampshire Administrative Rules Adm 609.02.)

B. Bid Protest Appeals

A person who claims to be aggrieved by the informal resolution of a matter may request resolution by way of an adjudicative proceeding under New Hampshire Administrative Rules Adm 200 either (1) if corrective action was taken, then within 15 days of the notice of the corrective action; or (2) if an informal meeting or an informal telephone communication was held, within 15 days of the notice of conclusions. Any appeal of the decision rendered shall be in accordance with the provisions of RSA sections 541:3 through 541:9. (New Hampshire Administrative Rules Adm 609-02.)

C. Contract Disputes

The same process outlined above regarding award decisions applies to other decisions of the Division of Plant and Property Management.

D. Suspension and Debarment

Bids, quotations, and proposals will be disqualified for any of the reasons set forth at New Hampshire Administrative Rules Adm 604.04, Disqualification. Included among these reasons is a failure to possess a vendor code number; failure to be in good standing with the New Hampshire secretary of state; having been convicted of, or pleaded guilty to, a specific prohibited bidding practice; debarment in any other state, by the federal government, or in New Hampshire; and a variety of other enumerated disqualifying non-conformities.

V. Administrative and Judicial Review

A. Administrative Review

Under RSA chapter 541, Rehearings and Appeals in Certain Cases, a motion for rehearing of any order or decision made by any state department or official must be made within 30 days after such order or decision is made. (RSA § 541:3.) The motion must set forth every ground upon which it is claimed that the decision or order complained of is unlawful or unreasonable. (RSA § 541:4.) The state department or official must within ten days grant or deny the rehearing. (RSA § 541:5.)

B. Judicial Review

Within 30 days after an application for rehearing is denied, or if the rehearing is granted, within 30 days after the decision on such rehearing, the applicant may appeal to the Supreme Court of New Hampshire by petition. (RSA § 541:6.) The petition must briefly state the nature of the proceeding before the state department or official and set forth the order or decision complained of, and the grounds upon which the same is claimed to be unlawful or unreasonable upon which the petitioner will rely in the Supreme Court. (RSA § 541:7.)

VI. Extent of State's Adoption or Adaptation of ABA Model Procurement Code

New Hampshire has partially adopted the American Bar Association (ABA) Model Procurement Code. (See the New Hampshire survey response to the National Association of State Procurement Officials 2018 Survey of Statement Procurement Practices.)

VII. Cooperative Purchasing

A. Authority

Under RSA chapter 53-A, any powers, privileges, or authority of a public agency can be exercised jointly with any other public agency of the state. A public agency is any political subdivision of the state or of an adjoining state and any quasi-municipal corporation, including but not limited to school districts, school administrative units, village districts, regional water districts, and special districts. (RSA § 53-A:2.)

B. Requirements

The attorney general will review all agreements to ensure compliance with state law. Appropriate action by ordinance, resolution, or other action pursuant to law of the governing bodies of the participating public agencies shall be necessary before any such agreement may enter into force. (RSA § 53-A:3(I).) The agreement must specify:

(a) Its duration;
(b) The precise organization, composition and nature of any separate legal or administrative entity created thereby together with the powers delegated thereto, provided such entity may be legally created;
(c) Its purpose;
(d) The manner of financing the joint or cooperative undertaking and of establishing and maintaining a budget therefor;

(e) The method to be employed in accomplishing the partial or complete termination of the agreement and for disposing of property upon such termination;
(f) Any other necessary and proper matters.

(RSA § 53-A:3(II).) If the agreement does not establish a separate legal entity it must also contain:

(a) Provision for an administrator or a joint board responsible for administering the joint or cooperative undertaking. In the case of a joint board all public agencies party to the agreement shall be represented.
(b) The manner of acquiring, holding and disposing of real and personal property used in the joint or cooperative undertaking.

(RSA § 53-A:3(III).)

New Jersey Procurement Rules and Regulations

Prepared by Kristopher Berr
Del Duca Lewis
Email: kjb@delducalewis.com

I. Statutory Reference

A. Procurement/Purchasing Statutes

Title 52, chapters 32 through 40, of the New Jersey Statutes contains statutes relevant to state procurement. Pursuant to these statutes, the Department of the Treasury, Division of Purchase and Property (DPP) administers procurements in accordance with the procurement rules defined in the New Jersey Administrative Code (NJAC), as discussed below.

The DPP provides centralized procurement and related services to agencies of the executive branch of state government. Its primary mission is the timely and effective procurement of contracts for goods and services necessary for the daily operation of state government. (NJAC § 17:12-1.1.) Information about New Jersey's procurement program and contracting opportunities can be found at the DPP's website, https://www.nj.gov/treasury/purchase.

Procurements by local boards of education under the Public School Contracts Law, New Jersey Statutes Annotated (NJSA) section 18A:18A-1 *et seq.*, or those by the New Jersey Turnpike Authority (chapter 9 of title 19 of the NJAC) are outside the authority of the DPP. It should therefore be noted that different rules may apply to those types of procurements.

II. Regulations

The basic procedures for procurement are contained in the NJAC in sections 17:12-1.1 to -9.6. The relevant provisions of the NJAC are organized as follows and discussed in more detail below:

Subchapter 1.	Description of Organization; Means of Procurement
Subchapter 1A.	Procurement Methodology
Subchapter 1B.	Terms and Conditions
Subchapter 2.	Advertised Procurement Procedures
Subchapter 3.	Protest Procedures

Subchapter 4.	Complaint and Audit Procedures
Subchapter 5.	Political Contribution Compliance Review Process
Subchapter 6.	Debarment, Suspension, and Disqualification of a Person(s)
Subchapters 7 & 8.	(Reserved)
Subchapter 9.	Distribution and Support Services Unit, Surplus Computer Distribution Program

III. Source Selection

A. DPP's Procedures for Formal, Advertised, Competitive Procurement

By statutory mandate, all state procurements are required to be conducted through a public advertisement for bids. (NJSA § 52:34-6.) This mandate is applied through section 17:12-1A-1 of the NJAC, pursuant to which "all procurements shall be effected through advertised procurement procedures." (NJAC § 17:12-1A.1.)

The DPP may structure the solicitation for award to two or more bidders in order to meet the state's anticipated needs, consistent with certain criteria, including (1) anticipated quantities of goods required; (2) the agency's need for prompt access to maintenance, repair parts, and service; (3) the agency's need for cost-efficient, timely local deliveries; (4) the agency's need for materials, supplies, services, or equipment compatible with those previously purchased; (5) the agency's need for standardization of equipment, interchangeability of parts, or continuation of services; (6) safety, environmental, or technological needs; or (7) purchase of a particular product or purchase from a particular source.

1. Advertising

Under NJSA sections 52:34-6 and -7 and NJAC section 17:12-2.1, it is generally required that all agency procurements exceeding $25,000 be publicly advertised. The notice of bid opportunity is to be placed in newspapers and other media, such as the DPP's website, so as to give the best notice to prospective bidders. (See generally NJSA § 52:34-12.)

However, even above the $25,000 threshold, there are a number of exceptions to public advertising requirements, which are addressed in Section III.B below.

2. Requirements for Bidding

To be eligible for consideration for award of a contract in accordance with NJAC section 17:12-2.2, a bidder's proposal must comply with a number of requirements, including the following:

1. The proposal must be enclosed and sealed. For electronic submission, sealing shall be as described in the request for proposals (RFP).
2. The proposal must be timely submitted.
3. The proposal must be signed by a representative of the bidder.
4. The proposal must contain all certifications, forms, and attachments required by the RFP.
5. If required, the proposal must be accompanied by bid security in the specified amount and form.
6. The proposal must include all RFP-required pricing information.
7. The proposal must be preceded by the bidder's attendance and registration at any pre-proposal conference and/or site inspection for which attendance and

registration is mandatory pursuant to the RFP, unless waived by the director of the DPP.

The full list is set forth at NJAC section 17:12-2.2(a). Importantly, if a proposal fails to include all required information, it "shall be subject to automatic rejection." (NJAC § 17:12-2.2(b).)

3. Bid Security and Bid Performance Security

Under NJAC section 17:12-2.4, the DPP may require bid security "when appropriate, based upon a review of market conditions and an evaluation of potential risk to the State." A bidder's failure to submit the required bid security with its proposal is a cause for automatic rejection.

The director of the DPP may also determine that performance security is warranted for a particular contract and, if so, set the amount of security necessary to protect the state's interests. A contractor's failure to submit the required performance security is sufficient cause for the director to cancel the contract and assess the contractor for any costs incurred by the state. (*Id.* § 17:12-2.5.)

4. Receipt of Proposals

NJAC section 17:12-2.6 provides that proposals must be timely received before the announced deadline and at the designated location. All other proposals are to be rejected. However, the director may extend the time for bid opening under certain, limited circumstances, including inclement weather or where the vendor notifies the DPP of a documentable cause of delay to its proposal submission. (*Id.*) Promptly after the deadline for submission of proposals, the opening and reading of proposals shall be conducted. In the context of RFPs that have a negotiation component, only the names and addresses of the bidders will be publicly announced at the proposal opening.

After award of a contract, all proposals are considered public documents under the Open Public Records Act, NJSA section 47:1A-1 *et seq.*, unless an exemption is applicable. The burden is on the bidder to establish the basis for an exemption.

5. Evaluation of Proposals

According to NJAC section 17:12 2.7, proposals are evaluated either by an evaluation committee appointed by the director of the DPP or by a DPP staff member. Under either method, proposals will be evaluated for a determination of competitive range. (NJAC § 17:12-2.7(f).) Competitive range bidders will be further evaluated on the basis of price and the evaluation criteria set forth in the RFP and will prepare a written recommendation for the director's consideration. (*Id.*) The director may accept, modify, or reject the recommendation and will issue a notice of intent to award to all participating bidders. (*Id.* § 17:12-2.7(g).)

Where the RFP documents set forth evaluation criteria but fail to assign weights to each such criterion, the evaluators are required to determine and document the weighted criteria. (*Id.* § 17:12-2.7(b).)

As part of their evaluation, the DPP's evaluators may make written requests to bidders to clarify portions of their proposals. (*Id.* § 17:12-2.7(e).) However, the clarification process serves only to clarify ambiguities, and is not an opportunity for bidders to supplement, change, or correct its proposal. Any attempt by a bidder to supplement, change, or correct its proposal is to be disregarded by the DPP evaluators. (*Id.*)

If the RFP includes a negotiation component, the RFP must state that the state may negotiate with bidders. Only bidders whose proposals are determined to be in the competitive range are eligible for negotiations. The evaluators may conduct several rounds of negotiations with bidders and may elect to request the submission of best and final offers. (*Id.* § 17:12-2.7(j).)

6. Bypassing Low Bidder for Poor Past Performance

In evaluating proposals, the director of the DPP may bypass a lower price proposal due to the lower price bidder's poor performance on current or prior state contracts. (*Id.* § 17:12-2.8.) In making this determination, the director takes into consideration the frequency and seriousness of the bidder's poor performance and other information the director may solicit, including information from agency records or from the bidder itself. The bypassed bidder must receive notice of the decision to bypass and may challenge the decision. (*Id.*)

7. Lowest Price, Responsive Procurements

In lieu of conducting a procurement based upon weighted evaluation criteria, the DPP may also structure a procurement to award contracts to the bidder that submits the lowest price, responsive proposal. (*Id.* § 17:12-2.9.) For this method of procurement, the DPP will define in the RFP the factors that establish responsiveness and must specify that award will be made to the lowest price proposal meeting the responsiveness criteria. (*Id.* § 17:12-2.9(b).) The DPP may not bypass a lower priced responsive proposal, except for poor performance pursuant to NJAC section 17:12-2.8. Clarifications and negotiations pursuant to NJAC section 17:12-2.7 are both permitted.

8. Tie Proposals

If two or more proposals are tied with respect to price and other evaluation criteria, NJAC section 17:12-2.10 provides that the tie is to be broken by the following factors, in order of priority: (1) tie-breaking provisions listed in the RFP; (2) a usable cash- or volume-based discount that renders one proposal more favorably priced; (3) delivery advantage, specifically shorter proposed time frames for delivery and/or closer proximity to the point of delivery; (4) active registration as an approved small business; and (5) in-state location. If these factors do not break the ties, multiple awards may be made. (*Id.* § 17:12-2.10(b).)

9. Preference Laws: Out-of-State Vendors

NJAC section 17:12-2.13 allows the director of the DPP to apply a preference for in-state bidders in the evaluation and award of state contracts. The director must provide notice of the DPP's intent as to in-state preference in the language of the RFP.

Moreover, pursuant to NJSA section 52:32-1.4, the director is required to apply a reciprocal preference against an out-of-state bidder whose home state applies an in-state preference. However, the director is free to waive this requirement where doing so would be in the best interest of the state and under certain limited circumstances.

B. Exceptions to Formal, Advertised, Competitive Procurement

While formal, advertised, competitive procurement is the state's primary method of source selection as discussed above, NJAC section 17:12-1A.2 provides certain exceptions pursuant to which formal, advertised, competitive procurement procedures do not apply, including contracts between state agencies, contracts awarded by the DPP after the state treasurer has approved a waiver of advertising requirements, cooperative procurement agreements with other states, and DPP procurements that allow the use of federal supply schedule contracts. A complete listing of such exceptions is set forth at NJAC section 17:12-1A.2(a).

IV. Bid Protests and Contract Disputes

A. Bid Protests

Broadly speaking, there are two kinds of protests available: (1) a pre-award protest of the terms, conditions, or specifications of an RFP, and (2) a post-award protest to an award decision.

1. Pre-Award Protests

A vendor that intends to submit a proposal in response to an advertised RFP may submit a written protest to the director of the DPP setting forth in detail any grounds to challenge the RFP. (NJAC § 17:12-3.2.)

Protests must be filed during the period of time after the DPP has formally responded to questions posed during the RFP-established question and answer period, but in sufficient time to permit the DPP to review the merits and take action prior to the deadline for proposal submission. (*Id.* § 17:12-3.2(b).) The director may disregard any protest filed fewer than seven business days prior to such deadline. (*Id.*)

To be considered on its merits, a protest must identify the solicitation number for the particular procurement; identify the specification(s) at issue and state the specific grounds for challenging such specification(s), "including all arguments, materials, or other documentation that may support the protester's position that the specification should be changed"; and include a statement as to whether the protester requests an opportunity for in-person presentation and the reason for the request. Any protest that does not contain all of these item may be disregarded. (*Id.*)

After receipt of a timely pre-award protest, the director shall issue a final written decision on the protest prior to the public opening and reading of proposals. (*Id.* § 17:12-3.2.) The director may resolve the protest by amending the RFP and extending the deadline for proposal submission, by canceling the procurement, or by any other appropriate means. (*Id.* § 17:12-3.2(d).) The director's decision constitutes the final agency decision pursuant to NJAC section 17:12-3.1(b).

2. Post-Award Protests

A bidder who has submitted a proposal in response to an RFP may submit a written protest to the director concerning either (1) the rejection of its proposal, when such rejection is based upon the bidder's failure to comply with NJAC section 17.12-2.2; (2) the notice of award of a contract; or (3) the DPP's cancellation of an RFP after the opening of proposal. (*Id.* § 17:12-3.3.) Any such protest must be filed within ten business days following the bidder's receipt of written notification that its proposal is non-responsive or of notice of award. An untimely protest may be disregarded by the director. (*Id.*)

To be considered, a protest must identify the solicitation number for the particular procurement; identify the specific grounds for challenging the decision, "including all arguments, materials, or other documentation that may support the protester's position that the contract award should be overturned"; and include a statement as to whether the protester requests an opportunity for oral presentation and the reason for the request.

The director may disregard a protest not containing all of these items. (*Id.* § 17:12-3.3(b).) Upon receipt of a timely protest, the DPP is required to refrain from awarding the contract until a final decision on the merits has been rendered by the director, except in circumstances where the failure to proceed with the contract will result in substantial cost to the state or where required by public exigency. (*Id.* § 17:12-3.3(c).)

The director is required to issue a final, written decision on the basis of the written protest record and the report of the hearing, if any, that is held on the matter. (*Id.* § 17:12-3.3(d).) The director's decision constitutes a final agency decision pursuant to NJAC section 17:12-3.1(b).

3. Discovery Procedures in Protests

When a protest is received, the DPP may request "any and all records and documents deemed appropriate and relevant to the issues and arguments set forth in the protest." (*Id.* § 17:12-3.4.) The bidder must promptly provide the requested records to the DPP upon request, and its failure to do so may constitute a sufficient basis for the DPP to deny the protest. (*Id.*)

B. Bid Protest Appeals

Final agency decisions of protests are appealable to the New Jersey Superior Court Appellate Division. (*Id.* § 17:12-3.1(b).)

C. Contract Disputes

1. State Claims against Contractor

a. Performance Issues

NJAC section 17:12-4.2 establishes the "means of assuring prompt action" in cases where the state "claims that a State contractor's performance fails to meet contract requirements, and establishing a record that documents a contractor's poor performance in cases where a contractor's performance fails to meet contract requirements." Under NJAC section 17:12-4.3, the state agency involved in the contract is required to promptly notify the DPP's Contract Compliance and Audit Unit (CCAU) of any failure by a contractor to comply with the terms and conditions of the contract. Notification must be in writing. Under NJAC section 17:12-4.3(b), the following alleged breaches of contract terms by the contractor are to be reported to CCAU:

1. Failure by the contractor to deliver goods or services at the time and place or in the manner, quantity or quality specified;
2. Demand for prices other than those specified in the contract;
3. Delivery of unauthorized substitutes or ungraded material where grading is required;
4. Sale of goods that are not authorized by the contract;
5. Failure to install goods; improper installation;
6. Any other failure to comply with contract specifications or failure to achieve a satisfactory rating for the service provided under the contract if quality assurance surveys are performed;

7. Conflict of interest; and
8. Failure to comply with any relevant legal or contractual requirement.

b. Time Frames

NJAC section 17:12-4.4 governs the time frame for resolution of agency complaints to CCAU. As soon as possible after receipt of the complaint, CCAU will inform the contractor of the complaint in writing. The contractor must reply to the complaint within ten days of its receipt and may cure the alleged deficiency in performance or submit a corrective action plan. If the contractor elects to cure or submit a corrective action plan, CCAU may take those steps into account in determining whether the complaint will be decided adversely to the contractor, but such steps will not necessarily invalidate the complaint.

The contractor or complainant are entitled to file an appeal to the director of the DPP within ten business days of receipt of CCAU's initial determination. If the director finds that a complaint against a contractor is valid, the contractor must be notified of the deadline for the contractor to cure the performance deficiencies.

c. Resolution of Complaints

Under NJAC section 17:12-4.5, a CCAU-adjudicated complaint appealed to the director is to be resolved by written decision on the basis of the director's review of the written record. The director may also require the complainant and/or respondent to make an in-person presentation, including the presentation of additional documentation in support of its position.

The director may review the record or conduct a hearing himself or herself, or designate a hearing officer. Where a hearing officer is appointed, he or she must make an advisory report to the director, and the parties will have ten business days to provide the director with written comments on the report. Thereafter, the director must make a written decision. The director's decision shall constitute a final agency decision appealable to the appellate division of the superior court.

The period during which a complaint is being handled administratively does not stop the running of any limitations period in the New Jersey Contractual Liability Act, NJSA section 59:13-1 *et seq*.

d. Effect of Contractor Noncompliance with Contract Provisions

NJAC section 17:12-4.6 clarifies that the CCAU complaint procedures discussed above shall not preclude the contracting agency from rejecting noncompliant goods and services. The contracting agency must report any such decisions to the DPP immediately.

If the director determines that a contractor's noncompliance with the contract "affects or may affect the health, safety, or welfare of the State or its citizenry," then the director may contact the contractor directly to obtain compliance. (NJAC § 17:12-4.7.) If the contractor does not immediately resolve the issue, then the director may retain a replacement contractor, and charge all excess costs to the noncomplying contractor. (*Id.*)

In addition, under NJAC section 17:12-4.8, the director may terminate a contract with a noncomplying contractor and immediately purchase (or direct the using agency to purchase) goods or obtain services from another source, making the defaulting contractor liable to the state for any difference in price. This right is triggered by either of the following circumstances: (1) refusal of the contractor to bring goods or services into compliance as required by the director or CCAU; (2) refusal of the contractor to answer inquiries by the DPP or failure to respond to a formal complaint within ten days of receipt; or (3) rejection of goods under NJAC section 17:12-4.6.

Upon continued or willful failure to perform, the director may suspend or debar the contractor (as discussed in Section IV.D below).

2. Contractor Claims against the State

The State of New Jersey, through the Contractual Liability Act, NJSA section 59:13-1 *et seq.*, has waived its sovereign immunity from liability arising out of state contracts. However, there is no recovery against the state for punitive or consequential damages arising out of a contract, nor is there any recovery against the state for claims based upon implied warranties or upon contracts implied in law. (NJSA § 59:13-3.) The statute confers jurisdiction to hear such claims on the courts and provides that all such claims will be heard by a judge, sitting without a jury. (*Id.* § 59:13-4.)

a. Claims Process and Litigation

It is the responsibility of the contractor to "promptly" notify the state in writing of any situation or occurrence that could "potentially result in the submission of a claim" against the state. (*Id.* § 59:13-5.) Generally, a notice of claim for breach of contract must be filed with the contracting agency within 90 days after accrual. (*Id.*) A notice of claim must include the name of the claimant, the nature of the claim, specific reasons for making the claim, and the total dollar amount of the claim, if known. After the expiration of 90 days from the date that the notice of claim is received by the contracting agency, the claimant may file suit in the courts. (*Id.*)

Any contract claim will be barred if the contractor/claimant (1) fails to notify the appropriate contracting agency within 90 days of accrual of the claim; (2) fails to file suit (a) within two years of accrual of the claims or (b) within one year after completion of the contract, whichever may be later; or (3) the claimant has accepted any award, compromise, or settlement made by the state. (*Id.*)

Even so, judges of the superior court have the discretion to permit a claimant who fails to file a timely notice of claim to file such notice at any time within one year after the accrual if the state has not been substantially prejudiced by the late filing. (*Id.* § 59:13-6.) Application to the court for permission to file a late notice of claim must be made by motion and based upon affidavits setting forth sufficient reason for the failure to file a timely notice of claim. (*Id.*)

b. Successful Claims

According to NJSA section 59:13-8, prejudgment interest does not accrue on contractor claims against the state, but the court, in its discretion, may award prejudgment interest in connection with claims arising out of state construction projects.

Under NJSA section 59:13-9, whenever any claim is settled or reduced to final judgment in a court, it must be certified by the attorney general to the state treasurer, who then must pay the claim out of any funds available to the department or other agency against which the claim was made.

D. Suspension and Debarment

1. Grounds for Debarment

Under NJAC section 17:12-6.3, the director of the DPP shall debar a person for any of the following causes:

1. Commission of a criminal offense as an incident to obtaining or attempting to obtain a public or private contract, or subcontract thereunder, or in the performance of such contract or subcontract;
2. Violation of the Federal Organized Crime Control Act of 1970, or commission of embezzlement, theft, forgery, bribery, falsification or destruction of records, perjury, false swearing, receiving stolen property, obstruction of justice, or any other offense indicating a lack of business integrity or honesty;
3. Violation of the Federal or State antitrust statutes, or of the Federal Anti-Kickback Act (18 U.S.C. 874, 40 U.S.C. 276b, c);
4. Violation of any laws governing the conduct of elections of the Federal Government, State of New Jersey or of its political subdivision;
5. Violation of the "Law Against Discrimination" (P.L. 1945, c.169, N.J.S.A. 10:5-1 et seq., as supplemented by P.L. 1975, c.127), or of the act banning discrimination in public works employment (N.J.S.A. 10:2-1 et seq.) or of the act prohibiting discrimination by industries engaged in defense work in the employment of persons therein (c.114, L. 1942, N.J.S.A. 10:1-10 et seq.);
6. Violation of any laws governing hours of labor, minimum wage standards, prevailing wage standards, discrimination in wages, or child labor;
7. Violation of any laws governing the conduct of occupations or professions or regulated industries;
8. Violation of any laws which may bear upon a lack of responsibility or moral integrity;
9. Willful failure to perform in accordance with contract specifications or within contractual time limits, including, but not limited to, failure to accept purchase orders and maintain prices or any terms and conditions as bid;
10. A record of failure to perform or of unsatisfactory performance in accordance with the terms of one or more contracts, provided that such failure or unsatisfactory performance has occurred within a reasonable time preceding the determination to debar and was caused by acts within the control of the person debarred;
11. Violation of contractual or statutory provisions regulating contingent fees;
12. Any other cause affecting responsibility as a State contractor of such serious and compelling nature as may be determined by purchase and property to warrant debarment, including but not limited to, making a material false representation in a bid, even if such conduct has not been or may not be prosecuted as violations of such laws or contracts;
13. Debarment by some other department or agency in the Executive Branch;
14. Any offer or agreement to pay or to make payment either directly or indirectly, any fee, commission, compensation, gift, gratuity, or other thing of value of any kind to any State officer or employee or special State officer or employee, as defined by N.J.S.A. 52:13D-13b and e, in the Department of the Treasury or any other agency with which such

vendor transacts or offers or proposes to transact business, or to any member of the immediate family as defined by N.J.S.A. 52:13D-13i, of any such officer or employee, or any partnership, firm, or corporation with which they are employed or associated, or in which such officer or employee has an interest within the meaning of N.J.S.A. 52:13D-13g;

15. Failure by a vendor to report to the Attorney General and to the Executive Commission on Ethical Standards in writing forthwith the solicitation of any fee, commission, compensation, gift, gratuity or other thing of value by any State officer or employee or special State officer or employee;
16. Failure by a vendor to report in writing forthwith or failure to obtain a waiver from the Executive Commission on Ethical Standards, who may undertake, directly or indirectly, any private business, commercial or entrepreneurial relationship with, whether or not pursuant to employment, contract or other agreement, express or implied, or sell any interest in such vendor to, any State officer or employee or special State officer or employee having any duties or responsibilities in connection with the purchase, acquisition or sale of any property or services by or to any State agency or any instrumentality thereof, or with any person, firm or entity with which he or she is employed or associated or in which he or she has an interest within the meaning of N.J.S.A. 52:13D-13g;
17. Influence or attempt to influence or cause to be influenced, any State officer or employee or special State officer or employee in his or her official capacity in any manner which might tend to impair the objectivity or independence of judgment of said officer or employee;
18. Cause or influence or attempt to cause or influence, any State officer or employee or special State officer or employee to use, or attempt to use, his or her official position to secure unwarranted privileges or advantages for the vendor or any other person.

2. Conditions Affecting Debarment

The existence of any of the causes above shall not necessarily require debarment. (NJAC § 17:12-6.4.) Rather, the decision to debar shall be made only in the discretion of the director and must include consideration of all mitigating factors. (*Id.*) The standard of proof necessary to justify debarment depends upon the nature of the offending conduct, as more fully set forth in NJAC section 17:12-6.4.

3. Procedure Relating to Debarment

NJAC section 17:12-6.5 requires that the director furnish to a party proposed for debarment a written notice setting forth the reasons for the proposed debarment, and indicating that such party will be afforded an opportunity for a hearing. All such hearings are to be conducted in accordance with the provisions of the Administrative Procedures Act. However, where another department or agency has imposed debarment upon a party, the director may also impose a similar debarment without affording an opportunity for a hearing. In that situation, the director must first furnish notice of the proposed similar debarment to the party and afford the party an opportunity to present information to explain why the proposed similar debarment should not be imposed in whole or in part.

Debarment shall be for a reasonable, defined period of time that generally shall not exceed five years. Debarment for an additional period is also possible, if the party is given written notice and an opportunity to present information on his or her own behalf.

Debarment may be removed, or the debarment period may be reduced, in the discretion of the director upon the submission by the debarred party of a "good faith application under oath" supported by documentary evidence establishing good cause for relief. Such good cause may include newly discovered evidence, reversal of conviction, or change in ownership/control of the company. (*Id.* § 17:12-6.5.)

4. Grounds for Suspension

Pursuant to NJAC section 17:12-6.6, suspension shall be based upon the same causes justifying debarment under section 17:12-6.3. Unlike debarment, which requires a hearing, the director shall suspend "upon adequate evidence" that cause for debarment exists, where such suspension is in the public interest. (*Id.* § 17:12-6.6.) To justify suspension, the finding of cause must be based upon adequate evidence, and not upon unsupported accusations. (*Id.* § 17:12-6.7.)

5. Procedures for Suspension

NJAC section 17:12-6.8 requires that within ten days after the effective date of the suspension, the director must provide the suspended party with a written notice stating that a suspension has been imposed and its effective date; setting forth the reasons for the suspension; stating that the suspension is for a temporary period pending the completion of an investigation and such legal proceedings as may ensue; and indicating that, if such legal proceedings are not commenced or the suspension removed within 60 days of the date of such notice, the party will be given a statement of the reasons for the suspension and an opportunity for a hearing, or a statement declining to give such reasons and setting forth the director's position regarding the continuation of the suspension.

A suspension may not continue beyond 18 months from its effective date unless civil or criminal action regarding the alleged violation has been initiated within that period or a debarment action has been commenced. (*Id.* § 17:12-6.8.) If either has begun, the suspension may continue until the proceedings are completed. A suspension may include all known affiliates of a person. (*Id.*)

6. Extent of Suspension or Debarment

According to NJAC section 17:12-6.9, the exclusion from state contracting through debarment, suspension, or disqualification extends to all state contracting and subcontracting within the control or jurisdiction of the director, including any contracts that use state funds. Nevertheless, the director may grant an exception from total exclusion after determining that this step, with respect to a particular state contract, is essential to the public interest. The director is required by NJAC section 17:12-6.11 to supply to the state treasurer a monthly list of all persons debarred, suspended, or disqualified in accordance with the procedures described above.

V. Administrative and Judicial Review

The information on administrative and judicial review is set forth fully above. With respect to judicial review, the New Jersey Rules of Court provide that an appeal may be taken as of right from any final agency decision. (New Jersey Court Rule 2:2-3.) Appeals must be taken within 45 days of the agency's decision. (*Id.* 2:4-1(b).)

The appellate division performs only a limited review of agency decisions in the area of public procurement. (*Van Note-Harvey Associates, P.C. v. New Jersey School Development Authority*, 407 N.J. Super. 643, 648 (N.J. Super. Ct. App. Div. 2009).) New Jersey "jurisprudence recognizes that the Legislature purposefully conferred broad discretion on the Director of the Division of Purchase and Property to determine 'which bid will be most advantageous to the State.'" (*In re Jasper Seating Co., Inc.*, 406 N.J. Super. 213, 222 (N.J. Super. Ct. App. Div. 2009) (quoting *Commercial Cleaning Corp. v. Sullivan*, 47 N.J. 539, 548 (1966)).) Courts will intervene only in rare instances when "an agency action is clearly inconsistent with its statutory mission or with other State policy." (*George Harms Construction Co. v. New Jersey Turnpike Authority*, 137 N.J. 8, 27 (1994).) A reviewing court "may not substitute its own judgment for the agency's, even though the court might have reached a different result." (*In re Stallworth*, 208 N.J. 182, 194 (2011) (citations omitted).) Therefore, "[b]road latitude and discretion is afforded to the agency, and the court 'will not interfere in the absence of bad faith, corruption, fraud or gross abuse of discretion.'" (*Van Note-Harvey Associates, P.C. v. New Jersey School Development Authority*, 407 N.J. Super. 643, 648 (N.J. Super. Ct. App. Div. 2009) (quoting *Commercial Cleaning Corp. v. Sullivan*, 47 N.J. 539, 549 (1966).) Thus, it is well settled that an award of a contract pursuant to the director's authority "will not be disturbed absent a showing of bad faith, corruption, fraud or gross abuse of discretion." (*State v. Ernst & Young, L.L.P.*, 386 N.J. Super. 600, 619 (N.J. Super. Ct. App. Div. 2006) (citing *Commercial Cleaning Corp. v. Sullivan*, 47 N.J. 539, 549 (1966).)

VI. Extent of State's Adoption or Adaptation of ABA Model Procurement Code

New Jersey's statutory and regulatory scheme does not follow the American Bar Association (ABA) Model Procurement Code.

VII. Cooperative Purchasing

A. Authority

As an exception to the standard competitive bidding requirements discussed above, NJSA section 52:34-6.2(a) authorizes the director of the DPP to enter into cooperative purchasing agreements with one or more other states, or political subdivisions of other states, for the purchase of goods and services. The director is also empowered under NJSA section 52:34-6.2(b) to purchase goods and services through any contract awarded through a cooperative purchasing agreement.

B. Requirements

1. Joining Cooperative Agreements

The requirements for cooperative purchasing are set forth at NJAC sections 17:12-1A.3 and -1A.4. Under NJAC section 17:12-1A.3(a), the director may enter into a cooperative purchasing agreement with one or more other states, with one or more political subdivisions of another state or of New Jersey, or with a nationally recognized and accepted cooperative procurement entity in which one or more other states participate.

In order for the director to permissibly enter into such a cooperative agreement, the cooperative agreement must provide for the combined requirements of the cooperating parties to be, procured through an advertised competitive bidding process. (NJAC § 17:12-1A.3(b).) However, the director is not required to join the cooperative agreement prior to the time when cooperating parties undertake the competitive bidding process. Rather, the director may enter into the cooperative agreement either prior to, during, or after an advertised competitive procurement is conducted. (*Id.* § 17:12-1A.3(a).)

Before joining a cooperative agreement for the purchase of goods or services, the director must determine that the cooperative agreement is the most cost-effective contractual solution. (*Id.*) Cost-effectiveness must be determined by considering pertinent factors, such as (1) whether the cooperative agreement provides for pricing lower than current state contract pricing, which will afford material cost savings; (2) whether the cooperative agreement provides pricing lower than the pricing for comparable goods or services in other state or public entity contracts; (3) whether the cooperative agreement provides for expanded product or service availability; (4) the ability to avoid the cost and time of a state procurement; (5) whether the cooperative agreement provides for goods or services through vendors with a record of satisfactory performance; (6) whether the cooperative agreement provides for lower minimum purchase requirements; (7) whether the cooperative agreement provides a comparatively better quality of goods or services; and (8) administrative cost factors required to participate in the cooperative agreement.

Where the director determines that a cooperative agreement is the most cost-effective solution, he or she may enter into the agreement only after reviewing and approving the specifications and proposed contractual terms and conditions between the vendor and cooperating parties; and requiring the vendor to execute an addendum containing standard state contracting terms and conditions, and any other terms that the director determines make the cooperative agreement more favorable to the state. (*Id.* § 17:12-1A.3(c).) The director must also provide public notice of the agreement. (*Id.*)

2. Leading a Cooperative Agreement

In addition to joining a cooperative agreement, the director may also lead, sponsor, conduct, solicit, award, and/or administer a cooperative agreement. (*Id.* § 17:12-1A.4(a).) Any contract procured through such a cooperative agreement must be procured through advertised procurement procedures. (*Id.* § 17:12-1A.4(b).) The procurement documents are required to set forth the combined requirements of the cooperative purchasing participants and must specify that each jurisdiction participating in a contract is solely responsible for the payment of the purchase price and cost of purchases made by it under the terms of any resultant contract. (*Id.* § 17:12-1A.4(c).) If the director procures contracts on behalf of a nationally recognized and accepted cooperative procurement entity, then the director is permitted to utilize a contract structure whereby the director awards a master agreement to one or more contractor(s), with all participating entities joining the master agreement via execution of a participating addendum.

New Mexico Procurement Rules and Regulations

Prepared by Joshua Grabel
Dickinson Wright PLLC
Email: jgrabel@dickinsonwright.com

I. Statutory Reference

A. Procurement/Purchasing Statutes

The relevant sections of the New Mexico Statutes Annotated of 1978 (NMSA) are as follows:

§§ 13-1-21 to 13-1-199.	Procurement Code and resident and veterans' preferences
§§ 13-1B-1 to 13-1B-7.	Alternative Fuel Acquisition Act
§§ 13-1C-1 to 13-1C-7.	State Use Act—preference for persons with disabilities
§§ 13-4-1 to 13-4-43.	Public works contracts
§§ 13-7-1 to 13-7-13.	Health Care Purchasing Act

B. Other Applicable Statutes

The relevant NMSA sections are listed below:

§§ 10-16-1 to 10-16-18.	Governmental Conduct Act
§§ 10-16A-1 to 10-16A-8.	Financial Disclosure Act
§§ 10-16B-1 to 10-16B-4.	Gift Act
§ 22-21-1.	Prohibited sales by school personnel
§§ 30-23-1 to 30-23-7.	Misconduct by public officials
§§ 30-24-1 to 30-24-2.	Bribery of public officer or public employee

Note: Municipal ordinances should also be consulted. Home rule municipalities that enact their own purchasing ordinances are exempt from the state Procurement Code.

II. Regulations

The Procurement Code and related regulations are found at the New Mexico Administrative Code (NMAC) website, https://www.generalservices.state.nm.us/state-purchasing/resources-and-information/, and are listed in the table below.

Part 1.4.1	Procurement Code Regulations
Part 1.4.2	Resident Business and Manufacturer Preferences
Part 1.4.3	Resident Contractor Preference
Part 1.4.7	Suspension or Debarment of Bidders, Offerors, or Contractors
Part 1.4.8	Use of Competitive Sealed Proposals for Construction and Facility Maintenance, Services, and Repairs
Part 1.5.7	Design and Build Project Delivery Systems
Part 1.5.8	Construction Management Services
Part 1.5.25	State Agencies Lease-Purchasing of Real Property

Local public bodies, including counties, municipalities, and school districts, may adopt procurement ordinances and regulations to govern their purchases so long as they are consistent with the requirements of the Procurement Code. Local public bodies, except home rule municipalities, must comply with the Procurement Code, but are not required to purchase through the state purchasing agent. Home rule municipalities may adopt their own purchasing ordinances and, if they do, they are exempt from the state Procurement Code.

Vendors must comply with all federal and state laws, rules and regulations, and executive orders of the governor pertaining to equal employment opportunity. Vendors must also comply with Executive Order No. 2007-049, requiring certain vendors to provide health insurance coverage for employees, and Executive Order No. 2009-049, requiring certain vendors to provide the state information concerning pay equity.

III. Source Selection

The state purchasing agent is the purchasing authority for most purchases by state government entities. State agencies, through their central purchasing offices, are permitted to make purchases of professional services, small purchases, and emergency purchases. Local public bodies, the judicial and legislative branches, and state educational institutions are not required to purchase through the state purchasing agent.

The Procurement Code requires that all procurement be achieved by competitive sealed bid, competitive sealed proposals, small purchases, sole source procurement, emergency procurements, existing contracts (primarily federal and state price agreements), purchases from antipoverty program businesses, and procurements under the Educational Facility Construction Manager At Risk Act.

Competitive Sealed Bids: An invitation for bids (IFB), containing the specifications for the items or services to be procured, contractual terms and conditions, evaluation criteria to determine product acceptability, and instructions for submitting bids, is used to initiate a competitive sealed bid procurement. Notices of IFBs are published through an online procurement portal available on the website for the New Mexico General Services Department located at https://www.generalservices.state.nm.us/state-purchasing/online-procurement/. Potential vendors can register on the procurement website and receive notifications related to potentially relevant procurements.

Bids must be submitted via the online portal. New Mexico also offers a specific "Response Guide" that addresses many questions that potential bidders may have in pursuing a project in New Mexico, which is available at https://www.generalservices.state.nm.us/state-purchasing/resources-and-information/#Vendors. Each bid, except for those portions for which a bidder has made a written request for confidentiality, is subject to public inspection. A contract solicited by competitive sealed bids must be awarded to the lowest responsible bidder. No negotiation is permitted except to avoid rejection of all bids under certain circumstances.

Competitive Sealed Proposals: Procurements of professional services, a design and build project, or when the purchasing office determines that use of competitive sealed bids would not be practicable or advantageous to the government entity may be achieved using competitive sealed proposals. A request for proposals (RFP) is used to initiate a competitive sealed proposal procurement. The RFP must contain the specification for the services or items to be procured, contractual terms and conditions, campaign contribution disclosure forms, and instructions for submitting proposals. The RFP must contain evaluation factors and their relative weights. Offerors submitting proposals may be allowed to discuss their proposals with the procuring entity and may be allowed to revise proposals after submission and prior to award for the purpose of obtaining best and final offers. Special provisions apply to design and build projects and qualifications-based proposals for architects, engineers, landscape architects, and surveyors. Contracts are awarded to offerors whose proposals are most advantageous to the government entity, considering the evaluation factors. RFPs are also available to be found and submitted through the New Mexico procurement portal and the electronic process outlined therein.

A guide for how to proceed with RFPs is also available at https://www.generalservices.state.nm.us/state-purchasing/resources-and-information/.

Notices of active RFPs for the state of New Mexico are available at https://www.generalservices.state.nm.us/state-purchasing/active-itbs-and-rfps/active-procurements/.

A. Small Purchases

A government entity may procure services or items having a value less than $20,000 by issuing a purchase order to a contractor based on best obtainable price. For small purchases of nonprofessional services, construction, or tangible personal property exceeding $20,000 but not exceeding $60,000, at least three businesses must be contacted in writing to request a quote for the purchase, and the lowest acceptable quote must be awarded the contract. Small purchases of most professional services not exceeding $60,000 may be purchased by negotiation without quotes.

B. Sole Source Procurement

A contract may be awarded without competitive sealed bids or competitive sealed proposals when the purchasing authority determines, in writing, that there is only one source for the procurement and that other similar services, construction, or property cannot meet the intended purpose of the contract. At least 30 days before a sole source contract is awarded, the purchasing authority must post the proposed award on its website. A qualified potential contractor who is not awarded the contract may protest the proposed award.

C. Emergency Procurement

A purchasing authority may make emergency procurements when emergency conditions as defined by statute and regulation exist. An "emergency condition" is a condition that creates a threat to public health, welfare, safety, or property, including floods, epidemics, riots, essential equipment failures, or similar events.

D. Procurement under Existing Contracts

A purchasing authority may purchase without competitive bids or proposals from contractors with current federal supply contracts at a price equal to or less than the federal supply contract price or from contractors with a current price agreement with the state purchasing agent or another state or a central purchasing office.

E. Resident Preferences

Resident businesses, resident veteran businesses, resident contractors, and resident veteran contractors are given from 5 percent to 10 percent of their bids, points, or weight of factors preferences. To be eligible for the preferences, the business or contractor must receive a certificate from the New Mexico Taxation and Revenue Department after meeting the residency requirements of NMSA section 13-1-22.

F. Contracts

In general, there are two types of purchases made by governmental entities: term contract and open-market purchase. A term contract is entered to purchase items in demand throughout the year, including vehicles, tires, office equipment, and services. These contracts are generally entered into for one year but may extend to four years. Open-market purchases are those for a one-time purchase. The State Purchasing Office establishes statewide price agreements for property and services commonly used by governmental entities. It can also enter into agency-specific price agreements.

IV. Bid Protests and Contract Disputes

A. Bid Protests

Any bidder or offeror who is aggrieved by a solicitation or award of a contract, including a sole source procurement, may protest to the purchasing authority that has control and administration of the procurement. (See NMSA § 13-1-172.) For a state procurement, that may be either the state purchasing agent or central purchasing office of the state agency. The protest must be submitted in writing within 15 calendar days after knowledge of the facts or occurrences giving rise to the protest. Protests are generally governed by the New Mexico Procurement Code. (NMAC §§ 1.4.1.90–1.4.1.93.)

The protest must include the name and address of the protestant, the solicitation number, the statement of the grounds for protest, and supporting exhibits, evidence, or documents to substantiate the claim, and it must specify the ruling requested from the purchasing authority.

Protests of state procurements are subject to the state Procurement Code regulations. Other central purchasing offices may adopt their own regulations governing protests. Under the state regulations, all other bidders or offerors are given notice of a protest and are automatically parties to the protest. The purchasing authority may require parties to submit briefs or other statements of positions and may, but is not required to, hold an evidentiary hearing on the protest.

B. Bid Protest Appeals

Appeals from protests are taken to the state district court pursuant to NMSA section 39-3-1.1 and the associated Rule of Civil Procedure, Rule 1-074 NMRA, which generally govern appeals from administrative agency decisions. Appeals may be taken only from final agency action. The appeal is a review on the record and is not a de novo proceeding. A notice of appeal must be filed with the district court within 30 days after the date of the final decision of the agency. The appeal may be taken to the district court for the county in which the agency's principal office is located or the district court of any county in which a hearing was conducted. A party may seek review of a final district court action by writ of certiorari to the New Mexico Court of Appeals, which may exercise its discretion in granting review. A party may seek further review by writ of certiorari to the New Mexico Supreme Court.

C. Contract Disputes

1. Contract Claims

There is no special procedure for contract claims in New Mexico. Contracts may contain arbitration or mediation provisions, and generally establish jurisdiction and venue in New Mexico district courts. Pursuant to NMSA section 37-1-23, governmental entities, except municipalities, are immune from actions based on contract unless there is a written contract, and all claims on written contracts must be brought within two years from the time of accrual. Claims on municipal contracts must be brought within three years.

2. Contract Claims Appeals

Final decisions of district courts on contract claims may be appealed to the court of appeals. Notices of appeal must be filed with the district court and court of appeals within 30 days of the final decision of the district court. Review of the court of appeals' decision is by writ of certiorari to the New Mexico Supreme Court.

D. Suspension and Debarment

The purchasing authority may recommend the suspension or debarment of a business after notice to the business. The decision to suspend may be made by the purchasing authority, but the decision to debar must be made by the governing authority of the state agency or local public body. Debarment may not exceed three years and suspension may not exceed three months, except that if a bidder or offeror has been charged with a criminal offense that is a cause for debarment, the suspension must be in effect until the criminal charge is resolved. Causes for debarment or suspension must have occurred within three years of the procurement and, pursuant to NMSA section 13-1-178, include the following:

> (1) criminal conviction of a bidder, offeror or contractor for commission of a criminal offense related to obtaining unlawfully or attempting to obtain a public or private contract or subcontract, or related to the unlawful performance of such contract or subcontract;

(2) civil judgment against a bidder, offeror or contractor for a civil violation related to obtaining unlawfully or attempting to obtain a public or private contract or subcontract, or related to the unlawful performance of such contract or subcontract;

(3) conviction of a bidder, offeror or contractor under state or federal statutes related to embezzlement, theft, forgery, bribery, fraud, falsification or destruction of records, making false statements or receiving stolen property or for violation of federal or state tax laws;

(4) conviction of a bidder, offeror or contractor under state or federal antitrust statutes relating to the submission of offers;

(5) criminal conviction against a bidder, offeror or contractor for any other offense related to honesty, integrity or business ethics;

(6) civil judgment against a bidder, offeror or contractor for a civil violation related to honesty, integrity or business ethics;

(7) civil judgment against a bidder, offeror or contractor pursuant to the Unfair Practices Act [Chapter 57, Article 12 NMSA 1978];

(8) violation by a bidder, offeror or contractor of contract provisions . . . of a character that is reasonably regarded by the state purchasing agent or a central purchasing office to be so serious as to justify suspension or debarment action, including:

(a) willful failure to perform in accordance with one or more contracts; or

(b) a history of failure to perform or of unsatisfactory performance of one or more contracts; provided that this failure or unsatisfactory performance has occurred within a reasonable time preceding the decision to impose debarment; and provided further that failure to perform or unsatisfactory performance caused by acts beyond the control of the contractor shall not be considered to be a basis for debarment;

(9) any other cause that the state purchasing agent or a central purchasing office determines to be so serious and compelling as to affect responsibility as a contractor; or

(10) for a willful violation by a bidder, offeror or contractor of the provisions of the Procurement Code.

The terms "bidder," "offeror," and "contractor" include principals, officers, directors, owners, partners, and managers of the bidder, offeror, or contractor.

Notice of the proposed debarment or suspension must be provided to the business. If requested by the business, a hearing must be held prior to suspension or debarment. Regulations governing state debarment and suspension are found at NMAC part 1.4.7.

A final decision to debar or suspend may be appealed to the district court pursuant to NMSA section 39-3-1.1 and Rule 1-074 NMRA. Review of a district court decision may be sought by writ of certiorari to the New Mexico Court of Appeals and Supreme Court.

V. Administrative and Judicial Review

A. Administrative Review

As discussed above, there is no administrative process for disputes related to contract formation (aside from compliance with the Procurement Code) or performance.

Courts of general jurisdiction, primarily district courts and the appellate courts, hear public contract disputes subject to the Rules of Civil Procedure and the Rules of Appellate Procedure. New Mexico appellate decisions are available at https://coa.nmcourts.gov/home/formal-opinions/.

B. Judicial Review

- *State ex rel. Regents of Eastern New Mexico University v. Baca*, 2008-NMSC-047, 144 N.M. 530, 189 P.3d 663: Unsuccessful bidder could not circumvent statutory procedures for judicial review of administrative decision by filing declaratory judgment action having first filed a bid protest. Declaratory judgment action may be appropriate even when there is an administrative remedy if issues raised are purely legal and do not require any fact-finding by the administrative entity.
- *RMCI, General Contractors, Inc. v. Albuquerque Bernalillo County Water Utility Authority*, No. 31,058, 2014 WL 2451202 (N.M. Ct. App. Apr. 27, 2014): Unsuccessful bidder's complaint for declaratory judgment and injunctive relief dismissed as moot. Plaintiff did not exhaust administrative remedies and failed to properly protest award of the contract. By the time the district court acted on the complaint, the contract was final and performance started. The request for injunctive and declaratory relief was therefore moot.
- *State ex rel. Educational Assessments Systems, Inc. v. Cooperative Educational Services of New Mexico, Inc.*, 1993-NMCA-024, 115 N.M. 196, 848 P.2d 1123: Procurement Code provides an adequate legal remedy and writ of quo warranto was not a proper remedy.
- *Planning & Design Solutions v. City of Santa Fe*, 1994-NMSC-112, 118 N.M. 707, 885 P.2d 628: City violated its procurement ordinance by failing to award contract to business with highest points, adding a criteria not included in the RFP, and then rejecting all bids; actions were arbitrary and capricious. Court held that the city breached an implied contract to fairly consider each bid in accordance with its rules and that the bidder was entitled to reliance damages, the expenses incurred in preparing and submitting a bid.
- *Trace v. University of New Mexico Hospital*, 355 P.3d 103 (N.M. Ct. App. 2015): Case manager contract was subject to the Procurement Code and was not exempt as a litigation expense under NMSA section 13-1-98(R) even though the case manager was appointed by the workers compensation judge.
- *City of Albuquerque v. New Mexico Public Regulation Commission*, 2003-NMSC-028, 134 N.M. 472, 79 P.3d 297: Public service company could recover costs of complying with local ordinances to place utilities underground by tariff that required the costs to be borne by the municipality, the customer, or a combination. The tariff does not violate the Procurement Code; it is within the exception in NMSA section 13-1-98(D) for purchases of publicly provided or publicly regulated electricity, which includes purchase of facilities.
- *James Hamilton Construction Co. v. State*, 2003-NMCA-067, 133 N.M. 627, 68 P.3d 173: Unsuccessful bidder's protest was untimely when not filed within 15 days of the preliminary award. Unsuccessful bidder knew or should have known that the competitor's bid was not signed as of that date.
- *Bradbury & Stamm Construction v. Board of County Commissioners of Bernalillo County*, 2001-NMCA-106, 131 N.M. 293, 35 P.3d 298: County required to apply resident preference formula in NMSA section 13-4-2(E) in bids for public

works contracts. Bidder substantially complied with administrative procedures when it filed its protest with a senior buyer of the county and filed an appeal in district court after receiving a "determination" from the county on the resident preference question.

- *Davis & Associates, Inc. v. Midcon, Inc.*, 1999-NMCA-047, 127 N.M. 134, 978 P.2d 341: Procurement Code does not bar a disappointed bidder from pursuing a common-law or equitable action against another bidder whose protest resulted in the unjust denial of a party's bid. However, merely filing a protest challenging the other party's bid does not support an actionable claim. See also *Resource Lighting, Inc. v. Rohde, May Keller, McNamara Architecture, P.C.*, No. 30,013, 2011 WL 10976716 (N.M. Ct. App. Sept. 7, 2011).
- *Hamilton Roofing Co. v. Carlsbad Municipal Schools Board of Education*, 1997-NMCA-053, 123 N.M. 434, 941 P.2d 515: When court ruled that a construction contract had been improperly awarded and declared the contract void, contractor was entitled to compensation for actual expenses incurred under the contract plus some profit pursuant to NMSA section 13-1-182.
- *BC&L Pavement Services, Inc. v. Higgins*, 2002-NMCA-087, 132 N.M. 490, 51 P.3d 533: Bidder's failure to be licensed at the time that bid was submitted was proper grounds for rejection of bid. Bidder was not prejudiced by purchasing agent's failure to send written notification; oral notification was given and bidder filed a timely protest.
- *Campos de Suenos, Ltd. v. County of Bernalillo*, 2001-NMCA-043, 130 N.M. 563, 28 P.3d 1104: County was immune under NMSA section 37-1-23 from suit by party claiming an implied-in-fact contract with the county to purchase its ballpark. Writings containing some of the terms of a contract were not a "valid written contract" necessary to allow suit against the county for its breach.

VI. Extent of State's Adoption or Adaptation of ABA Model Procurement Code

New Mexico largely adopted the American Bar Association (ABA) Model Procurement Code in 1984. Since that time, the state has added design-build and construction management project delivery methods, but has not adopted other infrastructure delivery methods. It has also placed additional restrictions on the use of sole source and emergency procurements. The state requires state agencies and local public bodies to name chief procurement officers and recently established certification requirements for chief procurement officers.

VII. Cooperative Purchasing

A. Authority

Cooperative procurement is authorized in New Mexico pursuant to NMSA sections 13-1-135 and 13-1-136. Cooperative purchasing agreements providing for mutually held funds or involving public funds or property included in NMSA section 11-1-4 must be entered under the Joint Powers Agreements Act, NMSA sections 11-1-1 through 11-1-7. Purchases made pursuant to a cooperative agreement in New Mexico are not subject to any provisions of the Procurement Code other than those in NMSA sections 13-1-135 through 13-1-137.

B. Requirements

Any cooperative procurement agreement in New Mexico shall clearly specify the purpose of the agreement and the method by which the purpose will be accomplished. Any power exercised under a cooperative procurement agreement entered into pursuant to this subsection shall be limited to the central purchasing authority common to the contracting parties, even though one or more of the contracting parties may be located outside the state. An approved and signed copy of all cooperative procurement agreements entered into pursuant to this subsection shall be filed with the state purchasing agent. A cooperative procurement agreement entered into pursuant to this subsection is limited to the procurement of items of tangible personal property, services, or construction. (See NMSA §§ 13-1-135 through 13-1-137.)

New York Procurement Rules and Regulations

Prepared by C. Scott Maravilla
Federal Aviation Administration
Email: cmaravilla@hotmail.com

I. Statutory Reference

A. Procurement/Purchasing Statutes

New York public procurement is centralized and overseen by the Office of General Services (OGS). Additional information about the OGS Procurement Services Group can be found on its website at https://ogs.ny.gov/procurement. Public procurement is governed by article 11, State Purchasing, of the New York Code. (New York State Finance Law § 160 *et seq*.) The table of contents for the relevant statutory provision is as follows:

§ 160.	Definitions
§ 161.	State procurement council
§ 162.	Preferred sources
§ 163.	Purchasing services and commodities
§ 163-A.	Vendor preparation of specifications for technology procurements; prohibitions
§ 163-B.	Environmentally-sensitive cleaning and maintenance products
§ 164.	Exemptions
§ 165.	Purchasing restrictions
§ 165-A.	Iran divestment
§ 166.	Requirements for financed equipment acquisition or financed creation or improvement of information technology systems and related research and development
§ 167.	Transfer and disposal of personal property
§ 168.	The management of surplus computer equipment

B. Other Applicable Statutes

- State Finance Law, article 7, section 112 (State financial accounting systems; approval of contracts)

- Public Officers Law, article 4, sections 73 (Business or professional activities by state officers and employees and party officers); 73-A (Financial disclosure); 73-B (Advertisements by elected government officials and candidates made with public funds; prohibited); 74 (Code of ethics)
- Executive Law, article 6, section 94 (Joint commission on public ethics; functions, powers, and duties; review of financial disclosure statements; advisory opinions; investigation and enforcement)
- Civil Service Law, article 7, title C, section 107 (Prohibition against certain political activities; improper influence)
- Legislative Law, article 1-A, sections 1-A–1-V (Lobbying Act)
- Economic Development Law, article 4-C, sections 140–146 (Procurement Opportunities Newsletter)
- Education Law, article 8, section 355 *et seq*. (Powers and duties of trustees—administrative and fiscal functions), and article 124, City University of New York, section 6218 (Education contracts and purchases)
- Civil Practice Law and Rules, article 5, section 506 (Where special proceeding commenced), and article 78, sections 7801–7806 (Proceeding against body or officer)

II. Regulations

The New York State Finance Law establishes a State Procurement Council (Council) to "continuously strive to improve the state's procurement process." (New York State Finance Law § 161.) The Council is a 21-member body, which includes the OGS commissioner, the state comptroller, the director of the budget, the chief diversity officer, and the commissioner of economic development. The Council evaluates and makes recommendations to the OGS commissioner for the "development of specifications for commodities and services" to be procured through centralized contracts. The Council also establishes and maintains procurement guidelines for direct purchases from vendors by state agencies, and identifies to the commissioner any deficiencies in products or services received by state agencies from centralized contracts. The OGS commissioner may, when he or she deems it necessary, adopt the Council's recommendations by promulgating rules and regulations. These rules and regulations can be found at New York Compilation of Codes, Rules, and Regulations title 9, section 250.0 *et seq*. The table of contents for the relevant rules is as follows:

§ 250.0. Operating principles, purpose, intent, and applicability.
§ 250.1. Definitions.
§ 250.2. General provisions for purchasing commodities.
§ 250.3. Investigations.
§ 250.4. General provisions for purchasing services.
§ 250.5. Process for conducting State procurements.
§ 250.6. Discretionary buying thresholds.
§ 250.7. Method of procurement.
§ 250.8. Public notice.
§ 250.9. Soliciting and accepting offers.
§ 250.10. Letting of contracts.
§ 250.11. Reasonableness of results.

§ 250.12. Purpose of preferred sources.
§ 250.13. Preferred status.
§ 250.14. Public list of services and commodities provided by preferred sources.
§ 250.15. Priority accorded preferred sources.
§ 250.16. Prices charged by the Department of Correctional Services.
§ 250.17. Prices charged by agencies for the blind, other severely disabled, and veterans' workshops.
§ 250.18. Partnering with preferred sources.
§ 250.19. Procedure for agency non-centralized printing purchases.
§ 250.20. Special procedures for printing purchases.

III. Source Selection

Among the permissible procurement methods used by New York State agencies are invitations to bid (IFBs) and requests for proposals (RFPs). The preferred means of procurement is by competition. These formal competitive methods of procurement are used for purchases of services and commodities not available from preferred sources or from OGS Centralized Contracts if the purchase exceeds $85,000, $50,000 if by another state agency, and $100,000 if by a small business or one certified pursuant to article 15-A of the Executive Law, or are recycled or remanufactured commodity or technology. Otherwise, acquisitions made up to the discretionary buying thresholds are not subject to competition, but must comply with the advertising requirements under Economic Development Law article 4-C (purchases in excess of $15,000 must be advertised). Agencies must comply with their own internal policies and procedures governing non-competitive purchases, which should include an assessment as to whether a formal competitive process or a less formal competitive process meets the agency's needs. New York regulations also require preapproval by the Office of the State Comptroller for contracts exceeding $50,000. For OGS, the preapproval limit by the comptroller is set at $85,000.

A. IFB

This method is used when the method of award is based on lowest price only. Solicitation of formal sealed bids is due at a specific date and time. There is a public opening and reading of bids. The agency reviews the bid submissions to ensure completeness and accuracy. Beginning with the apparent low bid, the agency then verifies that the winning bid meets the mandatory requirements and specifications of the IFB and that the winning bidder is responsible. If the apparent low bidder is not found to be responsive or responsible, the agency rejects the bid and reviews the next-lowest bid. Once the agency reviews and verifies the lowest responsive and responsible bidder(s), it makes the award(s) accordingly.

B. RFP

RFPs are used for the procurement of services or technology in situations where price is not the sole determining factor, and the award will be based on a combination of cost and technical factors—in other words, a best-value award determination. The RFP describes in general terms the needs of the state and allows offerors to propose solutions. Award is made to the highest-ranked responsible offeror based on technical and financial evaluation criteria set forth in the RFP establishing best value for the state. "Best value" is defined under the regulations as "the basis for awarding contracts for services to the offeror which optimizes quality, cost and efficiency, among responsive and responsible offerors. Such basis shall reflect, wherever possible, objective and quantifiable analysis."

IV. Bid Protests and Contract Disputes

The cognizant administrative process for dispute resolution of bid protests is that established by the procuring state agency. Where the procuring state agency is OGS or the dispute is related to a centralized contract, vendors may administratively resolve disputes, complaints, or inquiries related to bid solicitations, contract awards, or contract administration on both an informal and formal basis under the OGS New York State Procurement (NYSPro) Dispute Resolution Procedures (revised in September 2014). The procedures apply to both bid protests and contract disputes. Finally, the procedures are not intended "to limit or impair the rights of any vendor or contractor to seek and pursue remedies of law through the judicial process."

A. Informal Dispute Resolution

1. Centralized Contract

In a dispute involving a centralized contract, the parties agree to use their best efforts to resolve the matter expeditiously. Performance of those aspects of the contract not in dispute will continue. Primary responsibility for resolution rests with the state agency contract coordinators, the contractor's account executive, and the state and local government regional general manager.

2. Authorized User Dissatisfaction

Where the state agency is dissatisfied with the vendor's products, the parties will use their best efforts to resolve the matter "amicably."

3. Negotiations

If negotiations between the agency and the vendor fail to result in a resolution after 14 business days, the matter is elevated to the state contract administrator and the contractor's senior vice president. They agree to use their best efforts to resolve the matter within 14 business days. This section does not prevent a party from seeking equitable remedies, including injunctive relief.

4. Extension of Time

The informal period may be used for as long as the parties are making progress.

B. Formal Dispute

1. Solicitation

The protest of a solicitation must be filed no later than ten business days prior to the date proposals are due. If the time is less than ten days, protests must be filed 24 hours prior to the receipt deadline.

2. Award

The protest of the award of a contract must be filed within ten business days after the challenging party knew or should have known of the facts that form the basis of the formal dispute, but not filed later than ten business days after award.

3. Administration

Formal contract disputes must be filed within 20 business days after the disputing party knew or should have known of the facts that form the basis of the contract dispute.

4. Standing

Only an interested party has standing to file a protest or contract dispute. An "interested party" is defined as an actual or prospective bidder or offeror whose direct economic interest will be affected by an award or failure to award. An actual bidder or offeror may file a protest of an award. In the case of a contract dispute, it is the "awarded contractor for the subject contract."

5. Form and Filing

The formal dispute must be in writing and include the name, address, email address, fax, and telephone number of the filing party; solicitation or contract number; detailed statement of the legal and factual grounds for the protest, including a description of resulting prejudice to the filer; copies of relevant documents; request for a ruling by the agency; statement as to the form of relief requested; all information establishing that the filer is an interested party; and all information establishing the timeliness of the formal dispute. The formal dispute must be filed with the director, NYSPro, OGS.

6. Stay of Procurement

NYSPro may, at its discretion, suspend, modify, or cancel the disputed procurement/contract action prior to the issuance of the formal dispute decision.

7. Hearing

No formal hearing is provided for under the Dispute Resolution Procedures. However, NYSPro may require the filer to participate in a conference call with OGS to discuss the formal dispute.

8. Decision

A decision stating the reasons on which it is based and informing the filer of his or her right to appeal, if unfavorable, shall be sent by regular mail within 30 business days of receipt of the dispute. The director of NYSPro may extend the time frames at his or her discretion.

C. Appeal

A filer who is dissatisfied with the formal dispute determination may file a written appeal with the New York chief procurement officer. The decision of the director of NYSPro is a final and conclusive agency determination, unless appealed.

1. Deadline

An appeal must be received by the chief procurement officer no more than ten business days after the filer's receipt of the NYSPro determination.

2. Form and Filing

The appeal shall not include new facts and information unless requested in writing by the chief procurement officer.

3. Hearing

The procedure provides that the chief procurement officer shall "hear and make a final determination on all appeals."

4. Decision

The decision on the appeal shall be issued within 20 business days of receipt.

D. Suspension and Debarment

There are no statutes, regulations, or procedures that that govern suspension or debarment except for those purchases where prevailing wages must be paid. (See article 8 of the Labor Law.)

V. Administrative and Judicial Review

A. Administrative Review

New York does not have an administrative agency that hears appeals from final agency action on bid protests and contract disputes.

B. Judicial Review

Article 78 of the Civil Practice Law and Rules allows for the use of a special proceeding in New York Supreme Court[1] to challenge a determination of a state agency. A special proceeding under article 78 is not available when the vendor seeks money damages. Litigation before the New York Court of Claims is the appropriate venue in such instances.

A vendor may bring an article 78 proceeding when it seeks to overturn an adverse decision of a state government official or agency, and may initiate the proceeding in a competitive bidding process. The vendor brings its action against the entity or individual that issued the final decision. A vendor cannot seek redress of an administrative decision unless it is final. If the administrative agency's rules provide for an appeal process that the vendor did not avail itself of, the article 78 proceeding is subject to dismissal for failure to exhaust administrative remedies.

The statutory enumerated questions the court may consider include whether a rational basis supports the decision, whether the action taken was arbitrary or capricious, whether substantial evidence supports the decision, or whether the state official or agency acted in excess of its jurisdiction. The court confines its review to the

1. The New York Supreme Court is the state trial court, not the highest court in the state (which is the New York Court of Appeals).

established administrative record. The court may grant the relief sought or deny and dismiss the petition on the merits or with leave to renew.

An article 78 special proceeding must be commenced in the New York Supreme Court in any county within the judicial district where the respondent officer or agency made the determination that the petitioning vendor seeks to challenge or where the principal office of the respondent is located. Different venue rules apply to proceedings against certain officers and agencies, including the commissioner of education and the comptroller. Appeals of an order or judgment from the state Supreme Court go to the Appellate Division of the New York Supreme Court and then to the court of appeals.

VI. Extent of State's Adoption or Adaptation of ABA Model Procurement Code

New York reports that it has partially adopted the American Bar Association (ABA) Model Procurement Code. (See the 2015 Survey of State Procurement Practices, compiled by the National Association of State Procurement Officials.)

VII. Cooperative Purchasing

A. Authority

Local governments and political subdivisions are not subject to New York State procurement law. They are governed by their own municipal laws. New York, however, provides local governments with the means of leveraging purchase power with other municipalities. These methods include "piggybacking" on existing contracts and cooperative purchasing. "Piggybacking" is an exception to the competition requirements under the General Municipal Law (GML).[2] Section 16 of the GML allows New York local governments and political subdivisions to use existing contracts of the United States or another state or local entity so long as the award was made to the "lowest responsible bidder" or on the basis of best value.[3] In addition to the limitations to federal, state, and local public contracts and low-cost or best-value awards, the contract must also be available for use by other state and local governments and political subdivisions.

Cooperative purchasing involves in two or more entities entering into a public contract for goods and services.[4] In New York, these include cities, villages, counties, school districts, and Boards of Cooperative Educational Services.[5]

B. Requirements

To elect cooperative purchasing for procurements, state and local entities must first enter into an intergovernmental cooperative agreement. The agreement must be approved by a majority vote of each party's governing body. It must also provide,

2. N.Y. Gen. Mun. Law § 103(1).

3. GML § 103(16) contains a sunset provision where it will expire and be deemed repealed on July 31, 2021, pursuant to L.2012, ch. 308, § 2.

4. N.Y. Gen. Mun. Law §§ 119-n & 119-o.

5. New York State OGS, *Procurement for Municipalities*, https://ogs.ny.gov/procurement/procurement-municipalities (last visited June 1, 2022).

among other requirements, a means for the equitable allocation of revenue, financing, and operating costs. The cooperative agreement also needs to address the handling of personnel including termination and compensation, and establish responsibility between the governments or political subdivisions "for the establishment, operation and maintenance of the joint service." Finally, the parties must enumerate the means for resolving disputes that may arise with respect to payments and sharing expenses.

North Carolina Procurement Rules and Regulations

Prepared by Jackson W. Moore
Smith, Anderson, Blount, Dorsett, Mitchell & Jernigan, L.L.P.
Email: jmoore@smithlaw.com
and
Jeffrey J. Truitt
General Counsel, BitGreen Inc.

I. Statutory and Other References

A. Procurement/Purchasing Statutes

The relevant sections of the North Carolina General Statutes are as follows:

§§ 143-48 through 143-63.	Purchases and Contracts (Goods and Services)
§§ 143-128 through 143-135.9.	Public Construction; Procedure for Letting and Performing Public Contracts
§§ 143B-1350 through 143B-1364.	Information Technology Procurement
§§ 115D-58.14 through 115D-58.15.	Community College Procurements
§§ 116-31.10 through 116-31.12.	University of North Carolina Procurement
§ 131E-23(d).	Hospital Authority Procurements
§§ 153A-158 through 153A-165.	County Acquisition of Property
§ 153A-427.	Regional Solid Waste Management Procurements
§ 157-9.	Housing Authority Procurements
§ 159B-11.	Joint Municipal Power Agencies

The North Carolina General Statutes may be found at the following address: https://www.ncleg.gov/Laws/GeneralStatutes.

State agencies are subject to the procurement requirements established by article 3 of chapter 143 of the North Carolina General Statutes, sections 143-48 through 143-64. The secretary of the Department of Administration (secretary) is responsible for administering the state's program for acquisition of goods and services with the exception of information technology. (North Carolina General Statutes §§ 143-49,

143B-1350(a).) The secretary is authorized and responsible for adopting and carrying out certain rules and procedures necessary to promote sound purchasing management, including contract award protest procedures. (North Carolina General Statutes § 143-53.) Administration of the procurement program for state agencies has been delegated to the state purchasing officer (SPO) who reports to the secretary. (01 North Carolina Administrative Code (NCAC) 05A.0101.)

The state chief information officer (state CIO) is responsible for establishing policies and procedures for information technology procurement for state agencies. (North Carolina General Statutes §§ 143B-1322(a), 143B-1350(a).) The term "information technology" or "IT" is broadly defined by the General Assembly. (North Carolina General Statutes § 143B-1320(11).)

State agencies seeking to procure or obtain IT goods and services must comply with part 4 of chapter 143B of the General Statutes. (North Carolina General Statutes §§ 143B-1350 through -1362.) State agencies covered by article 15 of chapter 143B are required to use IT contracts established by the Department of IT. (North Carolina General Statutes § 143B-1351(a). See North Carolina General Statutes § 143B-1325(c) (listing participating agencies).) The state CIO has the authority to cancel or suspend any agency IT procurement that occurs without state CIO approval. (North Carolina General Statutes § 143B-1350(a).)

Local governments may use the contracts offered by the Department of IT without complying with otherwise applicable competitive bidding requirements. (North Carolina General Statutes § 143B-1351(b).)

The Department of Health and Human Services, in cooperation with the state CIO, is responsible for coordinating health IT policies and programs within the state. (North Carolina General Statutes § 143B-139.4D.)

State agencies seeking to contract to obtain services of a consultant or advisory nature must obtain the governor's approval, subject to certain exceptions. (North Carolina General Statutes §§ 143-64.20 through 143-64.24.)

B. Other Applicable Statutes, Regulations, and Executive Orders

1. Statutes Governing Improper Influence over Public Procurement

State Government Ethics Act (North Carolina General Statutes §§ 138A-1 through 138A-45.)

Legislative Ethics Act, Code of Ethics (North Carolina General Statutes §§ 120-85.1 through 120-106.)

Lobbying Law (North Carolina General Statutes §§ 120C-100 through 120C-800.)

Anti-bribery statutes (North Carolina General Statutes §§ 14-217 and 14-218): Under North Carolina's anti-bribery statute, it is a Class F felony for any office holder or candidate or nominee for such office who, except in payment of his or her legal salary, fees, or perquisites, receives or consents to receive, directly or indirectly, "anything of value or personal advantage, or the promise thereof, for performing or omitting to perform any official act" that is within the scope of his or her official authority and was connected with the discharge of his or her legal duties, or with the express or implied understanding that his or her official action, or omission to act, is to be in any degree influenced thereby.

Public officers or employees benefiting from public contracts (North Carolina General Statutes § 14-234): Public officers and employees are generally prohibited from deriving benefits from contracts they are making or administering, including soliciting or receiving any gift, reward, or promise of reward, including a promise of future employment, in exchange for recommending, influencing, or attempting to influence the award by a contract by the public agency. (North Carolina General Statutes § 14-234(a).) There are various definitions and limitations in the scope of this prohibition found at North Carolina General Statutes section 14-234(a1). There are various exceptions found at North Carolina General Statutes sections 14-234(b) and 14-234(d1) through (d5).

Prohibition on misuse of confidential information (North Carolina General Statutes § 14-234.1): It is a crime for a public officer or employee to use non-public information received by the officer in his or her official capacity to gain any pecuniary benefit or acquire a pecuniary interest in any property or transaction or intentionally aid another to gain a pecuniary benefit.

Prohibition of use of purchasing power for private gain (North Carolina General Statutes § 143-58.1.)

Regulations of gifts and favors (North Carolina General Statutes § 133-32): It is a crime for a contractor, subcontractor, or supplier to make gifts or favors to a North Carolina state officer or employee, or for the officer or employee to willfully receive or accept any gift or favor from a contractor, subcontractor, or supplier to the state agency, if the state employee is involved in preparing plans, specifications, or estimates for public contracts; awarding or administering public contracts; or inspecting or supervising construction. There are various exceptions found at North Carolina General Statutes section 133-43(d).

2. North Carolina False Claims Act

The North Carolina False Claims Act (NCFCA) parallels the federal False Claims Act. The NCFCA is codified at North Carolina General Statutes sections 1-605 through 1-618. The NCFCA, like the federal False Claims Act, exposes any person or business that submits fraudulent claims to treble damages, statutory penalties, and civil investigative demands. (See generally *State ex rel. Stein v. Kinston Charter Academy*, 2021-NCSC-163 (Dec. 17, 2021).)

The NCFCA makes liable any person who (either alone or as part of a conspiracy) knowingly submits a false or fraudulent claim; makes or uses a false record or statement that is "material" to a false or fraudulent claim; delivers to the state less than all state money or property he or she is obligated to deliver; creates or delivers a document certifying receipt of property used or to be used by the state and, intending to defraud the state, makes or delivers the receipt without "completely knowing that the information on the receipt is true"; purchases, or receives as a pledge, public property from a state official who cannot lawfully sell or pledge the property; uses a false record or statement "material" to an obligation to transmit money to the state; or knowingly conceals or knowingly and improperly avoids or decreases an obligation to pay or transmit money or property to the state. (See North Carolina General Statutes § 1-607(a).)

Under North Carolina General Statutes section 1-606(2), a "claim" includes any request or demand for money or property made to a state officer or employee. A "claim" also includes any request or demand to a private party for money that will be used to advance a state program or interest if the state provides any portion of the money to the person making the request or demand or if the state agrees to reimburse the recipient for any portion of the money or property requested or demanded. The definition of "knowingly" in North Carolina General Statutes section 1-606(4) makes one liable if he or she actually knows he or she is submitting false information or acts "in deliberate ignorance" or "in reckless disregard" of the truth or falsity of the information provided.

Pursuant to North Carolina General Statutes section 1-607(a), a person who violates the NCFCA is liable for three times the state's damages, plus the costs of bringing the civil action, plus a civil penalty of between $5,500 and $11,000 for each violation, subject to adjustments for inflation. A court may limit these damages to not less than twice the state's damages under certain circumstances. (North Carolina General Statutes § 1-607(b).)

The NCFCA authorizes the attorney general to issue a civil investigative demand, an administrative subpoena requiring the person to produce documents or objects for the attorney general's inspection and copying. (North Carolina General Statutes § 1-614.) The NCFCA creates a class of potential qui tam plaintiffs who can collect money if they successfully "blow the whistle" on fraud. (North Carolina General Statutes §§ 1-608 through 1-611.) The NCFCA also creates a private action for retaliation against "[a]ny employee, contractor, or agent who is discharged, demoted, suspended, threatened, harassed, or in any other manner discriminated against in the terms and conditions of employment" because of lawful actions done by that person in furtherance of an action brought under the act or to stop the violation of the act. Relief for successful claimants includes reinstatement, two times the amount of back pay, interest, litigation costs, and reasonable attorneys' fees. (North Carolina General Statutes § 1-613.)

3. Procurement Preferences and Offshoring Constraints

a. Domestic Preferences

Preference is given to North Carolina products and citizens and articles manufactured in the state of North Carolina where quality and price is not sacrificed. (North Carolina General Statutes § 143-59(a).) Where a North Carolina preference cannot be given, the state shall give preference to the extent permitted by law to products or services manufactured or produced in the United States. (North Carolina General Statutes § 143-59A.)

b. Reciprocal Preferences

For determining the low bidder on state contracts valued at more than $25,000, a nonresident's bid may be increased by the same percentage that the bidder's home state gives preference to bidders in that state. (North Carolina General Statutes § 143-59(b).)

c. Limitations on Purchases from Certain Foreign Vendors

State contracts cannot be made with certain "tax haven countries" or vendors who refuse to collect certain taxes required by state law. (North Carolina General Statutes § 143-59.1.)

d. No Contracting with Those Convicted of Certain Crimes

Vendors cannot contract with the state if any officer, director, or owner of the vendor has been convicted of a federal or state securities laws. (North Carolina General Statutes § 143-59.2(a).) Vendors must certify to this fact in connection with bids. Giving a knowingly false certification is a Class I felony, and contracts entered into in violation of the statute are void. (North Carolina General Statutes § 143-59(b), (c).)

e. Contracts Performed Outside the United States

A vendor submitting a bid shall disclose in a statement, provided contemporaneously with the bid, where services will be performed under the contract sought, including any subcontracts, and whether any services under that contract, including any subcontracts, are anticipated to be performed outside the United States. (North Carolina General Statutes § 143-59.4.)

f. Preferences to the Blind and Severely Disabled

Preferences are provided to the blind and severely disabled for the operation of vending machines on state property, as well as highway vending facilities. (North Carolina General Statutes §§ 111-41, 111-48.) North Carolina General Statutes sections 143-48.2 and 143-129.5 specify that under certain circumstances, state agencies or a city, county, or other governmental entity may purchase goods and services directly from a nonprofit work center for the blind and severely disabled.

g. Preference for Department of Correction Products

This preference statute controls the sale of prison industry products and prohibits their sale to the private sector. All agencies are directed to give preference to Department of Correction products in purchasing articles, products, and commodities that are needed and are manufactured or produced within the state prison system and offered for sale to them by the Department of Correction. Products available from the private sector are to be purchased only when it is determined that the Correction Enterprises product will not satisfy the requirement or will not be available when needed. Correction Enterprises is required to keep the price of products substantially in accord with that paid by governmental agencies for similar products of equivalent quality. (North Carolina General Statutes § 148-134.)

II. Regulations

Relevant sections of the NCAC are listed below:

Tit. 01, 5B .0101 through .1903.	Division of Purchase and Contract; Purchasing Procedures
Tit. 01, 5D .0101 through .0209.	Division of Purchase and Contract; Consulting Contracts
Tit. 01, 30I .0101 through .0310.	Minority Business Participation Goals for Construction Projects
Tit. 09, 06B .0101 through .1402.	Office of Information and Technology Services; Procurement; Debarment; Protests; Cooperative Purchasing

The secretary is authorized and responsible for adopting and carrying out the state's procurement rules with the exception of IT procurements, which are regulated by the state CIO. Administration of non-IT procurements is delegated to the SPO, who reports to the secretary. The Purchase and Contract Division (P&C) is the central non-IT purchasing authority for all state agencies. Its website offers information about its duties and authorities at https://ncadmin.nc.gov/about-doa/purchase-and-contract. P&C had previously made available online its May 2013 Agency Purchasing Manual.

The manual was removed from the website in 2017 and "is not a valid resource or a valid representation of P&C's specific policies."[1]

Procurements are publicized online via the Interactive Purchasing System (IPS) at https://www.ips.state.nc.us/ips/Default.aspx, which lists solicitations from all state departments and campuses, plus public schools and some local governments. Provisions of the state's Administrative Code governing purchase and contract appears at title 1 (Administration), chapter 5 (Purchase and Contract), at http://reports.oah.state.nc.us/ncac.asp.

III. Source Selection

The general methods of procurement include the following:

A. State Non-IT Procurements

1. Non-IT Purchasing/Delegation Benchmarks

The secretary of administration, through the SPO, establishes procedures for state agencies to bid and contract for non-IT goods and services valued at or below certain benchmarks established by statute. (North Carolina General Statutes § 143-53(a)(2).) Procurement transactions over an applicable benchmark must be handled by or delegated by the SPO and must follow the competitive bidding procedure defined by North Carolina General Statutes section 143-52, which includes sealed offers solicited by P&C via advertisements. (01 NCAC 05B.0301(3).)

Bid value benchmarks for each state department, institution, and agency (other than the University of North Carolina or state community colleges) are set by the director of P&C following the director's consultation with the state budget officer and the state auditor. (North Carolina General Statutes § 143-53.1.)

The expenditure benchmark for the president of the University of North Carolina or a special responsibility constituent institution (North Carolina General Statutes § 116-30.1) with respect to competitive bid procedures shall be no greater than $500,000. The Board of Governors for the University of North Carolina sets the benchmark for the president and each constituent institution. (North Carolina General Statutes § 116-31.10(a); 01 NCAC 05B.0301(2)(b).)

The State Board of Community Colleges, in consultation with the Department of Administration, can increase or decrease the purchasing/delegation benchmark for each of its constituent community colleges, up to a maximum purchasing/delegation of $100,000. (North Carolina General Statutes §§ 143-53.1, 115D-58.14(c).)

For non-IT purchases over $5,000 up to the agency's or university's benchmark, P&C regulations require the agency to seek competition and issue solicitation documents requesting or inviting offers using standard terms and conditions issued by P&C, unless prior written approval is obtained from P&C. (01 NCAC 05B.0301(2)(a).) Agency purchases exceeding $10,000 and university purchases exceeding $25,000 shall be advertised on IPS. (01 NCAC 05B.0301(b), 05B.0316.)

For the purchase of equipment, materials, and supplies in excess of an agency's benchmark, competitive sealed bids generally are required, as is advertising for a

1. The Purchasing Manual was withdrawn as stated at this link: https://files.nc.gov/ncdoa/pandc/Documents/Contract-Administration-and-Monitoring-Guide/Withdrawal-of-State-Procurement-Manual_02.2021.pdf (all links in this chapter were active as of July 22, 2021).

minimum of ten days and a public opening of bids. (North Carolina General Statutes §§ 143-52, 143-52.1; 01 NCAC 05B.0309, 05B.0310(3).) The SPO will review a proposed contract before award.

For service contracts, agencies and universities shall solicit sealed offers. After the agency or university opens and evaluates the offers, it shall prepare a written recommendation for award. If the contract exceeds the applicable benchmark, the agency or university shall submit all offers and the recommendation to P&C for review. P&C shall approve the recommendation or take other action deemed necessary by the SPO. P&C's decision shall be sent to the agency; the using agency shall award the contract for services. (North Carolina General Statutes § 143-52(a); 01 NCAC 05B.0301(3)(b).)

The Contract Management Section within P&C (CMS) shall assist state departments, agencies, and institutions to establish formal contract administration procedures and to act as a general resource for agencies on issues related to procurement, including contract drafting, solicitation and bid evaluation procedures, contract negotiation, and other matters as directed by the SPO. (North Carolina General Statutes § 143-50.1(d).)

CMS is required to participate in, assist in the preparation of, and review all proposed solicitations for supplies, materials, printing, equipment, or contractual services that exceed $1,000,000. This includes a review of proposed contracts to ensure they are in proper legal form, contain all clauses required by law, and require performance that will accomplish the intended purposes of the proposed contract. (North Carolina General Statutes § 143-50.1(b).)

CMS is required to notify the attorney general of pending contracts for "contractual services" costing more than $5,000,000. The term "contractual services" means work performed by an independent contractor requiring specialized knowledge, experience, expertise, or similar capabilities wherein the service rendered does not consist primarily of acquisition by the state of equipment or materials or the rental of equipment, materials, and supplies. Such contracts are not valid unless signed by an appropriate representative from the attorney general's office assigned to review the contract. (North Carolina General Statutes § 143-49(3a).)

2. Small Purchasing of Non-IT Goods and Services

A small purchase is defined as the purchase of commodities, services, or printing, not covered by a term contract, involving an expenditure of public funds of $5,000 or less. The executive officer of each agency or university, or his or her designee, must prepare, in writing, purchasing procedures for making small purchases. The agency using the goods shall award contracts for small purchases. The SPO may require that a copy of the small purchase procedures be sent to P&C. (01 NCAC 05B.0301(1).)

3. Non-IT Sole Source Procurement/Waiver of Competition

Under certain conditions, competition may be waived for procurements under the agency's delegation or benchmark. Conditions permitting waiver include situations where a needed product or service is available from only one source of supply, emergency action is indicated, competition has been solicited but no satisfactory offers received, or personal or particular professional services are required. (North Carolina General Statutes § 143-53(b)(3); 01 NCAC 05B.1401.) Any waiver of competition for the purchase of goods or services in excess of the benchmark set by North Carolina General Statutes section 143-53.1 requires the secretary's approval. (North Carolina General Statutes § 143-53(a)(5).)

4. Design-Build/Public-Private Partnerships

North Carolina authorizes the use of construction management at risk contracts, design-build, design-build bridging, and public-private partnership contracts on public projects. Detailed requirements are specified for each contract vehicle. (North Carolina General Statutes §§ 143-128.1, 143-128.1A, 143-128.1B, 143-128.1C.)

5. Prequalification in Public Construction Contracts

For public construction or repair projects equal to or exceeding $500,000, the general rule is that each contract be awarded to the lowest responsible bidder after advertisement and the receipt of sealed bids. (North Carolina General Statutes § 143-129(b).)

Public owners may "prequalify" bidders for particular construction or repair work under certain circumstances. Prequalification is defined as "[a] process of evaluating and determining whether potential bidders have the skill, judgment, integrity, sufficient financial resources, and ability necessary to the faithful performance of a contract for construction or repair work." (North Carolina General Statutes § 143-135.8(f).) Bids submitted by bidders not prequalified will be deemed non-responsive. (North Carolina General Statutes § 143-135.8(d).)

Governmental entities who choose to prequalify bidders must adopt a transparent, objective, and uniform policy before advertising the contract for which the entity intends to prequalify bidders. (North Carolina General Statutes § 143-135.8(b), (c).) The policy must allow all bidders who meet the prequalification criteria to be prequalified in time to bid on the project and must clearly state the prequalification criteria and the assessment process of the criteria to be used.

There also must be a process for a bidder to protest the agency's denial of the bidder's prequalification. The protest process must be completed before the opening of bids and, further, must allow bidders who become prequalified as a result of the protest sufficient time to submit a bid for the project. Finally, the prequalification policy must notify denial of prequalification to a bidder upon the bidder's request. (North Carolina General Statutes § 143-135.8(c).)

Prequalification is specifically prohibited when selecting construction managers at risk, design-builders, preliminary designers for design-build bridging projects, and private developers for public-private partnership contracts. (North Carolina General Statutes § 143-135.8(f).)

6. Emergency Purchasing of Non-IT Goods and Services

Pursuant to North Carolina General Statutes section 143-57 and 01 NCAC 5B.1602, an agency may make purchases of commodities, printing, or services in the open market in cases of "emergency or pressing need." A pressing need is one arising from unforeseen causes including, but not limited to, delay by contractors, delay in transportation, breakdown in machinery, or unanticipated volume of work. Emergencies are defined as situations that endanger lives, property, or the continuation of a vital program and that can be rectified only by immediate, on-the-spot purchases or rental of commodities, printing, or services.

Agencies may negotiate with potential vendors to acquire the commodity, service, or printing needed at the best possible price, delivery, terms, and conditions. A solicitation document requesting or inviting offers will be issued, including standard language, terms, and conditions issued by P&C, unless circumstances prohibit their use. (01 NCAC 5B.1602(b).)

When action becomes necessary because of an emergency or pressing need and the expenditure is over the agency's benchmark or delegation, prior verbal approval must be obtained from P&C if time permits. Subsequently, whether or not such prior approval was possible, if the expenditure is over the agency's benchmark or delegation, an explanation of the emergency or pressing need purchase must be reported in writing to P&C. (01 NCAC 5B.1602(c).)

B. State IT Procurements

1. Benchmarks for IT Procurement

The state CIO is responsible for establishing policies and procedures for IT procurement for state agencies. (North Carolina General Statutes § 143B-1350(a); 09 NCAC 06B.0201.) The general IT purchasing delegation/benchmark is $25,000 unless special authorization is authorized by the state CIO. (09 NCAC 06A.1303.) This delegation is for all state agencies. IT procurements above $25,000 require approval of the IT Procurement Office. Agencies are responsible for establishing written procurement policies and procedures under their delegated authority.

2. IT Procurement Process

The purchasing agency manages the IT procurement process of requesting or inviting an offer. (09 NCAC 06B.0301(a).) All IT purchases involving the expenditure of state funds shall be competitively bid in conformity with principles of "best value," which is a multi-factor analysis to determine which proposal offers the best tradeoff between price and performance, where quality is considered an integral performance factor. (See North Carolina General Statutes § 143-135.9; 09 NCAC 06B.0301(b).)

The purchasing agency determines the best-value method through development of one of several bidding methods, including (but not limited to) requests for information to gather information to prepare a solicitation of offers; invitations for bid when the best-value recommendation is based on the lowest price or highest qualified and technically acceptable selection method; requests for quotation for contracting with one or a limited group of vendors for purchases of specific goods and services or small purchases of goods, or pursuant to a waiver of competition; and requests for proposal when negotiations or a ranking of offers is needed and will not be based solely on the lowest price-technically acceptable source. (09 NCAC 06B.0302(1)(b).) The IT regulations also allow for simultaneous or separate evaluations of technical and price provisions. (09 NCAC 06B.0302(1)(b).)

The purchasing agency shall develop, advertise, and publish its solicitation for offers, hold scheduled conferences or site visits, receive offers, and conduct a public bid opening. The purchasing agency must advertise and publish solicitations for purchases exceeding the general delegation as established by the state CIO for no fewer than ten calendar days. (09 NCAC 06B.0314(a), (b).) The purchasing agency's evaluation committee then shall evaluate and rank offers in accordance with the stated solicitation selection method and evaluation criteria. (09 NCAC 06B.0302(1)(c)–(h).) Award is made by the agency to the responsive and responsible offeror whose offer is determined to be the most advantageous and best value to the state, using all evaluation criterial set forth in the solicitation. (09 NCAC 06B.0302(1)(i).)

3. Sole Source Procurement/Waiver of Competition for IT Procurements

The state CIO may limit or waive competition if the purchasing agency submits a written request demonstrating, to the state CIO's satisfaction, facts supporting one or more of the 16 supporting conditions found at 09 NCAC 06B.0901(b), including indications requiring emergency action, competition is limited or unavailable, or personal or particular professional services are required. (09 NCAC 06B.0901(a).)

Negotiations are also available to purchasing agencies. Purchasing agencies shall conduct negotiations under its general delegation for IT procurement. (09 NCAC 06B.0316.) Negotiations exceeding the purchasing agency's delegation are permitted if the purchasing agency receives prior approval to negotiate from the state CIO. (09 NCAC 06B.0316(a).) If the purchasing agency conducts negotiations with only one offeror, the purchasing agency shall document the reasons for the lack of competition as part of the procurement record. (09 NCAC 06B.0316(b), .1402.)

Exemptions may be granted by the state CIO where limited competition, waiver of competition (see 09 NCAC 06B.0901), special delegation (see 09 NCAC 06B.1303, .1304), exemption, or an emergency purchase is permitted by rule.

4. Emergency Purchasing of IT Goods and Services

An agency may purchase IT goods or services on the open market in cases of emergency or pressing need. (09 NCAC 06B.1302(a).) Prior verbal approval shall be obtained from the state CIO when the estimated expenditure is over the purchasing agency's delegation unless the purchase must be made outside of business hours or when state offices are otherwise closed. Subsequently, a written report to the state CIO is required by the purchasing agency explaining the nature of the emergency or pressing need. (09 NCAC 06B.1302(b).)

5. Debriefing of IT Procurement Awards

Agencies may debrief successful or unsuccessful offerors for IT procurements by personal meeting or by written or electronic communication. (09 NCAC 06B.0405(a).) All competing offerors may request a debriefing by submitting a written request to the purchasing agency within three business days from notice of award date. (09 NCAC 06B.0405(c)(3).) Debriefings may not include point-by-point comparisons of the debriefed offeror's proposal with those of offerors or reveal any information not then available for public inspection or properly designated as confidential. (09 NCAC 06B.0405(b).) Debriefings shall include review of the committee's evaluation of the vendor's proposal/offer under the terms of the solicitation, including specific items identified in 09 NCAC 06B.0405(c)(5).

IV. Bid Protests and Contract Disputes

A. Bid Protests of Non-IT Awards

01 NCAC 05B.1519 establishes protest procedures that apply to non-IT contract awards with an actual or estimated dollar value over the agency's benchmark. For non-IT contract awards awarded by the secretary above the agency's benchmark, the disappointed offeror shall submit a written request for a protest meeting within 30 calendar days from the date of contract award. The letter shall identify specific reasons and any supporting documentation for why the offeror has a concern with the award. If the letter does not contain this information or if the SPO determines that the protest is meritless so that a meeting would serve no purpose, the SPO may refuse the protest meeting within ten calendar days of receipt of the protest meeting request. (01 NCAC 05B.1519(6).)

To protest a non-IT contract awarded by an agency valued below the agency's benchmark, the offeror shall submit a written request for a protest meeting to the agency's executive officer within 30 calendar days from the date of the contract award.

The letter shall offer specific reasons and any supporting documentation for why the offeror has a concern with the award. If the letter does not contain this information, or if the agency executive officer determines that the protest is meritless and a meeting would serve no purpose, the executive officer may refuse the protest meeting request within ten calendar days of the receipt of the letter. (01 NCAC 05B.1519(a).)

1. Stay of Non-IT Awards during Protest

There is no statutory provision providing for a stay of a non-IT award.

2. Bid Protest Decision

If the protest meeting is granted, the executive officer or SPO will attempt to schedule it within 30 consecutive calendar days after receipt of the letter. Within ten days of the protest meeting, the executive officer or SPO will respond to the offeror in writing with the executive officer's or SPO's decision. A copy of the executive officer's letter will be forwarded to the SPO. (01 NCAC 05B.1519(a), (b).)

3. Appeals of Non-IT Bid Protests to the Office of Administrative Hearings

Agency or SPO decisions on non-IT bid protests may be appealed (unless the agency is specifically exempted) under the Administrative Procedure Act. (See North Carolina General Statutes § 150B-23; 26 NCAC 03.0101 through .0403.)

A contested case associated with a contract awarded by a state agency typically is made through North Carolina's Office of Administrative Hearings (OAH), which is governed by article 3 of the North Carolina Administrative Procedure Act. (See https://www.oah.nc.gov/.) Contested cases involving certain agencies are governed by article 3A of the Administrative Procedure Act. (*Homoly v. State Board of Dental Examiners*, 468 S.E.2d 481, 484 (N.C. Ct. App. 1996) ("[T]he contested case provisions of Article 3 do not apply to Article 3A agencies and the same is true conversely."), *review denied*, 471 S.E.2d 71 (N.C. 1996).)

The OAH is a quasi-judicial agency created under article III, section 11 of North Carolina's constitution. (See North Carolina General Statutes § 7A-750.) Although some agency statutes provide for shorter time periods, contested cases generally must be filed within 60 days after notice is sent by the agency of its decision to all persons aggrieved who are known to the agency. (See North Carolina General Statutes § 150B-23(f).) Electronic filing in contested cases is available. (See 26 NCAC 03.0101(c).)

Contested cases are heard before an appointed administrative law judge (ALJ), are governed by OAH rules, and are conducted as adversarial proceedings much like bench trials. (See North Carolina General Statutes §§ 150B-22 through 150B-37.) Mediated settlement conferences may be required by the chief ALJ. (See North Carolina General Statutes § 150B-23.1.) In many cases North Carolina's Rules of Civil Procedure and Rules of Evidence will apply. (See North Carolina General Statutes §§ 150B-33(b)(3a), 150B-33; 26 NCAC 03.0122.) Venue for a hearing is the county where any person resides whose property or rights are the subject of the hearing, or in the principal office of the agency, or any other county determined by the ALJ in his or her discretion to "promote the ends of justice or better serve the convenience of witnesses." (See North Carolina General Statutes § 150B-24.)

Under article 3 cases the aggrieved party must state facts tending to establish that the agency "substantially prejudiced the petitioner's rights and that the agency: (1) Exceeded its authority or jurisdiction; (2) Acted erroneously; (3) Failed to use proper procedure; (4) Acted arbitrarily and capriciously; or (5) Failed to act as required by law or rule." (See North Carolina General Statutes § 150B-23(a); *cf.* North Carolina General Statutes § 150B-51(b) (pleading requirements for article 3A proceedings).)

The decision of the ALJ is final, beginning with contested cases filed on or after January 1, 2012, and is subject to further judicial review. (See North Carolina General Statutes § 150B-34.) The ALJ is authorized to grant judgment on the pleadings or summary judgment.

B. Bid Protests of IT Contract Awards

NCAC title 09, 06B.1102(b) establishes protest procedures that apply to IT contract awards with an estimated value of $25,000 or more. Agencies may establish procedures to handle an offeror's protests for contracts with lesser dollar values. (01 NCAC 05B.1519(b); 09 NCAC 06B.1102(b).)

A disappointed offeror may deliver a written request for a protest meeting to the agency head or his or her designee within 15 calendar days from the date of contract award. The agency head shall furnish a copy of the written request to the state CIO within ten calendar days of receipt. The offeror's request shall contain specific reasons and supporting documentation regarding why there is a concern with the award. The agency head may deny the requested meeting if the agency head determines that a meeting would serve no purpose or if the protestor does not include the required information in its request. (09 NCAC 06B.1102(c)(1); 09 NCAC 06B.1102(d)(1).)

The agency shall schedule the meeting within 30 days after receipt of the letter of request, unless all parties agree to a later date. Within ten calendar days of the date of the protest meeting, the agency shall respond in writing to the offeror with an agency decision. (09 NCAC 06B.1102(c)(2); 09 NCAC 06B.1102(d)(2).)

1. Further Administrative Review by the State CIO after Protest Decision

If a party desires further review after receiving an agency bid protest decision of an IT procurement, a protesting party may, within 60 days from the date such decision is received, request a hearing and final decision by the state CIO in accordance with the Administrative Procedure Act and the rules of the state CIO. (09 NCAC 06B.1102(f).)

The rules for contested hearings before the state CIO can be found at NCAC title 09, 06B.1103 through .1121. Proceedings generally follow the North Carolina Rules of Civil Procedure and the General Rules of Practice for the Superior and District Courts, and hearings shall be conducted, as nearly as practical, in accordance with the trial division of the General Court of Justice. (09 NCAC 06B.1105(1), (4).) Any means of discovery available pursuant to the North Carolina Rules of Civil Procedure is allowed. (09 NCAC 06B.1111(b).) Motions, intervention, and subpoenas are available to litigants. (09 NCAC 06B.1113, .1114, .1115.) Sanctions may be issued by the hearing officer in certain circumstances. (09 NCAC 06B.1114.) The North Carolina Rules of Evidence generally apply. (09 NCAC 06B.1120.)

The hearing officer, if not the state CIO, shall issue a written recommended final agency decision. The state CIO shall make the final agency decision. (09 NCAC 06B.1107(b).) The report, the decision of determination of the state CIO upon review, shall be final unless further appeal is made to the courts under the provisions of chapter 150B of the General Statutes. (09 NCAC 06B.1107(d).)

C. Contract Claims

A centralized agency complaint service has been established within P&C to handle problems that arise between agencies and vendors. When a problem arises with a vendor, the agency should first contact the vendor directly to resolve the problem. If the problem is not resolved satisfactorily within a reasonable time period or becomes a recurring issue, the problem should be reported by the agency to P&C on a vendor complaint form. This process is detailed at https://files.nc.gov/ncdoa/fiscal/DOA-Vendor-Complaint-Policy-and-Procedures-Manual.pdf.

Once this information is received by P&C's agency complaint service, it will be logged into the system and directed to the appropriate purchasing group. A purchaser will then work with the vendor and the agency to resolve the complaint. P&C will contact the purchaser at the agency for additional information or to report progress in resolving the complaint.

Information regarding vendor performance is used in evaluating and awarding future contracts and in determining whether a vendor is performing responsibly. Information on the performance of a specific vendor may also be requested by agencies as they make their own procurements.

D. Suspension and Debarment

1. Default, Disqualification, and Debarment

Pursuant to NCAC title 01, 5A.1520 (and NCAC title 09, 06B.1206 for IT contracts), the agency that issued the solicitation document resulting in the contract may find a contractor in default for failing to perform in accordance with the contract requirements, terms, and conditions. If a contractor is found in default of a contract, the agency that issued the solicitation document resulting in the contract may take action, immediately if necessary, to purchase the needed commodities, printing, or services on the open market and charge any additional cost for the commodities, printing, or services and expense for doing so to the defaulting contractor.

If an agency finds a contractor in default, such action and the circumstances are reported by the agency to P&C in writing and to the Office of Information Technology Services in the case of IT contracts. (01 NCAC 5A.1520; 09 NCAC 06B.1206.) This does not limit any other remedies that may be available to the state or agency.

P&C may remove the defaulting contractor from any mailing lists that may be utilized and debar the contractor from doing business with the agency, or any agency, for a period of time at the discretion of P&C.

2. Debarred Vendor List

The North Carolina Department of Administration offers links to the state's Procurement Rules along with quick reference links to current statewide contracts. P&C also has a listing of actions taken by the state, which includes suspensions and debarments, at https://ncadmin.nc.gov/documents/nc-debarred-vendors.

The state CIO, upon finding cause to debar a vendor, may remove the vendor from any distribution lists that may be utilized and may prohibit award of any contract to the debarred vendor for a period not to exceed one year. (09 NCAC 06B.1206(c).) Causes of debarment include conviction for commission of a criminal offense as an incident to obtaining a public or private contract or subcontract; conviction under state or federal statutes of embezzlement, theft, forgery, or similar crimes indicating a lack of business integrity or honesty; violation of the state Government Ethics Act or the Lobbying Law; and deliberate failure without good cause to perform a contract in accordance with the specifications or within the time limit provided in the contract. (09 NCAC 06B.1206(b).)

V. Administrative and Judicial Review

If the ALJ or state CIO issues an unfavorable ruling in connection with a non-IT or IT procurement, the unsuccessful party may pursue judicial review in North Carolina Superior Court. (North Carolina General Statutes § 150B-43. See generally *Aetna Better Health of North Carolina, Inc. v. North Carolina Department of Health & Human Services*, 2021-NCCOA-486 (Sept. 21, 2021).) Review is conducted without a jury, and venue is in Wake County, North Carolina, or the county where the aggrieved person resides. The superior court's standard of review is found in North Carolina General Statutes section 150B-51 and varies depending upon the circumstances. Appeals from the superior court go to the North Carolina Court of Appeals.

VI. Extent of State's Adoption or Adaptation of ABA Model Procurement Code

North Carolina has not formally adopted the American Bar Association (ABA) Model Procurement Code. However, elements of the Model Procurement Code appear in the General Statutes and accompanying regulations, and partial adoption of the Model Procurement Code is suggested by state procurement officials in their responses to the 2020 Survey of State Procurement Practices published by the National Association of State Procurement Officials (NASPO).[2] On July 16, 2014, the secretary of administration issued a detailed report,[3] after consulting with the University of North Carolina School of Government, examining "the feasibility of adopting provisions of the ABA Model Procurement Code." (See North Carolina General Statutes § 143-49(16).) While the report concluded that "no compelling reason exists to replace the existing law with the Model Code," it included several recommendations based on the Model Code that would better clarify the procurement process and the responsibilities of personnel and agencies involved in the procurement process. (See Report on the Feasibility of Adopting the American Bar Association Model Procurement Code at 1.) The report also includes a detailed "cross-walk" comparing the Model Code with then-current North Carolina procurement requirements. (*Id.* at 9–19.)

VII. Cooperative Purchasing

A. Authority

The secretary of administration is charged with establishing procedures to permit state government to join with any federal, state, or local governmental agency, entity, or subdivision, or any nonprofit organization, in cooperative purchasing plans, projects, arrangements, or agreements if the interest of the state would be served thereby. (North Carolina General Statutes § 143-49(17).)

---

2. The survey results may be found at NASPO, *2020 Survey of State Procurement Practices*, https://www.naspo.org/research-innovation/publications/survey-state-procurement-practices/ (last visited June 1, 2022).

3. The report may be found at Report on the Feasibility of Adopting the American Bar Association Model Procurement Code, https://www.ncleg.gov/documentsites/committees/govops/Full%20Commission/Previous%20Sessions/2014%20Meetings_Materials/06_August%202014/Mandated%20Reports/GenGov/GenGov_DOA_PurchaseContractRecommendation_2014.pdf (Report).

The state CIO is required to establish procedures to permit state and local government agencies to use the General Services Administration (GSA) Cooperative Purchasing Program to purchase IT awarded under GSA Supply Schedule 70, Information Technology, and under GSA's Consolidated Schedule containing IT special item numbers, as well as cooperative purchase agreements with respect to state IT procurement. (North Carolina General Statutes § 143B-1350(c)(4), (5).) The State IT Procurement Office website offers detailed instructions for agencies seeking to make purchases from the GSA schedule.[4]

One exception to the public bidding requirements of North Carolina General Statutes section 143-129 is for purchases made through "a competitive bidding group purchasing program, which is a formally organized program that offers competitively obtained purchasing services at discount prices to two or more public agencies." (North Carolina General Statutes § 143-129(e)(3).)

Governmental entities can also determine that it is in the best interest of the entity to waive further competition and purchase supplies, materials, or equipment from an entity that has, within the previous 12 months, after completing a public, formal bid process similar to that required by chapter 143, contracted to furnish the supplies, materials, or equipment to the United States or any federal agency; to the state of North Carolina or any agency or political subdivision of the state; or to any other state or any agency of political subdivision of that state, if the person or entity is willing to furnish the items at the same or more favorable prices, terms, and conditions as those provided under the contract with the other unit or agency. Certain notice requirements must be followed before approval of such a "piggyback" purchase, and approval must be made at a regularly scheduled meeting of the governing body. (North Carolina General Statutes § 143-129(g).)

B. Requirements

When an agency participates in a cooperative project with another governmental entity or with a nonprofit organization, goods and services necessary for the project shall be procured according to the procurement rules set by the SPO (for non-IT procurements) and the state CIO (for IT procurements). (01 NCAC 05B.1513; 09 NCAC 06B.1006.)

The SPO and state CIO may authorize acquisition of purchases within their authority, on behalf of the governmental entity or nonprofit organization, authorizing acquisition on the state's behalf under the provisions of another state or governmental entity, provided that the SPO or state CIO give "due consideration" to the differences in purchasing rules, regulations, and procedures of the contracting entity. In addition, the state CIO may authorize procurements under the provisions of the GSA Schedule 70 and Consolidated Schedule for Information Technology Purchases. (09 NCAC 06B.1006(1)–(3).)

4. State CIO instructions in connection with GSA procurements may be found at GSA Contract Purchasing Procedures for North Carolina, https://files.nc.gov/ncdit/documents/Statewide_Policies/GSA-Ordering-Procedures-2019-02-15.pdf.

North Dakota Procurement Rules and Regulations

Prepared by Jeff H. Eckland
Eckland & Blando LLP
Email: jeckland@ecklandblando.com
With assistance from Mark J. Blando, Vince Reuter, and Robert Dube[1]

I. Statutory Reference

The Office of Management and Budget (OMB) has the authority to purchase, lease, or otherwise arrange for most commodities and services required by the state. (North Dakota Century Code § 54-44.4-02 (2009).) The major exceptions include public improvements, public media, and materials and equipment related to the North Dakota Department of Transportation (NDDOT). (*Id.* § 54-44.4-02(1)–(4).) By statute, the OMB has created administrative rules for procuring and administering government contracts within its domain. (See North Dakota Administrative Code 4-12-01 to -16 (2004).) Moreover, it provides guidelines on subjects related to procurement on its website at https://www.omb.nd.gov/doing-business-state/procurement/procurement-laws-rules-guidelines.

The State of North Dakota gives the power to procure government contracts to counties, municipalities, and government agencies by statute according to the type of product or service sought, the professional skill required, or the amount of money required to effectuate the contract's ends. (See, e.g., North Dakota Century Code § 11-11-14 (2015) (Counties); *id.* § 40-05-01 (Municipalities).)

The OMB's State Procurement Office is responsible for operating this centralized purchasing service. It has provided a comprehensive website for all information related to its mission, located at https://www.omb.nd.gov/doing-business-state/procurement. For more general information, the OMB can be found at https://www.omb.nd.gov/, and the State of North Dakota at https://www.nd.gov/.

The North Dakota Constitution, and its statutes, laws, and rules, can be found by searching the North Dakota legislative branch's website, https://www.ndlegis.gov/.

A. Procurement/Purchasing Statutes

The relevant sections of the North Dakota Century Code are listed below:

1. Research, drafting, proofing, and citation assistance provided by Kenneth Cooper of Eckland & Blando.

State Purchasing Practices
§ 54-44.4 (2003)

Public Improvement Bids and Contracts
§ 48-01.2 (2017)

Architect, Engineer, and Land Surveying Services
§ 54-44.7 (2007)

Department of Transportation
§§ 24-02-16 to -34 (2017)

Purchasing Laws Relating to Printing and Newspapers
§ 46-01 to -02 (1999)

Purchasing by Counties
§ 11-11-14 (2015). Powers of board of county commissioners
§ 11-11-16 (1943). Board has power to erect, repair, and maintain buildings from current revenue
§ 11-11-17 (1999). Board of county commissioners may supervise the building or repairing of roads, bridges, and property of the county—Compensation
§ 11-11-26 (2015). When board shall advertise for bids
§ 11-11-27 (2015). Contents of advertisement—When bids may be opened—Lowest bidder accepted
§ 11-11-29 (1943). Contract—Form—Contents—Majority vote necessary—When payment made

Purchasing by Municipalities
§ 40-05-01 (2015). Powers of all municipalities
§ 40-05-05 (1993). Cities may contract for electrical energy or gas
§ 40-05-09 (1931). Purchase of firefighting equipment—How paid—Limitations
§ 40-05.1-06 (2017). Powers (home rule in cities)

Purchasing by Local School Boards
§ 15.1-09-34 (2021). Contracts by school boards—Bids—Penalty
§ 15.1-09-34.1 (2001). Vehicle and heating fuel—Purchases
§ 15.1-09-43 (1999). Purchase of schoolbus—Payment period
§ 15.1-09-50 (2005). Board of education of city of Fargo Powers

Purchasing by State Board of Higher Education
§ 15-10-17 (2021). Specific powers and duties of state board of higher education

Purchasing by Parks and Park Districts
§ 40-49-14 (2019). When yea and nay vote taken—Letting contracts—Debt limit—Bills, claims, and demands against board

Work Activity Center Contract Awards
§ 25-16.2-01 (2011). Work activity center—Definition

§ 25-16.2-02 (2011). Direct bidding with work activity centers for highway grade stakes

§ 25-16.2-03 (2011). Contract requirement

Lease-to-Purchase Agreement

§ 54-06-17 (1975). Certain rental-purchase-type agreements authorized

Cooperative Purchasing between Government Bodies

§ 54-40.3-01 (1993). Joint powers agreements—General Authority

§ 54-40.3-02 (1993). Clarification of constitutional authority and effect of other statutes—Construction

Purchasing from Federal Government

§ 21-06-08 (1945). Authority to contract with the federal government—Delegation of authority

Vendor Preference and Sealed Bid Laws

§ 44-08-01 (2001). Preference to North Dakota bidders, sellers, and contractors

§ 44-08-01.1 (2005). Bids to be sealed—Designation of time and place for opening—Preference for tie bids

§ 44-08-02 (2015). Resident North Dakota bidder, seller, and contractor defined

B. Other Applicable Statutes

The relevant sections of the North Dakota Century Code are listed below:

Contracts and Obligations Statutes

§§ 9-01 to 9-16 (1943). General contract law

Occupational and Professional Licensing Requirements

§ 43-07-11.1 (2019). Contracts with state

§ 43-07-12 (2019). Bids to show license issued

Employee Preference Laws

§ 43-07-20 (1995). Employment preference in contract

Contractor's Retention of Funds

§ 43-07-23 (2007). Allowable retention of estimates—Interest on retainage

Legislative Lobbying

§ 54-05.1 (1951)

State Audit Laws

§ 54-10-19 (2009). Supervision of public institutions and private institutions with which state has dealings

Claims against the State (Sovereign Immunity)

§ 32-12.2 (2013)

Executive orders can be found by searching the archive on the governor of North Dakota's website at https://www.governor.nd.gov/executive-orders.

The attorney general issues advisory opinions, when requested by state officers, on legal questions relating to the duties of such officers. (North Dakota Century Code

§ 54-12-01 (1997).) While not binding on the courts, these opinions "nonetheless [have] an important bearing on the construction and interpretation of a statute," and "are entitled to respect." (See *Edinger v. Governing Authority of Stutsman County Correctional Center*, 695 N.W.2d 447, 451 (N.D. 2005); *Haugen v. City of Berthold*, 267 N.W.2d 198, 200 (N.D. 1978).) Further, when necessary, the attorney general may determine the legality of all contracts, which should occur before a proposed contract is forwarded to the other party. (Contract Drafting and Review Manual 2 (2022), https://attorneygeneral.nd.gov/sites/ag/files/documents/Contract-Drafting-Manual.pdf.)

II. Regulations

By statute, the OMB has authority to adopt and enforce specific rules for the procurement of government contracts. (North Dakota Century Code § 54-44.4-04 (2003) (authority for promulgating article 4-12).)

The relevant rules of the North Dakota Administrative Code are listed below:

4-12-01 (2004). General Rules
4-12-02 (2004). Procurement Organization and Leadership
4-12-03 (2004). Delegation of Purchasing Authority
4-12-04 (2004). Ethics in Public Procurement
4-12-05 (2004). Bidders List
4-12-06 (2004). Specifications for Commodities and Services
4-12-07 (2004). Managing Contractual Risk
4-12-08 (2004). Competitive Solicitation Methods
4-12-09 (2013). Limited Competition, Noncompetitive, and Emergency Procurements
4-12-10 (2004). Mistakes in Bids or Proposals
4-12-11 (2004). Evaluation of Bids or Proposals
4-12-12 (2004). Contract Negotiations
4-12-13 (2004). Contract Administration
4.14-14 (2004). Resolution of Protested Solicitations and Awards
4-12-15 (2004). Intergovernmental Relations
4-12-16 (2004). Printing

III. Source Selection

A. Procurement Policy and Regulatory Definitions

1. State Bidding Policy: Lowest Responsible Bidder

North Dakota's competitive bidding statutes were "enacted for the benefit of the public and taxpayers to invite competition; to prevent favoritism, fraud, corruption, improvidence, extravagance, and collusion; and to secure the best work or supplies at the lowest price practicable." (*Danzl v. City of Bismarck*, 451 N.W.2d 127, 130 (N.D. 1990).)

Public improvements required by the state, its agencies, and its subdivisions are therefore generally awarded to the lowest responsible bidder. (North Dakota Century Code § 48-01.2-07 (2017).) Additionally, goods and services procured through the

OMB and its delegated agencies are generally awarded to the lowest responsible bidder. (*Id.* § 54-44.4-05(1) (2011).)

2. Types of Contracts and Selected Definitions

a. Construction Management at Risk

"[A] public improvement delivery method through which a construction manager provides advice to the governing body during the planning and design phase of a public improvement, negotiates a contract with the governing body for the general construction bid package of the public improvement, and contracts with subcontractors and suppliers for the actual construction of the public improvement." (*Id.* § 48-01.2-01(6) (2017).)

b. Design Services

"[A]rchitect services, engineer services, landscape architect services, or surveyor services." (*Id.* § 48-01.2-01(11).)

c. Design-Bid-Build

"[A] project delivery method in which design and construction of the project are in sequential phases, and in which the first project phase involves design services, the second project phase involves securing a contractor through a bidding process, and the third project phase provides for construction of the project by a contractor awarded the project." (*Id.* § 48-01.2-01(12).)

d. Lowest Responsible Bidder

"[T]he lowest best bidder for the project considering past experience, financial condition, past work with the governing body, and other pertinent attributes that may be identified in the advertisement for bids." (*Id.* § 48-01.2-01(19).)

B. Competitive Bids

By statute, certain contract types require competitive bidding through a sealed bid process. These include (1) contracts for construction of public improvements if the estimated cost exceeds $200,000 (North Dakota Century Code §§ 48-01.2-04 (2015), 48-01.2-02.1 (2019).); (2) most state purchasing contracts through the OMB (*Id.* § 54-44.4-05(1).); (3) state printing contracts. (*Id.* § 46-02-05.); (4) highway construction contracts exceeding $20,000. (*Id.* § 24-02-17.); and (5) concessions in public buildings or on public grounds. (*Id.* § 48-09-01.)

The details of public improvements and OMB purchasing contracts will be provided in this section, with printing, the NDDOT, and concessions discussed in Section III.C, Rules for Specific Contract Types.

1. Pre-Bid Notice Requirements (Advertisements)

a. Public Improvements

If the construction of a public improvement is estimated to cost in excess of $200,000, the government body must advertise the project for three consecutive weeks. (North Dakota Century Code §§ 48-01.2-04(1), 48-01.2-02.1.) Although the first publication should be at least 21 days before any of the bids are opened, a court may allow a "substantial compliance" standard to this timing requirement under exigent circumstances.

(See *Danzl v. City of Bismarck*, 451 N.W.2d 127, 129–30 (N.D. 1990) (disregarding the fact that some bids were literally opened ahead of a statutory requirement because of the large number of bids involved at the reading).) The advertisement must be published in the official newspaper of the political subdivision where the public improvement is sought, in a daily newspaper having a general circulation in the area where the project is located, and in a trade publication, electronic plan service, builders exchange, or other industry-recognized method of general circulation among the contractors so desired. (North Dakota Century Code § 48-01.2-04(1).)

There are two exceptions. First, the advertisement for a public improvement financed by special assessments need only be published once each week for two weeks in the official newspaper, with the first publication appearing at least 14 days before the bid opening. (*Id.*) Second, if the governing body declares an emergency situation, it may contract for the construction of a public improvement without advertising for bids. (*Id.* § 48-01.2-04(2).)

By statute, advertisements for public improvements must state "[t]he nature of the work and the type and location of the proposed public improvement"; "[w]hen and where the plans, drawings, and specifications may be seen and examined"; "[t]he place, date, and time the bids will be opened"; "[t]hat each bid must be accompanied by a separate envelope containing the contractor's license and bid security" (5 percent of the full amount of the bid); with exceptions on certain water supply projects, "that a bidder . . . must be licensed for the full amount of the bid," and that it will be rejected if a license is not obtained within 20 days after the bid is awarded; "[t]hat no bid may be read or considered if the bid does not fully comply with these requirements[,] and that any deficient bid submitted must be resealed and returned to the bidder immediately"; and "[t]hat the governing body reserves the right to reject any and all bids and rebid the project until a satisfactory bid is received." (*Id.* § 48-01.2-05.)

Certain contracts solicited by agencies or subdivisions may have more stringent advertising requirements. (See, e.g., *id.* § 11-11-26 (for fuel contracts in excess of $4,000 counties require advertisement or telephone solicitation from at least two suppliers); *id.* § 40-49-14 (park boards require advertisement for all contracts in excess of $50,000); *id.* § 24-02-19 (NDDOT requires advertisement for all contracts in excess of $20,000 (citing *id.* § 24-02-17)).) If there is any conflict between statutes governing the advertisement of bids, the two should be construed so that effect may be given to both provisions. (*Brusegaard v. Schroeder*, 201 N.W.2d 899, 905 (N.D. 1972).) If they are irreconcilable, however, the special provision should prevail and will "be construed as an exception to the general provision, unless the general provision" was enacted later, whereby that later provision prevails because it manifests the legislative intent to change the law. (*Id.*)

b. OMB Vendor List

There is no general advertisement requirement for the commodities and services procured through the OMB. Instead, the OMB creates and maintains "bidders lists" of vendors that desire to provide commodities and services to the state or its agencies and subdivisions. (North Dakota Century Code § 54-44.4-09(1) (2015).) "A vendor that wants to receive notice of solicitations for bids or proposals must apply to have its name placed on the bidders list for the type of commodities or services that the vendor sells." (North Dakota Administrative Code 4-12-05-01 (2004).) The OMB will then use the list to solicit bids for all commodities and services the state requires to be competitive. (North Dakota Century Code § 54-44.4-09(1).)

A person or company seeking to get on a bidders list and thus receive bid notices through the OMB must first become an approved vendor. (*Id.*) This requires filing a detailed application with the OMB. (*Id.* § 54-44.4-09(2).) Additionally, remaining on the bidders list requires the vendor to adequately update its information and respond to solicitations in accordance with OMB policy. (North Dakota Administrative Code 4-12-05-01.)

Finally, the OMB may award a bid to a vendor not on the list of approved vendors if the procurement officer makes a written determination that it is in the best interest of the state to receive that particular bid. The successful bidder, however, should become approved before the award, or within at least 60 days, unless it is deemed unnecessary after consultation between the procurement officer and the secretary of state. (North Dakota Century Code § 54-44.4-09(4).)

2. Competitive Bidding Requirements

a. Public Improvements

Government contracts for public improvements estimated to be in excess of $200,000 must be drawn to specification by an architect or engineer and be subject to competitive bidding. (*Id.* §§ 48-01.2-02, 48-01.2-04(1), 48-01.2-02.1.) Additionally, if the contract is segmented, each portion of the overall project must be bid on separately if that portion meets certain cost thresholds. (*Id.* § 48-01.2-06.)

All bids for public improvements must be accompanied by the contractor's license (See *id.* § 43-07-12.) and a bid security. (*Id.* § 48-01.2-05.) The "security must be in a sum equal to 5 percent of the full amount of the bid, and must be in the form of a bidder's bond. (*Id.*) If a successful bidder does not execute a contract within the 10 days allowed, the bidder's bond is forfeited to the governing body and the project awarded to the next lowest responsible bidder." (*Id.*)

After the contract requirements are properly solicited, and the time for responding has lapsed, all the bids will be opened and read aloud at the time and place specified in the advertisement. (*Id.* § 48-01.2-07.) The contract will then be awarded to the lowest responsible bidder. (*Id.*) Regardless of any bid received, however, the governing body reserves the right to reject any and all bids if it is unsatisfied, or there is an indication of noncompetitive collusion. (*Id.*) The competitive bidding process may then be reinitiated in full. (*Id.*)

Using the statutory definition of "lowest responsible bidder" (See *id.* § 48-01.2-01(19).), the procuring government body may exercise some discretion in awarding a public improvement contract other than merely price. (*Baukol Builders, Inc. v. County of Grand Forks*, 751 N.W.2d 191, 199 (N.D. 2008).) For example, factors such as the estimated time of completion, and the bidder's ability, capacity, reputation, experience, and efficiency may all be used to determine the award. (*Id.*; see also N.D. Op. Att'y Gen. 2002-F-04 (2002).)

The contractor may subcontract for all work within the agreement. (North Dakota Century Code § 48-01.2-22 (2017).) In doing so, however, it must advertise for the work publicly, and open bids from potential subcontractors. (*Id.*) Further, the governing body reserves the right to influence the selection of subcontractors, but only insofar as actual past experience dictates. (*Id.*)

b. OMB

Commodities and services purchased through the OMB are generally purchased under a competitive procurement process to the lowest responsible bidder. (*Id.* § 54-44.4-05(1).)

Depending upon the value and complexity of commodities or services to be purchased, the state procurement office and each purchasing agency will issue solicitations by one of the following methods: (1) "[s]mall purchase procedures, including an informal competitive process" (See Section III.B.3.a, Exceptions to Competitive Bidding, OMB.); (2) "[c]ompetitive sealed bids; (3) "[c]ompetitive sealed proposals"; or (4) a "[m]ultistep competitive process." (North Dakota Administrative Code 4-12-08-01 (2004).)

i. Competitive Bidding

With competitive bidding, invitations for sealed bids are issued that include the purchase specifications and all contractual terms and conditions. (*Id.* 4-12-08-03(1).) "At the specified date and time, a public bid opening will be held and each" timely submitted bid opened. (*Id.* 4-12-08-03(3).) After opening begins, negotiation is not permitted, and the award is "made to the responsible vendor with the lowest responsive bid, based strictly on the criteria set forth in the invitation for bids." (*Id.* 4-12-08-03(6).) Lastly, the procurement officer reserves the right to cancel all bids and "negotiate for a lower price with the successful bidder." (*Id.* 4-12-08-03(7).)

ii. Competitive Proposals

Competitive proposals are used for services, information technology, and equipment when competitive sealed bidding is not practicable or advantageous. (*Id.* 4-12-08-04(1).) Requests for proposals are issued to potential vendors found on the bidders list and include the work specifications, all contractual terms and conditions applicable to the procurement, and the relative importance of price and other factors. (*Id.* 4-12-08-04(2).) All proposals in accordance with the specifications should be returned to the designated place in the solicitation in a secured, unopened envelope. (*Id.* 4-12-08-12(1); see also North Dakota Century Code § 44-08-01.1 (2001) (general statutory requirement that bids for government contracts are sealed).) The state agency will issue a written receipt or a written note of rejection depending on whether the submission is timely. (North Dakota Administrative Code 4-12-08-1, 4-12-08-12(3) (2004).)

At the specified date and time, each proposal will be opened with only the names of the vendors disclosed. (*Id.* 4-12-08-04(4).) The evaluation of proposals includes meetings with each potential vendor and further negotiations toward the optimal agreement for performance and price. (*Id.* 4-12-08-04(7), (8) (citing *id.* 4-12-12 (rules for contract negotiations)).) After contract negotiations, and a vendor is selected, a notice is sent to all vendors offering their services. (*Id.* 4-12-08-04(9), (10).)

iii. Multistep Solicitation

A multistep solicitation for commodities or services may be used when an initial solicitation for an unpriced technical bid or proposal is useful to develop a shortlist of qualified vendors. (*Id.* 4-12-08-05(1).) This method is proper when it is not practical to prepare initially definitive purchasing descriptions that will be suitable to determine the award. (*Id.* 4-12-08-05(2).) Further, during the first phase of the multistep process, it is permissible for the procuring officer to hold discussions with the vendors on unpriced technical bids or proposals or hold conferences with all potential bidders or proposal offerors. (*Id.* 4-12-08-05(3).)

iv. Communications

Under both methods, all questions for clarification during the solicitation period are to be sent directly to the officer identified in the solicitation document. (*Id.* 4-12-08-08(1).)

Further, the opportunity for questions may be limited by the solicitation itself. (*Id.* 4-12-08-08(2).) If the response to the question contains material information that is not found in the solicitation, the procuring officer must distribute the response to all vendors. (*Id.* 4-12-08-08(3).)

v. Solicitation Amendments

The bid or proposal specifications may be amended at any time before the bids are opened. (*Id.* 4-12-08-09(1).) This includes amending the solicitation to extend the allowable time for bidding. (*Id.*) Further, the solicitation can be cancelled in whole or part if there are material changes in demand, the funds available to purchase the commodities or service, or anything else that makes the original solicitation inapplicable. (*Id.* 4-12-08-09(3).) The OMB must notify all potential vendors of material changes to the solicitation, and may require receipt of the amendment from those vendors in writing. (*Id.* 4-12-08-09(2), (3).)

vi. Presolicitation, Pre-Bid, or Preproposal Conferences

The OMB may request a presolicitation conference prior to issuing a competitive sealed solicitation to obtain comments and suggestions about optimal specifications. (*Id.* 4-12-08-10(1).) The OMB may specifically invite certain potential bidders or offerors of proposals to this conference, or provide public notice of it to all. (*Id.*) Attendance at such conference is not a mandatory condition for submitting a bid or proposal. (*Id.*)

A pre-bid or preproposal conference or a site inspection may be scheduled on the solicitation and conducted prior to the submission of sealed bids or proposals in response to a multistep process. (*Id.* 4-12-08-10(2).) This conference, however, may be mandatory for issuing a bid or proposal, and only those that attended eligible for the contract, if the information provided at the conference is necessary to adequately prepare the potential bidder or proposal offeror. (*Id.*) Any amendments discussed during a conference of this type must be later issued as a written amendment to all eligible bidders. (*Id.*)

vii. Ties or Limited Bids/Proposals Received

If two or more bidders offer equal prices or receive equal evaluation scores after any reciprocal preference is applied, the preferences are assigned in the following order: (1) bids submitted by North Dakota vendors; (2) approved vendors on the state bidders list; (3) bid or proposal that arrived earliest; and, finally, (4) a random drawing. (North Dakota Century Code §§ 44-08-01.1 (2005), 54-44.4-09(4); North Dakota Administrative Code 4-12-11-05 (2004).)

viii. One Bid/Proposal Received

When only one bid or proposal is received, the award may still be made but only after making a determination that the specifications were not too restrictive, that other bidders or proposal offerors had the reasonable opportunity to respond, and that the price submitted is fair and reasonable. (North Dakota Administrative Code 4-12-11-08(1).) Alternatively, the procurement officer may reject the bid or proposal and solicit again, or cancel the procurement. (*Id.*) Finally, if the price submitted by the lone bidder or proposal offeror is not fair and reasonable, but there is no time for resolicitation, the procurement may be conducted as a limited competitive or noncompetitive purchase. (*Id.* 4-12-11-08(2).)

3. Exceptions to Competitive Bidding

a. OMB

Statutory exceptions to the general competitive bidding process exist for goods and services procured through the OMB. By statute, the

> circumstances that may permit limited competitive, noncompetitive, or negotiated purchases include:
>
> a. The commodity or service is available from only one source.
>
> b. The commodity or service is to be purchased for experimentation or trial.
>
> c. No acceptable bid or proposal was received pursuant to a competitive bidding or competitive proposal process.
>
> d. Commodities are being purchased for over-the-counter resale.
>
> e. Acceptable commodities or services are produced or provided by correctional institutions or other government agencies . . . .
>
> f. The anticipated cost of purchasing specified commodities or services is less than an amount determined by the office of management and budget which would justify the expense of a competitive bidding or competitive proposal process.
>
> g. A used commodity is advantageous to the state and the commodity is available only on short notice.
>
> h. The commodity is a component or replacement part for which there is no commercially available substitute and which can be obtained only from the manufacturer.
>
> i. Compatibility with equipment currently owned by the state is essential to the proper functioning of that equipment.
>
> j. The agency provides documentation indicating that the services or the circumstances are of such a nature that deviation from the procurement procedure is appropriate.

(North Dakota Century Code § 54-44.4-05(2) (2011).) The OMB adopted rules to promote fair and equitable procurement of contracts in those circumstances outside of the competitive process. (*Id.* § 54-4.4-01.)

4. Limited Competitive Procurements

When circumstances arise making a fully competitive procurement process difficult or impossible, a limited competition process is allowed.

Limited-bidding competition may be appropriate when (1) "products or services exclusive to particular individuals or business entities are required and competition for the proprietary product or service exists"; (2) "circumstances require that commodities or services be provided by bidders or offerors within a specific geographic area," such as equipment requiring local service, onsite service within a specific time, or delivery of ready-mix concrete; or (3) "it is determined that a competitive sealed bid or competitive sealed process is impracticable or not in the best interest of the state." (North Dakota Administrative Code 4-12-09-02 (2012).) When using limited-bidding competition, the government agency must provide evidence necessary supporting full competition is impracticable or not in the best interest of the state. (*Id.*) Further, the purchasing agency must provide evidence necessary for an independent examination and determination of the material facts of the procurement. (*Id.*)

5. Noncompetitive Procurements

Competition may be waived when the commodity or service can only be obtained from a sole source, or the commodity or service is so unique that it does not have reasonable competition. (*Id.* 4-12-09-03 (2012).) When making this purchase, the government agency must make a written determination of the necessity for waiving competition by fully explaining why competition is impracticable or not in the best interest of the state. (*Id.*) Further, the purchasing agency must provide evidence necessary for an independent examination and determination of the material facts of the procurement. (*Id.*)

A noncompetitive procurement is not justified by (1) a lack of adequate advance planning; (2) administrative delays in the procurement; (3) improper handling of procurement requests; or (4) pending expiration of budget authority. (*Id.* 4-12-09-03.)

6. Emergency Procurement

For public improvements, competition for a public improvement contract estimated to be worth over $200,000 may be waived if a governing body declares an emergency situation. (North Dakota Century Code § 48-01.2-04(2).) In turn, the government body may contract for the construction of a public improvement without seeking bids. (*Id.*)

For contract procurement through the OMB, purchases may be made under emergency conditions in circumstances when there is insufficient time for usual competitive procurement methods and that involve public health, public safety, or when immediate expenditures are necessary. (*Id.* § 54-44.4-02(7).) An emergency procurement need not be made through regular competitive sealed bidding or proposals, but must be made with competition that is practicable in the circumstances. (*Id.*) When making an emergency purchase, the government agency must make a written determination explaining why the emergency exists and provide the evidence necessary for an independent examination into the material facts of the procurement. (North Dakota Administrative Code 4-12-09-04 (2021).)

C. Rules for Specific Contract Types

1. Contracting for Architect/Engineering Services

The procurement of an architect, engineer, construction management, or land surveying service contract is governed by a distinct set of rules. "'Architect, engineer, construction management, and land surveying services' are those professional services associated with the practice of architecture, professional engineering, professional land surveying, landscape architecture, interior design pertaining to construction, and construction management." (North Dakota Century Code § 54-44.7-01 (2001).) Duties falling to these professionals include "studies, investigations, surveys, evaluations, consultations, planning, programming, conceptual designs, plans and specifications, cost estimates, inspections, and other specialized services." (*Id.*) It is the policy of North Dakota that state agencies shall negotiate these contracts "on the basis of demonstrated competence and qualification for the particular type of services required." (*Id.* § 54-44.7-02.)

a. Competitive Bidding

A government agency requiring the services of an architect, engineer, construction manager, or land surveyor must first designate a selection committee with the purpose of selecting the best contractor. (*Id.* § 54-44.7-03(1).) This agency is responsible for developing a description of the proposed project, declaring the required professional services for that project, and preparing a formal and detailed invitation to firms for submission of bids. (*Id.* § 54-44.7-03(2).) This invitation must be published, and upon written request mailed to any interested party. (*Id.*)

Responses to this solicitation from interested professionals must not be less than 21 days after the publication. (*Id.* § 54-44.7-03(3).) Following receipt from all interested professionals, the committee will hold interviews with at least three qualified responders, or with whoever submitted bids if less than three responded. (*Id.* § 54-44.7-03(4).) After compiling this short list, the committee will evaluate each professional interviewed and rank the three most qualified professionals. (*Id.* § 54-44.7-03(5).)

The committee's report will then be sent to the governing body of the contracting agency for its evaluation and approval. (*Id.* § 54-44.7-03(6).) That body will negotiate a contract with the most qualified professional at a compensation that is fair and reasonable to the state. (*Id.* § 54-44.7-03(7).) Should the governing body become unable to negotiate a satisfactory contract with the most qualified professional, those negotiations will cease, and new negotiations will commence in the same manner with the next most qualified professional until a satisfactory contract has been negotiated. (*Id.*) If no agreement is reached then negotiations must be continued in the same manner until agreement is reached. (*Id.*)

b. Exceptions to Competitive Bidding

All state agencies securing architect, engineer, construction management, or land surveying services for projects for which the fees are estimated to be less than $35,000 can employ the professionals by direct negotiation and selection. (*Id.* § 54-44.7-03 (2017).)

i. Agricultural Exception

"For a public building in use by or to be used by the state agricultural experiment station in connection with farm or agricultural research operations, the plans, drawings, and specifications, with the approval of the state board of higher education, may be prepared by an engineer in the regular employment of that station." (*Id.* § 48-01.2-02.)

2. NDDOT

The NDDOT provides a unique and self-administered contract procurement system for roads, bridges, and other projects within the agency's statutory responsibility. More information can be found by searching its website at https://www.dot.nd.gov/business/bidinfo.htm.

A contract with the NDDOT will either require the contractor to furnish all equipment and materials, or the NDDOT will work with the OMB to purchase the necessaries separately. (North Dakota Century Code § 24-02-16 (1999).) The OMB then has the discretion of allowing the NDDOT to contract for the equipment and materials itself. (*Id.*) Regardless of who carries out the purchase, however, the contracts for equipment and materials must be efficient and economical. (*Id.*) Moreover, if purchased separately, the equipment and materials can be resold to the working contractor, and thus made a part of the contract, if the NDDOT finds it advantageous. (*Id.*)

a. Competitive Bidding

By statute, the NDDOT must publicly advertise for all contract work estimated to exceed $20,000. (*Id.* § 24-02-17.) The solicitation must state where the bidder may inspect the plans and specifications, with whom bids must be filed, and the time and place where bids must be opened. (*Id.* § 24-02-19.) Further, contractors must prequalify before being allowed to bid on any project involving a road or bridge. (NDDOT, *Standard Specifications for Road and Bridge Construction*, Vol. 1, § 102.01. Further information on qualifying and bid notifications can be found on the website located at https://www.dot.nd.gov/business/bidinfo.htm.) At the outset, the top three bidders will be retained, and subsequently the contract will be awarded to the responsible bidder submitting the lowest and best bid. (North Dakota Century Code § 24-02-23.) Lastly, the NDDOT may reject all bids if they are all deemed unsatisfactory. (*Id.*)

b. Exceptions to Competitive Bidding

If it is deemed in the best interest of the state, the NDDOT may do the work necessary for minor grading reconstruction on any state highway without letting a contract for such reconstruction work. (*Id.* § 24-02-18.) Alternatively, the director may contract with the county in which any such reconstruction project is located, to perform such reconstruction work on a cost basis. (*Id.*)

3. Purchasing Laws Relating to Printing and Newspapers

Purchases of printing materials are procured under the authority of the OMB but administered under a separate set of statutory laws. (*Id.* §§ 46-01-01, 46-01-02.) The OMB has the authority to (1) "[b]id all printing requisitions as requested and let all contracts and (2) [d]etermine the price of any legal notice or publication when requested by any state agency or department, or by any political subdivision. Its decision on the proper fee for the publication is binding and final, subject to review by the courts." (*Id.* § 46-01-02.)

4. Information Technology Purchases

The Information Technology Department (ITD) has the authority to procure government contracts related to information technology. (*Id.* § 54-59-05(5) (2021).) The ITD adopts the OMB Central Services Division purchasing procedures as standard for all technology purchases. (Information Technology Procurement Standard ¶ 1 (Jan. 11, 2004, rev. Feb. 23, 2016), https://www.ndit.nd.gov/standards/POL0020208.) Other state agencies must go through the ITD for all information and technology concerns. (*Id.* ¶ 7.)

D. Vendor Preferences

North Dakota has preference laws that must be applied when evaluating bids and proposals. By statute, a government purchase in North Dakota must give a preference to a resident North Dakota bidder equal to the preference given or required by the state of the nonresident bidder, also known as a "reciprocal preference." (North Dakota Century Code § 44-08-01 (2001).) A bidder is "resident" if it maintains a bona fide place of business within North Dakota for at least one year prior to the date the contract was awarded. (*Id.* § 44-08-02.)

North Dakota also has preference laws for certain commodities and services. (See, e.g., *id.* § 48-05-02.1 (coal), *id.* § 25-16.2-02 (construction stakes), *id.* § 54-44.4-07 (bio-based products).) Additionally, "if practicable, all state, county, and other political subdivision public printing" should be awarded to a resident of North Dakota. (*Id.* § 46-02-15.)

Finally, all construction contracts with the state, except those involving federal aid or where a preference would be contrary to law, must include a clause requiring the contractor to give preference to North Dakota residents in hiring, with preference given first to veterans. (*Id.* § 43-07-20.)

E. Affirmative Action and Nondiscrimination Obligations

The procurement of commodities and services by the OMB cannot be based upon discrimination because of race, religion, color, national origin, sex, age, marital status, pregnancy, parenthood, disability, or political affiliation. (North Dakota Administrative Code 4-12-04-07 (2004).)

IV. Bid Protests and Contract Disputes

The North Dakota Legislature enacted a statute authorizing suits arising upon contract to be brought in the district court against the state. (North Dakota Century Code § 32-12-02 (1979).) Actions are to be brought in the county in which the plaintiff resides, and a surety must be offered by the plaintiff to cover any costs that might later be rendered against him or her. (*Id.*)

Before a suit arising upon contract for the recovery of money is allowed in district court, however, it must first be presented to the department, institution, agency, board, or commission to which the claim arose. (*Id.* § 32-12-03.) Further, the neglect or refusal of the office to act on such claim for a period of ten days after its presentation for allowance must be deemed a refusal to allow the claim. (*Id.*)

A. Bid Protests

1. Public Improvements (Injunctive Relief)

The district court in North Dakota has original jurisdiction over bid protests for public improvement contracts involving injunctive relief. (*Baukol Builders, Inc. v. County of Grand Forks*, 751 N.W.2d 191, 195 (N.D. 2008) (citing North Dakota Constitution art. VI, § 8, and North Dakota Century Code §§ 27-05-06 and 32-23-01).)

A party with standing can protest the awarding of a public improvement contract in North Dakota by seeking an injunction in state court. (See *Danzl v. City of Bismarck*, 451 N.W.2d 127, 129 (N.D. 1990) (plaintiffs sought an injunction to prevent the awarding of a bid because the city of Bismarck allegedly violated a competitive statute); see also *Baukol Builders, Inc. v. County of Grand Forks*, 751 N.W.2d 191, 193 (N.D. 2008) (lowest bidder for public improvement construction contract seeks injunction against a county for allegedly violating a competition statute).) Further, any state taxpayer has standing to challenge a statute on the basis that state funds are being unlawfully dissipated. (*Danzl*, 451 N.W.2d at 129.)

A plaintiff may not generally recover damages against a public entity for violation of competitive bidding statutes, however, because the statutes were enacted to benefit the public and not intended to benefit contractors. (*Becker Electric, Inc. v. City of Bismark*, 469 N.W.2d 159, 160 (N.D. 1991) (citations omitted).) The *Becker* court recognized a possible exception. A monetary award may be possible if the contractor endured bid preparation costs and the bid was ultimately awarded to another because of fraud or collision. (*Id.* at 161.)

2. OMB

The OMB provides an administrative process for all bid protests. To initiate this process, a vendor will submit a written protest to the officer responsible for the procurement to dispute the awarding or intent to award the contract. (North Dakota Century Code § 54-44.4-12(1) (2003).) The protest must be detailed and clearly identify the nature of the protest. (North Dakota Administrative Code 4-12-14-02(1) (2004).) The protest must be submitted within seven calendar days after the protestor knows or should have known of the facts giving rise to the protest. (North Dakota Century Code § 54-44.4-12(1).)

During the time the protest is being considered, the award will be stayed, unless a written determination is made that award without delay is necessary to protect the interests of the state. Written notice of the protest and stay of award will be sent to the successful bidder or offeror. (*Id.* § 54-44.4-12(2); North Dakota Administrative Code 4-12-14-02(3) (2004).)

The procurement officer has seven calendar days to review the protest and render a decision, and may only extend the decision period by seven more days. (North Dakota Administrative Code 4-12-14-02(2).) If the protest is not resolved during this time, the procurement officer will send a written, detailed decision by mail, and also inform the protestor of the protestor's right to appeal. (North Dakota Century Code § 54-44.4-12(3).)

B. Bid Protest Appeals

1. Public Improvements (Injunctive Relief)

The Supreme Court of North Dakota has appellate jurisdiction over all bid protest appeals originally decided in inferior district courts. (North Dakota Constitution art. 6, § 2; North Dakota Century Code §§ 28-27-01 (appeals to supreme court), 28-27-02 (reviewable orders), 32-23-07 (review of declaratory judgment).) The Supreme Court of North Dakota may delegate a bid protest appeal to an intermediate appellate court at its discretion. (North Dakota Century Code § 27-02.1-01.)

2. OMB

A vendor may file an administrative appeal with the OMB for unfavorable decisions by the procurement officer. "An appeal must be filed in writing within seven (7) days after the" vendor receives the decision by the procurement officer. (*Id.* § 54-44.4-12(4).) The appeal must include a copy of the decision being appealed from and a basis for the appeal. (*Id.*)

During the time the appeal is being considered, the bid award will be stayed, unless a written determination is made that award without delay is necessary to protect the interests of the state. (North Dakota Administrative Code 4-12-14-03(1)(b) (2021).)

Within seven days the director of the OMB or the director's designee will mail a decision to the protesting vendor. (*Id.* 4-12-14-03(1)(a).) This decision will detail the reasons for the action taken and inform the vendor of its right to further judicial or administrative review. (*Id.* 4-12-14-03(1)(c).) This decision is considered final and conclusive. (*Id.* 4-12-14-03(1)(d).)

Remedies for a successful appeal include cancellation and reissue of a solicitation, amendment of a solicitation and evaluation criteria, and cancellation of a contract award. (*Id.* 4-12-14-03(2)(a).) When it is decided that the protesting bidder or offeror should have been awarded the contract under the solicitation, that bidder or offeror may not recover profits that it anticipates would have been made if that party had been originally awarded the contract. (*Id.* 4-12-14-03(2)(b).) Monetary relief must be referred to the Office of the Attorney General. (*Id.*)

C. Contract Disputes

Contracts involving government agencies or officials in North Dakota are generally interpreted under the same rules as contracts between private parties. (North Dakota Century Code § 9-07-01.) With public contracts, however, any ambiguity or uncertainty is interpreted against the private party. (*Id.* § 9-07-19.)

1. Public Improvements or the OMB

After a government contract has been entered into for a public improvement, the private contractor may sue the state or its agency for breach of that contract, but only after first presenting a claim to the director of the OMB. (*Id.* § 32-12.2-04(1).) The contractor must bring this claim "within one hundred eighty [180] days after the alleged injury is discovered or reasonably should have been discovered." (*Id.*) The written notice should state "the time, place, and circumstances of the injury, the names of any state employees known to be involved, and the amount of compensation or other relief demanded." (*Id.*) A contractor bringing a legal action against the state must serve the director of the OMB at the time the summons, complaint, or other legal pleading is served in the action. (*Id.* § 32-12.2-04(5).)

2. NDDOT (Arbitration)

All controversies arising out of a contract for the construction or repair of highways entered into through the NDDOT must be submitted to arbitration. (*Id.* § 24-02-26.) Moreover, any person who voluntarily enters into a contract for the construction or repair of highways is considered as having agreed to arbitration of all controversies arising out of that contract. (*Id.*)

a. Arbitration Board

The number of arbiters required is determined by the amount of the claim. For a claim for less than $100,000, only one arbitrator may be jointly selected by the parties, and for a claim greater than $100,000 the arbitration board should comprise three persons. (*Id.*) Unless a party submits the dispute to the American Arbitration Association, the party desiring arbitration of claims greater than $100,000 will serve a written demand upon the adverse party, designating an arbiter and detailing the claim. (*Id.* § 24-02-27.) The party served with the demand must respond within 30 days, and the response must designate a second arbitrator and must explain the respondent's position concerning each claim item. (*Id.*) The two arbiters will then select a third arbiter. (*Id.*) For claims less than $100,000 both parties will select the arbiter. (*Id.*) All problems organizing the arbiters will be dealt with through this section. (*Id.*)

"If either party refuses to submit to arbitration . . . that party must be deemed to have waived all claims and demands, and the arbitrators shall proceed to determine the controversies set forth by the moving party according to the justice of the case." (*Id.* § 24-02-29.) "Judgment must be entered upon the award of such arbitrators in all things the same as though the submission to arbitration has been signed by both parties." (*Id.*)

The arbitrators shall determine all controversies between the parties growing out of the contract, including the question whether it had been performed at the time claimed by the contractor and whether the additional work required by the director as specified has been done. (*Id.* § 24-02-31.) If it has not been done they shall specify the particulars in which it has not, give appropriate directions with reference thereto, and shall make a proper award for any extra work they find the contractor entitled to, making such award so far as it is practicable upon the basis of the contract price, having due regard to what is just and equitable between the parties under the facts and circumstances of the case. (*Id.*)

"If after the making of an award which requires the contractor to do further work, any controversies arise between the parties as to the doing of such work, the controversies may be submitted to the same arbitrators on five days' notice for further determination." (*Id.* § 24-02-32.)

b. Conditions Precedent to Arbitration

"No right exists to demand arbitration against the director [of the NDDOT] until certain conditions have been complied with." (*Id.* § 24-02-30.) The contractor must first "give the director notice in writing that the contractor claims the contract has been or will be performed fully on a day stated," and this may not be less than ten days after the giving of such notice. (*Id.*) At the time stated in the notice, the director will cause the work to be inspected, and if the director claims the work has not been completed, the director will "specify the particulars in which it is incomplete and then direct that it be completed accordingly." (*Id.*)

If the director considers further work necessary to bring the project up to the desired standard for acceptance, the director may specify any such additional work. (*Id.*) The contractor shall proceed with all reasonable dispatch, having due regard to weather conditions, with the speedily performance of the additional work. (*Id.*) "When the contractor claims in good faith, supported by affidavit furnished to the director, that the contractor has completed such additional work according to the specifications furnished to the contractor, and the director fails for ten (10) days to accept such work as completed, the contractor has the right to institute proceedings under this chapter." (*Id.*)

If the contractor believes it is entitled to additional compensation before the work is performed, the contractor must, "prior to beginning the work on which the claim will be based upon, notify the engineer in writing of the intent to make claim for additional compensation." (*Id.* § 24-02-26.1.)

"If the basis for the claim does not become apparent until the contractor has commenced work on the project[,] and it is not feasible to stop the work[,] the contractor [must] immediately notify the engineer that the work is continuing and that written notification of the intent to make claim will be submitted within ten calendar days." (*Id.*) Failure of the contractor to give the notification required and to maintain proper records and accounts may constitute a waiver of the claim. (*Id.*) Moreover, notification of the claim and proper records and accounts cannot be construed as evidence towards the validity of the claim. (*Id.*)

"A contractor submitting a claim for compensation . . . must do so in writing, not later than ninety (90) days after the department has submitted the final estimate to the contractor. The claim must state the monetary amount of the claim, the reason for the claim, when the loss was incurred, and a short statement of the factual situation under which the claim arose. The claim must be made under oath or equivalent affirmation." (*Id.*)

"The director shall act on claims of less than three (3) million dollars within sixty (60) days after the claim is served upon the director. The director shall act on claims greater than three (3) million dollars within one hundred eighty (180) days after the claim is served upon the director. The contractor and the director may negotiate a supplemental agreement for the claim items that are accepted by the director, and the director [will] immediately pay the contractor for any additional compensation resulting from the supplemental agreement. The contractor may demand arbitration on the remaining claim items within ninety (90) days after the contractor has been notified of the director's action." (*Id.*)

The contractor must "make available to the department and allow the department to examine and copy all of the contractor's records, documents, worksheets, and other data which are pertinent to the justification of the claim and to the substantiation of all costs related to the claim. The department shall also make available to the contractor all of the department's records, documents, worksheets, and other data which are pertinent to the department's response to the claim." (*Id.*)

c. Arbitration Procedure

After a board of arbitration has been appointed, a validity of agreement to arbitrate must be provided and the agreement "must provide for the entry of judgment upon the award by the district court of the county in which the improvement, or some part thereof, involved in the contract is located." (*Id.* § 24-02-28.) Moreover, the county must be specified in the submission, it must be executed by the director, and after submission of the arbitration agreement, the arbitration must proceed in accordance with the provisions of North Dakota's Uniform Arbitration Act, North Dakota Century Code chapter 32-29.3 (2021), unless a party submits the dispute to arbitration in accordance with the construction industry arbitration rules of the American Arbitration Association. (*Id.*) "If the rules of the American arbitration association conflict with North Dakota law, North Dakota law governs. The decision of the arbitrators must be in writing and must state the basis for the decision." (*Id.*)

d. Judgment against Director

"When judgment has been entered against the director, the same is not collectible or enforceable by execution, but if the same provides for the payment of money by the director, it must be paid in the same manner, to the same extent, and out of the same funds as though the claims thus established had been recognized and allowed without arbitration." The performance of the duty of the director with reference to payment or other compliance with such judgment may be enforced by mandamus proceedings in the district courts of the state." (*Id.* § 24-02-33.)

3. Suits by Subcontractors or Other Providers of Goods and Services

Any additional subcontractor who has furnished labor, materials, or supplies has the right to commence an action to recover against the contractor or surety furnishing the performance bond within one year of the date of the final acceptance of the project by the department. (See, e.g., *id.* §§ 48-01.2-11 (public improvements), 24-02-25.1 (NDDOT).)

4. Contract Claim Appeals

A party to a proceeding heard by an administrative agency may appeal from the order within 30 days after notice of the final determination has been given. (*Id.* § 28-32-42(1).)

The appeal should be taken to the district court designated by law, and if none is designated, then to the district court of the county where the hearing was held. (*Id.* § 28-32-42(4); see also *Cooke v. University of North Dakota*, 603 N.W.2d 504, 507 (N.D. 1999) (contractors can appeal unfavorable administrative decisions to the district court).) Only final orders are appealable. (North Dakota Century Code § 28-32-42(3).) A procedural order made by an administrative agency while a proceeding is pending before it is not a final order. (*Id.*)

In other words, for the district court to have subject-matter jurisdiction over claims against the state, the plaintiff must first strictly comply with all administrative requirements, including the timely notice, and exhaust all administrative remedies. (*Ungar v. North Dakota State University*, 721 N.W.2d 16, 22 (N.D. 2006).)

The procedure for obtaining administrative review of bid protest and other contract claims can be found by searching North Dakota's Uniform Rules of Administrative Procedure located at https://www.ndlegis.gov/information/acdata/html/98-02.html.

D. Suspension and Debarment

The state procurement manager of the OMB, after consultation with the attorney general, may suspend or debar any vendor from a bidders list for cause. (North Dakota Administrative Code 4-12-05-02 (2021).) The maximum time period for a suspension period must be less than six months, while the debarment period must be less than three years. (*Id.*)

Procedurally, the vendor will be given written notice that describes the term of the suspension or debarment, the vendor's right to make a written appeal within seven calendar days, and the reinstatement process. (*Id.*) After the vendor receives notice of suspension or debarment, the vendor should "submit a written explanation of the circumstances that were the cause of the suspension or debarment order, or may show that the circumstances have been corrected." (*Id.* 4-12-05-03.) "Frivolous protests may [also] be cause for suspension or debarment from consideration of contract award for a period of up to three (3) years. A written determination by the state procurement manager is required for this action." (*Id.* 4-12-14-03(3).)

V. Administrative and Judicial Review

A. Administrative Review

"Any party before an administrative agency who is aggrieved by the final order of the agency, including the administrative agency when the hearing officer is not the agency head or one or more members of the agency head . . . may file a petition for reconsideration" within 15 days after notice of a final decision has been given. (North Dakota Century Code § 28-32-40 (2021).) "Filing of the petition is not a prerequisite for seeking judicial review." (*Id.*)

B. Judicial Review

1. Public Improvement Bid Protests (Injunctive Relief)

The standard of review for bid protest cases involving injunctive relief is whether the lower court decision was clearly erroneous. (See *Baukol Builders, Inc. v. County of Grand Forks*, 751 N.W.2d 191, 200 (N.D. 2008) (concluding that district court did not err when deciding that Grand Forks County did not abuse its discretion when it awarded the contract to the second lowest bidder).)

"A court abuses its discretion if its decision is arbitrary, capricious, or unreasonable, or if it misinterprets or misapplies the law." (*Id.* at 201 (citation omitted).)

2. Review of Administrative Decisions

"A judge of the district court must review an appeal from the determination of an administrative agency based only on the record filed with the court." (North Dakota Century Code § 28-32-46 (2001).)

> [T]he court must affirm the order of the agency unless it finds that any of the following are present:
>
> 1. The order is not in accordance with the law.
> 2. The order is in violation of the constitutional rights of the appellant.
> 3. The provisions of this chapter have not been complied with in the proceedings before the agency.
> 4. The rules or procedure of the agency have not afforded the appellant a fair hearing.
> 5. The findings of fact made by the agency are not supported by a preponderance of the evidence.
> 6. The conclusions of law and order of the agency are not supported by its findings of fact.
> 7. The findings of fact made by the agency do not sufficiently address the evidence presented to the agency by the appellant.
> 8. The conclusions of law and order of the agency do not sufficiently explain the agency's rationale for not adopting any contrary recommendations by a hearing officer or an administrative law judge.
>
> If the order of the agency is not affirmed by the court, it must be modified or reversed, and the case shall be remanded to the agency for disposition in accordance with the order of the court.

(*Id.*; see also *id.* § 28-32-47 (reviewing agency's rulemaking powers).)

VI. Extent of State's Adoption or Adaptation of ABA Model Procurement Code

North Dakota is not a Model Procurement Code state.

VII. Cooperative Purchasing Agreements

A. Authority

North Dakota has adopted the use of cooperative purchasing agreements. (*Id.* § 54.4-13 (2013).) Under North Dakota Century Code section 54.4-13(1), the OMB is required to purchase commodities or services as requested by the State Board of Higher Education and the legislative and judicial branches. For the State Board of Higher Education, the OMB "shall make joint purchase" of commodities or services "of high common usage," when the State Board of Higher Education determines it to be "in the best interest of the state." (*Id.* § 54.4-13(2).) For non-State Board of Higher Education contracts, the OMB may, but is not required to, purchase services or commodities under joint purchasing agreements if "it is determined to be in the best interest of the state after consideration of price, contractual terms and conditions, and the availability of competition from approved vendors." (*Id.* § 54.4-13(3).) Further, North Dakota Century Code section 54-44.4-13(6) allows cooperative purchasing agreements to "include open-ended contracts that are available to other government entities, nonprofit organizations established on behalf of public entities, tribal agencies, or transportation providers determined to be eligible."

B. Requirements

Prior to entering into a cooperative purchasing agreement, the OMB "must determine that the contracts were awarded through full and open competition or source selection methods specified in [North Dakota Century Code §] 54-44.4-05." (*Id.* § 54-44.4-13(7).) The OMB shall also "send notice to approved vendors of the office's intent to make a cooperative purchase." (*Id.*) The OMB maintains a website that explains the cooperative purchasing agreement system and lists the available cooperative purchasing contracts at https://www.omb.nd.gov/doing-business-state/procurement/cooperative-purchasing. The OMB has also published a brochure, available at https://www.omb.nd.gov/sites/www/files/documents/doing-business-with-the-state/procurement/CooperativePurchasing.pdf, that further explains the process, although it contains much of the same information as the main website. There is not yet case law interpreting North Dakota Century Code section 54-44.4-13, so it remains unclear what rights and remedies are available to a disappointed bidder who would like to lodge a bid protest on a cooperative purchasing agreement contract.

Ohio Procurement Rules and Regulations

Prepared by Barbara A. Duncombe
Taft Stettinius & Hollister LLP
Email: bduncombe@taftlaw.com
With assistance from Sean A. Graves and Erin R. Davis

I. Statutory Reference

The Ohio Revised Code, Ohio Administrative Code (OAC), and Ohio Constitution govern public contracting in Ohio, although Ohio has no consolidated public contracting statute. Different rules apply to contracting with the state, counties, and municipal corporations. Ohio favors competitive bidding. Several sections of the state constitution apply to public contracts. Relevant sections include article I, section 2, the state's equal protection clause, article VIII, governing public debt and public works, and article XVIII, governing municipal corporations.

A. Procurement/Purchasing Statutes

State agencies and political subdivisions have different contracting authority.

1. Department of Administrative Services

The Ohio Department of Administrative Services (DAS) has many responsibilities outlined in Ohio Revised Code Annotated chapters 123, 124, and 125. Those responsibilities include providing centralized services for state agencies, boards, and commissions, as well as local governments and state universities. (See https://das.ohio.gov/.) DAS is given the authority to establish contracts for supplies and services for the use of these entities. (Ohio Revised Code Annotated § 125.02.)

2. Ohio Department of Transportation

Construction projects for the state highway system are overseen by the Ohio Department of Transportation (ODOT) and governed by Ohio Revised Code Annotated chapter 5525.

3. Counties

Counties, through their boards of commissioners, may provide for the procurement of equipment, stationery, and postage reasonably necessary for the proper and convenient conduct of county offices, and such facilities as will result in expeditious and economical administration of such offices. (Ohio Revised Code Annotated § 307.01(A).[1]) Ohio Revised Code Annotated section 153.12 *et seq.* and section 307.86 *et seq.* govern the construction contracts for such facilities. Boards of county commissioners may also construct and improve county roads. (Ohio Revised Code Annotated § 5555.02; see Ohio Revised Code Annotated § 5555.61 *et seq.*)

4. Municipal Corporations

Municipal corporations may also construct and improve public facilities. (Ohio Revised Code Annotated § 153.12 *et seq.*; Ohio Revised Code Annotated § 717.01.) The director of public service manages and supervises such projects. Ohio Revised Code Annotated section 735.05 *et seq.* govern this process for cities and Ohio Revised Code Annotated sections 735.273, 731.14, and 731.141 apply to villages. (See generally Ohio Revised Code Annotated tit. VII.)

5. Controlling Board

The Controlling Board is a legislative body composed of three members of the House of Representatives, three members of the Senate, and a president. (Ohio Revised Code Annotated § 127.12.) The Board provides oversight to ensure that funds appropriated by the legislature are used in accordance with legislative intent. Specifically, the Board has the power to make budgetary adjustments that are within the scope of the original legislative appropriation. (Ohio Revised Code Annotated § 127.17.) The Controlling Board may grant a waiver of competitive selection when it determines that an emergency or sufficient economic reason exists. (Ohio Revised Code Annotated § 127.16.) However, some types of supplies and services and certain sources are exempt from Controlling Board review. (Ohio Revised Code Annotated § 127.16; Ohio Controlling Board Manual § II, at 29 (rev. 2018), https://ecb.ohio.gov/documents/2018_ControllingBoardManual_4-4-18.pdf.) Generally, agencies must seek Controlling Board approval when the cumulative amount to be spent with a single vendor will exceed $50,000 per fiscal year and purchase does not follow competitive selection. (Ohio Revised Code Annotated § 127.16(B)(1).) "If the proposed purchase of a supply or service is not one of the exempt types and is not being procured from an exempt source or through the divisions of DAS listed above, then the final factor for determining the requirement for Controlling Board approval is whether the agency's fiscal activity with the vendor equals or exceeds the Controlling Board threshold." (Ohio Controlling Board Manual § II, at 30.)

II. Regulations

The pertinent regulations are found in the OAC. The following articles apply:

- OAC 123:2, Division of Equal Employment Opportunity for Construction/Contract Compliance Officer
- OAC 123:5, Division of Purchasing

1. Two Ohio counties have adopted an executive form of county government, as opposed to a Board of County Commissioners. Accordingly, under their home rule-based charters, both have unique procurement requirements and policies. For Cuyahoga County, see Cuyahoga County Office of Procurement and Diversity, https://opd.cuyahogacounty.us/ (last visited June 2, 2022), and for Summit County, see Summit County Purchasing Department, https://co.summitoh.net/departments/Purchasing.html (last visited June 2, 2022).

- OAC 164-1-32, Minority Business Enterprises
- OAC 4115, Purchases of Products and Services of Persons with Severe Disabilities Committee
- OAC 5101:9-4, Ohio Department of Job and Family Services, Procurement Standards and Procedures

III. Source Selection

A. Contracts with the State (DAS)

Ohio competitively awards state construction contracts. DAS's Division of Public Works primarily awards and oversees these projects, but other state agencies may enter into construction contracts in certain circumstances. (See Ohio Revised Code Annotated ch. 152. See also https://das.ohio.gov/.)

B. Competitive Bidding

Ohio law favors competitive bidding in contracts with the state and its agencies. (Ohio Revised Code Annotated ch. 153.)

1. Invitation to Bid

The awarding authority must first give public notice of the time and place that it will accept bids. (Ohio Revised Code Annotated § 153.06.) It must also publish notice once a week for three consecutive weeks in a newspaper of general circulation. (Ohio Revised Code Annotated § 153.07.) The date of the last publication must be at least eight days before bid opening. (Ohio Revised Code Annotated § 153.07.) In addition, the awarding authority must make all information about the project available for public inspection from the first day notice is published through the day bids are received. The awarding authority must maintain such information at the office designated to receive the bids. (Ohio Revised Code Annotated § 153.07.)

2. Bid Opening and Tabulation

After collecting the bids, the awarding authority opens them on the day and at the location named in the notice and then immediately tabulates the bids. (Ohio Revised Code Annotated § 153.08.)

3. Bid Evaluation and Contract Award

The awarding authority must evaluate the bids and award the contract to the *lowest responsive and responsible bidder*. (Ohio Revised Code Annotated § 153.08; Ohio Revised Code Annotated § 9.312.) The awarding authority must do this within 30 days of bid opening. (Ohio Revised Code Annotated § 153.08.) Contractors must provide a bid guaranty meeting the requirements of Ohio Revised Code section 153.54. The awarding authority will reject bids lacking a bid guaranty as non-responsive. (Ohio Revised Code Annotated § 153.08.)

4. Choosing Bidder Other Than the Lowest Responsive and Responsible

If the awarding authority believes that accepting the lowest responsive and responsible bid is not in the best interest of the state, then it may award the contract to one of the other bidders or reject all bids and re-advertise the procurement. (Ohio Revised Code Annotated § 153.09.)

5. Rejecting All Bids

The awarding authority may reject all bids, cancel the solicitation, and re-advertise the procurement. (Ohio Revised Code Annotated § 153.09.)

6. Absolute Deadline

Unless the awarding authority and bidders agree to extend the time for award, the awarding authority must award and execute a contract within 60 days of bid opening. Failure to satisfy this requirement invalidates all bids. (Ohio Revised Code Annotated § 153.12(A).)

7. Winning Bid Requirements

Before contract formation, the winning bidder must satisfy several requirements. For Ohio corporations, the winning bidder must (1) comply with the workers' compensation requirements of Ohio Revised Code Annotated chapter 4123 and (2) possess a valid certificate of compliance with affirmative action programs issued pursuant to Ohio Revised Code Annotated section 9.47. (Ohio Revised Code Annotated § 153.08.) In addition to those requirements, a nonresident corporation must also (1) certify that it is authorized to do business in Ohio and (2) file a power of attorney designating the secretary of state as its agent for accepting service of summons for any suit on a bond. (Ohio Revised Code Annotated § 153.08.) The attorney general must also approve the contract and any required bond. (Ohio Revised Code Annotated § 153.08.)

8. Contract Formation

If the awarding authority is the state, a state agency, or a political subdivision, the winning bidder must enter into a contract with the awarding authority within ten days of the award. (Ohio Revised Code Annotated § 153.54(D).) At that time, the contractor must also file a performance bond for the amount of the contract price. (Ohio Revised Code Annotated § 153.54(C).) If the winning bidder fails or refuses to sign the contract within ten days of the award, the winning bidder is liable for the lesser of the difference between that bidder's bid price and that of the next lowest bidder's price, a penal sum of 10 percent of the bid, or the awarding authority's re-solicitation costs. (Ohio Revised Code Annotated § 153.54(B)–(D).)

9. Notice to Proceed

After contract execution, the contractor may request a notice to proceed from the awarding authority. (Ohio Revised Code Annotated § 153.12(A).)

10. Restrictions on Contract Formation

The parties may not form a contract if the contract price exceeds the estimated cost of the project by more than 10 percent. (Ohio Revised Code Annotated § 153.12(A).) This rule also applies to projects involving multiple contracts where the total price for the project exceeds the estimated cost of the project by more than 10 percent. (Ohio Revised Code Annotated § 153.12(A).)

C. Non-ODOT Construction Guaranty Requirements

1. Bid Guaranties

Ohio Revised Code Annotated section 153.54 governs guaranty requirements for construction contracts with counties, municipal corporations, and state agencies other than ODOT. Contractors must include with their bids either a bid bond for the full amount of the bid or a certified check, cashier's check, or letter of credit for 10 percent of the bid. (Ohio Revised Code Annotated § 153.54(A).) Bid securities must be conditioned upon the bidder's entering a proper contract with the awarding authority. (Ohio Revised Code Annotated § 153.54(B)(1), (C).)

a. Failure to Form a Proper Contract

If the bidder fails to execute the contract, and the public owner awards the contract to the next lowest bidder, then the bidder and its surety are liable. Liability is the lesser of the contracting authority's increased cost or a 10 percent penalty. (Ohio Revised Code § 153.54(D).) If the contracting authority re-advertises the bid, then liability is a 10 percent penalty or the costs associated with re-soliciting the procurement, whichever is less. (Ohio Revised Code Annotated § 153.54(E).)

b. Bonds

Bid bonds serve as performance and payment bonds. They must indemnify the public owner against all damage suffered by the contractor's failure to perform the contract and the contractor's failure to pay legal claims for labor and materials furnished under the contract. (Ohio Revised Code Annotated § 153.54(B)(2).)

c. Checks and Letters of Credit

When the bid guaranty is a check or letter of credit, the winning bidder must submit performance and payment bonds for the amount of the contract. (Ohio Revised Code Annotated § 153.54(B)(2), (C)(1).)

2. Bond Withdrawal

Contractors may withdraw construction contract bid bonds without penalty under certain circumstances.

a. Substantial and Unintentional Error

Contractors may withdraw erroneous bids. This rule applies only to good faith bids that are significantly lower than the other bids. The contractor's error must have been caused by a substantial arithmetic error or an unintentional omission of a substantial quantity of work, labor, or material in the compilation of the bid. Contractors may not withdraw bids if withdrawal would result in an award to the same bidder on a different bid or if the error was based on poor judgment. Withdrawing bidders cannot supply material or labor to, or perform any work for, the winning contractor without approval from the contracting authority. (Ohio Revised Code Annotated § 9.31. See also Ohio Revised Code Annotated § 153.54(B).)

b. Multiple Awards

A contractor may withdraw its bid when the state or one of its political subdivisions accepts the contractor's bid for another project. This rule applies only where both contracts are for less than $500,000. (Ohio Revised Code Annotated § 153.54(G).) To do this, the bidder must certify that the total value of all its current contracts is less than $500,000. (Ohio Revised Code Annotated § 153.54(G).) The bidder's surety must also certify that the bidder cannot perform the subsequent contract without exceeding the bidder's bonding capacity. (Ohio Revised Code Annotated § 153.54(G).) Upon withdrawal, the contracting authority may either award the contract to the next lowest bidder or reject all bids and re-solicit the project. (Ohio Revised Code Annotated § 153.54(G).)

c. *Timing*

Contractors must submit their claims for withdrawal within two business days of the bid opening. (Ohio Revised Code Annotated § 9.31.)

d. *Contesting Withdrawal*

Contracting authorities may contest a bidder's right to withdrawal. Under Ohio Revised Code Annotated section 9.31, the contracting authority must hold a hearing within ten days following bid opening to challenge withdrawal. (Ohio Revised Code Annotated § 9.31.)

e. *Consequences of Withdrawal*

When a contractor withdraws its bid, the contracting authority may either award the contract to the next lowest bidder or reject all bids and re-advertise. (Ohio Revised Code Annotated § 9.31.) Contracting authorities may hold withdrawing bidders liable for costs associated with re-soliciting the procurement. (Ohio Revised Code Annotated § 9.31.)

3. Bond Reductions

Contracting authorities may reduce performance bonds for partial contract performance on public improvement construction contracts with the state, a political subdivision, or a state agency other than ODOT. The contracting authority may reduce a bond by 25 percent after 50 percent contract completion and 50 percent after 75 percent contract completion provided the contractor satisfies several other requirements. (Ohio Revised Code Annotated § 153.80(B)(1).) Those include (1) satisfactory and contractually compliant work; (2) no unresolved or disputed claims; and (3) contract pricing within 10 percent of the next lowest bid and the cost estimate for the project. (Ohio Revised Code Annotated § 153.80(B)(1).)

4. County and Municipal Road Construction Projects

County and municipal road construction contracts are subject to the same bonding requirements outlined above. (See Ohio Revised Code Annotated § 5555.61; Ohio Revised Code § 5559.13.)

D. State Highway Construction

1. ODOT

ODOT is responsible for the construction and repair of the state's highways. (Ohio Revised Code Annotated § 5501.11.)

2. Competitive Bidding Exceptions

The director of ODOT estimates the cost of each prospective project. (Ohio Revised Code Annotated § 5517.02(A).) ODOT may also bypass competition to (1) perform repair and maintenance work estimated to cost less than $30,000 per mile, exclusive of structures and traffic control signals; (2) construct any single structure or traffic signal estimated to cost less than $60,000; and (3) complete emergency bridge or road work. (Ohio Revised Code Annotated § 5517.02(B), (C).)

3. Competitive Bidding

ODOT must competitively let its contracts to the lowest competent and responsible bidder. (Ohio Revised Code Annotated § 5517.02(E).)

a. Invitation to Bid

The director of transportation must advertise ODOT procurements for two consecutive weeks in an appropriate newspaper. (Ohio Revised Code Annotated § 5525.01.) That notice must identify the due date for bids and a location for prospective contractors to review the project details. (Ohio Revised Code Annotated § 5525.01.)

b. Bid Guaranties and Information Accompanying Bids

Prospective contractors must submit bid guaranties with their bids. (Ohio Revised Code Annotated § 5525.01.) Each bidder must also furnish the director detailed information about all the bidder's pending work and any other information the director considers necessary. (Ohio Revised Code Annotated § 5525.01.) If a bidder fails to submit the required information and then fails or refuses to correct this error at the director's request, the bidder may forfeit its bid guaranty. (Ohio Revised Code Annotated § 5525.01.)

c. Bid Withdrawal

Bidders may withdrawal their bids without forfeiting their bid guaranty where there is a bid mistake. The bidder must make a written request to withdraw the bid within 48 hours after the bid deadline. This written request must include a sworn statement indicating the grounds for withdraw. To be withdrawn, a bid must be submitted in good faith and the mistake must be a clerical error, a substantial omission, or a miscalculation. The bid must also be substantially lower than the other bids. (Ohio Revised Code Annotated § 5525.01.)

d. Restrictions on Withdrawal

Bidders may not withdraw bids based on a mistake in judgment. If the director decides that the bid has not met the conditions for withdrawal, the director may award the contract to the low bidder, notwithstanding the allegations of mistake. If the low bidder refuses to sign the contract, the director may forfeit the bidder's bid guaranty. (Ohio Revised Code Annotated § 5525.01.)

e. Rejecting Bids

ODOT may reject any or all bids. (Ohio Revised Code Annotated § 5525.01.)

f. Contract Award

ODOT must award its contracts to the *lowest competent and responsible qualified bidder* within ten days after it opens the bids. (Ohio Revised Code Annotated § 5525.01. See also Ohio Revised Code Annotated §§ 5525.02 through 5525.09 (describing lowest competent and responsible qualified bidder).) Upon awarding the contract, ODOT must return the other contractors' bid guaranties. (Ohio Revised Code Annotated § 5525.01.) Although Ohio Revised Code Annotated section 9.312 does not specifically apply to ODOT, it is helpful in understanding the competent and responsible provisions of Ohio Revised Code Annotated section 5525.01.

g. Contract Formation

The winning bidder has ten days after receiving the award to contract for the work and to furnish both performance and repayment bonds. (Ohio Revised Code Annotated § 5525.01.) When the winning bidder enters a contract with the contracting authority, the contracting authority must then return the bidder's bid bond. (Ohio Revised Code Annotated § 5525.01.) If the winning bidder fails to comply with these rules, the bidder forfeits its bid bond as liquidated damages. (Ohio Revised Code Annotated § 5525.01.)

h. Payment and Performance Bonds

Before ODOT may execute a contract, the winning bidder must provide the director with payment and performance bonds. (Ohio Revised Code Annotated § 5525.16(A).) If the bidder is awarded the contract but fails or refuses to furnish the performance and payment bonds, then it forfeits its bid guaranty as liquidated damages. (Ohio Revised Code Annotated § 5525.01.) The performance bond must be for the estimated cost of the work, and it must be conditioned on the contractor's timely completion of the contract. (Ohio Revised Code Annotated § 5525.16(A)(1).) Performance bonds must indemnify the state against any damages resulting from the contractor's failure to adequately perform. (Ohio Revised Code Annotated § 5525.16(A)(1).) Payment bonds are conditioned on full payment by the contractor and all subcontractors for labor and materials used on the project. (Ohio Revised Code Annotated § 5525.16(A)(2).)

i. Contract Restrictions

ODOT may not enter into a contract for a price more than 5 percent above the estimated cost of the project. (Ohio Revised Code Annotated § 5525.10.) If the director receives no bids within the estimate, the director must cancel the solicitation. The director may then re-advertise the project using the same cost estimate or may revise the cost estimate. (Ohio Revised Code Annotated § 5525.10.)

j. Confidential Cost Estimate Exception

The director may keep ODOT's cost estimates confidential until the director receives all bids. (Ohio Revised Code Annotated § 5525.15.) The estimates remain confidential until the director publicly announces them at the bid opening. (Ohio Revised Code Annotated § 5525.15.) When ODOT uses this procedure, the prohibition against awarding contracts for 5 percent above the estimate does not apply. (Ohio Revised Code Annotated § 5525.15.) When the successful bid exceeds the cost estimate, the director must be satisfied that it is fair and reasonable before awarding the contract. (Ohio Revised Code Annotated § 5525.15.)

k. Foreign Corporations, Partnerships, and Persons

Ohio law prohibits contracts between ODOT and foreign corporations unless the secretary of state certifies the corporation to transact business in Ohio. (Ohio Revised

Code Annotated § 5525.18.) If ODOT awards the contract to a nonresident person or partnership, then ODOT may execute the contract only after the entity has filed a power of attorney with the secretary of state allowing the secretary to accept service of process for that person or entity. (Ohio Revised Code Annotated § 5525.18.)

4. Contractor Prequalification

Ohio Revised Code Annotated section 5525.02 requires ODOT to prequalify bidders for its road and highway projects. ODOT may not consider bids from non-qualified companies. (Ohio Revised Code Annotated § 5525.08.) Qualification is at the director's discretion. The director may consider equipment, past records, experience, personnel, and other matters deemed necessary by the director in determining a bidder's qualifications. (Ohio Revised Code Annotated § 5525.05.) Bidders must possess sufficient assets or working capital to assure satisfactory completion of the contract. (Ohio Revised Code Annotated § 5525.04.) In addition, winning contractors may not enter into subcontracts with non-qualified companies. (Ohio Revised Code Annotated § 5525.06.)

E. Non-Construction Source Selection Techniques

1. Architectural, Construction Management, and Other Professional Service Procurement

a. Governing Statutes

Ohio Revised Code Annotated sections 153.65 to 153.99 govern procurement of professional design services[2] by the state and its agencies.

b. Invitation to Bid

State agencies must publicly announce all projects that include estimated design services over $50,000. (Ohio Revised Code Annotated §§ 153.67, 153.71.) In those cases, state agencies must send announcements to each design firm qualified to perform the project or post an announcement with trade associations or media outlets. (Ohio Revised Code Annotated § 153.67(D).) The announcement must indicate the required contractor qualifications and how to respond. (Ohio Revised Code Annotated § 153.67(B)–(C).) State agencies must provide adequate opportunity for firms to submit statements of interest in the project. (Ohio Revised Code Annotated § 153.67(A).)

c. Firm Ranking

A state agency must select and rank the three firms most qualified to provide the design services it seeks. The contracting authority must determine these rankings based on a number of factors. These factors include a firm's qualification statement, a firm's contract statement, the contracting authority's discussions with a firm, and a firm's proposed technical approach to the project. (Ohio Revised Code Annotated § 153.69(A).) If the contracting authority determines that there are fewer than three qualified firms available, then it must rank only the qualified firms. (Ohio Revised Code Annotated § 153.69(A).)

---

2. Professional design services include those of architects, landscape architects, professional engineers, and surveyors. OHIO REV. CODE ANN. § 153.65 (2013).

d. Firm Selection and Contract Negotiation

After ranking the firms, the agency must attempt to negotiate a contract with the firm it considers the *most highly qualified* to perform the project. The agency must set compensation at a fair and reasonable rate. (Ohio Revised Code Annotated § 153.69(B).) If the contracting authority cannot reach a deal with the highest ranked firm, then it must attempt to negotiate with the next most qualified firm. This procedure continues until the parties execute a contract. (Ohio Revised Code Annotated § 153.69(D).) If the contracting authority cannot negotiate a contract with any of the ranked firms, then it must rank more firms and attempt to negotiate contracts with them. (Ohio Revised Code Annotated § 153.69(E).)

e. Emergency Exception

The provisions of Ohio Revised Code Annotated sections 153.65 to 153.99 do not apply when the public authority determines that there is an emergency requiring immediate attention. (Ohio Revised Code Annotated § 153.71(B).)

f. Firm Prequalification

The state and its agencies may prequalify professional design firms seeking to provide design services. (Ohio Revised Code Annotated § 153.68.) Agencies may require that each firm maintain a filed statement of its qualifications. (Ohio Revised Code Annotated § 153.68.) Qualifications include (1) competence, as indicated by training, education, and personnel experience; (2) ability of the firm to handle the required workload, as indicated by facilities, personnel, and equipment; (3) past performance as indicated by the evaluations by previous clients with respect to cost, quality, and prompt completion; and (4) any other relevant consideration. (Ohio Revised Code Annotated § 153.65.)

2. Employing a Construction Manager

Ohio Revised Code Annotated sections 9.33 to 9.332 apply where the state or a political subdivision wishes to employee a construction manager.

a. Invitation to Bid

Public owners must advertise contracts for the employment of construction managers in an appropriate newspaper. (Ohio Revised Code Annotated § 9.331(A).) The advertisement must contain a general description of the project, a statement of the specific services sought, and a description of the qualifications required by the project. (Ohio Revised Code Annotated § 9.331(B).)

b. Firm Ranking, Firm Selection, and Contract Negotiation

The public owner uses similar procedures mandated for state agencies seeking professional design services. (Ohio Revised Code Annotated § 9.332.)

c. Special Rules for Counties

A county may competitively let its construction manager procurements. Such procurements, however, are excepted from Ohio's competitive bidding requirements. (Ohio Revised Code Annotated § 307.86.)

F. Procurement of Goods and Non-Professional Services

1. DAS

The state agencies must make purchases of supplies and services over $50,000 through DAS. (Ohio Revised Code Annotated § 125.05.) DAS must competitively let such contracts to the *lowest responsive and responsible bidder*. (Ohio Revised Code Annotated § 125.11.) DAS must advertise posted in any electronic form the DAS director considers appropriate to sufficiently notify competing persons. (Ohio Revised Code Annotated § 125.07(A)–(D).) The advertisements must state when and where DAS will open bids, any bid conditions, the bid terms, and a list of the desired goods or services. (Ohio Revised Code Annotated § 125.07(B).)

2. Counties

A county must competitively bid its purchases of goods or non-professional services over $50,000. (Ohio Revised Code Annotated § 307.86.[3]) Counties must follow similar competitive procedures for goods and non-professional services that they follow for construction procurement. (Ohio Revised Code Annotated §§ 307.86–307.921.)

3. Municipal Corporations

Municipal corporations must purchase goods and services in accordance with Ohio Revised Code Annotated sections 731.14 to 731.15 in the case of a village, and Ohio Revised Code Annotated sections 735.05 to 735.06 in the case of a city. The procedures outlined in those sections mimic the competitive requirements for municipal construction procurement. (*Compare* Ohio Revised Code Annotated §§ 731.14 to 731.15, *with* Ohio Revised Code Annotated §§ 735.05 to 735.06.)

G. Bond Requirements

1. The State

DAS may require contractors to submit with their bids a bond payable to the state and conditioned on faithful and timely performance of the contract. (Ohio Revised Code § 125.38.)

2. Counties

Contractors must give a bid guaranty to provide goods or non-professional services over $50,000 to a county. (Ohio Revised Code Annotated § 307.88(A).) Bid guaranties must be conditioned on the execution of a contract conforming with the invitation to bid. (Ohio Revised Code Annotated § 307.88(A).) When a contracting authority accepts a bid, it may also require a performance bond identical to that required for state construction projects. (Ohio Revised Code Annotated § 307.89.)

---

3. For exceptions to this competitive bidding requirement, see OHIO REV. CODE ANN. § 307.86(A)–(N) (2020).

3. Municipal Corporations

Contractors must provide a sufficient bond, certified check, cashier's check, or money order with their bids for non-construction contracts with municipal corporations. This guaranty certifies that if the contracting authority accepts a contractor's bid, the contractor will fully perform. (Ohio Revised Code Annotated § 735.06.)

4. Bond Reduction

Contracting authorities may reduce performance bonds on contracts for goods and services with the state, a political subdivision, or a state agency other than ODOT. The contracting authority may reduce a bond by 25 percent after the contractor has performed 50 percent of the contract. (Ohio Revised Code Annotated § 9.313.) The contracting authority may reduce a performance bond by 50 percent after the contractor has performed at least 75 percent of the contract. (Ohio Revised Code Annotated § 9.313.)

H. Preferences and Set-Aside Programs

1. Local Construction Preferences

If a foreign construction contractor would receive a preference for similar work in its home state, then Ohio contracting authorities must prefer Ohio contractors in contracts involving the state or a state-supported institution. (Ohio Revised Code Annotated § 153.012.) The contracting authority's preference for an Ohio contractor must be identical to the preference provided by the foreign contractor's state. (Ohio Revised Code Annotated § 153.012.) The Ohio preference statute is reactive and does not disadvantage bidders from states that allow Ohio contractors to bid on their public works projects without penalty.

2. Non-Construction Preferences

Before DAS may award a supply contract, DAS must first determine if the offering is a U.S. domestic source end product. DAS must reject all goods not meeting this standard unless it determines that the goods or services involved are not sufficiently available in the United States. (OAC 123:5-1-06(A)(1).) Following a determination that products are domestic source end products, DAS gives preference to domestic Ohio bids for products produced or mined in Ohio or a border state. (OAC 123:5-1-06(A)(2).)

a. Contract Award

If there is sufficient competition, DAS may award the contract to the *lowest responsive and responsible bidder* from among bids offering goods produced or mined in Ohio. DAS may also award the contract to bidders from states bordering Ohio, as long as those border states do not penalize Ohio bidders in their procurement system. It may also award to contractors from other states or countries within North America as long as the bidder has a significant Ohio economic presence. (Ohio Revised Code Annotated § 125.09(C)(4)–(5).) DAS cannot make an award based on unannounced evaluation criteria whereby the variations from the instructions or specifications is substantial, affects the amount of the bid, and gives the bidder an advantage or benefit not allowed to other bidders. (*Cleveland Construction, Inc. v. Ohio Department of Administrative Services, General Services Administration*, 700 N.E.2d 54 (Ohio Ct. App. 1997).)

b. Lowest Responsive and Responsible from Non-Ohio Bidder

If the apparent *lowest responsive and responsible bidder* is not from Ohio or its bordering states, then DAS shall apply the following preferences: (1) if the apparent low bid offers a domestic source end product, apply a 5 percent increase to the price; (2) if the apparent low bid offers a foreign produce, apply a 6 percent increase to the price; and (3) if sufficient competition does not exist or all prices are determined to be excessive, DAS may cancel the bid, re-bid, or award the contract. (OAC Annotated 123:5-1-06(A)(3).) After application of these preferences, DAS may award to either the non-Ohio bidder or, if the administrator determines that the selection of the lowest Ohio bid does not result in an excessive price or a disproportionately inferior product or service, then DAS may award to the lowest and best Ohio bidder notwithstanding the lower price of the non-Ohio bidder. (OAC Annotated 123:5-1-06(A)(4).)

c. Buy American Certificate

All invitations to bid require bidders to execute a Buy American Certificate. The language of this certificate is found in OAC Annotated 123:5-1-06(B). Ohio invitations to bid also require certain Buy Ohio product and bidder information. This includes (1) the identity of any non-Ohio products being offered; (2) a representation that all other products are Ohio products; and (3) a representation that the bidder claims to qualify as offering an Ohio product or as having a significant Ohio presence. (OAC Annotated 123:5-1-06(C).)

3. Model Preference System

The director of DAS must publish, as a model act, a system of local preferences both for products mined or produced in Ohio and for Ohio contractors. (Ohio Revised Code Annotated § 125.11(E).) This act is similar to the system of preferences under which the state operates pursuant to Ohio Revised Code Annotated chapter 125 and Ohio Revised Code Annotated section 153.012. (Ohio Revised Code Annotated § 125.11(E).) Any county, township, or municipal corporation may, by resolution of its legislative authority, adopt this model system with respect to any contract for goods, services, or public improvements. (Ohio Revised Code Annotated § 307.90(B) (counties); § 505.103 (townships); § 717.21 (municipal corporations).)

4. Set-Aside Programs

a. Minority Business Enterprise Set-Asides

Ohio law establishes a set-aside program for minority business enterprises (MBEs).

b. DAS

The director of DAS must set aside 15 percent of its purchases for competition by MBEs. (Ohio Revised Code Annotated § 125.081(A).) Procedures within the set-aside are the same as for all other DAS purchases except that only MBEs compete. (Ohio Revised Code Annotated § 125.081(A).)

c. Other State Agencies

State agencies must also set aside 15 percent of their purchases for competition by MBEs. Procedures within the set-aside are the same as for all other agency purchases except that only MBEs compete. (Ohio Revised Code Annotated § 125.081(B).)

d. No MBE Bids

If no MBE submits a bid, the purchase is governed by the normal competitive procedures. In such cases, the contracting agency shall set aside additional purchases for which only MBEs may compete. The contracting agency must ensure that MBE set-asides equal approximately 15 percent of its total yearly expenditures. (Ohio Revised Code Annotated § 125.081(C).)

5. Encouraging Diversity, Growth, and Equity Program

The Ohio Code requires the director of DAS to establish a business assistance program known as the Encouraging Diversity, Growth, and Equity (EDGE) program. (Ohio Revised Code Annotated § 123.152(B).) The goal of the EDGE program is to make all state contracts, services, benefits, and opportunities available to businesses without discrimination based on race, color, religion, sex, national origin, disability, age, or ancestry. The program is designed to facilitate access to state government contracts and business services for EDGE-certified businesses.

6. EDGE Business Enterprise

"EDGE business enterprise" means a sole proprietorship, association, partnership, corporation, limited liability corporation, or joint venture certified as a participant in the EDGE program by the director of administrative services under the relevant section of the Ohio Revised Code. (Ohio Revised Code Annotated § 123.152(A).) The EDGE program establishes goals for state agencies in awarding contracts to certified EDGE businesses based on the availability of eligible program participants by region. EDGE procurement contracts apply to goods and services, professional services, information technology services, construction, architecture, and engineering. (Ohio Revised Code Annotated § 123.152.)

7. EDGE Eligibility

Businesses interested in becoming an EDGE-certified contractor must apply to the Ohio DAS Equal Opportunity Division for certification. To be considered eligible for certification, a business must be (1) a small business enterprise; (2) owned by a U.S. citizen and Ohio resident; (3) in business one year prior to applying for certification; and (4) at least 51 percent owned and controlled by a socially and economically disadvantaged business owner *or* economically disadvantaged business and located in a qualified census tract. (OAC 123:2-14-02.)

8. EDGE Benefits

EDGE-certified businesses are eligible for contract assistance, financial and bonding assistance, management and technical assistance, and protégé opportunities with industry mentors. (Ohio Revised Code Annotated § 123.152.)

IV. Bid Protests and Contract Disputes

A. Bid Protests

1. Award Other Than to the Lowest Responsive and Responsible Bidder

When a contracting authority awards a contract to other than the apparent low bidder, the contracting authority must notify the apparent low bidder of its decision.

(Ohio Revised Code Annotated § 9.312(A).) If the apparent low bidder files a written agency protest within five days, then the contracting authority must meet with the bidder before awarding the contract. (Ohio Revised Code Annotated § 9.312(B).) The contracting authority must affirm or reverse its initial decision before making its final award. (Ohio Revised Code Annotated § 9.312(B).)

2. Protest Letter

If a contractor decides to file a bid protest, the contractor should provide the agency with a thorough explanation of the relevant facts. A protest letter should present a complete narrative of the protest grounds, include documentary support and affidavits, and include legal analysis. The protest letter should also state whether the contractor seeks contract award or mere procurement re-solicitation. (See Ohio Revised Code Annotated § 9.312(B).)

3. Forum Selection and Standing

a. Proper Forum

If a disappointed bidder does not believe that the purchasing agency can adequately address its protest, then the bidder can file suit in one of two forums. If a disappointed bidder is seeking only equitable relief, then it may file in either the court of claims or the court of common pleas. If a bidder is seeking either damages or damages coupled with equitable relief, then it must sue in the court of claims. (See *Meccon, Inc. v. University of Akron*, 911 N.E.2d 933, 935 (Ohio Ct. App. 2009), *aff'd*, 933 N.E.2d 231 (Ohio 2010).)

b. Standing

There are four circumstances under which a party has standing to protest a bid. They are (1) contractors' associations whose members either are qualified to bid, and who did bid, or whose members sought to obtain work as subcontractors on the project; (2) contractors qualified to bid on department projects who purchased plans and who did bid as prime contractors; (3) contractors qualified to bid on department projects who purchased plans and sought to obtain contracts as subcontracts; and (4) Ohio taxpayers who are specially affected by the bid conditions. (*State ex rel. Connors v. Ohio Department of Transportation*, 455 N.E.2d 1331, 1331–32 (Ohio Ct. App. 1982).)

4. Remedies

a. Available Relief

Various relief is available when a contracting authority wrongfully awards a contract. First, the protesting bidder should seek a preliminary injunction or temporary restraining order to postpone or suspend award of the contract until resolution of the protest on the merits. Second, the disappointed bidder must seek a writ of mandamus that directs the purchasing agency either to award the contract to the bidder or to cancel the procurement and re-issue the invitation to bid. (See *CB Transportation, Inc. v. Butler County Board of Mental Retardation*, 397 N.E.2d 781 (Ohio Ct. Com. Pl. 1979).)

b. Damages

Depending on the circumstances, the disappointed bidder may seek damages. Proving damages, however, is very difficult. At least two Ohio courts have rejected the concept of monetary damages to recover lost profits in a bid protest action. (See

Cementech, Inc. v. Fairlawn, 109 Ohio St. 3d 475 (2010) (Ohio Supreme Court ruled that a wrongfully rejected bidder cannot recover its purported lost profits because it harms the taxpayers who the competitive bidding laws were intended to protect); *Hardrives Paving & Construction, Inc. v. City of Niles*, 650 N.E.2d 482 (Ohio Ct. App. 1994) (finding that monetary damages are against public policy because they work a hardship upon taxpayers).) However, where a rejected bidder can show it sought injunctive relief, which was denied, and later successfully proves that the public authority wrongfully rejected its bid, the Ohio Supreme Court has found that bidder is entitled to recover its bid preparation costs. (*Meccon, Inc. v. University of Akron*, 933 N.E.2d 231 (Ohio 2010).)

B. Contract Disputes

1. Pre-Completion Disputes

Resolution of disputes after award and during performance of a contract are governed by general contract principles. Like protests, there are two forums where disputes may be resolved—in the agency and in the court of claims. When a dispute first arises, the contractor should attempt to resolve it with the agency in the form of a claim. To be binding, administrative claim resolution procedures must be included in a contract. (A.H. Gaede, Jr. et al., *Fifty State Public Construction Contracting* § 37.26 (1st ed. 1996).)

2. Construction and Public Improvement Contracts

After exhausting the administrative remedies, a contractor may attempt to resolve its dispute in court. For construction contract disputes, contractors must file their claims with the court of claims. Contractor and purchasing agencies then have the choice of proceeding judicially or in an arbitration-type process. (Ohio Revised Code Annotated § 153.12(B).)

V. Administrative and Judicial Review

A. Standard of Review

1. Abuse of Discretion

Ohio courts presume that public officials perform their duties properly and legally. (*State ex rel. Shafer v. Ohio Turnpike Commission*, 113 N.E.2d 14 (Ohio 1953).) Courts do not interfere, therefore, with a proposed contract award unless there is a clear abuse of discretion. (*Dayton ex rel. Scandrick v. McGee*, 423 N.E.2d 1095 (Ohio 1981).) An abuse of discretion occurs only when the courts have found that (1) the bids have been altered materially after bid opening; (2) the contracting authority alters the bid evaluation criteria after bid opening; or (3) the contracting authority acts fraudulently, in bad faith, or with an unreasonable, arbitrary, or unconscionable attitude. (*Cleveland Construction, Inc. v. Ohio Department of Administrative Services, General Services Administration*, 700 N.E.2d 54 (Ohio Ct. App. 1997); *Dayton ex rel. Scandrick v. McGee*, 423 N.E.2d 1095, 1098 (Ohio 1981); *State ex rel. H.P. Clough & Co. v. Commissioners of Shelby County*, 36 Ohio St. 326 (1881).) A municipality may not award a contract based on unannounced criteria. (*Dayton ex rel. Scandrick v. McGee*, 423 N.E.2d 1095 (Ohio 1981).) Nor may a government entity waive bid requirements that destroy the competitive bidding process. (*Kokosing Construction Co. v. Dixon*, 594 N.E.2d 675 (Ohio Ct. App. 1991).) Where a public entity substantially complies with announced procedures expressly set forth in the bid proposal, no abuse of discretion occurs. (*Danis Clarkco Landfill Co. v. Clark County Solid Waste Management District*, 653 N.E. 2d 646 (Ohio 1995); *Kokosing Construction Co. v. Dixon*, 594 N.E. 2d 675 (Ohio Ct. App. 1991).)

2. Injunction Standard

Ohio courts consider and balance four factors to determine whether to grant a preliminary injunction or temporary restraining order to suspend any contract award until resolution of a bid protest. These factors include (1) the movant's likelihood of success on the merits of the claim; (2) whether the movant will suffer immediate and irreparable injury if the preliminary injunction is not issued; (3) any harm resulting to others if the preliminary injunction or temporary restraining order is issued; and (4) the public interest. (*Vanguard Transportation Systems, Inc. v. Edwards Transfer & Storage Co.*, 673 N.E.2d 182 (Ohio Ct. App. 1996); *Beasley v. East Cleveland*, 486 N.E.2d 859 (Ohio Ct. App. 1984). *See also* Ohio Revised Code Annotated § 2727.02; Ohio Rule of Civil Procedure 65.) Courts take a particular caution in granting injunctions in cases affecting a public interest where a court is asked to interfere with or suspend the operation of important works or control the action of another department of government. (*Danis Clarkco Landfill Co. v. Clark County Solid Waste Management District*, 653 N.E.2d 646 (Ohio 1995); *Leaseway Distribution Centers, Inc. v. Department of Administrative Services*, 550 N.E.2d 955 (Ohio Ct. App. 1988).)

VI. Extent of State's Adoption or Adaptation of ABA Model Procurement Code

There is no evidence to confirm that Ohio has adopted the American Bar Association (ABA) Model Procurement Code.

VII. Cooperative Purchasing

A. Authority

The State of Ohio permits cooperative purchasing, which allows certain governmental entities to avail themselves of existing cooperative purchasing agreements without themselves having to engage in competitive bidding.

Political subdivisions, including counties, municipal corporations, townships, special districts, and school districts, are permitted to utilize cooperative purchasing for the procurement of "equipment, materials, supplies or services" pursuant to Ohio Revised Code Annotated section 9.48.

Ohio regional councils of governments (COGs), which can include non-Ohio political subdivisions as members, may also engage in cooperative purchasing pursuant to Ohio Revised Code Annotated section 167.081.[4]

Similarly, Ohio Revised Code Annotated section 125.04 permits state institutions of higher education, governmental agencies, political subdivisions, county boards of elections, private fire companies, private nonprofit emergency medical service organizations, and chartered non-public schools to participate in contracts into which DAS has entered for the purchase of supplies and services.

---

4. The rules regarding COGs can be found generally in Ohio Rev. Code Ann. ch. 167.

B. Requirements

There has been considerable debate in Ohio about whether "construction services" are eligible for cooperative purchasing under Ohio Revised Code Annotated section 9.48. This debate was caused when, on August 13, 2019, the Ohio attorney general issued Opinion No. 2019-028 explaining that "construction services" may not be purchased using cooperative purchasing under Ohio Revised Code Annotated section 9.48 because that category of procurement is not specifically identified. However, Opinion No. 2019-028 also explains that political subdivisions who are members of regional COGs may procure construction services using cooperative purchasing under Ohio Revised Code Annotated section 167.081 so long as the cooperative purchasing contract (1) contains unit prices for material, labor, or services; (2) provides for the repair, enlargement, improvement, or demolition of a building or structure (e.g., construction services); and (3) was awarded pursuant to a competitive bidding procedure of a governmental entity that is a member of a multistate consortium of which the COG is also a member. (Ohio Revised Code Annotated § 167.081.)

Oklahoma Procurement Rules and Regulations

Prepared by Melissa J. Copeland[1]
Schmidt & Copeland, LLC
Email: missy@schmidtcopeland.com

I. Statutory Reference

This summary covers acquisitions made by agencies of the State of Oklahoma. These acquisitions are governed by the Central Purchasing Act codified at Oklahoma Statutes (OS) title 74, section 85.1 *et seq.*, the Public Competitive Bidding Act codified at OS title 51, section 101 *et seq.*, and, in part, the Public Finance Act codified at OS title 62, sections 34.11.1–34.33, respectively.

The state agency responsible for procurement functions of state agencies is the Office of Management and Enterprise Services (OMES). Although OMES is made up of several subdivisions, only three handle the various procurement responsibilities. They are Central Purchasing, Information Services, and Capital Assets Management. The procurement of construction services is handled by Capital Assets Management. Central Purchasing, with the state purchasing director at the helm, handles the procurement of all goods and services, including the procurement of information technology and telecommunications goods and services. Information Services is headed up by the state chief information officer (CIO). OS titles 62 and 74 and title 260 of the Oklahoma Administrative Code (OAC) provide that the CIO has the same power and authority regarding procurement of all information technology and telecommunications products and services for all state agencies as the state purchasing director.

A. Procurement/Purchasing Statutes

The State of Oklahoma has not codified all of its procurement statutes into one consolidated code. However, as mentioned above, all state agency acquisitions are governed by the Central Purchasing Act codified at OS title 74, section 85.1 *et seq.*, the Public Competitive Bidding Act codified at OS title 61, section 101 *et seq.*, particular statutes of the Public Finance Act codified at OS title 62, sections 34.11.1–34.33, and the Information Technology Consolidation and Coordination Act codified at OS title 62, section 35.1 *et seq.* With the exception of the procurement of construction, the procurement

1. Prior edition prepared by Ferris J. Barger, state purchasing director, Tracy Hird, Office of Management and Enterprise Services (OMES) deputy general counsel, Tim Tuck, OMES deputy general counsel, and Kendell Shropshire, OMES legal assistant.

of all goods and services by state agencies follows the Central Purchasing Act. The Public Finance Act and the Information Technology Consolidation and Coordination Act provide further instruction on the procurement of information technology goods and services. Construction procurement is governed by the Public Competitive Bidding Act.

The Central Purchasing Act applies to every state agency in whole or part with the exception of an enumerated few that are exempt from the act. Pursuant to OS title 74, section 85.3A, the Central Purchasing Act does not apply to county government, the Oklahoma State Regents for Higher Education, the institutions, centers, or other constituent agencies of the Oklahoma State System for Higher Education, OneNet, the Department of Public Safety gun range, and the state treasurer for certain purchases. Likewise, the Central Purchasing Act does not apply to political subdivisions. (See OS tit. 74, § 85.2(27), which excludes "political subdivision" from the definition of "state agency," and § 85.2(18) for a definition of "political subdivision.")

The table of contents of the Central Purchasing Act, OS title 74, section 85.1 *et seq.*, is set forth below:

§ 85.1.	Short Title
§ 85.2.	Definitions
§ 85.3.	Purchasing Division—Director—Employees—Encouragement of Certain Purchases—Conflict of Interest
§ 85.3A.	Exempted Entities—Participation in Advisory Committee
§ 85.5.	Powers and Duties of State Purchasing Director
§ 85.5.1.	Oklahoma Privatization Act
§ 85.5a.	State Purchase Card
§ 85.6.	Grade and Quality of Merchandise Delivered
§ 85.7.	Competitive Bid Procedures
§ 85.12.	Act Not to Affect Nonconflicting Procedures—Acquisitions Excluded
§ 85.12b.	Lease, Charter, or Contract for Use of Aircraft—Guidelines
§ 85.17A.	State Agencies Shall Reciprocate Bidding Preference—Awarding Contracts
§ 85.22.	Notarized Sworn Statement Attached to Competitive Bid
§ 85.33.	Registration of State Vendors Revolving Fund
§ 85.33A.	Contract Management Revolving Fund
§ 85.39.	Development and Promulgation of Internal Purchasing Procedures
§ 85.40.	Travel Expenses Incurred by Vendor Included in Contract Award
§ 85.41.	Contracts for Professional Services—Compliance with Act
§ 85.41A.	Emergency Acquisitions
§ 85.42.	Certain Contracts Prohibited—Contract Limitations
§ 85.43.	Annual Report of Acquisitions Exceeding Fifty Thousand Dollars—Contents
§ 85.44B.	Payment for Contracted Products or Services
§ 85.44C.	Unlawful Contract
§ 85.44D.1.	Requisition for Product or Service by Sole Source Contract
§ 85.44EE.	Disabled Veteran Business Enterprise Act

The table of contents of the Public Competitive Bidding Act, OS title 61, section 101 *et seq.*, is set forth below:

§ 101.	Short Title
§ 102.	Definitions
§ 103.	Competitive Bidding Required
§ 103.2.	Political Subdivision May Appoint Purchasing Agent
§ 103.4.	State Agency and School District Exclusion
§ 103.5.	Right of Way Clearance Contracts Below $50,000
§ 103.6.	Contracts Not Exceeding One Hundred Thousand Dollars Not Public Construction Contracts
§ 103.7.	Contracts by the Oklahoma Department of Wildlife Conservation
§ 103.8.	Justification for Contracting with Out-of-State Company
§ 104.	Bid Notices
§ 105.	Contents of Bid Notices
§ 106.	Bidding Documents to be on File
§ 107.	Requirements of Bids Exceeding Certain Amount
§ 108.	Written Statement under Oath to Accompany Bid
§ 109.	Late Bids
§ 110.	Opening of Bids
§ 111.	Time for Awarding of Contract
§ 112.	Bids, Contracts, Bonds open for Public Inspection
§ 113.	Execution of Contract—Bond—Insurance
§ 113.1.	Partial Payment—Retainage
§ 113.2.	Withdrawal of Retainage—Deposit of Securities
§ 113.3.	Interest—Rate
§ 114.	Conflict of Interest
§ 115.	Collusion among Bidders
§ 116.	Disclosure of Terms of Bids
§ 117.	Award to Other Than Lowest Bidder
§ 118.	Prequalification of Bidders
§ 119.	Rejection of Bids
§ 119.1.	Certain Contract to be Negotiated When No Bid Is Received
§ 120.	Assignment of Contracts
§ 121.	Change Orders or Addenda
§ 122.	Taxpayer Suits to Enjoin Execution of Unlawful Contracts
§ 123.	Supervisor's Certification to Accompany Invoices
§ 124.	Inspections
§ 125.	Accounting Procedure
§ 126.	Construction on Force Account Basis
§ 127.	Contracts Made by a Public Entity—Applicability
§ 128.	Insurance against Fire and the Elements
§ 129.	Exemptions—Contracts before August 1, 1974—Contracts for CompSource Oklahoma Pilot Programs

The table of contents of the pertinent statutes of the Public Finance Act, OS title 62, sections 34.11.1–34.33, are set forth below:

§ 34.24.1. Portal System for License Application—Reports—Exemptions
§ 34.25. Convenience Fee for Electronic or Online Transactions
§ 34.26. Electronic Portal System—Open-System Concept
§ 34.27. State Government Technology Applications Review Board
§ 34.28. Accessibility of Information Technology for Individuals with Disabilities
§ 34.29. Definitions
§ 34.30. Electronic and Information Technology Accessibility Advisory Council
§ 34.31. Escrow of Source Code Required for Acquisition of Customized Computer Software—Required Escrow Provisions
§ 34.31.1. Preference for Open Source Software
§ 34.31.2. Public Agency Utilization of State Technology Contracts
§ 34.32. Security Risk Assessment—Reports
§ 34.33. Authority to Develop, Design, and Construct State's Information Technology and Telecommunications Infrastructure and Security

B. Other Applicable Statutes

State Use Statutes (OS tit. 74, §§ 3001–3010): The legislature created the State Use Committee to administer a procurement program promoting meaningful and gainful employment opportunities for persons with severe disabilities. (OS tit. 74, § 3001 *et seq*.) Statutes require OMES to employ within the purchasing division a contracting officer, appointed by the state purchasing director with the advice of the State Use Committee, to solicit, develop, and negotiate contracts with qualified agencies and individuals for the program. The committee may certify qualified sheltered workshops and severely disabled individuals. The committee designates by regulation a procurement schedule of products directly manufactured, produced, processed, or assembled, and services directly performed, offered, or provided by a qualified entity, which the committee determines suitable for procurement by a state agency. Program funds are directly related to the amount of sales by the vendors. One percent of all sales to a state entity from a qualified vendor is deposited into the State Use Revolving Fund for the sole purpose of promoting the program.

Information Technology Consolidation and Coordination Act (OS tit. 62, §§ 35.1–35.9): This act was enacted with the purpose of consolidating the information technology structure, operations, and purchasing procedures of the state.

Online Bidding Act (OS tit. 74, §§ 85.45o–85.45s): This act allows for goods, services, and construction to be procured through electronic or online bidding.

Ethics Laws (OS tit. 74, ch. 62, app. 1): This appendix covers the ethics rules.

Open Records Act (OS tit. 51, §§ 24A.1–24.32): This act ensures and facilitates the public's right of access to and review of government records.

Purchases from Oklahoma Correctional Industries (OS tit. 57, § 549.1): All offices, departments, institutions, agencies, counties, cities, districts or political subdivisions, schools, colleges or universities, or any agency thereof, or any agencies of the state, which are supported in whole or in part by this state, may purchase the goods or services produced by the prison industries of the Department of Corrections through their properly authorized purchasing authority, or they may place a direct order without competitive bid with the prison industries of the Department of Corrections. State agencies shall make maximum utilization of such products, and no similar products shall be purchased by state agencies from any other source than the Department of Corrections except where goods or services are listed on the state use procurement schedule unless the Department of Corrections certifies to the state purchasing director that it is not able to provide products, and no claim therefor shall be paid without such certification.

II. Regulations

A. OMES

OAC title 260, chapter 115 governs procurement for goods and services. The table of contents of chapter 115 appears below:

B. OMES

OAC title 260, chapter 65 governs construction and properties. The table of contents of chapter 65 appears below:

Appendix B.	Formulas for Determining Single Present Worth, Present Worth Factor, and Present Worth Escalating Factor
Appendix C.	Suggested Equipment Life
Appendix D.	Evaluation of Total Life Cycle Cost

III. Source Selection

A. Formal Competitive Bidding—Sealed Bid Submission

1. Goods and Services

No state agency shall make acquisitions exceeding $50,000 without submission of requisition to the state purchasing director and submission of suppliers' sealed competitive bids or proposals to the state purchasing director pursuant to OS title 74, section 85.7(A). State agencies that have internal certified procurement officers and approved internal purchasing procedures may make acquisitions pursuant to applicable requirements of the Purchasing Act and utilizing a formal competitive solicitation process.

2. Information Technology Goods and Services

All state agency requisitions of information technology and telecommunications software, hardware, equipment, peripheral devices, maintenance, consulting services, high-technology systems, and other related information technology, data processing, telecommunications, and related peripherals and services must be submitted to the CIO pursuant to OS title 62, section 34.11.1(H)(1). This provision applies regardless of the dollar amount of the requisition.

3. Construction

All public construction contracts exceeding $100,000 and construction management trade contracts or subcontracts exceeding $50,000 shall be let and awarded to the lowest responsible bidder by open competitive bidding after solicitation for sealed bids pursuant to OS title 61, section 103(A). Construction contracts equal to or greater than $50,000 but less than $100,000 shall be let and awarded to the lowest responsible bidder by receipt of written bids pursuant to OS title 61, section 103(E).

B. Small Purchases—Open Market Acquisitions

1. Goods and Services

State agencies shall make acquisitions not exceeding $25,000 without competitive bidding so long as the acquisition is fair and reasonable pursuant to OS title 74, section 85.5(C)(11)(a).

2. Information Technology Goods or Services

(See Section III.A.1 above.)

3. Construction

Construction contracts for less than $10,000 may be negotiated with a qualified contractor without competitive bidding pursuant to OS title 61, section 103(D).

C. Emergency Procurement

1. Goods and Services

Competitive bidding and submission of a requisition to the state purchasing director is not required for emergency acquisitions by state agencies pursuant to OS title 74, section 85.41A. This applies to both acquisitions of information technology and non-information technology goods and services pursuant to OS title 62, section 34.11.1(H)(1).

2. Construction

Competitive bidding and publication of such notice is not required for emergency construction acquisitions if the governing body of a public agency declares by two-thirds majority vote of the members that an emergency exists, the chief administrative officer of a public agency without a governing body declares that an emergency exists, or the governing body of a public agency by two-thirds majority vote delegates the declaration of an emergency to the chief administrative officer for emergency construction contracts not exceeding $150,000 pursuant to OS title 61, section 130.

D. Sole Source Procurement

Pursuant to OS title 74, section 85.45j, an acquisition may be exempt from competitive bidding procedures as a sole source acquisition. Pursuant to the OMES Procurement Information Memorandum (PIM) Sole Source and Sole Brand Acquisitions, Central Purchasing provides sole source certification guidelines to aid in the determination of whether a sole source or sole brand is the proper acquisition method. This PIM also provides examples of supporting documentation to evidence the necessity of using the sole source or sole brand. The PIM can be found by going to https://oklahoma.gov/omes/services/purchasing/reference-guide/pims.html.

IV. Bid Protests and Contract Disputes

A. Bid Protests

A supplier may protest a contract award of goods or services by a state agency or the purchasing division to the state purchasing director. (OAC § 260:115-3-19.) A supplier may protest a construction contract award by a state agency or the Construction and Properties Department of Capital Assets Management to the state construction administrator. (OAC § 260:65-1-12.) All remedies available to suppliers through the sealed bid process pursuant to the Oklahoma Central Purchasing Act or the Public Building Construction and Planning Act are also available to online bidders in an online bidding process.

A supplier shall submit written notice to the state purchasing director or the state construction administrator of a protest of an award of contract by a state agency, the purchasing division or the Construction and Properties Department within ten business days of contract award. The protest notice shall state supplier facts and reasons for protest.

The state purchasing director or the state construction administrator shall review the supplier's protest and contract award documents. The state purchasing director may either respond to the protest or delegate the responsibility by written notice to the state agency that awarded the contract. However, this option is not available to the state construction administrator. Written notice of the decision by the state purchasing director, the state construction administrator, or the agency, if applicable, to sustain or deny the protest will be sent to the supplier within ten business days of receipt of the protest. An agency making an acquisition for goods and services pursuant to OS title 74, section 85.5(N) shall conduct all actions and bear all costs associated with the protest or appeal of a contract award.

B. Bid Protest Appeals

1. Supplier Appeal

The supplier may appeal a denial of protest by the state purchasing director to the director of OMES. The supplier shall file a written appeal within ten business days of the date of the state purchasing director's or state construction administrator's notice of denial.

2. Stay

With regard to goods and services protest appeals, OAC section 260:115-3-19(a)(3)(B) provides that the OMES director may enter an order staying contract performance upon such terms and conditions as the OMES director determines to be proper. Any request for a stay of contract performance must be made in writing and filed during the ten-business-day time period in which an appeal may be commenced to the OMES director. The director shall have continuing jurisdiction to modify any such orders during the pending of the appeal as appropriate.

3. Appeal Hearing

The director of OMES may hear the protest or assign the supplier's appeal to an administrative law judge the department retains. If the protest is assigned to an administrative law judge, the administrative law judge shall review the protest for legal authority and jurisdiction. If legal authority and jurisdictional requirements are met, the administrative law judge shall conduct an administrative hearing and provide proposed findings of fact and conclusions of law to the director. If the protest is heard by the director, the director shall have all powers granted by law, including all powers delegated to the administrative law judge. The director shall send written notice of the final order sustaining or denying the supplier's appeal to the parties. The cost of actions required by the provisions of the relevant statute, together with other necessary expenses incurred pursuant to the statute, shall be paid by the state agency responsible for the initial solicitation.

4. Conduct of Administrative Hearing

Administrative hearings shall be conducted in accordance with the Administrative Procedures Act (OS tit. 75, § 250 *et seq.*) and the following procedures:

Prehearing Conference: A prehearing conference shall be scheduled to determine the legal or factual issues that shall be limited to those brought by the supplier in its initial protest to the state purchasing director or state construction administrator.

Burden of Proof: The burden of proof shall be upon the supplier, which must prove its case by a preponderance of the evidence. A preponderance of the evidence is that evidence that, in light of the record as a whole, leads the administrative law judge to believe a fact is more probably true than not true.

Representation: Corporations must be represented by legal counsel in accordance with Oklahoma law. Legal counsel must be licensed or registered pursuant to the rules creating and controlling the Oklahoma Bar Association.

Proper Parties: In addition to the supplier protesting the contract award and OMES, the supplier awarded the contract and the state agency for which the bid was let may participate in the bid protest proceedings as a proper party.

Discovery: The conduct of discovery is governed by the Administrative Procedures Act, OS title 75, section 309 *et seq.*, and other applicable law.

5. Authority of the Administrative Law Judge

The administrative law judge may (1) establish a scheduling order; (2) establish reasonable procedures such as authorizing pleadings to be filed by facsimile or electronic mail; (3) rule on all interlocutory motions, including requests for a temporary stay of the contract award pending a final order from the director of OMES; (4) require briefing of any or all issues; (5) conduct hearings; (6) rule on the admissibility of all evidence; (7) question witnesses; and (8) make proposed findings of facts and conclusions of law to the OMES director.

6. Remedies

The administrative law judge may recommend that the OMES director deny the supplier's appeal or that the contract award be cancelled and rebid.

7. Supplier Appeal of OMES Director Denial

If the OMES director denies a supplier's appeal, the supplier may appeal pursuant to provisions of OS title 75, section 309 *et seq.*

C. Contract Disputes

1. Goods and Services (OAC § 260:115-9-1)

Whenever a supplier provides a state agency with defective products or fails to perform in accordance with contract requirements, a state agency shall notify the supplier in writing of the deficiency and include information necessary for the supplier to resolve the problem. If the state agency and supplier are unable to resolve the dispute, the state agency shall submit a written request for dispute resolution to the state purchasing director. If the state purchasing director resolves the dispute, the supplier and state agency shall be notified of the dispute resolution terms and conditions. If the supplier fails to meet the terms or conditions of the dispute resolution, the state purchasing director shall terminate the contract between the supplier and the state agency and may suspend the supplier. If the state agency fails to meet the conditions of the dispute resolution, the state purchasing director may order an audit of the state agency's acquisitions. If the state purchasing director determines that the supplier fails to meet the terms and conditions of the contract, the state purchasing director shall terminate the contract between the supplier and the state agency and may suspend the supplier. If the state purchasing director determines that actions of the state agency fail to meet the terms of the contract, the state purchasing director may order an audit of the state agency's acquisitions. If the state purchasing director terminates a contract between a supplier and a state agency, the attorney general of the State of Oklahoma, the state purchasing director, or the requisitioning agency may seek damages from the supplier. Damages may include additional cost to obtain the acquisition from another supplier, the cost of re-bidding the acquisition, and the cost of acquisition receipt delay.

2. Construction

For a description of how construction contract disputes are handled, see OAC sections 260:65-1-22 and 260:65-1-23.

D. Suspension and Debarment

1. Suspension

Supplier suspension from the suppliers list is governed by OAC section 260:115-3-21.

a. Cause for Suspension

The state purchasing director may suspend a supplier from the suppliers list and from submitting bids to the purchasing division or any other state agency subject to the Central Purchasing Act for the following reasons: (1) a supplier fails to post or allows to expire a bid bond, performance bond, or surety bond required in connection with an acquisition; (2) a supplier fails to perform pursuant to the contract; (3) a supplier provides acquisitions that fail to meet the requirements of the contract; (4) a supplier fails to deliver an acquisition pursuant to the contract; (5) a supplier fails timely to replace, at its own expense, acquisitions that fail to meet the requirements of the contract or that have latent defects; (6) a supplier provides the state purchasing director with false, misleading, inaccurate, materially deficient, or incomplete information on a bidder registration form; (7) a supplier fails to keep a bid firm for the period specified in the solicitation after the solicitation closing date; (8) a supplier fails to resolve a dispute with a state agency; (9) upon judgment by the appropriate regulatory authority or court of competent jurisdiction that a supplier engaged in discriminatory practices; (10) a supplier misrepresents, fails to provide, or allows to expire a professional certification required in connection with an acquisition; (11) a supplier colludes with other suppliers to restrain competitive bidding; (12) a supplier provides a state employee with a kickback; (13) the state purchasing director determines, in his or her sole discretion, that a supplier is no longer responsible or qualified to do business with the State of Oklahoma; (14) a supplier violates any provision of the Oklahoma Central Purchasing Act; (15) any other reason the state purchasing director determines appropriate; or (16) violation of applicable procurement ethics rules or laws.

b. Suspension Notice

The state purchasing director shall notify a supplier of the supplier's suspension within five business days of the state purchasing director's determination. The notice shall designate the suspension period that shall begin three business days from the date of the notice and shall expire no later than the end of the period specified in the notice.

c. Suspension Appeal

A supplier may appeal a suspension in writing to the state purchasing director within five business days of receipt of the suspension notice; however, the supplier shall be suspended during the appeal.

If a supplier appeals suspension by the state purchasing director, the state purchasing director shall affirm or deny the appeal in writing to the supplier. If the state purchasing director affirms the appeal, the supplier shall be reinstated to the supplier list. If the state purchasing director denies the supplier's appeal, the supplier may appeal to the OMES director pursuant to OS title 75, section 309 *et seq*. and the provisions of OAC section 260:115-3-19.

d. Suspension Period

The suspension period begins three business days from the date of the notice and shall expire no later than the end of the period specified in the notice.

e. Supplier Request for Reinstatement

A supplier that the state purchasing director suspends may request the state purchasing director to allow the supplier to register for the suppliers list before the end of the supplier's suspension period. The state purchasing director may consider reinstating the supplier upon submission by the supplier of documents that indicate a change of conditions.

f. Supplier Reinstatement

If the state purchasing director reasonably believes that the supplier demonstrates the ability to satisfy requirements for performance of state contracts, the state purchasing director shall send written notification of reinstatement.

2. Debarment

Supplier debarment is governed by OAC section 260:115-3-21. The state purchasing director may debar a supplier from the suppliers list and from submitting bids to the purchasing division or other state agencies subject to the Central Purchasing Act for a period of no more than three years.

a. Cause for Debarment

Fraud, Bribery, or Corruption: The state purchasing director may debar a supplier upon conviction of an individual or business entity guilty of a felony involving fraud, bribery, or corruption.

Gift, Donation, or Gratuity: The state purchasing director may debar a supplier upon conviction of an individual or business entity of a misdemeanor involving a gift, donation, or gratuity.

Anti-Kickback Act of 1974: The state purchasing director may debar a supplier upon conviction of an individual or business entity of a felony involving the Anti-Kickback Act of 1974.

Debarment by Federal Government Entities: This may be cause for debarment within the state.

b. Debarment Notice

If the state purchasing director debars an individual or business entity, the state purchasing director shall notify the individual or business entity in writing.

c. Debarment Considerations

The state purchasing director shall consider the following factors when considering debarment of an individual or business entity: disassociation, imputed business entity, imputed individual, time period, failure to respond to inquiries, or other factors.

d. State Purchasing Director Options

Upon completion of review of debarment records, the state purchasing director shall take an action affecting the individual or business entity, including declining to debar, suspension, or debarment.

e. Reinstatement after Debarment

A debarred individual or business entity may submit a written request for reinstatement to the state purchasing director. The state purchasing director shall consider information the individual or business entity provides to determine if the individual or business entity merits reinstatement to the suppliers list. The state purchasing director may approve or deny reinstatement of the individual or business entity to the supplier's list and shall provide written notice of the reinstatement approval or denial.

f. Supplier Appeal of State Purchasing Director Actions

A supplier may appeal a debarment or a denial of reinstatement by the state purchasing director to the director within ten business days of the date of the state purchasing director's notice of debarment or denial of reinstatement pursuant to OS title 75, section 309 *et seq*. and the provisions of OAC section 260:115-3-19.

3. Suspended/Debarred Vendor List

There is no online listing of suspended or debarred vendors.

V. Administrative and Judicial Review

A. Administrative Review

(See Section IV.B, Bid Protest Appeals, and Section IV.D, Suspension and Debarment.)

B. Judicial Review

Following an administrative decision, a supplier may appeal to the district court pursuant to OS title 75, section 318.

VI. Extent of State's Adoption or Adaptation of ABA Model Procurement Code

The State of Oklahoma has not adopted the American Bar Association (ABA) Model Procurement Code formally. While the State of Oklahoma has not enacted the ABA Model Procurement Code, Oklahoma has enacted several provisions, in both statute and rule, that are comparable to provisions found in the ABA Model Procurement Code.

VII. Cooperative Purchasing

A. Authority

"Cooperative contracts shall not be utilized unless the purchasing cooperative and its affiliated suppliers have complied with competitive bid requirements of this act and associated rules." (OS tit. 74, § 85.7(E).) A "purchasing cooperative" is defined as "an association of public entities working together to provide leverage in achieving best value and/or the best terms in contracts awarded through a competitive bidding process." (OS tit. 74, § 85.2(21).) The Public Competitive Bidding Act provides that "any school district, including a technology school district, may either participate in, sponsor, conduct or administer a cooperative purchasing agreement for the acquisition of any commodities or services with one or more public agencies in accordance with an agreement entered into between the participants. Such cooperative purchasing may include, but is not limited to, joint or multiparty contracts between public agencies and open-ended state public procurement contracts." (OS tit. 61, § 139.)

B. Requirements

Any cooperative contract must comply with the applicable provisions of Oklahoma law. In addition, the Public Competitive Bidding law provides that purchases made in accordance with OS title 61, section 139 shall be required to satisfy any procurement regulation, including the Central Purchasing Act, the Public Competitive Bidding Act, the Finance Act, related administrative rules, and federal regulations that may apply due to the federal source of the funding for the anticipated purchase.

Oregon Procurement Rules and Regulations

Prepared by Thomas A. Larkin and Grant N. Margeson
Sokol Larkin
Email: tlarkin@sokol-larkin.com, gmargeson@sokol-larkin.com

I. Statutory Reference

A. Procurement/Purchasing Statutes

Oregon's Public Contracting Code (PCC) contains three chapters. Oregon Revised Statutes (ORS) section 279A concerns public contracts, section 279B concerns the public procurement of goods and services, and section 279C concerns public improvement, architectural, engineering, land surveying, and related service contracts. The website of the Oregon State Legislature provides the full text of these statutes: https://www.oregonlegislature.gov.

A table of contents follows:

Chapter 279A Public Contracting—General Provisions

GENERAL PROVISIONS

§ 279A.005.	Short title
§ 279A.010.	Definitions for Public Contracting Code
§ 279A.015.	Policy
§ 279A.020.	Organization of Public Contracting Code
§ 279A.025.	Application of Public Contracting Code
§ 279A.030.	Federal law prevails in case of conflict

AUTHORITY

§ 279A.050.	Procurement authority
§ 279A.055.	Personal services contracts
§ 279A.060.	Local contract review boards
§ 279A.065.	Model rules generally; applicability to contracting agencies
§ 279A.070.	Rules
§ 279A.075.	Delegation

DISADVANTAGED BUSINESS ENTERPRISES, MINORITY-OWNED BUSINESSES, WOMEN-OWNED BUSINESSES, BUSINESSES THAT SERVICE-DISABLED VETERANS OWN AND EMERGING SMALL BUSINESSES

CONTRACT PREFERENCES

STATE PROCUREMENT

INTERGOVERNMENTAL RELATIONS

(Generally)

§ 279B.235.	Condition concerning hours of labor; compliance with pay equity provisions; employee discussions of rate of pay or benefits
§ 279B.240.	Exclusion of recycled oils prohibited

(Specifications in State Contracts)

§ 279B.270.	State contracting agencies to use recovered resources and recycled materials; notice to prospective contractors
§ 279B.275.	Purchase of goods containing recycled polyethylene material
§ 279B.280.	Use of recycled products when economically feasible
§ 279B.283.	Condition concerning use of conflict minerals

LEGAL REMEDIES

§ 279B.400.	Protests and judicial review of approvals of special procurements
§ 279B.405.	Protests and judicial review of solicitations
§ 279B.410.	Protests of contract award
§ 279B.415.	Judicial review of protests of contract award
§ 279B.420.	Judicial review of other violations
§ 279B.425.	Review of prequalification and debarment decisions

Chapter 279C Public Contracting—Public Improvements and Related Contracts

GENERAL PROVISIONS

§ 279C.005.	Definitions
§ 279C.010.	Applicability

ARCHITECTURAL, ENGINEERING, PHOTOGRAMMETRIC MAPPING, TRANSPORTATION PLANNING, LAND SURVEYING, AND RELATED SERVICES

§ 279C.100.	Definitions for ORS 279C.100 to 279C.125
§ 279C.105.	Contracts for architectural, engineering, photogrammetric mapping, transportation planning, or land surveying and related services; procedures
§ 279C.107.	Public disclosure of contents of proposals for architectural, engineering, photogrammetric mapping, transportation planning, or land surveying services; treatment of trade secrets and confidential information
§ 279C.110.	Selection procedure for consultants to provide services; use of pricing proposals; compensation; protests; applicability; rules
§ 279C.115.	Direct contracts for services of consultants
§ 279C.120.	Selection procedure for related services
§ 279C.125.	Architectural, engineering, photogrammetric mapping, transportation planning, and land surveying services selection process for local government public improvements procured through state agency; rules

PROCUREMENT OF CONSTRUCTION SERVICES

(General Policies)

§ 279C.300. Policy on competition

§ 279C.305. Least-cost policy for public improvements; requirement to file list of planned projects and estimated costs and to identify projects contracting agency intends to complete with own personnel and resources; required analysis; exceptions

§ 279C.306. Administrative enforcement of least-cost policy for public improvements; procedure; civil action

§ 279C.307. Limitations in procurement of personal services; exception

§ 279C.310. Limitation on contracting agency constructing public improvement

§ 279C.315. Waiver of damages for unreasonable delay by contracting agency against public policy

§ 279C.320. Contracts for construction other than public improvements

§ 279C.325. Limitation on contracting agency awarding contract to nonresident education service district

(Competitive Bidding; Contract Specifications; Exceptions; Exemptions)

§ 279C.330. "Findings" defined

§ 279C.332. Definitions for ORS 279A.065, 279C.307, 279C.335, 279C.337, and 279C.380

§ 279C.335. Competitive bidding; exceptions; exemptions

§ 279C.340. Contract negotiations

§ 279C.345. Specifications for contracts; exemptions

§ 279C.350. Exemption procedure; appeal

§ 279C.355. Evaluation of public improvement projects not contracted by competitive bidding

(Solicitation; Contract Award; Rejection)

§ 279C.360. Requirement for public improvement advertisements

§ 279C.365. Requirements for solicitation documents and bids and proposals

§ 279C.370. First-tier subcontractor disclosure

§ 279C.375. Award and execution of contract; determination of responsibility of bidder; bonds; impermissible exclusions

§ 279C.380. Performance bond; payment bond; waiver of bonds

§ 279C.385. Return or retention of bid security

§ 279C.390. Exemption of contracts from bid security and bonds

§ 279C.395. Rejection of bids

(Competitive Proposals)

§ 279C.400. Competitive proposals; procedure

§ 279C.405. Requests for information, interest, or qualifications; requirements for requests for proposals

§ 279C.410. Receipt of proposals; evaluation and award

§ 279C.412. Competitive quotes for intermediate procurements

§ 279C.414. Requirements for competitive quotes

(Prequalification and Disqualification)

§ 279C.430. Prequalification of bidders; rules

§ 279C.435. Effect of prequalification by Department of Transportation or Oregon Department of Administrative Services

§ 279C.440. Disqualification from consideration for award of contracts

§ 279C.445. Appeal of disqualification

§ 279C.450. Appeal procedure for decision to deny, revoke, or revise prequalification; hearing; costs; judicial review

(Remedies)

§ 279C.460. Action by or on behalf of adversely affected bidder or proposer; exception for personal services contract

§ 279C.465. Action against successful bidder; amount of damages; when action to be commenced; defenses

§ 279C.470. Compensation for contractor on contract declared void by court; exceptions; applicability

CONSTRUCTION CONTRACTS GENERALLY

(Required Contract Conditions)

§ 279C.500. "Person" defined

§ 279C.505. Conditions concerning payment, contributions, liens, withholding, drug testing

§ 279C.510. Demolition contracts to require material salvage; lawn and landscape maintenance contracts to require composting or mulching

§ 279C.515. Conditions concerning payment of claims by public officers, payment to persons furnishing labor or materials, and complaints

§ 279C.520. Condition concerning hours of labor; compliance with pay equity provisions; employee discussions of rate of pay or benefits

§ 279C.525. Provisions concerning environmental and natural resources laws; remedies

§ 279C.527. Inclusion of amount for green energy technology or woody biomass energy technology in public improvement contract; written determination of appropriateness; conditions, exemptions, and limitations; rules

§ 279C.528. State Department of Energy requirements and specifications; record keeping requirements; rules

§ 279C.530. Condition concerning payment for medical care and providing workers' compensation

§ 279C.535. Conditions concerning steel materials; rules

§ 279C.537. Condition concerning use of diesel engines in motor vehicles used in performing certain public improvement contracts; rules

(Hours of Labor)

§ 279C.540. Maximum hours of labor on public contracts; holidays; exceptions; liability to workers; rules

§ 279C.545. Time limitation on claim for overtime; posting of circular by contractor

(Retainage and Payments)

§ 279C.550. "Retainage" defined

§ 279C.555. Withholding of retainage

§ 279C.560. Form of retainage; procedures for holding and payment

§ 279C.565. Limitation on retainage requirements

§ 279C.570. Prompt payment policy; progress payments; retainage; interest; exception; settlement of compensation disputes

(Subcontractors)

§ 279C.580. Contractor's relations with subcontractors

§ 279C.585. Authority to substitute undisclosed first-tier subcontractor; circumstances; rules

§ 279C.590. Complaint process for substitutions of subcontractors; civil penalties

(Action on Payment Bonds and Public Works Bonds)

§ 279C.600. Right of action on payment bond or public works bond of contractor or subcontractor; notice of claim

§ 279C.605. Notice of claim

§ 279C.610. Action on contractor's public works bond or payment bond; time limitation

§ 279C.615. Preference for labor and material liens

§ 279C.620. Rights of person providing medical care to employees of contractor

§ 279C.625. Joint liability when payment bond not executed

(Termination or Suspension of Contract for Public Interest Reasons)

§ 279C.650. "Labor dispute" defined

§ 279C.655. Extension and compensation when work suspended

§ 279C.660. Compensation when contract terminated due to public interest

§ 279C.665. Contractual provisions for compensation when contract terminated due to public interest

§ 279C.670. Application of ORS 279C.650 to 279C.670

PREVAILING WAGE RATE

§ 279C.800. Definitions for ORS 279C.800 to 279C.870

§ 279C.805. Policy

§ 279C.807. Workforce diversity for public works projects

§ 279C.808. Rules

§ 279C.810. Exemptions; rules

§ 279C.815. Determination of prevailing wage; sources of information; comparison of state and federal prevailing wage; other powers of commissioner

§ 279C.817. Determination of applicability of prevailing wage rate; time limitation; hearing; rules

§ 279C.820. Advisory committee to assist commissioner

§ 279C.825.	Fees; rules
§ 279C.827.	Division of public works project; applicability of prevailing wage rate to divided projects
§ 279C.829.	Agreement with other state to pay less than prevailing rate of wage
§ 279C.830.	Provisions concerning prevailing rate of wage in specifications, contracts, and subcontracts; applicability of prevailing wage; bond
§ 279C.835.	Notifying commissioner of public works contract subject to prevailing wage; payment of fee
§ 279C.836.	Public works bond; rules
§ 279C.838.	Applicability of state and federal rates of wage; determination of site of project; determination of applicability of wage to transportation workers; waiver
§ 279C.840.	Payment of prevailing rate of wage; posting of rates and fringe benefit plan provisions
§ 279C.845.	Certified statements regarding payment of prevailing rates of wage; retainage
§ 279C.850.	Inspection to determine whether prevailing rate of wage being paid; civil action for failure to pay prevailing rate of wage or overtime
§ 279C.855.	Liability for violations
§ 279C.860.	Ineligibility for public works contracts for failure to pay or post notice of prevailing rates of wage; certified payroll reports to commissioner
§ 279C.865.	Civil penalties
§ 279C.870.	Civil action to enforce payment of prevailing rates of wage
§ 279C.875.	Criminal liability for intentional failure to pay prevailing wage; rules

II. Regulations

Contracting agencies, defined by ORS section 279A.010(1)(b), must follow the Attorney General Model Rules (Model Rules) for contracting or replace the Model Rules through a contract review board. (ORS § 279A.065.) The Model Rules remain subject to the Oregon Administrative Procedures Act, ORS chapter 183, and may be found at Oregon Administrative Rules (OAR) chapter 137, divisions 46, 47, 48, and 49, and at the following website: https://secure.sos.state.or.us/oard/displayChapterRules.action?selectedChapter=93.

Subject to two exceptions, state agencies defined in ORS section 279A.010(1)(mm) remain subject to Department of Administrative Services (DAS) rules. (ORS § 279A.140.) State agencies generally include Oregon executive bodies. The DAS website may be found at the following link: https://www.oregon.gov/das/Pages/index.aspx. (See also OAR 125-247-0010 *et seq.*)

The Oregon Cooperative Purchasing Program (OrCPP) (https://www.oregon.gov/das/procurement/pages/orcpp.aspx) allows qualified agencies and organizations to access, among other things, state contracts relating to the purchase of goods and services, procurement training opportunities, and unlimited advertising on the state's Oregon Buys e-procurement system, found at https://oregonbuys.gov/bso/. Additionally, a reciprocal interstate agreement allows access to designated State of Washington contracts. Agencies must first, however, determine whether Washington contracts meet their own purchasing rules and the requirements of ORS section 279 prior to use.

Oregon's Procurement Services (OPS) provides training, certification, and direction for public contracting in the State of Oregon. The OPS also maintains additional procurement-related information at its website: https://www.oregon.gov/DAS/Procurement/Pages/Index.aspx.

III. Source Selection

A. Competitive Sealed Bidding/Competitive Sealed Proposals

With certain specific exceptions, contracting agencies shall award public contracts for goods and services by competitive sealed bidding (under ORS § 279B.055) or competitive sealed proposals (under ORS § 279B.060). (ORS § 279B.050.)

B. Small Procurements

Any procurement of goods or services not exceeding $10,000 may be awarded in any manner deemed practical or convenient by the contracting agency. (ORS § 279B.065.) Contracts awarded under these procedures may be later amended to exceed $10,000, but procurements may not be artificially divided or fragmented so as to constitute a small procurement. (ORS § 279B.065(2).)

C. Intermediate Procurements

An "intermediate" procurement, between the amounts $10,000 and $150,000, may be awarded using the intermediate procedures set forth in ORS section 279B.070.

D. Sole Source Procurements

ORS section 279B.075 allows contracting agencies to award a contract without competition when the director of the DAS, the local contract review board, a state contracting agency with procurement authority under ORS section 279A.050, the state chief information officer (for certain goods or services and if the director has delegated the necessary authority to the state chief information officer), or a person designated in writing by either the DAS director, contract review board, or state contracting agency determines in writing that the goods or services are only available from one source and makes certain written findings in accordance with the statute.

E. Emergency Procurements and Special Procurements

The Oregon Legislature also enacted provisions allowing for emergency procurements (ORS § 279B.080) and other "special procurements" (ORS § 279B.085) under certain specified circumstances.

F. Professional Services

Generally, the procurement of services follows the source selection methods discussed above and adopts the same methods for the procurement of goods. However, architectural, engineering, land surveying, and related professional consulting services require procurement through the screening and selection procedures selected at the discretion of the state agency in question, subject to the general criteria set forth in ORS section 279C.110. The parties determine compensation for such professionals only after selecting the consultant. (ORS § 279C.110)

G. Construction Services

Except as specified in ORS section 279C.335, all public improvement contracts shall be procured through competitive bidding procedures, which are set forth in detail in ORS section 279C.300 *et seq*.

IV. Bid Protests and Contract Disputes

A. Bid Protests

1. Standing

A prospective bidder, proposer, or offeror for a public contract may file a protest with the contracting agency if it believes that the procurement process is contrary to law or that a solicitation document is unnecessarily restrictive, legally flawed, or improperly specifies a brand name. (ORS § 279B.405(2).)

A bidder or proposer may protest the award of a public contract or a notice of intent to award, whichever occurs first, where the bidder would be eligible for the contract award following a successful protest *and* one of the reasons for the protest set forth in ORS section 279B.410(1)(b) exists. The contracting agency must timely respond in writing to a protest, which response remains subject to judicial review in the manner provided by ORS section 279B.415.

2. Deadline

The timeliness of a bid protest depends on the rules enacted by the contracting agency involved and the subject of the protest. (ORS § 279B.405(3).) This timeline must be communicated to bidders, proposers, and offerors. (ORS § 279B.405(3).)

3. Grounds of Protest

A protest must contain sufficient information to identify the solicitation at issue; grounds that demonstrate how the procurement process is contrary to law or how the solicitation document is unnecessarily restrictive, legally flawed, or improperly specifies a brand name; evidence or supporting documentation; and the relief sought. (ORS § 279B.405(4).)

A contract-specific special procurement under ORS section 279B.085 must first be protested with the director of the Oregon DAS or the local contracting agency, as applicable, and seek judicial review before the contract is awarded. (ORS § 279B.400.)

4. Decision

The contracting agency must consider the protest and issue a written decision or otherwise notify the protestor that the protest is untimely or failed to meet the above requirements. The contracting agency must issue this decision in accordance with its own rules or the Model Rules no less than three days before bids, proposals, or offers are due. (ORS § 279B.405(5)–(6).)

5. Stay

If a party seeks judicial review, the agency may not proceed with the contract execution unless it determines that a compelling government interest in proceeding exists or that the goods and services are urgently needed, and these determinations are set forth in writing and immediately provided to the protesting bidder. The court may nonetheless stay the performance of the contract upon motion of the protestor if the court finds that the government's determination was not supported by substantial evidence or constitutes a manifest abuse of discretion. (ORS § 279B.405(9).)

B. Bid Protest Appeals

The agency's decision is subject to judicial review by the Circuit Court for Marion County, or the circuit court for the county in which the agency's principal offices are located, and only if the suit or writ of review is filed before the opening of bids, proposals, or offers. (ORS § 279B.405(7)–(8).)

The court shall give due deference to any factual decision made by the contracting agency and may not substitute its judgment for that of the agency, but shall review all questions of law de novo. (ORS § 279B.405(10).) The court may award costs and attorney fees to the prevailing party. (ORS § 279B.405(10)(c).)

C. Contract Disputes

Oregon contract claims and appeals proceed in accordance with the express terms of the underlying contract documents. Many public works contracts incorporate by reference the Oregon Department of Transportation's (ODOT's) Standard Specifications for Construction. These specifications impose multiple notice and claim requirements on persons performing in connection with a public works project. Accordingly, claimants must pay careful attention to any dispute resolution clauses in the underlying agreement. The following link provides access to the ODOT Standard Specifications for Construction: https://www.oregon.gov/odot/Business/Pages/Standard_Specifications.aspx.

Claimants should also consider Oregon's prompt payment (ORS § 279C.570 *et seq.*) and retainage (ORS § 279C.555) statutes when developing or filing a contract claim.

D. Suspension and Debarment

Agencies may exclude a prospective bidder or proposer from consideration for a contract award based on the reasons set forth in ORS section 279B.130(2). The agency must first, however, provide the bidder or proposer notice and a reasonable opportunity to be heard. Debarments may not exceed three years in duration. Related decisions may be appealed if the bidder or proposer notifies the agency of its appeal as provided in ORS section 279B.425 within three days of the bidder or proposer's receipt of debarment notice.

The Oregon DAS or a local review board hears debarment appeals. Within 30 days following the DAS's or board's receipt of a notice of appeal, the DAS or board must hold a hearing and issue a written decision concerning debarment. (ORS § 279B.425.) Aggrieved persons may appeal the DAS or board decision through a petition to the circuit court, filed within 15 days of the DAS or board decision. The circuit court may reverse a DAS or board decision only on finding that the decision was obtained through corruption, fraud, or undue means; that there was evident partiality or corruption to the substantial prejudice to the petitioner; or that there was evident material miscalculation of figures or mistakes operating to the substantial prejudice of the petitioner. (ORS § 279B.425.)

V. Administrative and Judicial Review

A. Administrative Review

The administrative review process is set forth above.

B. Judicial Review

The agency's decision is subject to judicial review by the Circuit Court for Marion County, or the circuit court for the county in which the agency's principal offices are located, only if the suit or writ of review is filed before the opening of bids, proposals, or offers.

VI. Extent of State's Adoption or Adaptation of ABA Model Procurement Code

Oregon's PCC was substantially amended in 2003 to closely model the American Bar Association's (ABA's) 2000 update of the Model Procurement Code for State and Local Governments.

VII. Cooperative Purchasing

A. Authority

Cooperative procurement is provided for in ORS section 279A.200 *et seq.*

B. Requirements

Pursuant to ORS sections 279A.205 and 279A.210, a contracting agency may participate in, sponsor, conduct, or administer a joint cooperative procurement, as defined in ORS section 279A.200(1)(e). A joint cooperative procurement contemplates that the members and their needs are known at the time of a bid. A joint cooperative procurement may not be a permissive cooperative procurement (ORS § 279A.210(2)), which is defined as a cooperative procurement in which the purchasing contracting agencies are not identified (ORS § 279A.200(1)(g)). Permissive or interstate cooperative procurements, defined in ORS section 279.200(1)(d) and (g), are not allowed for public improvements contracts. (ORS § 279A.205.) Public improvement is defined as a project for construction, reconstruction, or major renovation on real property by or for a contracting agency. (ORS § 279A.010(1)(cc).) But it does not include "[p]rojects for which no funds of a contracting agency are directly or indirectly used, except for participation that is incidental or related primarily to project design or inspection" or "[e]mergency work, minor alteration, ordinary repair or maintenance necessary to preserve a public improvement." (ORS § 279A.010(1)(cc).)

A joint cooperative procurement is valid if the solicitation and award process is an open and impartial competitive process and uses selection methods substantially equivalent to those in ORS sections 279B.055 (competitive sealed bidding), 279B.060 (competitive sealed proposals), or 279B.085 (special procurements), or uses a competitive bidding process substantially equivalent to the one in ORS chapter 279C; the solicitation and original agreement identifies the cooperative procurement group or each participating purchasing contracting agency and specifies the estimated contract requirements; and no material change is made in the terms, conditions, or prices of the contract between the contractor and the purchasing contracting agency from the terms, conditions, and prices of the original contract between the contractor and the administering contracting agency. (ORS § 279A.210.)

Protests regarding the procurement process, the contents of solicitation documents, or the award or proposed award of an original contract may be directed only to the administering contracting agency. (ORS § 279A.225.) Protests regarding the use of a cooperative contracting agency after the execution of an original contract must be directed to the purchasing contracting agency. (ORS § 279A.225.) In both cases, the protest must be in accordance with the provisions of ORS sections 279B.400 to 279B.425. (ORS § 279A.225.) The decision of a local contracting agency to use a cooperative procurement is reviewable in the circuit court of the county where the principal offices of the local contracting agency are located, and the decision of a state contracting agency to use a cooperative procurement is reviewable by the Circuit Court for Marion County or the circuit court of the county where the principal offices of the state contracting agency are located. (ORS § 279A.225.)

Pennsylvania Procurement Rules and Regulations

Prepared by Kristopher Berr
Del Duca Lewis
Email: kjb@delducalewis.com

I. Statutory Reference

A. Procurement/Purchasing Statutes

In Pennsylvania, procurement is governed by the Commonwealth Procurement Code, which is codified at Pennsylvania Consolidated Statutes title 62, section 101 *et seq*. The Procurement Code can be accessed online through the Pennsylvania General Assembly website at https://www.legis.state.pa.us.

Under the Code, the Department of General Services (DGS) is generally responsible for procurement and the establishment of procurement policy for supplies, services, and construction for the commonwealth's agencies and row offices, with certain exceptions. Further information about DGS can be found online at https://www.dgs.pa.gov/Pages/default.aspx. Note that while DGS is responsible for procurement on behalf of the commonwealth's executive and independent agencies, its scope of responsibility does not extend to "state affiliated entities," which include the Pennsylvania Turnpike Commission, the Pennsylvania Housing Finance Agency, the Pennsylvania Municipal Retirement System, the Pennsylvania Infrastructure Investment Authority, the State Public School Building Authority, the Pennsylvania Higher Educational Facilities Authority, and the State Systems of Higher Education. DGS is also not responsible for procurement for the commonwealth's unified judicial system, General Assembly, political subdivisions, or transportation authorities.

II. Regulations

DGS publishes a Procurement Handbook, which provides a standard reference to established policy, procedures, and guidelines for the procurement of supplies, services, and construction under the authority of the Procurement Code. The official version of the Procurement Handbook is published online only, and can be found at https://www.dgs.pa.gov/Materials-Services-Procurement/Procurement-Handbook/Pages/default.aspx.

The Procurement Handbook is composed of four main parts:

Part 1—Policies and Guidelines

Part 2—Procurement of Supplies Procedures
Part 3—Procurement of Services Procedures
Part 4—Procurement of Design and Construction Services

III. Source Selection

The general methods of procurement under the Procurement Code include:

A. Competitive Sealed Bidding

The Procurement Code designates competitive sealed bidding as the default method of source selection. (62 Pennsylvania Consolidated Statutes § 511.) This method is used where the supply, service, or construction requirements can be described using objective, measurable criteria to determine acceptability, and price is the only factor to differentiate responsive bids. (62 Pennsylvania Consolidated Statutes § 512(e).) Invitations for bids must be publicized and must set forth the objective criteria on which bids will be evaluated for acceptability, such as inspecting, testing, quality, or delivery. (62 Pennsylvania Consolidated Statutes § 512(c) and (e).) This method of procurement allows only limited discretion in the award process. Discretion is limited to determining bidder responsibility; determining bid responsiveness; and rejecting all bids. (See 62 Pennsylvania Consolidated Statutes § 512(g).) Unless all bids are rejected, DGS is required to award the contract to the lowest responsible bidder. (62 Pennsylvania Consolidated Statutes § 512(g).)

B. Competitive Sealed Proposals

The Procurement Code permits a procuring agency to utilize the competitive sealed proposal process where the contracting officer determines that competitive sealed bidding is impracticable or is not advantageous to the Commonwealth. (62 Pennsylvania Consolidated Statutes § 513(a).) Proposals are solicited through a request for proposals (RFP), which sets forth evaluation factors and their relative importance. (62 Pennsylvania Consolidated Statutes § 513(b) and (e).) Under this process, the agency may conduct discussions and negotiations with responsible offerors for the purpose of clarification and for obtaining best and final offers. (62 Pennsylvania Consolidated Statutes § 513(f).) The agency is required to select for contract negotiation the responsible offeror whose proposal is determined to be the most advantageous to the commonwealth. (62 Pennsylvania Consolidated Statutes § 513(g).) The agency's determination as to which proposal is the most advantageous is not based solely on price, but is instead based upon a consideration of the evaluation factors defined in the RFP. (62 Pennsylvania Consolidated Statutes § 513(g).)

C. Small Procurement

The Procurement Code authorizes procurements without formal bid procedures where the contract amount does not exceed certain dollar thresholds established by DGS. (62 Pennsylvania Consolidated Statutes § 514.) Those thresholds are subject to change from year to year and may be found in the Procurement Handbook. For example, effective January 1, 2021, no-bid procurement was available for construction contracts below the threshold of $20,692.

D. Sole Source Procurement

Pursuant to section 515 of the Procurement Code, Pennsylvania Consolidated Statutes title 62, section 515, sole source procurement is available where the contracting officer makes a written determination that one of the following conditions exists: (1) only a single contractor is capable of providing the supply, service, or construction; (2) federal or state law exempts the supply, service, or construction from the competitive procedure; (3) the total cost of the supply, service, or construction is less than the amount established by the department for small, no-bid procurements under section 514 (relating to small procurements); (4) it is clearly not feasible to award the contract for supplies or services on a competitive basis; (5) the services are to be provided by attorneys or litigation consultants selected by the Office of General Counsel, the Office of Attorney General, the Department of the Auditor General, or the Treasury Department; (6) the services are to be provided by expert witnesses; (7) the services involve the repair, modification, or calibration of equipment and they are to be performed by the manufacturer of the equipment or by the manufacturer's authorized dealer, provided the contracting officer determines that bidding is not appropriate under the circumstances; (8) the contract is for investment advisors or managers selected by the Public School Employees' Retirement System, the State Employees' Retirement System or a state-affiliated entity; (9) the contract is for financial or investment experts to be used and selected by the Treasury Department or financial or investment experts selected by the secretary of the budget; or (10) the contract for supplies or services is in the best interest of the commonwealth.

E. Emergency Procurements

The Procurement Code permits an agency to make an emergency procurement when (1) a threat to public health, welfare, or safety exists or (2) circumstances outside the control of the agency create an urgency of need that does not permit the expiration of time associated with formal competitive procedures. (62 Pennsylvania Consolidated Statutes § 516.) This type of procurement does not require a written contract, and the supplier may be paid based solely upon an invoice for the approved emergency services. (62 Pennsylvania Consolidated Statutes § 516.)

F. Multiple-Award Contracts

Section 517 of the Procurement Code, Pennsylvania Consolidated Statutes title 62, section 517, permits a procuring agency to enter into contracts on a multiple-award basis when the agency determines that one or more of the following is applicable: (1) it is administratively or economically impractical to develop or modify specifications for a myriad of related supplies because of rapid technological changes; (2) the subjective nature in the use of certain supplies and the fact that recognizing this need creates a more efficient use of the item; (3) it is administratively or economically impractical to develop or modify specifications because of the heterogeneous nature of the product lines; (4) there is a need for compatibility with existing systems; or (5) the agency should select the contractor to furnish the supply, service, or construction based upon best value or return on investment.

When one or more of the above circumstances exists, the purchasing agency is required to proceed using the procedures applicable to competitive sealed bidding (section 512) or competitive sealed proposals (section 513), whichever is appropriate.

G. Other

There are also specialized procurement procedures used for the following goods and services:

1. Services of accountants, clergy, physicians, lawyers, dentists, and other professional services (62 Pennsylvania Consolidated Statutes § 518)
2. Insurance and notary bonds (62 Pennsylvania Consolidated Statutes § 519)
3. Contracting for supplies manufactured by, and services performed by, persons with disabilities (62 Pennsylvania Consolidated Statutes § 520)
4. Procurement of design professional services (62 Pennsylvania Consolidated Statutes § 905)

IV. Bid Protests and Contract Disputes

A. Bid Protests

1. Standing

Any bidder, offeror, prospective bidder, prospective offeror, or prospective contractor who is aggrieved in connection with the solicitation or award of a contract has standing to protest. (62 Pennsylvania Consolidated Statutes § 1711.1(a).) However, protests relating to cancellation of invitations for bids or RFPs and protests relating to the rejection of all bids or proposals are not permitted. (62 Pennsylvania Consolidated Statutes § 1711.1(a).)

2. Form of Protest

A protest must be in writing and filed with the agency head, and must state all grounds upon which the protesting party asserts that the solicitation or award was improper. (62 Pennsylvania Consolidated Statutes § 1711.1(b)–(c).) Issues not raised are deemed waived.

3. Deadlines

a. Solicitation Protest

If a protest is submitted by a prospective bidder or offeror, the protest must be filed before bid opening or the proposal receipt date, as applicable. (62 Pennsylvania Consolidated Statutes § 1711.1(b).)

b. Award Protest

If a protest is filed by a bidder or offeror or a prospective contractor, the protest must be filed *within seven days* after the protestor knew or should have known of the facts giving rise to the protest, except that in no event may a protest be filed later than seven days after the date the contract is awarded. (62 Pennsylvania Consolidated Statutes § 1711.1(b).)

4. Stay of Procurement

Where a timely protest is submitted, the purchasing agency shall not proceed further with the solicitation or award of the contract, unless the agency head makes a written determination that the protest is clearly without merit or that award of the contract without delay is necessary to protect the substantial interests of the commonwealth. (62 Pennsylvania Consolidated Statutes § 1711.1(k).)

5. Evaluation Procedures

Within 15 days of the receipt of a protest, the contracting officer may submit a written response to the head of the purchasing agency. (62 Pennsylvania Consolidated Statutes § 1711.1(d).) The protester may file a written reply within ten days of the contracting officer's response. (62 Pennsylvania Consolidated Statutes § 1711.1(d).) After receipt of the protest and any response and reply, the head of the purchasing agency will evaluate the protest and issue a decision. (62 Pennsylvania Consolidated Statutes § 1711.1(e).) In performing his or her evaluation, the agency head shall review the protest and any response; request and review any additional documents deemed necessary; give the protester and the contracting officer reasonable opportunity to review and address any additional documents or information requested; and in his or her sole discretion, conduct a hearing.

6. Determination

Upon completion of his or her evaluation of the protest, the head of the agency shall issue a written decision with explanation within 60 days of the receipt of the protest, unless that period is extended with consent of the protester. (62 Pennsylvania Consolidated Statutes § 1711.1(f).) However, if the head of the purchasing agency determines the award was contrary to law, he or she may afford the following remedies: If the determination is made prior to execution of a contract, cancel the solicitation or proposed award, or revise the solicitation or proposed award to comply with law. If the determination is made after execution of a contract, and the awardee has not acted in bad faith or fraudulently, ratify or affirm the contract, if the agency determines that doing so is in the best interest of the commonwealth; modify the contract to comply with law, with the consent of all parties; or terminate the contract and compensate the awardee for any costs incurred under the contract prior to termination. If the determination is made after execution of a contract, and the awardee has acted in bad faith or fraudulently, ratify or affirm the contract, if the agency determines that doing so is in the best interest of the commonwealth, without prejudice to the agency's right to recover its damages; modify the contract to comply with law, with the consent of all parties; or declare the contract void. (62 Pennsylvania Consolidated Statutes § 1711.2.)

B. Bid Protest Appeals

1. Deadlines

Within 15 days of the mailing date of a decision by the agency denying the protest, the protester has the right to file an appeal in commonwealth court. (62 Pennsylvania Consolidated Statutes § 1711.1(g).) Any issues not raised in the protest are waived. (62 Pennsylvania Consolidated Statutes § 1711.1(g).)

2. Appeal Record

The record of determination for review by the court consists of the solicitation or award; the contract, if any; the protest; any response or reply; any additional documents or information considered by the head of the purchasing agency in evaluating the protest; the hearing transcript and exhibits, if any; and the final determination. (62 Pennsylvania Consolidated Statutes § 1711.1(h).)

3. Standard of Review

The commonwealth court considers the appeal, without a jury, on the record of determination (addressed above). (62 Pennsylvania Consolidated Statutes § 1711.1(i).) The purchasing agency's decision will be affirmed unless the court finds from the record that the determination is arbitrary and capricious, an abuse of discretion, or is contrary to law. (62 Pennsylvania Consolidated Statutes § 1711.1(i).)

4. Remedy

If the court sustains the appeal, it may enter an order affirming, modifying, vacating, setting aside, or reversing the decision. (62 Pennsylvania Consolidated Statutes § 1711.1(j).) If the court determines that the solicitation or the award is contrary to law, then the court is limited to canceling the solicitation or award and declaring any resulting contract void. (62 Pennsylvania Consolidated Statutes § 1711.1(j).)

C. Contract Disputes

1. Right to File Claim

A contractor may file a claim arising from its contract with the commonwealth by filing a written claim with the contracting officer within six months after the claim accrues. (62 Pennsylvania Consolidated Statutes § 1712.1.) Failure of a contractor to file a claim within this six-month time period shall be deemed a waiver. (62 Pennsylvania Consolidated Statutes § 1712.1.) The claim must state all grounds on which the contractor asserts that a controversy exists. (62 Pennsylvania Consolidated Statutes § 1712.1(c).)

2. Contracting Officer Determination

The contracting officer will review the claim and will generally issue a final determination within 120 days of receipt of the claim. (62 Pennsylvania Consolidated Statutes § 1712.1(d).) This time period may be extended by consent of the contracting officer and the contractor. (62 Pennsylvania Consolidated Statutes § 1712.1(d).) If the contracting officer fails to issue a final determination within the 120 days (unless extended by consent of the parties), the claim is deemed denied. (62 Pennsylvania Consolidated Statutes § 1712.1(d).) The determination of the contracting officer shall be the final order of the purchasing agency. (62 Pennsylvania Consolidated Statutes § 1712.1(d).) The contractor may thereafter file a statement of claim with the Commonwealth Board of Claims as explained below.

D. Appeals to the Board of Claims

1. Deadlines

Within 15 days of the mailing date of a final determination denying a claim or within 135 days of filing a claim, if no extension is agreed to by the parties (whichever occurs first), the contractor may file a statement of claim with the Board of Claims. (62 Pennsylvania Consolidated Statutes § 1712.1(e).) The agency must file its response within 30 days after the statement of claim is filed. (62 Pennsylvania Consolidated Statutes § 1725(b).)

2. Pleading Requirements

The contractor's statement of claim and the agency's response must be signed and verified, and the filing party must prove that it mailed a copy of its filing to the other party. (62 Pennsylvania Consolidated Statutes § 1725(a)–(b).)

3. Hearing

After the pleadings are complete, the Board will list the case for hearing as soon as practicable, but no earlier than 30 days after the close of pleadings. (62 Pennsylvania Consolidated Statutes § 1725(c).) The hearing before the Board is public and shall be governed by rules established by the Board. The Board's Rules of Procedure may be found at http://www.boc.state.pa.us/pdf/manual.pdf.

4. Decision

After considering the pleadings and the testimony given at the hearing, the Board issues opinion either dismissing the claim or ordering an award in favor of the claimant. (62 Pennsylvania Consolidated Statutes § 1725(e).)

5. Appeal to Commonwealth Court

The decision of the Board of Claims is appealable to the commonwealth court. The Board's decision must be appealed within 30 days in accordance with Pennsylvania Consolidated Statutes title 42, section 763.

E. Suspension and Debarment

Section 531 of the Procurement Code authorizes a purchasing agency to debar or suspend a person from the award of commonwealth contracts. (See 62 Pennsylvania Consolidated Statutes § 531(a).)

1. Cause for Suspension or Debarment

Pursuant to Pennsylvania Consolidated Statutes title 62, section 531(b), the causes for debarment or suspension include the following:

> (1) Commission of embezzlement, theft, forgery, bribery, falsification or destruction of records, making false statements or receiving stolen property.
>
> (2) Commission of fraud or a criminal offense or other improper conduct or knowledge of, approval of or acquiescence in such activities by a person associated with:
>
> (i) obtaining;
>
> (ii) attempting to obtain; or
>
> (iii) performing a public contract or subcontract.
>
> The person's acceptance of the benefits derived from the conduct shall be deemed evidence of such knowledge, approval or acquiescence.
>
> (3) Violation of Federal or State antitrust statutes.
>
> (4) Violation of any Federal or State law regulating campaign contributions.
>
> (5) Violations of any Federal or State environmental law.
>
> (6) Violation of any Federal or State law regulating hours of labor, minimum wage standards or prevailing wage standards; discrimination in wages; or child labor violations.
>
> (7) Violation of the . . . Workers' Compensation Act.

(7.1) Violation of [Pennsylvania laws] (relating to fraudulent traffic in Supplemental Nutrition Assistance Program (SNAP) benefits).

(8) Violation of any Federal or State law prohibiting discrimination in employment.

(9) Debarment by any agency or department of the Federal Government or by any other state.

(10) Three or more occurrences where a person has been declared ineligible for a contract.

(11) Unsatisfactory performance, including, but not limited to, any of the following:

> (i) Failure to comply with terms of a Commonwealth agency contract or subcontract, including, but not limited to: willful failure to perform in accordance with the terms of one or more contracts, a history of failure to perform or unsatisfactory performance of one or more contracts.
>
> (ii) Offering unbalanced bids.
>
> (iii) Failure to complete the work in the time frame specified in the contract.
>
> (iv) Being declared in default on prior work or project.
>
> (v) Failure to submit documents, information or forms as required by contract.
>
> (vi) Making false statements or failing to provide information or otherwise cooperate with the contracting agency, the Office of State Inspector General or other Commonwealth authorities.
>
> (vii) Discrimination in violation of laws or regulations in the conduct of business as a contractor.

(12) Any other act or omission indicating a lack of skill, ability, capacity, quality control, business integrity or business honesty that seriously and directly affects the present responsibility of a person as determined by the purchasing agency.

2. Standard and Basis of Decision

The decision to debar must be based upon substantial evidence that a cause for debarment (as explained above) has occurred, and must take into account the seriousness of the violation and any mitigating factors. (62 Pennsylvania Consolidated Statutes § 531(a).) Before a person may be debarred, he or she must be given notice of the potential for debarment and an opportunity to be heard. (62 Pennsylvania Consolidated Statutes § 531(c).) A debarment may be for a period of not more than three years. (62 Pennsylvania Consolidated Statutes § 531(a).) The head of the purchasing agency also has the authority to suspend a person from consideration for contract awards for a period of up to three months if there is probable cause for debarment. (62 Pennsylvania Consolidated Statutes § 531(a).)

3. Effect

Suspension or debarment of a person automatically prohibits all commonwealth agencies from awarding any contract to the person or renewing or extending any contract with the person unless the contracting officer determines that there are compelling reasons for the award, renewal, or extension and the head of the purchasing agency approves the determination. (62 Pennsylvania Consolidated Statutes § 531(f).)

4. Finality of Decision

A written suspension or debarment decision shall be deemed final and conclusive unless the person appeals to the commonwealth court within 30 days after receipt of the decision. (62 Pennsylvania Consolidated Statutes § 531(e).)

V. Administrative and Judicial Review

The complete administrative and judicial review processes applicable to bid protests and suspension and debarment proceedings are set forth above.

VI. Extent of State's Adoption or Adaptation of ABA Model Procurement Code

Pennsylvania self-reports that it has completely adopted the American Bar Association (ABA) Model Procurement Code. (See 2014 Survey of State Procurement Practices, compiled by the National Association of State Procurement Officials.)

VII. Cooperative Purchasing

A. Authority

1. Cooperative Purchasing Administered by DGS

Section 1902 of the Procurement Code, Pennsylvania Consolidated Statutes title 62, section 1902, authorizes DGS to enter into cooperative purchase agreements for the purchase of supplies, services, or construction for the use of local procurement units and/or state-affiliated entities. In accordance with this authority, DGS has established the COSTARS program, through which DGS enters into cooperative contracts that permit local procurement units and state-affiliated entities registering as COSTARS members to purchase goods and services directly from COSTARS vendors and contractors. More information about the COSTARS program can be found on the DGS website at https://www.dgs.pa.gov/COSTARS/.

Pursuant to section 1902, DGS is required to enter into cooperative purchasing contracts for the use of local public procurement units or state-affiliated entities if the number of contractors under a previously existing contract for the same supply or service is reduced to a single contractor. All such contracts are required to be awarded in accordance with section 517 (relating to multiple awards) using an invitation for bids.

2. Cooperative Purchasing Administered by the Purchasing Agency

In addition to cooperative purchasing administered by DGS, section 1902 also authorizes state and local procurement units to enter into, sponsor, conduct, and administer cooperative purchasing agreements with Pennsylvania local and state entities, the federal government, or other state entities, for the purchase of supplies, services, or construction.

Cooperative purchasing may be accomplished through a variety of contract types, including but not limited to joint or multiparty contracts between public procurement units or open-ended purchasing agency contracts that are made available to local public procurement units. (62 Pennsylvania Consolidated Statutes § 1902.)

B. Requirements

Pennsylvania procurement units are not required to comply with the competitive procurement obligations required by the Procurement Code where they participate in a cooperative purchase, provided that the administering federal, state, or local agency has complied with its own statutory and regulatory procurement requirements. Specifically, pursuant to section 1908, if the agency administering the cooperative agreement entered into the agreement in accordance with governing procurement law, then the Pennsylvania purchasing agency that participates in the cooperative purchase will also be deemed to have complied with its own procurement requirements.

In addition, chapter 28 of the DGS Procurement Handbook provides that before cooperative purchasing is authorized for a commonwealth agency, DGS must approve the procurement as the best value. To facilitate this determination, the agency must establish a business case to support the cooperative purchase rather than competitive bidding or competitive proposals.

Where contract disputes arise under cooperative purchasing agreements, section 1910(a) provides that procurement units subject to chapter 17 of the Procurement Code must resolve such disputes in accordance with chapter 17. (See Section IV, Bid Protests and Contract Disputes.)

With respect to local procurement units not subject to chapter 17 of the Procurement Code, section 1910(b) provides two options for dispute resolution. First, section 1910(b) authorizes such local units to contract with the Board of Claims to resolve controversies between the local public procurement unit and its contractors. Second, it also permits local procurement units to enter into agreements with their cooperative purchase partners, including the federal government, other state purchasing entities, or other Pennsylvania procurement units, to establish procedures or use existing procedures of the unit or activity to resolve controversies with contractors.

Puerto Rico Procurement Rules and Regulations

Prepared by María C. Cartagena-Cancel
McConnell-Valdés LLC
Email: mcc@mcvpr.com
With editorial assistance from José A. Irizarry-Castro
McConnell-Valdés LLC
Email: jic@mcvpr.com

I. Statutory Reference

A. Procurement/Purchasing Statutes

Enabling statutes authorize agencies in Puerto Rico to enter into agreements and contracts through competitive bidding or similar processes for the acquisition of goods and services necessary to carry out their delegated duties. Each agency adopts its own procurement regulations. The term "agency" encompasses the majority of the government, except the legislative and judiciary branches and other entities excluded from the definition set forth in the Uniform Administrative Act. (See Laws of Puerto Rico Annotated tit. 3, § 9603(a).)

Puerto Rico's judicial and legislative branches are responsible for their own procurement processes. Accordingly, the Office of Courts Administration has power to acquire goods and services. (See Laws of Puerto Rico Annotated tit. 4, § 24n.) To that end, the judicial branch adopts its own bids and procurement regulations. Similarly, the Legislative Assembly is responsible for its procurement processes and has promulgated regulations for the administration of the legislative branch and its dependencies. (See Laws of Puerto Rico Annotated tit. 2, § 553.)

As to municipalities, Act No. 107-2020 of August 14, 2020, known as the Municipal Code, authorizes them to acquire whatever equipment is necessary for the preparation and operation of any public work or facility, and to contract professional, technical, and consulting services that may be necessary to carry out the activities, programs, and operations of the municipality. (See art. 1.008.)

1. State Government Procurement

Although Puerto Rico agencies are empowered to acquire goods and services, the General Services Administration (GSA) was created for the purpose of offering auxiliary services to different government agencies. The Administration provides to the agencies, departments, and instrumentalities of the executive branch the means of acquiring supplies and nonprofessional services.

The General Services Administration Act (GSA Act), Act No. 73-2019, as amended, was enacted on July 19, 2019. Additionally, the Uniform Regulation for Purchases and Bids of Goods, Works, and Nonprofessional Services of the General Services Administration became effective on November 18, 2020.

The main objectives of the GSA Act are to centralize the purchases of goods and services for the Puerto Rico government and to simplify the procurement process with the purpose of achieving cost savings. The GSA Act applies to all dependencies and departments of the executive branch and all public corporations of the government of Puerto Rico, except to the Office of Government Ethics; Office of the Inspector General; University of Puerto Rico; State Elections Commission; Fiscal Agency and Financial Advisory Authority; Government Development Bank for Puerto Rico; Puerto Rico Public-Private Partnerships Authority; Puerto Rico Infrastructure Financing Authority; Puerto Rico Aqueduct and Sewer Authority; Puerto Rico Electric Power Authority; Puerto Rico Highway and Transportation Authority; Puerto Rico Cooperative Insurance Supervisory Public Corporation; Public Hospitals; State Insurance Fund Corporation; Metropolitan Bus Authority; and Public Buildings Authority.

The GSA Act's purchase and procurement processes do not apply to municipalities; the legislative branch; the judicial branch; private parties under an operations and management contract with a government entity; and government entities with public-private partnerships (only to the matters pertaining to the partnership agreement, unless otherwise provided in said agreement). Private operators may voluntarily use the GSA to procure goods and services.

Exempted entities of the executive branch must adopt regulations on purchases of goods and services and procurement procedures to be certified by the GSA. Government entities and exempted entities must create an annual procurement plan, detailing the needs and proposed purchases the entities will make. Purchases relating to the recovery and reconstruction of Puerto Rico must be carried out pursuant to the GSA Act and regulations. If federal regulations apply, these will preempt rules set forth by the GSA Act and regulations.

B. Other Applicable Statutes

1. Ethics Laws

The Anticorruption Code for the New Puerto Rico (Anticorruption Code), Act No. 2-2018, as amended, was enacted on January 4, 2018. Contractors, government employees, and officers are subject to the Anticorruption Code.

a. Contractor's Ethical Obligations

Ethical obligations and responsibilities of government contractors include, among others:

- Disclose all the information needed for the executive agencies to evaluate in detail any transactions and make correct and informed determinations.
- Observe the precepts and principles of excellence and honesty that cover his or her profession, in addition to the ethical standards or rules of the association or college of which he or she is a member and that regulate his or her trade or profession in the relationship with competitors as well as with the government of Puerto Rico and its employees or officials.

- Submit quotations based on a fair price for his or her services, considering experience, education, and technical skills.
- Commit to complete the work within the term agreed on, guarantee the quality of the services and goods provided, and charge for services upon presentation of an invoice the correction of which shall be certified.
- Refrain from offering or delivering to a public servant or former public servant of the executive agencies, or the members of his or her family unit, with whom said person wishes to enter into, or has entered into, a contractual, commercial, or financial relationship, directly or indirectly, any gift, items of monetary value, contribution, gratuity, favor, service, donation, loan, or share in any business entity or legal transaction. In the cases referring to a former public servant, the preceding prohibition shall be extended to one year from the date the public servant ceased duties in the executive agency.
- Collaborate with any investigation initiated by the government on business transactions, execution of contracts, or granting of government incentives to which he or she was a party or from which he or she benefited directly or indirectly.
- Avoid matters that could give rise to a conflict of interest or the appearance of a conflict of interest.
- Report any acts that violate the provisions of the Anticorruption Code.
- Refrain from establishing negotiations with the secretaries, heads of agencies, municipal executives, or executive directors of public corporations leading to the granting of undue advantage, privileges, or favors for their benefit, or the benefit of any other person, represented by them.
- Refrain from using confidential information acquired in the course or as a result of any task entrusted thereto under a contract by the government of Puerto Rico, for purposes other than the contracted task, or to obtain, directly or indirectly, any financial advantage or benefit for the contractor, a member of his or her family unit, or any other person, business, or entity.
- Refrain from requesting or obtaining confidential information from a current or former public servant to obtain, directly or indirectly, any financial advantage or benefit for the contractor, or for any other natural or juridical person; nor for purposes other than those of the contracted task.
- Refrain from accepting or maintaining contractual or business relations with a public servant or a member of his or her family unit that has the effect of impairing the independent judgment of the public official or servant in the performance of his or her official duties.
- Refrain from entering into contracts with executive agencies if there is any conflict of interests.
- Refrain from directly or indirectly request a public official, servant, or employee to represent his or her private interests, make efforts, or exert influence to obtain a contract, the payment of a claim, a permit, license, or authorization, or in any other matter, transaction, or proposal in which said person or his or her family unit has private interests, even when it concerns official actions of the public official, servant, or employee within the scope of his or her official authority.
- Do not induce a public servant or former public servant to violate the provisions of the Anticorruption Act.

b. Executive, Legislative, and Judicial Branches; Restrictions on Former Public Servants

The conduct of active and former public servants of the executive branch is governed by the provisions of the Puerto Rico Government Ethics Office Organic Act, No.

1-2012, as amended (Ethics Office Act). The Ethics Office Act contains the following prohibitions related to government procurement. A public officer or employee shall not

- accept or keep a job or contractual or business relations or responsibilities in addition to those of his or her public office or employment, whether it is in the government or in the private sector, which, although legally permitted, may have the effect of impairing his or her freedom of judgment in the performance of his or her official functions;
- accept or keep a job or contractual relations from which he or she obtains undue advantage with a private person or business that is regulated by or has contractual business or financial relations with the government agency for which he or she works, when the public servant is empowered to decide or influence the official actions of the agency with regard to such private person or business; or
- approve or recommend the execution of a contract in the name of the agency for which he or she works shall or intervene or participate in the execution of a contract with a private person or business in which he or she, or any member of his or her family unit, relative, partner, or housemate, has or has had directly or indirectly a monetary interest during the past two years before his or her appointment.

c. Prohibition against Granting Bids or Contracts to Persons That Have Been Convicted of Certain Crimes

Pursuant to section 3.4 of the Anticorruption Act, any natural or juridical person who has been convicted of (1) violating sections 4.2, 4.3, or 5.7 the Ethics Office Act; (2) committing any of the offenses against public service or public funds deemed felonies under sections 250 through 266 of Act No. 146-2012, as amended, known as the Penal Code of Puerto Rico; (3) any of the offenses classified under the Anticorruption Code; or (4) any other felony involving misappropriation of public funds or property, including, but not limited to, the offenses listed in section 6.8 of Act No. 8-2017, as amended, known as the Government of Puerto Rico Human Resources Administration and Transformation Act, shall be ineligible to contract or bid with any executive agency of the government of Puerto Rico for the period established in section 6.8 of Act No. 8-2017. If no such period is established, the person shall be ineligible for ten years from the date he or she finishes serving the sentence.

Every contract shall include a termination clause in the event that a person who entered into a contract with the executive agencies is convicted in the federal or state jurisdiction of any of the offenses that render the person ineligible to enter into contracts under the list above. It shall be certified in the contracts that the person has not been convicted in the federal or state jurisdiction of any of the aforementioned offenses. The duty to inform shall be of a continuous nature at all stages of the contracting process and the execution of the contract.

The Department of Justice shall establish a registry denominated the "Registry of Persons Convicted of Corruption," which shall include any person convicted of any of the following offenses:

- Offenses established in chapter IV of Act No. 1-2012, as amended, or similar offenses in previous or subsequent laws
- Offenses provided in sections 3.7 and 4.4 of the Anticorruption Code

- Sections 250 through 266 of the Penal Code of Puerto Rico, or similar offenses in previous or subsequent laws
- Any of the offenses listed in section 6.8 of the Government of Puerto Rico Human Resources Administration and Transformation Act, when the offense was committed in the exercise of a public function or whenever public funds or assets have been involved

2. Contracts Registry

Government and municipal entities must keep a registry of all contracts executed, including amendments thereto, and must remit a copy of the contract to the Office of the Comptroller within 15 days following the date of the execution. If the contract is executed outside Puerto Rico, this period is extended to 30 days. (See Laws of Puerto Rico Annotated tit. 2, § 97.)

It is not necessary to submit to the comptroller a copy of the following contracts:

- Personal services of a sporadic nature for a non-extendible term of less than six months, and at a cost of less than $2,000
- Personal services of a professional nature for a non-extendible term of one year or less, and whose services do not constitute a position or employment and its cost does not exceed $5,000
- Works at a cost not to exceed $2,000
- Those executed through public auctions, excepting those that are connected to construction projects or works
- Professional services with physicians and health professionals executed with government entities whose main objective is to provide medical services
- Any other type of contract that the comptroller may, by regulations to that effect, determine not to be sent to him or her

Noncompliance with these requisites is not in itself cause for declaring a legally valid contract or juridical business null. However, the law provides that no provision or consideration of services object of a contract may be demanded until this requisite is satisfied.

Every contract subject to registration shall contain a clear and conspicuous notice that shall read as follows: "No provision or consideration of services object of this contract may be demanded until the same has been filed for registration with the Office of the Comptroller pursuant to the provisions of Act No. 18 of October 30, 1975, as amended [§§ 97 and 98 of this title]."

C. Opinions of the Office of the Attorney General

By statute, the secretary of justice provides written opinions to the executive as well as to the legislature, whenever it is requested, on any issue of law regarding their respective positions. (See Laws of Puerto Rico Annotated tit. 3, § 71.)

Opinions by the secretary of justice can be found at the Puerto Rico Department of Justice website at http://www.justicia.pr.gov/opiniones-del-secretario/.

II. Regulations

The Spanish text of Puerto Rico procurement regulations can be found at app.estado.gobierno.pr/ReglamentosOnLine/ReglOnLine.aspx.

Bid processes are informal, and regulations and terms are established by the agencies (i.e., each agency has its own set of rules). (See Laws of Puerto Rico Annotated tit. 3, § 9642.) Consequently, there are a considerable number of regulations. Below is a listing of some of the Puerto Rico procurement regulations promulgated by the main government entities:

Agency/Government Entity/Public Corporation	**Regulation Number**
General Services Administration	Uniform Regulation for Purchases and Bids of Goods, Works, and Nonprofessional Services of the General Services Administration of the Government of Puerto Rico, Regulation 9230 of November 18, 2020
Health Insurance Administration	P.R. Regs. ASES REG. 5256 P.R. Regs. ASES REG. 7636
Medical Service Administration	P.R. Regs. ASEM REG. 5261 P.R. Regs. ASEM REG. 4170
Aqueducts and Sewers Authority	P.R. Regs. AAA REG. 2732 P.R. Regs. AAA REG. 5319 P.R. Regs. AAA REG. 5016
Public-Private Partnerships Authority	P.R. Regs. AAPP REG. 8968
Roads and Transportation Authority	P.R. Regs. ACT REG. 5263 P.R. Regs. ACT REG. 4500
Public Buildings Authority	P.R. Regs. AEP REG. 7812 P.R. Regs. AEP REG. 6131 P.R. Regs. AEP REG. 8511
Puerto Rico Power Electric Authority	P.R. Regs. AEE REG. 8518
Ports Authority	P.R. Regs. AP REG. 7476
Lands Authority	P.R. Regs. ATPR REG. 5656
Authority for the Financing of the Infrastructure of Puerto Rico	P.R. Regs. AFI REG. 5853
Puerto Rico Economic Development Bank	P.R. Regs. BDE REG. 7395
Tourism Company	P.R. Regs. TURISMO REG. 7598 P.R. Regs. TURISMO REG. 8844
Department of Agriculture	P.R. Regs. DA REG. 6632
Department of Education	P.R. Regs. DE REG. 7040 P.R. Regs. DE REG. 7545 P.R. Regs. DE REG. 7283 P.R. Regs. DE REG. 7934
Treasury Department	P.R. Regs. HACIENDA REG. 6514 P.R. Regs. HACIENDA REG. 6796

Department of Justice	P.R. Regs. JUSTICIA REG. 3661 P.R. Regs. JUSTICIA REG. 4174
Department of Family Affairs	P.R. Regs. FAMILIA REG. 5450 P.R. Regs. FAMILIA REG. 7757
Department of Housing	P.R. Regs. VIVIENDA REG. 6793
Department of Health	P.R. Regs. SALUD REG. 6584 P.R. Regs. SALUD REG. 5363
Department of Transportation	P.R. Regs. DTOP REG. 4764 P.R. Regs. DTOP REG. 5393 P.R. Regs. DTOP REG. 4830
Office of Courts Administration	P.R. Regs. SUPREMO REG. TRIB 6 P.R. Regs. OAT OAT-8 P.R. Regs. OAT OAT-10 P.R. Regs. OAT OAT-19 P.R. Regs. OAT OAT-20
Puerto Rico Office of the Commissioner for Municipal Affairs	P.R. Regs. OCAM REG. 7539

III. Source Selection

The invitation to bid could be in the form of a formal auction, request for proposals (RFP), or a hybrid process between a formal bid and RFP.

A. Traditional Bid Process

1. Invitation to Bid

The invitation provides general information about the bidding process. Typically, the invitation includes where and when (time and date) bids must be delivered; maximum time for bid acceptance; number of copies of the bid required; how the bid envelope should be marked; notice that bids must include a non-collusion form and a tax compliance certificate; a pricing sheet and reference form; a requirement that the bid be signed by an authorized individual; bonding requirements (performance or payment bonds), if any; and the amount of bid deposit, if any.

The agency's regulation may allow bidders to amend the offers prior to the opening of the tendered bids. In such cases, the amendment must be submitted in writing no later than the due date established by the agency to submit offers.

2. Presentation of the Offer

The offer may be withdrawn prior to the opening of the tendered bids. The envelopes are opened in public at the date and time advised in the invitation. Each bidder is entitled to examine the bids of its competitors. A bid that contains material variations from the government's specifications or that fails to include any required documentation could be rejected at this stage.

3. Evaluation and Adjudication

The agency's auction board or a designated committee shall make an award to the lowest responsive bidder, taking into consideration that the bid conforms to specifications, delivery terms, the ability of the bidder to fulfill and comply with the contract, financial responsibility of the bidder, business standing and integrity, and other conditions included in the bidding form. The bid could be awarded to a bidder who may not necessarily be the lowest bidder if deemed beneficial to the public interest.

B. Public-Private Partnerships

The Puerto Rico Public-Private Partnerships Act came into law on June 8, 2009, to promote the establishment of public-private partnerships for the creation of priority projects and, among other things, to further the development and maintenance of infrastructure facilities, to apportion between the Commonwealth of Puerto Rico and the contractor the risk involved in the development, operation, or maintenance of such projects, and to improve the services rendered and the functions of the government. (See Laws of Puerto Rico Annotated tit. 27, § 2601 *et seq.*)

To that end, the statute created the Public-Private Partnership Authority as a public corporation of the Commonwealth of Puerto Rico. The duties and powers of the Authority shall be discharged by a board of directors, which establishes the public policy of the Authority. (See Laws of Puerto Rico Annotated tit. 27, § 2604.)

The Public-Private Partnership Authority was designated as the sole government entity authorized and responsible for implementing the public policy on partnerships and for determining the functions, services, or facilities for which such partnerships are to be established. Accordingly, the Public-Private Partnership Authority has the specific power to evaluate the terms and conditions of each partnership contract and to make recommendations in connection therewith to the board of directors of the partnering government entity. (See Laws of Puerto Rico Annotated tit. 27, § 2605(b)(3).)

C. Requests for Proposals

Government agencies typically issue an RFP for the acquisition of technical services or sophisticated products based on additional criteria besides price. The RFP process allows negotiation before a contract is awarded.

The agency issues an RFP containing all the information and instructions necessary for companies to prepare their proposals. Subsequently, companies write and submit their proposals, paying close attention to specifications in the RFP, such as required work plan, staffing, and forms to be completed. Usually, a committee reviews the proposals and selects those deemed competitive enough to continue in the negotiation process. Therefore, negotiations begin between agency officials and the short-listed companies.

D. Bonds

Bid regulations typically require the issuance of a bid bond as well as a performance bond to ensure that the winning bidder executes the contract and provides the required surety bonds. The performance bond must be issued by an insurance company or a bank to guarantee satisfactory performance.

E. Mandatory Contract Provisions

Mandatory contract clauses are required by law and may also be required by agency procurement regulations (See Laws of Puerto Rico Annotated tit. 2, § 97(e); Laws of Puerto Rico Annotated tit. 3, § 8615.)

The following are brief summaries of mandatory provisions:

- Every contract subject to registration at the Office of the Comptroller must contain a clear and conspicuous notice that must read as follows: "No provision or consideration of services object of this contract may be demanded until the same has been filed for registration with the Office of the Comptroller pursuant to the provisions of Act No. 18 of October 30, 1975, as amended."
- The contract must include acceptance by the contractor of the norms established in the Anticorruption Code.
- Every contract shall include a termination clause in the event that a person who entered into a contract with the executive agencies is convicted in the federal or state jurisdiction of any of the offenses that render him or her ineligible to enter into contracts. It shall be certified in the contracts that the person has not been convicted in the federal or state jurisdiction of any of the offenses. The duty to inform shall be of a continuous nature at all stages of the contracting process and the execution of the contract.
- Government contracts usually require the following certifications:
    - Certification that the contractor has filed income tax returns during the past five tax years prior to the year in which the contract is to be executed and that it does not have outstanding tax debts with the Commonwealth of Puerto Rico of any sort or, if it has such debts, that the contractor is subject to and is complying with a payment plan
    - A certification from the Municipal Revenues Collection Center on the absence of any tax debt or the existence of a payment plan
    - A certification from the Department of Labor and Human Resources on the payment of unemployment insurance, temporary disability, or Social Security taxes or premiums, as applicable
    - A negative debt certification from the Child Support Administration; this requirement applies if the contractor is an individual
    - A certification that the contractor is not involved in any conflict of interest or of public policy
    - A certification that the contractor has not been convicted of offenses against public integrity, as defined in the Penal Code, or of embezzlement of public funds, and that he or she has not been found guilty of any such type of offense in the courts of the Commonwealth of Puerto Rico, the federal courts, or the courts of any jurisdiction of the United States
- The contract must include a clause stating that said documents have been attached to the contract.
- The contract must identify the legal provision authorizing its execution.
- There must be a clause providing for the corresponding withholdings established in the Internal Revenue Code.
- There must be a budget appropriation from which the fees of the contractor shall be paid.
- The contract must include a clause indicating that the contracting government entity may terminate the contract for professional services by giving notice

30 days prior to its being terminated, or within a lesser term, depending upon the services to be contracted.

- The contract must include a clause indicating that the agency may terminate the contract immediately in cases of negligence, dereliction of duties, or non-compliance by the contractor.
- The contract must include a clause stating that, if required, the necessary dispensation has been obtained from any government entity and that said dispensation shall become part of the contracting record.
- In contracts with individuals, a clause shall be included indicating that the contractor receives no payments or compensation for regular services rendered under a designation from any other public entity, except those authorized by law.
- In professional contracts, a clause shall be included under which the contractor accepts being knowledgeable of the rules of ethics of his or her profession and assumes responsibility for his or her own actions.

F. Socioeconomic Policies

1. Preference Procurement Act

On January 8, 2004, Puerto Rico passed Act 14. (Laws of Puerto Rico Annotated tit. 3, § 930 *et seq*.) The statute intends to promote the public policy of the Commonwealth of Puerto Rico to support the growth, development, and strengthening of Puerto Rican industry. More specifically, Act 14 pursues, among other objectives, to guarantee the greatest possible participation of Puerto Rican producers of goods and services in government purchases and to provide the necessary structures and mechanisms so that a greater number of local producers may access the government procurement market, whether through formal or informal auctions, open markets, contracts, or special procedures.

Section 930c of Act 14 states that, in any procurement of goods by the Puerto Rico government, preference shall be given to goods produced, manufactured, assembled, or packaged in Puerto Rico, or distributed by agents established in Puerto Rico, provided said goods and services meet the specifications, terms, and conditions established in the bidding notice or purchase order, and that their price, after applying the corresponding investment parameter, is the lowest or offers the conditions of quality, delivery, and availability of goods and services.

The statute provides for the creation of the Puerto Rican Industry Investment Board under the Puerto Rico Industrial Development Company. The Board is the government entity with authority to grant certificates of preference and to supervise the public entities in their full compliance with the norms of action, criteria, and other provisions of Act 14.

Pursuant to section 930d of Act 14, the Board classifies the services rendered in Puerto Rico as well as the articles extracted, produced, assembled, or packed in Puerto Rico, or distributed by agents established in Puerto Rico, taking into consideration whether the article or service is offered by a company conducting substantial operations in Puerto Rico according to the following factors: the added value in Puerto Rico, the number of jobs, the local payroll, the local capital, the research and development operations in Puerto Rico, and the country of origin of the materials used in the case of the purchase of products.

The Board assigns the corresponding investment parameter within the following items:

- Articles distributed by agents established in Puerto Rico, up to 2 percent
- Articles packed in Puerto Rico, up to 3 percent
- Articles assembled in Puerto Rico, up to 4 percent
- Articles that constitute Puerto Rican products, up to 10 percent
- Services rendered by small and medium-size companies or cooperative-based companies established in Puerto Rico, up to 2 percent

(See P.R. Regs. PRIDCO REG. 8488, *Reglamento General para Promover la Política de Preferencia en las Compras del Gobierno*, for details regarding the procedure that a company must follow to apply for a certification as well as the evaluation criteria.)

Board decisions granting a percentage discount must be made by resolution. Review of said resolution—according to the act and the regulations—may be undertaken by the Board motu proprio or at the request of a party.

Finally, Act 14 provides that secretaries of departments, heads of agencies, instrumentality chiefs, and the mayors shall oversee that the professional and technical personnel in charge of the drafting of specifications of articles to be purchased by the government, and of the acquisition of goods and services, perform their work taking into consideration the availability of goods and services provided by enterprises that operate in Puerto Rico.

IV. Bid Protests and Contract Disputes

A. Bid Protests

Losing bidders may file a motion for reconsideration within 20 days after adjudication of the bid or the RFP. The agency must consider the motion within 30 days of filing. If the agency makes a determination in its consideration, the term to petition the judicial review shall commence as of the date a copy of the notification of the decision of the agency settling the motion is filed. If the agency takes no action with respect to the motion for reconsideration within 30 days from its having been filed, it shall be understood that the motion was denied outright, and the term for judicial review shall commence to run as of that date. If the agency entertains the motion for reconsideration, it shall render its decision within 30 days. (See Laws of Puerto Rico Annotated tit. 3, § 9655.)

B. Bid Protest Appeals

The term for judicial review before the Puerto Rico Court of Appeals is 20 days from the date the copy of the agency's determination is filed in the administrative record. Typically, the reconsideration and the judicial review processes do not stay the execution of the contract.

C. Contract Disputes

The courts of Puerto Rico have jurisdiction to entertain government contract disputes. The government must comply with what was agreed upon independently of any change in government administration. (*Municipio de Ponce v. A.C.*, 153 D.P.R. 1 (2000).) A contract executed between a government and an individual is subject to the same rules of contractual interpretation that apply to contracts that are executed between private parties. (1978 Op. Sec. Just. No. 15; 1978 Op. Sec. Just. No. 2; 1977 Op. Sec. Just. No. 11; 1972 Op. Sec. Just. No. 17; *Municipio de Mayagüez v. Lebrón*, 167 D.P.R. 713 (2006); *Zequeira v. U.R.H.C.*, 83 P.R.R. 847 (1961); *Rodríguez v. Municipality*, 75 P.R.R. 449 (1953).)

D. Suspension and Debarment

Any natural or juridical person who has been convicted of (1) violating sections 4.2, 4.3, or 5.7 the Ethics Office; (2) committing any of the offenses against public service or public funds deemed felonies under sections 250 through 266 of Act No. 146-2012, as amended, known as the Penal Code of Puerto Rico; (3) any of the offenses classified under the Anticorruption Code; or (4) any other felony involving misappropriation of public funds or property, including, but not limited to, the offenses listed in section 6.8 of Act No. 8-2017, as amended, known as the Government of Puerto Rico Human Resources Administration and Transformation Act, shall be ineligible to contract or bid with any executive agency of the government of Puerto Rico for the period established in section 6.8 of Act No. 8-2017. If no such period is established, the person shall be ineligible for ten years from the date he or she finishes serving the sentence.

V. Administrative and Judicial Review

A. Administrative Review

The process of reviewing bids or RFP awards of an administrative agency begins within the agency itself. A non-winning bidder usually has the option of filing a motion for reconsideration within the administrative agency that issued the decision or filing a writ of administrative review before the Puerto Rico Court of Appeals.

B. Judicial Review

The judicial standards of review of bids and RFP awards are whether the agency action was arbitrary and capricious and whether the agency based its decision on substantial evidence. Under the arbitrary and capricious standard, courts must consider whether the decision was based on a consideration of the relevant factors and whether there has been a clear error of judgment. Pursuant to the substantial evidence standard of review, courts are required to uphold the agency's decision if it is reasonable, or the record contains such evidence as a reasonable mind might accept as adequate to support a conclusion.

1. Summary of Selected Decisions

The following are Puerto Rico Supreme Court opinions that have helped shape government procurement law in Puerto Rico:

a. Nullification or Termination of Government Contracts

Contracts executed in violation of the Municipal Law are null and void. A contractor cannot benefit from a municipality's ultra vires actions. (*Morales v. Municipio de Toa Baja*, 119 D.P.R. 682 (1987); *San Miguel, Etc. & Co. v. Municipio de Caguas*, 72 D.P.R. 391 (1951); *De La Cruz v. Gobierno de la Capital*, 68 D.P.R. 534 (1948); *Gayá v. Gobierno de la Capital*, 68 D.P.R. 281 (1948); *Torrellas v. Municipio de Yabucoa, y Carrasquillo, Interventor*, 62 D.P.R. 217 (1943); *Morales v. Municipio de Toa Baja*, 119 D.P.R. 682 (1941).)

Parties to a government contract may agree to include in their contracts a clause giving only one of them the power to put an end to the contractual relationship. To temper the rigors of unilateral cancellation, termination of the contract must not be allowed if there is bad faith or if there has been no change in the circumstances and conditions that gave rise to the contract in the first place. The government also has an obligation to pay for the work performed until the time of termination. (*Flores v. Municipio de Caguas*, 114 D.P.R. 521 (1983).)

The agreements between the plaintiff and municipal officers were null and void inasmuch as no public call for bids was made and neither was a budget previously approved for such purposes. Bidding requirements can only be waived if an emergency exists that requires the immediate delivery of materials, equipment, or the performance of services. To such effects, the mayor or the mayor's authorized representative must certify the facts or circumstances that warrant waiving bidding procedure. (*Hatton v. Municipio de Ponce*, 134 D.P.R. 1001 (1994).)

The fact that the bid had been awarded did not bar the Municipality Bid's Board from following the recommendations of its advisors and, if deemed necessary for the protection of the best interest of the municipality, to reverse the award of the bid. The rule in regard to this matter recognizes this power of the Board of Awards in order to avoid any possibility of favoritism, carelessness, extravagance, and corruption. (*Continental Construction Corp. v. Municipio de Bayamón*, 115 D.P.R. 559 (1984).)

b. When Is the Bid Award Binding?

The objective of provisions requiring contracts to be awarded to the lowest bidder is to prevent favoritism, corruption, extravagance, and improvidence in awarding contracts, and such provisions should be so construed as fairly and reasonably to accomplish such purpose. The bid award is not binding on a public agency until a formal contract is executed, and therefore the agency has the right to revoke the award at any time before a formal contract is entered into with the bidder. (*Cancel v. Municipio de San Juan*, 101 D.P.R. 296 (1973); *Justiniano v. E.L.A.*, 100 D.P.R. 334 (1971).)

c. Culpa in Contrahendo

Although an agency may set aside a bid award before the execution of the contract, it could be liable to the bidder under the culpa in contrahendo doctrine, which means "fault in negotiating." Under this doctrine, a party can be compensated for the expenses it incurred in reliance on the other party's offer to form a contract when the contract negotiations break down. In determining whether a party is liable under Puerto Rico law for its conduct during negotiations, the court must consider (1) the development of the negotiations; (2) how they began; (3) their course; (4) the conduct of the parties throughout them; (5) the stage at which they were terminated; and (6) the parties' reasonable expectations to form a contract, as well as any other relevant circumstance under the facts of the case. (*Producciones Tommy Muñiz v. COPAN*, 113 D.P.R. 517 (1982).)

d. Essential Conditions of the Invitation to Bid Are Part of the Contract

The essential conditions and terms of the invitation to bid accepted by the bidder to whom it is awarded should be read as if they were part of the final contract. Said essential terms and conditions may not be in conflict with the provisions of the contract. (*Banco de la Vivienda de Puerto Rico v. Pagán Insurance Underwriters*, 111 D.P.R. 1 (1981).)

e. Application of Preference Procurement Act Provisions

Pursuant to the Preference Procurement Act and its regulations, the percentage of preference granted by the Preference Board must be applied to each individual product selected by the Board. Said percentage does not apply to the bidder itself or to his or her products in general. The percentage of preference granted by the Board to each product shall be taken into consideration, in all government purchase processes, regardless of whether the purchase was made through a formal or informal bid, or in the open market. (*Mar-Mol Co. Inc. v. Administración de Servicios Generales*, 126 D.P.R. 864 (1990).)

f. Award Notification

The agency or municipality must send notification of the award to both successful and non-successful bidders. At a minimum, notification awards must include (1) names of the bidders that participated in the process and a summary of their respective offers; (2) grounds of the award; (3) defects, if any, of the unsuccessful bidders; and (4) the right to seek administrative and/or judicial review and the applicable term thereof. The term for seeking reconsideration and judicial review will not start to run unless the notification of the award complies with these minimum requirements. (*Punta Arenas Concrete, Inc. v. J. Subastas*, 153 D.P.R. 733 (2001); *IM Winner, Inc. v. Junta de Subastas del Gobierno Municipal de Guayanilla*, 151 D.P.R. 30 (2000); *RBR Construction, S.E. v. A.C.*, 149 D.P.R. 836 (1999).)

The term provided by section 3.19 of the Uniform Administrative Act, Laws of Puerto Rico Annotated title 3, section 9659, to request reconsideration of an adverse decision in a bidding proceeding begins to run from the date the bid is awarded and not when a particular offer of one of the bidders is rejected. (*Cotto v. Departamento De Educación*, 138 D.P.R. 658 (1995).)

g. Standing to Challenge Bid Award

Only bidders that have submitted offers during the bid proceedings are entitled to challenge the award. A person who was invited to the bidding process but merely participates in a bidders' meeting without submitting an offer is not considered a bidder. (*Velázquez v. Administración de Terrenos*, 153 D.P.R. 548 (2001).)

h. Taxes

Private companies contracted by an agency or instrumentality of the central, federal, or municipal government for the performance of construction work must pay municipal excise taxes even if the contracting agencies do not have to procure a permit from the Regulations and Permits Administration. (*Río Construction v. Municipality of Carolina*, 153 D.P.R. 615 (2001).)

i. Contract Shall Be Awarded to Lowest Qualified and Responsible Bidder

The agency, with its vast experience and expertise, is ordinarily in a better position than courts to determine the best bidder. The contracting agency can take into account relevant past performance information regarding a bidder's predecessor companies, key personnel, and major subcontractors, and must consider the currency, relevance, source, and context of the information, and general trends in a contractor's performance. The contract shall be awarded to the lowest qualified and responsible bidder and not merely to the lowest bidder. (*Empresas Toledo v. Junta de Subastas*, 168 D.P.R. 771, 778 (2006); *A.E.E. v. Maxon Engineering Services, Inc.*, 163 D.P.R. 434, 439 (2004).)

j. Enabling Statute Must Confer Authority

The Cardiovascular Center of Puerto Rico and the Caribbean acted in an ultra vires manner when it required that a cleaning services company deposit a bond as a jurisdictional requisite for judicial review of a bid award because its enabling statute does not confer such authority. (*Perfect Cleaning Services, Inc. v. Corporación del Centro Cardiovascular de P.R.*, 162 D.P.R. 745 (2004).)

k. Alter Ego

A judicial determination that a juridical person is an alter ego of another who is prevented from soliciting and contracting with government agencies prevents the alter ego from being awarded a bid in future government bid proceedings. (*Casco Sales v. Municipio de Barranquitas*, 172 D.P.R. 825 (2007).)

l. Public Records

After the bid award, the documents contained in the administrative file are considered public records subject to inspection by any citizen, pursuant to article 409 of the Puerto Rico Code of Civil Procedure, Laws of Puerto Rico Annotated title 32, section 1781 ("Every citizen has a right to inspect and take a copy of any public document of Puerto Rico, except as otherwise expressly provided by law."). The agency must allow the examination of the administrative file by the unsuccessful bidders with sufficient time prior to the applicable term to challenge the adjudication. (*Trans Ad de Puerto Rico, Inc. v. Junta de Subastas Autoridad*, 174 D.P.R. 56 (2008).)

m. Clarification Process during Procurement Proceedings

A hybrid proceeding, which meets all the characteristics of a formal bid but that also incorporates clarifications and participation mechanisms typical of an informal auction, is valid. The term "clarifications" should be construed broadly. Rather than being for the sole purpose of eliminating minor irregularities, informalities, or apparent clerical mistakes, clarifications should provide offerors the opportunity to clarify certain aspects of proposals. (*Caribbean Communications v. Policía de Puerto Rico*, 176 D.P.R. 978 (2009).)

VI. Extent of State's Adoption or Adaptation of ABA Model Procurement Code

The GSA Act, the Anticorruption Code, and the Preference Procurement Act adopt many of the provisions included in the American Bar Association (ABA) Model Procurement Code.

VII. Cooperative Purchasing

A. Authority

Article 24 of the GSA Act contains provisions designed to facilitate cooperative procurement among units of government.

B. Requirements

Government entities and exempted entities must create an annual procurement plan, detailing the needs and proposed purchases the entities will make. Suppliers must be registered with GSA in the Unified Registry of Suppliers of Professional Services or the Unified Bidders Registry to participate in the procurement process. All invoicing processes must be done electronically to safeguard the integrity of the information.

Rhode Island Procurement Rules and Regulations

Prepared by Robert E. Craven, Jr.
Adler Pollock & Sheehan
Email: rcraven@apslaw.com

I. Statutory Reference

A. Procurement/Purchasing Statutes

In Rhode Island, public contracts purchasing is generally managed by the chief procurement officer of the Department of Administration, Division of Purchases (DOP). The DOP's website can be found at https:/ridop.ri.gov. Purchasing is governed by General Laws of Rhode Island section 37-2-1 *et seq*. Relevant purchasing statutes are listed below:

§ 37-2-1. Purchasing Agent—Appointment—Duties.
§ 37-2-2. General Provisions.
§ 37-2-3. Supplemental General Principles of Law—Obligation of Good Faith.
§ 37-2-4. Applicability.
§ 37-2-5. Severability—Construction against Implicit Repealer.
§ 37-2-6. Determinations.
§ 37-2-7. Definitions.
§ 37-2-8. Rhode Island Foodstuffs.
§ 37-2-9. Authority and Duties of the Chief Purchasing Officer.
§ 37-2-9.1. Bidder Registration Fee.
§ 37-2-10. Distribution of Procurement Activities.
§ 37-2-11. Authority and Duties of the Purchasing Agent.
§ 37-2-12. Centralization of the Procurement Authority.
§ 37-2-13. Procurement Regulations.
§ 37-2-14. Relationship with User Agencies.
§ 37-2-15. Source Selection and Contract Formation—Statutory Provisions.
§ 37-2-16. [Reserved].
§ 37-2-17. Method of Source Selection.
§ 37-2-17.1. Rhode Island Vendor Information Program (RIVIP).

§ 37-2-17.2. Utilization of Department of Administration Rhode Island Vendor Information Program (RIVIP).
§ 37-2-18. Competitive Sealed Bidding.
§ 37-2-18.1. Reverse Auctions.
§ 37-2-18.2. Exemption from Competitive Bidding.
§ 37-2-19. Competitive Negotiation.
§ 37-2-20. Negotiations after Unsuccessful Competitive Sealed Bidding.
§ 37-2-21. Noncompetitive Procurements.
§ 37-2-22. Small Purchases.
§ 37-2-23. Cancellation of Invitation for Bids and Requests for Proposals.
§ 37-2-24. Responsibilities of Bidders and Offerors
§ 37-2-25. Prequalification of Contractors—General.
§ 37-2-25.1. Prequalification of Vendors for Electronic Reverse Auctions.
§ 37-2-26. Prequalification of Contractors—Roads—Department of Transportation.
§ 37-2-27. Prequalification—Construction Management.
§ 37-2-27.1. Procurement of Construction Manager at-Risk Services—Written Determination.
§ 37-2-27.2. Procurement of Construction Manager at-Risk Services—Owner's Program Manager.
§ 37-2-27.3. Procurement of Construction Manager at-Risk Services—Technical Review Committee.
§ 37-2-27.4. Procurement of Construction Manager at-Risk Services—Bidding of Subcontracts.
§ 37-2-27.5. Procurement of Construction Manager at-Risk Services—Public Records.
§ 37-2-28. Cost or Pricing Data.
§ 37-2-29. Cost Plus a Percentage of Cost.
§ 37-2-30. Cost Reimbursement Contracts.
§ 37-2-31. Use of Other Types of Contracts.
§ 37-2-32. Approval of Accounting System.
§ 37-2-33. Multi-Year Contracts.
§ 37-2-34. Right to Inspect Facilities—Right to Audit.
§ 37-2-35. Finality of Determinations.
§ 37-2-36. Reporting of Suspected Collusive Bidding or Negotiations.
§ 37-2-37. Report of Procurement Actions Taken under §§ 37-2-21 and 37-2-22.
§ 37-2-38. Issuance of Specifications.
§ 37-2-38.1. Certification by Building Commissioner.
§ 37-2-39. Responsibility for Selection of Methods of Construction Contracting Management.
§ 37-2-40. Bid Security.
§ 37-2-41. Contractors' Bonds.
§ 37-2-42. Price Adjustments.
§ 37-2-43. Contract Clauses and Their Administration.

§ 37-2-77. International Trade Agreements—Procurement Rules—General Assembly Approval.
§ 37-2-78. Severability.
§ 37-2-79. Establishment of the Rhode Island Strategic Purchasing Advisory Commission.
§ 37-2-80. Selection of Vendors and Services with Place of Business Located in Rhode Island.
§ 37-2-81. Authority to Conduct State and National Background Checks for Vendors with Access to Federal Tax Information.

B. Other Applicable Statutes

- Code of Ethics, General Laws of Rhode Island section 36-14-1 *et seq*.
- Award of Municipal Contracts Act, General Laws of Rhode Island section 45-55-1 *et seq*.
- Public Works Arbitration Act, General Laws of Rhode Island section 37-16-1 *et seq*.
- Actions against the State on Highway and Public Works Contracts, General Laws of Rhode Island section 37-13.1-1 *et seq*.
- Access to Public Records Act, General Laws of Rhode Island section 38-2-1 *et seq*.: This law is Rhode Island's equivalent of the federal Freedom of Information Act, 5 U.S.C. § 552.
- Green Buildings Act, General Laws of Rhode Island section 37-24-1 *et seq*.: This law was enacted in November 2009, adopting the Leadership in Energy and Environmental Design (LEED)-certified standard of the U.S. Green Building Council.
- General Laws of Rhode Island section 37-24-4: This law requires that all major facility projects for public agencies or school districts "be designed and constructed to at least the LEED-, LEED for Neighborhood Development-, and SITES- . . . certified or an equivalent high-performance green building standard."
- General Laws of Rhode Island section 37-24-4(c): Lesser green building standards may be applied if there is no appropriate LEED standard or practical application of the LEED standard for that type of building or renovation project.
- General Laws of Rhode Island section 37-24-6: The law offers protection from liability if the person, corporation, or entity made a good-faith attempt to achieve the required green building standard.
- General Laws of Rhode Island section 37-24-6: The law establishes the Rhode Island Executive Climate Change Coordinating Council. The Council is composed of officials from state agencies with responsibility and oversight relating to assessing, integrating, and coordinating climate change efforts.

II. Regulations

The DOP maintains and manages the rules, regulations, and general conditions of purchases (the "regulations"). Below is an index to the different sections of the regulations. Note that in the event that the federal government forms a trade agreement between the federal government and a foreign country to which Rhode Island—at the request of the federal government—is a party, the procurement rules of the international trade agreement shall not apply to Rhode Island unless the Rhode Island General Assembly expressly approves them. (General Laws of Rhode Island § 37-2-77.) Neither the governor nor the federal government can commit the state to alternate procurement rules. (*Id.*)

Key provisions of the regulations include (1) all public contracts must be approved by the DOP's chief purchasing officer (220-30-00 Code of Rhode Island Rules § 8.2(B)(2)(b)); (2) certain provisions of the regulations are incorporated into all state contracts (*Id.* § 8.2(D)); (3) both parties to a public contract have the obligation of "good faith" in the performance and enforcement of the contract (*Id.* § 8.2(F)(2)); and (4) a purchase order shall consist of the State of Rhode Island General Terms and Conditions of Purchase, a bid package, and contract documents (*Id.* § 8.4(C)).

Title 220, chapter 30, subchapter 00:

Part 1. General Provisions

Part 4. Vendor Qualification, Prequalification, and Solicitation

Part 5. Competitive Bid and Competitive Sealed Bid Review and Source Selection

Part 6. Negotiation

Part 8. Contracts

Part 9. Exceptions to Competitive Bidding Requirements

Part 12. Rhode Island Department of Transportation Projects

Part 13. General Conditions of Purchase

Part 14. Vendor Suspension and Debarment

Mandatory registration and use of the E-Verify program—a federal system aimed at verifying employee eligibility to work legally within the United States—was ended by Executive Order in 2011. Though legislation has been introduced before the General Assembly to reinstate the E-Verify program, it has been unsuccessful.

Some of Rhode Island's state agencies have promulgated additional purchasing rules, including, for example, the Narragansett Bay Commission (835-30-00 Code of Rhode Island Rules § 1.1 *et seq.*), the Rhode Island Student Loan Authority (*Id.*), the Rhode Island Turnpike and Bridge Authority (855-00-00 Code of Rhode Island Rules § 1.1 *et seq.*), and the Rhode Island Airport Corporation (800-00-00 Code of Rhode Island Rules § 6.1 *et seq.*).

III. Source Selection

A. Small Purchases

The DOP has delegated purchasing authority for small purchases to state agencies. Pursuant to General Laws of Rhode Island section 37-2-22, general procurements that do not exceed a single transaction limit of $5,000 or construction procurements that do not exceed a single transaction of $10,000 qualify as small purchases.

B. Rhode Island Vendor Information Program and Ocean State Procures

The Rhode Island Vendor Information Program (RIVIP) is an electronic vendor program that allows potential vendors online access to all invitations for bids and requests for proposals. General Laws of Rhode Island section 37-2-17.1 mandates that the RIVIP be readily accessible through public access stations located in the state capitol building in Providence, and in the city hall, town hall, or public library of each of the 39 cities and towns in Rhode Island. Further, General Laws of Rhode Island section 37-2-17.1(b) requires that online access to the RIVIP be provided to potential vendors. General Laws of Rhode Island section 37-2-17.1(c) allows the DOP to hold electronic reverse auctions on the RIVIP, in accordance with General Laws of Rhode Island section 37-2-25.1. The RIVIP can be accessed at https://ridop.ri.gov/.

As of publication, the DOP is in the process of phasing out the RIVIP and replacing it with a new e-procurement system called Ocean State Procures (OSP). Information regarding the OSP program, as well as future information regarding the phase-in process, is available at https://ridop.ri.gov/ocean-state-procures-osp/whats-new. The OSP can be accessed at https://ridop.ri.gov/ocean-state-procures-osp.

C. Contract Solicitation

General Laws of Rhode Island section 37-2-17 mandates that all state contracts shall be awarded through the following methods: competitive sealed offers, pursuant to General Laws of Rhode Island section 37-2-18; competitive negotiation, pursuant to General Laws of Rhode Island sections 37-2-19 and 37-2-20; noncompetitive negotiation, pursuant to General Laws of Rhode Island section 37-2-21; small purchase procedures, pursuant to General Laws of Rhode Island section 37-2-22; or reverse auctions, pursuant to General Laws of Rhode Island section 37-2-18.1.

D. Noncompetitive Negotiation

Pursuant to General Laws of Rhode Island section 37-2-21, public contracts may be awarded through noncompetitive procurement methods when there is only one source for the required supply, service, or construction item (as determined by the chief purchasing officer or purchasing agent),[1] or in an emergency situation when a threat to public health, welfare, or safety exists, provided that competition may still be incorporated into the process as is practicable under the circumstances.

Aside from small purchases, the use of particular source selection methods is not controlled by contract amounts. Rather, discretion is granted to the DOP to determine which source selection process is most appropriate for each contract. However, "[i]n instances where contracts are entirely supported by state funds and two (2) or more vendors or service providers are judged to be equal on all other factors," the DOP must select the vendor that is headquartered or maintains a principal place of business in Rhode Island or, secondarily, must select the entity that proposes a joint venture with such a vendor. (General Laws of Rhode Island § 37-2-80 (noting that this requirement shall not apply to contracts financed, in part or in whole, by the federal government).)

1. To award a contract on the basis of noncompetitive negotiation, the purchasing agent must determine—in writing—that (1) a single or sole source of procurement is involved; (2) the product, or market in which the product is sold, is noncompetitive in nature; or (3) collusive or exclusionary selling practices are in evidence. 220-30-00 R.I. Code R. § 6.4.

E. Competitive Bidding

1. Administration and Bid Specification

State purchases and the awarding of construction contracts are addressed by the DOP. The chief purchasing officer appoints a chief purchasing agent to oversee each public procurement project. The chief purchasing officer has adopted the state procurement regulations to provide a framework for the implementation of the law and to create a set of expectations for all public projects bidders.

Purchases and construction contracts for Rhode Island cities and towns are governed by the Award of Municipal Contracts Act, General Laws of Rhode Island section 45-55-1 *et seq*.

Notably, the Rhode Island Department of Transportation (RIDOT) has its own set of standard detailed bid specifications. These specifications are set forth in RIDOT's Standard Specifications for Road and Bridge Design. The specifications are several hundred pages in length and include the general requirements and covenants, as well as technical specifications. The most recent edition of the "Blue Book," as it is popularly known, was last amended by RIDOT in March 2018. Specifications are available on RIDOT's website, http://www.dot.ri.gov/business/bluebook.php, and may also be ordered directly from RIDOT in hard copy.

The Rhode Island judiciary has broad authority over its own administrative affairs, including judicial procurements. (See General Laws of Rhode Island § 8-15-4(d).) The Rhode Island judiciary subsequently adopted, and maintains, its own Judicial Purchasing Rules and Regulations, available at https://www.courts.ri.gov/PublicResources/purchasingrules/PDFs/Purchasing-Rules-Reg.pdf.

2. Bid/Proposal Procedures

Unless invitations are accessible through the RIVIP, solicitations for bids must be issued through public notice (i.e., newspaper) not less than seven days nor more than 28 days before the opening of bids. (General Laws of Rhode Island § 37-2-18(h).) The DOP can waive the 28-day maximum, if necessary. For services contracts in excess of $20,000, a bidders' conference may be held to establish the requirements and evaluation criteria to be used in the solicitation. (*Id.* § 37-2-61.)

Bids shall be opened publicly and an abstract made of all bid offerings. (*Id.* § 37-2-18(d).) The contract will be awarded "with reasonable promptness by written notice" given to the award recipient. (*Id.* § 37-2-18(e).) If all bids exceed the amount of funds available for the purchase, then a negotiated award may be granted. (*Id.* § 37-2-20(a), (b), (d).) Negotiations are conducted with the two or three lowest bidders to the sealed bid invitation and an award granted to the best offeror. (*Id.* § 37-2-20(b).)

Bidder security is required for all competitive sealed bids for construction contracts over $50,000. (*Id.* § 37-2-40(a).) However, security may be required for any project under $50,000 if the circumstances warrant. (*Id.*) The bidder's security must be in the form of a bond issued by a surety company or the cash equivalent. (*Id.*) The security must be equal to at least 5 percent of the amount of the bid. (*Id.* § 37-2-40(b).) Once the bids are opened, the security is irrevocable unless permission is granted to withdraw a bid. (*Id.* § 37-2-40(d).

If the purchasing agent determines that competitive sealed bidding is not practicable, the contract may be awarded by competitive negotiation. (*Id.* § 37-2-19.) This process requires public notice, submission of proposals, and written or oral discussions with all offerors. (*Id.* § 37-2-19(b)–(d).) An award is made based on considerations of price and the evaluation factors set forth in the request. (*Id.* § 37-2-19(e).)

The chief purchasing officer may provide for prequalification of suppliers and contractors, which are organized on a mailing list for solicitation purposes. (*Id.* § 37-2-25.) A contractor may be eliminated from the list or added to the list (i.e., deemed responsible or not responsible) between the time of bid opening or receipt of the offers and the granting of an award. (*Id.*) Prequalification is determined according to a list of criteria set forth in the general laws. (*Id.* §§ 37-2-26, 37-2-27.)

3. Exceptions to Competitive Bidding Requirements

Pursuant to state law, competitive bidding may not be required for the following purchases: (1) for contractual services where no competition exists, such as sewage treatment, water, and other public utility services; (2) when, in the judgment of the Department of Administration, food, clothing, equipment, supplies, or other materials to be used in laboratory and experimental studies can be purchased otherwise to the best advantage of the state; (3) when instructional materials are available from only one source; (4) where rates are fixed by law or ordinance; (5) for library books; (6) for commercial items that are purchased for resale; (7) for professional, technical, or artistic services; (8) for all other commodities, equipment, and services that, in the reasonable discretion of the chief purchasing officer, are available from only one source; (9) for interests in real property; (10) for works of art for museum and public display; (11) for books, maps, periodicals, newspaper or journal subscriptions, and technical pamphlets; (12) for licenses for use of proprietary or patented systems; and (13) for services of visiting speakers, professors, performing artists, and expert witnesses. (*Id.* § 37-2-54.)

Further, Rhode Island's three public institutions of higher education (i.e., the University of Rhode Island, Rhode Island College, and the Community College of Rhode Island) are exempt from the competitive bidding procedures outlined above for research or research-related activities funded with federal or other third-party funds. (General Laws of Rhode Island § 37-2-18.2.) However, the three schools remain "subject to rules and regulations promulgated by [the Rhode Island Board of Education (the board).]" (*Id.*; *id.* § 16-97-1(a) (As of January 1, 2013, the board of education "shall be responsible for and shall exercises the purposes, powers, and duties, . . . for the coordination of education from pre-k through higher education and shall set goals and policies for the effective coordination of these public education systems.").) The chair of the board of education shall consult with the chairs of several other pertinent educational councils "in developing agendas, goals, policies, and strategic plans for the board." (*Id.* § 16-97-1(g).) An annual report will be submitted to the governor and other government officials on the first of March. (*Id.* § 16-97-6.)

F. Construction Manager At-Risk Services

For some public projects, a "construction manager at-risk" (CMAR) or "construction management at-risk firm" is used as the management approach. (*Id.* § 37-2-7(31).) In this type of management, an entity "experienced in construction has the ability to evaluate and to implement drawings and specifications as they affect time, cost and quality of construction and the ability to coordinate and deliver the construction of the project within a guaranteed maximum price." (*Id.*)

From a procurement standpoint, every project utilizing the CMAR delivery method must be approved by both the DOP's chief purchasing officer and by the chief executive officer of the public entity undertaking the project. (*Id.* § 37-2-27.1.) Except for those involved in highway or heavy construction projects, both individuals must execute a written determination documenting the following: (1) that selection of a general contractor as the lowest responsive bidder based on a lump-sum, fixed-fee contract is not practicable and will not result in the best value for the state; (2) that the public entity has clearly identified in writing why the use of CMAR services is appropriate for the building project; (3) that the building project has an estimated construction value of $5,000,000 or more; (4) that written procedures are in place to ensure fairness in competition, evaluation, and reporting of results at every stage in the procurement process; (5) that detailed plans and procedures are in place to effectively procure and manage CMAR services, including the procurement of a qualified owner's program manager (OPM); and (6) that the public entity has a detailed, written plan with clearly identified procedures to monitor and approve all reimbursable costs. (*Id.* § 37-2-27.1(a), (b).) Further:

> When evaluating the procurement of construction manager at-risk services, the factors that may be considered in determining whether the general contractor method of construction management is not practicable or will not result in the best value for the state, public corporation, or public agency shall include:
>
> (1) Whether specifications can be prepared that permit award on the basis of either the lowest bid or the lowest-evaluated bid price;
>
> (2) Whether the available sources, the time and place of performance, and other relevant circumstances exist as are appropriate for the use of competitive sealed bidding;
>
> (3) The complexity of the project, including the existing or proposed infrastructure or structures, required demolition or abatement, adjacency to other structures or abutters, site constraints, building systems, uniqueness of design elements, or environmental implications;
>
> (4) The size, scope, and estimated cost of the project;
>
> (5) The adequacy of available documentation regarding the existing site, buildings, or structures; abutter infrastructure, buildings, or structures; or other documentation of as-built conditions;
>
> (6) Phasing or logistical challenges arising out of the need to maintain existing occupancy, continue existing operations, provide phased occupancy, or achieve more favorable project financing terms;
>
> (7) The anticipated impact of fast-tracked design and construction on project cost or schedule;
>
> (8) Potential to achieve optimal minority or woman business enterprise or other subcontractor or vendor participation required in accordance with any applicable state or federal laws;
>
> (9) The amount and type of financing available for the project, including whether the budget is fixed and the source of funding, for example, general or special appropriation, federal assistance monies, general obligation bonds or revenue bonds;
>
> (10) The administration or implementation of procedures required to comply with applicable regulations or statutes; and
>
> (11) Mitigating the potential claims against the state arising from the inherent risks associated with factors noted in subdivisions (3) through (10) of this subsection.

(*Id.* § 37-2-27.1(c).)

The OPM hired to oversee the project shall have at least seven years' experience in the construction and supervision of the construction of buildings of similar size and complexity. (*Id.* § 37-2-27.2.) In addition, the OPM shall not have been employed during the preceding year by the design firm, the CMAR firm, and/or the subcontractors associated with the project. (*Id.*) Prior to the engagement of an OPM, the DOP's chief purchasing officer must make the following determinations in writing: the state does not have the ability to prepare the requisite design or engineering specifications, bridging documents, or scope of work; the state cannot manage or supervise the work of specialty trade contractors and will not contract directly with such specialty trade contractors; it is in the state's best interest to retain a program manager to supervise and or monitor the activities of a general contractor; it is in the state's best interest to retain a program manager to supervise and or monitor the engineering and architectural services for a project; and/or the construction project has an estimated cost equal to or greater than $10,000. (220-30-00 Code of Rhode Island Rules § 8.11.)

When procuring CMAR services for a using agency—other than a public corporation or a public agency—the chief purchasing officer must appoint a five-member technical review committee composed of individual's from various state agencies. (General Laws of Rhode Island § 37-2-27.3.) The technical review committee is responsible for both drafting and evaluating the request for proposals used to procure the CMAR. (*Id.*) The committee is also responsible for prequalifying at least two firms as professionally and technically qualified for the project. (*Id.*) If the committee is unable to prequalify at least two firms, then the public entity must complete the project through the procurement of a general contractor. (*Id.*)

All subcontracts entered through the CMAR delivery method must utilize the RIVIP, described above, and all vendors must be prequalified as a responsible bidder or offeror. (*Id.* § 37-2-27.4.) All subcontract bids must be opened in public, and must be forwarded to the CMAR for evaluation and further negotiation where appropriate. (*Id.*)

All documents related to a construction project delivered through a CMAR, including, but not limited to, design documents, construction documents, bid documents, financial documents, and contract documents, shall be considered public records and be made available for public inspection in accordance with the Rhode Island Access to Public Records Act. (*Id.* § 37-2-27.5(a).) Information may only be withheld from public inspection if the CMAR firm or the relevant subcontractor specifically states in writing a description of the data or materials to be protected and the reasons why protection is necessary, and if the chief purchasing officer determines through a written determination that the records are not public. (*Id.*)

IV. Bid Protests and Contract Disputes

A. Bid Protests

Any actual or prospective bidder, offeror, or contractor who is aggrieved in connection with the solicitation or selection of an award of a public contract may file a protest with the DOP's chief purchasing officer. (*Id.* § 37-2-52(b).) The protest "or notice of other controversy" must be filed in writing within two calendar weeks of the date when the aggrieved person "knows or should have known" of the facts giving rise to the protest. (*Id.*) Once a protest is received, the chief purchasing officer shall "promptly" issue a written decision. (*Id.* § 37-2-52(c).) If the procurement is to proceed, notwithstanding the filing of a protest, then the chief purchasing officer is required to first issue an "adequately supported determination that continuation of the procurement is necessary to protect a substantial interest of the state." (*Id.* § 37-2-53.)

It is important to note that an aggrieved bidder need not avail itself of the DOP protest process and may proceed directly to court, as described below. However, an aggrieved bidder would be wise to utilize the DOP protest process, so that the subject project will be temporarily delayed to provide a "window of opportunity" for the aggrieved to seek injunctive relief in the state courts.

If the aggrieved bidder fails in the DOP bid protest process, then it has the option of filing a civil action to enjoin the award of a state or a municipal procurement contract in the state court. (See *id.* § 8-2-14(a).) If more than $5,000 is in dispute, the superior court has jurisdiction; for disputes less than $5,000, jurisdiction lies with the district court. (See *id.*) So long as the action is brought in good faith—and not to further the interests of a stranger to the record—Rhode Island taxpayers may also maintain an action to enjoin a municipal officer from abusing his or her powers by expending money without authority of law. (See *Paul Goldman, Inc. v. Burns*, 283 A.2d 673, 674–75 (R.I. 1971).) However, an aggrieved party will very rarely obtain an injunction against an award, because a statutory "presumption of correctness" applies to "[t]he decision of any official, board, agent, or other person appointed by the state concerning any controversy arising under or in connection with the solicitation or award of a contract." (General Laws of Rhode Island § 37-2-51.) The Rhode Island Supreme Court has instructed the superior court not to vacate an award or decision of the municipality absent compelling or unusual circumstances. (*Truk Away of Rhode Island, Inc. v. Macera Brothers of Cranston, Inc.*, 643 A.2d 811, 816 (R.I. 1994).) The Rhode Island Supreme Court, however, has recently reminded public owners that, even where the public bidding statute does not apply, they cannot act "'corruptly or in bad faith, or so unreasonably or arbitrarily as to be guilty of a palpable abuse of discretion.'" (*Kayak Centre at Wickford Cove, LLC v. Town of Narragansett*, 116 A.3d 250, 255 (R.I. 2015) (quoting *Paul Goldman, Inc.*, 283 A.2d at 676) (concerning a concession contract, which is not subject to state procurement law).)

Contractors who are prospective bidders and failed to bid on a public project due to union wage and hiring restrictions have standing to sue the state for violations of the State Purchases Act and would have had to include a 5 percent bond with the bid, subject to forfeiture, if those contractors refuse to sign a project labor agreement. (*Associated Builders & Contractors of Rhode Island Inc. v. Department of Administration*, 787 A.2d 1179, 1185 (R.I. 2002).) The Rhode Island Supreme Court held in *Associated Builders* that an awarding authority may include a project labor agreement as a bid specification in a public contract only when the awarding authority has demonstrated that: "(1) the size and complexity of the project are such that a [project labor agreement] supports the goals and objectives of the state purchases act, and (2) the [record] demonstrates that the awarding authority has conducted an objective, reasoned study using reviewable criteria in determining that the adoption of a [project labor agreement] helps to achieve the goals of the state purchases act." (*Id.* at 1189.)

B. Contract Disputes

1. Contract Claims

Any person, firm, or corporation that is a party to a contract with the state may bring a contract-based action against the state within three years of the date of project completion, with such action receiving a priority position on the superior court's calendar. (General Laws of Rhode Island § 37-2-49.) Damages in contract-based actions are limited to double that of the original contract amount. (*Id.* § 37-2-49(e).)

However, the Public Works Arbitration Act imposes an obligation to arbitrate disputes in certain public projects. (*Id.* § 37-16-2.) In the absence of an arbitration clause containing a specified arbitration method, all contracts between a public entity and a contractor for the construction, alteration, repair, or painting of any public building, sewer, highway, bridge, water treatment facility, or disposal facility project must provide a mandatory default arbitration provision. (*Id.*) The default public works arbitration provision requires the parties to designate one arbitrator each, with those two arbitrators then selecting a third "neutral" arbitrator. (*Id.*)

The clause allows for binding decisions and requires all decisions to be issued in writing and to be signed by the majority of the arbitrators. (*Id.*) Once the neutral is selected, General Laws of Rhode Island section 37-16-2 requires that the arbitration hearing occur not later than 15 days from that date of selection. If the parties cannot agree as to the appointment of the arbitrators, whether under the process described in the statutory arbitration provision or under another provision in the contract between the parties, then either party can petition the superior court to appoint a single arbitrator, as provided for in General Laws of Rhode Island section 37-16-7.

As an exception to the above process, any dispute exceeding $100,000 and associated with the construction of a highway or bridge shall be arbitrated only with the consent of the parties (arbitration is mandatory on highway or bridge projects when the dispute is less than $100,000). (*Id.* § 37-16-2(c).) Further, where the contract in such highway or bridge projects contemplates a method for choosing the arbitrator(s) that is different than what is provided General Laws of in Rhode Island section 37-16-2(b), the different method shall be used. (*Id.* § 37-16-2(e).)

2. Contract Claims Appeals

The Rhode Island Supreme Court, in accordance with regular civil practice in Rhode Island, will hear appeals from actions filed in superior court under General Laws of Rhode Island section 37-2-49. Following issuance of an order or entry of judgment on an award made under the Public Works Arbitration Act, an appeal may be taken in accordance with the procedure and law applicable to all other arbitration appeals in Rhode Island. (*Id.* § 37-16-25.) In all but the rarest circumstances, orders and judgments are unlikely to be overturned.

C. Suspension and Debarment

The DOP may disqualify a supplier, contractor, or subcontractor from participating in state procurements and further may debar or suspend those entities. (220-30-00 Code of Rhode Island Rules § 4.5(C); *id.* § 14.5.) Debarment results in the removal of the entity from state bidder lists, exclusion from all subsequent procurement opportunities, and termination from all outstanding contracts. (*Id.* § 14.3(A); *id.* § 14.5; 290-10-00 Code of Rhode Island Rules § 2.6 (five-year debarment on RIDOT projects).) Suspension involves the same sanctions as debarment, but for a limited period of time. (220-30-00 Code of Rhode Island Rules § 14.3(D).) A debarment or suspension order against part of a corporation usually constitutes debarment or suspension of all of its divisions and other organizational elements. (*Id.* § 14.5(A)(1).)

Further, the improper conduct of any individual associated with a contractor may be imputed to the contractor if that individual's performance occurred within his or her performance of duties for the entity, or with the entity's knowledge, approval, or acquiescence. (*Id.* § 14.5(A)(2).) If the entity accepts benefits from said improper conduct, then that will be evidence of the entity's knowledge, approval, and/or acquiescence. (*Id.*)

In addition to criminal offenses (including violation of state and federal antitrust and campaign contribution laws), Code of Rhode Island Rules title 220, chapter 30, subchapter 00, section 14.5(C)(2) provides the following justifications for debarment: (1) violation of the terms of a public agreement or transaction so serious as to affect the integrity of any agency program; (2) falsification of information on a bid submission or bidder registration form, subcontracting plan, or minority business enterprise utilization plan; (3) material nonperformance on two or more contracts, subject to the notice provisions set forth in section 13.20 of the chapter, if applicable; (4) debarment by the federal government; (5) withdrawal, without written permission of the purchasing agency, of two or more bids after an award has been announced; (6) commission of any act indicating a lack of business integrity or business honesty; (7) lack of competence, financial responsibility, or other limitations related to the ability of a vendor to provide goods and services; (8) failure to pay subcontractors for work performed and accepted in accordance with the Prompt Pay Statute, General Laws of Rhode Island section 42-11.1-3; or (9) any failure by a vendor to perform a contract in a workmanlike manner.

Code of Rhode Island Rules title 220, chapter 30, subchapter 00, section 14.5(B) provides the following justifications for suspension (including the above grounds for debarment): (1) an indictment or any public agency filing charging a criminal offense, conviction for which would justify debarment; (2) substantial evidence of willfully supplying materially false information incident to obtaining or performing any public contract or subcontract, or willful failure to comply with requirements imposed upon contractors or subcontractors by law or regulation; (3) suspension by the federal government; (4) substantial nonperformance on at least one contract; or (5) a finding of lack of responsibility pursuant to the regulations.

Further, a contractor may be subject to penalty, including suspension or debarment, for knowingly engaging a suspended or debarred subcontractor. (*Id.* § 14.5(D).)

An aggrieved party may seek review of a DOP administrative decision in the superior court if the dispute amount is in excess of $5,000, or the district court if it is below $5,000. (See General Laws of Rhode Island § 8-2-14(a).)

V. Administrative and Judicial Review

A. Administrative Review

Information regarding administrative review is set forth above.

B. Judicial Review

Recent and important judicial decisions include:

- *La Gondola, Inc. v. City of Providence by and through Lombardi*, 210 A.2d 1205 (R.I. 2019)—Reaffirming the "very high level of deference" and "the presumption of correctness" afforded to the decisions of public officials made in connection with the solicitation or award of a government contract.
- *Kayak Centre at Wickford Cove, LLC v. Town of Narragansett*, 116 A.3d 250, 254 (R.I. 2015)—Holding that General Laws of Rhode Island section 45-55-5, which details the procedure for competitive sealed bidding with respect to municipal contracts and which states "[t]he contract shall be awarded . . . to the responsive and responsible bidder whose bid is either the lowest bid price, or lowest evaluated or responsive bid price," is not applicable to concessions contracts.

- *H.V. Collins Co. v. Williams*, 990 A.2d 845 (R.I. 2010)—In a general contractor's challenge against the chief purchasing officer regarding the rejection of its low bid for a public construction project (which had been submitted two minutes late and had been immediately opened but ultimately rejected as untimely) the trial court found that the rejection of the bid was not an abuse of the purchasing officer's discretion and granted the defendants' motion for summary judgment, pursuant to the statutory presumption of correctness mandated by General Laws of Rhode Island section 37-2-51. The Rhode Island Supreme Court held that the appeal was moot because the construction project was near completion and the plaintiff sought only declaratory relief, rather than monetary damages.
- *Blue Cross & Blue Shield of Rhode Island v. Najarian*, 911 A.2d 706, 709 (R.I. 2006)—Confirming that "an award of attorneys' fees to a prevailing party wrongfully enjoined in the context of a public contract bid" is not required or mandatory.
- *Blue Cross & Blue Shield of Rhode Island v. Najarian*, 865 A.2d 1074 (R.I. 2005)—Even where an award violates the provisions of the State Purchases Act, a public official's contract award "is still to be given great deference as long as the authority did not act in bad faith, was not 'corrupt' and was not so arbitrary or capricious as to amount to a 'palpable abuse of discretion.'"
- *Aetna Bridge Co. v. Department of Transportation*, 795 A.2d 517 (R.I. 2002)—This is the seminal Rhode Island decision interpreting Rhode Island public works arbitration, setting out high standards for overturning public works arbitration awards and holding that "pass-through" claims on behalf of subcontractors are not arbitrable if no concomitant liability exists for the contractor.
- *Associated Builders & Contractors of Rhode Island, Inc. v. Department of Administration*, 787 A.2d 1179 (R.I. 2002)—On public contract projects, the state bears the burden of establishing that a project labor agreement is necessary and appropriate.
- *H.V. Collins Co. v. Tarro*, 696 A.2d 298 (R.I. 1997)—A public awarding authority is not precluded from taking into account factors beyond price when selecting best or superior bidders, and that authority is not necessarily required to award a contract to the lowest bidder who satisfies the minimum criteria announced in the project's request for proposals, as long as the authority's analysis is "sufficiently objective, measurable, and enunciated" in the request for proposals. This dispute involved a school and occurred under the Award of Municipal Contracts, Competitive Sealed Bidding Statute, General Laws of Rhode Island section 45-55-5.
- *Clark-Fitzpatrick v. Gill*, 652 A.2d 440 (R.I. 1994)—This public-contract-based action touches on several topics that typically reoccur in complex public project litigation under General Laws of Rhode Island section 37-13-1.1.
- *Truk Away of Rhode Island, Inc. v. Macera Brothers of Cranston, Inc.*, 643 A.2d 811 (R.I. 1994)—A Rhode Island court will not interfere with the award of a public contract "absent a showing that the [awarding authority] acted corruptly or in bad faith, or so unreasonably or arbitrarily as to be guilty of a palpable abuse of discretion."

VI. Extent of State's Adoption or Adaptation of ABA Model Procurement Code

Rhode Island has partially adopted the American Bar Association (ABA) Model Procurement Code (MPC). (National Association of State Procurement Officials, 2020

Survey of State Procurement Practices, https://www.naspo.org/research-innovation/publications/survey-state-procurement-practices/.) For example, consistent with the MPC, Rhode Island centralizes its procurement offices. (*Id.*) Like the MPC, Rhode Island allows single source bidding and informal competition ($5,000 or less). (*Id.*) The formal request for proposal process is triggered at $5,000. (*Id.*) The state has also started using an e-procurement system—Ocean State Procures—to promote statewide procurements and transparency through open and equal access to procurement opportunities. (*Id.*) In contrast to the MPC, the state does not have steps for review, approval, and pre-audit (by someone outside the central office). (*Id.*) Rhode Island does allow vendors to protest procurement decisions and file lawsuits. (*Id.*) Rhode Island also has permitted reverse auctions for solicitation. (See General Laws of Rhode Island § 37-2-18.1.)

VII. Cooperative Purchasing

A. Authority

In an effort to "insure that the state is supplying its real needs at the lowest possible cost," state law permits the chief purchasing officer to "enter into cooperative purchasing agreements with other governmental entities." (*Id.* § 37-2-54(j).) State law expressly authorizes purchasing cooperatives with respect to certain resources, such as electricity. (See, e.g., *id.* § 39-3-1.1; *id.* § 16-3.1-17 (permitting Rhode Island Board of Regents for Elementary and Secondary Education to engage in cooperative purchasing of food).) State law further permits "local governmental units to make the most efficient use of their powers by enabling them to cooperate with other localities on a basis of mutual advantage" to procure supplies and services. (*Id.* § 45-40.1-1.)

B. Requirements

State law does not address set requirements of general purchasing cooperatives. However, there is some guidance with regard to the cooperative purchasing of particular resources. With regard to electricity, for example, purchasing cooperatives "shall be considered to be associations of electricity consumers organized solely for the purpose of negotiating the purchase of electric power by members of the cooperative." (*Id.* § 39-3-1.1.) However, purchasing cooperatives created pursuant to this grant of authority "are specifically not required to be legal entities," though they may be if so desired, and are expressly "prohibited from engaging in resale of electric power." (*Id.*)

South Carolina Procurement Rules and Regulations

Prepared by Keith C. McCook[1]
South Carolina State Fiscal Accountability Authority
Email: kmccook@ogc.sc.gov

I. Statutory Reference

This summary covers acquisitions by governmental bodies governed by the South Carolina Consolidated Procurement Code. Only limited information is provided for acquisitions by other entities.

Except as noted otherwise, all citations are to the South Carolina Code of Laws and the South Carolina Code of Regulations.

The state agency with general oversight of government contracting is called the State Fiscal Accountability Authority (the Authority). The Division of Procurement Services (DPS, or the Division), a subdivision of this agency, serves as the state's central purchasing office. Extensive information about DPS is available at https://procurement.sc.gov/. The Authority's governing board promulgates the state's procurement regulations.

South Carolina's legislature, known as the South Carolina General Assembly, posts both the South Carolina Code of Laws and the South Carolina Code of Regulations on the internet at https://www.scstatehouse.gov/. All citations contained herein are to the law current through the 2020 legislative session.

A. Procurement/Purchasing Statutes

In large measure, South Carolina has consolidated its procurement laws into one code, the South Carolina Consolidated Procurement Code. Originally adopted in 1981, the Procurement Code is closely modeled after the American Bar Association's (ABA's) initial version of the Model Procurement Code for State and Local Governments. In 2000, the ABA updated the Model Code. South Carolina adopted the construction-related amendments in 2008. (Act 174, 2008 S.C. Acts 1524, 1526.)

The Procurement Code is codified at title 11, chapter 35 of the South Carolina Code of Laws in sections 11-35-10 through 11-35-5340 and is divided into the following 13 articles:

1. The author is currently employed by the State Fiscal Accountability Authority. The views expressed herein are entirely the author's and do not necessarily represent those of either the agency or the chief procurement officers.

Article 1. General Provisions
Article 3. Procurement Organization
Article 5. Source Selection and Contract Formation
Article 7. Specifications
Article 9. Construction, Architect-Engineer, Construction Management, and Land Surveying Services
Article 10. Indefinite Delivery Contracts
Article 11. Modifications and Termination of Contracts for Supplies and Services
Article 13. Cost Principles
Article 15. Supply Management
Article 17. Legal and Contractual Remedies
Article 19. Intergovernmental Relations
Article 21. Assistance to Minority Businesses
Article 23. Statewide Provisions

Absent some exceptions, all procurements are governed by the source selection procedures outlined in article 5, including construction. Article 9 provides additional rules applicable to construction.

A number of state agencies are not governed by the Procurement Code. For the most part, these entities might be characterized as quasi-governmental bodies. Examples include the South Carolina State Ports Authority and the South Carolina Public Service Authority (Santee Cooper). While most exempt entities are identified in section 11-35-710, a few others are exempted by their enabling legislation.

In a limited fashion, the Procurement Code applies to political subdivisions (e.g., municipalities, counties, and school districts). Larger school districts must adopt policies or procedures substantially similar to the Procurement Code. (South Carolina Code of Laws § 11-35-5340; South Carolina Code of Regulations 19-445.3000.) All other political subdivisions must adopt sound principles of appropriately competitive procurement. (South Carolina Code of Laws § 11-35-5320.) The law does not require these entities to publish their procurement rules; accordingly, they must be obtained by contacting the entity directly.

The South Carolina Department of Transportation is governed by two sets of rules, depending on the acquisition. Some acquisitions are governed by the Procurement Code, others by portions of title 57. (See generally *id.* § 11-35-710(A)(1).)

B. Ethics Laws

The Ethics, Government Accountability, and Campaign Reform Act of 1991 (Ethics Act), as amended, contains numerous provisions relevant to contracting with a South Carolina public entity. Originally enacted in 1991 as Act No. 248, the Ethics Act has been codified in chapter 17 of title 2 and chapter 13 of title 8 of the South Carolina Code of Laws. The following list identifies those provisions of particular relevance to procurement:

§ 8-13-100.	Definitions
§ 8-13-700.	Use of official position or office for financial gain; disclosure of potential conflict of interest

§ 8-13-705.	Offering, giving, soliciting, or receiving anything of value to influence action of public employee, member, or official, or to influence testimony of witness; exceptions; penalty for violation
§ 8-13-720.	Offering, soliciting, or receiving money for advice or assistance of public official, member, or employee
§ 8-13-725.	Use or disclosure of confidential information by public official, member, or employee for financial gain; examination of private records; penalties
§ 8-13-755.	Restrictions on former public official, member, or employee serving as lobbyist or accepting employment in field of former service
§ 8-13-760.	Employment by government contractor of former public official, member, or employee who was engaged in procurement
§ 8-13-775.	Public official, member, or employee with official function related to contracts not permitted to have economic interest in contracts
§ 8-13-790.	Recovery of amounts received by official or employee in breach of ethical standards; recovery of kickbacks
§ 8-13-795.	Receipt of award, grant, or scholarship by public official or family member
§ 8-13-1150.	Filing of statement by certain consultants
§ 8-13-1342.	Restrictions on contributions by contractor to candidate who participated in awarding of contract

Though somewhat dated, the following publication provides an excellent summary of the Ethics Act and the administrative opinions interpreting its provisions: Kelly J. Golden, *South Carolina Government Ethics: A Guide to the Ethics Reform Act of 1991* (1999). These administrative opinions, as well as a topical index, are available from the South Carolina State Ethics Commission at ethics.sc.gov. While not part of the Ethics Act, a related issue—gifts to governmental entities—is addressed in regulation 19-445.2165. Many South Carolina public entities require, as a condition of contracting, that offerors certify their compliance with the Ethics Act.

C. Public Records

South Carolina has a single public records law, the South Carolina Freedom of Information Act (FOIA). The act has been codified in title 30, chapter 4 of the South Carolina Code of Laws. The following sections are of particular interest:

§ 30-4-20.	Definitions
§ 30-4-30.	Right to inspect or copy public records; fees; notification as to public availability of records; presumption upon failure to give notice; records to be available when requestor appears in person
§ 30-4-40.	Matters exempt from disclosure

For acquisitions subject to the Procurement Code, FOIA is supplemented by the following section of the Procurement Code:

SECTION 11-35-410. Public access to procurement information.

(A) Procurement information must be a public record to the extent required by Chapter 4, Title 30 (The Freedom of Information Act), except as otherwise provided by this code, and with the exception that commercial or financial information obtained in response to a request for proposals [RFP] or any type of bid solicitation that is privileged and confidential need not be disclosed.

(B) Privileged and confidential information is information in specific detail not customarily released to the general public, the release of which might cause harm to the competitive position of the party supplying the information. Examples of this type of information include:

(1) customer lists;

(2) design recommendations and identification of prospective problem areas under an RFP;

(3) design concepts, including methods and procedures;

(4) biographical data on key employees of the bidder.

(C) The board shall promulgate regulations directing the public availability and disposition of documents submitted in response or with regard to a solicitation or other request where no award is made.

(D) For all documents submitted in response or with regard to any solicitation or other request, the person submitting the documents shall comply with instructions provided in the solicitation for marking information exempt from public disclosure. Information not marked as required by the applicable instructions may be disclosed to the public.

(E) A governmental body, with the approval of the appropriate chief procurement officer, may keep portions of a solicitation confidential and release the information to prospective offerors only upon execution of a nondisclosure agreement, provided the information is otherwise exempted from disclosure by law.

(F) If requested in writing before a final award by an actual bidder, offeror, contractor, or subcontractor with regard to a specific intended award or award of a contract, the procurement officer shall, within five days of the receipt of any such request, make documents directly connected to the procurement activity and not otherwise exempt from disclosure available for inspection at an office of the responsible procurement officer. Without otherwise limiting any other exemptions granted by law, and except as provided herein, documents of and documents incidental to proposed contractual arrangements, including those used for contract negotiations, are not exempt from disclosure after the date notice of intent to award is posted, unless the notice is subsequently canceled.

Three paragraphs warrant particular attention.

Paragraph (A): FOIA section 30-4-40(a)(5) provides an exemption from public release for "documents incidental to proposed contractual arrangements." Subject to a limited exception appearing in paragraph (a)(5)(c), this exemption ends "once a contract is entered into." In contrast, the exemption provided by section 11-35-410(A) does not expire.

Paragraph (D): Vendors concerned with the public availability of information included in their bid or proposal should pay careful attention to any applicable bidding instructions. The state's standard bidding instructions provide ample opportunity for vendors to protect their information, but strict compliance with the bidding instructions is important. Paragraph (D) allows any "[i]nformation not marked as required by the applicable instructions [to] be disclosed to the public." For additional information, consult the Division's FOIA Document Guide, published in the "legal" section of the Division's website.

Paragraph (F): The amount of time to protest is very short—far shorter than the amount of time agencies have to produce records under FOIA. To address this issue, paragraph (F) provides agencies with a much shorter response time when a public records request is made "before a final award by an actual bidder, offeror, contractor, or subcontractor with regard to a specific intended award or award of a contract." Offerors that expect to protest should be prepared to submit a FOIA request to the responsible procurement officer as soon as the state posts an award or intent to award, whichever is earlier. Their attorney should consider requesting redacted information pursuant to regulation 19-445.2200.

II. Regulations

The South Carolina Code of Regulations is organized into chapters, articles, and individual sections. The procurement regulations are codified in chapter 19, article 4 of this Code at 19-445.2000 through 19-445.3000, as well as 19-446. The following is a comprehensive list of those regulations.

19-445.2000.	State Procurement Regulations.
19-445.2005.	Internal Procurement Procedures; Procurement Records.
19-445.2010.	Disclosure of Procurement Information.
19-445.2015.	Unauthorized or Illegal Procurements.
19-445.2017.	Pre-Solicitation Procedures.
19-445.2020.	Certification.
19-445.2022.	Temporary Suspension of Authority; Audit.
19-445.2025.	Authority to Contract for Certain Services; Definitions.
19-445.2027.	Electronic Commerce.
19-445.2030.	Competitive Sealed Bidding—The Invitation for Bids.
19-445.2040.	The Official State Government Publication.
19-445.2042.	Pre-Bid Conferences.
19-445.2045.	Receipt, Safeguarding, and Disposition of Bids.
19-445.2050.	Bid Opening.
19-445.2055.	Bid Acceptance and Bid Evaluation.
19-445.2065.	Rejection of Bids.
19-445.2070.	Rejection of Individual Bids.
19-445.2075.	All or None Qualifications.
19-445.2077.	Bid Samples and Descriptive Literature.
19-445.2080.	Bid Reductions.
19-445.2085.	Correction or Withdrawal of Bids; Cancellation of Awards.
19-445.2090.	Award.
19-445.2095.	Competitive Sealed Proposals.
19-445.2097.	Rejection of Proposals.
19-445.2098.	Rejection of Individual Proposals.
19-445.2099.	Competitive Negotiations.

19-445.2100.	Small Purchases and Other Simplified Purchasing Procedures.
19-445.2105.	Sole Source Procurements.
19-445.2110.	Emergency Procurements.
19-445.2115.	Information Technology Procurements.
19-445.2120.	Cost or Pricing Data.
19-445.2122.	Price Reasonableness.
19-445.2125.	Responsibility of Bidders and Offerors.
19-445.2127.	Organizational Conflicts of Interest.
19-445.2130.	Prequalification of Supplies and Suppliers.
19-445.2132.	Prequalification for a Single Solicitation.
19-445.2135.	Conditions for Use of Multi-Term Contracts.
19-445.2137.	Food Service Contracts.
19-445.2140.	Specifications.
19-445.2141.	Commercial Products.
19-445.2143.	Contract Clauses and Administration.
19-445.2145.	Construction, Architect Engineer, Construction Management, and Land Surveying Services.
19-445.2150.	Surplus Property Management.
19-445.2152.	Leases, Lease/Payment, Installment Purchase, and Rental of Personal Property.
19-445.2155.	Intergovernmental Relations.
19-445.2160.	Assistance to Minority Businesses.
19-445.2165.	Gifts.
19-445.2180.	Assignment, Novation, and Change of Name.
19-445.2200.	Administrative Review Protective Orders.
19-445.3000.	School District Procurement Codes; Model.
19-446.	Representation in Proceedings.

Regulation 19-445.2010 warrants particular attention, as it restricts the disclosure of procurement information at certain points during the process applicable to competitive sealed proposals (CSPs).

A. Guidance for Agencies

South Carolina's central purchasing office does not publish a single, comprehensive procurement manual. Nevertheless, a vast amount of information is posted on the internet at https://procurement.sc.gov/.

Any lawyer undertaking to assist a client involved in a procurement governed by the Consolidated Procurement Code would be well served to spend an hour or more working his or her way through the Division's entire website. The following items are of particular relevance:

Public Record Access: The Division publishes a FOIA Document Guide that outlines how it responds to public records requests for procurement-related matters.

Standard Contract Clauses and Bidding Instructions: The Division publishes a "Compendium of Standardized Clauses Commonly Used by the Information Technology Management Office & State Procurement Office," which includes all the standard bidding instructions and standard contract terms used by DPS. It includes a variety of appendices of potential interest.

State Construction Guide: The Manual for Planning and Executing State Permanent Improvement Projects, which the Office of the State Engineer publishes, contains administrative guidance regarding construction acquisitions. This document is informally referred to as the OSE Manual.

III. Source Selection

The Procurement Code provides for a wide variety of source selection procedures, each of which is briefly summarized.

For all competitive selection procedures above the small-purchase threshold, excluding construction-related design services, the rules for competitive sealed bidding serve as the starting point. Accordingly, familiarity with the rules for competitive sealed bidding is essential.

A. Competitive Sealed Bidding (Invitation for Bids)

The basic rules governing competitive sealed bidding appear in South Carolina Code of Laws section 11-35-1520 and South Carolina Code of Regulations 19-445.2030 through -445.2090. Bids are invited using an invitation for bids (IFB). Prequalification is allowed, but unusual. An IFB must include all contractual terms and conditions applicable to the procurement. Adequate notice of an IFB must be provided at a reasonable time before bid opening. At a minimum, notice of an IFB must appear in the state's publication titled "South Carolina Business Opportunities" (SCBO). Bid are opened publicly, and bid tabulations are available immediately. Unless expressly authorized otherwise, bids must be accepted unconditionally and without alteration. Strict rules govern the withdrawal and correction of bids. If bids are opened, an award must be made to the lowest responsive and responsible bidder, absent a compelling reason to reject bids.

For contracts with a total or potential value of $100,000 or more, the state must post notice of its intent to award a contract for seven business days before entering into a contract. Such notice is provided by posting it at a location and on a date specified in the solicitation. In addition, the notice must be sent on the same day to all bidders responding to the solicitation. The posting date must appear on the face of the notice. Both the IFB and the notice must contain a statement of a bidder's right to protest and, pursuant to section 11-35-4210(8), the address of the appropriate chief procurement officer (CPO).

For construction, these rules are slightly modified. (See South Carolina Code of Laws § 11-35-3020.)

B. Negotiations after Unsuccessful Competitive Sealed Bidding

Negotiations are allowed if the bidding process is unsuccessful and an authorized official determines in writing that "time or other circumstances will not permit the delay required to resolicit." (*Id.* § 11-35-1540.) Bidding is unsuccessful if the bids received "are considered unreasonable," "are not independently reached in open competition, or the low bid exceeds available funds." (*Id.*) Negotiations are subject to the following limitations: all responsible bidders are allowed to participate, the negotiated price is below the price provided by the lowest responsible and responsive bidder, and "the negotiated price is the lowest negotiated price offered by any responsible and responsive offeror." (*Id.*) This process is governed by section 11-35-1540, except for construction acquisitions, which are governed by section 11-35-3020(d).

C. Fixed Price Bidding

Fixed price bidding is a variation of competitive sealed bidding characterized by multiple awards. Award is made to all bidders that meet a maximum price established in the IFB. Because award is made to all responsive and responsible bidders, the state may accept bids throughout the contract term. (*Id.* § 11-35-1525.)

D. Competitive Best Value Bidding

Best value bidding is a variation of competitive sealed bidding characterized by the evaluation of both price and non-price criteria. The IFB must identify all criteria to be used in determining award and must state the numerical weighting for each criterion. Price cannot be weighted at less than 60 percent. All non-price criteria must be evaluated before determining the effect of cost on the score of each bid. Once the evaluation is complete, all responsive bidders are ranked from most advantageous to least advantageous, with award made to the responsive and responsible bidder whose bid is determined, in writing, to be most advantageous to the state. The contract file must contain the basis on which the award is made and must be sufficient to satisfy external audit. (*Id.* § 11-35-1528.)

E. Reverse Auctions

Dubbed "competitive on-line bidding" by the statute, reverse auctioning is a variation of competitive sealed bidding. In order to proceed, the state must successfully register at least two bidders that have been determined responsible and have agreed to any terms, conditions, or other requirements of the solicitation. At a pre-set time, the state begins to accept real-time electronic bids. After the first bid is received, the lowest bid price must be posted electronically to the internet and updated on a real-time basis. The state continues to accept bids until a pre-set closing time, which may depend on a variable specified in the solicitation (e.g., time since the last bid was received). Until closing, a bidder may lower the price of its bid, as long as the new price is below the then-lowest bid. (*Id.* § 11-35-1529.)

F. CSPs

The CSP process relies on many of the basic rules that govern competitive sealed bidding. The differences appear primarily in section 11-35-1530 and regulation 19-445.2095.

Prequalification is allowed but rarely used. Proposals are solicited with a request for proposals (RFP). Between opening and award, access to information obtained in response to an RFP, concerning the number of offerors or their identity, or regarding the evaluation process, is highly restricted. (South Carolina Code of Regulations 19-445.2010 and -445.2095(C)(1).)

All factors to be considered in evaluating proposals, including their relative importance, must be identified in the RFP. Evaluation factors are usually assigned numerical weightings, but the weightings need not be provided in the RFP.

At the conclusion of the evaluation process, proposals must be ranked "from most advantageous to least advantageous," and only responsive proposals may be included in the final ranking. A proposal is responsive only if it "conforms in all material aspects to the . . . request for proposals." As a result, offerors that take exception with a solicitation's requirements cannot be considered for award.

Non-responsive offerors may be provided an opportunity to correct any deficiencies that make them non-responsive, but procurement staff has the option not to provide such an opportunity—and frequently choose not to do so.

After ranking, the procurement officer may award to the highest-ranked offeror, modify the solicitation and request best-and-final offers (BAFOs), or begin negotiations with the highest-ranked offeror.

If BAFOs are sought, they must be sought from all responsive offerors. Once received, BAFOs must be re-evaluated and re-ranked.

If negotiations are conducted, the state must first document its negotiation objectives. Negotiations may involve price and scope of work, provided that any changes are "within the general scope" of the RFP. (South Carolina Code of Laws § 11-35-1530(8)(a).) Negotiations are conducted sequentially, not simultaneously. In the vast majority of CSP procurements, negotiations are conducted only with the highest ranked offeror. If the procurement officer cannot negotiate "a satisfactory contract," negotiations may be conducted "with the second, and then the third, and so on, ranked offerors to the level of ranking determined by the procurement officer in his sole discretion." (*Id.*) If these negotiations are unsuccessful, the procurement officer may "reopen negotiations with any offeror with whom he previously negotiated." (*Id.* § 11-35-1530(8)(b).)

Regardless of the process used, the award decision must be made on the basis of criteria identified in the RFP. (*Id.* § 11-35-1530(9).) In addition, the file "must contain the basis on which the award is made and must be sufficient to satisfy external audit." (*Id.*)

G. Competitive Negotiations

Most of the rules governing competitive negotiations (CNs) appear in section 11-35-1535 and regulation 19-445.2099.

CN is far more flexible than CSPs and differs in several important respects. Responsiveness is not a pre-condition of evaluation, ranking, or negotiations. Proposals are evaluated, but not ranked, and negotiations are simultaneous, not sequential. Additional differences are reflected in the following summary.

Proposals are solicited with an RFP. Between opening and award, access to information obtained in response to an RFP, concerning the number of offerors or their identity, or regarding the evaluation process, is highly restricted. (South Carolina Code of Regulations 19-445.2010 and -445.2095(C)(1).)

All factors to be considered in evaluating proposals, including their relative importance, must be identified in the RFP. If price is an evaluation factor, the RFP "must state whether all evaluation factors other than cost or price, when combined, are significantly more important than, approximately equal to, or significantly less important than cost or price." (*Id.* 19-445.2099(E)(6).)

After evaluation, the state must identify those offerors that submitted the most promising offers, thus establishing a "competitive range." Ordinarily, the competitive range will include no more than three offerors.

After establishing the competitive range, but prior to the final selection process, the state must undertake at least two steps: minimal negotiations and one opportunity for proposal revisions. For each offeror in the competitive range, the state must identify and seek elimination of any undesirable terms, including any terms that do not conform to the RFP's material requirements. This process may result in the elimination of offerors from the competitive range. Once this process is concluded, any offerors still in the competitive range must be afforded an opportunity to amend their proposals.

A far more robust process is possible.

Prior to establishing the competitive range, and up until award, the state may ask an offeror to clarify information in its proposal, provided the communication does not involve any changes to terms that would bind the parties after contract formation.

Negotiations can be extensive and may involve bargaining about any terms of a proposed contract, including those stated in the solicitation—as long as the state does "not relax or change any material requirement of the solicitation." Changes to a material requirement can only be accomplished by issuing an amendment, and any amendment issued after opening must be issued to all offerors still in the competitive range. (*Id.* 19-445.2099(D)(4) & (H)(1)(g).)

Negotiations may vary considerably among offerors. While the state must document its pre-negotiation objectives, those objectives may differ for each offeror in the competitive range. With limited constraints, the scope and extent of negotiations are a matter of the procurement officer's judgment; similarly situated offerors must be given similar opportunities to negotiate, all offerors must be treated fairly and impartially, and the duty of good faith applies at each step in the process.

Offerors can be provided multiple opportunities to revise their proposals, either to document understandings reached during negotiations or to respond to an amendment. Likewise, multiple amendments can be issued, provided they do not exceed the general scope of the initial solicitation.

Once negotiations are complete, all offerors remaining in the competitive range must be afforded a final opportunity to submit a proposal revision. The state must then conduct a final evaluation to determine which proposal provides it the best value. In making this decision, the state may decide not to select either the lowest priced or the highest technically rated offeror; rather, the state can make tradeoffs among price and non-price factors in making its best value decision.

H. Sole Source

Absent an emergency, competition is required unless "there is only one source for the required" item. (South Carolina Code of Laws § 11-35-1560; South Carolina Code of Regulations 19-445.2105.) If a procurement is restricted to one vendor, the file must contain "an explanation as to why no other will be suitable or acceptable to meet the need." (South Carolina Code of Laws § 11-35-1560.) When deciding what is required and why no other vendor can meet the need, the state is limited by the prohibition against using "unduly restrictive" specifications. (*Id.* § 11-35-2730; South Carolina Code of Regulations 19-445.2105(E)(2).) "In cases of reasonable doubt, competition must be solicited." (South Carolina Code of Laws § 11-35-1560.)

For contracts in excess of $50,000, and absent an approval otherwise, notice of the intent to award without competition must be posted in SCBO for at least five business days before entering a contract. For contracts greater than $250,000, such notice must be posted at least ten business days before entering a contract.

I. Emergency

Under section 11-35-1570, contracts may be awarded without competition when there is an immediate threat to "public health, welfare, critical economy and efficiency, or safety" if the threat results from conditions "as may arise by reason of floods, epidemics, riots, equipment failures, fire loss, or such other reason as may be proclaimed by" an authorized official. (South Carolina Code of Regulations 19-445.2110(B).) Even if emergency conditions exist, the agency must be incapable of meeting its needs through normal procurement methods. Interpreting the relevant statute and regulations, the South Carolina Supreme Court has concluded that a "sudden, unexpected occurrence" is necessary to justify an emergency procurement. (*Sloan v. Department of Transportation*, 666 S.E.2d 236 (S.C. 2008).)

Even under emergency circumstances, a procurement must be conducted with "as much competition as is practicable." (South Carolina Code of Laws § 11-35-1570.) In addition, the scope of the procurement must be limited to those items "necessary to meet the emergency." (South Carolina Code of Regulations 19-445.2110(C).)

For emergency contracts in excess of $50,000, notice of the award must be posted in SCBO.

J. Auction and Bankruptcy

Under section 11-35-1575, the state may acquire supplies in an auction or bankruptcy sale. In order to participate, the state must evaluate several factors and, prior to the sale, "determine the maximum price that it can pay for each item desired."

K. Qualifications-Based Selection

For the acquisition of construction-related professional services, such as architecture and engineering services, the state uses a qualifications-based selection process. (South Carolina Code of Laws § 11-35-3020.) This process is similar to the federal Brooks Act, 40 U.S.C. § 1101 *et seq*.

L. Small Purchase Procedures

Pursuant to section 11-35-1550, small purchase procedures are available for acquisitions valued up to $100,000. Higher thresholds may exist for technical colleges and public institutions of higher learning.

M. Unsolicited Proposals

South Carolina has no established process for the consideration of unsolicited proposals.

Note: South Carolina has a substantial in-state vendor preference. Appearing in section 11-35-1524, this preference applies to both supplies and services. A preference is also provided for service contractors that use in-state subcontractors. The preferences do not apply to motor vehicles, construction, supplies, or services relating to construction, acquisitions conducted using CSPs, CNs, or acquisitions with a value exceeding certain thresholds.

IV. Bid Protests and Contract Disputes

A. Bid Protests

Section 11-35-4210(1)(a) grants to any "prospective bidder, offeror, contractor, or subcontractor who is aggrieved in connection with the solicitation of a contract" a right to protest. Protests must be received within 15 days of the date the solicitation is first advertised in SCBO, a government-issued publication used to provide public notice. (South Carolina Code of Laws § 11-35-1520(3); South Carolina Code of Regulations 19-445.2040.) SCBO is available on the internet at https://procurement.sc.gov/. Solicitation amendments may be protested within 15 days of the date they are issued, but only if the amendment is at issue. An amendment is not at issue unless it provides new or different information than a previously issued solicitation document. Posting of an award does not shorten the time to protest a solicitation.

Section 11-35-4210(1)(b) grants to any "actual bidder, offeror, contractor, or subcontractor who is aggrieved in connection with the intended award or award of a contract" a right to protest. To preserve this right, a protestant must "notify the appropriate chief procurement officer in writing of its intent to protest within seven business days of the date that award or notification of intent to award, whichever is earlier, is posted and sent in accordance with this code." If such notice has been timely filed, a protestant may file its actual protest within 15 days of the date the award notice was posted and sent. The date of posting must appear on the face of all award statements.

Protests of sole source and emergency contracts are governed by section 11-35-4210(1)(c). The time periods for protesting each are tied to the applicable public notice requirements discussed in Section III above.

In calculating the applicable time periods, the Procurement Code defines and differentiates between days and business days. Before you start counting, make sure you identify the applicable term. "Days" means "calendar days." "'Business day' means a day that is neither a Saturday, Sunday, nor a state or federal holiday." Section 11-35-310(13) provides the following general instructions: "In computing any period of time prescribed . . . by this code . . . , . . . the day of the . . . event . . . from which the designated period of time begins to run is not to be included. The last day of the period computed is to be included, unless it is a Saturday, Sunday, or a state or federal holiday, in which event the period runs to the end of the next day which is neither a Saturday, Sunday, nor such holiday." (South Carolina Code of Laws § 11-35-310(13).)

In furtherance of these protest rights, all solicitations, all award notices, and all notices regarding sole source and emergency contracts must include a statement of the protest rights granted by section 11-35-4210(1). (*Id.* §§ 11-35-1520(10), -1560(A), and -1570(B).) These documents must also include "[n]otice of the address of the appropriate chief procurement officer . . . ." (*Id.* § 11-35-4210(8).) As noted above, award statements must include the date of posting on their face. As a matter of course, the posting date for notices regarding sole source and emergency contracts is reflected by the date of its publication in SCBO.

The protest periods are not triggered by actual notice to those involved (i.e., receipt of the notice). Rather, the Procurement Code relies on constructive notice. Solicitations must be advertised in SCBO, as must all public notices regarding sole source and emergency contracts. Publication in SCBO serves as constructive notice. In competitive procurements, the constructive notice approach is furthered by requiring that solicitations specify the date on and location at which award notices will be posted. (*Id.* § 11-35-1520(10); South Carolina Code of Regulations 19-445.2090(B).) If the date of award will be delayed, notice of a time extension must be provided. Offerors are responsible for checking for award notices at the date and location specified.

Protests must be in writing and must be received by the appropriate CPO within the applicable time period. Time limits are strictly applied. The protest must "set forth the grounds of the protest and the relief requested with enough particularity to give notice of the issues to be decided." (South Carolina Code of Laws § 11-35-4210(2).)

Authority to review protests is split between three CPOs: the state engineer, the information technology management officer, and the materials management officer. Each is authorized to conduct an administrative review and issue a binding decision.

If a protest is filed, an automatic stay prevents the state from "proceed[ing] further with the solicitation or award of the contract until ten days after a decision is posted by the appropriate chief procurement officer, or, in the event of timely appeal to the Procurement Review Panel, until a decision is rendered by the panel." (*Id.* § 11-35-4210(7).) A process exists for lifting the automatic stay, but such requests are rarely granted.

Available remedies are identified in section 11-35-4310 and depend on whether a contract has formed prior to the protest.

Protestants bear the burden of proving their issues of protest. In conducting an administrative review, a CPO has the option of conducting an administrative hearing.

B. Bid Protest Appeals

A CPO's decision regarding a protest may be appealed to the Procurement Review Panel, which is a separate state agency. Any appeal must be filed within ten days of the date the CPO's decision is posted. Section 11-35-4210 requires the CPO to "post a copy of the decision at a time and place communicated to all parties participating in the administrative review, and the posted decision must indicate the date of posting on its face and must be accompanied by a statement of the right to appeal provided in section 11-35-4210(6)."

The appeal, referred to in the Procurement Code as a "request for review," must be directed to the appropriate CPO, who shall forward the request to the Procurement Review Panel, or submitted to the Panel directly. The request for review must be in writing, setting forth the reasons for disagreement with the decision of the CPO. As provided in each year's annual appropriations act, the request for review must be accompanied by a $250 filing fee made payable to the Procurement Review Panel.

The Panel provides a de novo administrative review. Witnesses testify as if no hearing took place before the CPO. Ordinarily, a transcript of any CPO hearing does not exist. While the documentary evidence relied upon by the CPO forms the initial record before the Panel, this evidence may be supplemented on appeal, and the existing record is subject to evidentiary objections.

C. Contract Disputes

1. Contract Claims

Article X, section 10 of the South Carolina Constitution provides that "[t]he General Assembly may direct, by law, in what manner claims against the State may be established and adjusted." Consistent with section 10, the General Assembly enacted section 11-35-4230, which creates an administrative review process for contract-related disputes. For controversies concerning a contract governed by the Procurement Code, this process is the exclusive means of resolving "controversies between a governmental body and a contractor . . . which arise under or by virtue of a contract between them including, but not limited to, controversies based upon breach of contract, mistake, misrepresentation, or other cause for contract modification or recission." (*Id.* § 11-35-4230(1).) (See generally *Unisys Corp. v. S.C. Budget & Control Board*, 551 S.E.2d 263 (S.C. 2001) ("[B]ecause a statute waiving the State's immunity must be strictly construed, the State can be sued only in the manner and upon the terms and conditions prescribed by the statute. The term 'exclusive means' must therefore be strictly construed to limit suits on contracts with the State to the forum provided in § 11-35-4230.

Application of the strict construction rule, contrary to Unisys's assertion, results in upholding the exclusivity provision of § 11-35-4230.") (citations omitted).)

To initiate resolution of a controversy, a party to the contract must submit "a request for resolution to the appropriate chief procurement officer in writing setting forth the specific nature of the controversy and the specific relief requested with enough particularity to give notice of every issue to be decided." (South Carolina Code of Laws § 11-35-4230(2).) Though not required by the statutes or regulations, a party responding to such a request should file a responsive pleading.

The state's general statutes of limitation do not apply to claims governed by this provision; instead, the following statute applies: "A request for resolution of contract controversy must be filed within one year after the date the contractor last performs work under the contract or within one year after the claim accrues, whichever is later; except that in the case of latent defects a request for resolution of a contract controversy must be filed within three years of the date the requesting party first knows or should know of the grounds giving rise to the request for resolution." (*Id.*)

A CPO "may award such relief as is necessary to resolve the controversy as allowed by the terms of the contract or by applicable law." (*Id.* § 11-35-4320.)

2. Contract Claims Appeals

A CPO's decision regarding a contract controversy may be appealed to the Procurement Review Panel, which is a separate state agency. Any appeal must be filed within ten days of the date the CPO's decision is posted. Section 11-35-4230 requires the CPO to "post a copy of the decision at a time and place communicated to all parties participating in the administrative review, and the posted decision must indicate the date of posting on its face and must be accompanied by a statement of the right to appeal provided in section 11-35-4230(6)."

The appeal, referred to in the Procurement Code as a "request for review," must be directed to the appropriate CPO, who shall forward the request to the Procurement Review Panel, or submitted to the Panel directly. The request for review must be in writing, setting forth the reasons for disagreement with the decision of the CPO. As provided in each year's annual appropriations act, the request for review must be accompanied by a $250 filing fee made payable to the Procurement Review Panel.

The Panel provides a de novo administrative review. Witnesses testify as if no hearing took place before the CPO. Ordinarily, a transcript of any CPO hearing does not exist. While the documentary evidence relied upon by the CPO forms the initial record before the Panel, this evidence may be supplemented on appeal, and the existing record is subject to evidentiary objections.

D. Suspension and Debarment

Section 11-35-4220 authorizes the appropriate CPO, upon administrative review, to suspend and debar a person from consideration for award of contracts.

Suspension is the "disqualification of a person to receive invitations for bids, requests for proposals, or the award of a contract by the State, for a temporary period pending the completion of an investigation and any legal proceedings that may ensue because a person is suspected upon probable cause of engaging in criminal, fraudulent, or seriously improper conduct or failure or inadequacy of performance which may lead to debarment." (*Id.* § 11-35-310(36).)

Debarment is a similar disqualification, but for "a specified period of time commensurate with the seriousness of the offense or the failure or inadequacy of performance." (*Id.* § 11-35-310(14).)

The causes for debarment or suspension are set by statute, but include the violation of an order issued by either a CPO or the Procurement Review Panel, and any other cause determined to be "so serious and compelling as to affect responsibility as a state contractor or subcontractor." (*Id.* § 11-35-4220(2).)

Any decision issued must state "the action taken, the specific reasons for it, and the period of debarment or suspension, if any." (*Id.* § 11-35-4220(3).) The decision and a statement of rights to appeal must be posted and furnished to the person affected. Any appeal must be filed within ten days of the posting.

V. Administrative and Judicial Review

A. Administrative Review

CPO decisions in a protest, debarment, or contract controversy may be appealed only to the Procurement Review Panel.

The Panel is a separate state agency created by the Procurement Code. (*Id.* § 11-35-4410.) The Panel has seven members, all appointed by the governor. Four members constitute a quorum. In the event of a tie vote, the CPO decision is considered final.

The Panel is not governed by the state's Administrative Procedures Act and has no formal rules of procedure. When a case is filed, a memorandum outlining the Panel's practices is sent to all the parties. This memorandum has remained unchanged for many years. A copy is available on the internet at the following URL, in the Legal section, under the heading General Information: https://procurement.sc.gov/.

The Panel has issued hundreds of decisions. These decisions are available on the internet at https://procurement.sc.gov/ and are treated by the Panel as precedent. These decisions are also available in the Westlaw database titled "South Carolina Procurement Decisions." Neither the website nor Westlaw are updated promptly. The most recent decisions can be requested directly from the Panel.

The Panel's orders serve as the final administrative decision.

B. Judicial Review

South Carolina does not have a court dedicated to governmental disputes, such as a court of claims. All appeals from the Procurement Review Panel go directly to the South Carolina Court of Appeals. (South Carolina Code of Laws § 11-35-4410(6).)

VI. Extent of State's Adoption or Adaptation of ABA Model Procurement Code

The South Carolina Consolidated Procurement Code, originally adopted in 1981, is closely modeled after the ABA's initial version of the Model Procurement Code for State and Local Governments. In 2000, the ABA updated the Model Code. South Carolina adopted the construction-related amendments in 2008. (Act 174, 2008 S.C. Acts 1524, 1526.)

VII. Cooperative Purchasing

A. Authority

The following discussion is limited to acquisitions by governmental bodies subject to the South Carolina Consolidated Procurement Code.

Intergovernmental agreements (i.e., agreements *between* public entities) are authorized by article 19 of the Consolidated Procurement Code. Intergovernmental agreements include both agreements that govern intergovernmental acquisitions (i.e., an acquisition by one public procurement unit from another public procurement unit) and those that govern cooperative purchasing (i.e., an acquisition "conducted by, or on behalf of, more than one public procurement unit").

Cooperative purchasing is governed by section 11-35-4810. The requirements for participating in a cooperative purchase are discussed in the next section. If the cooperative purchasing effort involves "an agreement entered into between" the governmental body and the other participating public procurement units, only article 19 of the Consolidated Procurement Code applies to that "contract[] between public procurement units." (South Carolina Code of Laws §§ 11-35-40(2), -4810(1), and -4880.)

B. Requirements

Generally, a governmental body can only participate in a cooperative purchase conducted by another public procurement unit if (1) the procurement is conducted in a manner that complies with one of the source selection procedures authorized by the Consolidated Procurement Code (e.g., articles 5 or 9) and (2) the governmental body complies with any other applicable provisions of the Procurement Code (e.g., contract type, contract duration approval, non-appropriations).

For cooperative purchasing undertaken with another state government, "source selection methods substantially equivalent to those" required by the Code may be used, but only if the applicable CPO determines in writing that the "contracts [were or will be] awarded through full and open competition, including use of [competitive] source selection methods *substantially equivalent* to those specified in Article 5 and, as applicable, Article 9 of this code, and consistent with the requirements of Section 11-35-2730 (Assuring Competition)." (*Id.* § 11-35-4810(2) & (3).)

Regardless of who conducts the procurement or what source selection procedures are used, any participation by a governmental body in a cooperative purchase must be approved by the applicable CPO. In order to grant approval, the CPO must determine in writing "that participation is in the interest of the State," and in making this determination, the CPO must evaluate and consider the impact on South Carolina businesses. Unless the procurement is conducted by the central procurement office of another state, the applicable CPO must also determine that the "entities responsible for the management and administration of the procurement . . . have in place appropriate and adequate internal controls to provide safeguards for the maintenance of a procurement system of quality and integrity with clearly defined rules for ethical behavior on the part of all persons engaged in the public procurement process." (*Id.* § 11-35-4810(3).)

Special rules apply to "multistate" procurements: "Thirty days' prior notice of a proposed multistate solicitation must be provided in accordance with Section 11-35-1520(3). Supplies acquired pursuant to such contracts may be distributed only through vendors with an in-state office, as defined in Section 11-35-1524(A)(6), when available; provided, however, that the provisions of this paragraph do not apply to public institutions of higher learning if the institution demonstrates a cost savings to the appropriate chief procurement officer in regard to the multistate solicitation and procurement." (*Id.* § 11-35-4810(4).)

South Dakota Procurement Rules and Regulations

Prepared by Jeff H. Eckland
Eckland & Blando LLP
Email: jeckland@ecklandblando.com
With assistance from Mark J. Blando, Vince Reuter, and Robert Dube[1]

I. Statutory Reference

The Office of Procurement Management (OPM) within the Bureau of Administration is generally responsible for the procurement of all supplies, materials, and equipment required by state agencies and institutions. The OPM can be contacted through the Bureau of Administration's website, located at https://boa.sd.gov/central-services/procurement-management/procurement-management-vendorInfo.aspx. Prior to June 1, 2022, prospective contractors had to register with the OPM through the "eschoolmall/mercury commerce" system. As of June 1, 2022, the OPM now requires online registration through its new ESM system at https://supplier.esmsolutions.com/registration#/registration/contactInformation/. At the time of publishing, OPM has not updated most of its internal references nor has it issued new guidance on how the new ESM system will differ, if at all, from the eschoolmall/mercury commerce system.

State procurement agencies include all agencies, departments, divisions, institutions, boards, and commissions of South Dakota state government. The OPM establishes statewide contracts for goods and authorizes small purchases and equipment leases by state agencies and institutions in compliance with state law.

South Dakota's statutes related to the procurement of government contracts can be found by searching https://sdlegislature.gov/Statutes/Codified_Laws/2034602.

A. Procurement/Purchasing Statutes

The relevant portions of the South Dakota Codified Laws are included in the lists below:

1. Generally

Chapter 5-18A. Public Agency Procurement—General Provisions

Chapter 5-18B. Procurement of Public Improvements

1. Research, drafting, proofing, and citation assistance provided by Kenneth Cooper and Thomas Harshaw of Eckland & Blando LLP.

Chapter 5-18C.	Procurement by Local Government Units
Chapter 5-18D.	Procurement by State Agencies
Chapter 5-14.	Public Buildings and Improvements

2. Bonds and Payments

Chapter 5-21.	Performance Bonds for Public Improvement Contracts
Chapter 5-22.	Liens Relating too Public Improvement Contracts
Chapter 5-26.	Prompt Payment Act

3. School District Purchases and Contracts

Chapter 13-20.	School District Purchases and Contracts
§ 13-49-15 (2016).	Purchasing and Contracting for Institutions—Incidental Powers of Board
§ 13-49-16 (2011).	Contracts Let in Accordance with Public Agency Procurement Law

4. Roads and Highways

Chapter 31-5.	State Highway Construction and Maintenance in General
§§ 31-12-12 to -17 (2018).	County Highway System Purchasing
Chapter 31-13.	Township Roads
Chapter 31-14.	County and Township Bridges and Culverts
Chapter 31-23.	Performance Bonds on Highway Contracts

B. Other Applicable Statutes

The relevant portions of the South Dakota Codified Laws are included in the lists below, unless otherwise noted:

1. South Dakota Constitution

Art. 3, § 27.	Sovereign Immunity

2. Contracts

Chapter 53-1.	Definitions and General Provisions
Chapter 53-2.	Parties to Contracts
Chapter 53-3.	Consent to Contracts
Chapter 53-4.	Duress, Fraud, Undue Influence, and Mistake
Chapter 53-5.	Objects of Contracts
Chapter 53-6.	Consideration for Contracts
Chapter 53-7.	Communication of Proposal and Acceptance
Chapter 53-8.	Oral and Written Contracts
Chapter 53-9.	Unlawful Contracts
Chapter 53-10.	Performance of Contracts

Chapter 53-11.	Extinction and Alteration of Contracts
Chapter 53-12.	Electronic Transactions

3. Uniform Commercial Code

Chapter 57A-1.	General Provisions
Chapter 57A-2.	Sales
Chapter 57A-2a.	Leases

4. Administrative Law

Chapter 1-26.	Administrative Procedure and Rules

5. Remedies

Chapter 21-1.	Damages
Chapter 21-2.	Damages for Breach of Contract
Chapter 21-8.	Injunction
Chapter 21-9.	Actions for Specific Performance
Chapter 21-11.	Revision of Contracts
Chapter 21-12.	Recission of Contracts
Chapter 21-24.	Declaratory Judgment
Chapter 21-29.	Writ of Mandamus
Chapter 21-30.	Writ of Prohibition
Chapter 21-32.	Remedies against the State
Chapter 3-21.	Liability of Public Entities and Public Officials

6. Legislative Lobbying

Chapter 2-12.	Lobbyists

C. Opinions by Attorney General

The attorney general of South Dakota is statutorily required to submit a written opinion upon all questions of law submitted by the state legislature, the governor, or another state agency. (South Dakota Codified Laws § 1-11-1.) While opinions by the attorney general are not binding on courts in South Dakota, they are entitled to weight when construing statutes. (*Rural Pennington County Tax Association v. Dier*, 515 N.W.2d 841, 844 (S.D. 1994) (citation omitted).)

Past opinions by the attorney general of South Dakota can be found on its website at https://atg.sd.gov/OurOffice/OfficialOpinions/opinions.aspx.

II. Regulations

Administrative Rules of South Dakota can be found by searching the state legislature's website located at https://sdlegislature.gov/Rules/Administrative. The relevant portions of the Administrative Rules are listed below:

A. Highway Construction Contracts

70:07:01:01 (2014).	Definitions
70:07:02:01 to :20 (2014).	Classification and Bidding Capacity Rating
70:07:03:01 to :05 (2014).	Bid Proposals
70:07:04:01 to :22 (2014).	Suspension and Debarment

III. Source Selection

A. Procurement Policy and Regulatory Definitions

1. State Bidding Policy: Lowest Responsible Bidder or Offeror

The purpose for requiring competitive bidding for government contract procurement in South Dakota is to "guard against favoritism, improvidence, extravagance, fraud, and corruption." (*Fonder v. City of South Sioux Falls*, 71 N.W.2d 618, 620 (S.D. 1955) (citation omitted).)

Absent an exception, a public contract will be awarded "to the lowest responsible and responsive bidder whose bid meets the requirements and criteria set forth in the invitation for bids." (South Dakota Codified Laws § 5-18A-5(7).) Alternatively, a public contract award will be made to the most responsible offeror whose proposal is deemed most advantageous to the state's needs. (*Id.* § 5-18A-7(6).)

2. Selected Regulatory Definitions

Design-Build Contract: "Any contract between a purchasing agency and a design-builder to furnish the architecture, engineering, and related services as required, and the labor, materials, and other construction services for a public improvement. A design-build contract may be conditioned upon future refinements in scope and price and may permit the purchasing agency to make changes in the scope of the project without invalidating the design-build contract." (*Id.* § 5-18A-1(9).)

Invitation for Bids (IFB): "Any document, whether attached or incorporated by reference, used for soliciting bids." (*Id.* § 5-18A-1(15).)

Performance Criteria: The "requirements for a public improvement, including[,] as appropriate, capacity, durability, production standards, ingress and egress requirements, building code requirements, or other criteria for the intended use of the public improvement, expressed in performance-oriented specifications or drawings suitable to allow the design-builder to make a proposal." (*Id.* § 5-18A-1(17).)

Public Improvement: "The process of building, altering, repairing, improving, or demolishing any public infrastructure facility, including any structure, building, or other improvements of any kind to real property, the cost of which is payable from taxes or other funds under the control of the purchasing agency, and includes any local improvement for which a special assessment is to be levied." (*Id.* § 5-18A-1(22).)

Resident: "Any person, partnership, association, limited liability company, foreign limited liability company, corporation, or foreign corporation licensed to do business within [South Dakota] that has maintained a substantial and bona fide place of business and has conducted business from within [South Dakota] for at least one year prior to the date on which a contract was awarded. The members of the partnership or association shall have been bona fide residents of the state for one year or more immediately prior to bidding upon the contract." (*Id.* § 5-18A-1(26).)

Surety: "A bond or undertaking executed by a surety company authorized to do business in the State of South Dakota and countersigned by an agent of the company resident in the State of South Dakota." However, the surety does not require a countersignature of a bid bond. (*Id.* § 5-18A-1(30).)

B. Procurement in South Dakota Generally

1. Registration Requirement

Corporations, partnerships, cooperatives, and business trusts are required to register with the South Dakota secretary of state, as outlined in South Dakota Codified Laws chapter 47 (2010), before transacting any business in the State of South Dakota. (See *id.* § 47-1A-1501 (corporations that are not registered in South Dakota must still file for a "certificate of authority" to transact business in South Dakota).) The various forms are available at the secretary of state's website, https://sdsos.gov/business-services/corporations/corporate-forms/default.aspx. Exceptions to the corporate registration requirement can also be found at South Dakota Codified Laws section 47-1A-1501.

2. OPM

The OPM uses a mandatory electronic bidder registration and solicitation response system to solicit formal sealed bids and proposals, as well as informal quotes for goods and some services being procured by state agencies. (South Dakota Codified Laws § 5-18D-4.)

A $50 annual registration fee is required and must be received by the OPM before a contractor can issue a bid. (See *id.* § 5-18D-7 (allowing the OPM to establish bidding fees).) To apply for any contract opportunity through this agency, the bidder must first register online at https://supplier.esmsolutions.com/registration#/registration/contactInformation/.

Through the registered bidders, the OPM creates the bidders' list for interested vendors. (*Id.*) Registered bidders receive email or fax notifications of sealed bid opportunities and can subsequently submit their responses electronically through the e-procurement system. Additionally, the OPM provides a detailed "Vendor's Manual" for prospective vendors at https://boa.sd.gov/central-services/procurement-management/docs/SDVendorManual_12-21-2021.pdf

C. General Methods of Awarding Contracts

By statute, there are generally five methods of awarding contracts for supplies, services, and construction services. Unless an exception applies, a contract will be awarded by:

1. Competitive sealed bids (South Dakota Codified Laws § 5-18A-5)
2. Competitive sealed proposals (South Dakota Codified Laws §§ 5-18A-6 to -7)
3. Limited or noncompetitive small purchases (South Dakota Codified Laws § 5-18A-11)
4. Noncompetitive sole source procurement (South Dakota Codified Laws § 5-18A-8)
5. Noncompetitive emergency procurement (South Dakota Codified Laws § 5-18A-9)

(South Dakota Codified Laws § 5-18A-3.) Exceptions to the general procurement process are found at section 5-18A-22.

1. Competitive Sealed Bids

Government agencies in South Dakota generally award contracts by using competitive sealed bids. (*Id.* § 5-18A-4.)

a. Public Notice Requirements

All public improvement contracts estimated to involve at least $100,000 must include public advertisements. (*Id.* § 5-18A-14.) Second, all public contracts for the procurement of supplies or services estimated to cost at least $25,000 must also include public advertisements. (*Id.*) Notably, a mere technical defect in the advertisement will not invalidate the eventual contract if there has been substantial compliance with the statute. (*Gridley v. Engelhart*, 322 N.W.2d 3, 6 (S.D. 1982).)

b. Competitive Bid Contents and Procedure

The IFB will include a purchase description, all contractual terms, and criteria for awarding the contract. (South Dakota Codified Laws § 5-18A-5.) Further, the procuring agency may require that a bond or an approved security is submitted with the bid as a guarantee that the bidder will enter into the contract. (*Id.* § 5-18A-35; see also *id.* § 5-18A-36 (special bond requirements for public improvement bids).) The procuring agency cannot, however, require that the bidder post that bond for longer than 30 days (for bids for services or public improvement) or 45 days (for bids for supplies) if the bid is not successful, and the bond will be returned upon the signing of the contract. (*Id.* § 5-18A-35.) A contractor may withdraw its bid before the time specified in the advertisement. (*Id.* § 5-18A-5(6).) Also, a contractor may modify its bid at any time before the time set in the IFB for the opening of all bids. (*Id.*)

c. Awarding the Contract with a Competitive Bid

At the deadline stated in the IFB, all bids are unconditionally accepted by the procuring agency. (*Id.* § 5-18A-5(5).) All bids are then evaluated solely on the criteria set forth in the IFB, and may include criteria other than price. (*Id.*) The procuring agency may waive technical irregularities that do not alter the price, quality, or quantity of goods or services offered. (*Id.* § 5-18A-5(6).) Waiving technical irregularities or other good-faith mistakes, however, must be supported in writing. (*Id.*) After bids have been received and opened, no "material change" can be made in any bid that may be more favorable to the successful bidder and also diverges from the original specifications. (*Gridley*, 322 N.W.2d at 8.)

After analyzing all the bids offered, the procuring agency will award the contract to the "lowest responsible and responsive bidder whose bid meets the requirements and criteria set forth in the invitation for bids." (South Dakota Codified Laws § 5-18A-5(7).) Courts will allow purchasing agencies a wide degree of discretion in choosing the best bid. (*Corner Construction Corp. v. Rapid City School District No. 51-4*, 845 F. Supp. 1354, 1358 (D.S.D. 1994).) The procuring agency's duty is to "carefully and honestly consider the terms of each bid, the needs of the county, and the responsibility of each bidder" upon the facts known at the time the contract is awarded. (*Id.* (quoting *In re McCain*, 68 N.W. 163, 164 (1896)).)

The purchasing agency must make a decision within 30 days after the bids are opened for contracts for services or public improvements and 45 days for contracts for supplies. (South Dakota Codified Laws § 5-18A-5.) Regardless of the bids received, however, if the procuring agency believes none of the bids are satisfactory, its decision may be to reject all bids and re-advertise. (*Id.*; see also *id.* § 5-18A-12 (all bids may be rejected if in the best interests of the agency).)

"If two or more competitive sealed low bids are found to be identical in price and product quality, and no resident bidder preference is applicable, the purchasing agency may: award the bid by lottery to one of the identical low bidders; or reject all the bids and re-solicit bid." (*Id.* § 5-18A-5(10).)

Finally, if the awarding bidder fails to enter into the contract before the time specified in the IFB, the purchasing agency may issue the contract to the next-lowest responsible bidder, and the original defaulting bidder will be responsible for any difference in price. (*Id.* § 5-18A-15.)

d. Noncompetitive Negotiation Exception

In the event that, after advertising for bids using the above procedure, no firm bids are received, the purchasing agency may nonetheless "negotiate the contract for the purchase of the supplies, services, or public improvement projects at the most advantageous price," but only if the specifications of the original bid are still met. (*Id.* § 5-18A-5(9).)

2. Competitive Sealed Proposals

Government agencies may choose to procure a contract through competitive sealed proposals if that "agency determines in writing that the use of competitive sealed bids is either not practicable or not advantageous." (*Id.* § 5-18A-6.)

a. Competitive Proposal Contents and Procedure

The competitive bid process begins with the government agency issuing a request for proposal (RFP) to all contractors responding to the public notice. (*Id.* § 5-18A-7(1).) The RFP will contain the importance of price and any other factors deemed important for that particular contract. (*Id.*) Further, "the procuring agency may require that a bond or an approved security is submitted with the proposal as a guarantee that the offeror will enter into the contract. (*Id.* § 5-18A-35.) The procuring agency cannot, however, require that the offeror post that bond for longer than 30 days if the proposal for services or public improvement is not successful or for longer than 45 days if the proposal for supplies is not successful, and the bond will be returned upon the signing of the contract. (*Id.*; see also *id.* ch. 5-21 (bond requirements for public improvement bids).)

As the proposals arrive to the procuring agency, that agency will open and record each proposal secretly to avoid disclosing its contents to competing offerors. (*Id.* § 5-18A-7(4).) The procuring agency may then begin confidentially discussing a potential contract with any responsible offeror who submitted a proposal determined to be reasonably likely to be selected for the award. (*Id.* § 5-18A-7(5).) While those discussions are confidential, "each offeror [is] accorded fair and equal treatment with respect to any opportunity for discussion and revision of its proposal." (*Id.*) In turn, a revision is "permitted after a submission and prior to an award for the purpose of obtaining the best and final offer." (*Id.*)

b. Awarding the Contract with a Competitive Proposal

The contract will be awarded to the offeror whose proposal is the "most advantageous to the purchasing agency" considering price and the RFP's evaluation factors. (*Id.* § 5-18A-7(6).) No other factors than those in the stated criteria can be used in the procuring agency's evaluation. (*Id.*) Like competitive bids, the purchasing agency reserves the right to reject any and all proposals and re-advertise for proposals if it finds all of the proposals unsatisfactory. (*Id.*; see also *id.* § 5-18A-12 (statute specifically stating that all proposals may be rejected if it is in the best interests of the agency).)

Additionally, if the awarding offeror fails to enter into the contract before the time specified in the RFP, the purchasing agency may issue the contract to the next-lowest responsible offeror, and the original defaulting offeror will be responsible for any difference in price. (*Id.* § 5-18A-15.)

3. Limited or Noncompetitive Small Purchases

South Dakota allows government agencies to streamline the procurement process if the purchase of services or supplies is estimated to fall under a certain price. Agencies have discretion for purchases estimated to cost less than $4,000. (*Id.* § 5-18A-11(2).)

All purchases estimated to be between $4,000 and $25,000 must follow limited competition procedures. (*Id.* § 5-18A-11(1).) First, the procuring agency must obtain at least three quotes from different vendors. (*Id.*) If three quotes cannot be obtained, the Bureau of Administration has the discretion to either approve the purchase, require additional quotes, or require that the purchase be advertised for bids. (*Id.*) Additionally, a state purchasing agency cannot circumvent the competitive bidding process by artificially dividing a large purchase into separate smaller ones. (*Id.* § 5-18A-11.)

4. Noncompetitive Sole Source Procurement

"A contract may be awarded for supplies or services without competition if the purchasing agency determines in writing that the supplies or services are of such a unique nature that the contractor selected is clearly and justifiably the only practicable source to provide the supplies or services." (*Id.* § 5-18A-8.) This determination will be based on either the uniqueness of the supplies or services, or the sole availability at the location required. (*Id.*) In these cases, the purchasing agency must negotiate for the most advantageous price, and the contract must include written verification that it is the sole source. (*Id.*) Sole source procurement under this section does not apply to construction services or construction equipment. (*Id.*)

5. Noncompetitive Emergency Procurement

A purchasing agency can make a noncompetitive emergency purchase if "there exists a threat to public health, welfare, or safety or for other urgent and compelling reasons." (*Id.* § 5-18A-9.) Before making the purchase, however, the government agency must first see whether renting is practicable under the circumstances, and it must still attempt to procure the contract with as much competition as practicable under the circumstances. (*Id.*)

The emergency prompting a noncompetitive purchase under this section cannot arise from the procuring agency's failure to abide by ordinary procurement procedures. (*Id.*) Moreover, the Supreme Court of South Dakota has held that a damaged road, when there are ways and means for temporary maintenance, is not an emergency that waives competition for a larger construction contract. (*Bak v. Jones County*, 210 N.W.2d 65, 68 (S.D. 1973); see also *Hamar Construction Co. v. Union County*, 248 N.W.2d 65, 67 (S.D. 1976) (a separate statute provides for emergency noncompetitive maintenance of bridges).)

D. Procurement of Public Improvements

By statute, the procurement of public improvements in South Dakota is governed by separate rules and contains unique obligations for private contractors. (See generally South Dakota Codified Laws ch. 5-18B.) A summary of the more basic rules follows.

1. Public Improvement Bid General Contents and Procedure

A competitive bid estimated at $100,000 must require a public advertisement of an RFP that contains plans and specifications. (*Id.* §§ 5-18A-14; 15-18B-1.) The bid process for public improvements begins with an RFP containing performance criteria, created by a dedicated and independent performance developer, which will determine the proposal selected for the contract award. (See *id.* §§ 5-18B-25 to -27.) All proposals delivered to the procuring agency must be sealed and remain unopened until the time set forth in the RFP. (*Id.* § 5-18B-33.) Further, the sealed proposals must identify each intended subcontractor and establish a maximum cost that the procuring agency will pay if there are no changes. (*Id.*) "Until a proposal is accepted, the drawings, specifications, and other information in the proposal remain the property of the person making the proposal," and "the purchasing agency [must] make reasonable efforts to maintain the secrecy and confidentiality of any proposal" and all information contained in any proposal. (*Id.* § 5-18B-34.)

a. Check or Bond Requirement

Each proposal sent to the procuring agency must include a certified check or cashier's check for 5 percent of the amount of the bid payable to that agency. (*Id.* § 5-18B-2.) Alternatively, the contractor may issue a bid bond for 10 percent of the bid's amount through a surety authorized to do business in South Dakota. (*Id.*) By statute, all bonds or checks issued as a guaranty on the contract must be returned within 30 days if the proposal is not accepted. (*Id.* § 5-18A-35.) The successful contractor, however, will have its bond or check returned upon the execution of the contract. (*Id.*) Previously, the procuring agency could waive the accompanying bond or check requirement for all projects estimated to cost $50,000 or less. (*Id.* § 5-18B-3.) However, effective July 1, 2021, the procuring agency is able to waive the accompanying bond or check requirement for public improvement contracts estimated to cost $100,000 or less. (*Id.* § 5-18A-14.) Additional and more detailed bond requirements, procedures, and rights in the event of a dispute are provided in a separate statute located at South Dakota Codified Laws chapter 5-21.

b. Resident Labor Requirement

South Dakota requires that labor for public improvements is performed substantially by South Dakota residents. Consequently, all proposals must certify that (1) no more than 20 percent of the cost of labor is being provided by nonresident subcontractors or, alternatively, (2) more than 20 percent of the cost of labor is being provided by nonresident subcontractors because resident contractors are not available at a competitive price. (*Id.* § 5-18B-6.)

c. Project Superintendent and Payment

"The purchasing agency may appoint a competent superintendent who may be the architect or engineer furnishing the plans and specifications for the public improvement." (*Id.* § 5-18B-14.) The superintendent must "report to the purchasing agency or board every thirty [30] days as to the progress and character of the work done by the contractor." (*Id.*) "Upon the reports of the superintendent, the purchasing agency" will make payments to the contractor during the process of construction to the extent provided by the contract. (*Id.*) Final payment to the contractor will be made within 30 days after the completion and acceptance of the public improvement by the purchasing agency. (*Id.*)

d. Design-Bid-Build Preference

For all public improvement contracts expected to exceed $100,000, the contractor must be a separate entity from the architect or engineer. (*Id.* § 5-18B-15.) Only emergency public improvements are exempted from this rule. (*Id.*)

e. Design-Build Contracts

Combining builder and architect or engineer services in a design-build contract, as an alternative to a design-bid-build contract, is available where the purchasing agency determines it is in the best interest of the state. A design-build contract may be justified if the agency needs a faster construction timeline, early cost commitments, the project is complex, or the project can be specified at an early stage. (*Id.* § 5-18B-20(2); see also *id.* § 5-18B-29 (elements of design-build RFPs).)

Additionally, before issuing the RFP, the purchasing agency must first establish and publish procedures for the solicitation and award of the contract. (*Id.* § 5-18B-20(1).) However, the purchasing agency must "follow the procedures of other laws governing public improvement construction contracts to the extent such laws are compatible with the use of design-build contracts." (*Id.* § 5-18B-20(3).)

Generally, to procure a design-build contract for public improvements, the purchasing agency must locate and mail RFPs to at least three qualified design-builders. (*Id.* § 5-18B-29 (with limited exceptions).) Additionally, all design-build proposals must be accompanied by a deposit or bond under the same public improvement contract requirements. (*Id.* § 5-18B-32; see also *id.* § 5-18B-18; *id.* ch. 5-21.) This deposit or security may be forfeited if the proposal is accepted but the design-builder fails to execute the design-build contract. (*Id.* § 5-18B-32.)

To be eligible for a design-build contract, the design-builder must first be authorized as an architect, engineer, or general contractor. (*Id.* § 5-18B-21.) This authorized design-builder may sublet responsibility for either construction or professional design services specific to the design-build contract to any person licensed and registered to provide professional design services in South Dakota. (*Id.* §§ 5-18B-22 to -24.)

2. Awarding the Public Improvement Contract

All proposals for public improvements should be submitted to the performance criteria developer for review. (*Id.* § 5-18B-35.) Before delivering the proposal, however, a contractor may ask for clarification for any item in the RFP, as long as the information in every proposal remains confidential. (*Id.*) Further, a contractor may withdraw the bid or proposal at any time prior to acceptance. (*Id.* § 5-18B-38.) At the deadline, when all the proposals have been received, the performance criteria developer will issue a written opinion on each proposal and relay the proposals to the purchasing agency for final review. (*Id.*)

The purchasing agency will then evaluate the proposals it receives along with the performance criteria developer's opinion according to the criteria and procedures set forth in the RFP. (*Id.* § 5-18B-36.) In doing so, the purchasing agency will first make an independent determination that the contract's procurement had adequate competition, and then accept the proposal it considers most advantageous to the purchasing agency. (*Id.* §§ 5-18B-35 to -36.)

The purchasing agency must further provide a written report detailing the reason why one proposal was selected over its competitors, which will be available to the public. (*Id.* § 5-18B-36.) As with all government bids or proposals, the purchasing agency reserves the right to reject any and all proposals and may re-solicit using the same or different criteria. (*Id.* § 5-18B-37.)

a. Public Improvement Contract Negotiations and Modifications

The state procuring agency may continue to negotiate for a price after the bid or proposal is received. "If the lowest responsive and responsible bid for a public improvement project exceeds the final estimated project cost, the [Bureau of Administration], acting on behalf of the state or any other purchasing agency, may negotiate with that low bidder for the construction of a public improvement at the most advantageous price." (*Id.* § 5-18B-5.)

Moreover, a contract for a public improvement may be amended or modified without issuing a new IFB or RFP if (1) the contract contains unit prices for the same type or class of work; (2) the change or extra work is necessitated by circumstances related to soils, utilities, or unknown conditions directly affecting the performance of the work that were not reasonably foreseeable at the time the underlying contract was let and the change or extra work is necessary to the completion of the public improvement; or (3) the sum of the proposed amendment or change order plus the sum of all other prior noncompetitive amendments or change orders, exclusive of modifications within this same subsection, does not exceed the following: (a) for contracts less than $500,000, the greater of $25,000 or 15 percent of the base contract; (b) for contracts greater than $500,000 but not more than $2,500,000, the greater of $75,000 or 10 percent of the base contract; and (c) for contracts greater than $2,500,000, the greater of $250,000 or 5 percent of the base contract. (*Id.* § 5-18B-19.)

E. Highways, Roads, and Bridges

1. Department of Transportation (State Trunk Highway Procurement)

The South Dakota Department of Transportation (SDDOT) is the agency responsible for the procurement of government contracts related to the state's trunk highway system. (*Id.* chs. 31-4 to -5.) The SDDOT's main website can be found at https://dot.sd.gov/; see also http://apps.sd.gov/HC65BidLetting/ebsbiddinginfo.aspx; http://www.sddot.com/pe/projdev/bidlet_contractor.asp (re: procurement of contracts).

a. Prequalification of Bidders

Bidding on SDDOT state highway projects begins with potential contractors qualifying for the right to bid. For all state highway projects estimated to be at least $250,000, a bidder must complete and execute a prequalification statement on forms furnished by the SDDOT. (Administrative Rules of South Dakota 70:07:02:04.) Forms can be located at https://dot.sd.gov/inside-sddot/forms-publications/forms. The application must be sent to a designated committee at least 14 days prior to the day of the letting. (*Id.* 70:07:02:06.) For more detailed instructions on how to prequalify, visit the SDDOT's website at https://apps.sd.gov/hc65bidletting/ebshowtobid.aspx.

b. Procedure for Bidding

The SDDOT will advertise future construction projects on its "Notice to Contractors" page. Prequalified contractors should download bid files from the SDDOT Bid Letting website located at https://apps.sd.gov/hc65bidletting/ebshowtobid.aspx. Accessing bidding files, and signing in to the plan holders list, will require obtaining a user ID and password from the SDDOT Bid Letting engineer. Contractors will also be required to register for digital signatures with a third-party bid repository company before submission. Per the SDDOT's website, registration for digital signatures may be done through Surety 2000 or SurePath. The link for Surety 2000 is https://surety2000.com/, and is valid as of the date of publication. The website also provides http://

web.insurevision.com/south-dakota-dot/ for SurePath customers, however this link is no longer valid as of the date of publication and no replacement has been provided.

Bidding files require the use of the South Dakota Electronic Bidding System (SDEBS), which is downloadable at http://apps.sd.gov/hc65bidletting/ebsInstall.aspx. The SDEBS Contractor Bidding User Manual is available at https://apps.sd.gov/HC65C2C/EBS/SDEBS%20Contractor%20Bidding%20User%20Manual.pdf.

Bids must be completed in their entirety utilizing the SDEBS, and submitted to the website as provided by the third-party bid repository company. Proposals that have been voided by the bidder will be disregarded. Thus, bidders may withdraw their bids from the third-party bid repository company website at any time prior to letting.

The proposal guaranty required and that must accompany each proposal is a certified check, cashier's check, or bank draft issued upon a national or state bank, or a bid bond issued in accordance with the laws of South Dakota. Bidders must execute the "Participation by Minority Contractors" or "Disadvantaged Business Enterprise (DBE) Assurance" and "Contractors Affidavit/Declaration" included in the bidding files provided by the SDDOT.

2. County Roads Procurement

County roads that are not designated "trunk highways" by the legislature are managed by the county in which the road sits. (South Dakota Codified Laws § 31-12-5.) In turn, the county board of commissioners has the power to procure contracts for the construction, improvement, maintenance, and repair of a county highway. (*Id.* § 31-12-6.) Public notice requirements for the procurement of county highway contracts in South Dakota cite the general competitive bid procedures.

3. Municipal Road Procurement

South Dakota Codified Laws section 31-12-31 was repealed in 2018; prior to its repeal it provided that the procurement of contracts regarding "secondary roads" within the control of individual townships could be performed through ordinary competitive bid processes. Since its repeal, a replacement statute has not been passed by the South Dakota Legislature.

4. Bridge Procurement

All bridges that do not fall within the immediate control of the SDDOT will be managed by the county where the bridge stands or will be placed. (*Id.* § 31-14-2.) Prior to 2018, if the cost was estimated to exceed $2,000, however, the final contract must have obtained SDDOT approval. (*Id.* § 31-14-12; see generally *id.* ch. 31-14.) However, South Dakota Codified Laws section 31-14-12 has been repealed and has not been replaced by the South Dakota Legislature.

F. Rules for Special Contract Types

1. School District Purchasing

Generally, a purchase by schools in South Dakota for improvements or supplies is performed through the procurement process as stated in South Dakota Codified Laws chapter 5-18A-D (2010) and sections 13-20-3 and 13-49-16 (board of regents must also use ordinary competitive bidding process). The plans and specifications, however, are designed by the school board. The process further allows for certain emergency purchases and requires the posting of a bond through the procedures mandated in South Dakota Codified Laws chapter 5-18A-D and sections 13-20-4, 13-20-7, and 13-20-7.1.

2. Purchases by Local Government

Special attention should be paid to any purchase of goods or services by a local government. While the competitive bidding process remains largely unchanged (but see South Dakota Codified Laws § 5-18C-6 (ordinary bid requirements do not apply to purchase of fuel by local government)), unique rules apply depending on the type of contract entered into. (See generally *id*. ch. 5-18C.)

3. Computer and Technology Purchases

The purchase of computer hardware and software is exempt from the competitive bidding process. (*Id*. § 5-18A-22(5); see also Op. S.D. Att'y Gen. No. 82-52 (1982) (Computer programs and software do "not fall within the bid requirements of state law.").) For information on how to contract for exempted hardware or software in South Dakota, visit https://boa.sd.gov/services/docs/ES-04_local_purchases.pdf.

G. South Dakota Vendor Preference Laws

South Dakota allows its government purchasing agencies to grant preferences toward a vendor if certain conditions are met. In turn,

> if all things are equal, including the price and quality of the supplies or services, a purchasing agency [will] give preference: (1) To a qualified agency if the other equal low bid or proposal was submitted by a business that was not a qualified agency; (2) To a resident business if the other equal low bid or proposal was submitted by a nonresident business; (3) To a resident manufacturer if the other equal low bid or proposal was submitted by a resident business that is not a manufacturer; (4) To a resident business whose principal place of business is located in South Dakota, if the other equal low bid or proposal was submitted by a resident business whose principal place of business is not located in the State of South Dakota; or (5) To a nonresident business providing or utilizing supplies or services found in South Dakota, if the other equal low bid or proposal was submitted by a nonresident business not providing or utilizing supplies or services found in South Dakota.

(*Id*. § 5-18A-25 (2010).)

Regardless of equality, a government purchasing agency will still grant a resident bidder a preference if the nonresident's state or foreign province grants a preference to the detriment of South Dakota residents. (*Id*. § 5-18A-26.) In such a case, the amount of preference South Dakota will give to its resident bidder is equal to the preference in the other state or province. (*Id*.) The OPM maintains a list of all states that have resident bidder preference laws and how those laws affect the bidding process in South Dakota. (*Id*. § 5-18A-27.)

H. Affirmative Action and Nondiscrimination Laws

The State of South Dakota requires that all contractors, and suppliers doing business with any state agency, department, or institution, provide a statement of nondiscrimination. By signing a paper bid or proposal, or submitting a bid or proposal through the electronic procurement system, the bidder certifies they do not discriminate in their employment practice with regard to race, color, creed, religion, age, sex, ancestry, national origin, or disability. (See OBM, *Vendor's Manual* 14 (rev. Dec. 2021), https://boa.sd.gov/central-services/procurement-management/docs/SDVendorManual_12-21-2021.pdf.) If the contract is estimated to exceed $5,000, and the services are not personal in nature, the policy in South Dakota is that minority business enterprises shall have the maximum practicable opportunity to participate in the performance of government contracts. (*Id.* at 15.) Thus, the contractor must agree to use his or her best efforts to carry out this policy in the award of subcontracts to the fullest extent consistent with the efficient performance of this contract. (*Id.*)

IV. Bid Protests and Contract Disputes

In the absence of an express statutory waiver, courts in South Dakota strictly adhere to the constitutionally mandated doctrine of sovereign immunity found in South Dakota Constitution article 3, section 27. (*Arcon Construction Co., Inc. v. South Dakota Cement Plant*, 349 N.W.2d 407, 410 (S.D. 1984).) Thus, a suit can only be maintained against the state if there is a statute or constitutional provision explicitly allowing it. (*Pourier v. South Dakota Department of Revenue & Regulation*, 778 N.W.2d 602, 605 (S.D. 2010); see also South Dakota Codified Laws § 31-2-34 (private individuals may sue the SDDOT for breaches of road construction contracts), and *id.* §§ 9-12-1 and 9-1-6 (permits suits for breaches of contracts against municipalities).)

Regardless of whether a specific statute exists, however, a municipality may still impliedly waive sovereign immunity for breach of an explicit contractual obligation when it is operating in a corporate or proprietary capacity. (*Blue Fox Bar, Inc. v. Yankton*, 424 N.W.2d 915, 917–18 (S.D. 1988).) Further, the Supreme Court of South Dakota has held that the enactment of the Uniform Commercial Code is a waiver of sovereign immunity for contract disputes involving goods because government entities are included in the definition of "organizations." (*Arcon Construction Co.*, 349 N.W.2d at 410.)

A. Bid Protests

1. Bid Protest Procedure

The procedure for formally protesting the awarding of a bid may be done administratively or judicially depending on the type of contract sought and the agency procuring the bid. For example, with design-build public improvement contracts, the purchasing agency must establish procedures in the RFP for all formal protests relating to the solicitation or award of the contract prior to letting the bid. (South Dakota Codified Laws § 5-18B-20; see, e.g., *S.J. Louis Construction, Inc. v. Lewis & Clark Regional Water System*, 585 F. Supp. 2d 1139, 1141 (S.D. 2008) (appeal from the dismissal of an administrative bid protest for a contract involving the installation of a pipeline).) Additional rules and procedure for filing an administrative action with the purchasing agency can be found at South Dakota Codified Laws chapter 1-26.

If a purchasing agency is not obligated to create an administrative tribunal, a private contractor can sue directly in the courts to seek injunctive relief. (See, e.g., *Winter Brothers Underground Inc. v. City of Beresford*, 652 N.W.2d 99, 102 (S.D. 2002) (a contract with a city government for underground sewer improvements).)

2. Standing for Bid Protests

Merely losing out on an award is not a sufficient injury for standing to seek injunctive relief in court. (*H & W Contracting, LLC v. Watertown*, 633 N.W.2d 167, 171 (S.D. 2001) (citing *Tri-State Milling Co. v. Board of County Commissioners*, 68 N.W.2d 104 (1995)).) However, standing for a bid protest exists if the losing bidder can show a prima facie case of "favoritism, improvidence, extravagance, fraud, or corruption." (*Id.* at 172.) Moreover, because the losing bidder is essentially stepping into the shoes of public interest, the remedy extends only to suits for declaratory or equitable relief seeking to compel compliance with the competitive bid laws. (*Id.* at 172–73.) Alternatively, a taxpayer, who theoretically pays for the government contracts, has standing based on the special injury to himself or herself. (*Id.*; see also South Dakota Codified Laws § 9-1-6 ("Any citizen or taxpayer residing within a municipality may maintain an action or proceeding to prevent, by proper remedy, a violation of any provision of statutes regarding municipal governments."); but see *Winter Brothers Underground Inc.*, 652 N.W.2d at 102 ("the mere payment of a sales tax by a consumer does not fit within the definition of a taxpayer.").)

3. Bid Protest Remedies

The form of relief applicable for a bid protest is an injunction and declaratory judgment to compel a government purchasing agency to comply with the mandatory competitive bid obligations. (*Winter Brothers Underground Inc.*, 652 N.W.2d at 102.) Because of the nature of the suit, a losing bidder cannot retrieve any monetary damages for its bid preparation. (*H & W Contracting*, 633 N.W.2d at 172–73.) While courts have not explicitly ruled them out, writs of mandamus or prohibition are very unlikely to apply in a bid protest because of the discretionary nature of awarding a bid and the alternative remedy of declaratory relief. (*Id.* at 175–76.)

B. Bid Protest Appeals

A bid protestor who has exhausted all administrative remedies within the agency and is still aggrieved can appeal for judicial review. (South Dakota Codified Laws § 1-26-30.) The requirement to exhaust all administrative remedies, however, does not apply to independent judicial writs enforceable in court. (*Id.*)

C. Contract Disputes

A contractor can sue a government agency for breach of contract if privity exists between the two entities. (*C & W Enterprises, Inc. v. Sioux Falls*, 635 N.W.2d 752, 757 (S.D. 2001).) Moreover, when a government agency enters into a contract with a general contractor, who in turn subcontracts certain work to another party under the express approval of that agency, privity exists between the government agency and the subcontractor for all work that the government has approved. (*Id.*)

D. Suspension and Debarment

For all contracts procured through the OPM, a vendor will be removed from the bidders' list for failure to pay the required registration fee. (See OBM, *Vendor's Manual* 8 (rev. Dec. 2021, https://boa.sd.gov/central-services/procurement-management/docs/SDVendorManual_12-21-2021.pdf. Moreover, the OPM can suspend a vendor from consideration for any contract for up to three months, or debar that vendor for up to three years, for certain acts of noncompliance. (South Dakota Codified Laws

§ 5-18D-12.) The SDDOT has its own criteria for suspension and debarment, which can be found at Administrative Rules of South Dakota 70:07:04:01 to :12.

V. Administrative and Judicial Review

A. Administrative Review

The administrative review process is set forth above.

B. Judicial Review

The judicial review process is set forth above.

VI. Extent of State's Adoption or Adaptation of ABA Model Procurement Code

South Dakota is not a Model Procurement Code state. South Dakota law governing the procurement of government contracts is located in several different chapters of the South Dakota Codified Laws, and the OPM establishes statewide contracts for goods and authorizes small purchases and equipment leases by state agencies and institutions in compliance with state law.

VII. Cooperative Purchasing

A. Authority

South Dakota has adopted the use of cooperative purchasing agreements. (South Dakota Codified Laws § 5-18A-37 (2010).) Under South Dakota Codified Laws section 5-18A-37, "any purchasing agency may enter into agreements with purchasing agents" in South Dakota, any other states, or with the federal government wherein "any of the parties may agree to participate in, administer, sponsor, or conduct purchasing transactions under a joint agreement or contract for the purchase of supplies or contractual services." Purchasing agencies may also work with other states or the federal government to "develop uniform purchasing specifications on a regional or national level to facilitate cooperative interstate purchasing transactions." (*Id.*) This letter can no longer be found and no replacement can be found.

B. Requirements

The South Dakota Bureau of Administration maintains a website, listing the purchasing agreements in which it participates through the National Association of State Purchasing Officials (shorthanded as NASPO ValuePoint), at https://boa.sd.gov/central-services/procurement-management/procurement-management-naspo-contracts.aspx. South Dakota has not issued pertinent guidance on how a contractor can qualify for a contract under a cooperative purchasing agreement but it directs any questions regarding the program to the OPM. Further, there is not yet case law interpreting South Dakota Codified Laws section 5-18A-37, so it remains unclear what rights and remedies are available to a disappointed bidder who would like to lodge a bid protest on a cooperative purchasing agreement contract.

Tennessee Procurement Rules and Regulations

Prepared by Erica Bell Vick, David R. Esquivel, and Ramon J. Ryan
Bass, Berry & Sims PLC
Email: evick@bassberry.com; desquivel@bassberry.com; ramon.ryan@bassberry.com

I. Statutory Reference

A. Procurement/Purchasing Statutes

The Tennessee Central Procurement Office is charged with the responsibility of procuring all materials. The statutes that govern the public procurement practices in the state of Tennessee are within Tennessee Code Annotated title 12, chapter 3.

These statutes can be accessed at the following website address: http://www.lexisnexis.com/hottopics/tncode/. A table of contents of these purchasing statutes is set forth below:

Part 1: Applicability of Chapter

§ 12-3-101.	Items purchased by central procurement office.
§ 12-3-102.	Exemptions for purchases of certain departments, institutions, and agencies.
§ 12-3-103.	Professional service contracts.
§ 12-3-104.	Transfer of equipment between departments.

Part 2: General Provisions

§ 12-3-201.	Definitions
§ 12-3-202.	State network telephone service for state university and college students.

Part 3: Purchases and Contracts for Goods and Services

§ 12-3-301.	Written acquisition plan, provision of data, and agency amendment.
§ 12-3-302.	Prohibited statements or agreements regarding willingness to meet low bid.
§ 12-3-303.	Execution by agency heads and exceptions.
§ 12-3-304.	Void contracts and liability.
§ 12-3-305.	Management of contracts, guidelines, maximum liability, and certification.

§ 12-3-306. Registration with department.
§ 12-3-307. Procedural and administrative accountability requirements.
§ 12-3-308. Nondiscrimination and contracts with religious organizations.
§ 12-3-309. Prohibited contracts and appeals process.
§ 12-3-310. Call center contracts.
§ 12-3-311. Noncompetitive purchases and contracts for non-construction and non-engineering projects or services.

Part 4: Delegation of Purchasing Authority

§ 12-3-401. Delegation of purchasing authority.

Part 5: Competitive Solicitations

§ 12-3-501. Competitive sealed solicitations.
§ 12-3-502. Public advertisement of solicitation and examination of responses.
§ 12-3-503. Informal solicitation rules.
§ 12-3-504. Goods and services from single supply source.
§ 12-3-505. Purchase of goods to meet emergency.
§ 12-3-506. Negotiation with vendors who maintain pricing agreements with United States.
§ 12-3-507. Competitive negotiation and best interest of state.
§ 12-3-508. Utility contracts.
§ 12-3-509. Receipt of goods and services.
§ 12-3-510. Procurement records shall be open and accessible.
§ 12-3-511. Availability of funds.
§ 12-3-512. Cooperative purchasing agreements with other states or local governments.
§ 12-3-513. Competitive reverse auction process.

Part 6: Cost Principles and Audits

§ 12-3-601. Cost or pricing data, inaccuracies, and exceptions.
§ 12-3-602. Inspection of contractors and audits.
§ 12-3-603. Cost principles and regulations.

Part 7: Procurement and Limitation of Liability

§ 12-3-701. Limitation of liability.

Part 8: Procurement Specifications and Scopes of Work

§ 12-3-801. Open and competitive soliciting.
§ 12-3-802. Specifications for goods and services.
§ 12-3-803. Modifications to specifications.
§ 12-3-804. Use of standard specifications.
§ 12-3-805. Recommended specifications.
§ 12-3-806. Remanufactured goods.

Part 12: Local Governments

The statutes that govern procurement by and within the governing bodies of the counties of the state of Tennessee are found within Tennessee Code Annotated title 5, chapter 14. A table of contents of these purchasing statutes is set forth below:

Part 1: County Purchasing Law of 1957

Part 2: County Purchasing Law of 1983

§ 5-14-203.	Limits on purchases.
§ 5-14-204.	Bidding—Exceptions.
§ 5-14-205.	Expenditures under $10,000.
§ 5-14-206.	Stricter requirements—Regulations.
§ 5-14-207.	Bid specifications for purchases of chemical products.

The statutes that govern procurement by and within the governing bodies of cities and towns, municipalities, and by city managers in the state of Tennessee are found within Tennessee Code Annotated title 6, chapters 19, 35, and 56. A table of contents of these purchasing statutes is as follows:

Chapter 19: Powers under City Manager—Commission Charter

§ 6-19-104.	Purchasing and contract procedures.

Chapter 35: City Manager: Administration of City Affairs under Modified Manager—Council Charter

§ 6-35-205.	Purchasing.

Chapter 56: Fiscal Affairs

§ 6-56-301.	Short title.
§ 6-56-302.	Application of part.
§ 6-56-303.	Limits on purchases.
§ 6-56-304.	Advertising and bidding—Exceptions.
§ 6-56-305.	Advertising and bidding—Expenditures of less than $2,500.
§ 6-56-306.	Additional authority of municipal governing body.
§ 6-56-307.	Bid specifications for purchases of chemical products.

B. Other Applicable Statutes

The statutes governing public contracts are found in Tennessee Code Annotated sections 12-4-101 through 12-4-1007.

Ethics and lobbying is governed by Tennessee Code Annotated sections 3-6-101 through 3-6-309. The Tennessee Ethics Commission Act of 2006 governing ethics and lobbying issues is one of the provisions of the code in this section.

Bribery is a Chapter 16 offense against the administration of government. (See Tennessee Code Annotated §§ 39-16-101 through 39-16-108.)

II. Regulations

Regulations are promulgated pursuant to the statutory authority of Tennessee Code Annotated section 12-3-701(d). Pertinent regulations may be found as follows: Official Compilation Rules & Regulations of the State of Tennessee 0690-03-01.01 through 0690-03-01.28. Furthermore, the rules of the Central Procurement Office regarding purchasing, supplies, materials, equipment, and services are also available online at https://www.tn.gov/generalservices/procurement/central-procurement-office--cpo-/library-.html. The Central Procurement Office has created a Procurement Procedures Manual that is available online at https://www.tn.gov/content/dam/tn/generalservices/documents/cpo/cpo-library/Procurement_Procedures_Manual_of_the_CPO_final_copy_04.01.19.pdf.

III. Source Selection

The general methods of procurement include the following:

A. Informal Solicitations and Small Purchases

Pursuant to Tennessee Code Annotated section 12-3-503(a), the Procurement Commission may authorize the chief procurement officer (CPO) to establish informal solicitation and small purchase rules, policies, and procedures for purchases not exceeding $50,000 or $10,000, respectively, if all of the members of the Procurement Commission agree. The CPO must solicit quotes or proposals from at least three vendors. (See Purchasing Procedures Manual §§ 6.4.1–6.4.2.)

B. Invitation to Bid

An invitation to bid (ITB) is a procurement method where a contract is awarded to one or more bidders. (Official Compilation Rules & Regulations of the State of Tennessee 0690-03-01.02(kk).)

C. Request for Proposals

A request for proposals (RFP) is a written solicitation for written proposals to provide goods or services to the state. (Official Compilation Rules & Regulations of the State of Tennessee 0690-03-01-.05(2).)

D. Emergency Purchases

An emergency purchase may occur when there is a serious and unexpected situation that poses an immediate risk to health, life, property, or environment that calls an agency to action; such action entails the need to secure goods or services to carry out an emergency response. (See Purchasing Procedures Manual § 6.1.1.) All emergency purchases shall, if practicable, be made by competitive procurement. (Tennessee Code Annotated § 12-3-505.)

E. Competitive Negotiation

Pursuant to Tennessee Code Annotated section 12-3-507, competitive negotiation may occur when it is in the best interest of the state to competitively negotiate a contract. The state's policies provide for the safeguarding of the information and provide fairness to the vendors in the negotiation process.

F. Sole Source

A sole source procurement is one where only one vendor possesses the unique and singularly available capability to meet the requirement of the solicitation, such as technical qualifications, ability to deliver at a particular time, or services from a public utility, or a situation where a particular supplier or person is identified as the only qualified source available to the requisitioning authority. (See Purchasing Procedures Manual §§ 6.2.1–6.2.4.) A sole source procurement must be approved by the CPO, and the justification for awarding a sole source contract must be in writing. (Purchasing Procedures Manual §§ 6.2.1–6.2.4; see also Tennessee Code Annotated § 12-3-504.)

G. Reverse Auction

A reverse auction is a competitive real-time internet procurement process that allows purchase orders and contracts to be awarded to the respondent or respondents offering the lowest price. (See Tennessee Code Annotated § 12-3-513.) This procurement method is available when the minimum response is greater than $100,000 and the number of approved online respondents is greater than five. (See Purchasing Procedures Manual § 6.6.2.)

H. Request for Information

A request for information (RFI) is a solicitation sent to a broad base of potential suppliers for the purpose of developing strategy, building a database, or preparing for an RFP or a request for qualifications (RFQ). (Official Compilation Rules & Regulations of the State of Tennessee 0690-03-01.02(ccc).)

I. RFQ

An RFQ is a written solicitation containing a list of qualifications that must be met before a vendor may propose in response to an RFP. The appropriate response to an RFQ is a written response from a vendor. (Official Compilation Rules & Regulations of the State of Tennessee 0690-03-01.02(eee).)

J. Negotiation with Vendors Who Maintain a General Services Administration Price Agreement

Subject to the rules of the Central Procurement Office, the CPO may negotiate with a vendor who maintains a General Services Administration (GSA) pricing agreement with the United States or any agency thereof; however, the price under any contract executed under this authority cannot exceed the price contained in the GSA contract with the vendor. (Tennessee Code Annotated § 12-3-506.)

K. Purchase or Contract for Utilities and Services

Subject to its rules, the Central Procurement Office shall purchase or contract for all telephone, telegraph, electric light, gas, power, postal, and other services for which a rate for the use thereof has been established by a public authority, in such manner as the CPO deems to be in the best interest of the state. (Tennessee Code Annotated § 12-3-508.)

L. Proprietary Procurement

Proprietary procurements may be made for a service or a product that is manufactured and marketed by a person having the exclusive right to provide the service or manufacture or sell the product in which resellers are granted the right to sell. All proprietary procurements, regardless of the dollar amount, require the CPO's prior approval. (Official Compilation Rules & Regulations of the State of Tennessee 0690-03-01-.05(7).)

M. Tennessee Rehabilitative Initiative in Correction

All state agencies are required to purchase from Tennessee Rehabilitative Initiative in Correction (TRICOR) provided such items and services are certified by the

Procurement Commission as being of satisfactory quality, reasonable in price, and available in accordance with Tennessee Code Annotated section 41-22-119.

N. Central Nonprofit Agency

All state agencies are required to purchase from the central nonprofit agency when such items and services are certified by the Procurement Commission as to quality, availability, and fair market price in accordance with Tennessee Code Annotated section 71-4-701 *et seq*. This shall not apply when the commodities or services are available from any agency of the state, or where the Procurement Commission determines that the commodities or services do not meet the reasonable requirements of a department, institution, agency, or political subdivision of the state.

O. Blind Services

All purchases made by any agency of the state, whether or not through the purchasing division of the Department of General Services, shall be made from an agency of the State of Tennessee or a nonprofit workshop for the blind in Tennessee, operating under the approval of the Department of Human Services and the Division of Services for the Blind. (See Tennessee Code Annotated § 71-4-204.) The products or services must comply with applicable federal standards and specifications for such services and be priced in accordance with prices provided by such standards. (See Tennessee Code Annotated § 71-4-205.)

IV. Bid Protests and Contract Disputes

A. Bid Protests

1. Deadlines

A protest must be submitted within seven calendar days after the earlier of the notice of award or intent to award the contract is issued or knowledge of any other matter with regard to which a protest may lie—for example, a solicitation requirement that advantages one proposer over another. (See Tennessee Code Annotated § 12-3-514(b).)

2. Standing

Any respondent who has submitted a response to a solicitation and who claims to be aggrieved in connection with the solicitation, award, or proposed award of a contract may protest to the CPO. (Tennessee Code Annotated § 12-3-514(b).)

3. Form and Filing

The protest must be in writing. (See Tennessee Code Annotated § 12-3-514(b).)

The signature of an attorney or protesting party on a protest constitutes a certificate by the signer that they have read the document, and to the best of their knowledge, the document is well grounded in law and fact. (See Tennessee Code Annotated § 12-3-514(c).)

The protesting party must post a protest bond with the protest. (Tennessee Code Annotated § 12-3-514(d).) The amount of the protest bond will be 5 percent of the lowest bid or cost proposal; 5 percent of the maximum or estimated maximum liability; 5 percent of the estimated maximum revenue if the contract at issue will be revenue producing to the state; or in the case of a no-cost contract, an amount to be determined by the CPO. The protesting party will have an opportunity to oppose payment of the protest bond prior to the bond being payable to the state upon a finding that the protest was signed, before or after appeal to the CPO or protest committee, in violation of the provisions regarding the certification of protest documents; the protest has been brought or pursued in bad faith; the affected state agency has suffered damages resulting in a loss of funding, increased expenditures, or a disruption in services; the protest was filed in bad faith or in violation of the provisions regarding certification of protest documents; the protest was not upheld; the protest did not state on its face a valid basis for protest; or for any other reason approved by the protest committee. (Tennessee Code Annotated § 12-3-514(e).) The state shall hold the protest bond for 11 calendar days after the date of the final determination of the CPO. If a protesting party appeals the CPO's determination to the protest committee, then the CPO shall hold the protest bond until instructed by the protest committee to either keep the bond or return it to the protesting party. (See Tennessee Code Annotated § 12-3-514(f).) If, at the time of filing notice of a protest, the lowest bid is less than $1,000,000, a minority or small business protesting party may submit a written petition for exemption to the protest bond requirement. (See Tennessee Code Annotated § 12-3-514(g).)

4. Stay of Procurement

A stay of the solicitation, award, or proposed award will be granted upon receipt of a protest and the accompanying protest bond. The stay must not be lifted unless, after giving the protesting party an opportunity to be heard, the CPO or the protest committee makes a written determination that the continuation of the procurement process or the award of the contract without further delay is necessary to protect the interests of the state. (See Tennessee Code Annotated § 12-3-514(b), (i).)

5. Decision

The CPO has authority to resolve a protest and is required to do so within 60 calendar days after a protest is filed. The final determination of the CPO shall be made in writing and submitted to the protesting party, the protest committee, and the comptroller of the treasury.

B. Bid Protest Appeals

After the final determination of the CPO or if the CPO fails to resolve the protest within 60 calendar days, then the protesting party may request that the protest committee meet to consider the protest. A request for consideration before the protest committee shall be made in writing within seven calendar days from the date of the CPO's final determination or within seven calendar days following the CPO's failure to resolve the protest within 60 calendar days after receipt of the protest. (Tennessee Code Annotated § 12-3-514(h).)

C. Contract Disputes

If a protest is received by the state subsequent to a contract executed pursuant to a procurement process, then the Tennessee Claims Commission has exclusive jurisdiction to determine all monetary claims against the state, including, but not limited to, claims for the negligent deprivation of statutory rights pursuant to Tennessee Code Annotated section 9-8-307(a)(1)(N). (See Tennessee Code Annotated § 12-3-514(g).)

D. Suspension and Debarment

All contracts subject to procurement rules and regulations must contain a provision concerning the circumstances under which a contracting party may be considered debarred or suspended from doing business with the state. (See Official Compilation Rules & Regulations of the State of Tennessee 0690-03-01-.17(2)(t).) That provision shall serve as certification that the contractor is not presently debarred, suspended, or otherwise declared ineligible by a state or federal agency; has not been convicted of or had a civil judgment rendered against the contracting party within the past three years from the commission of fraud or a similar criminal offense in connection with a public transaction; is not presently indicted or otherwise criminally or civilly charged with any similar offense; and has not, within the past three years, had one or more public transactions terminated for cause or default.

V. Administrative and Judicial Review

A. Administrative Review

The administrative review process is detailed above. (See Sections IV.A–B.) A protesting party must exhaust all administrative remedies before initiation of judicial review. (Tennessee Code Annotated § 12-3-514(j).)

B. Judicial Review

Protest decisions are appealed by common law writ of certiorari to the chancery court from the protest committee. The scope of review in the proceedings is limited to the record made before the protest committee and involves only an inquiry into whether the protest committee exceeded its jurisdiction, followed an unlawful procedure, or acted illegally, fraudulently, or arbitrarily without material evidence to support its action. (Tennessee Code Annotated § 12-3-514(l).)

VI. Extent of State's Adoption or Adaptation of ABA Model Procurement Code

Tennessee has not adopted the American Bar Association (ABA) Model Procurement Code in whole or in part.

VII. Cooperative Purchasing

A. Authority

The statute governing cooperative purchasing is found in Tennessee Code Annotated section 12-3-1205.

B. Requirements

Any local government of the state may participate in, sponsor, conduct, or administer a cooperative purchasing agreement with one or more other local governments to procure supplies, services, or construction in accordance with an agreement entered into between the participants. This includes, but is not limited to, a multi-party contract between local governments. Where a city is required to advertise and receive bids, it is sufficient that the purchasing entity comply only with its own purchasing requirements. (Tennessee Code Annotated § 12-3-1205(a).)

Any local government of the state may participate in a cooperative purchasing agreement with one or more out-of-state governmental entities to the extent allowed by the other state's laws for the procurement of goods, supplies, services, or equipment, or with an agency of the United States, to the extent allowed by federal law, in accordance with an agreement entered into between or among the participants. Such goods, supplies, services, or equipment must be procured in a manner that constitutes competitive bidding and are advertised, evaluated, and awarded by a governmental entity and made available for use by other governmental entities. (Tennessee Code Annotated § 12-3-1205(b)(1).)

Any local government within Tennessee may participate in a master agreement by adopting a resolution accepting its terms. If a participant to the master agreement is required to advertise and receive bids, it is sufficient that the purchasing entity complied with its own requirements. The participant is required to acquire and maintain documentation that the purchasing entity complied with its own purchasing requirements. (Tennessee Code Annotated § 12-3-1205(b)(2).)

Tennessee Code Annotated section 12-3-1205(b)(4) lists the items that are excluded under this authorization: (1) the purchase of new or used motor vehicles (unless manufactured for a special purpose as defined in Tennessee Code Annotated § 12-3-1208)—under this section, motor vehicle does not include farm tractor, mower, earth-moving machinery, construction machinery, or other similar machinery or equipment; (b) the purchase of construction, engineering or architectural services, and construction materials—"construction materials" does not include materials used in the operation of a municipal utility system; and (c) the purchase of fuel or fuel products and lubricating oils.

Authorization for exercising joint purchasing authority with an agency of the United States under Tennessee Code Annotated section 12-3-1205(b)(1) does not include the authority to purchase construction machinery utilized in construction or on construction sites. (Tennessee Code Annotated § 12-3-1205(b)(5).) A municipality may participate in a cooperative purchasing agreement with the Central Procurement Office and a public institution of higher education to procure goods and services. This type of cooperative purchasing must be awarded through full and open competition. (Tennessee Code Annotated § 12-3-512.)

Texas Procurement Rules and Regulations

Prepared by Sandy D. Hellums-Gomez[1]
Husch Blackwell, LLP
Email: sandy.gomez@huschblackwell.com

I. Statutory Reference

A. Overview—State Purchasing Statutes

The Office of the Comptroller of Public Accounts Statewide Procurement Division (SPD)[2] is responsible for general purchasing of products and services for Texas state agencies, except for information technology and telecommunications products. Along with other procurement and contracting methods, the Comptroller's Office establishes and operates multiple award schedule contracts (TXMAS contracts). The Office also establishes and manages cooperative contracts for goods and services such as office equipment (other than information technology and telecommunications products and services), credit or merchant cards, food, fleet services, and related products, and similar other commodities and services.

The Texas Legislature has delegated certain purchasing authority to a number of state agencies for specialized or unique procurement requirements. These delegations have been in effect for many years. Examples of agencies granted delegations of purchasing authority include the Texas Lottery Commission, the Health and Human Services Commission, and the Texas Department of Transportation. SPD has also delegated purchasing authority for the following types of procurements:

- One-time purchases of goods that do not exceed $50,000
- Purchases of services that do not exceed $100,000
- Direct publications
- Purchases of perishable goods
- Distributor purchases
- Fuel, oil, and grease purchases
- Internal repair purchases
- Emergency purchases

1. Prior editions prepared by Cheryl Burtzel.
2. *See* Office of the Comptroller, *Purchasing*, https://comptroller.texas.gov/purchasing/ (last visited June 2, 2022).

The general provisions of Texas state agency purchasing law are found in chapter 2155'of title 10 of the Texas Government Code.[3] A table of contents for Texas Government Code chapter 2155 is set forth below:

---

3. Texas Constitution and Statutes, https://statutes.capitol.texas.gov/ (last visited June 2, 2022).

SUBCHAPTER E. MASTER BIDDERS LIST

§ 2155.261.	Applicability
§ 2155.262.	Uniform Registration Form
§ 2155.263.	Centralized Master Bidders List
§ 2155.264.	Agency Solicitation of Bids or Proposals for Acquisition over $25,000
§ 2155.265.	Access to Master Bidders List
§ 2155.266.	Registration and Renewal Fee
§ 2155.267.	Rules and Procedures regarding Master Bidders List
§ 2155.268.	Use of State Agency Bidders List
§ 2155.269.	Waiver
§ 2155.270.	Agency Assistance with Bidders List Issues

SUBCHAPTER F. INSPECTION AND CERTIFICATION OF GOODS OR SERVICES; AUDITS

§ 2155.321.	Definitions
§ 2155.322.	Inspection and Certification
§ 2155.323.	Audit of Financial Information
§ 2155.324.	Purchase Audit
§ 2155.325.	Purchase Audit after Issuance of Warrant
§ 2155.326.	Audit by State Auditor
§ 2155.327.	Interagency Purchases and Transactions

SUBCHAPTER G. PAYMENT PROVISIONS

§ 2155.381.	Invoice
§ 2155.382.	Payment by Warrant
§ 2155.383.	Advance Payments to State or Federal Agency
§ 2155.384.	Authority to Pay Charges
§ 2155.385.	Credit Cards
§ 2155.386.	Prepayment for Library Materials by Institution of Higher Education
§ 2155.387.	Payment for Road Construction Materials Delivered by Vehicles Exceeding Weight Limits

SUBCHAPTER H. PURCHASING PREFERENCES

§ 2155.441.	Preference for Products of Persons with Mental Retardation or Physical Disabilities
§ 2155.442.	Preference for Energy Efficient Products
§ 2155.443.	Preference for Rubberized Asphalt Paving
§ 2155.444.	Preference to Texas and United States Products and Texas Services
§ 2155.4441.	Preference under Service Contracts
§ 2155.445.	Preference for Recycled, Remanufactured, or Environmentally Sensitive Products
§ 2155.446.	Purchase and Use of Paper Containing Recycled Fibers
§ 2155.447.	Purchase of Recycled Oil

§ 2155.448.	Expenditures for Recycled, Remanufactured, or Environmentally Sensitive Commodities or Services
§ 2155.449.	Preference for Products and Services from Economically Depressed or Blighted Area
§ 2155.450.	Preference for Products of Facilities on Formerly Contaminated Property
§ 2155.451.	Vendors That Meet or Exceed Air Quality Standards
§ 2155.452.	Preference for Contractors Providing Foods of Higher Nutritional Value
§ 2155.453.	Certain Contracts for Homeland Security or Law Enforcement Technology

SUBCHAPTER I. MULTIPLE AWARD CONTRACT SCHEDULE

§ 2155.501.	Definitions
§ 2155.502.	Development of Multiple Award Contract Schedule
§ 2155.503.	Rules
§ 2155.504.	Use of Schedule by Governmental Entities
§ 2155.505.	Historically Underutilized and Small Businesses
§ 2155.506.	Reporting Requirements
§ 2155.508.	Internet Availability
§ 2155.509.	Notice regarding Procurements Exceeding $25,000
§ 2155.510.	Rebates

B. Other Applicable Statutes

- Purchasing Methods (Texas Government Code § 2156.001 *et seq.*)
- Purchasing: Purchase of Automated Information Systems (Texas Government Code § 2157.001 *et seq.*)
- Purchasing: Miscellaneous Provisions for Purchase of Certain Goods and Services (Texas Government Code § 2158.001 *et seq.*)
- Historically Underutilized Businesses (Texas Government Code § 2161.001 *et seq.*)
- Ethics, Reporting, and Approval Requirements for Certain Contracts (Texas Government Code § 2261.251 *et seq.*)
- Professional Services Procurement Act (Texas Government Code ch. 2254)
- Interagency Cooperation Act (Texas Government Code ch. 771)
- Interlocal Cooperation Act (Texas Government Code ch. 791)
- Contracting and Delivery Procedures for Construction Projects (Texas Government Code ch. 2269)
- Building Construction and Acquisition and Disposition of Real Property (Texas Government Code ch. 2166)

II. Regulations

Regulations regarding general state agency purchasing requirements are promulgated pursuant to the statutory authority of Texas Government Code section 2155.0012 and are found in the Texas Administrative Code, title 34, part 1, chapter 20. In addition, the State of Texas Procurement and Contract Management Guide provides agencies with a framework for the statewide purchasing process.[4] Each state agency is also required to post its contract management handbook establishing "consistent contracting policies and practices to be followed by the agency" online and to submit a link to the web page for these procedures to the Texas comptroller.[5]

III. Source Selection

The basic methods of procurement for state agencies include:

A. Informal Bidding

This method is used for purchases under $25,000. Bids are solicited by telephone, facsimile, email, letter, posting on electronic commerce networks, or other means, and may be written or faxed by a designated closing date. There is no formal opening and reading of bids. Award is made to the lowest responsive and qualified bidder.

B. Invitation for Bid

An invitation for bid (IFB) or other formal procurement methods must be used for purchases over $25,000. A written solicitation of formal sealed bids is published, and bid responses are due at a specific date and time. There is a public opening and reading of bids. Award will be made to the lowest responsive, qualified, and responsible bidder. Price generally is the determinative criterion.

C. Competitive Sealed Proposals

This form of source selection is used when the comptroller or other state agency determines that other procurement processes are not practicable or advantageous to the state. The request for proposals (RFP) describes applicable background information, the specifications for the goods or services to be procured, needs of the state, evaluation criteria, the procurement time line, terms and conditions, and other information. Offerors submit written proposals describing their proposed solution(s), pricing, qualifications, and other information required by solicitation. Award is made to the highest-ranked, qualified, and responsible offeror based on evaluation criteria set forth in the RFP.

D. Request for Qualifications

Requests for qualifications (RFQs) are utilized for the procurement of professional services.[6] Professional services include those (1) within the scope of the practice of accounting, architecture, landscape architecture, land surveying, medicine, optometry, professional engineering, real estate appraising, or professional nursing; (2) provided in connection with the employment or practice of a person licensed in fields identified

---

4. State of Texas Procurement and Contract Management Guide, Version 2.1 (2022), https://comptroller.texas.gov/purchasing/publications/procurement-contract.php (last visited June 2, 2022).

5. Tex. Gov't Code § 2261.256 (2015); Texas Comptroller, *State Agency Contract Management Procedures*, https://comptroller.texas.gov/purchasing/sb20/procedures.php (last visited June 2, 2022).

6. Tex. Gov't Code ch. 2254.

by statute; or (3) provided by an interior designer.[7] RFQs are awarded on the basis of demonstrated competence and qualifications to perform and a fair and reasonable price.[8] For a limited number of services, architectural, engineering, and land surveying, the agency must select the vendor based on competency alone and then may negotiate a price.[9]

E. Reverse Auctions

These are real-time bidding events that are internet-dependent and are conducted at a prescheduled time and internet location in which multiple suppliers, anonymous to each other, submit bids for designated goods or services. Once the auction is closed, the state evaluates the bids and awards to the lowest responsive and responsible vendor.

F. Alternative Delivery Methods

Alternatives are available for the procurement of construction services. Building construction is generally controlled by the Texas Facilities Commission and the preferred selection process is the lowest and best bid method.[10] However, the state may use any contracting method allowed pursuant to Texas Government Code chapter 2269.[11] Chapter 2269 allows the use of alternative delivery methods for public works contracts including design-build, construction manager at risk, and job order contracting, among others.[12]

G. Multiple Award Contract Procedure

A multiple award contract is available for use by state agencies in accordance with applicable procedures. This procedure may be used only after the director of the Comptroller's Office SPD or a state agency's purchasing director has made a written determination that its use is in the best interest of the state of Texas. In arriving at a determination, the following factors shall be considered: (1) the quality, availability, and reliability of the supplies, materials, equipment, or service and their adaptability to the particular use required; (2) the ability, capacity, and skill of the bidder; (3) the sufficiency of the bidder's financial resources; (4) the bidder's ability to provide maintenance, repair parts, and service; (5) compatibility with existing equipment; (6) the need for flexibility in evaluating new products on a large scale before becoming contractually committed for all use; and (7) any other relevant factors. (34 Texas Administrative Code § 20.46.) The Comptroller's Office maintains multiple award schedules for goods and services that are not categorized as automated information systems; the Texas Department of Information Resources (DIR) maintains multiple award schedule contracts for information technology goods and services and for telecommunications-related goods and services. The Multiple Award Schedule notice must be posted on the Electronic State Business Daily for purchase from a multiple award schedule contract with a total value exceeding $25,000. (34 Texas Administrative Code § 20.210.)

---

7. *Id.* § 2254.002(2).
8. *Id.* § 2254.003(a).
9. *Id.* § 2254.003(b).
10. *Id.* § 2166.253.
11. *Id.* § 2166.2525.
12. *Id.* ch. 2269.

Note: The summary of procurement methods presented above is a very simplified overview of the procurement methods frequently used by Texas state agencies. Please note that (1) there are other processes, especially when specialized or unique products or services are to be procured; (2) extensive subtleties to implementation of these processes exist; and (3) there other issues to consider when participating in state agency-related procurements. Further, additional procedures and requirements applicable to procurements by local governments (counties, municipalities, special purpose districts, and elementary and secondary schools) are found in other Texas statutes and codes and are not discussed in this summary.

IV. Bid Protests and Contract Disputes

A. Bid Protests

1. Generally

Texas Government Code section 2155.076 states, in effect, that the Comptroller's Office and each state agency shall develop and adopt protest procedures regarding purchasing issues. State agencies that are not subject to the Texas Administrative Procedure Act (Texas Government Code § 2001.001 *et seq.*) shall provide public notice of its proposed and adopted protest rules and provide a procedure for public comment on the proposed rules.

The bottom line is that procurement protest procedures vary from state agency to state agency. Procurement participants should check the rules and protest procedures published by the agency conducting a procurement. In many cases, these rules can be found on the agency's website or, for those agencies subject to the Texas Administrative Procedure Act, in the Texas Administrative Code provisions applicable to the agency in question (and found on the website of the secretary of state of Texas). Many state agencies have adopted protest procedures similar to the sample process appearing in Section IV.B.

2. Sample Procurement Protest Process—Comptroller's Office

The Comptroller's Office procurement protest rules for its Texas Procurement and Support Services (TPASS) procurements are found in section 20.384 of title 34 of the Texas Administrative Code.

Any actual or prospective bidder, offeror, or contractor who considers himself or herself to have been aggrieved in connection with the solicitation, evaluation, or award of a contract by TPASS may formally protest to the director of TPASS.

Protests must be received by the director of TPASS within ten working days after the protesting party knows, or should have known, of the occurrence of the action that is protested

3. Necessary Elements

The protest must be in writing and must contain the following: (1) specific identification of the statutory or regulatory provision that the protesting party alleges has been violated; (2) specific description of each action by TPASS that the protesting party alleges to be in violation of the statutory or regulatory provision(s) at issue; (3) a precise statement of relevant facts; (4) a statement of any issues of law or fact that the protesting party contends must be resolved; (5) a statement of the argument and authorities that the protesting party offers in support of the protest; and (6) a statement that copies of the protest have been mailed or delivered to the using agency and all other identifiable interested parties.

The protest must be sworn by an individual authorized to sign contracts on behalf of the vendor. The protest, in order to be considered "filed," must be received by the director of TPASS within the deadline specified in Section IV.A.2 above. Copies of the protest must be mailed or delivered to the using agency (if the Comptroller's Office is conducting the procurement on behalf of another agency) and other interested parties.

4. Stay of Procurement

Once a timely protest has been filed, the state shall not proceed further with the solicitation or award of the contract unless the chief clerk, after consultation with the director of TPASS and the using agency, makes a written determination that the contract must be awarded without delay, to protect the best interests of the state.

5. Hearing

No hearing is required under the rules.

6. Decision Process

At the *first stage*, the director of TPASS may settle and resolve the dispute over the solicitation or award of a contract at any time before the matter is submitted on appeal to the general counsel of the Comptroller's Office. The director may solicit written responses to the protest from other interested parties.

At the *second stage*, if the protest is not resolved by mutual agreement, the director shall issue a written determination that resolves the protest. If the director determines that no violation of statutory or regulatory provisions has occurred, then the director shall inform the protesting party, the using agency, and other interested parties of that determination by letter that sets forth the reasons for the determination. If the director determines that a violation of any statutory or regulatory provision has occurred in a situation in which a contract has not been awarded, then the director shall inform the protesting party, the using agency, and other interested parties of that determination by letter that details the reasons for the determination and the appropriate remedy. If the director determines that a violation of any statutory or regulatory provisions has occurred in a situation where a contract has been awarded, then the director shall inform the protesting party, the using agency, and other interested parties of that determination by letter that details the reasons for the determination. This letter may include an order that declares the contract void.

B. Bid Protest Appeals

The protesting party may appeal a determination of a protest by the director to the general counsel of the Comptroller's Office.

An appeal must be received in the office of the general counsel by not later than ten working days after the date on which the director has sent written notice of determination of the protest. An appeal is limited to review of the director's determination. The appeal must be in writing, must be mailed or delivered to the using agency and all other interested parties, and must contain a certified statement that such copies have been provided.

The general counsel may refer the matter to the chief clerk of the Comptroller's Office or may issue a written decision that resolves the protest. If the general counsel refers the matter to the chief clerk, the following requirements shall apply: (1) the general counsel shall deliver copies of the appeal and any responses by interested parties to the chief clerk; (2) the chief clerk may consider any documents that agency staff or interested parties have submitted; (3) the chief clerk shall issue a written letter of determination of the appeal to the parties that shall be final; (4) in a subsequent open meeting conducted by the chief clerk under Texas Administrative Code title 34, section 20.383, the chief clerk shall inform the Statewide Procurement Advisory Council of any such recent determinations by the chief clerk on any contract awards made in any open meeting attended by the Council; and (5) a written decision issued by either the chief clerk or the general counsel shall be the final administrative action of the Comptroller's Office.

Protests or appeals not timely filed shall not be considered unless good cause for delay is shown or the chief clerk determines that an appeal raises issues that are significant to agency procurement practices or procedures in general.

C. Contract Disputes (Texas Government Code § 2260.001 *et seq.*)

This process applies to disputes between a vendor and a Texas state agency (including institutions of higher education) involving alleged breach of a written contract for goods and services *except* contracts subject to section 210.221 of the Texas Transportation Code. This process does not apply to (1) a county, municipality, court of a county or municipality, special purpose districts, or other political subdivisions of the state of Texas (Texas Government Code § 2260.001(4)); (2) a claim for personal injury or wrongful death arising from a breach of contract (Texas Government Code § 2260.002(1)); or (3) a contract executed or awarded on or before August 30, 1999 (Texas Government Code § 2260.002(2)).

1. Process

Contractors may make a claim against a unit of state government for breach of contract between the unit of state government and the vendor. The defending state agency or unit of state government may assert counterclaims. This procedure is exclusive and is a prerequisite to suit on a contract claim. (Texas Government Code § 2260.005.)

Claim Deadline: Written notice of a breach of contract claim must be provided to the allegedly breaching unit of state government not later than the 180th day after the date of the event giving rise to the claim. Notice must state with particularity (1) the nature of the alleged breach; (2) the amount the contractor seeks as damages; and (3) the legal theory of recovery.

The defendant state governmental unit must provide written counterclaims, if any, to the contract no later than the 60th day after the date of the notice of claim was received from the vendor. Failure to assert counterclaims within the 60-day period results in waiver of the right to assert the counterclaim.

2. Negotiation (Texas Government Code § 2260.052)

The chief administrative officer or, if designated in the contract at issue, another officer of the unit of state government shall examine the claim (and counterclaim, if any). Negotiation must begin no later than the 120th day after the date the claim is received. Each unit of state government with rulemaking authority shall develop rules to govern the negotiation and mediation of a claim under this statute. Those state governmental bodies that do not have rulemaking authority shall follow the rules adopted by the attorney general of Texas.

3. Limitation on Damages (Texas Government Code § 2260.003)

Damages recoverable on a claim for breach of contract under this statute are capped at the amount equal to the sum of (1) the balance due and owing on the contract price; (2) the amount or fair market value of orders or requests for additional work made by the state to the extent that the orders or requests for additional work were actually performed; and (3) any delay or labor-related expense incurred by the contractor as a result of an action of or a failure to act by the state or a party under the control or supervision of the state.

Damages may *not* include the following: (1) consequential or similar damages (except as described in item (3) in Section IV.C.3 immediately above); (2) exemplary damages; (3) any damages based on an unjust enrichment theory; (4) attorneys' fees; or (5) home office overhead.

a. Payment of Claim (Texas Government Code § 2260.054)

Money appropriated to the state governmental unit for either payment of contract claims or for payment of the contract that is the subject of the claim are the only funds that may be used to pay any claim amount awarded to a contractor under this process. If the existing appropriations are insufficient to pay the full amount of the claim or settlement, the unit of state government may seek additional appropriations to pay the balance of the claim or settlement. Note, however, that the Texas Legislature is in Regular Session only once every two calendar years.

D. Suspension and Debarment

1. Vendor Performance Program

The Comptroller's Office administers a vendor performance tracking program as required by statute. It is initiated by a written determination by the State Purchasing Division director after consultation with the state purchasing agent(s) or agency procurement officer(s), the Office of Legal Services, and, where practicable, the vendor who is to be suspended. A notice of the suspension shall be sent to the suspended vendor and shall provide that (1) the suspension is for the period necessary to complete an investigation into possible debarment, but not longer than 120 days; (2) bids or proposals will not be solicited or considered from the vendor during the period of suspension; and (3) the suspended person may request a hearing. The suspension remains in effect during any appeals.

2. Debarment

The Comptroller's Office may debar a vendor for a time period that reflects the severity of the vendor's action (or inaction) and the damage to the state's interest. The following factors are considered at minimum: (1) the number and severity of the vendor's performance problems in relation to the volume of goods or services provided; (2) the effectiveness of corrective actions taken by the vendor; and (3) the age and relevance of past performance information at the time it is used. Overall, when in the best interest of the state, a vendor may be debarred for any of the following:[13] (1) a history of unsatisfactory performance of a contract, or a history of failure to perform contracted services; (2) stating an unwillingness to honor a binding bid; (3) knowingly and intentionally supplying false information in order to appear responsive to a solicitation, to obtain a contract, or

13. The State of Texas vendor information is available online at https://comptroller.texas.gov/purchasing/vendor/ (last visited June 2, 2022).

to qualify for a bid preference; (4) knowingly or intentionally conferring or offering to confer any gift, gratuity, favor, or advantage, present or future, upon any employee of a state agency who exercises any official responsibility for an acquisition; (5) conviction of any felony charge of fraud, bribery, collusion, conspiracy, federal or state antitrust laws, or other criminal offense in connection with the bidding upon, award of, or performance of any contract for goods and services with any state agency; (6) violation of state ethics laws; (7) failure to comply with terms and conditions of existing contracts; (8) notice of debarment activities from other governmental entities; or (9) any cause indicating that the individual or firm is not a responsible vendor.

3. Debarment Process

Vendors are notified of the proposed debarment in writing delivered to the vendor's address of record. The notice will state the reasons for the debarment action. A vendor may submit a written appeal to the proposed debarment to the Comptroller's Office director of procurement within ten business days following the notification of the proposed debarment.

The current list of vendors debarred from doing business with the State of Texas can be found at https://comptroller.texas.gov/purchasing/programs/vendor-performance-tracking/debarred-vendors.php.

Please note that the revisions to procurement laws in 2015 included additional requirements for additional contract monitoring, accountability, and vendor performance reporting. Additional administrative rules and agency guidance are expected as implementation of the procurement law revisions and requirements proceeds.

V. Administrative and Judicial Review

A. Administrative Review

The administrative review process applicable to bid protests at the Comptroller's Office and suspension and debarment proceedings are set forth above.

B. Judicial Review

There is limited judicial review available to vendors under the protest procedures generally in place at Texas state agencies. Due to the limited access to judicial review in most state agency procurement protest procedures, there is minimal judicial precedent to review for guidance on these issues. In many cases, sovereign immunity will bar access to the courts for review of a state agency procurement protest.

Attorney General Opinion No. GA-0685 (2008) discusses in part whether there is recourse available to a vendor to compel a state agency to reconsider the application of a bid preference. Any statutes applicable to a particular state agency as well as any rules adopted by the agency must be reviewed to determine what recourse might be available when a bidder believes bidding preferences were applied incorrectly.

VI. Extent of State's Adoption or Adaptation of ABA Model Procurement Code

The State of Texas has not adopted the American Bar Association's (ABA's) Model Procurement Code for State and Local Governments.

VII. Cooperative Purchasing

A. Authority

Purchasing may also be accomplished via cooperative methods.[14] The comptroller may utilize compacts, interagency agreements, or cooperative purchasing agreements with other state governments, agencies of other states, or other governmental entities.[15] Procuring goods and services via a cooperative agreement often results in a more efficient process, but has additional statutory requirements of its own.

B. Requirements

State agencies may contract with another agency for the provision of services, materials, and equipment. When utilizing an interagency cooperation contract, the participating agencies must enter into a written agreement specifying the kind and amount of services or resources to be providing, the cost basis, and maximum cost.[16] The agreement must also certify the following: (1) the services are necessary and essential; (2) it serves the interest of efficiency and economy; (3) there are no lowest responsible bidder requirements; and (4) it does not exceed the parties' duties, responsibilities, or appropriated funds.[17] Similarly, an agency of the state may contract with local governments for similar purposes.[18] In addition to the limitations of chapter 791, a state agency purchasing services through an interlocal contract must comply with the requirements of chapter 2161.[19]

In addition to interlocal purchasing authority, the state maintains cooperative purchasing systems that are widely used by entities throughout Texas. DIR[20] has responsibility for procurement and management of contracts for information technology and telecommunications products and services.[21] These contracts include cooperative contracts made available to Texas state agencies and to Texas cities, counties, school districts, post-secondary educational institutions (universities, community colleges, and the like), and other local governmental entities. DIR cooperative contracts also have been made available to other state or local governmental bodies throughout the United States. The statutory changes passed during the 2015 Regular Session of the Texas Legislature included limitations on the dollar amount for procurements made by state agencies through the cooperative contracting vehicles offered by DIR.[22]

---

14. Tex. Gov't Code § 2156.181(a).
15. *Id.*
16. *Id.* § 771.002(1).
17. *Id.* §§ 771.003, 771.010.
18. *Id.* § 791.001 *et seq.*
19. *Id.* § 791.011(g).
20. DIR, https://dir.texas.gov/ (last visited June 2, 2022).
21. DIR also is responsible for information resource and telecommunications planning and policies generally applicable to Texas state agencies. It also promulgates standards and guidelines for use and deployment of information technology, data management, and information security for state agencies.
22. State agencies may not contract to purchase information technology commodity items (commercial software, hardware, or technology services) through a DIR cooperative contract if the value of the contract exceeds $1 million. Purchasing methods other than a cooperative contract must be used if the value of the contract will exceed $1 million. Acts 2015, 84th Leg., Reg. Sess., ch. 326 (S.B. 20) (effective Sept. 1, 2015).

The state comptroller also oversees Texas SmartBuy, a central procurement cooperative for non-information technology goods and services.[23] Agencies and local governments participate in the membership purchasing program. Agencies are able to leverage the statewide buying power and enter into established TXMAS contracts for a wide range of goods and services. Local governments and state-funded nonprofit organizations also utilize the cooperative through interlocal agreements.

Despite the convenience and economic benefit of cooperative purchasing, there are some limits on its usage. Cooperative purchasing may not be utilized for engineering or architectural services.[24] When purchasing through a cooperative method, entities should be mindful to consider multiple vendors or suppliers and independently confirm vendor proposals and contract terms. This will ensure that the entity obtains the best value through this procurement process.

23. *See* Tex. Gov't Code § 2155.061.

24. *Id.* § 2156.181(a-1).

Utah Procurement Rules and Regulations

Prepared by Brian D. Bolinder
Richards Brandt Miller Nelson
Email: brian-bolinder@rbmn.com

I. Statutory Reference

Utah law on construction contracting by state and local government agencies is loosely based on the Model Procurement Code, as originally adopted in 1980. The Utah Procurement Code has been substantially amended in each legislative session since 2012. Statutory language forms the foundation for regulations issued by the Division of Facilities Construction and Management (DFCM) and the Utah Department of Transportation (UDOT). Municipalities may adopt ordinances dealing with all aspects of construction contracting, and those sources must be consulted for local variations from the information provided below. The primary sources for this chapter are Utah's statutes, case law, and agency regulations. This author is unaware of any secondary sources on this topic. National continuing legal education (CLE) providers occasionally offer CLE seminars on distinct topics relevant to this subject matter.

A. Procurement/Purchasing Statutes

State agency processes for procurement are generally set forth in the Utah Procurement Code, codified as Utah Code Annotated section 63G-6a *et seq*.

B. Other Applicable Statutes and Rules

1. Prevailing Wage Requirements

Except in limited circumstances, Utah law prohibits a political subdivision of the state from requiring its contractors, subcontractors, and suppliers to pay "a predetermined amount of wages or wage rate; or a type, amount, or rate of employee benefits." (Utah Code Annotated § 34-30-14(2)(a)(i), (ii).) The prohibition "does not apply when federal law requires the payment of prevailing or minimum wages to persons working on projects funded in whole or in part by federal funds." (*Id.* § 34-30-14(2)(b).) However, political subdivisions of the state are authorized to create housing authorities that in turn may "agree to any conditions attached to federal financial assistance relating to the determination of prevailing salaries or wages or payment of not less than prevailing salaries or wages or compliance with labor standards in the development or administration of projects" and "include in any contract awarded or entered into in connection with a project stipulations requiring that the contractor and all subcontractors comply with requirements as to minimum salaries or wages." (*Id.* § 35A-8-407(2)(i).) Utah law also authorizes communities to create community development and renewal agencies, which may grant tax incentives to businesses and industries to participate in a community development plan. Receipt of incentives is conditioned, in part, on achieving wage goals for jobs created by the industry or business, "which shall be at least 110% of the prevailing wage of the county where the project area is located." (*Id.* § 17C-4-109(3)(d).)

2. License Requirements

The requirements to obtain a Utah contractor's license are found at Utah Code Annotated section 58-55-301 *et seq*. The process to prequalify vendors may request information on licenses and certifications. (*Id.* § 63G-6a-410(4)(b)(iii).) UDOT permits contractors who are not licensed in Utah to bid on federal-aid UDOT projects, "provided that such contractor, prior to undertaking any construction under that bid, shall be licensed in Utah." (Utah Administrative Code Rule 916-1-5.) Otherwise, "[e]ach bidder must comply with the laws of Utah relative to the licensing of contractors. A contractor's license is required prior to the submission of a bid . . . ." (*Id.*) Note that the Division of Water Resources defines a "responsible contractor" as one who is licensed. (Utah Code Annotated § 73-10-27.) Note further, absent a statutory exception, it is unlawful for a contractor not licensed in Utah to bid on any construction project in Utah. (*Id.* § 58-55-501(8).)

3. Prompt Payment Act

Utah's "Prompt Payment Act" is at Utah Code Annotated section 15-6-1 *et seq*. Absent the existence of a dispute between the state agency and its contractor, payments are due on the date required by the contract or no later than 60 days after "receipt of the invoice covering the delivered items or services." (*Id.* § 15-6-2(1).) Overdue payments earn interest at 2 percent above the Internal Revenue Service refund rate then in existence at the time of the overdue payment. (*Id.* § 15-6-3.) "Any interest that remains unpaid at the end of any 60-day period or that remains unpaid at the end of any specified period provided by contract shall be added to the principal amount of the debt and shall accumulate interest." (*Id.* § 15-6-3(2).) "Upon payment by an agency of the state of Utah or by an agency of the United States, a business which has acquired under contract, property or services in connection with its contract with such an agency from a subcontractor or supplier, shall pay such subcontractor or supplier within 30 days after payment from such agency." (*Id.* § 15-6-5.) Interest accrues at the rate of 15.5 percent per year beginning 31 days after the prime contractor is paid, and is due the subcontractor or supplier "who is not paid within 45 days after the business receives payment from the agency, unless otherwise provided by contract." (*Id.*)

4. Insurance Requirements

a. Liability Insurance for Asbestos Contractors

No specific statutes require unique insurance for asbestos contractors.

b. Worker's Compensation Insurance

Utah's Worker's Compensation Act is at Utah Code Annotated section 34A-2-101 *et seq.*

c. Public Liability and Property Damage Insurance

This form of insurance is typically required by contract. (See, e.g., UDOT Standard Specifications for Road and Bridge Construction § 00820, ¶ 1.17.)

d. Commercial General Liability Insurance

This form of insurance is typically required by contract. (See *id.*)

II. Regulations

General regulatory guidance is at Rule 33-1 *et seq.* of the Utah Administrative Code. Specific guidance may be found in the Utah Administrative Code, Rule 23-1 *et seq.* for DFCM projects, and at Rule 916-1 *et seq.* and the Standard Specifications for Road and Bridge Construction (2020 ed.) for UDOT projects.

III. Source Selection

A. General Procurement

1. State Agency Processes

a. Competitive Bidding (Utah Code Annotated § 63G-6a-601 et seq.)

"A procurement unit may award a contract by the bidding process in accordance with the rulemaking authority." (Utah Code Annotated § 63G-6a-602.) The invitation for bids (IFB) must describe what is sought, must include "the objective criteria that will be used to evaluate the bids," and must also include the contractual terms and conditions applicable to the procurement. (*Id.* § 63G-6a-603(2).) Public notice of the IFB must be given "at least seven consecutive days" before the bid opening date. (*Id.* § 63G-6a-112(1)(a).) Bids are opened publicly at the bid opening time, and "the name of each bidder and the amount of each bid" is published. (*Id.* § 63G-6a-606(3)(a).) Utah abides by the firm bid rule. (*Id.* § 63G-6a- 604(2).) But, bidders may correct an immaterial error in a bid. (*Id.* § 63G-6a-114.) Rules and regulations regarding correction or withdrawal of erroneous or mistaken bids are published and mirror federal standards. (See Utah Administrative Code Rule 23-1-606 for DFCM projects; UDOT Standard Specifications for Road and Bridge Construction § 00120.) Bids shall be evaluated based on the "objective criteria" used in the IFB and "to achieve the greatest long-term value to the state and the procurement unit." (Utah Code Annotated § 63G-6a-606(1).) No criteria may be used in bid evaluation that are not set forth in the IFB. (*Id.* § 63G-6a-606(2).) The contract must be awarded to the lowest responsive and responsible bidder whose bid meets the objective criteria of the solicitation. (*Id.* § 63G-6a-606(3)(a).)

b. Request for Proposals (Utah Code Annotated § 63G-6a-701 et seq.)

A procurement unit may solicit proposals, using a request for proposals (RFP), in lieu of bids in accordance with rulemaking authority rules. (*Id.* § 63G-6a-702(a).) However, procurement of architect-engineer services is governed by Utah Code Annotated section 63G-6a-1501 *et seq.* An evaluation committee evaluates and scores proposals based on the criteria listed in the proposal and may use an expert or consultant to understand a technical issue if a procurement unit approves. (*Id.* § 63G-6a-707.) Provisions are in place to ensure impartiality of the evaluation committee. (*Id.*) The deliberations of the evaluation committee may be held in private. (*Id.*) Evaluation of proposal cost is prohibited until after the recommendation is issued based on the scores of all criteria other than cost unless a procurement official waives the prohibition by a written statement indicating why waiving the provision is in the best interests of the procurement unit. (*Id.*) At the conclusion of the evaluation process, the evaluation committee must prepare a written statement recommending the award of the recommended proposal, containing the score awarded by the committee and explaining how the recommended proposal provides the best value to the procurement unit. (*Id.*) The requirement of a written statement is not required for awards to construction managers or general contractors if the award is based solely on the qualifications and management fee to be paid. (*Id.*) The process provides for the possibility of best and final offers pursuant to a specific process. (*Id.* § 63G-6a-707.5.) Rules 23-1-701 through -719 of the Utah Administrative Code govern DFCM's proposal evaluation and award process. UDOT's process is described in sections 00120 and 00515 of the Standard Specifications for Road and Bridge Construction.

c. Award without Competition and Single-Source Procurement

A contract may be awarded

> for a procurement item without engaging in a standard procurement process if the chief procurement officer or the head of the procurement unit . . . determines in writing that: (a) there is only one source for the procurement item; (b) transitional costs are a significant consideration in selecting a procurement item; and the results of a cost-benefit analysis demonstrate that transitional costs are unreasonable or cost-prohibitive, and that the award of a contract without engaging in a standard procurement process is in the best interest of the procurement unit; or (c) the award of a contract is under circumstances . . . that make awarding the contract through a standard procurement process impractical and not in the best interest of the procurement unit.

(*Id.* § 63G-6a-802.) DFCM regulations authorize sole source procurement "if (a) there is only one source for the procurement item; (b) the award to a specific supplier, service provider, or contractor is a condition of a donation or grant that will fund the full cost of the supply, service, or construction item; or (c) the procurement item is needed for trial use or testing to determine whether the procurement item will benefit the procurement unit." (Utah Administrative Code Rule 23-1-801(2).) Sole source procurements over $50,000 are required to be published; however, sole source procurements under $50,000 may be published at the discretion of the director. (*Id.* Rule 23-1-801(7).) Publication requirements are waived for public utilities, where the award is a condition of a donation or grant, when the circumstances are clear there can only be one source, or other circumstances determined in writing by the director. (*Id.*) Sole source procurement can be contested prior to the closing of the public notice period, which contest will be investigated by the director. (*Id.* Rule 23-1-801(8) & (9).)

d. Prequalification of Bidders

"A procurement unit may establish an approved vendor list for a specific, fully defined procurement item; or a future procurement item that is not specifically and full defined" (Utah Code Annotated § 63G-6a-507(3)(a)), but only after complying with the detailed process for obtaining vendor statements of qualification described in section 63G-6a-410 of the Utah Code. UDOT requires contractors to be prequalified (Utah Administrative Code Rules 23-1-401, 916-2-1 *et seq.*), except for contracts under

$3,000,000. (*Id.* Rule 916-2-3(1).) UDOT reviews the qualification status of its contractors at least annually. (*Id.* Rule 916-2-3(3).)

e. Bond Requirements

The Utah Procurement Code requires a bid bond "of at least 5% of the amount of the bid . . . for all competitive bidding for construction contracts." (Utah Code Annotated § 63G-6a-1102.) Payment and performance bonds of 100 percent of the price for the construction project are also required. (*Id.* § 63G-6a-1103(1)(a), (b).) Agencies may, by administrative rule, waive requirements for bid, performance, and payment bonds "for circumstances in which the procurement officer considers any or all of the bonds to be unnecessary to protect the procurement unit." (*Id.* § 63G-6a-1103(3).)

If the state or a political subdivision of the state fails to obtain a payment bond, it shall, upon demand of a subcontractor or supplier who has furnished labor or material to the project, promptly pay the subcontractor or supplier. Further, the subcontractor or supplier has a direct right of action against the state or political subdivision for the unpaid value of labor or material furnished to the project. The claimant must give written notice by certified or registered mail to the public entity within 90 days after last furnishing labor or material, stating "a designation of the construction project and its location, the amount claimed, and the name of the party for whom the labor was performed or to whom the material was supplied." (*Id.* § 14-1-19.) The claimant must file its action no later than one year after the date it last furnished the labor or material to the project. (*Id.*)

f. Multiple Primes

DFCM may award contracts to multiple prime contractors through the use of a multiple award contract. (Utah Administrative Code Rule 33-13-203(5)(b).) UDOT authorizes two prime contractors who are separately prequalified to submit a single bid on UDOT projects. (*Id.* Rule 916-1-4(3)(b).)

g. Design-Build

Design-build contracts are specifically authorized by Utah law. (Utah Code Annotated § 63G-6a-1205(4)(i)(i).) Specific guidance for DFCM design-build contracts is at Rule 23-1-1307 and for UDOT contracts at Rule 916-3-1 *et seq.* of the Utah Administrative Code.

h. Financing Arrangements

State construction is financed with appropriated funds. However, DFCM regulations anticipate that some construction may occur with non-appropriated funds, and establishes procedures for ensuring that the source of non-appropriated funds will formally commit to providing the funds. (Utah Administrative Code Rule 23-24-1 *et seq.*) There is currently one privately funded toll road in Utah, the Adams Avenue Parkway.

2. Local Processes

Counties and municipalities are free to adopt any section of the Utah Procurement Code. (Utah Code Annotated § 63G-6a-107.4.) And, a "procurement unit" can include local governments, districts, special service districts, conservation districts, public corporations, or a public transit district. (*Id.* § 63G-6a-103(62).) Counties and municipalities must award improvement projects for Class B and Class C roads to the lowest responsible bidder, when the estimated cost of the project exceeds the bid limit established by section 72-6-109 of the Utah Code. (*Id.* § 72-6-108.) The resulting contracts are expressly subject to the Utah Procurement Code. (*Id.* § 72-6-108(5).) Local ordinances should be consulted to determine the preferred method for awarding contracts, which likely will be by sealed bid, and will closely resemble procedures used in state procurements. Absent such guidance, the IFB or RFP will designate the criteria for award of the contract. Municipalities have wide discretion in awarding contracts, even in the context of sealed bids. In *Cal Wadsworth Construction v. City of St. George*, 898 P.2d 1372 (Utah 1995), the court wrote:

> In deciding which bid to accept, the city may consider a variety of factors other than the amount of the bid, including the experience, skill, ability, and honesty of the bidders . . . . Thus, a municipality is not bound to accept a bid simply because it is the lowest. This is true even when the advertisement indicates that the municipality will contract with the lowest bidder . . . . Because the local decision makers are in the best position to decide which bid is best for the municipality, courts will not interfere with their judgment unless fraud, dishonesty, collusion, or lack of good faith is involved.

(See also *Clayton v. Salt Lake City*, 387 P.2d 93 (Utah 1963) (public authority "must have wide latitude in which to exercise its judgment" in obtaining best value for construction dollars).)

B. Architect/Engineering Procurement

1. State Agency Process

Architect-engineer services must be procured by the procedures set forth at Utah Code Annotated section 63G-6a-1501 *et seq.* "A procurement unit seeking to procure design professional services shall publicly announce all requirements for those services and negotiate contracts for design professional services on the basis of demonstrated competence and qualification for the type of services required, and at fair and reasonable prices." (Utah Code Annotated § 63G-6a-1502(1).) Firms are encouraged to submit a statement of qualifications. A request for statement of qualifications may include "work history and experience," "performance ratings," "quality assurance or quality control plan," "quality of . . . past work product," how and when the professional services will be delivered, "financial solvency," and the firm's "management plan . . . key personnel and subconsultants." (*Id.* § 63G-6a-1502.5.) But the statement of qualifications cannot include "a request for a price or a cost." (*Id.*) Evaluation committees must publish selection criteria and use those criteria, or the criteria published in the announcement of a proposed contract, in awarding a contract. The evaluation committees must evaluate at least three firms, and must select at least three of the "most highly qualified." (*Id.* § 63G-6a-1503.) The procurement officer awards a contract to a "qualified design professional" in an amount "that the procurement officer determines in writing to be fair and reasonable . . . . In making the determination . . ., the procurement officer shall take into account the estimated value, scope and professional nature of the services; and the complexity of the project or services." (*Id.* § 63G-6a-1505.) If the procurement officer is unable to successfully negotiate a contract with the highest scoring design professional, discussions will be terminated and negotiations commenced with the second-highest scoring, qualified design professional, and so on. If a contract cannot be negotiated with any of the three design professionals, the procurement officer "shall select additional design professionals, and . . . shall continue discussions in accordance with this part until an agreement is reached." (*Id.* Refer to Rule 23-1-1501 *et seq.* of the Utah Administrative Code for the specific procedures used by DFCM to procure architect and engineer services.)

2. Local Government

Procurement units are required to adopt any or all provisions and ordinances for the procurement of architect-engineer services contained in the Utah Procurement Code. (Utah Code Annotated § 63G-6a-107.4.) Municipalities have likely adopted unique procedures. (See, e.g., Salt Lake City Code § 3.24.040.)

C. Preferences

1. Minority Business Enterprises

Utah has no minority or disadvantaged business entity assistance requirements separate from those that may be required on federal or federally assisted projects.

2. Women-Owned Enterprises

Utah has no such preferences.

3. Small Business

Utah has no such preferences.

4. Local Preference

a. Preference for Providers of State Products

Bidders who provide products "produced, manufactured, mined, grown, or performed in Utah" are entitled to the same preference on Utah contracts "as against those bidders offering [products from] any state that gives or requires a preference to procurement items produced, manufactured, mined, grown, or performed in that state." (Utah Code Annotated § 63G-6a-1002.)

b. Preference for Resident Contractors

"When awarding contracts for construction, an issuing procurement unit shall grant a resident contractor a reciprocal preference over a nonresident contractor from any state that gives or requires a preference to contractors from that state" in an amount "equal to the amount of the preference applied by the state of the nonresident contractor." (*Id.* § 63G-6a-1003(2)(a), (b).)

5. Other Preferences

a. Purchase of Prison Industry Goods

"An applicable procurement unit may not purchase any goods or services provided by the correctional industries division from any other source unless" the prison industry goods do not meet the reasonable requirements of the procurement unit, the goods or services cannot be supplied within a reasonable time, or the cost of the prison industry goods is not competitive with other sources. (*Id.* § 63G-6a-804(4)(a).)

b. Purchase from Community Rehabilitation Programs

A "community rehabilitation program" "means a program that is operated primarily for the purpose of the employment and training of persons with a disability by a government agency or qualified nonprofit organization which is an income tax-exempt organization under . . . the Internal Revenue Code." (*Id.* § 63G-6a-805(c).) "[E]ach procurement unit shall purchase goods and services produced by a community rehabilitation program using the preferred procurement contract list . . . if: (a) the good or service offered for sale by a community rehabilitation program reasonably conforms to the needs and specifications of the procurement unit; (b) the community rehabilitation program can supply the good or service within a reasonable time; and (c) the price of the good or service is reasonably competitive with the cost of procuring the good or service from another source." (*Id.* § 63G-6a-805(7).)

IV. Bid Protests and Contract Disputes

A. Bid Protests

1. Forum and Procedures

Under the Utah Procurement Code, bid protests must be filed with the protest officer.

For protests involving counties or local or municipal procurements, protesters will most likely seek a preliminary injunction or temporary restraining order in situations where the protester believes the procuring municipality may have ignored or disregarded solicitation provisions. (See *Cal Wadsworth Construction v. City of St. George*, 898 P.2d 1372 (Utah 1995).)

2. Protests to the Protest Officer

a. Standing

"[P]rotest may be filed with the protest officer by a person who: (a) has standing; and (b) is aggrieved in connection with a procurement or an award of a contract." (Utah Code Annotated § 63G-6a-1602(1).)

b. Timeliness of Protest

A protest shall be filed before the opening of bids or the closing date for proposals, or within seven days after the protester "knows or first has constructive knowledge of the facts giving rise to the protest" if the protester did not know and should not have known of the facts giving rise to the protest before bid opening or the closing date of a proposal, or the procurement is other than a standard procurement. (*Id.* § 63G-6a-1602(2)(b).) Failure to meet these deadlines precludes the protester from filing a protest, or filing "an action or appeal challenging a solicitation or award of a contract before an appeals panel, a court, or any other forum." (*Id.* § 63G-6a-1602(7)(a), (b).) Utah's courts enforce these deadlines. (*Alpine Orthopaedic Specialists, LLC v. Utah State University*, 2011 UT App 294, 263 P.3d 501.)

c. Content of Protest

At a minimum, the protest must include the protester's mailing address, email address, and "a concise statement of the facts and evidence" explaining how the protestor is "aggrieved," "providing the grounds for" the protest, and "supporting the protestor's claim of standing." (Utah Code Annotated § 63G-6a-1602(4)(a).) Protesters desiring a hearing should include their request in the protest, as a hearing is not mandatory. (*Id.* § 63G-6a-1603(3).)

d. Procedures

The protest officer must follow the procedures in the Utah Procurement Code in deciding the protest. (*Id.* § 63G-6a-1603.) The protest officer shall summarily dismiss the protest if it is not timely or does not comply with section 63G-6a-1602 of the Utah Code. (*Id.* § 63G-6a-1603(1), (2).) If the protest is timely and meets the requirements of the code, the protest officer may "dismiss the protest if the protest officer determines that the protest alleges facts that, if true, do not provide an adequate basis for the protest; uphold the protest without holding a hearing if the protest officer determines that the undisputed facts of the protest indicate that the protest should be upheld; or hold a hearing on the protest if there is a genuine issue of material fact that needs to be resolved in order to determine whether the protest should be upheld." (*Id.* § 63G-6a-1603(3).) If the protest officer holds a hearing, he or she has authority to subpoena witnesses and compel their attendance at the hearing, and subpoena documents; may obtain additional factual information; and may take testimony from experts, the person filing the protest, representatives of the procurement unit, and "others to assist the protest officer to make a decision on the protest." (*Id.* § 63G-6a-1603(4)(a).) The protest officer is not bound by the rules of evidence at the hearing. (*Id.* § 63G-6a-1603(4)(b).) The protest officer may allow interested parties to intervene. (*Id.* § 63G-6a-1603(4)(c). See Rule 33-16-301 of the Utah Administrative Code.) The hearing must be recorded (although the method of recording the hearing is not specified) and the protest officer must "preserve all records and other evidence relied upon in reaching the protest officer's written decision until the decision, and any appeal of the decision, becomes final." (Utah Code Annotated § 63G-6a-1603(4)(d)(i), (ii).)

The protest officer must issue a written decision "promptly" but no later than 30 days after the filing of the protest, unless the parties agree otherwise. If no decision is issued by this 30-day deadline, the protest is deemed denied. (*Id.* § 63G-6a-1603(6)(a) & (9).) The decision must "state the reasons for the action taken; inform the protestor of the right to judicial or administrative review . . . and indicate the amount of the security deposit or bond required under section 63G-6a-1703" of the code. (*Id.* § 63G-6a-1603(6)(b).) The protest officer shall "mail, email, or otherwise immediately furnish a copy of the decision to the protestor." (*Id.* § 63G 6a 1603(6)(c).) The decision "is effective until stayed or reversed on appeal." (*Id.* § 63G-6a-1603(7).) "A determination . . . by the protest officer regarding an issue of fact may not be overturned on appeal unless the decision is arbitrary and capricious or clearly erroneous." (*Id.* § 63G-6a-1603(10).)

e. Appeals

Adverse decisions from the protest officer may be appealed to the Utah State Procurement Policy Board. (*Id.* § 63G-6a-1702.)

3. Remedies

a. Before Award

The filing of a timely protest and any resulting appeals precludes the procurement unit from proceeding with the solicitation or award of the contract "until all administrative and judicial remedies have been exhausted or until the chief procurement officer . . . makes a written determination that the award of the contract without delay is in the best interest of the procurement unit or the state." (*Id.* § 63G-6a-1903(1), (2).) If the solicitation or proposed award "is in violation of law," the solicitation or award must be canceled or revised. (*Id.* § 63G-6a-1909.)

b. After Award

Absent fraud or bad faith on the part of the successful offeror, the contract may be ratified, if doing so is in the best interest of the procurement unit, or terminated, with the successful offeror receiving expenses reasonably incurred under the contract, including a reasonable profit. (*Id.* § 63G-6a-1907.) If the successful offeror acted fraudulently or in bad faith, "the contract may be declared null and void," or "ratified and affirmed" if to do so is in the best interest of the procurement unit. The procurement unit reserves the right to seek damages from the contractor. (*Id.* § 63G-6a-1907(1)(b).)

c. Bid and Proposal Costs

"If a protest is sustained administratively or upon administrative or judicial review and the protesting bidder or offeror should have been awarded the contract under the solicitation but is not, the protestor is entitled to" bid and proposal costs and appeal costs plus any appropriate equitable relief. (*Id.* § 63G-6a-1904(1).)

d. Unsuccessful Protests

If a procurement appeals panel or "other appellate body" does not sustain a protest, the unsuccessful protester must "reimburse the conducting or issuing procurement unit for all expenses that the conducting or issuing procurement unit incurred in defending the appeal, including personnel costs, attorney fees, other legal costs, the per diem and expenses paid by the conducting or issuing procurement unit to witnesses or appeals panel members, and any additional expenses incurred by the staff of the conducting or issuing procurement unit who have provided materials and administrative services to the procurement appeals panel for that case." (*Id.* § 63G-6a-1904(2).)

B. Bid Protest Appeals

1. Utah Procurement Policy Board and Procurement Appeals Panels

a. Composition

The Utah Procurement Code does not specify the composition of the Procurement Policy Board. However, the Utah Administrative Code requires the board to have 15 voting members and a non-voting secretary. (Utah Administrative Code Rule 33-2-4.)

A procurement appeals panel is appointed by the chair of the Procurement Policy Board, and consists of "at least three individuals, each of whom is a member of the board," or their designees. The appointing officer also appoints one of the members to serve as the coordinator of the panel. (Utah Code Annotated § 63G-6a-1702(5).) The procurement appeals panel cannot include a person "employed by the procurement unit responsible for the solicitation, contract award or other action complained of." (*Id.* § 63G-6a-1702(5)(f).)

b. Timeliness of Protests

The protester may appeal the protest officer's adverse decision to the Procurement Policy Board. The notice of appeal must be filed within seven days after service of the decision (by personal service, email, or regular mail) or within seven days after the protest is deemed denied. (*Id.* § 63G-6a-1702(2).)

c. Contents of the Appeal, Posting Security

The notice of appeal must include the appellant's address and email of record and a copy of the written decision from which the appeal is taken, with a certificate of service to all parties of record. The appeal cannot include grounds for the protest that were not presented to the protest officer. (*Id.* § 63G-6a-1702(3).) In addition, the appellant must pay a security deposit or post a bond with the office of the protest officer within the same seven-day deadline for filing an appeal. The amount of the bond was subject to interpretation under the prior version of the code and implementing regulations. (See *FirstDigital Telecom, LLC v. Procurement Policy Board*, 2015 UT App. 47, 345 P.3d 767.) However, the 2017 amendments to the code include detailed guidance for calculating the deposit/bond amount. (Utah Code Annotated § 63G-6a-1703.) Utah Code Annotated section 63G-6a-1703(2) includes additional guidance for calculating the deposit/bond amount. The protest officer retains the deposit/bond until the protest and any appeal is final. (*Id.* § 63G-6a-1703(4).) If the protestor prevails, the deposit/bond is returned, with any interest accrued on the deposit. (*Id.*) The deposit/bond will be forfeited to the state's General Fund if the protester does not prevail, and if the procurement appeals panel deems the protest frivolous or filed to harass or delay the procurement. (*Id.* § 63G-6a-1703(5).) Failure to post a deposit/bond, or posting a deposit/bond late or in an insufficient amount, will result in dismissal of the appeal. (*FirstDigital Telecom*, 2015 UT App. 47, 345 P.3d 767.)

d. Procedures

The panel is required to "conduct an informal proceeding on the appeal within 30 days after the day on which the procurement appeals panel is appointed." (Utah Code Annotated § 63G-6a-1702(6).) The panel is limited to considering the appeal "solely" in light of the protest decision, the record considered by the protest officer, and the hearing record, if held. (*Id.* § 63G-6a-1702(7).) The panel may hold an informal hearing and ask questions and receive responses regarding the appeal, but may not otherwise take additional evidence or consider any additional ground for the appeal and the rules of evidence do not apply. (*Id.* § 63G-6a-1702(6)(b) & (14).) The panel "shall uphold the decision of the protest officer, unless the decision is arbitrary and capricious or clearly erroneous." (*Id.* § 63G-6a-1702(9)(d).) The panel must "issue a written decision on the appeal; and mail, email, or hand-deliver the written decision on the appeal to the parties to the appeal and to the protest officer" within seven days after concluding the proceeding. (*Id.* § 63G-6a-1702(6).)

e. Remedies

If the panel reverses the protest officer's decision, the panel "shall remand the matter to the protest officer, to cure the problem or render a new decision," or "may recommend action that the protest officer should take." (*Id.* § 63G-6a-1702(12)(a).) But the panel "may not order that a contract be awarded to a certain person; a contract or solicitation be cancelled; or any other action be taken other than the action described in Subsection (12)(a)." (*Id.* § 63G-6a-1702(c).)

f. Appeal

An adverse decision from the Procurement Policy Board may be appealed to the Utah Court of Appeals. (*Id.* § 63G-6a-1802.)

2. Utah Court of Appeals

A protester—and, in some circumstances, the procurement unit—may appeal an adverse decision of the chair of the Procurement Policy Board or the decision of the procurement appeals panel by filing a notice of appeal with the Utah Court of Appeals within seven days after the decision. (*Id.* § 63G-6a-1802(1)(b).) The Utah Rules of Appellate Procedure apply to appeals filed with the Utah Court of Appeals. (Utah Rules of Appellate Procedure 1 & 18.) The court "shall consider the appeal as an appellate court; may not hear the matter as a trial de novo; and may not overturn a finding, dismissal [or] decision . . . unless the finding, dismissal [or] decision . . . is arbitrary and capricious or clearly erroneous." (Utah Code Annotated § 63G-6a-1802(4).) Specifically, "[a] determination of an issue of fact by a procurement appeals panel may not be overturned on appeal, unless the determination is arbitrary and capricious or clearly erroneous." (*Id.* § 63G-6a-1705.)

C. Contract Disputes

1. Dispute Procedures

There is no statute requiring the state and its agencies to adopt specific dispute procedures. But the form contracts include clauses to address contractor claims. (See, e.g., UDOT Standard Specifications for Road and Bridge Construction §§ 00747, 00777.) The DFCM has published a dispute resolution process as well. (Utah Administrative Code Rule 23-26.) Claimants must participate in this administrative dispute process precedent to seeking judicial review. (*Id.* Rule 23-26-6.)

2. Administrative Remedies/Exhaustion

Generally, "[a] party aggrieved may obtain judicial review of final agency action," but "only after exhausting all administrative remedies available." (Utah Code Annotated § 63G-4-401(1), (2); *Republic Outdoor Advertising, LC v. Utah Department of Transportation*, 2011 UT App 198, 258 P.3d 619.)

3. Court Jurisdiction and Venue

Utah's district courts have jurisdiction over contractor claims against the state. (Utah Code Annotated § 63G-7-501.) Venue of those claims lies in the county where the claim arose or in Salt Lake County. (*Id.* § 63G-7-502.)

4. Arbitration

Utah's Uniform Arbitration Act is at Utah Code Annotated section 78B-11-101 *et seq.* The act only applies where the parties have an agreement to arbitrate a dispute. (*Id.* § 78B-11-104.) The standard form contracts of state agencies do not provide for arbitration of disputes.

5. Alternative Dispute Resolution

Utah's Alternative Dispute Resolution Act is at section 78B-6-201 *et seq.* "The purpose . . . is to offer an alternative or supplement to the formal processes associated with a court trial and to promote the efficient and effective operation of the courts of this state by authorizing and encouraging the use of alternative methods of dispute resolution to secure the just, speedy, and inexpensive determination of civil actions filed in the courts of this state. (*Id.* § 78B-6-203.) Presumably, if a contractor has filed suit to resolve a dispute, the act would allow the court to refer the dispute to a form of alternative dispute resolution.

6. Sovereign Immunity Issues

Utah's Governmental Immunity Act is at Utah Code Annotated section 63G-7-101 *et seq*.

a. Contracts

"Immunity from suit of each governmental entity is waived as to any contractual obligation." (*Id.* § 63G-7-301(1).) Moreover, general contract claims against the state and its agencies are not subject to the notice and timeliness requirements of the Governmental Immunity Act.

b. Torts

Generally, "[a] governmental entity, its officers, and its employees are immune from suit, and immunity is not waived, for any injury proximately caused by a negligent act or omission of an employee committed within the scope of employment . . . ." (*Id.* § 63G-7-201(4).) Claimants cannot recover punitive damages from a governmental entity. (*Id.* § 63G-7-603(1)(a).)

c. Construction Liens

Preconstruction and construction liens may not be recorded against public property. (*Id.* § 38-1a-103.)

7. Construction Claims

a. Standard Specifications

"A contractor may increase the contract price only in accordance with the terms of the contract." (*Id.* § 63G-6a-1206.5.) And, "[a] procurement unit may include in a contract terms that provide for: (1) incentives, including bonuses; (2) payment of damages, including liquidated damages; or (3) penalties." (*Id.* § 63G-6a-1210.) Therefore, claim procedures are covered in contract clauses. (See, e.g., UDOT Standard Specifications for Road and Bridge Construction § 00820; Utah Administrative Code Rule 23-26-1 *et seq.*) The methods by which a contractor may be compensated for changes in the scope of work, changes in the time of performance, suspensions of work, and differing site conditions are also governed by standard clauses. (UDOT Standard Specifications for Road and Bridge Construction § 01282.) Utah courts will look to specific contract clause language to determine if a contractor qualifies for additional compensation. (*Meadow Valley Contractors, Inc. v. Utah Department of Transportation*, 2011 UT 35, 266 P.3d 671 (contract notice of claim provision strictly enforced against claimant contractor).)

b. Liability for Specification Defects (Spearin Doctrine)

In Utah, "[w]e recognize the validity of the proposition . . . that if plans and specifications are so deficient or defective that a contractor encounters conditions different from those as represented or reasonably to be anticipated, he should be entitled to recover for extra costs incurred in dealing with those different conditions." (*R.C. Tolman Construction Co. v. Myton Water Association*, 563 P.2d 780, 782 (Utah 1977).) Bidders are entitled to rely on the accuracy of plans and specifications furnished by public entities. (*Jack B. Parson Construction Co. v. Utah Department of Transportation*, 725 P.2d 614 (Utah 1986).) "A contractor of public works who, acting reasonably, is misled by incorrect plans and specifications issued by the public authorities as the basis for bids and who, as a result, submits a bid which is lower than he would have otherwise made may recover in a contract action for extra work or expenses necessitated by the conditions being other than represented." (*Thorn Construction Co. v. Utah Department of Transportation*, 598 P.2d 365, 368 (Utah 1979) (quoting *Souza & McCue Construction Co. v. Superior Court of San Benito County*, 370 P.2d 338, 339 (Cal. 1962)).)

c. Changes Clause

A contractor is entitled to compensation and a time extension when changes in the scope of work cause the contractor to incur additional costs and increase the time required to complete the contract. Public agencies will seek to strictly enforce contractual clauses requiring the contractor to give notice of such claims to the public owner. (*Meadow Valley Contractors, Inc.*, 2011 UT 35, 266 P.3d 671.)

d. Differing Site Conditions/Disclaimers

In Utah, a contractor is entitled to recover the costs and expenses it incurs as the result of site conditions being other than as represented on the plans and specifications, or other than as represented by an authorized agent of the public owner. (*Thorn Construction Co. v. Utah Department of Transportation*, 598 P.2d 365 (Utah 1979).) This conclusion remains valid notwithstanding boilerplate language in the specifications that attempts to shift responsibility for determining the accuracy of specific representations as to site conditions from the public entity to the bidder. "[A] general disclaimer or reference to other materials is ineffective to qualify a specific misleading representation; the general duty such a disclaimer imposes is superseded by a specific, positive misstatement, and the bidder is not required to search further for the facts." (*Jack B. Parson Construction Co. v. Utah Department of Transportation*, 725 P.2d 614, 617 (Utah 1986).) But a specific disclaimer, such as "The soil report was obtained only for the engineer's use in the design and is not a part of the contract documents. The log of borings is provided for contractor's information but is not a warrant of subsurface conditions," precludes the contractor from relying on subsurface data provided with the bid documents. (*Frontier Foundations, Inc. v. Layton Construction Co.*, 818 P.2d 1040, 1042 (Utah Ct. App. 1991).) If the information is not included in the plans and specifications, and the contractor does not rely on the erroneous information in preparing its bid, the contractor is not entitled to recover. (*L.A. Young & Sons Construction Co. v. Tooele County*, 575 P.2d 1034 (Utah 1978).)

e. Delays

Contract clauses grant the contractor an extension of time to complete the contract in situations where delays are due to the activities of the public owner or are caused by events over which the contractor has no control and are not the contractor's fault. (UDOT Standard Specifications for Road and Bridge Construction § 00555, ¶ 1.13, Work Suspensions.)

f. Liquidated Damages

Liquidated damages provisions are enforceable in Utah when the fixed amount is a "reasonable forecast of just compensation" for damages resulting from breach, and such damages are, by their nature, "very difficult of accurate estimation." (*Reliance Insurance Co. v. Utah Department of Transportation*, 858 P.2d 1363 (Utah 1993) (quoting

Restatement of Contracts § 339 (1932)).) "Whether an amount was a reasonable forecast is determined by looking at the contract, not at the time of its breach, but rather at the time of its formation." (*Id.* at 1367.) Similarly, the second prong of the *Restatement* test is examined in light of facts known at contract formation, not at the time breach occurred. (*Id.* at 1368.) The doctrine of substantial completion is not a defense against the imposition of liquidated damages, when the liquidated damages clause specifically requires all contract work to be completed and warns that liquidated damages will be assessed if any work remains incomplete past the scheduled completion date. (*Id.* at 1370.) Liquidated damages clauses are not subject to heightened judicial scrutiny, are "reviewed in the same manner as other contractual provisions," and will only be invalidated if the terms are unconscionable. (*Commercial Real Estate Investment, L.C. v. Comcast of Utah II, Inc.*, 2012 UT 49, ¶ 38, 285 P.3d 1193, 1202.)

g. No Damages for Delay

Utah's courts will enforce "no damages for delay" clauses in construction contracts where the delay is not the result of fraud or active interference, is not of such duration as would justify the delayed party in abandoning the contract, is caused by events specifically within the scope of the clause, or is not a delay caused by events not within the parties' contemplation to be included in the clause at the time the parties entered the contract. (*Western Engineers, Inc. v. Road Commission*, 437 P.2d 216 (Utah 1968).) There, the court enforced a contract clause between the state road commission (now UDOT) and its consulting engineers that said: "The consulting engineer agrees to prosecute the work continuously and diligently, and that no charges or claims for damages will be made by them for any delay or hindrances, of any cause whatsoever . . . . Such delays . . . shall be compensated for by an extension of time . . . ." The court held the clause was not ambiguous and wrote: "Delays that could reasonably be foreseen could have been specifically provided for in the contract. It was for the unforeseen delays that the clause was included to protect the State and compensate the plaintiffs for such delays." (*Id.* at 218.) "In other words, damages cannot be awarded for delays contemplated by the parties and should be controlled by the contractual remedies, unless the delays can be said to be so excessive and unreasonable as to fall outside the scope of the contract and warrant an additional recovery in quantum meruit." (*Allen-Howe Specialties Corp. v. U.S. Construction, Inc.*, 611 P.2d 705, 709 (Utah 1980).)

h. Contract Interpretation Rules

Utah courts attempt to determine the intentions of the contracting parties when interpreting a contract. (*John Call Engineering, Inc. v. Manti City Corp.*, 743 P.2d 1205 (Utah 1987).) "If the contract is in writing and the language is not ambiguous, the intention of the parties must be determined from the words of the agreement . . . . A court may only consider extrinsic evidence if, after careful consideration, the contract language is ambiguous or uncertain . . . . A contract provision is ambiguous if it is capable of more than one reasonable interpretation . . . . Whether ambiguity exists in a contract is a question of law." (*Winegar v. Froerer Corp.*, 813 P.2d 104, 108 (Utah 1991).) If the court determines a contract is ambiguous, the court may consider extrinsic evidence as an aid to interpreting the contract. (*Ward v. Intermountain Farmers Association*, 907 P.2d 264 (Utah 1995).) "Although the terms of an instrument may seem clear to a particular reader—including a judge—this does not rule out the possibility that the parties chose the language of the agreement to express a different meaning. A judge should therefore consider any credible evidence offered to show the parties' intention." (*Id.* at 268.) "Only if extrinsic evidence does not resolve the ambiguity is it appropriate to construe the document against its drafter." (*General Security Indemnity Co. of Arizona v. Tipton*, 2007 UT App 109, 158 P.3d 1121, 1123.)

i. Cost Issues

"A rulemaking authority may, by rule, establish the cost principles to be included in a cost-reimbursement contract to determine incurred costs for the purpose of calculating a reimbursement." (Utah Code Annotated § 63G-6a-1206(1)(a).) On DFCM contracts, cost and pricing data is required for contracts that "expressly allow price adjustments." (Utah Administrative Code Rule 23-1-1209.) UDOT requires contractors to submit certified cost and pricing data in support of contractor claims. (UDOT Standard Specifications for Road and Bridge Construction § 00777, ¶ 1.17.) The books and records of contractors and subcontractors are subject to audit for a period of six years after final payment. (Utah Code Annotated § 63G-6a-1206.3(1), (3), (4).) The total cost method of proving damages is disfavored. (*Highland Construction Co. v. Union Pacific Railroad Co.*, 683 P.2d 1042 (Utah 1984).)

8. Statutes of Limitations on Contract Claims

a. Contractor Claims against State and Local Agencies

The statutes of limitations are as follows: six years for breach of a written contract (Utah Code Annotated § 78B-2-309); four years for open account for the sale of goods or labor or materials; four years "upon a contract, obligation, or liability not founded upon an instrument in writing" (*Id.* § 78B-2-307); and four years for most torts. (*Id.*)

b. Claims against Counties, Cities, or Incorporated Towns

Statutes of limitation on contract claims against counties, cities, or incorporated towns are the same as stated in the previous section.

c. Statutory Bond Claims

The limitations period is one year after the date the claimant last furnished labor, material, equipment, or services for which the claim is made on the bonded project. (*Id.* § 63G-6a-1103.)

d. Statute of Repose

Utah's architects' and builders' statute of repose is at section 78B-2-225 of the Utah Code, and requires that an action for breach of contract or warranty "for acts, errors, omissions, or breach of duty arising out of or related to the design, construction, or installation of an improvement, regardless of whether based in tort, contract, warranty, strict liability, product liability, indemnity, contribution, or other source of law" against a provider of relevant services be "commenced within six years after the date of completion or abandonment of an improvement." (*Id.* § 78B-2-225(1)(b) & (3)(a).) "All other actions by or against a provider shall be commenced within two years from the earlier of the date of discovery of a cause of action or the date upon which a cause of action should have been discovered through reasonable diligence. If the cause of action is discovered or discoverable before completion of the improvement or abandonment of construction, the two-year period begins to run upon completion or abandonment." (*Id.* § 78B-2-225(4)(a).) But, "[n]otwithstanding Subsection (4)(a), an action may not be commenced against a provider more than nine years after completion of the improvement or abandonment of construction. In the event the cause of action is discovered or discoverable in the eighth or ninth year of the nine-year period, the injured person shall have two additional years from that date to commence an action. (*Id.* § 78B-2-225(4)(d).) In *Willis v. DeWitt*, 2015 UT App 123, 350 P.3d 250, the Utah Court of Appeals held that Utah's statute of repose was not subject to challenge on grounds of equitable tolling by application of a discovery rule. In that matter, the claimant's contract claims were not brought within six years of the completion of construction as required by statute and were therefore time-barred. (*Id.*)

e. State and Local Agency Claims against Contractors and Design Professionals

Statutes of limitation on contract claims against contractors and design professionals brought by state or other governmental entities are the same as stated in Section IV.C.8.a. (Utah Code Annotated § 78B-2-115.)

9. Additional Issues

a. Apparent Authority

Contract clauses and regulations typically establish the scope of actual and apparent authority granted to the project engineer. For example, on UDOT projects, the engineer "decides all questions regarding the quantity, quality, and acceptability of materials furnished and work performed, work progress, contract interpretation, project final acceptance, and acceptable contract completion." (UDOT Standard Specifications for Road and Bridge Construction § 00727, ¶ 1.6.) The project engineer is expressly authorized to issue all interpretations dealing with project acceptance and completion. (*Id.*) More specifically, the UDOT project engineer "decides the extent to which the work will be accepted and remain in place when a contract item does not meet contract requirements but is adequate to serve the design purpose." (*Id.* ¶ 1.8. See *Meadow Valley Contractors, Inc. v. Utah Department of Transportation*, 2011 UT 35, 266 P.3d 671.)

b. Architect/Engineer Decision

The UDOT project engineer is empowered to investigate all claims of differing site conditions, changes in the work, requests for time extensions, and other claims and to render a decision. A Claim Board of Review will review the decision if requested in writing by the contractor. But UDOT's regulations are silent on the standard of review, and research reveals no case law on point on this issue.

c. Notice

Contract clauses and regulations require the contractor to promptly notify the public owner in writing of situations that the contractor believes constitute changes to the work, differing site conditions, or grounds for time extensions or other similar claims. The rules and clauses typically state that failure to provide the required notice constitutes waiver of the claim. (See, e.g., UDOT Standard Specifications for Road and Bridge Construction § 00777, ¶ 1.13, Differing Site Conditions and New Work.) Public agencies will seek to strictly enforce contractual clauses requiring the contractor to give notice of claims to the public owner. (*Meadow Valley Contractors, Inc.*, 2011 UT 35, 266 P.3d 671.)

D. Debarment and Suspension

1. Statutory Authority

The Utah Procurement Code authorizes a procurement official to debar or suspend a contractor. (Utah Code Annotated § 63G-6a-904(1).) Contractors may be debarred for a period not exceeding three years. (*Id.*) Contractors may be suspended "if there is probable cause to believe that the person has engaged in any activity which might lead to debarment." (*Id.*) A suspension may not be for a period exceeding three months unless an indictment has been issued for an offense that would be a cause for debarment. (*Id.* § 63G-6a-904(2).)

2. Due Process Requirements

Before debarring or suspending a person, the chief procurement officer or head of a procurement unit must consult with the procurement unit and its legal counsel; give the person at least ten days' written notice of the reasons for potential debarment or suspension, and notice of the required hearing; and hold an informal hearing. (*Id.* § 63G-6a-904(1).)

At the hearing, the chief procurement officer or head of a procurement unit may subpoena witnesses and compel their attendance; subpoena documents for use at the hearing; obtain additional factual information; and take testimony from experts and witnesses to assist in reaching a decision. (*Id.* § 63G-6a-904(1)(c).) The rules of evidence are inapplicable.

The chief procurement officer or head of a procurement unit must record the hearing, and preserve the evidence relied upon in reaching a decision until the decision is final. (*Id.*)

3. Grounds for Debarment or Suspension

Section 63G-6a-904(3) lists the following grounds for suspension or debarment:

> (a) conviction of a criminal offense as an incident to obtaining or attempting to obtain a public or private contract or subcontract or in the performance of such contract or subcontract;
>
> (b) conviction under state or federal statutes of embezzlement, theft, forgery, bribery, falsification or destruction of records, receiving stolen property, or any other offense indicating a lack of business integrity or business honesty which currently, seriously, and directly affects responsibility as a contractor for the procurement unit;
>
> (c) conviction under state or federal antitrust statutes;
>
> (d) failure without good cause to perform in accordance with the terms of the contract;
>
> (e) a violation of [chapter 6a of the Utah Code]; or
>
> (f) any other cause the procurement official determines to be so serious and compelling as to affect responsibility as a contractor for the procurement unit, including debarment by another governmental entity.

Prior rules expressly considered a contractor's consistent failure to pay subcontractors as grounds for debarment.

4. Agency Rules

DFCM's debarment and suspension procedures are provided in Utah Code section 63G-6a-904. UDOT has adopted rules that provide for and expand upon the grounds for suspension or debarment, set forth factors that the agency will consider in setting the duration of debarment, and establish a minimum debarment duration of six months but no more than three years, which require the agency to treat the action as an informal administrative proceeding, and grant the contractor limited appeal rights. (Utah Administrative Code Rule 907-67-1 *et seq.*)

V. Administrative and Judicial Review

A. Administrative Review

Information regarding administrative review by the chief procurement officer and the Utah Procurement Policy Board is set forth above.

B. Judicial Review

Information regarding circumstances when judicial review is available is set forth above. Additional select relevant judicial decisions are set forth below:

- No contractor may "act as agent or commence or maintain any action in any court of the state for collection of compensation for performing any act for which a license is required . . . without alleging and proving" that he or she was a properly licensed contractor when the contract sued upon was entered into, and when the alleged cause of action arose. (Utah Code Annotated § 58-55-604.) Utah's courts have created exceptions to this rule in situations where the public is protected from the harm the licensing statutes are designed to prevent. (*American Rural Cellular, Inc. v. Systems Communication Corp.*, 890 P.2d 1035 (Utah Ct. App. 1995).)
- Out of state contractors may not maintain an action in Utah courts unless an application for authority to conduct business in Utah is filed with the Corporations Division of the Utah Department of Commerce. (Utah Code Annotated § 16-10a-1502(1).)
- Economic loss rule: In Utah, the economic loss rule immunizes design professionals and contractors from tort liability for purely "economic" losses arising from the negligent performance or breach of a contract. (*Davencourt at Pilgrims Landing Homeowners Association v. Davencourt at Pilgrims Landing*, 2009 UT 65, 221 P.3d 234; Utah Code Annotated § 78B-4-513.) In *Maack v. Resource Design & Construction, Inc.*, 875 P.2d 570 (Utah. Ct. App. 1994), the court wrote: "The 'economic loss rule' is the majority position that one may not recover 'economic' losses under a theory of nonintentional tort." Economic loss is defined as: "[D]amages for inadequate value, costs of repair and replacement of the defective product, or consequent loss of profits—without any claim of personal injury or damage to other property . . . as well as 'the diminution in the value of the product because it is inferior in quality and does not work for the general purposes for which it was manufactured and sold.'" (*Id.* (quoting *East River SS Corp. v. Transamerica Delaval, Inc.*, 476 U.S. 858, 866–75 (1986)).) The *Davencourt* court confirmed the status of the economic loss rule in Utah, stating, "[t]he economic loss rule remains in force and should be applied in accordance with our precedent." (2009 UT 65, 221 P.3d at 243.)
- Architects and engineers are required to exercise the care, skill, and diligence of design professionals in good standing. (*Wessel v. Erickson Landscaping Co.*, 711 P.2d 250 (Utah 1985).) "Except as provided in Subsections (2) and (6), an action for defective design or construction may be brought only by a person in privity of contract with the original contractor, architect, engineer, or the real estate developer." (Utah Code Annotated § 78B-4-513.) Design professionals who contract with the state and its agencies are not necessarily agents of the state for purposes of establishing liability for negligent design. Claims against design professionals must be asserted within the time provided by

Utah's architects' and builders' statute of repose. (*Id.* § 78B-2-225; *Willis v. DeWitt*, 2015 UT App 123, ¶ 8, 350 P.3d 250.) Any attempt by design professionals to contractually limit their liability to contractors or subcontractors is unenforceable in Utah, if the claim arises "from services performed by the design professional in connection with the development of land." (Utah Code Annotated § 13-8-2.)

VI. Extent of State's Adoption or Adaptation of ABA Model Procurement Code

The Utah Procurement Code is at chapter 6a of title 63G of the Utah Code and is loosely based on the American Bar Association (ABA) Model Procurement Code (2000). However, Utah has omitted large portions of the Model Procurement Code, revised the language, and reorganized those parts of the Model Procurement Code that Utah has adopted.

VII. Cooperative Purchasing

Cooperative procurement in Utah is governed by Utah Code title 63G, chapter 6a, section 2105. (Utah Code Annotated § 63G-6a-2105.) Pursuant to Utah statute, the chief procurement officer may enter into a cooperative procurement and/or a contract that is awarded as a result of cooperative procurement with another state, a cooperative purchasing organization, or a public entity inside or outside of Utah. (*Id.* § 63G-6a-2105(1).)

A. Authority

In addition to being allowed to participate in, sponsor, conduct, or administer a cooperative procurement with another Utah procurement unit or public entity in Utah if specific requirements are met, a Utah procurement unit may purchase under a cooperative purchasing organization if (1) each party enters into an agreement describing the rights and duties of each party; (2) the procurement meets all other procurement requirements; (3) the solicitation clearly discloses it as a cooperative procurement and identifies each party that may purchase; and (4) each party to the cooperative procurement signs a participating addendum describing the rights and obligations under any resulting contract. (*Id.* § 63G-6a-2105(4).)

B. Requirements

In order for a Utah procurement unit to enter into a contract awarded as a result of cooperative procurement, the procurement unit must be specifically identified in the resulting contract as an entity allowed to make purchases under the contract and sign a participating addendum. (*Id.* § 63G-6a-2105(5).) However, the requirement of a signed participating addendum is waived if the solicitation includes a statement indicating the resulting contract is issued for the benefit of public entities, nonprofit organizations, and agencies of the federal government. (*Id.* § 63G-6a-2105(2).)

Regional solicitations for the procurement of a procurement item within a specified geographical region of Utah is permitted if a plan is developed by the chief procurement officer that defines the boundaries, items, and solicitations, and that requires the responding entity to offer similar warranties and submit to similar obligations standard to other state cooperative contracts. (*Id.* § 63G-6a-2105(7).) However, those regional solicitation items may only be obtained after the expiration of any state cooperative agreement providing the same item. (*Id.*)

Vermont Procurement Rules and Regulations

Prepared by William T. Clark[1]
Downs Rachlin Martin PLLC
Email: wclark@drm.com

I. Statutory Reference

A. Procurement/Purchasing Statutes

The Department of Buildings and General Services has an Office of Purchasing and Contracting that manages the acquisition of material, equipment, supplies, fuel, and printing for all state agencies and oversees the bidding and contracting process to ensure compliance with laws and regulations. Various forms related to procurement can be obtained at https://bgs.vermont.gov/purchasing-contracting/forms.

The Vermont Statutes can be obtained online at https://legislature.vermont.gov/statutes/.

The statutes specifically on procurement are located in title 29, Public Property and Supplies.

See also chapter 49, Department of Buildings and General Services, which has the following provisions:

Subchapter 1: General Provisions

§ 901.	Repealed. 1987, No. 243 (Adj. Sess.), Section 37, eff. June 13, 1988
§ 902.	Duties of commissioner of buildings and general services
§ 903.	Requisition for supplies and materials
§ 903a.	Alternative purchasing sources
§ 904.	Surplus property; acceptance and distribution
§ 905.	Centralized purchasing of school equipment and supplies
§ 906.	Stationery and office supplies
§ 907.	Manner of payment of bills for purchases
§ 908.	Price-fixing illegal; penalty
§ 909.	State purchase of food and agricultural products

1. Second edition prepared by Andrew Victor; first edition prepared by Jessica Oski and Dominic N. Dagbanja.

Subchapter 2: State Purchasing of Apparel, Footwear, or Textiles

§ 921. Application of subchapter; definitions
§ 922. Bids for the sale of apparel, footwear, or textiles
§ 923. Exception
§ 924. Repealed. 2011, No. 139 (Adj. Sess.), Section 51, eff May 14, 2012
§ 925. Complaints of noncompliance with subchapter; investigations of complaints
§ 926. Determinations of noncompliance with subchapter
§ 927. Consequences of noncompliance with subchapter
§ 928. Coordination with other jurisdictions

See also chapter 59, Surplus Property, which has the following sections:

§ 1551. The state agency for surplus property
§ 1552. Authority and duties
§ 1553. Power of commissioner of buildings and general services to require bond
§ 1554. Transfer charges
§ 1555. Acquisition and distribution of surplus commodities
§ 1556. State surplus property
§ 1557. Transfer charges and credits

II. Regulations

The secretary of administration has responsibility to issue, rescind, and maintain administrative bulletins. Only those bulletins appearing on the secretary's website (https://aoa.vermont.gov/bulletins) are officially "in-force." Current addendums are listed below the bulletin to which they apply. Any bulletin that is not on the secretary's website is considered rescinded or replaced by other policies or procedures.

This list of bulletins, available at https://aoa.vermont.gov/bulletins, is below:

- Bulletin 2.3, State Vehicles (Purchase/Usage)—Effective February 21, 2016
- Bulletin 3.3, Delegation of Authority—Effective July 1, 2002
  - Addendum 3.3—Issued April 17, 2015
- Bulletin 3.4, Employee Travel & Expense Policy—Effective July 1, 2014
- Bulletin 3.5. Procurement and Contracting Procedures—Effective July 1, 2016; revised December 16, 2019
- Bulletin 5, Policy for Grant Issuance and Monitoring—Effective December 26, 2014
  - Bulletin 5 Guidance and Procedures
- Bulletin 7.14, Equipment Revolving Fund—Effective September 25, 2015
- Bulletin 10.0, Policy & Procedures Pertaining to ARRA [American Recovery and Reinvestment Act of 2009] Accountability and Transparency—Issued March 11, 2010
- Bulletin 17.10, Employment of Private Legal Counsel—Effective October 1, 2003

There are also policies, procedures, and other documents available at https://bgs.vermont.gov/purchasing, which are summarized below:

III. Source Selection

A. Requisition for Supplies and Materials

When any governmental agency needs to make purchases, including but not limited to all fuel, supplies, materials, and equipment, the commissioner of buildings and general services will purchase the items either by advertising for bids or by letters of inquiry, and the contract for those items will be awarded to the person whose bid or quotation is in the best interest of the state. The commissioner of buildings and general services may reject any or all bids or quotations and, with the approval of the secretary of administration, procure items in such manner as may be in the best interest of the state. When purchasing any items, the commissioner of buildings and general services, in any determination of the best interest of the state, considers (1) specified quality; (2) price; (3) ease of access of supply; (4) incidental administrative costs; (5) proven reliability of bidder; (6) use of recycled materials or products; (7) minimizing the creation, by the state, of solid waste; (8) the extent to which the usage of the item involves the generation of pollutants; (9) life-cycle costs, if required under the state agency energy plan, as implemented; (10) the interests of the state relating to the proximity of the supplier and the costs of transportation, and relating to the economy of the state and the need to maintain and create jobs in the state; and (11) the use of railroads and the increased revenues returning to the state from its railroad-leasing program.

Other specific considerations include the following:

1. Recycled Material

The commissioner, in the commissioner's discretion, may spend up to 10 percent more for comparable products that are made of recycled materials. If products made of recycled materials are to cost more than 10 percent more than comparable products, the commissioner shall receive consent of state entities that are to use the product before completing the order for the materials in question.

2. Vermont Bidders

Whenever any business or industry located in Vermont and employing citizens of this state submits a bid and the item has not been purchased from them, the commissioner of buildings and general services must record the reason for assigning the order as he or she did. This report is a public record available to any interested person. All bids or quotations are kept on file in the commissioner's office and open to public inspection.

3. Alternative Fuel Vehicles

The commissioner of buildings and general services, when purchasing vehicles for state use, will consider vehicles using alternative fuels when the alternative fuel is suitable for the vehicle's operation, is available in the region where the vehicle will be used, and is competitively priced with traditional fuels.

4. Bids for the Sale of Apparel, Footwear, or Textiles

Any bidder for the sale of apparel, footwear, or textiles must certify that each supplier at the point of assembly of the goods complies with all applicable wage, health, labor, environmental, and safety laws; legal guarantees of freedom of association; building and fire codes; and laws relating to discrimination in hiring, promotion, and compensation on the basis of race, disability, national origin, gender, sexual orientation, and affiliation with any political, nongovernmental, and civic group except when federal law precludes the state from attaching the procurement conditions provided in the relevant statute. These bidders must also certify that the suppliers comply with all human and labor rights treaty obligations that are shared by the United States and the country in which the goods are assembled, including obligations with regard to forced labor, indentured labor, slave labor, child labor, involuntary prison labor, physical and sexual abuse, and freedom of association. Prior to the awarding of a contract, a bidder for the sale of apparel, footwear, or textiles must submit a list of the names and addresses of suppliers at the point of assembly of goods subject to the bid process. If, after complying with the filing requirements, a bidder is awarded a contract, that contractor must, during the term of the contract, promptly inform the commissioner of any change in the information furnished to the commissioner pursuant to the relevant law. The commissioner may accept a bid from and award a contract to a supplier who has not met the above requirements if, after reasonable investigation by the commissioner, it appears that the required unit or item of supply or brand of that unit or item is procurable by the state from only that supplier or under other extraordinary circumstances.

B. Contracting Requirements under Bulletin 3.5

The requirements are available at https://aoa.vermont.gov/bulletins/3point5.

1. Contracts for Less Than $15,000

While a competitive solicitation process is preferable, the state may enter into a contract for $15,000 or less without a standard competitive solicitation process. At the time the contract is executed, the employee in charge of the contracting process must place in the official contract file a written explanation for selecting the contractor.

2. Contracts Greater Than $15,000 but Not More Than $100,000

The state may enter into a contract over $15,000 but not more than $100,000 following either a standard bid or a simplified bid process. A "simplified bid process" means that the agency has developed a specific and detailed statement of work for the service or product desired and has solicited written price quotations from vendors providing the specified services or products. The statement of work to be performed and request for price quotations must be provided in a timely manner to at least three potential bidders. If the agency is unsure whether the contract will fall below the $100,000 threshold, in order to avoid rebidding the work, the use of a standard bid process is recommended.

3. No-Cost Contracts

In situations where the state is seeking services for which it will not have to pay, and which may even produce revenue for the state, a standard bid process is to be used.

4. Information Technology and Information Security Contracts

The secretary of the Agency of Digital Services, also referred to as the state chief information officer (CIO), must review all requests for proposals (RFPs) for information technology or information security prior to their posting. The CIO must review and approve all information technology and information security contracts with a cost of $500,000 or more, unless the secretary of administration has waived this requirement or the secretary of administration has approved a contracting plan that includes information technology contracts.

5. Contracts for Installation, Maintenance, and Support or Training Services

Any contract that involves the contractor's personnel coming onto state property to provide service, maintenance, training, or technical support related to existing equipment should be developed as a contract for services. All such contracts must include Attachment C: Standard State Contract Provisions and comply with all other applicable state contracting provisions. Any contract for the purchase of a product, commodity, equipment, or software that also involves the contractor's personnel coming onto state property to install or service the purchased item or to train state personnel in the use of the item purchased should be developed as a commodities contract by submitting a requisition to the Division of Purchasing and Contract Administration, Department of Buildings and General Services. Any contract for the license of proprietary software, regardless of whether that also includes the contractor's personnel coming onto state property to install or service the purchased item or to train state personnel in the use of the item purchased, should be developed as a contract for services. All such contracts must therefore include Attachment C: Standard State Contract Provisions and comply with all other applicable provisions of Bulletin 3.5. With such contracts, the vendor will usually have a standard licensing agreement that the vendor will want to incorporate into the contract. Such standard licensing agreements often contain terms that are inconsistent with Attachment C and should be reviewed by the Office of Attorney General.

6. Marketing Contracts

Any contract for services relating to marketing with a value of greater than $15,000 requires the prior approval of the chief marketing officer (CMO), Agency of Commerce and Community Development. For marketing contracts valued at $15,000 or less, supervisors must refer to and comply with applicable statewide marketing guidelines, policies, and standards issued by the CMO. A marketing contract includes advertising (print, radio, television, and web/internet, but does not include recruiting); collaterals (brochures, fact sheets, folders, etc.); website design (not to include technical components); trade shows and events; direct mail campaigns; and sponsorships.

7. Contracts Greater Than $100,000

The state may enter into a contract greater than $100,000 only after adherence to standard bid processes as outlined in Bulletin 3.5.

C. The Standard Bidding Process

1. RFP

All state-issued RFPs are developed based on standardized requirements and are usually on standard forms.

2. Public Notice regarding the Standard Bid

The opportunity to bid for the proposed work is broadly publicized. Solicitations include posting on the Electronic Bulletin Board (EBB), which is operated by the

Agency of Commerce and Community Development as part of the Vermont Business Assistance Network. (See https://www.vermontbusinessregistry.com/.) Other methods of solicitation may include advertising in newspapers, direct mailings to potential vendors, direct mailings to vendors that are on a prequalified list, and/or publication in trade journals. The time between the initial public notice and the opening of bids is usually at least two weeks. For relatively complex work, additional time is usually permitted to allow potential vendors a reasonable opportunity to obtain the documents and prepare a responsive bid.

3. Contractor Selection and Documentation

The bid most responsive to the selection criteria established in the bid documents is usually the one that is accepted. Sometimes a contract selection committee is established to review the bids and make a written recommendation. At minimum, the agency will post public notification of its decision on the EBB. A complete copy of the bid documents, vendors solicited, price quotations, bids received, and any written selection justifications is kept in the contract file. For cost-based bids, when other than the lowest bid is accepted, documentation concerning the quality of services, products, or other relevant considerations offered by a higher-priced vendor that justify the award of the contract to the higher-priced vendor is also kept in the contract file. For qualifications-based selection processes, documentation of the basis for ranking each bidder's qualifications must be kept in the contract file. If a reasonable person might conclude that a contractor was selected for improper reasons, the state will disclose that fact in writing to the attorney general and the secretary and document the reasons why selecting the desired contractor is still in the best interests of the state.

4. Conferences and Adjustments to Bid Documents

For large or complex work, the agency soliciting the contract may hold a pre-bid conference where agency staff can review with potential vendors the scope of services for the work and other content of the bid documents. Any change to the interpretation of the bid documents resulting from a pre-bid conference, or from any other information upon which the agency intends bidders to rely, such as responses to bidders' questions, will be broadly publicized, including at minimum a notice on the EBB.

5. Bid Opening

A public bid opening and reading of bids is required for contracts over $100,000. Two staff members from the agency administering the bid process will be in attendance at the bid opening. Bids that have not been received prior to the established time for the receipt of bids are returned unopened to the bidder. With the approval of the attorney general, the state agency administering the bid process can waive technical noncompliance when doing so is in the best interest of the state. Such waivers will be fully documented and included in the contract file.

6. Prequalified Bidding

In order to streamline the bidding process in cases where a type of work is routinely bid on, for efficiency reasons, an agency may establish a list of prequalified vendors. A prequalified vendor is one who has been determined by an agency to be generally qualified to perform a type of work that is routinely put out to bid by the agency. All vendors who are determined qualified to perform the type of work for which the prequalification list has been established, and who so request it, will be included on the list by the agency.

At least once in a two-year period, agencies using a prequalified bidding process will publicly solicit the opportunity to be placed upon the list. The agency will establish clear criteria for the qualifications that, if met, allow potential vendors to be included on the prequalification list. Additionally, during the period between formal list revisions, the agency must maintain an ongoing process that allows additional vendors to request review and inclusion on the prequalification list.

When soliciting bids from a prequalified list, the public notice requirement will include the restriction that bidding is limited to those on that prequalification list and provide information as to how vendors can be included on this list in the future.

7. Qualification-Based Selection

With the prior approval of the secretary, in situations where the contract sought is for professional design services, such as architects or engineers, a qualification-based selection process may be used. The first consideration in this process is the selection of the most qualified vendor who can meet the contract requirements; the second consideration is cost. Vendors are ranked by qualification, then cost is negotiated with the most qualified bidder; if this negotiation is not satisfactory to the state, cost is negotiated with the next most qualified bidder, and so on, until a satisfactory agreement is reached and a contract negotiated. The qualification-based selection is required for contracts that are supported by certain federal funds if (1) the contract is for engineering and design services; (2) the contract is for $100,000 or more; and (3) the services relate directly to a highway construction project. Under these circumstances, the prior approval of the secretary is not required.

8. Exceptions and Waivers

a. Sole Source

In extraordinary circumstances, negotiating with only one contractor may be appropriate. Examples of when a sole source contract might be appropriate include when time is critical for performance of the required services (such as emergency repairs) and/or when only one contractor is capable of providing the needed service or product. In other than in emergency circumstances, a sole source contract usually requires approval by the secretary of administration.

b. Waivers

The secretary of administration may waive certain contracting requirements on a case-by-case basis pursuant to a written request from an agency. A waiver request must describe in detail the basis for the request and the specific component(s) of the contracting process for which the waiver is sought. Approval of the waiver must be granted prior to the signing of the contract by either the state or the contractor. Copies of all waivers granted by the secretary and the requests submitted are retained in the contract file.

c. Contracting Plans

For specific classes of contracts exhibiting characteristics that cannot reasonably be accommodated within the usual and customary contracting procedures, the secretary may approve a written contracting plan that provides an acceptable alternative to any requirement. Such an example might be contracts with multiple training specialists that provide a particular kind of training to a specific group, such as police officers or casework specialists, and that takes place frequently on an annual basis, but for which an exact time or number of trainings cannot be predicted accurately.

IV. Bid Protests and Contract Disputes

A. Bid Protests

There are no specific rules on bid protests.

B. Bid Protest Appeals

There are no specific rules on bid protest appeals.

C. Contract Disputes

1. Contract Claims

The state must initiate an investigation when there is reason to believe that a violation of procurement law has occurred. The investigation will be initiated by sending a certified letter to the contractor that is the subject of the complaint or whose supplier is the subject of the complaint. In making a determination of whether a violation of law has occurred, the state may take into account any factors, information, sources of information, and materials deemed reliable and relevant, as determined on a case-by-case basis. The state may employ an independent monitor to investigate a complaint. The determination of whether a party subject to a complaint is in compliance with law is solely that of the state. After rendering a determination, the commissioner of building and general services will promptly inform the complainant and contractor in writing. If, in the opinion of the commissioner, a contractor that has been determined to be not in compliance with law does not make good-faith efforts to change its practices or use its bargaining position with an offending supplier to change the supplier's practices, the commissioner may take appropriate remedial action, including barring the contractor from bidding on future state contracts or terminating the state's contract with the contractor.

2. Contract Claims Appeals

An appeal against a governmental agency is undertaken by filing with the clerk of the administrative body within 30 days of the date of the decision appealed from. Upon the filing of the notice of appeal, the clerk of the administrative body or other appropriate officer then provides to the appellant a list of all interested parties, with instructions to serve a copy of the notice upon each of them. A copy of the notice is to be served by the appellant upon the clerk of the superior court and upon each of the interested parties in accordance with that rule. Each appellee must cause its appearance to be entered with the clerk of the superior court within 20 days after the service of the notice of appeal. An appeal does not itself stay enforcement of the agency decision. If the agency does not grant a stay, the court, after the filing of the notice of appeal, may, upon motion, stay the agency decision and make such other orders as are necessary to preserve the rights of the parties upon such terms and conditions as are just.

D. Suspension and Debarment

If, in the opinion of the commissioner, a contractor that has been determined to be not in compliance with law does not make good-faith efforts to change its practices or use its bargaining position with an offending supplier to change the supplier's practices, the commissioner may take appropriate remedial action, including barring the contractor from bidding on future state contracts or terminating the state's contract with the contractor.

V. Administrative and Judicial Review

A. Administrative Review

In order to promote compliance with laws and regulations relating to contracting, the Department of Finance and Management and Department of Buildings and General Services will conduct management reviews of performance relative to the policy and requirements of law. (See https://aoa.vermont.gov/bulletins/3point5. See also Section IV.C.1, Contract Claims, above.)

B. Judicial Review

Any action or failure or refusal to act by a state agency may be reviewed if such review is otherwise available by law, such as Vermont's Administrative Procedures Act. (See, e.g., Vermont Statutes Annotated tit. 3, §§ 800–849.) Rule 75 of the Vermont Rules of Civil Procedure may also provide an avenue for judicial review of an agency's action or failure to act.

VI. Extent of State's Adoption or Adaptation of ABA Model Procurement Code

Vermont has not adopted the American Bar Association (ABA) Model Procurement Code for State and Local Governments. As demonstrated above, government contracting in Vermont follows a relatively simplified regime, which affords discretion and flexibility to state agencies. There is no indication at the time this summary went to press that Vermont was considering the Model Procurement Code.

VII. Cooperative Purchasing

A. Authority

Vermont has authorized cooperative purchasing. (See Vermont Statutes Annotated tit. 24, § 4901.) Any one or more municipalities may contract with other municipalities to perform any governmental service, provided that the legislative body of each municipality approves the contract and the expenses for such services are included in the municipal budget.

B. Requirements

Vermont requires that the interlocal contract set forth fully the purposes, powers, rights, objectives, and responsibilities of the contracting parties. (See Vermont Statutes Annotated tit. 24, § 4902.) Vermont permits interlocal contracts to transfer a local service power previously exercised by one municipality to another municipality. (Vermont Statutes Annotated tit. 24, § 4902.)

Virginia Procurement Rules and Regulations

Prepared by John S. Pachter, Edmund M. Amorosi, and Michael T. Gwinn
Smith Pachter McWhorter PLC
Email: jpachter@smithpachter.com, eamorosi@smithpachter.com, and mgwinn@smithpachter.com

I. Statutory Reference

A. Procurement/Purchasing Statutes

Adopted in 1982, the Virginia Public Procurement Act (VPPA) is codified at Virginia Code section 2.2-4300 *et seq*. A table of contents follows.

§ 2.2-4331.	Contract pricing arrangements.
§ 2.2-4332.	Workers' compensation requirements for construction contractors and subcontractors.
§ 2.2-4333.	Retainage on construction contracts.
§ 2.2-4334.	Deposit of certain retained funds on certain contracts with local governments; penalty for failure to timely complete.
§ 2.2-4335.	Public construction contract provisions barring damages for unreasonable delays declared void.
§ 2.2-4336.	Bid bonds.
§ 2.2-4337.	Performance and payment bonds.
§ 2.2-4338.	Alternative forms of security.
§ 2.2-4339.	Bonds on other than construction contracts.
§ 2.2-4340.	Action on performance bond.
§ 2.2-4340.1.	Statute of limitations on construction contracts.
§ 2.2-4340.2.	Statute of limitations on architectural and engineering contracts.
§ 2.2-4341.	Actions on payment bonds; waiver of right to sue.
§ 2.2-4342.	Public inspection of certain records.
Article 3.	**Exemptions and Limitations.**
§ 2.2-4343.	Exemption from operation of chapter for certain transactions.
§ 2.2-4343.1.	Permitted contracts with certain religious organizations; purpose; limitations.
§ 2.2-4344.	Exemptions from competition for certain transactions.
§ 2.2-4345.	Exemptions from competitive sealed bidding and competitive negotiation for certain transactions; limitations.
§ 2.2-4346.	Other exemptions for certain transactions.
Article 4.	**Prompt Payment.**
§ 2.2-4347.	Definitions.
§ 2.2-4348.	Exemptions.
§ 2.2-4349.	Retainage to remain valid.
§ 2.2-4350.	Prompt payment of bills by state agencies.
§ 2.2-4350.1.	Prohibition on payment without an appropriation; prohibition on IOUs.
§ 2.2-4351.	Defect or impropriety in the invoice or goods and/or services received.
§ 2.2-4352.	Prompt payment of bills by localities.
§ 2.2-4353.	Date of postmark deemed to be date payment is made.
§ 2.2-4354.	Payment clauses to be included in contracts.
§ 2.2-4355.	Interest penalty; exceptions.
§ 2.2-4356.	Comptroller to file annual report.
Article 5.	**Remedies.**
§ 2.2-4357.	Ineligibility.
§ 2.2-4358.	Appeal of denial of withdrawal of bid.
§ 2.2-4359.	Determination of nonresponsibility.

Virginia's primary purchasing department, the Department of General Services' (DGS's) Division of Purchases and Supply (DPS), has additional procurement-related information on its website at https://dgs.virginia.gov/procurement.

B. Other Applicable Statutes

Statutes relating to lobbying rules and registration requirements are available at Virginia Code section 2.2-418 *et seq*. Virginia's Ethics in Public Contracting standards relating to procurement integrity are set forth in VPPA section 2.2-4367 *et seq*. Other Virginia statutes related to procurement integrity include (1) the State and Local Government Conflict of Interests Act (Virginia Code § 2.2-3100 *et seq*.); (2) the Virginia Governmental Frauds Act (*Id*. § 18.2-498.1 *et seq*.); and (3) statutes related to bribery (*Id*. §§ 18.2-438 and 18.2-446 *et seq*.). Contractors who defraud the commonwealth are subject to penalties for violations of law, including under the Virginia Fraud against Taxpayers Act, section 8.01-216.1 *et seq*., Virginia's equivalent to the federal False Claims Act. The Virginia Freedom of Information Act, codified at section 2.2-3700 *et seq*. of the Virginia Code, permits access to public records of public agencies, subject to certain exceptions.

II. Regulations

Virginia has promulgated an Agency Procurement and Surplus Property Manual (APSPM) to establish the rules and regulations for procurement. The regulations cover a wide range of topics, including competitive sealed bidding, competitive negotiation, sole source procurement, contract administration, and appeals and disputes. The APSPM regulations can be found at https://dgs.virginia.gov/procurement/policy-consulting--review/policy/.

Virginia also has published a Vendor's Manual, which is also available at https://dgs.virginia.gov/procurement/policy-consulting--review/policy/, to guide vendors seeking to do business with the commonwealth. The Vendor's Manual, which is maintained by the DGS's DPS, provides information about agency purchases of non-technology goods and nonprofessional services.

Guidance for information technology procurements is available at the Virginia Information Technologies Agency website, https://www.vita.virginia.gov/.

The DGS's Division of Engineering and Buildings maintains information about the procurement of construction and professional services for the commonwealth, which is available at https://dgs.virginia.gov/engineering-and-buildings/.

III. Source Selection

A. Competitive Sealed Bidding

Competitive sealed bidding is the preferred method for acquiring goods, nonprofessional services, insurance, and construction for public use when the cost is expected to exceed $100,000. (Virginia Code § 2.2-4303(A), (D), and (G). Further details about this procurement method are available at chapter 6 of the APSPM.)

B. Competitive Negotiation

The VPPA requires the use of competitive negotiation for the procurement of all professional services. (Virginia Code § 2.2-4303(B).) This method may also be used for goods and professional services when it is not practically or fiscally advantageous to use competitive sealed bidding, as provided for in Virginia Code sections 2.2-4302.2 and 2.2-4303. (Further details about this procurement method are outlined in chapter 7 of the APSPM. See also Section III.D, Professional Services, below.)

C. Sole Source Procurement

A sole source procurement is authorized when there is only one source practicably available for the goods or services requested. (Virginia Code § 2.2-4303(E).) All sole source procurements in excess of $50,000 must be approved by the agency head. (More information is available at chapter 8 of the APSPM.)

D. Professional Services

Because they are services and not goods, the procurement of professional services is not handled by DPS. In large part, these service contracts are procured by the DGS's Division of Engineering and Building for construction and building-related projects (architects, engineers) and other agencies on an as-needed basis. Professional services include work performed by an independent contractor in the practice of accounting, actuarial services, architecture, land surveying, landscape architecture, law, dentistry, medicine, optometry, pharmacy, and professional engineering. (See APSPM chapter 4, § 4.23 for further details.) Architectural and professional engineering contracts for multiple projects are subject to additional terms and limitations. (Virginia Code § 4303.1.)

E. Construction Services

Procurement of construction for "capital outlay projects" is governed by the rules of the Construction and Professional Services Manual, issued by the DGS's Division of Engineering and Buildings. (See *id.* § 2.2-1132.)

F. Design-Build/Construction Management

Unlike many states that prohibit design-build in public contracts, Virginia allows its use, albeit with restrictions and special procedures. Design-build contracts are governed by Virginia Code section 2.2-4378 *et seq.* A careful review of the requirements is recommended. (*Id.*)

Virginia also permits the use of design-build in certain contexts under the Public-Private Education Facilities and Infrastructure Act of 2002 (PPEA) and the Public-Private Transportation Act of 1995 (PPTA). The PPEA authorizes a public entity to enter into a comprehensive agreement with a private operator to develop a qualifying project. (*Id.* § 56-575.1 *et seq.*) A qualifying project is (1) an education facility; (2) a building or facility for principal use by a public agency; (3) any improvement or equipment needed to enhance the public safety and security of a building used by a public entity; (4) utility and telecommunications infrastructure; (5) a recreational facility; (6) technology infrastructure, services, and applications; (7) any service designed to increase productivity or efficiency of a public entity; (8) any technology, equipment, or infrastructure to provide wireless broadband services to schools, businesses, or residential areas; (9) improvements to unimproved state or local real estate; or (10) any solid waste management facility. (*Id.*) Notably, the PPEA is exempt from the VPPA's stringent Review Board requirements. Despite this exemption, the public agency must still follow procedures that are (1) consistent with procedures for competitive sealed bidding or (2) consistent with competitive negotiation. (*Id.* § 56-575.16.) Use of the latter procedure requires approval by the governor or department secretary. (*Id.*) The PPTA was enacted to spur innovative solutions to Virginia's transportation and traffic problems in a more timely and less costly fashion. (*Id.* § 33.2-1800 *et seq.*) Like the PPEA, the PPTA is exempt from the VPPA's rigorous Review Board requirements.

IV. Bid Protests and Contract Disputes[1]

A. Bid Protests

Within certain limits, disappointed bidders or offerors may file a bid protest. Potential bidders or offerors may protest sole source or emergency contracts only. (*Id* § 2.2-4360.) The protest must be filed no later than ten days after public notice of the award or announcement of the decision to award, whichever occurs first. If a protest depends in whole or in part on information contained in public procurement records subject to inspection, the protest time expires ten days after those records are available for inspection. (*Id.*)

The following protest grounds will not be considered: (1) an allegation that the selected awardee is not a responsible bidder or offeror; (2) a challenge to the validity of the terms or conditions of the invitation to bid or request for proposal. (*Id.*) The protest must contain the basis for the protest and the relief sought. (*Id.*)

In response to the protest, the agency must issue a decision in writing within ten days stating reasons. (*Id.*) The decision is final unless the protester appeals within ten days of receipt by filing an administrative appeal or instituting legal action. (*Id.* See also *id.* §§ 2.2-4364 and 2.2-4365.) Pursuant to Virginia Code section 2.2-4360(b), if the agency determines before award that the selection decision was arbitrary or capricious, the public body shall cancel the proposed award or revise it to comply with the law. If award has been made but performance has not begun, the performance of the contract may be enjoined. Where performance has begun, the public body may declare the contract void on finding it is in the best interest of the public. The contractor shall be compensated for its cost of performance but will not be entitled to lost profits. *Note*: the prohibition against injunction after performance has begun does not apply to a circuit court's exercise of equitable powers on appeal of a protest decision. (*MFS Network Technologies v. Commonwealth*, 33 Va. Cir. 406 (Va. Cir. Ct. 1994).)

Pending final determination of protest or appeal, the validity of a contract awarded and accepted in good faith shall not be affected. (Virginia Code § 2.2-4361.) Contract award need not be delayed for the time allowed for protest, but in the event of timely protest or legal action, no further action to award the contract will be taken without written determination that it is necessary to protect the public interest or unless the bid or offer would expire. (*Id.* § 2.2-4362.)

A disappointed bidder or a bidder denied withdrawal of a bid may bring legal action in the appropriate circuit court instead of an administrative appeal. (*Id.* §§ 2.2-4360 and 2.2-4364.) While the protester need not resort to administrative appeal remedies, those procedures, once invoked, shall be exhausted before instituting legal action unless the public body agrees otherwise. (*Id.* § 2.2-4364(F).)

---

1. Note that localities, such as cities and counties, may have their own procurement rules and regulations, which should be consulted if a locality is a contracting party.

B. Bid Protest Appeals

Pursuant to Virginia Code section 2.2-4365, a public body may establish administrative procedures for hearing protests of awards, appeals from refusals to allow withdrawal of bids, appeals from disqualifications and determinations of nonresponsibility, and appeals of contract disputes during performance. Procedures shall provide for a hearing before a disinterested person or panel, an opportunity to present information, and issuance of a written decision containing findings of fact. (See *W.M. Schlosser Co., Inc. v. Board of Supervisors of Fairfax County*, 245 Va. 451 (Va. 1993) (county employee is not a disinterested person).) The findings of fact shall be final and conclusive unless (1) fraudulent, arbitrary, or capricious; (2) so grossly erroneous as to imply bad faith; or (3) in the case of denial of prequalification, not based on proper criteria. No determination on an issue of law shall be final if timely legal action is instituted. The DGS/DPS Procurement Appeals Board provides an impartial review of any Virginia agency's procurement of goods. (Virginia Code § 2.2-4365; APSPM ch. 11, § 11.2.) Appeals relating to service contracts may be handled by certain agencies, provided the *Schlosser* criteria are met.

C. Contract Disputes

1. Contract Claims

A contract claim must be filed in writing with the agency within 60 days after final payment to be timely. (Virginia Code § 2.2-4363.) Written notice of such claim must be given at the time of the occurrence upon which the claim is based. Time frames in which the agency must render a decision on a claim may vary by contract. (*Id.*) In the case where no time frame is specified, the claimant may pursue legal action in circuit court after a period of 90 days of the submission of the claim if no decision is rendered before then. (*Id.*) An agency's failure to render a decision within 90 days or such other time as may be provided by contract shall be considered a deemed denial. (*Id.*) A contractor may bring an action involving a contract dispute with a public body in the appropriate circuit court. (*Id.* See also *XL Specialty Insurance Co. v. Commonwealth*, 47 Va. App. 424 (Va. Ct. App. 2006) (sovereign immunity only waived for those entities in privity of contract with Virginia (i.e., contractors and not sureties)).)

2. Contract Claims Appeals

A contractor may appeal the agency's decision on a contract claim by using the agency's administrative procedures if available, or by appealing directly to the circuit court having jurisdiction. (Virginia Code §§ 2.2-4363, 2.2-4364, and 2.2-4365.) An agency may establish an administrative procedure for hearing "appeals from decisions on disputes arising during performance of a contract." (*Id.* § 2.2-4365.)

Appeals of agency decisions are to the circuit courts. (*Id.* See also *Viking Enterprise, Inc. v. County of Chesterfield*, 277 Va. 104 (Va. 2009) (procedural requirements for filing suit against counties and other entities that can be harmonized with the VPPA remain in effect for such appeals).) An appeal of the circuit court's decision shall be to the Virginia Supreme Court and not the court of appeals. (*Allstar Towing, Inc. v. City of Alexandria*, 231 Va. 421 (Va. 1986).)

Note: The VPPA encourages the use of alternative dispute resolution (ADR) to resolve contract disputes. (Virginia Code § 2.2-4366.) Contractors entering into the ADR process must also meet any deadlines relating to a formal claim submission. However, the results of ADR procedures such as arbitration are not binding on the commonwealth. (*Id.*)

D. Suspension and Debarment

Virginia's debarment statute permits the exclusion of prospective contractors from contracting for particular types of supplies, services, insurance, or construction for defined periods of time. (*Id.* § 2.2-4321.) The agency must have written debarment procedures in place. (*Id.*) A debarment action may be based on a contractor's unsatisfactory performance for a public body. (*Id.*)

V. Administrative and Judicial Review

A. Administrative Review

The procuring agency may provide an "administrative procedure for hearing (i) protests of a decision to award or an award, (ii) appeals from refusals to allow withdrawal of bids, (iii) appeals from disqualifications and determinations of nonresponsibility, and (iv) appeals from decisions on disputes arising during the performance of a contract, or (v) any of these." (*Id.* § 2.2-4365.) Beyond this agency review and the review of goods procurements by DGS/DPS, there are no other entities, such as a board of contract appeals, that offer further administrative relief or publish procurement decisions.

B. Judicial Review

A contractor or the public body may institute judicial review within 30 days of receipt of the agency's written decision. (*Id.* § 2.2-4365(B).) A petitioner must establish that the agency's decision was not (1) an honest exercise of discretion, but rather was arbitrary or capricious, or (2) not in accordance with the Constitution of Virginia, applicable state law or regulation, or the terms or conditions of the solicitation. (*Id.* § 2.2-4364(A).) In the case of denial of prequalification, the petitioner must show the decision was not based on applicable criteria. If the court reverses a finding that the apparent low bidder was nonresponsible, the court may direct the public body to award the contract to that bidder. (*Id.*)

If injunctive relief is granted, the court, on request of the public body, shall require the posting of reasonable security to protect the public body. (*Id.* § 2.2-4364(D).) As stated above, a contractor has the right to appeal an agency's decision on a claim to the appropriate circuit court.

A contractor may appeal the circuit court's decision to the Virginia Supreme Court, and not the intermediate court of appeals. Opinions from the Virginia Supreme Court are available at https://www.vacourts.gov/scndex.htm.

VI. Extent of State's Adoption or Adaptation of ABA Model Procurement Code

The VPPA, originally adopted in 1982, is based on the American Bar Association's (ABA's) 1980 version of the Model Procurement Code for State and Local Governments.[2]

---

2. Virginia Procurement Law Study Advisory Committee, Office of the Secretary of Administration and Finance, Virginia Procurement Law Study Final Report 13 (1980) ("In developing the proposed legislation, the Advisory Committee relied heavily upon the Model Procurement Code published by the American Bar Association."); Maria J.K. Everett,

VII. Cooperative Purchasing

A. Authority

The VPPA allows for any public body to "participate in, sponsor, conduct, or administer a joint procurement agreement on behalf of or in conjunction with one or more other public bodies . . . for the purpose of combining requirements to increase efficiency or reduce administrative expenses in any acquisition of goods, services, or construction." (Virginia Code § 2.2-4304(A).) It also allows for a public body to purchase from "another public body's contract or from the contract of the Metropolitan Washington Council of Governments or the Virginia Sheriffs' Association," with some exceptions. (*Id.* § 2.2-4304(B).)

B. Requirements

Cooperative procurements cannot be used for contracts for architectural or engineering services. (*Id.*) Cooperative procurements cannot be used for construction contracts except for sole source or emergency procurements awarded under Virginia Code section 2.2-4304; the installation of artificial turf and track surfaces; stream restoration; or stormwater management practices, including all associated and necessary construction and maintenance. (*Id.*) Information technology or telecommunications goods or services procured through cooperative purchasing must first be approved by the chief information officer of the commonwealth. (*Id.*)

Special Joint General Laws Subcommittee Studying the Virginia Public Procurement Act, Overview of the Virginia Public Procurement Act 4 (2013) ("The VPPA is based on the American Bar Association's Model Procurement Code.").

Washington Procurement Rules and Regulations

Prepared by Karl F. Oles and Danika Duffy
Stoel Rives LLP
Email: karl.oles@stoel.com

I. Statutory Reference

Washington does not have a single common statutory scheme for contracts issued by public agencies. There are common principles, but different types of public agencies may have different statutory powers. The actual authority for contracting is found in the specific chapters applicable to the various public agencies. See Table 1 below for a partial list. Moreover, public agencies generally have broad discretion to set their own contracting procedures and contract terms.

Washington public procurement law includes a jumble of statutes that sometimes overlap in their application. Finding all statutes applicable to a particular procurement can be a challenge. The relevant agency is often, but not always, a good source of information about the governing law.

The comments made here are intended for general information. In any particular case, reference should be made to specific applicable statutes, and care must be taken to determine whether the relevant statutes have been amended or affected by agency regulations or judicial decisions.

A. Procurement/Purchasing Statutes

Chapters 39.04 and 39.26 of the Revised Code of Washington (RCW) contain or reference many of the statutory requirements with general application. Chapter 39.04 applies broadly to the State of Washington and all state agencies and "municipalities," which include any city, county, town, municipal district, "or other public agency authorized by law to require the execution of public work." (RCW § 39.04.010(3).) Chapter 39.26 applies to state agencies but not to local agencies. For ease of understanding, references to "agency" below include all state and local entities, unless specified otherwise.

TABLE 1
Selected Agency Competitive Bidding Statutes
(Section numbers are to the Revised Code of Washington)

Public Works Contracts (state and local agencies)	Ch. 39.04
Procurement of Goods and Services (state agencies)	Ch. 39.26
Correctional Facilities (GC/CM option)	§ 39.04.220
Counties	§§ 36.32.235–.240
Fire Districts	§§ 52.14.110–.130
First-Class Cities	§§ 35.22.620–.650
Higher Education Institutions	§ 28B.10.350
Hospital Districts	§ 70.44.140
Port Districts	§§ 53.08.120–.135
Public Stadium Authorities	§§ 36.102.050–.060
Public Utility Districts	§§ 54.04.070–.092
School Districts	§ 28A.335.190
Second-Class Cities	§ 35.23.352
Washington Department of Transportation	§§ 47.28.030–.110
Water/Sewer Districts	§ 57.08.050
Water Pollution Control Facilities	§§ 70.150.020–.050

B. Other Applicable Statutes

Other statutes frequently affecting contracting decisions and claims involving public agency procurement include:

1. Contractor Registration

Persons and entities that offer to improve real estate are required to register under RCW section 18.27.020. "Contractor" is broadly defined (RCW § 18.27.010). Contractors must post a bond (RCW § 18.27.040) and provide evidence of insurance or financial responsibility to cover costs of property damage or personal injury (RCW § 18.27.050). Registration at the time the contract is formed is a prerequisite to filing of a suit for recovery on the contract (RCW § 18.27.080).

2. Prevailing Wage and Labor Hours Requirements

Under RCW section 39.12.020, workers on public works projects must be paid wages at least equal to the prevailing wages for their trade paid in the locality where the work is performed, as set by the Washington Department of Labor and Industries (L&I). Apprentices may be paid lower rates. Contractors are required to file various documents with L&I demonstrating intent to pay the appropriate wage rates and certificates that the wages have been paid. (RCW § 39.12.040.) Workers are required to be paid overtime for more than eight hours worked in a calendar day. (RCW § 49.28.010.) Contractors on projects estimated to cost more than $1 million are required to submit information regarding prefabricated and project-specific items produced outside the state of Washington. (RCW § 39.04.370.)

3. Public Disclosure Law

Construction documents, including bid documents submitted to an agency, are public records subject to disclosure under the Public Records Act, RCW chapter 42.56. (See also RCW § 39.26.030, which provides that bids to state agencies are protected from public disclosure until the public agency announces the successful bidder.) The Public Disclosure Law contains an exception for valuable formulae. (See RCW § 42.56.270(1).)

4. Worker Safety Requirements

Worker safety requirements are defined in the Washington Industrial Safety and Health Act, RCW chapter 49.17, and Washington Administrative Code (WAC) chapter 296-155. General contractors have a nondelegable duty that extends to all employees on a jobsite to ensure compliance with regulations promulgated under the act. (*State v. P.B.M.C., Inc.*, 114 Wash. 2d 454, 464 (1990).) Jobsite owners owe the same duty if they retain the right to control the manner in which independent contractors and their employees perform their work. (*Neil v. NWCC Investments V, LLC*, 229 P.3d 837 (Wash. Ct. App. 2010).)

5. Apprenticeship Requirements

Requirements have been established for minimum labor utilization percentages by participants in state-certified apprenticeship programs. (RCW § 39.04.300 *et seq.*) For example, after 2012, for new contracts of $1 million or more by school districts or four-year colleges, the specifications must require that at least 15 percent of the labor hours be performed by apprentices. (RCW § 39.04.320(1)(d)(iii).)

6. Retainage

Most public improvement contracts must provide for, and the public owner must retain, an amount not to exceed 5 percent of monies earned by the prime contractor as a trust fund for persons and entities performing work on the project, for equipment and material suppliers, and for the state with respect to taxes that may be due from the contractor. (RCW § 60.28.011(1).) Funds may be withheld from payments by the general contractor to subcontractors as well. (RCW § 60.28.011(5).)

There are exceptions, including projects supported by federal transportation funds, for which no amount need be retained. (RCW § 60.28.011(1)(b).) At the contractor's option, funds can be held by the agency, put in escrow, or held in an interest-bearing account. (RCW § 60.28.011(4).) The prime contractor may file a bond for all or a portion of the contract retainage. (RCW § 60.28.011(6).)

Most claimants must file a pre-claim notice to preserve their rights to the retainage fund. (RCW § 60.28.015.) Claims must be submitted within 45 days of the completion of the work. (RCW § 60.28.011(2).) If no claims have been properly made against the retained funds or against the performance bond on the contract, the funds are released 60 days after completion of all contract work. (RCW § 60.28.011(3).) However, that distribution is not allowed until after the Washington Department of Revenue, the Employment Security Department, and L&I certify that all taxes have been paid. (RCW § 60.28.051.)

There are several provisions allowing for the early or partial release of retained funds. (See RCW § 60.28.011(3) (when retainage equals 100 percent of the work remaining).

RCW § 60.28.011(6) (bond), and RCW § 60.28.011(7) (relating to delayed completion). See Section IV.C.2 below for information about disputes regarding retainage.)

7. Performance and Payment Bonds

On public contracts over $150,000, the contractor must post a performance and payment bond to secure its faithful performance and its obligation to pay those performing the work and certain taxes. (RCW § 39.08.010.) With some exceptions, the bond must be for the full contract price. (RCW § 39.08.030.) Most claimants must file a pre-claim notice (RCW § 39.08.065) and submit a timely claim after the project is complete (RCW § 39.08.030). Note that the deadlines for the pre-claim notice and the bond claim are different from those for project retainage. Under RCW section 39.26.190, bidders who regularly do business with the state may file an annual performance bond in lieu of furnishing individual bonds. (See Section IV.C.3 below for information about disputes regarding performance and payment bonds.)

C. Additional Resources

The Construction Section of the Washington State Bar Association (WSBA) conducts an annual seminar of current issues and topics relevant to the construction practitioner. Copies of the seminar manuals (and other materials) are available from the WSBA.

The Washington State Department of Enterprise Services (DES) provides training in public procurement issues. Beginning July 1, 2015, no agency employee may execute or manage contracts unless the employee has met the requirements as set by the department. (RCW § 39.26.110.) Training materials are available online.

II. Regulations

The DES regulations are found in title 200 of the WAC. Chapter 200-300 contains general regulations about bidding and award procedures. Chapter 200-305 establishes debarment procedures pursuant to RCW section 39.26.200. Chapter 200-320 contains regulations allowing competitive bidding of services customarily and historically provided by state employees.

III. Source Selection

A. Construction (Public Works)

1. Public Works Defined

"Public works" are defined in RCW section 39.04.010(4) as all "work, construction, alteration, repair, or improvement other than ordinary maintenance, executed at the cost of the state or of any municipality, or which is by law a lien or charge on any property therein." Certain work performed under RCW section 36.102.060 (related to public stadiums) is excluded from the definition of public works.

2. Selecting Contractors for Public Works Contracts

There are a number of different processes available for a given public agency to select a contractor to perform public works: competitive bidding, quotes from a small works roster, self-performance using employees of the agency, emergency contracts, the general contractor/construction manager (GC/CM) method, design-build, job order contracting, performance-based contracts for energy equipment and services, and lease-to-own arrangements. Some of these are explained more fully below.

a. Competitive Bidding

There is a strong public policy in Washington favoring competitive bidding. (*Platt Electric Supply, Inc. v. City of Seattle*, 555 P.2d 421, 425–26 (Wash. Ct. App. 1976).) However, each different type of public agency has its own statutory authority for conducting competitive bid competitions.

The objectives served by competitive bidding are to prevent fraud, collusion, favoritism, and improvidence and to enable the state to obtain the best work or supplies at the most reasonable price. (*Gostovich v. City of West Richland*, 452 P.2d 737, 740 (Wash. 1969).) A secondary purpose is to provide a fair forum for bidders, which ensures impartial treatment for bid participants and thus promotes the interests of the public. (*A.A.B. Electric, Inc. v. Stevenson Public School District No. 303*, 491 P.2d 684, 685 (Wash. Ct. App. 1971).)

i. Bidding Process

Typically, the statute requires that any contract for an expected price of over a minimum threshold (e.g., $50,000) be advertised ahead of time in a newspaper of general circulation. The bid opening must be at least a certain number of days after the first advertisement is made. The bid must be on the bid form prescribed by the public agency. A bid bond or certified check is usually required by the statute, equal to at least 5 percent of the bid amount.

For projects over $1 million, one hour after the bids are due, each bidder must submit a listing of the subcontractors who will perform any work in the heating, ventilation, and air-conditioning (HVAC), plumbing, or electrical disciplines or else list itself as the entity to perform the work. (RCW § 39.30.060(1).) General contractors normally can name only one subcontractor for each trade. (RCW § 39.30.060(2).) Thereafter the bidder cannot substitute a different subcontractor "in furtherance of bid shopping." (RCW § 39.30.060(3).) Hiring a subcontractor at a higher cost than that of the listed subcontractor has been held not to constitute bid shopping. (See *ETCO Services, LLC v. Killian Co.*, 528 F. App'x 698 (9th Cir. 2013) (unpublished).) Bids are typically opened after the bidders' subcontractor listings are received. Failure to supply the required information renders the bid nonresponsive. (RCW § 39.30.060(2).) Subcontractors claiming bid shopping may sue the general contractor for damages, but not the public agency. (RCW § 39.30.060(3).)

Generally, anyone may submit a bid for consideration. However, some public entities are allowed to prequalify bidders (i.e., to limit the bid process to firms that have previously submitted materials establishing their qualifications to perform the specific type of work). (See RCW § 54.04.085 for electrical facility contracts and RCW § 47.28.070 for highway projects.) Prequalification is also permitted for subcontractors under the GC/CM contracting procedure. (RCW § 39.10.400.)

Contracts entered into in violation of public bid laws are void and unenforceable. (See *Platt Electric Supply, Inc. v. City of Seattle*, 555 P.2d 421, 431 (Wash. Ct. App. 1976).)

If the contract includes trench excavation more than four feet deep, the bid must include an estimate of the cost of such work. (RCW § 39.04.180.)

ii. Award, Withdrawal

An award is typically made on the lowest responsive proposal from a responsible bidder. There is no statutory definition of a "responsive bid," but it is generally understood to be any bid that was timely submitted and offers to perform the work as advertised (i.e., the prescribed bid form is completely filled out with no omissions, additions, changes, or qualifications, and all required enclosures are submitted (such as the bid bond and subcontractor listing)). (See *Farmer Construction v. State*, 656 P.2d 1086, 1088 (Wash. 1983).) Late bids may be accepted if they were mailed on time (*Gostovich v. City of West Richland*, 452 P.2d 737, 739 (Wash. 1969)) or where no advantage or benefit not enjoyed by other bidders accrues as a result. (See *R.W. Rhine, Inc. v. Tacoma*, 536 P.2d 677 (Wash. Ct. App. 1975); *Quinn Construction Co. v. King County Fire Protection District No. 26*, 44 P.3d 865 (Wash. Ct. App. 2002).) Bids must be signed, because otherwise the bidder might not be bound by the bid. (*A.A.B. Electric, Inc. v. Stevenson Public School District No. 303*, 491 P.2d 684 (Wash. Ct. App. 1971). But see *Eastside Disposal v. Mercer Island*, 513 P.2d 1047 (Wash. Ct. App. 1973), and *Farmer Construction v. State*, 656 P.2d 1086 (Wash. 1983) (holding that an unsigned bid may be accepted where accompanied by a signed bid bond, particularly where they reference each other).) Any addenda to the original advertisement must usually be acknowledged. Failure to submit post-bid documents required by the bid advertisement may result in a determination that the bidder is not responsive.

Bidder responsibility is covered by RCW section 39.04.350. To be considered responsible, the bidder must be registered as a contractor under RCW chapter 18.27, have a current state unified business identifier (UBI) number, and be licensed under RCW title 51 (workers' compensation and employment security) and RCW title 82 (Department of Revenue). The bidder also must not be disbarred under RCW section 39.06.010 (employer and tax records violations) or RCW section 39.12.065(3) (prevailing wage violations). General contractors are required to verify that subcontractors meet the same requirements. (RCW § 39.06.020.) Supplemental responsibility criteria may be added by an agency at its discretion. (RCW § 39.04.350(3).) The social responsibility of the bidder may be considered. (*National Electric Contractors Association v. Pierce County*, 667 P.2d 1092 (Wash. 1983).) Model supplemental criteria have been prepared by the Capital Projects Advisory Review Board (CPARB) and are available at https://des.wa.gov/sites/default/files/public/documents/About/CPARB/AdminDocs/BidderResponsibilityGuidelines_11-16-17.pdf . Any criteria must be relevant to the contractor's performance of the particular project. (RCW § 39.04.350(3).)

Once bids are submitted, negotiations are not allowed to permit a bidder to change a nonresponsive bid into a responsive bid. (See *Hanson Excavating Co. v. Cowlitz County*, 622 P.2d 1285 (Wash. Ct. App. 1981); *Platt Electric Supply, Inc. v. City of Seattle*, 555 P.2d 421, 431 (Wash. Ct. App. 1976).) Reformation of a contract pricing provision was not allowed in *Red-Samm Mining Co. v. Port of Seattle*, 508 P.2d 175 (Wash. Ct. App. 1973).

Federal Comptroller General and Board of Contract Appeals decisions are considered useful precedent in determining the outcome in particular fact situations in the absence of specific Washington statutory or case law precedent.

In any competitive bidding process for public works in which a bid is received from a contractor residing in some other state that provides a percentage bidding preference for in-state bidders, a comparable preference disadvantage must be applied to the bid of that contractor. (RCW § 39.04.380(3).)

RCW section 39.04.015 allows negotiations for state agency contracts where the low bid exceeds available funds. There are limits on this authority. For example, for contracts of more than $5 million, the amount by which the bid exceeds the available funds cannot exceed 1 percent. (RCW § 39.04.015(2).)

A bid by a contractor is an offer to contract and does not create a contract until the agency has accepted it. (*Hadaller v. Port of Chehalis*, 986 P.2d 836, 839 (Wash. Ct. App.

1999).) There is no requirement that the lowest bid be accepted. Unless prohibited by statute, an agency may reject all bids, for any reason. (*Mottner v. Town of Mercer Island*, 452 P.2d 750, 753 (Wash. 1969).)

To be capable of acceptance, the bid must be unambiguous and in full compliance with all bid material requirements. Where the bid contains a minor irregularity, the agency has the discretion to waive the irregularity. The test of whether an irregularity is minor (as opposed to material) is "whether it gives a bidder a substantial advantage or benefit not enjoyed by other bidders." (*Gostovich v. City of West Richland*, 452 P.2d 737, 740 (Wash. 1969).) Generally, a minor irregularity is one that is merely a matter of form or has no effect on price, quantity, quality, or delivery and that can be corrected without affecting the relative standing of the bidders or otherwise prejudicing the other bidders. (*Id.*) Bids that contain material regularities must be rejected. (See *A.A.B. Electric, Inc. v. Stevenson Public School District No. 303*, 491 P.2d 684, 686 (Wash. Ct. App. 1971).)

Under most enabling statutes, a contractor's bid is secured by a bid bond or certified check, which is returned if the bidder executes the contract upon receiving notice of award. Where a bidder has made a mistake, such as failing to include the cost of an important element of the work in its bid amount, the bidder may seek to withdraw its bid without forfeiting the bid bond. There is no statutory provision establishing standards for withdrawal of bids upon allegation of a mistake, but guidance was provided in *Puget Sound Painters, Inc. v. State*, 278 P.2d 302, 304 (Wash. 1954), where a bidder was allowed to withdraw its bid without penalty where the mistake was in good faith, was without gross negligence, would have resulted in substantial detriment to the bidder, and was identified to the government promptly, and where the government would not suffer substantial hardship as a result. In contrast, judgmental mistakes such as underestimating the cost of labor or materials will not entitle the bidder to relief. (See *Peter Kiewit Sons' Co. v. Washington State Department of Transportation*, 635 P.2d 740 (Wash. Ct. App. 1981).)

Any bidder that establishes a mistake and withdraws its bid cannot participate in a rebid of the same project. (RCW § 39.04.107.) Bidders who chose to perform notwithstanding a mistake cannot obtain reformation of the resulting contract. (See *Red-Samm Mining Co. v. Port of Seattle*, 508 P.2d 175 (Wash. Ct. App. 1973).)

b. Alternative Public Works Contracting Procedures

The legislature has determined that the traditional process of awarding public works contracts in a lump sum to the lowest responsible bidder is a fair and objective method of selecting a contractor. However, under certain circumstances, alternative public works contracting procedures may best serve the public interest if such procedures are implemented in an open and fair process based on objective and equitable criteria. These alternative procedures include the GC/CM method, design-build contracting, and job order contracting. These alternative procedures are authorized, on a trial basis, in RCW chapter 39.10, which is scheduled to expire at the end of June 2031. (RCW § 39.10.490.)

i. GC/CM

GC/CM contracts are governed by RCW sections 39.10.340–.410. For projects that involve complex scheduling, phasing, or coordination, such as an occupied facility that must continue to operate during construction, agencies may conduct a request for proposals process to select the general contractor early during the design process so that the contractor can participate in such activities as design review and subcontract package development. (RCW § 39.10.340.) Award of the contract is based on a combination of the quality of the proposal plus the price offered for general conditions and profit, as described in the request for proposals. (RCW § 39.10.360.) A maximum allowable contract cost is negotiated late in the design process. (RCW § 39.10.370.)

Subcontracts under the GC/CM process are awarded by a competitive bid process. (RCW § 39.10.380.) Prequalification of the subcontractors is allowed. (RCW § 39.10.400(1).) If the GC/CM seeks to self-perform part of the work, it must compete with prospective subcontractors; in such cases, the bid process is conducted by the public owner. The work performed by the GC/CM may not exceed 30 percent of the total project price. (RCW § 39.10.390(3).)

In 2010, the legislature authorized an alternative selection method for electrical and mechanical subcontracts over $3 million on GC/CM projects. (RCW § 39.10.385.) In 2014, the legislature added special provisions for heavy civil contracts to multiple sections of the statute. (See, e.g., RCW § 39.10.340(6).)

ii. Design-Build

Design-build contracts are governed by RCW sections 39.10.300–.330 and are permitted for capital projects over $2 million where the construction activities are highly specialized, use of design-build will promote innovation and efficiency, or where design-build offers significant savings in project delivery time. A single firm is selected for both design and construction of the project. This reduces owner responsibility for design errors, allows for a shorter duration from commencement of design to completion of construction, and reduces disputes between the owner, architect, and contractor. However, the owner has less control over the design than in traditional design-bid-build.

iii. Job Order Contracting

Public agencies may use a job order contract for public works projects if a determination is made that the use of job order contracts will benefit the public by providing an effective means of reducing the total lead time and cost for certain kinds of projects, such as minor repair and renovation of public facilities where public bidding of each separate repair/renovation project might be inefficient.

Job order contracts are authorized by RCW sections 39.10.420–.460 and may be used if an agency expects to have multiple small projects and it determines that the job order method will promote efficiency by eliminating burdensome bidding procedures for each small job. (RCW § 39.10.420(3).) Contracts can be up to $4 million per year for up to three years. (RCW § 39.10.440(1).) Selection is based on proposals measured against evaluation factors disclosed ahead of time. (RCW § 39.10.430.) At least 90 percent of the work must be subcontracted. (RCW § 39.10.440(4).)

c. Miscellaneous

There are several alternative selection methods permitted for contracts under $350,000, termed "small works." All state agencies, and local agencies if authorized by their enabling legislation, are permitted to establish a small works roster under RCW section 39.04.155. The roster lists contractors who have responded to the public agency's advertisement, which must be given at least once each year. For any particular project, the agency invites firms from the roster to submit quotes, and the lowest responsive quote wins. The opportunity to compete must be either given to all firms on the roster or rotated on an equitable basis. These small works contracts need not be advertised to the public. Under legislation established in 2009, an agency may adopt procedures to encourage the participation of small firms. (RCW § 39.04.155(5).)

Enabling legislation for agencies typically permits award of contracts under a threshold amount (such as $75,000) without advertising. (See RCW § 39.04.190.) Quotes must be obtained from at least three bidders, with the results made available for public inspection. For very small contracts (e.g., contracts below $7,500), enabling legislation may permit award of a contract without any competition at all.

Enabling legislation may also permit an agency to perform the work with its own forces. This authority is typically limited to small contracts.

Performance-based contracts for energy equipment and services are allowed under RCW section 39.35A.030. A request for proposals process is used to select the "best" proposal based on published criteria, then the agency negotiates a contract for installation of the desired work.

Under RCW sections 39.04.020 and 39.04.280, agencies can adopt procedures to award contracts without competition if an emergency exists. An "emergency" is defined as unforeseen circumstances beyond the control of the agency that present a threat to proper performance of essential functions or will likely result in material loss or damage to property, bodily injury, or loss of life. (RCW § 39.04.280(3).) A written finding must be made and made available for public inspection. (RCW § 39.04.280(2)(b).)

Under RCW section 43.52.565, operating agencies (aka joint operating agencies (JOA)) may employ a competitive negotiation process to select a contractor to perform work on nuclear power plants. This allows a JOA to select a contractor on the basis of both price and other factors and to negotiate with more than one contractor before making a selection decision. Under the Interlocal Cooperation Act, RCW chapter 39.34, a public agency may contract with any other state or local agency to perform services that the Washington agency is authorized to procure.

d. Procurement of Architect and Engineering Services

Contracts for architectural or engineering (A/E) services (architects, engineers, land surveyors, and landscape architects) are governed by RCW chapter 39.80, which requires that contracts be advertised and the "most highly qualified" firm selected. (RCW § 39.80.050(1).) Minority- and women-owned firms shall be provided maximum practicable opportunity to compete for the contracts. (RCW § 39.80.040.) The agency then is required to negotiate the price and other terms of a contract with the selected firm. (RCW § 39.80.050(1).) If the agency is unable to negotiate a satisfactory contract with the firm selected at a price the agency determines to be fair and reasonable, negotiations with that firm shall be formally terminated, and the agency may select other firms in accordance with RCW section 39.80.050 until an agreement is reached or the process is terminated. Compliance is not required where an emergency exists. (RCW § 39.80.060.)

Two or more public agencies may enter into a contract providing for the joint utilization of A/E services if the agency contracting with the A/E firm complies with the requirements for such contracts under chapter 39.80 and if the services to be provided to the second agency are related to, and within the general scope of, the services the A/E firm was selected to perform for the first agency. An agreement providing for such joint utilization of A/E services must be entered into prior to the commencement of procurement of the services. (RCW § 39.34.030.)

The legislature has adopted alternative licensing provisions for persons with military service training, except where the licensing board determines that the training was not substantially equivalent to the state's regular licensing requirements.

(See RCW § 18.08.500 (architects), § 18.43.190 (engineers and land surveyors), and § 18.96.230 (landscape architects).)

B. Goods, Equipment, and Services

As with construction contracts, there is no uniform statutory authority governing the acquisition of goods, equipment, and services by public agencies. Each type of agency has its own rules. (See Table 1.)

1. DES

Most state purchases or leases of goods, equipment, and services are conducted by the DES (formerly the Department of General Administration). In 2012, the state legislature adopted comprehensive provisions for acquisition of goods, equipment, and services as RCW chapter 39.26. The DES may delegate acquisition authority to other state agencies, but such delegation does not relieve the agency from conformance with DES standards. (RCW § 39.26.090(5).)

As far as possible, all purchases of or contracts for goods and services by state agencies must be based on a competitive solicitation process. (RCW § 39.26.120(1).) Agencies must provide public notice for all competitive solicitations. (RCW § 39.26.150(1).) Emergency purchases are authorized without bids (as under prior law) in circumstances that are unforeseen and beyond the control of the agency, and either present a serious threat to the proper performance of "essential functions" or else may pose a risk of personal injury or damage to property. (RCW § 39.26.130.) Sole source contracts are permitted after public notice, subject to approval by the DES. (RCW § 39.26.140.)

Under section 39.26.160(2), the bidder's ability, capacity, skill, character, integrity, reputation, judgment, experience, prior performance, efficiency, and other relevant information may be considered in determining the successful bidder. The solicitation must clearly set forth the requirements and criteria that the agency will apply in evaluating submissions. (RCW § 39.26.160(4).) Limited negotiations are permitted with the lowest responsive and responsible bidder in order to determine whether the bid may be improved. (RCW § 39.26.160(6).)

Bid submissions and evaluations are exempt from disclosure until the agency announces the apparent successful bidder. (RCW § 39.26.030(2).)

Performance bonds may be required, or firms may post an annual bond if they do regular business with the state. (RCW § 39.26.190.)

Cooperative purchasing is authorized between agencies or under master or convenience contracts entered into by one agency and made available to other agencies. (RCW §§ 39.26.060–.070.)

As noted below, the DES has authority to debar contractors, by written decision after notice and an opportunity to be heard, for causes such as conviction of a crime in the obtaining or performing of a public contract; conviction or (in a civil case) judicial determination with respect to a charge of fraud, embezzlement, or other offense indicating lack of business integrity; or failure to perform prior contracts. (RCW § 39.26.200(2).)

2. Other Agency Acquisitions

Public agencies are usually required by their individual statutory provisions to use competitive bids for purchase of equipment and supplies. Exemptions are provided in RCW section 39.04.280, permitting waiver of the requirements for competitive bidding of purchases that are clearly and legitimately limited to a single source of supply, involving special facilities or market conditions, emergencies, and insurance or bonds. The public agency must adopt written policies implementing this section. In each case, the public agency must record and make open to public inspection the factual basis for the exemption. (RCW § 39.04.280(2)(a).) An emergency is defined as presenting a real, immediate threat to the proper performance of essential functions or will likely result in material loss or damage to property, bodily injury, or loss of life. (RCW § 39.04.280(3).)

Some municipalities are authorized to purchase materials, equipment, supplies, and services without advertisement and formal sealed bidding, usually below a maximum dollar threshold (see, e.g., RCW § 36.32.245(3), relating to county purchases). For such cases, RCW section 39.04.190 provides a uniform process for informal bidding. The agency may establish a list of interested vendors and then, when a specific contract is to be let, secure telephonic or written quotations from at least three vendors on the list. The agency must post a list of purchases made under this procedure. (RCW § 39.04.200.)

Under RCW section 39.04.160, public contracts entered into by the state are subject to the requirements of RCW chapter 39.19 relating to minority- and women-owned businesses. RCW section 39.19.060 requires state agencies and higher education institutions to adopt plans that include specific measures to afford the maximum practicable opportunity for such businesses to directly and meaningfully participate in the execution of public contracts for construction and goods and services.

IV. Bid Protests and Contract Disputes

A. Bid Protests

Disappointed bidders may protest the award of a contract. Procedures are established by each agency, either in regulations or through the bid documents. The process is typically very quick, as once the contract is executed, the disappointed bidder cannot obtain damages or force termination of the contract. (See *Peerless Food Products v. State*, 835 P.2d 1012, 1015–16 (Wash. 1992) (holding that permitting damages serves the bidder's interest alone and is contrary to the public interest the competitive bidding laws were designed to protect).) The disappointed bidder can obtain only injunctive relief preventing the agency from entering into the contract with anyone else. (*Id.*; see also *Mottner v. Town of Mercer Island*, 452 P.2d 750, 752–53 (Wash. 1969).) Thus, contrary to cases in other jurisdictions allowing recovery by disappointed bidders for improper agency action on various theories, damages are not awarded to disappointed bidders in Washington.

Many agencies adopt administrative procedures that allow protesting bidders to air their grievances prior to award of the contract. (See, e.g., *Edwards v. City of Renton*, 409 P.2d 153 (Wash. 1965).)

B. Bid Protest Appeals

Once the contract is entered into, injunctive relief is not available. (*Dick Enterprises, Inc. v. Metropolitan King County*, 922 P.2d 184 (Wash. Ct. App. 1996).) This can create a "race to the courthouse" atmosphere, where agencies may seek to shortcut the protest process and bidders may seek to get into court before the process is completed. In response, the legislature has enacted RCW section 39.04.105, which prohibits execution of the contract until two days after the protest decision is given, allowing the disappointed protester an opportunity to seek an injunction preventing execution of the contract.

The standard of judicial review for a bid protest is whether the agency was arbitrary, capricious, or contrary to law. (See *Equitable Shipyards, Inc. v. State*, 611 P.2d 396 (Wash. 1980).) Deference will be given to an agency where it is making a decision based on its specialized experience. (See *Everett Concrete Products v. Department of Labor & Industry*, 748 P.2d 1112 (Wash. 1988).) If a bid protest is not upheld, the court judgment may be appealed like other judgments.

C. Contract Disputes

1. Contract Claims

Washington has no administrative system devoted to public contracts parallel to the federal boards of contract appeals. Claims arising from public contracts are resolved in the state trial courts (or in federal courts if jurisdiction exists). Venue for such claims may be limited by statute. (See, e.g., RCW § 4.92.010 (claims against the state), or § 36.01.050 (claims against a county).)

Under RCW section 39.04.240, attorney fees are recoverable pursuant to RCW sections 4.84.250–.280 for actions involving public works contracts. Attorney fees may also be recoverable pursuant to contract provisions. Under RCW section 4.84.330, one-sided fee provisions in contract cases are reciprocal.

2. Retainage Claims

Foreclosure of a claim against public contract retainage is governed by RCW section 60.28.030, which requires suit to be filed within four months after filing of the lien claim. The claimant must also serve the summons and complaint on the contractor within this time period. (See *Galvanizer's Co. v. State Highway Commission*, 509 P.2d 73 (Wash. Ct. App. 1973).) The claimant may keep a claim alive by refiling every four months. (See *Shope Enterprises, Inc. v. Kent School District*, 702 P.2d 499 (Wash. Ct. App. 1985).) Venue for the foreclosure is proper in the county where the lien claim was filed. (RCW § 60.28.030. But *cf. Keystone Masonry, Inc. v. Garco Construction, Inc.*, 147 P.3d 610, 614–15 (Wash. Ct. App. 2006) (venue for public contract retainage claim was varied by agreement).)

The public agency need only respond as to the amount held, identify all claims filed against the funds, and withhold payment pending the outcome of the suit. (RCW § 60.28.030.)

Priority of liens among the Department of Revenue, employees of the contractor, and other parties is governed by RCW section 60.28.040. The public agency may also withhold from release of retainage for claims the public body may have against the contractor. (RCW § 60.28.021.)

3. Claims regarding Performance and Payment Bonds

In order to pursue a claim against the general contractor's bond, a claimant is required to file a notice with the public agency within 30 days after completion of the work or delivery of the supplies. (RCW § 39.08.030.) The statute provides a form of notice, which must be signed by the person or by the agent of a business entity making the claim. Using the statutory form should be sufficient. In *Williams v. Athletic Field, Inc.*, 261 P.3d 109 (Wash. 2011), a private lien case, the Washington Supreme Court held that a mechanics' lien that substantially followed the statutory form was sufficient to establish a valid claim of lien.

The bond requirement on public projects gives rise to legal issues that are familiar from private projects as well; for example, the issuer of the bond may assert suretyship defenses if the contractor's scope of work has been increased without its consent. (See, e.g., *United Pacific Casualty Insurance Co. v. Port of Everett*, 46 P.2d 736 (Wash. 1935).) Typically, however, the bond form includes prior consent for increases due to changes authorized by the contract.

Once a bond claim has been perfected, it may be enforced by a lawsuit against the surety that issued the bond. The statute does not provide for any particular venue or time limit, so normal rules about venue and normal statutes of limitations will presumably apply, though both may be varied by the terms of the bond itself. (See *Honeywell, Inc. v. Babcock*, 412 P.2d 511 (Wash. 1966) (court enforced limitation of action clause in payment bond on private project).)

4. Claims regarding Prompt Payment of Invoices, Withholding for Claims, Interest, and Attorney Fees

Public agencies are required to pay uncontested invoices timely and must pay interest at the rate of 1 percent per month if they neglect this obligation. (RCW § 39.76.011(1).) What counts as timely payment depends on a number of factors, including when the invoice is received, when the goods or services are provided, whether there is a good-faith dispute about the amount due, and whether the agency is waiting for federal funding to arrive. (RCW § 39.76.011(2).) If the agency disputes the amount of the invoice, it must provide written notice explaining the basis for its position and the remedial acts the contractor must perform to be entitled to payment. (RCW § 39.76.011(2)(b).)

Contractors on public projects are required to pay their subcontractors not later than ten days after receiving payment from the agency for the subcontractors' work. (RCW § 39.04.250(1).) If there is a good-faith dispute, the agency or the contractor may withhold up to 150 percent of the amount in dispute. (RCW § 39.04.250(2).) Interest accrues on wrongfully withheld payments. (RCW § 39.04.250(3).)

5. Notice Requirements for Claims

In 2003, the Washington Court of Appeals ruled that notice requirements in contracts strictly limiting the time period for providing notice and documentation of claims by contractors would be enforced. (*Mike M. Johnson, Inc. v. County of Spokane*, 78 P.3d 161 (Wash. Ct. App. 2003).) This ruling was controversial, causing debate as to whether notice requirements should be strictly enforced, even when no prejudice resulted to the public owner from the lack of notice. Legislation has been proposed to modify the application of such contract provisions, but has not been adopted.

A number of cases have been decided by Washington courts in subsequent years regarding notice requirements, including *Weber Construction, Inc. v. County of Spokane*, 98 P.3d 60 (Wash. Ct. App. 2004), and *American Safety Casualty Insurance Co. v. City of Olympia*, 174 P.3d 54 (Wash. 2007). Generally, a public agency owner may reserve its rights to reject a claim as untimely while negotiating with the contractor. On the other hand, it is possible to waive contractual claim procedures by conduct. (See *Shepler Construction, Inc. v. Leonard*, 306 P.3d 988 (Wash. Ct. App. 2013) (parties waived arbitration by litigating).)

The court of appeals has ruled that there is no automatic flow-down of a time limitation on claims to a subcontract unless it is clearly and unequivocally incorporated into the subcontract in a general and unlimited manner. (*Waldner Consulting, Inc. v. Miller Contracting, Inc.*, 152 Wash. App. 1015 (2009) (Division 2, unpublished opinion). See also *Northwest Infrastructure, Inc. v. PCL Construction Services*, 172 Wash. App. 1019 (2012) (Division 1, unpublished opinion) (holding that the owner's issuance of a unilateral change order to resolve an untimely claim restarted the claim notice period for the contractor).)

D. Suspension and Debarment

The director of the DES may debar a contractor from bidding on any state agency contracts for up to three years. (RCW § 39.26.200(1)(b).) Debarment may be justified by criminal offenses incident to the contracting process, conviction for embezzlement or other offenses indicating a lack of business integrity, multiple violations of the Federal Labor Relations Act, deliberate failure without good cause to perform contract provisions, or a recent record of violating ethical standards. Affected contractors may seek relief either in court or through the state Administrative Procedures Act, RCW chapter 34.05.

There is a statutory procedure that may be followed to disqualify a contractor from participation in a particular public contract bid. The public agency must provide a written determination with reasons, an opportunity to supplement the record, and a delay of any award until two business days after the final decision is received by the bidder in order to permit the disappointed bidder an opportunity to seek judicial review. (See RCW § 39.04.350(2).) Individual public agencies have also adopted procedures for debarment or suspension of contractors, and the practitioner should review those for application in specific circumstances.

V. Administrative and Judicial Review

Washington has no specialized administrative or judicial bodies for the review of disputes about public contracts.

VI. Extent of State's Adoption or Adaptation of ABA Model Procurement Code

The Washington statutory scheme does not follow the American Bar Association (ABA) Model Procurement Code.

VII. Cooperative Purchasing

A. Authority

There was a Washington State Purchasing Cooperative under the DES, but it was discontinued in 2013.

RCW section 39.26.060(1) provides:

> On behalf of the state, the [DES] may participate in, sponsor, conduct, or administer a cooperative purchasing agreement for the procurement of any goods or services with one or more states, state agencies, local governments, local government agencies, federal agencies, or tribes located in the state, in accordance with an agreement entered into between the participants. The

cooperative purchasing may include, but is not limited to, joint or multiparty contracts between the entities, and master contracts or convenience contracts that are made available to other public agencies.

Convenience contracts are addressed in RCW section 39.26.070.

B. Requirements

RCW section 39.26.060(2) provides, "All cooperative purchasing conducted under this chapter must be through contracts awarded through a competitive solicitation process."

Entities engaging in cooperative purchasing must sign Washington's Master Contracts Usage Agreement—a one-time agreement allowing qualifying organizations to use Washington State master contracts. For references to enabling regulations, see https://des.wa.gov/services/contracting-purchasing/purchasing/master-contracts-usage-agreement.

West Virginia Procurement Rules and Regulations

Prepared by Eric Whytsell
Stinson LLP
Email: eric.whytsell@stinson.com

I. Statutory Reference

A. Procurement/Purchasing Statutes

The relevant portions of the West Virginia Code are set forth below:

§ 5A-3-1 *et seq.*	Purchasing Division
§ 8-12-10.	Powers of Municipalities: Purchasing; Competitive Bidding
§ 5-22-1 *et seq.*	Government Construction Contracts
§ 5-22A-1 *et seq.*	Design-Build Procurement Act
§ 5G-1-1 *et seq.*	Procurement of Architect-Engineering Services

The Purchasing Division of the West Virginia Department of Administration is the state agency responsible for the procurement of goods and services for state government. In addition, the Purchasing Division administers various statewide programs including the West Virginia State Agency for Surplus Property; the Inventory Management Program; and the Travel Management Unit. The Division's website is http://www.state.wv.us/admin/purchase/default.html.

The table of contents of the West Virginia statutes governing the Department of Administration's Purchasing Division follows:

Chapter 5A. Department of Administration.

Article 3.	Purchasing Division.
§ 5A-3-1.	Division created; purpose; director; applicability of article; continuation.
§ 5A-3-1a.	Prescription drug products.
§ 5A-3-2.	Books and records of director.
§ 5A-3-3.	Powers and duties of Director of Purchasing.
§ 5A-3-3a.	Additional exemptions from purchasing requirements.
§ 5A-3-3b.	Exemption of facilities providing direct patient care services that are managed, directed, controlled, and governed by the secretary of the Department of Health and Human Resources.

§ 5A-3-21.	[Repealed.]
§ 5A-3-22.	[Repealed.]
§ 5A-3-23.	[Repealed.]
§ 5A-3-24.	[Repealed.]
§ 5A-3-25.	[Repealed.]
§ 5A-3-26.	[Repealed.]
§ 5A-3-27.	[Repealed.]
§ 5A-3-28.	Financial interest of secretary, etc.; receiving reward from interested party; penalty; application of bribery statute.
§ 5A-3-29.	Penalty for violation of article.
§ 5A-3-30.	Statement of purpose; obtaining money and property under false pretenses or by fraud from the State; penalties; definition.
§ 5A-3-31.	Corrupt actions, combinations, collusions, or conspiracies prohibited; penalties.
§ 5A-3-32.	Power of director to suspend right to bid; notice of suspension.
§ 5A-3-33.	Review of suspension by secretary.
§ 5A-3-33a.	[Repealed.]
§ 5A-3-33b.	Scope.
§ 5A-3-33c.	Duties.
§ 5A-3-33d.	Grounds for debarment.
§ 5A-3-33e.	Debarment procedure.
§ 5A-3-33f.	Effects of debarment.
§ 5A-3-34.	Authority over inventories and property.
§ 5A-3-35.	Submission of annual inventories.
§ 5A-3-36.	Inventory of removable property.
§ 5A-3-37.	Reciprocal preference; preference for resident vendors for certain contracts.
§ 5A-3-37a.	[Repealed.]
§ 5A-3-38.	[Repealed.]
§ 5A-3-39.	[Repealed.]
§ 5A-3-40.	[Repealed.]
§ 5A-3-40a.	[Repealed.]
§ 5A-3-41.	[Repealed.]
§ 5A-3-42.	[Repealed.]
§ 5A-3-43.	State agency for surplus property created.
§ 5A-3-44.	Authority and duties of state agency for surplus property.
§ 5A-3-45.	Disposition of surplus state property; semiannual report; application of proceeds from sale.
§ 5A-3-46.	Warehousing, transfer, etc., charges.
§ 5A-3-47.	Department of Agriculture and other agencies exempted.
§ 5A-3-48.	Travel rules; exceptions.
§ 5A-3-49.	[Repealed.]
§ 5A-3-50.	Acquiring and disposing of vehicles and aircraft.
§ 5A-3-51.	Maintenance and service to vehicles and aircraft.

§ 5A-3-52.	Division; fund.
§ 5A-3-53.	Enforcement of travel management regulations.
§ 5A-3-54.	[Repealed.]
§ 5A-3-55.	[Repealed.]
§ 5A-3-55a.	[Repealed.]
§ 5A-3-56.	Preference for the use of domestic steel products in state contract projects; exceptions; civil penalties.
§ 5A-3-57.	Buy American task force; study; report.
§ 5A-3-58.	Creation of the Purchasing Improvement Fund.
§ 5A-3-59.	Small, women, and minority-owned businesses.
§ 5A-3-60.	Annual purchasing training.
§5A-3-61.	Standardization.
§5A-3-62.	Prohibited contract clauses.

B. Other Applicable Statutes

1. Preference for Use of Domestic Aluminum, Glass, and Steel in Public Works Contracts

Only domestic aluminum, glass, or steel products shall be supplied for a public works contract or subcontract, unless a spending officer determines, in writing, after the receipt of offers or bids, that the cost of domestic aluminum, glass, or steel products is unreasonable or inconsistent with the public interest or that such domestic products are not produced in sufficient quantities to meet the contract requirements. This applies to any public works contract estimated to cost more than $50,000; and in the case of steel, any public works contract estimated to cost more than $50,000 or requiring more than 10,000 pounds of steel products. Regulation mandates that a price differential in excess of 20 percent between domestic and foreign sources is considered unreasonable. (West Virginia Code § 5-19-1 *et seq*. See also related regulations at West Virginia Code of State Rules § 148-10-1 *et seq.*)

2. West Virginia Jobs Act

West Virginia Code section 21-1C-1 *et seq.*: Pursuant to the legislative findings for this act, residents of local labor markets should be employed for the construction of public improvement projects that directly utilize taxpayer funding, in whole or in part. The act requires employers to hire at least 75 percent of employees for public improvement construction projects from the local labor market. (West Virginia Code § 21-1C-4.)

3. Wages for Construction of Public Improvements

The West Virginia Legislature repealed the state's prevailing wage statute in 2015. Bills to reestablish the prevailing wage for certain state contracts have been introduced, most recently in February 2022, but the prevailing wage law remains repealed.

4. Prohibition on Contracting with Party in Default with State

A state agency may not grant or renew any contract with any party who is in default with the Bureau of Employment Programs, Unemployment Compensation Division, with regard to required quarterly reports, payments, interest, and penalties. (West Virginia Code § 5A-3-10a(b).)

5. Lobbying

West Virginia Code section 6B-3-1 *et seq.* sets forth registration and other requirements, including registration fees, for those engaging in any lobbying activity. Persons must register before engaging in any lobbying activity, or within 30 days after being employed as a lobbyist, whichever occurs first.

6. Ethics Commission

West Virginia Code section 6B-2-1 *et seq.*: The Ethics Commission is the body charged with proposing and administering rules pertaining to conflicts of interest of, and disclosure of financial interests by, public officials, including receiving, initiating, and investigating complaints of alleged violations.

7. Pay-to-Play Law

Under West Virginia Code section 3-8-12(d), a person entering into a contract with the state may not (1) directly or indirectly make any contribution to any political party, committee, or candidate for public office in the state of West Virginia or to any person for political purposes or use during the period of negotiation or performance of the contract; or (2) solicit any contributions for any purpose during any period.

II. Regulations

The Purchasing Division Procedures Handbook provides valuable information on procedures for state procurement. The Handbook is current as of July 1, 2020, and is available online at http://www.state.wv.us/admin/purchase/handbook/2020/handbook.pdf.

Relevant portions of the West Virginia Code of State Rules are listed below:

§ 148-1-1 *et seq.*	Purchasing Division
§ 148-11-1 *et seq.*	Design-Build Procurement Regulations

III. Source Selection

All requisitions for commodities and services over $25,000 must be submitted to the Purchasing Division for formal competitive bidding. The Purchasing Division will review the bid specifications; select prospective bidders (in addition to those recommended by the agency); advertise in the *West Virginia Purchasing Bulletin*; request and receive bids; evaluate bids; and award the purchase to the lowest responsible bidder. The general methods of procurement include the following:

A. Emergency Purchasing

West Virginia Code section 5A-3-15: The director may authorize, in writing, a state spending unit to purchase in the open market, without filing requisition or estimate, specific commodities for immediate delivery to meet bona fide emergencies arising from unforeseen causes, including delays by contractors, delays in transportation, and unanticipated volume of work. A report of any such purchase, together with a record of the competitive bids upon which it was based, must be submitted at once to the director by the head of the state spending unit concerned, together with a full account of the circumstances of the emergency. Such report must be entered on a record and will be open to public inspection.

B. Small Purchasing

The director of purchasing may purchase up to $25,000 on the open market but will, wherever possible, obtain at least three competitive bids; the director may authorize spending units to purchase commodities, printing, and services on $2,500 or less without competition. (West Virginia Code § 5A-3-11.) In accordance with the West Virginia Code of State Rules, the Purchasing Division has delegated the ability to process procurements of $25,000 or less to state agencies. (West Virginia Purchasing Division Procedures Handbook § 5.1.)

C. Sole Source Procurement

The director may make a direct (sole source) award if (1) the spending unit requests a direct award in writing; (2) the spending unit provides written justification showing that the direct award is in the best interest of the state; (3) the spending unit provides written confirmation that competition is not available because there is no other source for the commodity or service, or that no other source would be willing or able to replace the existing source without a detrimental effect on the spending unit, the existence of a detrimental effect being determined by the director in his or her sole discretion; (4) the director publicly advertises a notice of intent to make a direct award without competition in the state's official bid notification system, as well as any other public advertisement that the director deems appropriate, for no less than ten business days; and (5) no other vendor expresses an interest in providing the commodity or service in question. (West Virginia Code § 5A-3-10c.)

D. Solicitation of Bids

The Purchasing Division utilizes various methods to solicit competition from responsible vendors. The two most often used for goods and services are requests for quotations (RFQs) and best value procurement (requests for proposals (RFPs) and expressions of interest (EOIs)), but there are special procedures for procurement in regard to architectural and engineering services, design-build contracts, and construction contracts. Commodities may also be procured through reverse auctions.

1. RFQs

This method is used to acquire most commodities and services, including construction. When the RFQ method is used, competitive bids are received, properly evaluated, and an award is made to the lowest responsible bidder who meets specifications, in accordance with West Virginia Code section 5A-3-11(e). Similarly, under West Virginia Code section 5-22-1(c), an RFQ for construction projects exceeding $25,000 in total cost must be awarded to the lowest qualified responsible bidder. In both cases, the award is completely objective, going to the lowest bid submission meeting the required specifications (also referred to as mandatory requirements). If a mandatory requirement is not met, then that bid is disqualified. After a proper evaluation, if an award is made to other than the lowest responsible bidder, a thorough written justification signed by the evaluator(s) must be inserted into the file and retained for public record and inspection.

2. Best Value Procurement

This method involves the use of RFPs and is the method used when the method of achieving an objective is not well known, making the development of mandatory requirements difficult to acquire services where the specifications or scope of work may not be well defined. Under this method, the lowest price is not the sole factor in determining the award. Best value procurement techniques include RFPs and EOIs, and are used to solicit proposals from potential bidders, taking into consideration the vendors' ability, resources, experience, and proposed methods to provide the required services. Best value procurement awards are awarded to the highest scoring responsive and responsible bidder based on criteria set forth in the solicitation and information contained in the proposals submitted in response. The award is based upon a subjective technical evaluation, where the agency first determines that all mandatory requirements have been met. It then assigns a subjective point value to the vendor's response to the non-mandatory specifications, followed by an objective point value based on the vendor's cost proposal and the cost score evaluation formula. Those criteria include, but are not limited to, price and the total cost of acquiring, operating, maintaining, and supporting a commodity or service over its projected lifetime, as well as technical criteria (e.g., evaluated technical merit, past performance, relative technical merit, utility of novel or unrequested items offered, and evaluated probability of timely, high-quality performance that accomplishes the business objectives set forth in the solicitation). (West Virginia Code § 5A-3-10b.)

a. RFPs

(i) Use: RFPs are limited to procurements with a minimum estimated value of $100,000 unless the director approves their use for small purchases in writing.

(ii) Format: All RFPs must follow the standard format defined by the Purchasing Division, which is provided in the Purchasing Division Procedures Handbook. An RFP template is available at http://www.state.wv.us/admin/purchase/forms.html.

(iii) Evaluation Criteria: All evaluation criteria must be clearly defined in the specifications section and be based on a 100-point total score, with technical criteria comprising 70 points and cost 30 points.

(iv) Proposal Format and Content: Proposals must consist of two distinct parts: technical and cost. The cost portion is to be sealed in a separate envelope and will not be opened until after the technical evaluation has been approved by an internal review committee.

(v) Proposal Submission: The vendor is responsible for submitting a complete and accurate proposal (both technical and cost) to the Purchasing Division by the specified bid opening date and time. Acceptable delivery methods include faxed bids provided the entirety of the faxed bid is received by the Purchasing Division prior to the bid opening date and time; hand delivery of paper bids; and paper bids delivered by the U.S. Postal Service or other courier. Bids delivered by U.S. Postal Service or other courier are only considered received when the Purchasing Division has the physical possession of the bid.

(vi) Technical Bid Opening: The Purchasing Division will open only the technical proposals on the date and time specified in the RFP. The Purchasing Division representative will read aloud the names of those who responded to the solicitation and confirm that the original package contained a separately sealed cost proposal.

(vi) Technical Evaluation: After the technical bids are opened, the evaluation committee will begin its technical evaluation, which must be completed prior to the cost bid opening. The evaluation committee must review the technical proposals, ensure compliance with mandatory requirements of the RFP, assign appropriate points using the RFP Technical Scoring Spreadsheet, and make a final written consensus scoring recommendation as soon as possible using the RFP Technical Evaluation Committee Scoring Memorandum (WV-112).

(viii) Cost Bid Opening: Once the technical evaluation is approved by the internal review committee, the Purchasing Division will schedule a time and date to publicly open and read aloud the cost proposals. The agency and the vendors will be notified of this date.

(ix) Cost Evaluation, Approval, and Award: After the cost proposals have been opened, the agency evaluation committee will review the cost proposals and using the cost formula assign an appropriate cost score to each proposal that has not been disqualified. The evaluation committee will then combine the technical and cost scores to make a final consensus recommendation for contract award to the Purchasing Division. Assuming the Purchasing Division concurs with the recommendation, the contract will be processed for award.

b. EOIs

(i) Use: The Purchasing Division uses EOIs primarily in the selection of architectural and engineering services, where the EOI method of procurement is required for projects estimated to exceed $250,000 in cost. Additional procedures for selection of these professional services are required in accordance with West Virginia Code section 5G-1-1 *et seq.*; these procedures are designed to select on the basis of demonstrated competence and qualification.

(ii) Format: For projects expected to exceed $250,000, state agencies must use a standard EOI format, which is provided in the Purchasing Division Procedures Handbook.

(iii) Evaluation and Award: After the bid opening of EOI responses, the evaluation committee must complete the following steps: initial evaluation to develop a "short list" (minimum of three firms) of firms best qualified to perform the desired service; interview of firms on short list; ranking the short list in order of preference; and negotiating a contract with the highest ranked firm first, moving down the list until a satisfactory contract is negotiated.

3. Reverse Auctions

Reverse auctions may be used to procure commodities (but not services), if the director determines their use would be fair, economical, in the best interests of the state, and the commodities to be procured are subject to low price volatility; have common specifications that are not complex; vary little between suppliers; are sourced primarily based on price with limited ancillary considerations; require little collaboration from suppliers; and are sold by a large, competitive supply base. A "reverse auction" is defined as a process by which bidders compete to provide commodities in an open and interactive market. Reverse auction bids are opened and made public upon receipt by the director, and then bidders are given the opportunity to submit revised bids until the bidding process is complete. The contract is awarded to the lowest responsible bidder. (West Virginia Code § 5A-3-10d.) All reverse auctions must be preceded by the prequalification of vendors. (West Virginia Code of State Rules § 148-1-11.3.) Prequalified vendors are granted access to participate in the reverse auction and may submit bids until the time for bidding has expired. (West Virginia Code of State Rules § 148-1-11.4.) The lowest responsible bidder within the time period allowed for the reverse auction will be awarded the contract. (West Virginia Code of State Rules § 148-1-11.5.)

4. Design-Build

This is a best value procurement tool that combines project design and construction within a single contract when applied to building renovations and new construction. The Design-Build Procurement Act and accompanying regulations (West Virginia Code § 5-22A-1 *et seq.*; West Virginia Code of State Rules § 148-11-1 *et seq.*) set forth specific instances in which this process may be utilized. Agencies must obtain a letter of approval from the Design-Build Board, which is chaired by the secretary of the Department of Administration, prior to issuing an invitation for qualifications. (West Virginia Code of State Rules § 148-11-5.)

5. Construction Contracts

A public entity must solicit bids for every construction project exceeding $25,000. Following the solicitation of bids, the construction contract will be awarded to the lowest qualified responsible bidder who furnishes a sufficient performance and payment bond. "Lowest qualified responsible bidder" means the bidder that bids the lowest price and that meets, at a minimum, all the following statutory requirements in connection with the bidder's response to the bid solicitation. The bidder must certify that it (1) is ready, able, and willing to timely furnish the labor and materials required to complete the contract; (2) is in compliance with all applicable laws of the state; and (3) has supplied a valid bid bond or other surety authorized or approved by the public entity. For contracts valued in excess of $250,000 for the construction, alteration, decoration, painting, or improvement of a new or existing building or structure, the apparent low bidder must submit a list of all subcontractors who will perform more than $25,000 of work on the project including labor and materials. This provision does not apply to other construction projects such as highway, mine reclamation, water, or sewer projects. Failure to submit the subcontractor list within one business day after the deadline for submitting bids will result in disqualification of the bid. (West Virginia Code § 5-22-1 *et seq.*)

IV. Bid Protests and Contract Disputes

A. Bid Protests

The Purchasing Division's Legislative Rules and Regulations (West Virginia Code of State Rules § 148-1-1 through § 148-1-11) provide participating vendors with the right to protest specifications and purchase order awards. (See West Virginia Code of State Rules § 148-1-8.)

1. Form and Filing

Protests based on bid specifications must be submitted no later than five working days prior to bid opening. Protest of purchase order or contract awards must be submitted no later than five working days after the award. The vendor is responsible for knowing the bid opening and award dates. Protests received after these dates may be rejected at the option of the director.

All protests will be submitted in writing to the Purchasing Division and contain the following information: the name and address of the protestor; the requisition, purchase order, or contract numbers; a statement of the grounds of protest; supporting documentation (if necessary); and the resolution or relief sought. Failure to submit this information will be grounds for rejection of the protest by the director of the Purchasing Division.

2. Stay

Continuation or delay of the purchase order or contract award while the protest is considered is at the discretion of the purchasing director.

3. Decision

The director or his or her designee will review the matter of protest and issue a written decision. A hearing may be conducted at the option of the purchasing director or assigned designee. (West Virginia Code of State Rules § 148-1-8, subsec. 8.2.1.)

4. Judicial or Administrative Proceeding

The Purchasing Division may refuse to review any protests when the matter involved is the subject of litigation before a court of competent jurisdiction; if the merits have previously been decided by a court of competent jurisdiction; or if it has been decided in a previous protest by the Purchasing Division. (West Virginia Code of State Rules § 148-1-8, subsec. 8.2.2.)

B. Bid Protest Appeals

After the director issues a final decision, a protestor may file a writ of mandamus or a writ of prohibition within the original jurisdiction of either a West Virginia circuit court or the Supreme Court of Appeals. (West Virginia Code §§ 51-1-3, 51-2-2(c)(2); see, e.g., *Wiseman Construction Co., Inc. v. Maynard C. Smith Construction Co., Inc.*, 779 S.E.2d 893 (W. Va. 2015) (syl. pt. 1).)

C. Contract Disputes

The West Virginia Legislature renamed the West Virginia Court of Claims the Legislative Claims Commission in 2017. The Commission hears claims against the state for monetary damages, including all contract claims against the state or any of its agencies. (West Virginia Code § 14-2-13.) The Commission's Rules of Practice and Procedure may be found at https://claims.wvlegislature.gov/rules-of-practice-and-procedure/.

1. Form and Filing

To begin the contract claims process, the claimant shall file written notice with the clerk of the Commission that shall include sufficient detail to identify the claimant;

circumstances giving rise to the claim; the substance of the claim; and the state agency concerned. The clerk shall then send a copy of the notice to the state agency concerned, and a copy to the Office of the Attorney General. Note that if a claim arises under existing appropriations, the legislature's Joint Committee on Government and Finance must first approve the placement of the claim on the Commission's docket. (West Virginia Code § 14-2-19.)

2. Government Response

The attorney general must, within 20 days after a copy of the notice has been furnished his or her office, file with the clerk a notice in writing, either denying the claim, requesting postponement of proceedings to permit negotiations with the claimant, or otherwise setting forth reasons for further investigation of the claim, and furnish the claimant or claimant's counsel of record a copy thereof. Otherwise, after said 20-day period, the Commission may order the claim placed upon its regular docket for hearing.

3. Negotiations

During negotiations and pending hearing, the state agency, represented by the attorney general, shall, if possible, reach an agreement with the claimant regarding the facts upon which the claim is based so as to avoid the necessity for introducing evidence at the hearing. If the parties are unable to agree upon the facts, an attempt shall be made to stipulate the questions of fact in issue.

4. Briefing

Claimants or their counsel, and the attorney general, may file with the Commission, for its consideration, a brief on any question involved in a claim, provided a copy of said brief is also presented to and furnished the opposing party or counsel. Reply briefs shall be filed within 15 days.

5. Witnesses

Claimants and state agencies desiring to have subpoenas for witnesses must file with the clerk a memorandum in writing giving the style and number of the claim and setting forth the names of such witnesses, and thereupon such subpoenas shall be issued and delivered to the person requesting the same. Requests for subpoenas for witnesses must be furnished the clerk in advance of the hearing date so such subpoenas may be issued in ample time before the hearing. The party by whom or at whose instance the witness is subpoenaed shall pay witness fees and mileage (where transportation is not furnished to any witness subpoenaed by or at the instance of either the claimant or the state agency).

6. Discovery

All discovery shall be conducted in accordance with the provisions of West Virginia Code section 14-2-15. Discovery may be used in a case pending before the Commission in the same manner that discovery is conducted pursuant to the Rules of Civil Procedure for trial courts of record, Rules 26 through 36. The Commission may compel discovery and impose sanctions for a failure to make discovery, in the same manner as a court is authorized to do under the provisions of Rule 37 of the Rules of Civil

Procedure for trial courts of record: provided that the Commission shall not find a person in contempt for failure to comply with an order compelling discovery.

7. Hearing

The Commission shall conduct a hearing to disclose all material facts and issues of liability and may examine or cross-examine witnesses. The Commission may call witnesses or require evidence not produced by the parties; the Commission may call expert witnesses and compensate those experts for their services in an amount not to exceed $3,500 per expert; the Commission may stipulate the questions to be argued by the parties; and the Commission may continue the hearing until some subsequent time to permit a more complete presentation of the claim. It also may stipulate the questions to be argued by the parties; and may continue the hearing to permit a more complete presentation of the claim. (West Virginia Code § 14-2-16.)

8. Commission's Determination

After the close of the hearing, the Commission shall consider the claim and conclude its determination, if possible, within 60 days. (West Virginia Code § 14-2-16.) The clerk of the Commission shall collect and edit the approved claims, awards, and statements, prepare them for submission to the legislature in the form of an annual report, and prepare them for publication. Claims and awards shall be separately classified as follows: (1) approved claims and awards not satisfied but referred to the legislature for final consideration and appropriation; (2) approved claims and awards satisfied by payments out of regular appropriations; (3) approved claims and awards satisfied by payment out of a special appropriation made by the legislature to pay claims arising during the fiscal year; and (4) claims rejected by the Commission with the reasons therefor.

a. Awards Arising under Existing Appropriations

If the Commission determines the claim arising under existing appropriations should be paid, the court shall certify the award to the appropriate state agency, the state auditor, and the governor. The governor may then instruct the auditor to pay the award and to charge the amount to the proper appropriation. (West Virginia Code § 14-2-19.)

b. Awards Arising under Special Appropriations

The legislature may make a special appropriation for the payment of claims against the state accrued or arising under the ensuing fiscal year. If the Commission approves a claim arising under such appropriation, the clerk shall certify the claim and award to the state auditor. The auditor shall issue his or her warrant to the treasurer in favor of the claimant. (West Virginia Code § 14-2-20.)

c. Awards Arising under Past Appropriations

If the awarded damages relate to a past appropriation, the clerk certifies to the Department of Administration, Division of Finance a list of awards recommended by the court to the legislature for appropriation. The governor then includes the awards in his proposed budget. (West Virginia Code § 14-2-23.) Payment is then contingent on the legislature's confirmation of the award and appropriation of money, which can take up to two years.

9. Shortened Procedures

Under certain limited circumstances, if the relevant agency concurs in the claim, and the claim does not arise under an appropriation for the current fiscal year, is less than $3,000, and has been approved by the attorney general, the Commission may conduct a shortened procedure. (West Virginia Code § 14-2-17.) There is a similar shortened procedure for road condition claims. (West Virginia Code § 14-2-17a.)

10. Appeals Process

Although the Claims Commission is part of the legislative branch, its decisions may be challenged by filing a writ of mandamus or a writ of prohibition within the original jurisdiction of either a West Virginia circuit court or the Supreme Court of Appeals. (West Virginia Code §§ 51-1-3, 51-2-2(c)(2) & (c)(4); see *Wiseman Construction Co., Inc. v. Maynard C. Smith Construction Co., Inc.*, 779 S.E.2d 893 (W. Va. 2015) (syl. pt. 1).)

D. Suspension and Debarment

1. Grounds for Debarment

The Department of Administration Purchasing Division sets out the grounds for debarment in West Virginia Code section 5A-3-33d. Grounds for debarment are conviction of an offense involving fraud or a felony offense in connection with obtaining or attempting to obtain a public contract or subcontract; conviction of any federal or state antitrust statute relating to the submission of offers; conviction of an offense involving embezzlement, theft, forgery, bribery, falsification or destruction of records, making false statements, or receiving stolen property in connection with the performance of a contract; conviction of a felony offense demonstrating a lack of business integrity or business honesty that affects the present responsibility of the vendor or subcontractor; default on obligations owed to the state; the vendor is not in good standing with a licensing board, in that the vendor is not licensed when licensure is required by the law of this state, or the vendor has been found to be in violation of an applicable licensing law after notice, opportunity to be heard, and other due process required by law; the vendor is an active and knowing participant in dividing or planning procurements to circumvent the $25,000 threshold requiring a sealed bid or otherwise avoid the use of a sealed bid; or violation of the terms of a public contract or subcontract.

2. Debarment Procedure

Debarment procedure is outlined in West Virginia Code section 5A-3-33e. The director first obtains lists of vendors declared ineligible under federal laws and regulation and lists of vendors who are in default on state obligations. The director then initiates debarment proceedings with respect to such vendors, except when good cause is shown, which includes evidence that the vendor has become responsible. The director may also initiate debarment proceedings if he or she finds probable cause for debarment for any ground set forth in West Virginia Code section 5A-3-33d. Additionally, the director will initiate debarment proceedings when any state agency requests debarment of a vendor and the director finds that probable cause for debarment exists.

The vendor will be notified by certified mail, return receipt requested, of the reasons for the proposed debarment in sufficient detail to put the vendor on notice of the conduct or transactions upon which the proposed debarment is based; the causes relied upon for the proposed debarment; that within 30 working days after receipt of the notice, the vendor may submit in writing information and argument in opposition to the proposed debarment; the procedures governing debarment decision-making; and the potential effect of the proposed debarment. In the event a vendor wishes to contest the debarment decision, the director will decide the matter in accordance with the provisions of West Virginia Code section 29A-5-1 *et seq*. Debarment may be in part or in full, extending either to all commodities and services of the vendor, or limited to specific commodities or services.

3. Effects of Debarment

The effects of debarment are outlined in West Virginia Code section 5A-3-33f. Unless the director determines in writing that there is a compelling reason to do otherwise, the state and its subdivisions may not solicit offers from, award contracts to, or consent to subcontract with a debarred vendor during the debarment period. The contracting officer may not exercise an option to renew or otherwise extend a current contract with a debarred vendor, or a contract that is being performed in any part by a debarred subcontractor, unless the director approves the action in writing, based on compelling reasons for exercise of the option or extension.

The director may reduce the period or extent of debarment, upon the vendor's request supported by documentation, for (1) newly discovered material evidence; (2) reversal of the conviction or judgment upon which debarment was based; (3) elimination of the causes for which the debarment was imposed; or (4) other good cause shown, including that the vendor has become responsible. The director may extend the debarment period for an additional period if the director determines that the extension is necessary to protect the interests of the state.

4. Suspended Vendor List

In the event that a vendor fails to honor any contractual term or condition, the director may suspend, for a period not to exceed one year, the right of a vendor to bid on state purchases when there is reason to believe the vendor has violated any of the provisions, terms, or conditions of a contract, the purchasing statutes, or the rules and regulations of the Department of Administration. (West Virginia Code § 5A-3-32.) Vendors will be notified of their suspension by a letter posted by certified mail describing the reason for the suspension. (West Virginia Code § 5A-3-32.) A suspended vendor may appeal the decision of the director to the secretary of administration, who has the authority to set aside the suspension. (West Virginia Code § 5A-3-33.)

The following are adequate grounds for suspension: a vendor has exhibited a pattern of poor performance in fulfilling his or her contractual obligations to the state; the vendor has breached any contract entered into pursuant to the provisions of West Virginia Code section 5A-3-1 *et seq.*, or Legislative Rule; or the vendor has been convicted of any federal, state, or local crime punishable as a felony, directly related to the performance of a contract entered into pursuant to West Virginia Code section 5A-3-1 *et seq.*, or Legislative Rule. A list of vendors debarred by the West Virginia Purchasing Division may be found at http://www.state.wv.us/admin/purchase/debar.html.

V. Administrative and Judicial Review

A. Administrative Review

West Virginia's Purchasing Division is responsible for procurement of goods and services for the state government. All bid protests must be submitted to the Purchasing

Division. The purchasing director will review the protest, may conduct a hearing, and ultimately issue a written decision.

Information about the Purchasing Division is available at http://www.state.wv.us/admin/purchase/default.html.

B. Legislative Review

Created by an Act of the Legislature in 2017, the West Virginia Legislative Claims Commission hears claims against the state for money damages. Awards are made subject to final approval by the legislature. Upon request, the Commission also issues advisory opinions to state agencies.

Information about the Claims Commission, including summaries of its decisions, is available at https://www.wvlegislature.gov/Joint/courtofclaims.cfm.

C. Judicial Review

Disappointed bid protestors and claimants may file a writ of mandamus or a writ of prohibition under the original jurisdiction of either the circuit courts or the Supreme Court of Appeals. (West Virginia Code §§ 51-1-3, 51-2-2(c)(2) & (c)(4); see *Wiseman Construction Co., Inc. v. Maynard C. Smith Construction Co., Inc.*, 779 S.E.2d 893 (W. Va. 2015) (syl. pt. 1).)

Information about the West Virginia judicial system is available at http://www.courtswv.gov/.

VI. Extent of State's Adoption or Adaptation of ABA Model Procurement Code

The West Virginia statutory scheme does not follow the American Bar Association (ABA) Model Procurement Code.

VII. Cooperative Purchasing

A. Authority

In addition to statewide contracts (i.e., those between the state and a vendor and used by state agencies and some political subdivisions to purchase frequently used commodities and services), West Virginia law provides authority for "piggybacking" contracts/cooperative purchasing in West Virginia Code section 5A-3-19 and at West Virginia Code of State Rules section 148-1-7.8. "Piggybacking" and "cooperative purchasing" are terms that describe the use by West Virginia state agencies and political subdivisions of and/or adoption of an existing contract of another public entity, including federal agencies and agencies of other states.

B. Requirements

The requirements contained in the Code and the Rules have been compiled into the Cooperative Purchasing Request, Justification, and Approval form (WV-40), which is used by agencies to request permission to use cooperative purchasing. The form may be accessed at http://www.state.wv.us/admin/purchase/Documents/WV40.pdf. The authority to engage in cooperative purchasing does not apply to procurements of $25,000 or less.

Wisconsin Procurement Rules and Regulations

Prepared by Jeff H. Eckland
Eckland & Blando LLP
Email: jeckland@ecklandblando.com
With assistance from Mark J. Blando, Vince Reuter, and Robert Dube[1]

I. Statutory Reference

The Department of Administration has the general authority to contract for goods and services on behalf of all agencies in the state of Wisconsin. (See Wisconsin Statutes § 16.71(1) (2015).) These duties may be delegated, however, to any government agency, except contracts for information technology and telecommunications, which must be approved by the Department of Administration. (See *id.* § 16.71(1m).) Wisconsin's judicial and legislative branches are responsible for their own contracting duties. (See *id.* § 16.74 (2015).)

Wisconsin law governing the procurement of government contracts is located in several different chapters, sections, and subsections, according to the subject matter of the contract, and the government unit with authority over that subject matter.

The Wisconsin Constitution, Wisconsin Statutes, and Administrative Code can be found by searching the Wisconsin State Legislature Legislative Reference Bureau's website at https://legis.wisconsin.gov/LRB/.

A. Procurement/Purchasing Statutes

The relevant portions of the Wisconsin Statutes are listed below:

1. General State Procurement Statutes

§ 16.70 *et seq.* (2015).	Department of Administration, Purchasing

2. General Municipality Law

§ 66.0131 (1999).	Local Governmental Purchasing
§ 66.0135 (1999).	Interest on Late Payments
§ 66.0301 *et seq.* (2017).	Intergovernmental Cooperation
§ 66.0901 *et seq.* (2017).	Public Works, Contracts, Bids

1. Research, drafting, proofing, and citation assistance provided by Kenneth Cooper of Eckland & Blando LLP.

3. Procurement of Printing Services or Paper

§ 35.01 *et seq.* (2015).Publication and Distribution of Laws and Public Documents

4. Construction and Engineering Contracts

§ 13.48 (2013).	Long-Range Public Building Program
§ 13.488 (2017).	Building Commission; Powers and Duties
§ 84.001 *et seq.* (2001).	State Trunk Highways; Federal Aid
§ 85.01 *et seq.* (2005).	Department of Transportation
§ 779.135 (2005).	Construction Contracts, Form of Contract
§ 779.14 (2017).	Public Works, Form of Contract, Bond, Remedy
§ 779.15 (2005).	Public Improvements; Lien on Money, Bonds, or Warrants Due the Prime Contractor; Duty of Officials

B. Other Applicable Law

The relevant portions of the Wisconsin Statutes are listed below, unless noted otherwise:

1. Wisconsin Constitution Provisions

Art. I, § 12.	Interference with Contracts
Art. I, § 13.	Takings
Art. I, § 18.	Prohibition on Public Funds to Religious Bodies
Art. IV, § 25.	Stationery and Printing
Art. IV, § 27.	Suits against State
Art. VIII.	Finance

2. Administrative Procedure and Review

§ 227.01 *et seq.* (2019).	Administrative Procedure and Review
§ 68.001 *et seq.* (1975).	Municipal Administrative Procedure

3. Causes of Action

§ 895.46 (2013).	Tort Claims

4. Wisconsin Uniform Commercial Code

§ 402.101 *et seq.* (2019).	Wisconsin Uniform Commercial Code

5. Other Governmental Units

§ 62.15 (2017).	Cities—Public Works

6. Public Records and Open Meetings

§ 19.21 *et seq.* (2017).	Public Records and Property
§ 19.81 *et seq.* (1983).	Open Meetings of Government Bodies

7. Other Contracting Requirements

§ 985.01 *et seq*. (2016). Publication of Legal Notices, Official State Newspaper

8. Lobbying Laws

§ 13.61 *et seq*. (1989). Regulation of Lobbying

9. Ethics and Anti-Bribery Statutes

a. *Public Official Code of Conduct*

§ 19.41 *et seq*. (2015). Code of Ethics for Public Officials and Employees

b. *Bribery and Misconduct*

§ 946.10 *et seq*. (2019). Bribery and Official Misconduct

c. *Criminal Penalties*

§ 19.58 (2003). Criminal Penalties for Public Officials
§ 939.50(1)(h) (2019). Bribery as a Class H Felony
§ 939.50(3)(h) (2019). Penalty for Class H Felony

10. Managing Bid Documents and Records

§ 19.35 (2015). Access to Records; Fees
§ 19.36 (2017). Limitations upon Access and Withholding
§ 19.48 (2015). Duties of the Government Accountability Board

11. Appropriations and Budget Management

§ 20.901 (2015). Departmental Cooperation
§ 20.915 (1983). State Motor Vehicles and Aircraft

12. Employment Regulations

§ 103.49 (1999). Wage Rate on State Work

13. Affirmative Action Policies

§ 16.283 (2013). Disabled Veteran-Owned Businesses
§ 16.285 (2013). Women-Owned Businesses
§ 16.287 (2013). Minority-Owned Businesses

C. Opinions of Attorney General

By statute, the Wisconsin attorney general provides written opinions upon all questions of law submitted to him or her by the legislature or by the head of any department of state government and, under certain circumstances, to district attorneys and county corporation counsel. (See Wisconsin Statutes § 165.015 (1983); see also *id.*

§ 165.25(3).) Attorney general opinions on the meaning of a statute are accorded persuasive value when Wisconsin appellate courts have not yet definitively answered the question. (*Schill v. Wisconsin Rapids School District*, 786 N.W.2d 177, 205 (Wis. 2010).) Thus, while they may, Wisconsin courts are not obligated to follow the attorney general's opinion. (*State ex rel. Krueger v. Appleton Area School District Board of Education*, 898 N.W.2d 35, 45 n.14 (Wis. 2017).)

II. Regulations

The secretary of the Department of Administration is empowered by statute to promulgate rules for administering the department. (See Wisconsin Statutes § 16.004(1) (2017).) Wisconsin's Administrative Rules can be found at https://docs.legis.wisconsin.gov/code/admin_code.

Below is a listing of the Wisconsin Administrative Rules relating to the procurement of government contracts:

Wisconsin Administrative Code [Adm] ch. 5 (2015).	**Procurement Requisitions**
§ 5.01.	Authority
§ 5.02.	Definitions
§ 5.03.	Initiating Procurement Actions
§ 5.04.	Request for Purchasing Authority
Wisconsin Administrative Code [Adm] ch. 6 (2015).	**Definitions**
Wisconsin Administrative Code [Adm] ch. 7 (2015).	**Solicitation of Bids and Proposals**
§ 7.01.	Standard Terms and Conditions
§ 7.02.	Special Conditions of Bid
§ 7.03.	Specifications
§ 7.04.	Amendments to Request for Bids or Proposals
§ 7.05.	Bidders List
§ 7.06.	Publication of Notice
§ 7.07.	American-Made Materials
§ 7.08.	Bonds and Sureties
§ 7.09.	Competitive Negotiation
§ 7.10.	Noncompetitive Negotiation
Wisconsin Administrative Code [Adm] ch. 8 (2015).	**Bidding Process and Exceptions to Bidding**
§ 8.01.	Simplified Bidding
§ 8.02.	Withdrawal and Modification of Bids
§ 8.03.	Basis for Awards as a Result of Bidding

§ 8.04.	Public Opening and Reading of Bids and Proposals
§ 8.05.	Waiver of Bidding for Sealed Bids
§ 8.06.	General Waiver
§ 8.07.	Recordkeeping Documentation
§ 8.08.	Exceptions to Bidding
Wisconsin Administrative Code [Adm] ch. 9 (2015).	**Bidders List Registration Fee and Subscription Service**
§ 9.01.	Authority
§ 9.02.	Purpose
§ 9.03.	Definitions
§ 9.04.	Fee
§ 9.05.	Bidders List Registration Fee
§ 9.06.	Subscription Fee
§ 9.07.	Refunds
Wisconsin Administrative Code [Adm] ch. 10 (2015).	**Contractual Services**
§ 10.01.	Authority
§ 10.02.	Purpose
§ 10.03.	Definitions
§ 10.035.	Cost-Benefit Analysis
§ 10.037.	Continued Appropriateness of Contracting
§ 10.038.	Submittal of Cost-Benefit Analysis
§ 10.039.	Effective Date
§ 10.04.	Prior Approval
§ 10.05.	Justification
§ 10.06.	Competitive Bidding
§ 10.07.	Waivers
§ 10.08.	Competitive Negotiation
§ 10.09.	Noncompetitive Negotiation
§ 10.10.	Disclosure
§ 10.11.	Purchase Orders
§ 10.12.	Contract Administration
§ 10.13.	Delegation of Authority
§ 10.14.	Performance of Contractors
§ 10.15.	Appeals
§ 10.16.	Exceptions

Wisconsin Administrative Code [Adm] ch. 20 (2015).	**Selecting and Contracting Architect/Engineer Services**
§ 20.01.	Authority
§ 20.02.	Definitions
§ 20.03.	Convening of Selection Committee
§ 20.04.	Selection Procedures
§ 20.05.	Selection by Nomination
§ 20.06.	Selection by Advertisement
§ 20.07.	Eligibility and Qualification Review
§ 20.08.	Interview
§ 20.09.	Contract Processing
§ 20.10.	Performance Reporting

Wisconsin Administrative Code [Adm] ch. 21 (2015).	**Advertising, Bidding, and Award of Construction Contracts**
§ 21.01.	Authority
§ 21.02.	Definitions
§ 21.03.	Advertising
§ 21.04.	Issuance of Addenda
§ 21.05	Submittal and Receipt of Bids
§ 21.06.	Withdrawal of Bids
§ 21.07.	Bid Opening
§ 21.08.	Rejection of Bids
§ 21.09.	Award of Contracts

Wisconsin Administrative Code [Adm] ch. 50 (2015).	**Contract Compliance**
§ 50.01.	Authority
§ 50.02.	Purpose
§ 50.03.	Definitions
§ 50.04.	Contract Provisions
§ 50.05.	Affirmative Action Plan
§ 50.06.	Compliance Review
§ 50.07.	Records
§ 50.08.	Complaint Procedure
§ 50.09.	Investigations
§ 50.10.	Hearings

III. Executive Orders

The governor of Wisconsin may issue executive orders, and they may be found at https://evers.wi.gov/Pages/Newsroom/Executive-Orders.aspx.

IV. Source Selection

A. Procurement Policy and Regulatory Definitions

1. State Bidding Policy

The competitive bidding process is the preferred method for selecting suppliers of goods and services to the state of Wisconsin. (See Wisconsin Administrative Code Adm § 10.06; *see also* Wisconsin Statutes § 16.75 (2021) (alternatives to competitive bidding are provided as exceptions).) The state and its agencies are permitted to use competitive bidding when the cost exceeds $25,000 and are required to do so when the cost exceeds $50,000. (Wisconsin Statutes § 16.75(b) (2021).) This is performed by either (1) soliciting sealed bids, to be opened publicly at a certain date, or (2) soliciting bids through an electronic auction. (*Id.*) Simplified acquisition procedures are available for contracts of $25,000 or less, or when some other statutory exception to competitive bidding exists. (*Id.*)

Unless a statutory exception applies, all government contracts for materials, supplies, equipment, and contractual services to be provided to any agency shall be awarded to the "lowest responsible bidder." (*Id.*) This takes into consideration life-cycle cost estimates (defined in Wisconsin Statutes § 16.75(1m)), the location of the agency, the quantities of the articles to be supplied, their conformity with the specifications, the purposes for which they are required, and the date of delivery. (*Id.*)

2. Legal and Public Notice Requirement

All procurements with an estimated cost over $25,000 must be advertised. (*Id.*) Notice will be posted at least seven days before bids are due. (*Id.*) Agencies post requests for proposals (RFPs) and bids on Wisconsin's procurement website, VendorNet, which can be located at https://vendornet.wi.gov/.

3. Selected Regulatory Definitions

Competitive Bidding: "offer of prices by individuals or firms competing to supply specified goods." (Wisconsin Administrative Code Adm § 6.01(5) (1986).)

Lowest Responsible Bidder: "the person or firm submitting the competitive bid with the lowest price that meets the specifications contained in the requests for bids. In establishing the lowest responsible bidder, all of the following factors may be considered: the financial ability to provide the services required or to complete the contract; the skill, judgment, experience, and resources to complete the contract; the necessary facilities, staff, personnel, and equipment to complete the contract; the demonstrated ability to satisfactorily perform the work or provide the materials in a prompt, conscientious manner; the demonstrated ability to comply in situations where the award is contingent on special considerations subject to the nature of the services or contract required; and any other factor determined to be relevant in assessing the bidder's ability to supply as required." (*Id.* § 6.01(9).)

Solicitation: "the process of notifying prospective bidders that the state wishes to receive bids or proposals on goods. The process may consist of public advertising, the mailing of requests for bids, posting of notices, telephone calls to prospective bidders, verbal notices, or any other means that makes the state's intentions known to potential suppliers." (*Id.* § 6.01(15).)

Specification: the "description of what the procuring agency requires and, consequently, what a bidder must offer to be considered for an award. A specification may be a description of the physical or functional characteristics, or the nature of a supply. It may include a description of any requirement for inspecting, testing, or preparing a supply item for delivery, the necessary performance criteria, and a description of the procedures to be followed when submitting and evaluating bids." (*Id.* § 6.01(16).)

B. Competitive Bidding

1. Sealed Bid Process

The sealed bid process is the preferred method for procuring contractual services, and shall be used in every case that permits the preparation of specifications or standards. (See *id.* § 10.06 (1983).) All requests for sealed bid proposals must specify the unique specifications for the particular project, and the condition that it will be awarded to the lowest responsible bidder. (See *id.* § 7.03 (1986).)

Procedures for the sealed process are found in the official State Procurement Manual, issued by the Department of Administration, State Bureau of Procurement, and found through VendorNet at https://doa.wi.gov/ProcurementManual/Documents/PRO-304.pdf. Significantly, receipt of a bid by the mail system does not constitute a receipt of a bid by the purchasing office. (Department of Administration, State Procurement Manual: The Procurement Process (2019).) Bidders may withdraw their bid at any time prior to opening. (*Id.*) Also, bidders may adjust bids after submission, but before being opened, by requesting that their bid be returned. Bidders then may resubmit the bid after making the desired changes. (*Id.*) All bids will be opened and recorded by the state. (See Wisconsin Administrative Code Adm § 8.04-07 (1986).)

2. Simplified Bidding Procedures

"Simplified bidding" is an alternative to the general sealed bidding process for bid proposals with an estimated cost of $25,000 or less. (See Wisconsin Statutes § 16.75(1)(c) (2021); see also *id.* § 16.75(1)(b)(3) (simplified bidding also available by auction).) With simplified bidding, unless impracticable, bids are either solicited from three or more vendors, or requests are directly delivered to three or more vendors. (See Wisconsin Administrative Code Adm § 8.01(a), (b) (1986).) The agency receives price quotations from these vendors, and after considering the quoted price from the vendor best able to supply, it enters into the contract. (See *id.* § 8.03.)

3. Waiver of Bidding Process

"Any procurement of contractual services that is not made by competitive bidding requires a waiver . . . ." (*Id.* § 10.07(1) (1983).) A waiver request must "contain a complete explanation of why competitive bidding cannot be used and the proposed" procedure. (*Id.*) Waivers will be authorized when in the best interest of the state. (*Id.* § 8.05(1).) For procurements estimated at $10,000 or less, one of the following conditions may justify a request to waive normal bidding processes:

1. Uniqueness: A product or service is one of a kind or from only one supplier.
2. Discount: The purchase of used equipment offers a significant discount.

3. Patent or Propriety: The product provides the state a superior or necessary utility that cannot be obtained by others.
4. Intrinsic Value: The product is unique as determined by its historic, artistic, or educational value.
5. Emergency: The risk of human suffering or substantial damage requires immediate action.

(*Id.* § 8.05(2).) Bids estimated at $10,000 or more cannot be delegated to the Department of Administration. (*Id.* § 8.05(1).) Further, repetitive and similar transactions between the state and one vendor may be consolidated into a general request for prior approval and therefore bypass the sealed bidding process. (*Id.* § 8.06.)

C. Negotiations

1. Competitive Negotiation

Competitive negotiation, also known as an RFP, is used to solicit proposals when an award cannot be made strictly on specifications or price. Procuring agencies will develop an RFP that clearly and concisely defines the problem to be solved, explains the desired outcomes or goals, and states the evaluation factors and relative importance of each. (See *id.* § 10.08 (1986).)

2. Noncompetitive Negotiation (Sole Source Supplier)

Agencies may use noncompetitive negotiation during procurement when the good or service is only found with a sole source. (See *id.* § 10.09 (1983).) Before entering an award by noncompetitive negotiation, the agency must demonstrate that a noncompetitive situation exists, that the price is equitable, that the situation requires procurement in this manner, and that noncompetitive negotiation is in the best interests of the state. (*Id.*)

D. Emergency Procurement

Procurement policies may be waived by the governor or his or her designee if there exists an emergency threatening the public health, safety, or welfare, and the waiver is necessary to meet that emergency. (Wisconsin Statutes § 16.75(6)(e) (2021).) In such a situation, the contract should still be made with as much competition as practicable. (*Id.*) The governor or his or her designee must then file an official statement describing the issue with the Department of Administration. (*Id.*)

E. Special Rules for Specific Contract Types

1. Architect/Engineering Service Contracts

Wisconsin law provides a selection process to determine architects or engineers for projects that have been approved by the state Building Commission. (See *id.* § 16.867 (2018).) If the estimated cost of the project is less than $5,000,000, a selection committee may utilize the simplified selection by nomination procedure. (Wisconsin Administrative Code Adm § 20.04 (2006).) Here, the department solicits architects/engineers by posting a detailed advertisement on VendorNet, and the architect/engineer responds through a letter of interest detailing his or her qualifications. (*Id.* § 20.05.) The selection committee evaluates all of the interested candidates and recommends a first and second architect/engineer to the department for the contract. (*Id.*) The secretary considers the recommendations and issues an approval or disapproval. (*Id.*)

For projects of $5,000,000 or more, however, the committee shall follow the selection by advertisement procedure. (*Id.* § 20.04(2).) This requires advertising on VendorNet and the official state newspaper with necessary information including, among other things, (1) project description, estimated project budget, and schedule, and (2) criteria used in ranking architects/engineers to qualify for the interview process. (*Id.* § 20.06(1).) In addition to the advertisement, the department may solicit for proposals through trade publications, or directly to architects/engineers if it is deemed necessary to ensure an adequate number of qualified bids. (*Id.* § 20.06(2).)

Bid selection occurs on the date stated in the advertisement. (*Id.* § 20.07(1).) The architects/engineers are first screened to determine whether the minimum qualifications exist. (*Id.* § 20.07(2).) Next, they are evaluated by the following criteria: past performance; production capabilities; current workload of state projects under contract by the architect/engineer; experience or specialization; geographic proximity; and any other pertinent information. (*Id.* § 20.07(3).)

The selection committee will interview architects/engineers it determines are the best qualified, and forward their recommendation for the firms receiving the two highest scores to the secretary of the Department of Administration. (*Id.* § 20.08.) The agency will then conduct negotiations to finalize a contract. (*Id.*)

2. Construction Contracts

The Department of Administration has the power to adopt rules and implement the advertising and award of contracts for construction projects. (Wisconsin Statutes § 16.855(15) (2018).) RFPs, which must include all drawings and specifications, are commonly advertised at least 30 days before the bid opening. (Wisconsin Administrative Code Adm § 21.03 (2010).)

Contractors who wish to compete for the contract must submit a completed bid, in a sealed and unopened envelope, by the appropriate deadline. (*Id.* § 21.05.) All bids must include the contractor's proposed price, acknowledgment of receipt of any addenda, the signature of the bidder, and a bid guarantee. (*Id.* § 21.08(1).) The bid guarantee must be a properly executed Department of Administration form of bid bond, a bank certified check, or a cashier's check. (*Id.* § 21.02(3).) The bid bond must equal 10 percent of the highest combination of the base bid and any alternate bids submitted. (*Id.*) Bid proposals may be withdrawn and resubmitted without prejudice at any time before bid opening. (*Id.* § 21.06.) The bidder must make a written request for withdrawal on company letterhead, or appear in person to request withdrawal. (*Id.*)

Construction contracts will be awarded to the lowest qualified responsible bidder. (*Id.* § 21.09(1).) "Final determination" of which bidder is the lowest responsible bidder "is vested with the department." (*Id.*) "In cases where the bidding documents provide a formula for [bid evaluation] in conjunction with the base and alternate bids," that formula will be used. (*Id.* § 21.09(2).) Factors that may be used by the department in evaluating bids include, but are not limited to, low net annual operating cost; low unit cost of capacity; highest performance per unit or cost; or annual maintenance and service costs. (*Id.* § 21.09(3).) Determinations on the winning bid may only be considered on the specifications located in the bid, unless it is in the state's best interest to do otherwise. (*Id.* § 21.09(5).) Final award "will not be finalized until the required performance payment bond and certificate of insurance has been received." (*Id.* § 21.09(7).)

F. American and Wisconsin Vendor Preferences

When all other factors are substantially equal, the state must purchase products that were substantially manufactured in the United States. (Wisconsin Statutes § 16.754(2) (1987).) There are limited exceptions, including when the goods are for commercial resale. (*Id.* § 16.754(3).) For example, if the vendor under consideration for a government contract is not a Wisconsin domiciliary, and the department determines that the state, foreign nation, or subdivision in which that vendor is a domiciliary grants it preference because of that status, the department or any agency shall grant a preference to another vendor that is a Wisconsin domiciliary. (*Id.* § 16.75(1)(a)(2).)

G. Affirmative Action and Nondiscrimination Obligations

All entities doing business with Wisconsin agree to comply with regulations related to nondiscrimination and the affirmative hiring of women, minorities, and handicapped persons. (Wisconsin Administrative Code Adm § 50.04 (1999).)

Contractors must agree that in connection to the work performed under their state contract, they will utilize an equal opportunity employment policy whereby they will not discriminate against any employee or applicant for employment because of age, race, religion, color, handicap, sex, physical condition, developmental disability, sexual orientation, or national origin. (*Id.* § 50.05.)

The contractor must also agree to take affirmative action to ensure equal employment opportunities. (*Id.*) This requirement applies to all classifications of individuals included in the nondiscrimination requirement except for sexual orientation. (*Id.*) The contractor shall strive to develop a workforce that is proportional to the percentage of minorities, women, and handicapped persons in the relevant labor market. (*Id.* § 50.03.) Additionally, the contractor must submit its affirmative action plan and the plan of any subcontractors to the department of administration. (*Id.* § 50.04(1)(b), (c).) Knowledge of the company's affirmative hiring plan must be shared with employees and potential employees in sufficient detail to allow them to take advantage of it. (*Id.* § 50.05.)

With legislative and judicial branch purchasing, the purchasing department must ensure that 5 percent of the total amount expended in each fiscal year is paid to minority business. (Wisconsin Statutes § 16.75(3m)(b) (2021).) A "minority business" means a sole proprietorship, partnership, limited liability company, joint venture, or corporation that (1) is at least 51 percent owned, controlled, and actively managed by a minority group member or members who are U.S. citizens or persons lawfully admitted to the United States for permanent residence, and (2) is currently performing a useful business function. (*Id.* § 200.49.) The purchasing agency may not, however, accept a proposal under this section that is more than 5 percent higher than the most advantageous offer. (*Id.* § 16.75(3m)(b).) Lastly, all contractors must report to the agency any amount of the contract that was subcontracted to minority businesses. (*Id.* § 16.75(3m)(c).)

V. Bid Protests and Contract Disputes

A private entity does not have a constitutional right to sue the state absent consent. (See *Cords v. State*, 214 N.W.2d 405, 410 (Wis. 1974).) The state has, however, consented to suit through the establishment of a specific claims procedure. (See *State v. P.G.*

Miron Construction Co., Inc., 512 N.W.2d 499, 501 (Wis. 1994) (citing administrative procedures available under Wisconsin Statutes § 16.007 (2005), once exhausted, lead to judicial review).)

A. Bid Protests

The State of Wisconsin provides administrative tribunals for bid disputes. By rule, any bidder or proposer who is aggrieved by a solicitation or notice of intent to award a contract may protest to the procuring agency. (See Wisconsin Administrative Code Adm § 10.15(1) (1986).) To do so, the protestor must file a written notice of intent to protest with the head of the procuring agency within five working days after issuance of the solicitation or the letter of intent to award a contract. (*Id.*) The protestor must then serve the written protest upon the head of the procuring agency within ten working days after issuance of the letter of intent to award a contract. (*Id.*) The head of the procuring agency, or designee, has the authority to settle and resolve a protest. (*Id.* § 10.15(2).) "If the protest is not resolved by mutual agreement, the head of the procuring agency, or designee, shall issue" a written decision, a copy of which is furnished to the protestor. (*Id.* § 10.15(3), (4).)

B. Bid Protest Appeals

In addition to the bid protests themselves, the State of Wisconsin provides administrative tribunals for appealing an earlier administrative bid-protest decision. By rule, a protestor may appeal the decision of the procuring agency to the secretary. (See *id.* § 10.15(5).) The protestor must first allege a violation of a statute or a provision of the Administrative Code to the secretary within five working days of that decision. (*Id.*) The secretary or designee "shall [then] take necessary action to settle and resolve the protest and shall promptly issue a written decision which shall be furnished to the protestor." (*Id.*) A protestor who wishes to obtain a rehearing must file a written petition for rehearing with the Department of Administration within 20 days after service of the order. (See Wisconsin Statutes § 227.49(1) (1985).)

Proceedings instituted by a timely protest immediately cease any solicitation or award of the contract until a decision is finally rendered, or the secretary makes a written determination that the award of the contract is necessary to protect a substantial interest of the state. (Wisconsin Administrative Code Adm § 10.15(6) (1986).)

C. Contract Disputes

1. Contract Claims

After a legitimate government contract has been entered into, a private contractor may sue the State of Wisconsin or an empowered state agency for a breach of that contract, but only after first making an administrative claim, having that claim refused, and posting a bond to indemnify the state against all costs incurred in the suit if the state prevails. (Wisconsin Statutes § 775.01 (1979).) Additionally, a subcontractor who is a third-party beneficiary under the government contract retains the same rights as the primary contractor under both Wisconsin Statutes section 16.007 and section 775.01. (See *CleanSoils Wisconsin, Inc. v. Department of Transportation*, 599 N.W.2d 903, 909 (Wis. Ct. App. 1999) (finding that a third-party subcontractor could bring suit to recover a debt owed by the state, but could not bring suit for unjust enrichment).)

a. Exhausting Administrative Remedies for Contract Claims

A Wisconsin claims board receives, investigates, and makes recommendations on all claims of $10 or more against the state or a state agency. (Wisconsin Statutes § 16.007(1) (2005).) In this administrative tribunal, after a claim has been made, the board gives a claimant at least ten days' written notice of the opportunity to contest the state's official position on a contract. (*Id.* § 16.007(3).) The claims board has relaxed evidentiary rules, but must provide the claimant the opportunity to argue its position. (*Id.* § 16.007(2).) To help in its decision, the board may summon and compel the attendance of witnesses, require the production of documents, and require sworn testimony. (*Id.* § 16.007(3).)

The board will then report its findings and recommendations to the Wisconsin Legislature. (*Id.* § 16.007(5).) If the board unanimously recommends payment of $10,000 or more, the legislature will set in motion a bill to compensate the private contractor for the state's debt. (*Id.* § 16.007(6) (citing Wisconsin Statutes § 799.01(1)(d)).) If the amount the board concludes should be paid is $10,000 or less, however, the legislature does not have to draft a new spending bill, and the board will pay the claim with its own designated funds. (*Id.*)

b. Contract Claims and Sovereign Immunity

All "claims" under Wisconsin Statutes section 775.01 must still comport with more general notions of sovereign immunity. Claims for damages based on contracts must be reasonably fixed monetary sums based on the contract or other fixed data. (See *Koshick v. State*, 706 N.W.2d 174, 178 (Wis Ct. App. 2005) (citing 26 C.J.S. *Debt* §§ 1, 4 (2001)).) Similarly, a "claim" under Wisconsin Statutes section 775.01 does not cover suits for unliquidated damages, amounts based on unascertainable projections such as lost profits, or actions where the sum must be derived from extraneous evidence. (*Id.*) Lastly, equitable remedies such as specific performance and unjust enrichment are barred by the state's sovereign immunity. (See *Brown v. State*, 602 N.W.2d 79, 88 (Wis. Ct. App. 1999) (specific performance); *CleanSoils Wisconsin, Inc. v. Department of Transportation*, 599 N.W.2d 903, 910 (Wis. Ct. App. 1999) (unjust enrichment).)

c. Declaratory Judgment

If the suit against the state or agency involves a violation of a statute in addition to, or in conjunction with, the breach of contract, then a private contractor may initiate a declaratory judgment action. (See Wisconsin Statutes § 227.41 (2013).) In this administrative proceeding, a contractor petitions the agency to issue a declaratory ruling under the statute. (*Id.*) If the final result of that hearing "adversely affects the substantial interests of any party," the contractor may appeal to the judiciary. (See *id.* § 227.52 (2019); see also *Wisconsin Department of Revenue v. Hogan*, 543 N.W.2d 825, 829 (Wis. Ct. App. 1995) ("not all decisions, orders, or determinations that might fit within a literal reading of [the statute] are subject to judicial review"; they must be "final and complete" and determine "the further legal rights of the party seeking review") (citations omitted).)

d. Contract Claim Appeals to Judiciary

A contractor denied damages by an administrative claims board has the right to appeal to the judiciary by statute. (See Wisconsin Statutes § 775.01 (1979).) The contractor will commence this action "by filing with the clerk of court a bond, not exceeding $1,000, with two [2] or more sureties, to be approved by the attorney general," that the contractor will indemnify the state if he or she should lose. (*Id.*)

D. Suspension and Debarment

The suspension and debarment of private contractors in Wisconsin are performed either through the state or agency doing the purchasing, or another agency enforcing a Wisconsin law applying to that contract. (See Wisconsin Administrative Code Adm § 24.05 (2011); see also Wisconsin Administrative Code Trans § 504.05 (2012); see also Wisconsin Administrative Code DWD § 294.05 (2000).) Generally, an agency can debar a private contractor for any of the enumerated reasons in the rule. (Wisconsin Administrative Code Trans § 504.05 (listing fraud, collusion, violation of federal or state statutes, embezzlement, theft, a history of failure to perform, and violation of the contract terms amongst many others).) The debarment procedure is intentionally informal, and hearings are reserved only for matters that can be contested, which does not include criminal convictions. (*Id.* § 504.05(3).) The agency can extend the debarment to any affiliates specifically named with the contractor who have been duly notified. (Wisconsin Administrative Code Adm § 24.05(1)(c).)

The agency's rule may provide the opportunity and procedure for administrative appeal. (See, e.g., Wisconsin Administrative Code DWD § 294.05(5)(a) ("Any party to the action may request a copy of the proposed findings of fact and order and appeal it within [twenty] 20 calendar days to present oral or written arguments to the designated representative."); but see Wisconsin Administrative Code Trans § 504.05 (appeals not mentioned).) The period for debarment is commensurate with the seriousness of the cause, but generally cannot exceed three years. (See Wisconsin Administrative Code Trans § 504.05(7) (2012).) A less serious punishment of suspension is generally limited to six months. (*Id.* § 504.06(4).)

The agency will maintain a list of debarred and suspended contractors, may not have contact with any of the listed contractors, and must also see that it is not involved in any government contract as a subcontractor. (See *id.* § 504.04.)

VI. Administrative and Judicial Review

A. Administrative Review

Contractors can appeal administrative decisions by right through an administrative tribunal. In short, a contractor may file a written request with the agency for hearing and have the right to that hearing if a substantial interest of that contractor is injured, the legislature did not exclude that interest from protection, the injury is specific to that claimant, and there is a dispute of material fact. (Wisconsin Statutes § 227.42 (2017).)

All parties to the administrative review are provided an opportunity to the hearing after reasonable notice. (*Id.* § 227.44(1).) All interested parties are allowed the opportunity to be heard and present or rebut evidence. (*Id.* § 227.44(2), (3).) The administrative tribunal has relaxed evidentiary rules, and has the power to compel testimony or documentation through a subpoena. (*Id.* § 227.45(1), (6m).) The agency will designate and empower a hearing examiner to administer these statutory rules, make rulings throughout the dispute, and authorize an official decision for the outcome. (*Id.* § 227.46(1), (2m).) This decision is final for the purposes of judicial review. (*Id.* § 227.46(2m).)

B. Judicial Review

A decision by the hearing examiner that adversely affects the substantial interests of the contractor is subject to judicial review. (*Id.* § 227.52 (2019).) Moreover, contractors are required first to engage the official administrative process before being allowed access to the judicial remedy. (See *State v. Outagamie County Board of Adjustment*, 628 N.W.2d 376, 390 (Wis. 2001).) A court will review an administrative agency's decision when (1) a final decision exists; (2) it is "made in writing accompanied by findings of fact and conclusions of law"; (3) it adversely affects "the substantial interest of any person"; and (4) "review is sought by a person aggrieved by the decision." (*Madison Landfills, Inc. v. Department of Natural Resources*, 509 N.W.2d 300, 304 (Wis. Ct. App. 1993); see also *Mailen v. Wisconsin Educational Approval Board*, 823 N.W.2d 840 (Wis. Ct. App. 2012).)

Contractors can request judicial review by serving a petition personally or through "certified mail upon the agency or one of its officials, and filing the petition in the office of the clerk of circuit court for the county where the judicial review proceedings are to be held." (Wisconsin Statutes § 227.53(1)(a)(1) (2019).) Service and filing must be within 30 days of the agency decision. (*Id.*)

The standard of review for an administrative decision is whether it was arbitrary or unreasonable. (*Glacier State Distribution Services, Inc. v. Department of Transportation*, 585 N.W.2d 652, 656 (Wis. Ct. App. 1998) (citation omitted).) An agency decision is arbitrary or unreasonable if it lacks a rational basis or resulted from unconsidered, willful, or irrational decision-making. (*Id.*) In fact, even where an agency's decision is against the great weight and clear preponderance of the evidence, it will not be reversed if "substantial evidence"—meaning relevant evidence that a reasonable mind might accept as adequate to support a conclusion—supports it. (*Mews v. Wisconsin Department of Commerce*, 676 N.W.2d 160, 164 (Wis. Ct. App. 2004) (citation omitted).) Finally, the contractor's failure to raise an issue before the administrative agency "generally constitutes waiver of that issue." (*State v. Outagamie County Board of Adjustment*, 628 N.W.2d 376, 390 (Wis. 2001).)

VII. Extent of State's Adoption or Adaptation of ABA Model Procurement Code

Procurement in Wisconsin is not modeled after the American Bar Association's (ABA's) initial version of the Model Procurement Code for State and Local Governments.

VIII. Cooperative Purchasing

A. Authority

Wisconsin permits the use of cooperative purchasing agreements under Wisconsin Statutes section 16.73 (2001). Under that statute, the Department of Administration may enter into joint purchase contracts with a municipality or a group of municipalities and municipalities may enter into joint purchase agreements with one another. (Wisconsin Statutes § 16.73(1).) The joint purchase contracts cannot cover construction contracts, but may cover the "purchase of materials, supplies, equipment, permanent personal property, miscellaneous capital or contractual services." (*Id.*) Further, "[w]hen it is in the best interest of the state and consistent with competitive purchasing practices," the Department of Administration can enter into cooperative purchasing agreements with other state governments or the federal government for the same areas as Wisconsin Statutes section 16.73(1). (*Id.* § 16.73(4)(a).)

B. Requirements

The Department of Administration, State Bureau of Procurement, maintains a website, available at https://doa.wi.gov/Pages/StateEmployees/CooperativePurchasing.aspx, that provides explanations on what entities can use cooperative purchasing agreements, what products are available, and where to find cooperative purchasing agreements. Wisconsin's cooperative purchasing agreements are available on VendorNet. Wisconsin has not posted guidance on how an interested bidder can become eligible to bid on cooperative purchasing agreements. Further, there is not yet case law construing the statute indicating what remedies are available to disappointed bidders.

Wyoming Procurement Rules and Regulations

Prepared by
John L. Skari, Jr.
Hassan & Cables, LLC
Email: john@hassancables.com
and
Eric Whytsell
Stinson LLP
Email: eric.whytsell@stinson.com

I. Statutory Reference

A. Procurement/Purchasing Statutes

The relevant sections of the Wyoming Statutes are included below:

§ 9-2-3204.	General Services Division
§ 9-2-3209.	Purchasing for legislature and judiciary; approval; requirements
§§ 9-2-3004 and 9-2-3006.	Procurement for capital construction projects
§ 9-23-101 *et seq.*	Professional Architectural, Engineering, and Land Surveying Services Procurement Act
§ 16-3-114.	Judicial review of agency actions; district courts
§ 16-6-602.	Payment of agency accounts; interest
§ 16-6-701 *et seq.*	Construction contracts with public entities

The Wyoming Department of Administration and Information (DAI) website offers information on the state's procurement statutes and regulations at https://ai.wyo.gov/divisions/general-services/purchasing. Purchases are made in accordance with statutory regulations through a comprehensive system of specifications, competitive sealed bidding, competitive negotiation, and noncompetitive negotiation. Awards are made to the lowest responsive and responsible bidder, unless criteria other than price are considerations of the award.

Effective October 1, 2020, all construction-related purchases and bid/request for proposal (RFP) solicitations became the responsibility of the Wyoming State Construction Department (SCD). (Wyoming Statutes § 9-2-3006.) The SCD website offers construction bid forms, documents, and the rules relating to agency procurement of professional services, capital construction project materials and services, and alternate design and construction delivery methods for capital construction projects. (See https://stateconstruction.wyo.gov/procurement.)

Both the DAI General Services Division's Procurement Section and SCD use a web-based bid system that requires vendors to register with Public Purchase, an e-procurement service available at https://www.publicpurchase.com/gems/register/vendor/register.

B. Other Applicable Statutes

The relevant sections of the Wyoming Statutes are included below:

§ 6-5-101 *et seq.*	Bribery and other offenses by public officials.
§ 6-5-105.	Prohibits requiring a contractor to deal with a particular person in procuring any goods or service required in submitting a bid to or fulfilling a contract with any government. Provision in an invitation to bid or contract document that violates this section is voidable.
§ 9-13-101 *et seq.*	Ethics and Disclosure Act proscribes nepotism, misuse of office, and other misconduct by government officials, including receiving gifts or private benefits from holding of an office.
§ 9-13-102(a)(vi).	Exceptions to definition of "gift" including printed information; gifts of nominal value for special occasions; awards, loans, gifts, gratuity or discounts not exceeding $250 in value, and food and beverage.
§ 9-23-106(d).	Prohibition on gratuities, kickbacks, and contingent fees in contracts for professional services.
§ 9-23-107.	Civil penalty for gratuities, kickbacks, and contingent fees relating to contracts for professional services.

II. Regulations

The DAI, through its General Services Division, adopts rules governing procurement, management, control, and disposal of all of supplies and services required by agencies and standard forms and procedures requiring that agencies award bids or contracts through the use of competitive sealed bidding, competitive negotiation, noncompetitive negotiation, or small-purchase procedures. (See Wyoming Statutes § 9-2-3204.)

The General Services Division's Procurement Section promulgates the State Purchasing Rules. These Purchasing Rules apply to all agencies, offices, departments, boards, commissions, or operating units of the executive branch of government except those noted in Wyoming Statutes section 9-2-3204(b). These excluded entities, including the University of Wyoming, community college districts, school districts, and, with certain exceptions, the Wyoming Department of Transportation, generally have their own procurement and purchasing services departments and their own rules and procedures. (See, for the University of Wyoming: http://www.uwyo.edu/procurement/, and, for the Wyoming Department of Transportation: https://www.dot.state.wy.us/home/business_with_wydot/purchasing.html.)

The Wyoming SCD, in conjunction with the agencies identified below, adopts rules and regulations necessary to implement the selection procedures under the Professional Architectural, Engineering, and Land Surveying Services Procurement Act. (Wyoming Statutes § 9-23-105(e).) These rules apply to any agency: school district, state office, department, board, council, commission, separate operating agency, institution, or other instrumentality or operating unit of the state excluding the University of Wyoming, community college districts, the Wyoming business council, and the Wyoming Department of Transportation. (Wyoming Statutes § 9-23-102(a)(i).)

The Wyoming Administrative Code governing the Purchasing Division is as follows:

DAI

PURCHASING DIVISION
State Procurement Rules

CHAPTER. 1 GENERAL PROVISIONS
Section 1. Authority
Section 2. Coverage
Section 3. Interpretation
Section 4. Enforcement
Section 5. Purchasing Policies
Section 6. Responsibility for Agency Functions
Section 7. Savings Clause

CHAPTER 2. LIMITATIONS ON PROCUREMENT
Section 1. Procurement Policies
Section 2. Emergency Purchases

CHAPTER 3. PREFERENCES
Section 1. Applicable Preferences
Section 2. Bidders and Proposers

CHAPTER 4. PROTEST
Section 1. Protest
Section 2. Notification of Protest by Bidder or Proposer
Section 3. Action by State on the Notification of Protest
Section 4. Formal Resolution of Protest
Section 5. Commencement of Action
Section 6. Time and Place of Hearing
Section 7. Service and Filing
Section 8. Default
Section 9. Hearing Officer
Section 10. Authority of Hearing Officer
Section 11. Final Decision

The Procurement Section of the DAI General Services Division makes the Wyoming Purchasing Procedures Manual, available at https://drive.google.com/file/d/1kx2XmYgr5i7sTV2-4huF9YZmppqFEMBv/view.

DAI Procurement Section Purchasing Procedures Manual (Oct. 2021)

SECTION NO.	SUBJECT
1. Procurement	
1(a)	Procurement up to $2,500.00 (Total to Pay)
1(b)	Procurement $2,500.00 to $15,000.00 (Total to Pay)
1(c)	Procurement $15,000.00 and Up
1(d)	Payment Vouchers
1(e)	Requisitioning Supplies, Materials, Equipment, or Services
1(f)	Purchase Order (PO)
1(g)	Change Orders
1(h)	Contracts
1(i)	Emergency Purchases
2. Bidding Process	
2(a)	Request for Proposal (RFP)
2(b)	Amendments to Invitation for Bids/Requests for Proposals
2(c)	Bid Exception Approval Requests Exceeding $15,000.00
2(d)	Bidder Registration
2(e)	Preference to Wyoming Resident Bidders
2(f)	Printing Preference
2(g)	Moving Expenses
2(h)	Use or Purchase of Meat
2(i)	Purchases Using Federal Funds
2(j)	Exemption from Taxes
2(k)	Notice of Intent to Award
2(l)	As Needed Contracts
2(m)	Public Records Request

The SCD Emergency Rules are available online at https://drive.google.com/file/d/1flAx6QT-8BppxvRiCdbMhXErfB-PY8aL/view.

Wyoming SCD Emergency Rules (Effective Oct. 1, 2020)

SECTION NO.	SUBJECT
1. General Provisions	
1	Authority
2	Definitions

2. Procurement of Professional Services	
1	Authority
2	Applicability
3	Submission of statements of qualifications
4	Issuance of requests for proposals (RFPs)
5	Firm interviews
6	Award of contract
7	Emergency selection
8	Emergency contract
3. Procurement by Competitive Bidding, Competitive Negotiation, or Noncompetitive Negotiation	
1	Authority
2	Applicability
3	General provisions
4	Choice of procurement process
5	Bid waivers
6	Emergency contracting
7	Noncompetitive negotiation
8	Competitive negotiation
9	Bidder prequalification for competitive sealed bidding
10	Prequalification term, status notification, and revocation
11	Request for review of denial of prequalification application
12	Advertising for competitive sealed bids
13	Procuring agency's addenda to bid advertisements
14	Requests for clarifications of bid advertisements
15	Access to plans and bid documents
16	Prebid conferences and site visits
17	Content of competitive sealed bids
18	Bid security
19	Bid submission, modification, and withdrawal
20	Principles for evaluating bids, price or quantity discrepancies, and bid irregularities
21	Evaluation of bids and award of contract
22	Cancellation of a bid advertisement
23	Cancellation of an award of a contract
4. Alternate Design and Construction Delivery Methods	
1	Authority
2	As-needed contracts

3	Construction manager at-risk (CMAR)
4	Design-build
5	Construction manager agent
5. Post-Award Project Performance	
1	Authority
2	As-needed contracts
3	Contract management
4	Payments
6. Dispute Resolution and Bidder or Firm Discipline	
1	Authority
2	Judicial review
3	Informal dispute resolution
4	Contractor or firm discipline

III. Source Selection

A. Voucher: General Accounting Expenditures Document

Agencies are authorized to procure supplies, materials, or services up to a total expenditure of $2,500 by issuing a General Accounting Expenditures (GAX) document. (Purchasing Procedures Manual § 1(d).) The GAX document is based on an invoice from the vendor and constitutes a straight request for payment from the State Auditor's Office without prior approval of the Procurement Section. A requisition must be processed for agency purchases of supplies, materials, equipment, or services involving total expenditures exceeding $2,500 for commodities or $1,500 for services. (Purchasing Procedures Manual § 1(e).)

B. Purchase Order

Agencies accomplish most commodity or service purchases by issuance of a numbered purchase order. The Procurement Section is the only agency authorized to issue a purchase order, which authorizes a vendor to deliver goods or services and assurance that payment will be made. (Purchasing Procedures Manual § 1(f).)

C. Contract/Master Service Agreement

Agencies use this method when ordering goods or services used repeatedly or on a continuing basis, and/or when more than one payment will be required to fulfill the agreement. (Purchasing Procedures Manual § 1(h).) Whenever an agency has a need to contract for goods or service and more than one payment will be required, a master service agreement (MSA) shall be issued by the Procurement Section. (Purchasing Procedures Manual § 1(h).) All requests for MSAs must be submitted on a requisition. Agencies may extend or amend contracts by mutual written agreement of the parties provided the original terms and conditions remain unchanged. Contracts are typically in effect for one year and may be extended one year at a time for a total contract period not to exceed three years. (Purchasing Procedures Manual § 1(h).)

D. Small Purchasing

Agencies may make purchases of $2,500 or less, or up to $15,000 or less on approval of the Department, using small-purchase procedures established by the Department. (Wyoming Statutes § 9-2-3204(b)(iv)(E).) Agencies are encouraged to get competitive quotes from at least three vendors, when possible.

E. Competitive Sealed Bidding

In procurements of supplies or services valued in excess of $15,000, competitive sealed bidding is used. (Wyoming Statutes § 9-2-3204(b)(iv)(A).) This allows agencies to secure acceptable products at the lowest possible cost to the taxpayers of the state. (Wyoming Statutes § 9-2-3204(b)(iv)(A).) In competitive sealed bidding, agencies award contracts to the responsible private-sector bidder making the lowest bid if the private-sector bidder's bid is not more than 5 percent higher than the lowest responsible non-private-sector bidder. (Wyoming Statutes § 9-2-3204(b)(iv)(G).)

F. Competitive Negotiation

If the use of competitive sealed bidding is not feasible or practical, the principal representative must submit a written determination to the Department. If approved by the Department, contracts may be awarded by competitive negotiation. (Wyoming Statutes § 9-2-3204(b)(iv)(B); Purchasing Procedures Manual § 1(c).) Elected state officials may contract for supplies or services for their office by competitive negotiation without department approval if the contract is for $25,000 or less and the elected state official determines that competition is not feasible. (Wyoming Statutes § 9-2-3204(b)(iv)(B).)

G. Noncompetitive Negotiation

Agencies may use noncompetitive negotiation only when competition is not feasible, as determined in writing by a principal representative and approved by the governor or his or her designee for prior approval. (Wyoming Statutes § 9-2-3204(b)(iv)(C); Purchasing Procedures Manual § 1(c).) The governor has designated the director of the DAI to make this determination. Elected state officials may contract for supplies or services for their office by noncompetitive negotiation without the approval of the governor or his or her designee if the contract is for $25,000 or less and the elected state official determines that competition is not feasible. (Wyoming Statutes § 9-2-3204(b)(iv)(C).)

H. Emergency Procurement

Emergencies or exceptions must be verbally authorized by the program manager prior to an agency making any commitment to vendors in an amount exceeding $15,000. As follow-up, the agency must write a letter reiterating the situation and forward it to the Procurement Office. (Purchasing Procedures Manual § 1(i).) Bid exception approval is required for contracts exceeding $15,000.

I. Professional Services/Capital Construction Projects

Procurement of professional services and capital construction projects pursuant to Wyoming Statutes sections 9-2-3004 and 9-2-3006 shall be conducted through the use of competitive negotiation, noncompetitive negotiation, or competitive sealed bidding. (Wyoming Statutes § 9-2-3004; SCD Emergency Rules chs. 2 and 3.)

1. Professional Services

A firm seeking to provide professional services may submit a statement of qualifications (updated every two years) to be placed on a list maintained by the SCD. For a project with fees of $50,000 or less, the Department may request statements of qualifications in preparation for the specific project. For projects with fees greater than $50,000, the procuring agency shall request a statement of qualifications by publishing notices in a newspaper of general circulation. (SCD Emergency Rules ch. 2, § 3.)

The procuring agency shall then review the statements of qualifications and submit an RFP for the project, giving preference to resident firms. (SCD Emergency Rules ch. 2, § 4.) The procuring agency shall then hold interviews with not less than three firms that provided proposals in accordance with Wyoming Statutes section 9-23-105(b). (SCD Emergency Rules ch. 2, § 5.)

The procuring agency must then consider the factors under Wyoming Statutes section 9-23-105(f)(i) (ability of professional personnel, past performance, ability to meet time requirements, location, current and projected workloads, volume of work previously awarded, and equitable distribution of contracts among qualified firms) in determining the firm to which to award the contract and enter into contract negotiations. (SCD Emergency Rules ch. 2, § 6.)

Any of these provisions may be waived by the procuring agency if following the provision would endanger the health, welfare, or safety of the public under the circumstances. (SCD Emergency Rules ch. 2, § 7.)

2. Capital Construction Projects

Contracts for capital construction project materials or services with an anticipated value of $50,000 or less must be procured through competitive negotiation. (SCD Emergency Rules ch. 3, § 8; Wyoming Statutes § 9-2-3006.) Contracts for capital construction project materials or services with an anticipated value of greater than $50,000 shall be procured through competitive sealed bidding. (SCD Emergency Rules ch. 3, §§ 9–21; Wyoming Statutes § 9-2-3006.) Bid waivers may be obtained if the principal representative of the procuring agency determines that competitive negotiation or competitive bidding is not feasible or practical and seeks the necessary approvals. (SCD Emergency Rules ch. 3, § 5; Wyoming Statutes § 9-2-3006.)

The competitive negotiation process for capital construction projects is set forth in SCD Emergency Rules chapter 3, section 8. The process for competitive sealed bidding is set forth in SCD Emergency Rules chapter 3, sections 9 through 21.

A procuring agency experiencing an emergency situation may, in accordance with these rules, procure services or materials without adhering to the notice, bid, and negotiation requirements in the rules. (SCD Emergency Rules ch. 3, § 6.)

IV. Bid Protests and Contract Disputes

A. Bid Protests

Protest of specific procurements may be made by the bidders, proposers, or qualified potential bidders or proposers for up to ten calendar days following the notice of intent to award the contract or purchase order by the state. (Wyoming Rules and Regulations AI PD ch. 4, § 1.) Protests must be made in writing to:

State Procurement
Department of Administration and Information
701 West 21st Street
Cheyenne, Wyoming 82002

The Procurement Section will then record the protest and, on agreement of the parties, schedule and conduct an informal meeting for the purpose of attempting an informal resolution. (Wyoming Rules and Regulations AI PD ch. 4, § 3.) At the conclusion of the informal resolution meeting, the protestors may request, in writing, a formal protest hearing if the protest is not resolved. (Wyoming Rules and Regulations AI PD ch. 4, § 4.) Formal protest requests are extremely rare.

Upon written request of a formal hearing, the Procurement Section shall commence proceedings to consider the protest in an order to show cause. Any bidder or proposer or qualified potential bidder or proposer may seek to intervene in a bid protest hearing upon written motion stating the reasons why intervention is sought. (Wyoming Rules and Regulations AI PD ch. 4, § 5.) The hearing shall be held no less than 20 days after service of the notice of hearing to the bidder or proposer. Hearings are conducted in Cheyenne, unless upon motion and for good cause another location is preferable. Hearings may be postponed upon motion and a showing of good cause by any party. (Wyoming Rules and Regulations AI PD ch. 4, § 6.)

Upon receipt of the hearing officer's recommendation, the director of the DAI shall issue a final decision in the protest. In the event the director determines that procurement procedures were violated, the director may take reasonable action to remedy the violation, including rescinding the notice of intent to award and reissuing a request for bid or proposal. (Wyoming Rules and Regulations AI PD ch. 4, § 11.)

B. Contract Disputes

The SCD has an informal dispute resolution procedure for contracts awarded under the Professional Architectural, Engineering, and Land Surveying Services Procurement Act. (SCD Emergency Rules ch. 4, § 3.) A bidder or firm may file a written request for informal dispute resolution with the SCD within ten days from the acceptance or rejection of a bid; notice of exclusion from consideration on an RFP; or notice of project award. Upon receipt, the SCD and the procuring agency, if applicable, "shall meet with the requestor to discuss the issues in the request"; this meeting may be in person, over the phone, or by any other means. (SCD Emergency Rules ch. 4, § 3.)

V. Administrative and Judicial Review

A. Administrative Review

The administrative review process is set forth above.

B. Judicial Review

Subject to the requirement that administrative remedies be exhausted, any person adversely affected in fact by a final decision of an agency in a contested case, or by other agency action or inaction, or a rule adopted by an agency, is entitled to judicial review in the district court for the county in which the administrative action or inaction was taken. (Wyoming Statutes § 16-3-114(a).) The district court may hold unlawful and set aside agency action, findings, and conclusions found to be (1) arbitrary, capricious, an abuse of discretion, or otherwise not in accordance with law; (2) contrary to constitutional right, power, privilege, or immunity; (3) in excess of statutory jurisdiction, authority or limitations, or lacking statutory right; (4) without observance of procedure required by law; or (5) unsupported by substantial evidence in a case reviewed on the record of an agency hearing provided by statute. (Wyoming Statutes § 16-3-114(c)(ii).)

"It is the responsibility of the public agency, which is charged with contracting, to accept that bid which, in its judgment, would provide the best project for the money. Inherent to its duties, presumed superior knowledge, and expertise, the responsible public authority must have wide latitude in which to exercise its judgment as to the best means of accomplishing that objective, and courts are reluctant to enjoin such administrative functions in the absence of dishonesty, fraud, collusion, or lack of good faith. The money amount of the bid is not the sole criteria. There must also be conformity with the bidding specifications. It is a general rule that bids for public contracts must substantially comply with the requirements of the specifications for bidding and the directions to prospective bidders. The determination as to whether these requirements are satisfied and the awarding of a contract are acts of discretion which will be enjoined only if done illegally, arbitrarily, capriciously, or unreasonably." (*State v. Weisz & Sons, Inc.*, 713 P.2d 176, 185–86 (Wyo. 1986).)

"The competitive bidding process is designed primarily to protect the public's interest in ensuring that the government will not pay too high a price for goods and services, and irregularities in that process will seldom provide a basis for a claim for damages." (*Lariat Diesel Corp. v. Wyoming Department of Transportation*, 86 P.3d 266 (Wyo. 2004).) The Wyoming Supreme Court recently held that neither a citizen nor a former member of the Wyoming House of Representatives had standing to challenge legislation authorizing two construction projects without complying with the competitive bidding or other safeguards set forth in Wyoming Statutes section 9-2-3204. (*Allred v. Bebout*, 409 P.3d 260 (Wyo. 2018).)

Review of any final judgment of the district court may be obtained by appeal to the Wyoming Supreme Court. (Wyoming Statutes § 16-3-115.)

VI. Extent of State's Adoption or Adaptation of ABA Model Procurement Code

The Wyoming statutory scheme does not follow the American Bar Association (ABA) Model Procurement Code.

VII. Cooperative Purchasing

A. Authority

Wyoming Statutes section 16-1-101 provides the authority to enter into cooperative purchasing agreements:

> In exercising, performing or carrying out any power, privilege, authority, duty or function legally vested in any one (1) or more of them by Wyoming law, the

state of Wyoming, and any one (1) or more of its counties, municipal corporations, school districts, special districts, public institutions, agencies, boards, commissions and political subdivisions, and any officer or legal representative of any one (1) or more of them, may cooperate with and assist each other, and like entities or authorities of other states, the United States and the Eastern Shoshone and Northern Arapaho Tribes of the Wind River Reservation.

B. Requirements

Cooperative purchasing "may be informal or subject to resolution, ordinance or other appropriate action, and may be embodied in a written agreement specifying purposes, duration, means of financing, methods of operations, termination, acquisition and disposition of property, employment of executive and subordinate agents, reciprocation of governmental immunity protections or other limitations of liability. . . ." (Wyoming Statutes § 16-1-101.)

Wyoming has exercised this authority by entering into a number of contracts through the National Association of State Procurement Officials' ValuePoint. In addition, individual agencies may choose to enter into cooperative purchasing agreements on a case-by-case basis. For example, the Northeast Wyoming Board of Cooperative Educational Services (NEW BOCES), https://www.newboces.com/, is a member of the Association of Educational Purchasing Agencies.